The Psychology of
Criminal Conduct

THE WILEY SERIES IN CLINICAL PSYCHOLOGY

Series Editors

Fraser N. Watts
MRC Applied Applied Psychology Unit
Cambridge, UK

J. Mark G. Williams
Department of Psychology
University College of North Wales, Bangor, UK

Severe Learning Disability and Psychological Handicap
John Clements

Cognitive Psychology and Emotional Disorders
J. Mark G. Williams, Fraser N. Watts, Colin MacLeod and Andrew Mathews

Community Care in Practice: Servives for the Continuing Care Client
Edited by Anthony Lavender and Frank Holloway

Attribution Theory in Clinical Psychology
Freidrich Försterling

Panic Disorder: Theory, Research and Therapy
Edited by Roger Baker

Measuring Human Problems: A Practical Guide
Edited by David Peck and C. M. Shapiro

Clinical Child Psychology: Social Learning, Development and Behaviour
Martin Herbert

The Psychological Treatment of Insomnia
Colin A. Espie

The Challenge of Severe Mental Handicap: A Behaviour Analytic Approach
Edited by Bob Remington

Microcomputers and Clinical Psychology:
Issues, Applications and Future Developments
Edited by Alastair Ager

Anxiety: Theory, Research and Intervention in Clinical and Health Psychology
Robert J. Edelmann

Innovations in the Psychological Management of Schizophrenia:
Assessment, Treatment and Services
Edited by Max Birchwood and Nicholas Tarrier

Psychological Aspects of Depression:
Toward a Cognitive–Interpersonal Integration
Ian H. Gotlib and Constance L. Hammen

The Psychology of Criminal Conduct: Theory, Research and Practice
Ronald Blackburn

The Psychology of Criminal Conduct

Theory, Research and Practice

Ronald Blackburn

University of Liverpool
and
Ashworth Hospital, Liverpool, UK

JOHN WILEY & SONS

Chichester · New York · Brisbane · Toronto · Singapore

National   01243 779777
International (+44) 1243 779777

Reprinted February 1994, September 1996, March 1997

First published in paperback July 1995

Reprinted November 1997, July 1998, January 1999

Other Wiley Editorial Offices

John Wiley & Sons, Inc., 605 Third Avenue,
New York, NY 10158-0012, USA

Jacaranda Wiley Ltd, 33 Park Road, Milton,
Queensland 4064, Australia

John Wiley & Sons (Canada) Ltd, 22 Worcester Road,
Rexdale, Ontario M9W 1L1, Canada

John Wiley & Sons (SEA) Pte Ltd, 37 Jalan Pemimpin #05-04,
Block B, Union Industrial Building, Singapore 129809

Library of Congress Cataloging-in-Publication Data:

Blackburn, Ronald.
    The Psychology of criminal conduct : theory, research, and practice /
Ronald Blackburn.
      p.   cm. — (The Wiley series in clinical psychology)
    Includes bibliographical references and index.
    ISBN 0-471-91295-6 (ppc)
    1. Criminal psychology.   2. Criminal behavior.   I. Title.
    II. Series.
    HV6080.B547   1993
    364.3'01'9—dc20   92–23728
                                                                      CIP

British Library Cataloguing in Publication Data:

A catalogue record for this book is available from the British Library

ISBN 0-471-91295-6 (cloth)
ISBN 0-471-96175-2 (paper)

Typeset in 10/12pt Palatino from author's disks by Text Processing Department,
John Wiley & Sons Ltd, Chichester
Printed and bound in Great Britain by Bookcraft (Bath) Ltd

Contents

Series Editor's Preface

Professional psychologists working with offenders need to draw together two somewhat different foundations for their work. On the one hand, they need to make use of methods of assessment and intervention which are not dissimilar from those used with other people with psychological disorders. They also need to be aware of the contribution to the understanding of crime that has been made by psychology and other disciplines. Both are dealt with here in a balanced way. Those who come to professional work with offenders from a broad background in professional psychology will find here the background information on offenders that they will need. Equally, those with a background in the scientific study of crime will find here an indication of the lines on which professional work with offenders has proceeded.

The application of psychology to forensic decision making is a branch of the discipline which is growing rapidly. Scientific research is proceeding apace, and there is a fast-growing body of professional psychologists skilled in work with offenders. This book reflects the growing strength of professional psychology in this area, providing the reader with a thorough, authoritative, and judicious review of the relevant literature. Though other comprehensive volumes on forensic applications of psychology are available, there is no other current book which has a consistency of approach that comes from having been written by a single, leading figure in the field. The book is also unusually international in its orientation, taking account of the different legal systems that operate in different countries.

The scientific study of crime, draws on many discipline, just as professional work with offenders draws on the contributions of various different professions. Though this book in the Wiley Series in Clinical Psychology takes psychology as its focal discipline, I hope it will be of interest to a wide range of other disciplines and professions concerned with crime and offenders.

FRASER WATTS
Series Editor

Preface

When Fraser Watts first suggested that I write a book on antisocial behaviour for clinical psychologists it seemed like a good idea. Having taught clinically oriented courses on criminal behaviour and forensic applications of psychology to clinical trainees for several years, I had long been frustrated by the lack of a comprehensive text. Also, as a result of a growth in services for mentally disordered offenders during the past decade, the number of clinical psychologists working at the interface of the criminal justice and mental health systems is now increasing. The opportunity to correct a hiatus in the psychological literature therefore seemed timely.

Had I forseen the task involved, my enthusiasm would have been muted, particularly since the resulting textbook is more ambitious in scope than was originally intended. Assembling in a single text the essential background material for clinical practitioners preparing for work with offenders confronted me squarely with the artificiality of our academic and administrative categories. Offenders diverted to mental health settings are not a distinctly defined group, either in terms of their mental health problems or their offending, and the interests and concerns of clinical psychologists working in these settings frequently coincide with those of psychologists working in penal and educational contexts. Understanding how psychological dysfunction sometimes contributes to crime also presupposes a knowledge of the many other factors involved. Moreover, there is no clear boundary between psychological approaches to crime and those of other behavioural and social scientists. In this respect, clinical psychologists working with offenders need to be applied criminologists as much as mental health specialists.

The primary aim of the book remains, therefore, to summarise the theoretical and empirical basis for clinical psychological practice, but I have attempted to set this more broadly in the context of the psychology of crime. I have also made occasional forays into the territory of sociologists, lawyers, philosophers and psychiatrists, but fully acknowledge my status as amateur in these areas. Some of my conceptions are undoubtedly muddled or simplistic. However, my purpose has been to draw attention to questions which must be raised in attempts to explain or intervene in criminal behaviour rather than to provide answers. I have also tried to emphasise that psychological practice is inevitably constrained not merely by psychological theories and research findings, but also by the wider intellectual climate in which these emerge.

The book falls broadly into two parts. The first half covers basic concepts in criminal justice and the study of crime, and examines the nature of offending from sociological and psychiatric as well as psychological perspectives. The major psychological theories are critically appraised, and research on the biological, familial and social, and individual correlates of offending are reviewed. The second half focuses on topics of particular concern to practitioners. Theoretical concepts and research on violence, mental disorder and crime, and sexual offending are examined, and the forensic contribution of psychologists to criminal justice investigation, prediction, and decision making evaluated. The final chapters review psychodynamic, behavioural and cognitive approaches to offender rehabilitation, the treatment of dangerous offenders, preventive approaches, and the efficacy and ethics of intervention.

A textbook purports to summarise the state of knowledge, and is essentially a journey through the writings and products of others. This is reflected in the lengthy bibliography. It would be foolish to pretend that this represents a wholly objective selection from the extensive literature, and my own biases and enthusiasm for the social cognitive trends in recent research and intervention will be apparent. Nevertheless, I hope I have avoided theoretical parochialism. Given the broad scope of the book, I also hope it will be of some use to psychologists more generally, including those undertaking courses on psychology and law or embarking on criminological research, as well as to other mental health and criminal justice professionals who draw on psychological conceptions of crime.

The solitary pursuit of writing a book is not accomplished in isolation from the influence and support of others, and I am pleased to acknowledge my gratitude to several people. Among the teachers, colleagues, and students who fostered and shaped my interests in offenders, I would particularly like to mention Tony Black, who encouraged my earliest clinical and research efforts at Broadmoor Hospital, and Gordon Trasler, whose clarity of thinking on the subject of psychology and crime did much to kindle my own enthusiasm. I am indebted to David Farrington, Clive Hollin, James McGuire, Ron Tulloch, and Norman Wetherick for taking the time to read drafts of several chapters, and for providing helpful comments which removed some of the warts. Needless to say, they are not responsible for the blemishes which remain. I am also grateful to Fraser Watts, the Series Editor, and Wendy Hudlass, of John Wiley & Sons, not only for their patience in tolerating missed deadlines, but also for encouraging me to complete the project through periods of waning enthusiasm. Finally, I must thank my wife, Celia, for her support and tolerance during what has been a long haul.

RON BLACKBURN
Liverpool, October 1992

Chapter 1

Crime, Criminology, and Psychology

INTRODUCTION

This book describes the contribution of psychology to our understanding of crime and its control. It does so from the standpoint of psychology as not only a behavioural and a social science, but also an applied discipline which seeks to resolve problems of individuals and the social systems in which they are embedded. This is not to imply that crime can be understood as a wholly psychological phenomenon, nor that psychology has pivotal answers to questions of how to control and prevent crime. These issues are beyond the competence of any single discipline. Any claims to "scientific" solutions to "the crime problem" are also disingenuous, since the kinds of conduct a society chooses to penalise by law, and how it deals with offenders, are determined by normative ethical systems. Science can inform these systems, but cannot replace them.

The study of crime has engaged the interest of many academic disciplines. Building on centuries of philosophical debate, systematic attempts to explain crime emerged from the developing biological and social sciences in the late nineteenth century. Anthropologists, statisticians, and economists have contributed to the analysis of crime, but the major theories have come from sociology, psychology, and psychiatry. Yet, despite the overlapping concerns of these disciplines, their theories have developed against a background of mutual disinterest, if not antipathy. This partly reflects longstanding ideological disputes between those who blame crime on the inherent corruptness of the human individual and those who attribute it to the corrupting influences of an inequitable society. However, even within disciplines, there has always been ambivalence about whether to pillory or romanticise the criminal.

The interest of psychologists in crime and the law dates from the advent of psychology as an empirical discipline. Lightner Witmer, who pioneered clinical psychology, taught courses on criminal behaviour at the University of Pennsylvania before founding the first psychological clinic in 1896

(McReynolds, 1987), and G. Stanley Hall described research on delinquents in a major text on adolescence in 1904. The empirical study of courtroom behaviour was extolled soon afterwards by the publication of Munsterberg's *On The Witness Stand* in 1908. Witmer's clinic also provided a model for the first child-guidance clinic for delinquents, the Chicago Juvenile Psychopathic Institute, which was set up in 1909 with William Healy, a psychiatrist, and Grace Fernald, a psychologist as its first professional staff. Educational, clinical, and prison psychologists subsequently established roles in providing services to the courts, penal institutions, and individual offenders, and psychology was the largest single source of criminological research dissertations in American universities during the first half of the century (Brodsky, 1972). Nevertheless, crime has always been a minority interest among psychologists.

During the last two decades, however, interest in the legal system has surged (Monahan and Loftus, 1982), as witnessed by the formation of psychology and law sections within both the British Psychological Society and the American Psychological Association, and the publication of specialist journals, as well as more than a dozen texts addressing psychology and law issues (e.g. Haward, 1981; Müller, Blackman and Chapman, 1984; Weiner and Hess, 1987). Not only is the behaviour of witnesses, victims, or legal officials of psychological interest, legal settings are recognised as fertile ground for testing theories about issues such as recognition and memory, decision-making, or attitude change. Although British courts make less use of psychologists as expert witnesses than those in America, psychologists have established a forensic role in both criminal and civil proceedings. Other contributions to the legal process include the selection and training of police and magistrates, the development of stress management procedures for police officers, and advice to legal review bodies, for example, on the interrogation of child witnesses, or use of the polygraph in "lie-detection".

Applications of psychology to law now draw on virtually all specialist fields of experimental and applied psychology, and are so diverse as to defy a single title, or coverage in a single text. *Psycholegal studies* are directed more towards law enforcement and the criminal justice system than to criminal behaviour, and this dual focus was recognised in the title of the Division of Criminological and Legal Psychology formed within the British Psychological Society in 1977 to represent several converging interests. However, the primary concern of this book is with psychological conceptions of criminal conduct and the application of psychological principles and methods to interventions with offenders. The focus is hence on *criminological psychology*, and broader aspects of the psychology and law interface are discussed only where they are pertinent to understanding criminal behaviour.

Crime is a legal concept, and "a crime (or offence) is a legal wrong that can be followed by criminal proceedings which may result in punishment" (Williams, 1978). Criminology is the study of such acts, the laws which define them as criminal, and the means by which society seeks to control and prevent them. Crime, however, is not a distinct category of behavioural phenomena, since the criminal law does not relate to a circumscribed area of human conduct. Moreover, criminology is not a unified discipline. Psychologists and psychiatrists study criminal behaviour for what it reveals about individual human propensities, whereas sociologists study crime for what it says about society. The remainder of this chapter therefore considers the nature of criminal law, criminal justice, and criminology.

CRIMINAL LAW AND THE CRIMINAL JUSTICE SYSTEM

Criminal law is the body of laws defining offences and how offenders are to be dealt with. Much of the law in England and Wales, the United States, and British Commonwealth countries is embodied in statutes enacted by the legislatures, but originates in common law, which was the law common to England after unification by the Normans, and which exists as a tradition of judicial decisions. These systems differ from each other and from those of Scotland and continental European countries, and there are also variations between American states. However, all advanced systems penalise conduct described in Anglo-American law as treason, murder, aggravated assault, theft, robbery, burglary, arson, and rape. Ellis (1987) suggests that this universal concern with harmful behaviour has an evolutionary basis, since all animals living in groups react negatively to victimisation of their members.

Law as a system of social rules

A law states a contingency; it specifies that a particular act will be followed by a legal penalty. However, the acts forbidden by law and the penalties prescribed are diverse, and definitions of law are as problematic as those of health and disease.

Functionally, the criminal law is similar to other systems of rules. Both explicit and tacit rules control behaviour in many settings, and facilitate shared goals by regulating the activities of group members. In games, committees, conversations, or in the course of particular relationships, for example, behaviour follows rule-like prescriptions of what should and should not happen, which are dictated by the customs, conventions, traditions and mores of the particular social unit. Sociologists and social psychologists conceptualise such rules as *norms*, which are the prevailing standards about the usual, expected, and permissible ways of doing things, as embodied in the shared beliefs and practices of group members. Without such standards, acts could not meaningfully be identified as deviant, nonconforming, or antisocial.

However, the concept of norm does not denote a single kind of belief or standard (Gibbs, 1972). Customs merely describe what is common and expected, while some norms, such as sexual mores, are evaluative and prescribe what is acceptable. Also, there is rarely complete consensus about evaluations, expectations, or other normative elements within a social unit, and normative judgements are typically applied conditionally according to setting and the age, sex, or status of participants. A particular form of behaviour can therefore rarely be said to be *the* norm for a group without qualification.

Some philosophers of law argue that laws are merely generalised predictions of what the courts will do in cases brought before them, but Mannheim (1965) regards them as normative insofar as they are imperatives prescribing how citizens should act. Sutherland and Cressey (1970) propose four characteristics which distinguish criminal law from other forms of social imperative. First, it is *political*, in that it is defined by the state, and applies to all citizens. Second, it defines crimes in terms of *specific* acts; the 1968 Theft Act, for example, states that "A person is guilty of theft if he dishonestly appropriates property belonging to another with the intention of permanently depriving the other of it". Third, it is applied with *uniformity* to all citizens within the jurisdiction, regardless of status. Fourth, it stipulates *penal sanctions* which can be enforced coercively by authorised agents of the state. While coercion is absent from much law enforcement, and some laws are rarely enforced, the *potential* for coercive enforcement is the most distinguishing feature of a law, compared with other normative rules (Gibbs, 1972).

What kind of rules or norms, then, does the law seek to enforce? Clearly, some normative standards are maintained without the threat of legal sanction for violation. The law is only minimally concerned with *customs and traditions*, for example, which are largely maintained informally, although traditions of dress are enforced by legal proscriptions against "indecency". Traditions of racial segregation are also enforced by law in some states, while challenged by law in others. *Religion* was historically an influence on law, although this declined following the secularisation of the modern state. Some religious influences persist, but mainly because they coincide with commercial or political interests. For example, the repeal of Sunday trading laws in Britain and America is constantly resisted by an alliance of religious fundamentalists and commercial concerns which seek to minimise business competition. In recent times, most western states have enacted laws on matters such as abortion, homosexuality, birth control, or suicide, contrary to the teachings of the dominant religions. In Christian countries, the Ten Commandments have never, in fact, provided more than a partial guide to what should be condemned by the state. For example, adultery is not a crime in law, except in some American states, but bigamy is universally criminal in monogamous societies.

The relation of law to *morality* has long been debated. An old legal distinction is that between offences which are *mala in se*, or inherently moral wrongs, and *mala prohibita*, which are acts deemed crimes for the convenience of the state. This distinction is related to a longstanding philosophical distinction between *natural law* and positive or merely human law (Mannheim, 1965). The concept of natural law attempts to identify universal standards of morality, and invokes notions of "divine" or "ideal" law, or what is fundamentally good in human nature. The search for such an absolute yardstick was undermined by the development of science, but notions of "rights" and "justice" nevertheless imply some basic nonlegal principles to which the law must appeal.

Whether the law *should* enforce morality surfaced as an issue following the proposals of the Wolfenden Committee in 1957 to decriminalise homosexual behaviour occurring in private between consenting adults. Some jurists followed John Stuart Mill and argued that the criminal law should function primarily to prevent individuals harming others, and should not concern itself with private morality. Others objected that the criminal law is based on morality, and that it should continue to enforce moral principles. The debate clearly involves competing assumptions about law and society, and reflects the lack of consensus about the functions of law. Certainly, there are many laws which derive from moral objection, particularly those relating to sexual behaviour, drug use, or gambling, which often create *victimless crimes* involving no harm to others. However, Mannheim (1965) suggests that law and morality represent overlapping but distinguishable sets of normative standards. In particular, the law is mainly concerned with overt action and compliance, and not covert motives, and focuses on prohibiting the commission of acts, and not exhortations to desirable behaviour. There are, however, some instances in which acts of omission are crimes, such as failure to feed one's children.

As a system of rules, then, the law overlaps with other normative elements governing behaviour. Walker (1987) summarises the functions of the law in relation to society, and identifies fourteen areas of concern. These are the protection of people from intended or unintended harm or exploitation, the prevention of behaviour which is "unnatural" or offensive, the discouragement of public disorder, the protection of property and of social institutions, such as marriage, the prevention of public inconvenience, the collection of revenue, the defence of the state, the enforcement of "compulsory benefits", such as the attendance of children at school, the prevention of unreasonable discrimination, and the enforcement of justice. While Walker suggests that central to these is the smooth running of society, and the preservation of order, it is clear that no single principle determines which type of conduct is a proper subject for the criminal law.

The nature of crimes and criminal responsibility

Given the cultural and historical relativity of the law, it is not surprising that lawyers find it difficult to identify what crimes have in common, other than that they are acts attracting legal punishment. Crimes are offences against the community, and distinct from *torts*, which are civil wrongs against individuals. Torts entail the initiation of proceedings by the injured party rather than state officials, and are redressed by the award of damages rather than punishment. This is not a firm distinction, since an offender convicted of a serious crime may also be required to pay civil damages to the victim.

While crimes are acts which harm the community, they encompass not only the most injurious behaviours, but also many with trivial effects, and the legal consequences for an offender range from the death penalty to a fine. Traditionally, serious and petty crimes have been distinguished in terms of felonies versus misdemeanours, or since 1967 in Britain, "indictable" versus "summary" offences, but these distinctions are mainly procedural, resting on the level of court in which an offence may be tried. Most offenders are tried in lower or summary courts, such as magistrates' or sheriff's courts, only more serious offences being dealt with in higher courts before a jury (now the Crown Court in England).

Crimes are not clearly distinguished by criteria of social disapproval. A behaviour contrary to law must first have been evaluated negatively by at least one person, i.e. the member of the legislature who introduces a statute, but the evaluation is not necessarily widely shared. The law prohibiting robbery, for example, probably coincides with condemnation of such behaviour by a majority of the population, but the same cannot be said for victimless crimes, or crimes carrying little moral opprobrium, such as road traffic offences. *White-collar crimes*, which cover violations of laws related to the conduct of business or trade as well as occupational crimes against organisations, may actually involve practices which are acceptable within a particular business setting, despite their consequences for the consumer.

Nevertheless, although crimes are not synonymous with moral rules, there is a significant moral element in the legal requirements for establishing the liability of a defendant to penal sanction. A basic common law principle is expressed in the Latin maxim *actus non facit reum nisi mens sit rea* (an act does not make a person guilty unless the mind be guilty). The essential elements of a crime are thus a voluntary act (*actus reus*) and an intention to commit the act (*mens rea*). These are positive elements, and have to be proved. The *actus reus* requirement excludes involuntary movements, such as those during an epileptic fit or somnambulism, and there must be a causal relationship between the harmful effect and the action of a defendant. Some lawyers argue that the requirement of *mens rea*, or the guilty mind, is that a person is legally punishable only if moral guilt can be imputed. However, while this may have been the reason for its introduction into the common law, Hart (1968) argues that this is no longer so, and that what is required by modern criminal law is that the act is legally, and not morally wrong. The moral principle is that it is unjust to punish people who could not help doing what they did. This reflects the law's view that human beings are able to freely choose their actions, and forms the basis for excusing conditions (mistake, accident, provocation, duress, or insanity) which may exculpate someone accused of a crime.

Criminal responsibility therefore means that the conditions for liability to legal punishment have been established. However, the term "responsibility" has been troublesome since it is used in several senses in both everyday language and the law (Fincham and Jaspars, 1980). Some writers assume that criminal responsibility is equivalent to "free will" (MacDonald, 1955), or moral responsibility (Wootton, 1959), and argue that it is an anachronistic basis for dealing with offenders. The ambiguous notion of "diminished responsibility", which appeared in the English Homicide Act of 1957, further implies that responsibility refers to a varying psychological capacity. The problem is that "legal responsibility" collapses several meanings into one.

Hart (1968) offers a conceptual analysis which identifies four basic senses of responsibility: (1) *causal* responsibility (for producing an outcome); (2)

role responsibility (for certain duties or obligations arising from a particular role); (3) *capacity* responsibility (the ability to understand, reason, and control conduct); (4) *liability* responsibility (for certain consequences). He divides the latter into legal liability (for legal punishment) and moral liability (for blame or praise). Responsibility as liability is the most important use in law, and its essential meaning relates to answering (i.e. responding to) or rebutting charges which if established carry liability to punishment. Other meanings of responsibility provide the criteria or conditions for this. Thus, causing some act or omission and having the necessary psychological capacity are conditions under which a person may be held legally responsible.

The demonstration of *mens rea* is therefore a condition of legal responsibility, but the criteria for this element of a crime have always been vague. For example, in American law, the criteria for first degree murder are acting with malice, premeditation, deliberation, and intent to kill. The Model Penal Code of the American Law Institute in 1962 proposed that *mens rea* elements should be limited to evidence of acting purposefully, knowingly, recklessly or negligently, and in England, the Law Commission has made similar recommendations. However, this focus on the state of mind of an accused person brings out a critical difference between the legal conception of human behaviour and that of some schools of psychology. For behaviourists, inferred intentions lack causal status. They merely refer to verbal discriminations of the variables about to produce behaviour, and are by-products of environmental contingencies (Skinner, 1978). Some psychologists therefore follow Wootton (1959) in suggesting that the law should dispense with *mens rea*, and focus on what an offender did, and how its repetition might be prevented (Black *et al.*, 1973; Feldman, 1977; Blackman, 1981; Crombag, 1984). However, this utilitarian view assumes that preventive measures can be determined scientifically or pragmatically, and ignores the deciding role of cultural norms. In some countries, for example, prevention is ensured by removal of the offending limb! Moreover, the reliance of the law on inferences of intent is based on everyday attributional processes, which in the view of contemporary social psychologists exert significant control over conduct (Fincham and Jaspars, 1980; Bandura, 1986; Ajzen, 1987).

To focus on what a person did to the exclusion of questions of why would also remove consideration of mitigating circumstances. It would lead to a requirement of *strict liability*, which already obtains for bigamy, statutory rape (sexual intercourse with a female under the age of consent), and "public welfare" offences such as road traffic offences or selling adulterated food. Strict liability removes standards of distributive justice from legal decision-making, and any extension would result in an excessively harsh system of punishment.

The evolution of the criminal law

Sanctions are applied within a group when normative violations are strongly disapproved or impede the attainment of group goals. Noncompliance with customs and convention attracts, at most, informal sanctions of disapproval or ostracism, but in specific groups, as well as nonliterate societies, sanctions may include expulsion from the group for violations of the mores or ethical rules.

Written rules emerge when competition between individuals or groups cannot be resolved by informal procedures, and in developed societies these include formal sanctions which are universally applicable. These initially allowed an aggrieved individual to retaliate, but since vendettas or blood feuds detract from social order, a further development was the specification of compensation or restitution. The earliest known example of such a written legal system is the Code of Hammurabi, King of Babylon, which dates from about 2200 BC. This is inscribed on a stele, now in the Louvre, and details the law on such matters as rental agreements, husband–wife obligations and rights, and the use of contracts. It abolished private retribution, and specifies penalties for particular wrongs, such as amounts payable in restitution for theft. However, it contains several severe penalties, and embodies the *lex talionis*, i.e. the principle of "an eye for an eye".

A system of civil law obtains when redress is formally adjudicated by an authoritative figure, and a common view is that criminal law evolved from civil law when wrongs became identified as offences against the community rather than individuals, and punishment was administered on behalf of the state. Legal sanctions may be instituted when the majority in a community has rational concerns about particular conduct, or is antagonised by infractions of valued customs or mores (Sutherland and Cressey, 1970). These possibilities assume a *consensus* within the group as to what behaviour should be formally sanctioned. However, *conflict theory* within sociology (Quinney, 1974) maintains that developed societies are composed of groups with incompatible interests. Laws are enacted to preserve the sectional interests of those who hold power or who have powerful advocates. The ruling groups thus secure their interests at the expense of the underprivileged, whose behaviour becomes a target for legal penalties. Even when behaviour is proscribed ostensibly in the common interest, as in laws against murder, assault, or rape, it is defined selectively so that such conduct on the part of the dominant group goes unpunished. The English law against rape, for example, was only recently extended to sexual coercion in marriage.

Some laws have clearly emerged to protect the interests of particular groups. The trespass laws, for example, were introduced in the fifteenth century to protect the warehouses of the developing English merchant classes, and in more recent times there have been laws against cattle rustling, motor theft, and racial and sexual discrimination. However, *radical criminologists*, who maintain a Marxist analysis of social structure and conflict, argue that the emergence of the criminal law at the end of the middle ages was a victory not simply of a particular interest group, but also of the economic and social ethic of individualism which shaped the subsequent function of laws in capitalist society (Taylor, Walton, and Young, 1973). Such a monolithic account may underestimate the alternative influences on the development of the law in the middle ages, since the Protestant Ethic has always had to accommodate other religious and moral influences. For example, justice in the thirteenth century was presided over by ecclesiastics, and through them, the Canon Law of the English Church exerted a considerable influence on the development of common law (Dreher, 1967). By the fourteenth century, when the term 'crime' first gained currency, and when the basic principles of modern criminal law were established, there was already a firm moral influence on the law.

Although sociologists such as Taylor et al. (1973) assert that the law creates crimes, the law is not clearly separable from other social institutions. Mechanisms for social control become centralised and formalised by those in powerful positions, but laws are made and changed because of public opinion or the activities of pressure groups, as well as the policies of government. Similarly, the operation of the criminal justice system is highly dependent on factors such as budgetary constraints or administrative pressures for results, and laws lacking public support are difficult to enforce. Unpopular laws may, in fact, produce new forms of problem behaviour, as happened when the Volstead Act created Prohibition in America. The law, then, is in constant interaction with law enforcement agencies, government, the mass media, and criminal behaviour itself.

The criminal and juvenile justice systems

The law in action is more than a catalogue of written proscriptions, and is determined by the agents of criminal justice, who comprise the police, court officials, and penal administrators. For example, judicial decisions in particular cases become part of the body of laws, and the police may enforce some statutes rarely or not at all, while zealously enforcing others. These agents exercise considerable discretionary powers of arrest, prosecution, and sentencing, which may result in bias and unevenness in the application of law. Indeed, it has been suggested that the increased volume of crime in the United States has created such pressures on the criminal justice system that "triage justice" prevails (Stone, 1984).

The concept of justice is concerned with the evaluation of the moral rightness of a person's fate, and the courts administer the law to this end. However, the ideal aim of the law is to maintain social order in the interests of the community at large, and the criminal justice system has both a preventive and a punitive function. The *preventive function* is justified by appeal to two traditional principles. The first is that of *parens patriae*, in which the state assumes "parental" responsibility for citizens in need of care and protection, as seen in the compulsory hospitalisation of mentally disordered people. The second is the assumption by the state of police powers to protect its citizens from law-breakers or those who are a danger to others. This is seen in both the assumed deterrent effect of legal punishment on potential offenders, and in powers accorded to the police and courts to detain people not convicted of offending, but considered at risk for doing so. The blurring of these two principles in European and American legislation underlies much of the recent attention given to the detention of mentally disordered offenders (Chapter 10).

The *punitive function* of criminal justice arises from the rights of the state to impose sanctions on those who violate the criminal law. Legal punishment entails the infliction of suffering, loss, or disablement on a convicted offender by an official who is legally authorised to inflict that punishment, and may take the form of capital or corporal punishment, detention in an institution, monetary fines, or restriction of movement within the community. While imprisonment is the central feature of the penal system, fewer than 5% of adult offenders are sent to prison. Most first-time offenders receive fines, probation orders, community service orders, or suspended sentences, and less than a third of these are subsequently reconvicted.

The use of prison as a punishment option is of relatively recent origin, and until the eighteenth century, dungeons and jails were used mainly for those awaiting trial or public punishment. Modern prisons originate in the efforts of eighteenth century Quakers to reform the "houses of correction", which led to the setting up of the first penitentiaries in Philadelphia and New York in the 1820s. The notion that prisons should be places of reform did not develop until later in the century. It was reflected in the establishment of the first reformatory for young offenders in Massachusetts in 1846, while in Britain, the antecedents of Approved Schools (now Community Homes) were set up by the Reformatory Schools Act of 1854.

Since the late nineteenth century, most countries have operated separate systems for criminal and juvenile justice. A *delinquent* is one who has committed an act which would be criminal if committed by an adult, which is defined by a lower age limit varying from fifteen to eighteen, depending on jurisdiction. However, delinquency also includes misbehaviour such as running away from home or truancy, which is based on the status of being a minor (hence *status offences*). Juvenile justice originates from a quasi-medical model which saw youthful offenders as sick and in need of intervention, such as probation in the community, to halt and correct the disorder, the basic philosophy of the juvenile court being that the community assumes guardianship responsibilities (*parens patriae*). Conflict theorists see the development of a separate system for controlling the antisocial behaviour of the young as a means of protecting the power and privilege of the industrial middle classes. Binder (1987), on the other hand, suggests that the system was motivated by humanitarian concerns, and was the outcome of changing conceptions of childhood and adolescence. The emergence of juvenile delinquency legislation in Canada, for example, reflected the activities of key "moral entrepreneurs" and not the involvement of an industrial ruling class (Hagan and Leon, 1977).

The aim of the juvenile court is, then, to decide how the child may be helped or rehabilitated. This, however, deprives the child of *due process of law*, i.e. the right to be represented by counsel, to cross-examine witnesses, and to refuse to testify against oneself. As a result of Supreme Court decisions in the United States in the 1960s, there has been greater recognition of the legal rights of children, reflected in changes in juvenile statutes and court procedures (Binder, 1987). At the same time, attempts have been made to minimise legal intervention both in America (Austin and Krisberg, 1981) and

Britain (Tutt, 1984), by, for example, the use of police cautions of youthful offenders, or by diverting them to community schemes rather than bringing them before the courts. Within the United Kingdom, this development has been most marked in Scotland, where juvenile justice was decriminalised following the Kilbrandon Report in 1964, and the juvenile court was replaced by a system of less formal hearings. In contrast, Scotland imprisons more adult criminals than any other western European country, with the exception of Northern Ireland.

PENAL PHILOSOPHIES

The terms "penitentiary", "reformatory", and the American concept of "correctional system" are reminders of the moral influences on the development of the penal system. Penal policy has never been formally predicated on any single function, and sentencing practices typically vary with the political climate. Some lawyers argue that punishment is crucial to demonstrate social denunciation of wrongdoing, but Hart (1968) notes that this is the function of criminal legislation, not punishment. However, legal punishment has several purposes, underlying which are the three justifying philosophical positions of *retribution*, *utilitarianism*, and *reformation* (Bean, 1981).

Retribution and the justice model

The notion that punishment should be inflicted in proportion to the harm done underlies the *lex talionis*, but legal retribution differs from revenge in that the penalty is exacted by the state rather than an aggrieved victim. Punishment expresses the moral disapproval of the state for law-breaking, but its severity is determined by standards of what is just and fair. This position was taken by Kant, who argued that criminals should be treated as rational people who accept the consequences of their action, and that punishment preserves the dignity of offenders.

Retribution looks backward to the offence itself, and questions of the explanation for the crime, or the future effects of punishment are irrelevant to the moral function of punishment. It is thus distinct from rehabilitation, which focuses on the offender, or deterrence, which is concerned with the utility of punishment from society's viewpoint. The retributivist position in the form of the "justice" or "just deserts" model gained considerable acceptance among penologists during the 1970s. In America, the Committee for the Study of Incarceration (Von Hirsch, 1976) recommended adoption of the "principle of commensurate deserts", which proposes that punishment should be dictated by the harm done and the culpability of the offender, and that it should serve the interests of justice, not crime control.

Although this principle has appealed to many liberals as the only defensible justification for punishment, it is inherently conservative. It assumes individual responsibility, and a social consensus about what is morally appropriate. However, it fails to take account of either the adverse conditions of imprisonment, or of individual variations in what is experienced as punishing. The model has nonetheless been adopted in several American states, which have abandoned use of the indeterminate sentence (Austin and Krisberg, 1981; Hudson, 1987), and has also been influential in Britain, where indeterminate sentencing has never been widely used. The 1991 Criminal Justice Bill, for example, asserts that a primary aim of penal policy is to "make the punishment fit the crime".

Utilitarianism

Utilitarianism provided the basis for the *classical school of criminology*, and was the product of the Age of Enlightenment. Punishment in the eighteenth century was excessively harsh and capricious, and was not governed by due process or conceptions of human rights (Toch, 1979). Utilitarians reacted by articulating a theory of legal punishment based on concepts of human rationality and the social contract.

In his *Essay on Crime and Punishment*, which appeared in 1764, the Italian legal theorist Beccaria proposed that the basically self-seeking nature of human beings can lead to the disruption of social order through interference with the personal welfare and property of others. This can be deterred by legal punishment, but this should be proportional to the harm involved, and governed by due process. The aim of punishment is prevention, rather than suffering or compensation, and it is directed towards the individual act. Individual motives or circumstances are not considered. Bentham elaborated on these proposals in his *Introduction to the Principles of Morals and Legislation*, published in 1789. His motivational theory views human behaviour, including crime, as directed at the attainment of pleasure and the avoidance of pain. This is subject to rational calculation, and self-interest can be made to coincide with the collective interest through the judicious use of rewards and punishments. The ethical "principle of utility" equates moral good with the greatest happiness of the greatest number. Legal punishment should promote the happiness of the community, and "prevent mischief" by applying sufficient pain to outweigh the pleasure of a crime. Bentham developed a complex catalogue of crime-related punishments based on a "felicific calculus" of the relative badness of specific acts.

Like retribution, then, utilitarianism focuses on the crime rather than the criminal. However, the two philosophies are irreconcilable in terms of the criteria for the degree of punishment to be inflicted, since what is socially useful is not necessarily just. Punishment for utilitarians is a means to an end, and looks to the future rather than the past. It pays no attention to individual rights. It should be just sufficient to dissuade the individual offender from repeating criminal acts (individual or *special deterrence*), or to intimidate would-be offenders from crime (*general deterrence*). Deterrence is thus derived from utilitarianism as a psychological theory of the effects of actual or threatened punishment, or as a sociological theory of social control.

While these views significantly influenced the development of criminal justice, they were too simple to translate readily into practice, and the courts found it too restrictive to apply punishments without considering the circumstances of the offender, or the likely effects of imprisonment. During the late nineteenth century, *neo-classicism* emerged as lawyers modified the earlier classicism with notions of "extenuating circumstances", and "partial responsibility", a development which Foucault (1978) attributes to a need to identify the individual who is a danger to society. While classical notions of free will and responsibility remained, this entailed a focus on criminals as individuals. As Taylor et al. (1973) note: "The neo-classicist took the solitary rational man of classicism and gave him a past and a future".

Reformation and rehabilitation

The individualisation of punishment entailed by neo-classicism coincided with the philosophy of rehabilitation, which emerged towards the end of the nineteenth century (Martin, Sechrest and Redner, 1981). This was a fusion of earlier concepts of reformation with the determinism of the new positivist sciences. Reformation was intrinsic to the medieval ecclesiastical view of penance as expiation of a wrong through suffering, and the avowal that the wrongdoer would in future refrain from sin. The eighteenth century Quakers also believed that solitude enabled the criminal to reform through contemplation of past wrongs. Reformation was consistent with the development of the juvenile justice system, which viewed legal intervention as an opportunity to prevent a child becoming criminal.

In Britain, the Gladstone Committee of 1895 recommended that imprisonment should involve efforts to make offenders physically and morally better than when they went in. The means for reforming offenders were to include moral instruction, and the availability of work and education. However, where reformation assumed free will, rehabilitation was particularly influenced by the introduction of psychoanalytic treatment into the prison system. Psychodynamic theories also influenced the development of the probation service.

Rehabilitation assumes that crime results from personal deficiencies or maladjustment. Attention is therefore focused on the individual criminal rather than the crime. It is not an alternative to punishment, since the law aims to prevent first offences and not simply reoffending by convicted criminals, but the legal sanction provides the occasion and means to help the individual adjust to society. However, the length of sentence may be indeterminate, to allow time for change, while release may be dependent on "cure", or the reduction of dangerousness as judged by "experts", such as psychiatrists or psychologists.

While reformation was inspired by the moral convictions of the Victorians, rehabilitation has been increasingly attacked by the political right as a "soft option", and by the left, which sees indeterminate sentencing as an interference with individual rights. Moreover, rehabilitation has often been an excuse for extended but nontherapeutic custodial measures (Allen, 1959). In 1962, the Model Penal Code of the American Law Institute specified the objectives of law as "to give fair warning of the nature of the conduct declared to constitute a crime", and "to promote the correction and rehabilitation of offenders". During the 1970s, however, evidence accumulated to suggest that rehabilitation schemes were largely ineffective in reducing recidivism (Martinson, 1974; Brody, 1976), and that the claims of clinicians to be able to judge dangerousness could not be substantiated (Monahan, 1981). Sociologists also argued that "treatment" of individual offenders or families diverted attention from the social inequalities which were largely responsible for crime (Balch, 1975). Rehabilitation has thus come to be seen as not only unsuccessful, but also misguided and coercive. The result has been a shift in penal policy away from goals of reformation to retribution and deterrence. However, the permanence of these trends remains to be seen. Hudson (1987) suggests that the justice model has failed to achieve a more just system of legal punishment, and as will be seen in Chapter 15, rehabilitation is far from dead.

Purposes of imprisonment

Although fewer than 5% of convicted offenders receive a custodial sentence, incarceration represents the most severe form of crime control, short of execution. Given the competing goals of legal punishment, there is no unanimity on the justification for imprisonment nor on the purposes it achieves, and many argue that its effects are largely negative (Bartollas, 1990). For example, high reconviction rates for ex-prisoners appear to suggest that prisons neither rehabilitate nor deter, and it is commonly suggested that they are not only "schools for crime", but also have harmful effects on the physical and psychological wellbeing of inmates.

The discrediting of rehabilitation resulted in a reappraisal of the purposes of prisons, and what they could reasonably be expected to achieve. Retributivist philosophies emphasised punishment for harm done, the primary consideration in imprisonment being to provide humane care and containment, but rehabilitation was not entirely abandoned as a penal policy. Morris (1974) argued that retribution and deterrence are the proper goals of imprisonment, and that it is inappropriate to mix these with attempts to reform. Nevertheless, he suggested that rehabilitation should be offered on a voluntary basis. He proposed that the guiding principles in imprisonment should be facilitated change rather than coerced cure, and graduated testing of fitness for freedom rather than parole predictions of suitability for release. Others, however, emphasise the utilitarian goals of imprisonment. Clarke (1985), for example, contends that the evidence does not justify attempts to change individuals, and that it is more practicable to focus on deterrence, incapacitation, and situational prevention.

In Britain, reconviction rates within two years of release from prison have been relatively stable since the 1970s at about 60% for adult males, and about

40% for females, although the figures are highest for young offenders and those previously imprisoned (Bottomley and Pease, 1986). Zamble (1990) also estimates that in Canada, reconviction rates within three years have been stable at 40 % to 50% during the past two decades. Such figures do not unequivocally favour a deterrent effect (Chapter 4). However, most first-time prisoners do not reoffend (Andenaes, 1974; Walker, Farrington and Tucker, 1981), suggesting that imprisonment may be a deterrent or reforming experience for some. While some studies find that imprisonment is less effective in reducing recidivism than noncustodial sentences (Newton, 1980), there appears to be an interaction between type of sentence and type of offender. In a six-year follow-up of English prisoners, for example, Walker and Farrington (1981) found that type of sentence made little difference to the likelihood of reoffending among the most recidivist, more than 85% being reconvicted regardless of type of sentence. Among first offenders, however, reconviction rates were higher for those given probation or suspended sentences than for those imprisoned or fined. Evidence favouring a criminalising effect of imprisonment is therefore slender, despite the popular view that prisons are schools for crime, and it may be only the least competent prisoners who acquire new criminal skills (Walker, 1983).

Imprisonment clearly serves the function of *incapacitation* insofar as offenders are temporarily prevented from committing further crimes, except against other prisoners or prison staff. There is therefore some interest in the possible effects on crime rates of increasing sentences generally (collective incapacitation) or for particular groups (selective incapacitation). Since imprisonment interrupts a criminal career, incapacitative effects depend on the individual crime rate and the duration of incarceration relative to career length. Incapacitation research therefore estimates the effects on crime rates of alternative sentences from offence histories of imprisoned offenders (Brody and Tarling, 1980: Blumstein, 1983: Farrington, Ohlin and Wilson, 1986).

Estimates of the amount of crime reduction, given longer sentences, vary widely, since they depend on assumptions about the average annual crime rate of individual offenders, how far their criminal activities would be replaced to satisfy "the market", and how much crime is committed by offenders not apprehended. However, an inevitable concomitant of longer sentences is an increased number of those in prison. For example, Brody and Tarling (1980) estimated that for two samples in England, where the average sentence length is less than a year, minimum mandatory sentences of 18 months would have reduced their offending by between 17% and 25%, but at a cost of more than a fourfold increase in the time spent in prison. They also estimate that a reduction of six months in sentences would increase convictions by 1.6%, while reducing time in prison by 40%.

While there is a case for the selective incapacitation of high-rate or dangerous offenders, the problem is to identify these in advance. Brody and Tarling (1980) found that although a small group of 52 dangerous offenders committed proportionately more of the subsequent violent crimes, increasing sentences by five years would have prevented violent reoffending by only nine of them. This is consistent with other findings on the difficulty of predicting dangerousness (Chapter 12). Incapacitation strategies therefore raise problems of justice and fairness. Moreover, the overall effect on the crime rate of changes in sentence length is minimised by the fact that most offenders are not sent to prison.

THE STUDY OF CRIME

The concept of crime in criminology

The fact that crimes do not constitute natural or homogeneous behavioural categories poses particular difficulties in identifying the subject matter of criminology and for constructing theories of "crime" or "criminal behaviour". Additional problems arise because many crimes are not detected or reported, while biases in the criminal justice system may determine who is adjudicated criminal (Chapter 2). The appropriate focus for the attention of criminologists has therefore been debated at some length (Mannheim, 1965; Bottomley, 1979; Young and Matthews, 1992).

A basic issue is whether criminology should be confined to the study of crime as legally defined (*legalism*), or whether it should also include antisocial conduct which is harmful but not illegal (*anti-legalism*). Some early criminologists took the anti-legalist view, proposing a notion of "natural crime" as antisocial behaviour which is universally regarded as harmful. Sellin (1938) also argued that the law could not prescribe the terms of a scientific discipline, and that universal categories could be found in the study of "conduct norms". A similar view is expressed by Gottfredson and Hirschi (1990), who argue that crimes are only one of several forms of behaviour which attract social sanctions, and that they share with deviance, sin, and recklessness a common cause in unrestrained self-interest.

Much sociology has followed this direction, seeing crime under the more general heading of *deviance*, or norm violation. Some sociologists and psychologists also argue that the study of crime must go beyond behaviour which is processed as criminal since criminal acts are less likely to be prosecuted when committed by members of powerful groups, such as business corporations or the police (Sutherland, 1945; Monahan, Novaco and Geis, 1979; Box, 1983). Schwendinger and Schwendinger (1970) further suggest that what is identified as antisocial must relate to concepts of human rights, and that criminology should include the study of such phenomena as imperialism, racism, or sexism. Another objection to a concern with criminal behaviour as a meaningful target comes from the *labelling* perspective in the sociology of deviance. This is summed up in the notion that "Deviance is not a quality that lies in behaviour itself, but in the interaction between the person who commits an act and those who respond to it" (Becker, 1963). From this perspective, the analysis of deviant behaviour focuses on how it is defined and reacted to, particularly by the agents of law enforcement. Paradoxically, this leads to a focus on legally adjudicated offenders.

Defending legalism, Vambery (1941) objected that claims of an absence of a scientific basis for a distinction between crime and noncrime could encourage the making of arbitrary laws in totalitarian societies. Firm support came from Tappan (1947), who suggested that concepts of what was antisocial rested on capricious value judgements, which were less precise than legal definitions of crime. He argued that legally defined crime is a significant field of study, and that "only those are criminals who have been adjudicated as such by the courts". However, many investigators now define delinquency in terms of self-reported acts which are legally punishable, but which have not necessarily come to legal attention (Chapter 2). Welford (1975) offers a less stringent defence, suggesting that some acts are intrinsically criminal insofar as they are universally condemned, and that the appropriate units of concern to criminology are serious crimes, not victimless or status crimes. However, this is a selective form of legalism.

Binder (1988) notes the continuing lack of unanimity, but takes issue with psychologists who equate antisocial behaviour with delinquency, stressing that delinquency cannot be defined in nonlegal terms. However, the debate centres on the conceptual boundaries of crime as a *behavioural* phenomenon. Conflict and radical criminologists object that this ignores crime as a *societal* phenomenon. Hartjen (1972), for example, argues that the legal definition of what is criminal depends on powerful sectional interests, and that the priority for the study of crime must lie with analysis of the political development of the criminal law. This view underlies the development of the *sociology of law*, which replaces the study of lawbreaking with the analysis of lawmaking. This explicitly political approach is concerned with "working towards penal change in a deliberately self-conscious fashion" (Bottomley, 1979). Criminology thus becomes a normative rather than a scientific discipline, or as Rock (1979) puts it, "a form of secular theology".

However, while criminal behaviour as legally defined lacks a psychological unity, one common feature is the *knowledge* of the lawbreaker that it attracts legal punishment. Since lawbreaking is in this respect only quantitatively different from other forms of rule violation which attract social sanctions, such as cheating, *rulebreaking* is a meaningful and nonarbitrary theoretical focus for criminological psychology. For example, stealing or aggression by young children is not criminal, but as will be discussed later, has similar antecedents to, and is associated with later delinquency. This does not equate antisocial behaviour with crime and delinquency, since any similarities must be established empirically. Nevertheless, while crime must be defined by a legal conception, those who study it cannot be bound by such a conception.

Schools of criminology

Although psychologists have been slow to recognise it, all scientific observations are "theory laden", and theories are also value laden (Kurtines, Alvarez and Azmitia, 1990). Similarly, people's views about crime causation and control are embedded in conceptual networks linking political ideology, moral reasoning, and personality characteristics, which fall into clusters of conservative or liberal beliefs (Carroll et al., 1987). While formal theories of crime and criminal justice do not always relate to ideological systems in any simple fashion, they nevertheless rest on at least implicit assumptions about human nature and society. Criminological theories are therefore distinguished by their philosophical underpinnings, and can be divided into classical, neo-classical, positivist, and antipositivist schools.

As described earlier, the *classical* school was the product of utilitarian philosophies. However, the assumption that human behaviour is always freely willed and rational was questioned by *neo-classicists*, who saw a need to consider individual circumstances surrounding a crime. The neo-classical revision has remained the basis for criminal justice practice throughout this century, but, in contrast, criminology has been dominated by *positivism*.

Positivism is the view that the human sciences should follow the methods of the natural sciences, and be concerned with positive "facts" rather than metaphysical issues. As in psychology, its application in criminology rests on the premise that human behaviour is determined and subject to natural laws. Positivist criminology began with the work of nineteenth century statisticians, but assumed an initially biological emphasis in the work of the Italian physician and anthropologist, Lombroso. Lombroso's *Criminal Man* first appeared in 1876, and developed the notion that criminal behaviour was the result of congenital impulses, the most prevalent type of offender being the "born criminal". Such an individual was biologically primitive, and an "atavistic" remnant of early human ancestry. He was said to show "stigmata" of primitive development, such as receding forehead, prominent eyebrows and jawbone, and physical asymmetries, as well as psychological stigmata in the form of insensitivity to pain, lack of moral sense, and reckless hedonism. Although Lombroso later suggested that only a minority were "born criminals", he identified a category of "criminaloids", whose deviance resulted from environmental pressures on a "weak nature".

Positivists objected to the classical doctrine of free will and responsibility, arguing that the use of proportionate punishment did not protect society from dangerous criminals because it failed to address the causes of crime. They proposed a scientific focus on the individual offender, rather than the criminal act, since criminals were essentially pathological characters. Criminality as the tendency to commit crimes was the target of attention. The early positivists suggested that penal policy should be directed towards changing or incapacitating the offender rather than punishing specific acts, and Lombroso advocated indeterminate sentences. Born criminals were not amenable to change, but others might be reformed, and identification of these and of criminals who were dangerous required methods of classification and treatment. This accorded status to the "experts" who could carry out these activities.

Criminology developed prior to the First World War as a result of an alliance of positivists with social statisticians and psychiatrists. Garland (1985) notes that a crisis in penal policy in Britain at the time made politicians receptive to the potential of a scientific approach to crime. While some positivists favoured environmental determinism, Lombroso's focus on individual abnormality rather than social conditions was more acceptable to the establishment. Although criminology had no institutional base in Britain until the creation of the first university chair and the Home Office Research Unit in the 1950s, its development was largely due to psychiatrists and psychologists. In contrast, its growth in the United States was dominated by positivist sociologists, perhaps because of greater readiness in American culture to blame the social order (Binder, 1988). One consequence of this is a marked ethnocentrism in much of the criminological literature, to the extent that crime sometimes appears to be an invention of American society!

Positivism in philosophy and social science came under attack in the 1950s. Logical positivism failed to provide adequate criteria for the development of science because it did not take account of the cognitive activities of the scientist or the social influences on scientific theories (Brown, 1977). It was challenged within psychology (Heather, 1976), and in criminology, criticisms came from humanistic sociologists (Matza, 1964), conflict theorists (Quinney, 1974), and radical criminologists (Taylor et al., 1973). These critiques portray positivism as dehumanising, as encouraging unjust penal policies in the guise of rehabilitation, and as aligned with an inequitable social system. Specifically, the main targets are determinism, individualisation, correctionalism, and the treatment of deviance as irrational. It is argued that in assuming determinism, positivism treats people as passive, denying them the power of choice and creativity. It also treats individuals and social groups as atomistically discrete entities, ignoring processes of mutual interaction. In focusing on the individual offender, it uncritically accepts the *status quo* in society, and assumes a moral consensus from which the criminal has deviated. Similarly, in treating the deviance of individuals and families as pathology, it implies that the law provides basic criteria of normality, while ignoring economic and political influences on the creation of law. Further, in searching for causal antecedents, positivism ignores the meaning of the deviant act, which may be rational problem-solving from the offender's viewpoint.

The alternative proposed by radical criminologists is a politically oriented criminology which seeks social change in a socialist direction. It adopts a "soft determinism", seeing deviance as the outcome of conscious choice against the background of the changing economic and political demands of advanced industrial society. The focus for criminology is the social context of the criminal act, how others react to it, and how the deviant reacts to rejection, and how political and historical factors shape the dialectical exchange between individual and society. No explicit recommendations are made about how the criminal justice system should deal with crime prior to the coming of the equitable society.

Radical criminology has been criticised by sociologists, including some sympathetic to its political stance (Schichor, 1980, Colvin and Pauly, 1983). It is seen to overemphasise the political nature of crime by "pathologising" society, while adopting a romantic notion of criminals, and assuming unconstrained freedom on the part of those with power and authority. It also neglects empirical research in favour of ideological treatises, and its simplistic analyses of the relations between crime, criminal justice, and capitalism, are not supported by differences in the distribution of crime between capitalist societies. Moreover, it rests on premises which make it subjective and unfalsifiable as a theory.

Young (1986) acknowledges the lack of impact of radical criminology, attributing this to a takeover by "left idealism", which simply inverts positivism and neglects both crime and criminals. He argues the need for a new "radical realist criminology", which "takes crime seriously" and recognises its impact on the vulnerable. This more pragmatic *left realism* (Young and Matthews, 1992) retains the political objectives and basic assumptions about crime of the earlier radical project, and proposes no new theoretical perspective. However, it seeks an accommodation with more traditional sociological theories of crime, while maintaining that these are "partial" theories, and that crime must be seen in terms of an interaction between offender, victim, the state, and the public. It also argues that criminological theory should be more integrated with practical interventions in law and order issues, giving particular priority to crime prevention, the democratisation of the criminal justice system, and the effects of crime on victims. However, it remains hostile to liberal reform and individualism, and forecloses on anything but a sociological level of analysis.

In addition to the radical critique of traditional criminology, reactions against positivism have followed several trends. One is a revival of classicism and an interest in rational decision-making and deterrence (Cornish and Clarke, 1986), while another is the adoption of the "justice" model (Von Hirsch, 1976). More liberal approaches are seen in attempts to minimise criminal justice intervention through decriminalisation of victimless offences, and diversion of young offenders to community oriented programmes (Tutt, 1984). Positivism, however, remains the philosophy of mainstream criminology, as well as psychology. Gottfredson and Hirschi (1987) re-examine the criticisms of positivism, and suggest that the alignment with particular theories, penal policies, or political ideologies was a consequence of zeal on the part of early positivists, but that none of these is entailed by commitment to positivism. They define this as "the scientific approach to crime where science is characterised by methods, techniques, or rules of procedure rather than by substantive theory or perspective", and see no incompatibility between positivism and classical theories of choice. The adequacy of positivism as a methodological prescription, however, remains questionable. This is discussed further below.

Acts, dispositions, and the explanation of criminal behaviour

It has been noted that both classicism and antipositivism are concerned with criminal *acts*, while positivism focuses on an individual's *tendency* to commit crimes. The distinction is critical in considering causes of "crime", but a source of much confusion. It is bound up with the "person–situation" debate in psychology, and since the causal role of persons and situations is an issue in criminology, this debate merits some attention.

At the centre of the debate has been the explanatory utility of the notion of personality *traits*, and indeed of the concept of personality itself. The meaning of the term "personality" has always been clouded by its everyday use as a summary of qualities people *have* which make them distinctive. A person may be said to have (or be) an "interesting" or "antisocial" personality. Personality in this context is simply an evaluative abstraction, but it is often reified and treated as some mystical entity which exists beyond social behaviour, emotions, cognitive processes, or whatever. Personality theorists focus on aspects of psychological functioning thought to determine variation between people, and offer a confusing array of definitions of "personality". However, as Hall and Lindzey (1970) note, such definitions are dictated by theory, and "...it is impossible to define personality without coming to agreement concerning the theoretical frame of reference within which personality will be viewed". Strictly, then, there is no such "thing" as personality, and it is more appropriately viewed as an area of inquiry. The area is broadly the study of behavioural regularities which distinguish and differentiate between individuals (i.e. dispositions or traits), and the processes and structures which a theory postulates as responsible for those regularities.

Mischel (1968) concluded that the empirical data did not justify conceptualising personality in terms of "broad response dispositions". Behaviourists took this as support for the situational control of behaviour, although the more common view is that behaviour depends on person–situation interactions. Mischel has subsequently modified his position (Mischel, 1984), and the controversy has subsided in the wake of interactionism, but many psychologists remain wary of trait concepts. However, questions of their utility are as much conceptual as empirical (Alston, 1975; Levy, 1983).

Whether behaviour is a function of the person or the situation depends on what is meant by *behaviour*. Although this is the most frequently used term in the psychological lexicon, it is the least frequently defined, and it is often used to mean both an *act* and a *tendency*. Consider the statements: (1) A hit B at school; and (2) A is aggressive. Both refer to "behaviour", but (1) describes a specific act, while (2) denotes a tendency or *disposition* to repeat aggressive acts. The claim that behaviour is a function of the situation usually refers to specific acts. However, a specific act or occurrence must be (at least) a function of the situation, because it depends on environmental opportunities and conditions: A could not have hit B without B's presence in that particular context. It is therefore tautologous to say that behaviour is "situationally specific", because what identifies a specific act is the situational context in which it occurs.

On the other hand, if "behaviour" means a tendency, it is clearly a property of the person; it is something he or she carries around with them, which is the product of their prior history. Terms such as "sociable" or "aggressive" have the same status as "agoraphobic" or "pedophilic". All describe tendencies or capacities residing in the person, which are manifest only under relevant conditions. Certain situations determine whether the person acts on that tendency, but the person possesses the tendency, regardless of whether it is performed. In this respect, the "person–situation" debate has been conducted at cross-purposes between experimenters concerned with responses to specific situations, and clinicians and trait theorists interested in lifestyles.

Acts and tendencies therefore call for different kinds of explanation. A specific act is a function of the situation *and* the person. The situation is necessary to provide the conditions and opportunities for action, but only the person has the power to produce that action. However, when a person acts on some tendency, the situation is merely the occasion for its expression, not the cause. To take an analogy, water realises the disposition of salt to dissolve in water, but the disposition derives from the chemical properties of salt, not the contact with water.

However, specific acts are of psychological interest only as exemplars of some more general class of behaviour, since science is not concerned with unique and unrepeatable occurrences. In the individual case, a specific act is usually of interest only insofar as the person has a tendency to repeat it. If a "situational analysis" reveals that the reason A hit B at school was to defend himself from B's unjustified assault, and A is not in the habit of hitting people, A's behaviour is not of further concern. If, on the other hand, this is the umpteenth time A has hit someone at school, then we must enquire why A has this aggressive tendency. Behaviourists object that if this "behaviour" is confined to school, it is a "specific response", not a trait. But the focus is on a disposition. It may be a narrower disposition than that usually described by trait terms, but, as Alston (1975) notes, if the only objection to traits is their breadth, it is a simple matter to narrow them. This is precisely the interactionist solution. Thus, rather than describing people as "aggressive", it may be more useful to distinguish the kind of response shown in particular situations, such as "verbally aggressive when criticised". This is nonetheless still trait description. There is, then, nothing problematic about traits as dispositions, since dispositional terms are indispensable to all law-like statements.

A further issue is their predictive utility. Traits are weak predictors of specific acts, and the typical validity coefficient is a correlation (r) of 0.30. This is usually taken to mean that variation in the trait accounts for 9% (i.e. r^2) of the predicted behaviour. However, according to Ozer (1985), it means that a common variable accounts for 30% (i.e. r) of the variance in the trait measure and the criterion, hardly a trivial amount. Nevertheless, traits summarise *average* and likely behaviour, and cannot reasonably be expected to predict single acts, unless other conditions are known (Ajzen, 1987). When measures of generalised traits are related to relevant behaviours averaged over settings, validity coefficients well above the 0.30 level are obtained (Hogan, Desoto and Solano, 1977; Kenrick and Funder, 1988). Traits, then, predict aggregated and not specific behaviours, and provide a useful first step in describing a person's behavioural repertoire.

Since traits refer to *capacities*, and not invariant behaviour, they are not sufficient to account for a particular act, which requires reference to a person's beliefs or expectancies relevant to the situation. This is the thrust of Mischel's critique. However, if there is consistency of behaviour across situations in the average, this must be explained by reference to generalised tendencies.

Personality theorists increasingly appeal to cognitive–motivational variables to account for these (Olweus, 1979; Epstein and O'Brien, 1985; Cantor, 1990).

Theories of criminal behaviour vary in whether they focus on *crime*, as the aggregate of criminal activities, *crimes*, as specific criminal acts or events, or *criminality* as a disposition to engage in such acts (Hirschi and Gottfredson, 1988; Gottfredson and Hirschi, 1990). Most psychological theories of "crime" attempt to account for criminality, or extended involvement in criminal activity, rather than criminal acts. This is exemplified in the work of Eysenck (1977), who sees criminality as "...a continuous trait of the same kind as intelligence, or height or weight". Those who repeat criminal acts are most likely to be extreme with respect to such a trait, and the concern is with the prior causes of the individual's antisocial disposition. Possession of the trait to a pronounced degree constitutes a necessary, and for some theorists a sufficient, cause of criminal acts, but acts themselves, and the context in which they occur, receive little attention. The emphasis is thus on *distal* causal factors. This kind of explanation has been described as "historical" or "genetic" (Burt, 1925; Sutherland and Cressey, 1970).

Neo-classicists and antipositivists, on the other hand, are concerned with criminal acts, and the focus is on *proximal* factors, i.e. the more immediate circumstances surrounding the commission of a crime. Sutherland and Cressey (1970) note that this focus may be "mechanistic", "situational", or "dynamic". These distinctions parallel the concepts of "person", "situation", and "person–situation interaction", and those who focus on criminal acts typically object to a "dispositional" approach to crime and a concern with distal factors, such as biological makeup or early family environment (Gibbons, 1971; Hough, Clarke and Mayhew, 1980; Haney, 1983; Tutt, 1984). Gibbons (1971), for example, suggests that some criminal acts are little more than a response to provocations and attractions in the immediate environment.

It should be apparent from the foregoing discussion, however, that to contrast "situations" and "dispositions", or proximal and distal factors as *causes* of "crime" is a false dichotomy. Clearly, early family experience cannot itself explain why an adult commits a specific criminal act. Equally clearly, some people have strong criminal dispositions, which can only be explained by prior history, not the immediate situation. Nor is the manifestation of this disposition in a specific act "caused" by the situation, since the act requires an actor with the capacity to act and to find certain situations "provoking" or "attractive". As Sutherland and Cressey (1970) note, proximal factors are not separable from the prior life experiences of the criminal, since "... the situation is defined by the person in terms of the inclinations and abilities he has acquired".

It is similarly a false dichotomy to assert that "criminogenic social conditions" *rather than* "dispositional variables" explain criminality (Haney, 1983). Social conditions are among the factors which account for the dispositions a person has, but do not in themselves account for criminal acts, since people respond differently to the same conditions. This is not to deny the relevance of social conditions or circumstances to the explanation of criminal behaviour, but as will be discussed shortly, we need to be clear about the meaning of "explanation.

The focus of explanation

As well as disagreeing about whether to focus on offences or offenders, criminologists also differ over the kinds of cause to seek. Sarbin (1979) draws an old philosophical distinction between original or *efficient causes*, and effective or *formal causes*. Efficient causes are the antecedents of criminal acts, which are in principle no different from those of any form of behavioural variation between people. Formal causes relate to the conditions by which an act or person becomes *classified* as criminal. These are of particular interest to radical criminology, which sees the criminal law as the formal cause of crime. Walker (1987) regards this as a "medieval way of talking", and the implication that people would stop killing or stealing if these ceased to be crimes is clearly absurd. Nevertheless, the distinction directs attention to the social organisations and decision-making processes which determine whether or not lawbreakers become involved in the criminal justice system. Criminal justice decision-making has recently been of interest to social psychologists (Konecni and Ebbesen, 1982), and receives some attention in Chapter 2. However, the efficient causes of criminal behaviour are the main concern of this book.

A problem facing early positivists who examined the background characteristics of criminals was the multiplicity of antecedents which emerged. Burt (1925), for example, detected more than 170 characteristics in the family, personality, and social background of delinquents. He concluded that delinquent behaviour is multiply determined, and that a single cause was unlikely to be found. Criminogenic influences thus vary from one offender to another, the excess of such influences or their combination being the decisive factor. This is consistent with the commonsense notion that the same event, such as a traffic collision, can result from several different circumstances. It has, however, led to protracted debate about the relative merits of "multiple factor" versus single theory approaches to the explanation of crime. The former is illustrated by the Cambridge Study on Delinquent Development (hereafter referred to as "the Cambridge study"), which has identified a number of personal and social correlates of delinquency from a long-term follow-up of a sample of London boys, and which began as an atheoretical (or multi-theoretical) search for predictors (West, 1982; Farrington and West, 1990). Such an approach risks an unrestricted eclecticism, and underestimates the influence of theory on observation.

The alternative is a single theory which can accommodate several factors or variables. For example, Trasler (1978) proposes that the common feature of crimes is a failure to inhibit proscribed action, and that the focus should be on the psychological processes involved, and the biological and social factors influencing them. Crime, however, includes such disparate behavioural phenomena that the possibility of a single kind of explanation encompassing all crimes seems remote. One solution is to reduce the heterogeneity of criminal behaviour by dividing offenders or offences into types or subgroups, and many investigators have followed this strategy (Chapter 3). Gottfredson and Hirschi (1990) criticise this approach on the grounds that crimes constitute a conceptual unity, and are susceptible to a single general explanation. However, events comprising a conceptual unity at one level of abstraction may nevertheless fall into distinguishable classes at another, and as Walker (1987) notes, the search for a unifying theory of crime is equivalent to looking for a single theory of disease.

Free will and determinism

As well as being an issue between schools of criminology, the question of free will versus determinism is also commonly identified as a source of tension between law and psychology. The law adopts the classicist view that people are free agents who can be held morally, and hence criminally responsible, while psychology as a positivist discipline assumes determinism, which in its extreme form negates the notion that people are blameworthy. Blackman, Müller and Chapman (1984) see this as a "basic paradigm clash", and assert that "...a deterministic analysis is, of course, made more plausible by increasing empirical support for its general position". This view is gratuitous, since the issue is a metaphysical one which is not susceptible to empirical resolution, nor has it proved tractable in the extensive philosophical debate.

Neither free will nor determinism has a consistently agreed meaning, but the main theoretical positions are hard determinism, soft determinism, and libertarianism (Sappington, 1990). Hard determinism holds that human behaviour is completely determined by factors outside the conscious person, and choice is irrelevant. This is the position of classical psychoanalysis and radical behaviourism. It equates determinism with predictability, and assumes that knowledge of the present should allow us to predict future outcomes. But there is no evidence in psychology, nor even in the physical sciences, that complete predictability is likely to be universally attainable.

A further difficulty with the assumption that all behaviour has an external cause is that it would seem to eliminate rational deliberation. Scientists who espouse determinism cannot claim exemption from determination of their own actions as scientists. Thus, neither the experiments they carry out nor the conclusions drawn from them could be rationally chosen. Some, however, argue that rationality is consistent with determinism because the available options are not themselves chosen (Norrie, 1986).

The latter argument is consistent with soft determinism, which views freedom and determinism as compatible. Thus, people make choices, but these choices are always constrained. Despite the association of determinism with positivism, many positivists have accommodated this position, which is now uncontroversial in psychology. Garland (1985) notes that some early criminological positivists advocated the view that free will is an illusion, but it is nevertheless one which motivates human action, a view taken by some psychologists more recently. This allowed the notion of responsibility to be retained, and made positivism acceptable to neo-classicists in England.

The libertarian view goes further, and while not seeing behaviour as wholly unconstrained, argues that human choices are not entirely predictable. Free does not mean uncaused, since this would imply chance, and those who argue for freedom of choice usually imply a special kind of cause which would allow a person the possibility of having chosen a course of action other than that actually undertaken. The special cause is to be found in the capacity of autonomous agents to make a purposeful, intentional choice. Glaser (1977), for example, proposes that "Thought always has much determination by the input of learning from experience...but it also has, at times, some free creativity in its output." Bandura (1986) also views freedom as "the exercise of self-influence", which operates deterministically on behaviour, and which determines personal freedom to avail oneself of many options. This comes about through the causal efficacy of thought. People are thus partial authors of their situations.

Sappington (1990) sees recent libertarian theories in psychology as an attempt to put the notion of free will on a scientific footing. Given that people have the capacity to generate novel choices, and can choose among these for goals to guide their behaviour, knowledge of them should facilitate the scientific task of prediction. Whether human choice is ever wholly autonomous, or whether the traditional criterion of "could have chosen otherwise" can ever be tested, remain significant problems for the libertarian view, but the gap between psychology and law may be less than behaviourists have maintained.

PHILOSOPHY OF SCIENCE AND THE EXPLANATION OF CRIME

Causal explanation and scientific method

There is little reason to believe that singular types of crime have singular antecedents, or that singular causes uniformly lead to singular forms of criminal conduct. However, the reason this is problematic is the positivist concern with identifying the causal antecedents of which criminal acts are an effect. In fact, within positivism, *cause* and *explanation* do not have the meanings commonly attributed to them. To understand the limits of positivism, and the alternative positions, the use of these terms needs to be examined.

As an attempt to apply the methods of natural science to human behaviour, positivism adopts "the standard view of science" (Manicas and Secord, 1983). The premise of determinism is that all events have an antecedent cause. Science deals with observable facts, and theoretical terms must be translated into observables by means of operational definitions. Its task is to discover regularities between antecedent causes and their consequential effects, leading to the specification of universal laws. The acid test of a law (or theory) is its ability to predict future events from knowledge of the causal antecedents.

Explanation is deduction from laws. If a phenomenon belongs to a particular class of events, it is explained by invoking the causal events specified by the law as applicable to all members of that class.

The concept of cause is not widely used in modern science, but Harré (1985) distinguishes two basic meanings. The first equates cause with *generation*. A cause in this sense is a power or capacity to generate an effect. The effect is produced because of the generative mechanism which makes it possible. Thus, gunpowder explodes because of its chemical structure. The application of a detonator simply *enables* the capacity to be realised. The effect is hence a *natural necessity*. In the second use, cause is equated with temporal *succession*. A cause is simply an event which precedes the effect in time, and is purely a statistical relation. This use derives from Hume, who maintained that entities or objects do not have a specific nature we can detect. What we detect are "constant conjunctions of sense impression". Any attribution of a reason for the connection is an inference deriving from our assumption that the future resembles the past. Cause in the sense of generation is thus merely a *logical necessity*, and hence an illusion.

Hume's concept of cause is the basis of empiricism, and is central to positivism. To ask "why" the conjunction occurs is a metaphysical, and hence inappropriate question. It will be noted that explanation in this context does not refer to generative mechanisms. Further, explanation is symmetrical with prediction, the only difference being that explanation refers back from effect to antecedent, while prediction refers to future effects from a given cause.

Positivism has been particularly influential in psychology, being adopted most unequivocally in radical behaviourism. While Skinner prefers to substitute "functional relation" between dependent and independent variables for "cause and effect connection", the alternative terms "merely assert that different events tend to occur together in a certain order" (Skinner, 1953). Prediction is achieved by analysing these relations, and control of behaviour by manipulating the causes. As reaffirmed by Zurriff (1985), behaviourism is a psychological version of positivism, the ability to predict and control behaviour being the pragmatic test of its validity.

Within the philosophy of science, objections to positivism come from several sources, which can be divided into *anti-naturalism* and *realism* (Bhaskar, 1979; Manicas, 1987). The radical criminologist critique of positivism is based on the espousal of an agency conception of human behaviour. The concern here is with the utility of the deductivist aspect of positivism for explaining crimes as behavioural events. This is a complex issue, but some of the recent views advanced in philosophy, psychology, and criminology will be briefly indicated.

Anti-naturalism

The anti-naturalists include neo-Wittgensteinian philosophers of science (see Keat, 1971), who argue that human behaviour is not amenable to analysis by the methods of the natural sciences. A particular objection of this group is to the Humean concept of causality as applied to human behaviour. They argue that rather than being *law-governed*, human action is *rule-following*. Regularities in behaviour derive from intentional agency, which reflects the capacity of humans to self-consciously monitor their behaviour in accordance with rules. Some in this group accept that the positivist version of science is appropriate for the physical sciences, but reject the assumption that observations are theory-neutral on the psychological grounds that "facts" as cognised are dictated by theory, and gain their meaning only through the prior theoretical conceptions of the observer (Hanson, 1958). This rejects the behaviourist distinction between what is "observable" and what is not, because we interpret behaviour before we describe it. Associated with anti-naturalism is the hermeneutic tradition, which sees the concern of social science as interpretation of the social meanings of action through understanding, or *verstehen*.

The notion that the goal of social science is understanding, rather than explanation by laws, derives from the earliest challenges to positivism, and was imported into psychology by Allport in the form of the distinction between *nomothetic* and *idiographic* approaches to the study of personality. This has been understood as a contrast between explaining behaviour by reference to general laws applicable to all people and understanding the unique attributes of an individual. Holt (1962) dismissed this as a false dichotomy, arguing that a unique description would call for a unique vocabulary of neologisms, and he considered neither term to be useful. The distinction has nonetheless persisted. Marceil (1977) suggests that Allport confounded *theory* (individuals have unique attributes) with *method* (study individuals rather than groups), and that while Allport intended a theoretical use of the term idiographic, it is often used ambiguously to refer to the study of the single case. However, general law-like statements in psychology are intended to apply to *particular* relevant instances, and single case analyses may still be nomothetic, as is, for example, *functional analysis* in clinical psychology (Owens and Ashcroft, 1982).

An anti-naturalist analysis of explanation is presented by Walker (1987). He rejects the positivist assumption of the symmetrical relation of explanation and prediction, pointing to explanations which do not entail prediction, such as an engineer's account of the collapse of a bridge. He distinguishes *likelihood* explanations, the general laws or probability statements of science, from *possibility* explanations. The latter are essentially historical narratives, which take particular account of reasons, but in which each event in a sequence may be explicable in terms of different laws or likelihood explanations. Likelihood explanations are appropriate for accounts of regularities, but not for irregular or unexpected events, such as a crime. For Walker, the generalisations of social science are typically low-level correlations, which can rarely specify the *necessary* conditions for a criminal event, still less the *sufficient* conditions. Possibility explanations are therefore appropriate for the social sciences, and especially criminology.

Walker considers it unreasonable to expect the explanation of crime to be "scientific". Bottomley (1979) also takes the view that what is most commonly required in criminology is *retrospective* explanation for a particular case or group of cases which renders them *intelligible* "with an intelligibility that is compatible with the subjective meaning of the behaviour for the actors involved". This entails an analysis of motives and reasons, and such explanations need not depend on empirical generalisations. This approach focuses on the criminal event, and accepts the unpredictability of much criminal behaviour.

Bottomley's argument is not dissimilar to that of some clinicians. T. Mischel (1964), for example, argued that Kelly's personal construct theory is consistent with the metaphor of rule-following, and that to understand a patient's constructs is to view action from the patient's perspective. This explains behaviour, while permitting prediction, but the general laws or knowledge of statistical regularities available to the clinician cannot provide this explanation or prediction, because they do not reflect the patient's *own* rules.

Both Bottomley and Mischel, then, see little use for general laws in accounting for human action. However, there is no obvious reason why understanding of an act should exclude explanation by reference to general principles. Moreover, while an offender's action may derive from idiosyncratic personal rules, it seems unlikely that it will be wholly immune to explanation in terms of general theories about how humans acquire and utilise rules, and how these undergo change. Such theories can be likelihood explanations without taking positivist form, and this view is developed in critical (or transcendental) realist philosophy.

Critical realism

The realist view of science is elaborated by Bhaskar (1979), and several writers explore its implications for psychology (Locke, 1972; Wetherick, 1979; Manicas and Secord 1983; Secord, 1983; Manicas, 1987). It accepts the anti-naturalist position regarding the primacy of agency accounts of human behaviour, but holds that the positivist view of science is incorrect. The physical and social sciences have different objects of enquiry, but they share common methodological principles. The main target of criticism is the Humean account of cause, and its implications for causal explanation.

Realism starts with the argument that the world is made up of real, though often non-observable entities, which achieve material effects because they possess *causal powers* to generate these effects. The concern of science is to construct and empirically confirm theoretical models of these causal properties. The causal antecedents of positivist "laws" are simply the activating or enabling conditions which permit the realisation of an entity's powers. They explain only as integral parts of a causal process. Causal explanation thus consists of answering the question "why?", and not merely "how?". However, explanation is not the same as prediction, since causal powers exist as capacities or tendencies which are only realised in the presence of enabling conditions. As the world outside the laboratory is an *open system*, these cannot be reliably predicted. Explanation, rather than prediction and control, is thus the goal of science, and explanatory power rather than falsifiability is the appropriate test of a theory's utility.

The causal powers which enable humans to act on the world reside in consciousness and the capacity to form models of the world, to reason, and to think. Reasons in the form of motives, intentions, and beliefs, are causes in a generative, non-Humean sense, and their analysis requires attention to ordinary language accounts which people offer in explanation of their behaviour. While the generative mechanisms of behaviour may be sought at physiological or sociological levels, this does not entail either dualism or reductionism. Mind depends on brain, but is "...a real emergent power of matter whose autonomy, though real, is nevertheless circumscribed" (Bhaskar, 1979).

The realist strategy for theorising and research differs radically from that of positivism, and claims to offer a more accurate account of what scientists actually do. With regard to the explanation of crime, it has rather different implications from the approach of the anti-naturalists. First, understanding of action by reference to its subjective or symbolic meaning is insufficient because this does not identify the beliefs and motives which constitute the reason for action. It is hence not a causal explanation. Second, the distinction between nomothetic and idiographic is seen to be false. Psychology is a nomothetic science, but explanation of the individual's behaviour involves both the use of causal laws and an analysis of the individual's biography, personal characteristics, and subjective interpretations of the situation. As Secord (1983) points out, this implies different roles for the pure and applied psychologist. Laboratory experiments appropriately explain the capacities or causal powers of people in general, but only identify what people *can* do, not what they *will* do in the open world. Whether capacities are realised depends on the presence of enabling and constraining conditions, which include incapacities or liabilities. The task for applied psychologists is to identify the internal and external conditions relevant to the exercise of powers identified by experimental study. In the psychological study of crime, the realist analysis implies that the focus of explanation is the intentions, goals, and belief systems of offenders, the conditions under which they develop, and the personal and situational characteristics which activate them.

The realist view is in agreement with Bottomley's emphasis on understanding criminal events, and the unpredictability of much crime. However, it also demands a causal explanation in terms of the characteristics of criminal actors. Such an analysis differs from that of the positivist, which leads to a muddled conception of how criminal behaviour occurs, and which fails to clarify what is to be explained. To illustrate, Hirschi (1978) presents a positivist analysis of the concept of cause in explaining delinquency. He denies that cause is a *force*, seeing it simply as a "nonspurious correlate" of delinquency. The major causes of delinquency are factors such as sex, age, race, social class, or educational performance. However, somewhat inconsistently, he goes on to argue that it is arbitrary to distinguish "causes that *produce* an effect...and causes that *prevent* an effect" (italics added). He later states that the delinquent *act* is "...determined by all causes present at the moment it is committed", but adds that his preferred theories "...locate the immediate causes of delinquent acts in the desires of the actor and his evaluation of the situation" and that "...such causes provide reasons and motives...". Hirschi's concept of cause as correlate thus makes no distinctions between age, sex, and educational performance on the one hand, and desires and evaluations on the other. From the realist critique, it should be apparent that only desires and evaluations *produce* the act, since they are the reasons *and* the causes. Age, sex, or educational performance cannot produce the act, although they provide conditions which enable the person to have particular desires and beliefs.

The positivist confusion over causes and enabling conditions is particularly apparent in much of the prediction research in criminology (Chapter 12). Factors such as age or sex, in fact, merely predict the *tendency* to commit delinquent acts. It requires a theory of what it means to be young, male, black, working class, and so forth, to explain how such a tendency develops, but we still need to identify the conditions which enable it to be realised as a delinquent act. This tendency has been the focus of positivist accounts of crime for over a century, but has not been clearly differentiated from delinquent acts themselves. However, Hirschi and Gottfredson (1988) recently state that: "...we must distinguish between two important concepts, crime, an event, and criminality, a characteristic of persons...the distinction...reminds us that criminality need not find expression in crime, and that crimes require more than criminals". Their theory remains positivistic, but this concept of criminality has something of the realist notion of a capacity (or liability) which may or may not be exercised in the open world.

This brief incursion into current philosophy of science has aimed to clarify what kind of theory is most likely to permit an adequate explanation of crime. Although philosophy cannot provide the substance of scientific theories, it provides the methodological rules for determining what constitutes science or knowledge. As will be seen, most psychological theories of criminal conduct have so far been positivistic, but cognitive and social learning theorists are increasingly concerned with the capacities which determine human agency (Trower, 1984; Bandura, 1986). Toch (1987) suggests that the analysis of crime should entail individual case studies in which motives and meanings enter into explanations of the individual's behaviour which are informed by more general principles from social learning theory and psychoanalysis. While he describes this as "supplementing positivism", such an approach is a move away from mechanistic determinism.

PSYCHOLOGY AND CRIMINOLOGY

Psychology and psychiatry have traditionally been concerned with which individuals become criminal and why, and sociology with which segments of the population. It might therefore appear that explanations of crime require an academic division of labour between these disciplines. However, within criminology, the three disciplines have been divided by sapiential power struggles and mutual distrust. This antipathy is seen, for example, in the description of clinical approaches to offenders as "correctionalism", and in the contemptuous dismissal of psychological perspectives on delinquency as "the inheritance of the meek and of marginal relevance to the development of either criminology or social policy" (Parker and Giller, 1981). In contrast, Lilly, Cullen and Ball (1989) and Young and Matthews (1992) castigate psychological approaches as *too* relevant to policies on the questionable grounds that attempts to understand individual offenders encourage conservative ideologies and punitive practices, and deny that crime has anything to do with society. Such antagonism is misguided. It represents a narrow disciplinary imperialism which denies the legitimacy of a psychological level of analysis, but neither psychology nor sociology can provide autonomous accounts of criminal behaviour.

These divisions go back to the origins of the three disciplines. Psychiatry emerged from the "alienism" or "psychological medicine" of the mid-nineteenth century, and had established itself as a profession in Europe and America by the time that psychology and sociology appeared as distinct academic disciplines at the turn of the century. Not only did psychiatry provide many basic concepts for the newly developing criminology, it also aspired to provide evidence on the mental state of all accused persons coming before the courts (Garland, 1985). Psychology in Britain, however, had little interest in crime, being mainly concerned to establish itself as an experimental science independent of philosophy. Hearnshaw (1964) traces the first psychological approach to delinquency in Britain to a book published in 1853 by Mary Carpenter, wife of a prominent physiologist, but until the influential work of Burt (1925), most of the early psychological research on criminals was carried out by prison physicians. However, although reflecting an outgrowth of psychoanalysis rather than academic psychology, psychologists were involved in setting up the Institute for the Study and Treatment of Delinquency in 1931, and subsequently the Psychopathic Clinic (later the Portman Clinic; Glover, 1960), and the early development of criminology in Britain was influenced by both psychology and psychiatry to an extent that Wootton (1959) described as "lopsided".

In the United States, the early influences on criminology were also psychological and psychiatric, as seen in interests in the adjustment of juvenile delinquents (Hall, 1904), intelligence and crime (Goddard, 1914), and psychodynamic theory (Healy and Bronner, 1936). These were eclipsed with the development of sociological approaches at the University of Chicago, and from about 1930, American criminology became dominated by sociology. Wheeler (1962) noted that this was due partly to psychiatry's disinterest in other academic disciplines, and partly to the concern of sociology to establish its own academic respectability and to avoid reduction to psychology. A significant consequence was the development within sociology of its own brand of social psychology, which aimed at the explanation of individual criminal conduct, while disguising its similarity to psychological and psychiatric explanations.

It is sometimes maintained that the distinctive contributions of these disciplines lie in different *units of analysis*. Blau (1981), for example, suggests that the study of *crime rates* is the province of sociologists who examine comparative rates and distributions of offences in relation to social structures, such as economic or ecological factors. The study of *individual criminals* is the focus of psychologists, who relate criminal behaviour to the personal attributes, histories, or immediate situations of offenders. However, this confuses units of analysis with *explanatory factors* (Bottomley, 1979). Aggregate rates of offending cannot be divorced from the characteristics of individuals responsible for them. A correlation of crime rate with levels of poverty or slum housing, for example, does not mean that poverty and housing conditions directly cause criminal behaviour, since the association may be mediated by individual characteristics correlated with these conditions. It is also an "ecological fallacy" to assume that aggregate level correlations reflect individual level correlates (Robinson, 1950). Similarly a correlation between personal characteristics and offending may result from unmeasured macro-social phenomena. Sociological and psychological mechanisms may therefore enter into both crime rates and the actions of individual criminals. It is the *kind* of explanatory factor, i.e. societal structures or properties of individuals, which provides the basis for a division of labour.

In practice, the approaches of these disciplines to crime overlap, since sociologists also study attributes of individuals, such as attitudes and individual behaviour in the form of self-reported delinquency. There is also a middle ground of interest in the form of social psychology or micro-sociology. Secord (1986) distinguishes three forms of social psychology in sociology: (1) *psychological sociology*, which relates macro-social phenomena to individual attributes, such as social roles; (2) *symbolic interactionism*, which focuses on the meanings imposed on interactions by the social situation, and which sees meaning as a social rather than an individual product, and (3) *ethnomethodology*, which also focuses on how actors interpret situations, but which emphasises the uniqueness of contextually-defined meanings. The latter two emphasise subjective methods of observation, and "...the situated, culture-bound, language-impregnated, historical nature of human action". All of these have played a significant part in the sociology of deviance, but until recently, psychological approaches to crime drew mainly on psychodynamic theory or on behavioural models derived from animal learning rather than social psychology.

However, despite attention to group processes, social psychology within psychology has emphasised objective experimentation, and retains the focus of the parent discipline on the individual. Implicitly, this endorses *methodological individualism*, i.e. the philosophical position that social phenomena can be accounted for by the dispositions, beliefs, resources, and interrelations of individuals. This implies that sociology is the study of groups deriving their characteristics from the individuals composing them, but this position is now rejected by many philosophers of science (Manicas, 1987). Representing collectivism, Bhaskar (1979) argues that society is not merely the creation of the people in it, because there are structures which pre-exist them. Society is an abstraction which is only present in human action, but action always expresses and utilises social forms, such as language, economic conditions, or class structure. Societal phenomena are thus real, and affect the individuals who contribute to them. On this view, sociology is not the study of group phenomena, but rather the study of how social structures provide the conditions for human action. The appropriate concern of psychology is with the cognitive and emotional properties people possess which enable them to relate to a social world which shapes those properties, but which is influenced by human agency.

This view of psychology is represented most clearly in the *reciprocal determinism* of social cognitive theory, which views humans as intentional agents who act on reasons and beliefs, and in which personal factors, behaviour, and environmental influences operate interactively as determinants of each other (Bandura, 1986). This contrasts with the unidirectional determinism of behaviourism, which treats behaviour as the *movement* of a passive body, rather than the *action* of an intentional agent to achieve a purpose (McGinn, 1979). Morris et al. (1987) argue that contemporary behaviourism assumes a person–environment interaction, but that applied behaviour analysts adopt a unidirectional environmental determinism for pragmatic reasons, because only the environment can be altered to affect behaviour. Nevertheless, in a thorough defence of behaviourism, Zurriff (1985) suggests that it cannot cope readily with the explanation of action, because an action language and a response language "categorise the world in different ways, and the two resulting systems are not easily related". This is a salutary judgement on the limits of behaviourism in accounting for human social behaviour, and correspondingly for understanding criminal conduct.

Psychological theories of crime remain predominantly individualistic. However, a psychological analysis of crime cannot avoid issues about the nature of human action and the relationship of the individual to society. For example, some theories explain delinquency in terms of social learning, but as Colvin and Pauly (1983) observe, the way in which behaviour is shaped by rewards and punishments is itself shaped by social structures which determine the patterns and availability of reinforcers to people in different social positions. Sociological and psychological theories of crime therefore provide incomplete accounts of the same phenomena.

Chapter 2

The Measurement and Distribution of Crime

INTRODUCTION

Statistical analyses of the distribution of offences have featured prominently in criminological research since the early nineteenth century. Like epidemiology in medicine, this research derives its impetus from a concern with control and prevention, and accords with sociological interest in the ecological and demographic correlates of crime. Epidemiology has generally been ignored by psychologists, partly because of the lower status of field studies relative to controlled experiments, but also because of its implicitly medical terms of reference (Cooper and Shepherd, 1973). However, such research complements the study of individual criminal behaviour, and psychological theories need to accommodate the known population characteristics and natural history of crime.

Until the 1950s, knowledge of crime drew largely on official data sources, but the existence of a "dark figure" of unrecorded crime and undetected criminals has long been known. Doubts about the validity of official statistics have led to wider use of alternative sources, including semi-official data, such as insurance company records, participant observation in delinquent groups, criminal biographies, and *in situ* observations of criminal activity, such as shoplifting. However, apart from official records, the most frequently used measures are self-reports of offending or of the experience of victimisation in community samples. This chapter examines the methods of identifying crimes and criminals, and what they reveal about the characteristics of offenders.

THE MEASUREMENT OF CRIME

For many purposes, crime is measured by counting criminal events or offenders, although it will become apparent that whether an event qualifies as a crime, or a person as a criminal, depends on complex decision processes. The *crime rate* is the aggregate number of crimes per unit of population, but this is the product of *prevalence*, the number of persons committing crimes at any one time, and frequency or *incidence*, the number of crimes committed per offender (Farrington, Ohlin and Wilson, 1986). Adoption of these epidemiological terms recognises that variations in crime rates between groups or over time may reflect changes in prevalence, incidence, or both.

Prevalence and incidence relate to a particular unit of time, and the temporal dimension is also reflected in the notion of *criminal careers*. This concept assumes that involvement in deviant behaviour entails entry into a social role which develops over time, and which like conventional occupational roles is governed by social systems and rules determining career adoption and progress. The more specific term *career criminal* implies an involvement in crime sufficiently intensive and extensive to constitute a way of life. Luckenbill and Best (1981) question the analogy with conventional occupational careers, since deviant careers may be short-lived, are not necessarily central to working life, and are not governed by accepted rules prescribing resources required, sequence of progression, or time of departure. However, from the criminal career perspective, different components of criminal activity, such as initial involvement, frequency, and termination, require different explanations (Blumstein, Cohen and Farrington, 1988).

Distinctions between types of crime, or types of offender, commonly rely on legal offence categories, although these may be grouped pragmatically, for example, in comparing property offences with those against persons. However, legal categories are no more than crude approximations to behavioural categories, and have only limited utility for psychological research. Systematic attempts to classify offences and offenders are described in Chapter 3.

Crimes are also distinguished in terms of *seriousness*. While this is often judged from the harm implied by a particular offence category, psychometric scaling of offence seriousness was initiated by Thurstone (1927), and developed by Sellin and Wolfgang (1964). The latter found that judges, police, and college students were able to rate the seriousness of offences using category or ratio scales, and agreed closely in their rankings, offences involving personal injury or material loss being judged more serious. Replications suggest substantial consistency in the ordering of offences across methods (Walker, 1978), social groups (Rossi et al., 1974), cultures (Normandeau, 1970), and time (Krus, Sherman and Krus, 1977), pointing to a normative consensus on offence severity, which transcends western society. This has implications for establishing the role of consensus as opposed to conflict in criminal law, and also for policies on sentencing and resource allocation within criminal justice agencies. However, judgements of crime seriousness vary with age and education, and consensus may have been overestimated as a result of artifacts of scale construction and measurement (Cullen et al., 1985). Studies of cognitive representations of aggressive acts also suggest that "seriousness" is not unidimensional, and that people distinguish acts by their justifiability, degree of provocation, or probability of occurrence, rather than by a simple continuum of severity (Forgas, 1986).

Official statistics

The most accessible information on crime rates comes from official statistics of crimes recorded by the police. However, before a crime is recorded, it must be known and reported, and the reporting of a crime is probably the most important decision made in the criminal justice system. Most nontraffic encounters between police patrolmen and juveniles in American cities are initiated by citizens (Black and Reiss, 1970; Lundman, Sykes, and Clark, 1978), and between 77% and 96% of recorded crimes in Britain come to light through reports from the public (Bottomley and Pease, 1986). However, not all offences reported are recorded by the police, and what ends up in the statistics also depends on the behaviour of the official agencies. Statistics are thus socially constructed, and reflect a filtering of complex events through a set of people with their own aims and preoccupations (Bottomley and Pease, 1986).

Criminal statistics are published annually by most western governments. In England and Wales, these are derived from monthly returns by police forces to the Home Office of "notifiable" (or indictable) offences recorded, under eight headings (Table 2.1). In the United States, similar data have been published since 1930 in the FBI *Uniform Crime Reports* (UCR). These divide offences into two parts, Part 1 covering the more serious, or index offences (Table 2.2). Differences between more and less "serious" crimes are somewhat arbitrary, and in Britain, notifiable offences include property crimes of which more than a third involve losses of less than £25. In America, however, larceny involving amounts of less than $50 is a Part 2 offence.

Table 2.1   Notifiable offences recorded by the police in England and Wales in 1988

Offence category	Offences (thousands)	Percentage of total	Rate per 100 000 population	Change in rate since 1979 (%)	Clear-up rate (%)
Violence against the person	158.2	4.3	315	+63.2	75
Sexual offences	26.5	0.7	53	+20.5	75
Robbery	31.4	0.8	63	+152.0	23
Burglary	817.8	22.0	1628	+47.2	29
Theft	1931.3	52.0	3844	+33.5	34
Fraud and forgery	133.9	3.6	266	+10.8	71
Criminal damage	593.9	16.0	1182	+81.3	24
Other	22.7	0.6	45	+150.0	96
Totals	3715.8	100.0	7396	+43.4	35

Source: This information is based on data which appears in *Criminal Statistics England and Wales 1988* (Home Office, 1989), and is adapted with the permission of the Controller of Her Majesty's Stationery Office, London.

Table 2.2   Index crimes recorded by the police in the United States in 1988

Offence category	Offences (thousands)	Percentage of total	Rate per 100 000 population	Change in rate since 1979 (%)	Clear-up rate (%)
Murder and nonnegligent manslaughter	20.9	0.2	8.4	−13.4	70
Forcible rape	92.5	0.7	38	+8.4	52
Robbery	543.0	3.9	221	+1.1	26
Aggravated assault	910.0	6.5	370	+29.4	57
Burglary	3218.1	23.1	1309	−13.4	14
Larceny-theft	7205.9	55.3	3135	+4.5	20
Motor vehicle theft	1432.9	10.3	583	+15.3	15
Totals	13923.1*	100.0	5664	+1.8	21

*Excludes arson. Source: United States Department of Justice, Federal Bureau of Investigation (1989), *Uniform Crime Reports 1988*, Washington, DC: US Printing Office.

During 1988, police in England and Wales recorded a total of 3 785 000 notifiable offences (Home Office, 1989a; this figure has subsequently risen to over five million). This represents a fall of 5% over 1987, but an increase of 43% since 1979, and a threefold increase over two decades. As can be seen from Table 2.1, property offences make up the bulk of the total, crimes against the person (violence, sex offences and robbery) comprising only 6%. It will also be noted that increases in offending are not uniform across categories. While robbery more than doubled in a decade, sexual offences increased by only a fifth. However, offence categories are not homogeneous. Within the theft category, theft from vehicles increased by 123% between 1979 and 1988, while thefts from shops rose by 6% during the same period. These gross figures, however, conceal wide variation across police forces.

Differences in crime definitions make comparisons across countries tenuous, but property crimes in the United States also make up more than three quarters of the total (Table 2.2). The rate of total serious crimes appears to be lower than in Britain, and increases over the decade from 1979 are notably smaller in the United States. Violent crimes, on the other hand, account for a higher proportion of the total, and the rates are substantially higher than those in Britain. For example, the 1988 rates for homicide and rape were respectively 1.2 and 5.7 per 100 000 in England and Wales, but 8.4 and 37.6 in the United States.

The tables also show the *clear-up rates*, which are the proportion of offences for which a suspect has been proceeded against. Overall, slightly more than a third of offences recorded in Britain was cleared-up in 1988, and although this represents an increase in absolute terms in recent years, the proportion of the total has been declining. This does not necessarily reflect a decline in police efficiency. The identification of a suspect depends more on what is reported to the police than on the detective work portrayed in fiction (Bottomley and Pease, 1986), and the higher clear-up rates for crimes against the person reflect the more ready identification of the offender by the victim in these instances.

Recorded crimes do not coincide with the number of individuals offending, since some offenders commit multiple offences, and some offences are committed by groups. Nevertheless, low clear-up rates suggest that *known offenders* represent only a minority of those committing crimes. In 1988, 527 000 people were cautioned or found guilty of indictable offences in England and Wales, 85% being male, and 47% under the age of 21 (Home Office, 1989a). Theft accounts for the largest single category (49%), while 13% were violent offenders, and 2% sexual offenders. However, a similar number was found guilty of nonindictable (summary) offences, while motoring offenders made up 40% of the total of 1 777 000 offenders. Although fewer motoring offenders have appeared in court since the introduction of fixed penalties in 1986, the situation has changed little since Wootton (1959) observed that "the typical criminal of today is the motorist".

The number of known serious offenders amounted to just over 1% of the population of England and Wales in 1988. However, from 1977 data on the proportion of offenders in each age group with a first conviction for a standard list offence (broadly similar to indictable offences), Farrington (1981) estimated that the *cumulative prevalence* of offenders in the population was 11.7% and 2.1% of males and females respectively up to age 17, 21.8% and 4.7% up to 21, and 43.6% and 14.7% over the lifespan. These may be overestimates, but they nevertheless indicate that a substantial proportion of the population is likely to be convicted of a crime during their lifetime. On the other hand, longitudinal studies suggest that only a minority of those convicted become repeated offenders. Wolfgang, Figlio and Sellin (1972) found that of 10 000 boys born in Philadelphia in 1945, 35% had been arrested for nontraffic offences by age 18, about a third being for index offences, but only 6% of the sample became recidivists. These accounted for 52% of all offences, and over 70% of all serious violent offences. A survey by the Home Office (1987) similarly found that nearly a third of a sample of English boys born in 1953 was convicted of a standard list offence by age 28, but only 6% for six or more offences, and these accounted for 70% of the convictions of the group. Very similar findings have been reported from Sweden by Stattin and Magnusson (1991).

Self-reported criminal behaviour

In self-report studies, individuals record their involvement in crime by means of anonymous questionnaires or interviews which enquire about the performance of particular acts during a specified period. Most research has focused on adolescents, and the majority typically describe engaging in illegal acts at some time, few of which have come to the attention of the police. For example, Williams and Gold (1972) found that 88% of a sample of 13 to 16 year old American adolescents admitted to one or more chargeable offences during the preceding three years, but only 9% had been caught by the police, and only 3% of delinquent acts had resulted in a police contact.

Such surveys reveal that few young males have *never* violated the law, and this is sometimes claimed to indicate that virtually everyone is a criminal. However, what is indicated is a continuum of involvement in crime, and prevalence varies with type of offence, being relatively low for more serious criminal acts. In the Cambridge study, 69% of boys admitted to breaking the windows of empty houses, but only 9% to breaking into a building to steal. Similarly, while a majority of boys report getting into fights, only a minority describe using weapons (West and Farrington, 1973; Hardt and Peterson-Hardt, 1977; Hindelang, Hirschi and Weis, 1981). Williams and Gold (1972), in fact, found that 60% of their sample had a zero score on a rating of offence seriousness.

Self-report measures clearly uncover many offences not known to the police, but some studies find that those achieving high scores are more likely to be apprehended, and that officially known delinquents achieve higher scores than nondelinquents. West and Farrington (1973) found that almost half of those with high self-report scores at age 16 already had an official conviction, compared with 11% of low scorers, and 44% of the remaining high scorers went on to acquire a conviction by the age of 21, in contrast to 15% of lower scorers. Overall, 70% of high scorers became official delinquents in the long run. Self-reported delinquency is not therefore independent of official delinquency, and correlations of about 0.5 have been obtained in several studies (Hindelang, Hirschi and Weis, 1981). On the other hand, a high correlation cannot be assumed. In one American study, only one of 23 youths reporting 20 or more index of fences over three years had an arrest for an index offence (Dunford and Elliott, 1984).

Self-report scales contain several sources of measurement error, and until recently there was little standardisation of content, number of items, or response format. Items merely sample the universe of potentially illegal behaviour, emphasising less serious acts, and summary measures typically have highly skewed distributions. Also, problems of recall are likely to attenuate reliability, although short-term retest reliabilities of 0.85 to 0.99 have been reported (Singh, 1979; Huizinga and Elliott, 1986).

Validity studies have utilised reports from informants, lie detectors, social desirability scales, and checks of self-reported police contacts with official records (Singh, 1979; Hindelang et al., 1981). While concurrent validity appears to be sufficiently high for some reliance to be placed on self-reported delinquency scales, their freedom from response sets remains to be established. Gibson (1975) suggested that they are strongly influenced by acquiescence, and Huizinga and Elliott (1986) think it probable that at least 20% of respondents conceal or forget their delinquencies, while as many again may exaggerate them. Validity may also be unequal across samples. Hindelang et al. (1981), for example, found that black adolescents were more likely than whites to under-report offences known to the police. As Huizinga and Elliott (1986) observe, the psychometric properties of self-report delinquency scales match those of measures commonly used in social psychology, but a measure of countable events must be judged more stringently than measures of attitude.

Self-reports have advantages over official measures for some purposes, and may be adequate for the domain of content tapped, but this is not the same as that of the official statistics (Hindelang, Hirschi and Weis, 1979). Thus, official measures tend to identify the worst offenders, self-reports the less serious. Nevertheless, the two probably diverge more on the overall rate of offending than on the prevalence of offenders.

Victimisation surveys

Crime surveys entail interviews with community samples concerning their experience of being victims of crimes during the preceding six or twelve months, and have been carried out at local and national level in several countries. The first nationwide survey in the United States in 1967 involved 10 000 households, and annual National Crime Surveys (NCS) of 132 000 American households have been conducted since 1972 (Block and Block, 1984). The British Crime Surveys (BCS) of 1982 (Hough and Mayhew, 1983), 1984 (Hough and Mayhew, 1985), and 1988 (Mayhew, Elliott and Dowds, 1989) have involved interviews with one person over the age of 16 in some 11 000 households in England and Wales, and initially 5000 in Scotland.

Considerably more victimisation is revealed by crime surveys than by the official statistics. The 1982 BCS, for example, estimated four times more household crimes (burglary, car theft, vandalism) and five times more personal crimes (assaults, robberies, personal thefts, sexual offences) than recorded by the police, although a third of all reported victimisations involve theft of or from, or damage to a motor vehicle. These may underestimate the volume of crime. Not only do surveys exclude some offence categories, such as shop thefts or victimless crimes, victims probably fail to report all crimes to interviewers, particularly those involving domestic disputes. However, much of the "dark figure" appears to consist of minor offences resulting in little or no personal damage or material loss.

Although most motor thefts are reported to the police, the reporting rate for other thefts is low, and overall, only about a third of offences is reported. Skogan (1977) found that 84% of crimes not reported to the police in the 1973 NCS involved losses of less than $50, and the most common reasons given for not reporting crimes in both American and British surveys are that the offence was too trivial, or that the police were unlikely to be able to do anything about it. Subjective ratings of the seriousness of offences also correlate significantly with the degree of reporting (Hough and Mayhew, 1985). Nevertheless, some serious crimes go unreported, possibly to avoid the stress of litigation (Skogan, 1977). The 1984 BCS enquired about reasons in instances where a crime was reported. A third of respondents referred to an obligation to inform the police, a third emphasised personal advantages, such as recovering property, while 16% indicated a desire for retribution.

However, the "dark figure" is also partly the result of underrecording of crimes due to police discretion when handling complaints. For example, in the 1988 BCS, 75% of reported thefts from vehicles, 65% of burglaries, and only 38% of robberies appeared in the criminal statistics. Some of the apparent underrecording may reflect different classifications of incidents by the police, but Bottomley and Pease (1986) suggest three main reasons why an incident may not be recorded as a crime. First, the complaint may be false, mistaken, or subsequently withdrawn. Second, the police judge that the incident is trivial, the participants are to blame, it is unlikely to be cleared-up, or the perpetrator was a child. Third, ambiguities in official definitions may lead to several offences being counted as one. Some offences are also written off as "no crime", although the overall rate in England and Wales is only about 6%. There is, however, regional variation in underrecording and write-off, reflecting organisational practices. For example, Nottinghamshire has recorded the highest crime rate in England over several years, but Farrington and Dowds (1985) found that higher levels of victimisation accounted for less than a third of the higher recorded rates. The discrepancy reflected differences in the recording of trivial offences, and in a more ready acceptance of admissions to offences by offenders.

Crime surveys are subject to sampling errors, since interviews are usually held with only one household member, and hence miss high risk groups, such as young males, commuters, or tourists, and estimates of low base rate crimes, such as rape, are particularly prone to error (Block and Block, 1984; Mayhew, Elliott and Dowds, 1989). They also depend on accuracy of recall, as well as willingness of victims to report their experiences. While offence descriptions are often more discriminating than those used in official statistics, the coding of offences depends on the interpretation of both victim and interviewer. Depending on the offence category, then, crime surveys may be subject to a degree of both over- and under-reporting. However, they provide much information not available in official statistics, such as the fact that most victims of crime are young, poor, or from ethnic minorities. They also help to demystify crime by bringing out the relatively trivial nature of much criminal behaviour (Bottomley and Pease, 1986).

The utility of crime measures

Ideally, the gathering of statistics about crime serves a number of purposes, such as the formulation of social policy, the evaluation of the criminal justice system, or the construction of theories (Nietzel, 1979). However, it is clear that the official statistics are an unreliable guide to the occurrence of criminal events, and some therefore argue that no reliance can be placed on them. Box (1981), for example, asserts that official data are not valid measures of criminal activity, since they are "... merely the sedimentation of all those discretionary decisions which comprise the administration of justice...".

Such a conclusion is questionable, since not only is validity a matter of degree, it must also be judged in terms of what is being measured, and for what purpose. Block and Block (1984) note that there is no "real" number of criminal occurrences which exists independently of the decision processes of victims or criminal justice agents, and official statistics, self-reports, and crime surveys do not capture identical phenomena. They nevertheless overlap. The reliability, and hence validity, of the official statistics is attenuated by several sources of error, but comparisons with crime surveys indicate that although official data grossly underestimate the overall crime rate, the discrepancies are maximal for relatively minor offences, and negligible or slight for some offences such as homicide or auto-theft. Hindelang (1974a) also showed that crime survey and UCR data agreed in both the rank order and geographical distribution of crime categories, and that official data are valid measures of the *relative* distribution of crime. When offence seriousness and frequency are taken into account, self-report and official data also show a significant degree of convergence (Hindelang et al., 1981). Official statistics cannot therefore be dismissed as wholly invalid, and their validity may be adequate for some purposes.

Their limitations must nonetheless be recognised, particularly when considering changes in crime levels. With the exception of Japan, all industrialised countries have recorded radical increases in crime during the past three decades, especially Britain and the United States (Rutter and Giller, 1983). However, much of the rise may be illusory, and serious crime was probably more endemic in pre-industrial society than in the twentieth century (Lane, 1974). The increase since the 1950s may reflect procedural factors, such as changes in legislation, as much as substantive changes in offending behaviour. Farrington and Bennett (1981), for example, estimated that in England and Wales the Theft Act of 1964 and the Criminal Damage Act of 1968 inflated the number of findings of guilt for indictable offences by 21%, as a result of the reclassification of many previously nonindictable offences. The recorded increase in violent offences may also be partly a result of "net-widening" through a lowering of the threshold for recording minor offences as violent (Bottomley and Pease, 1986). Although serious violence (i.e. that endangering life) has more than doubled in Britain during the past two decades, it has declined to about 7% of the total of violent crimes, while less serious violence has increased five fold.

Increases also reflect changes in reporting by victims. From 1981 to 1987, crimes known to the police in England and Wales increased by 41%, but during the same period the BCS found an increase of 30% (Mayhew et al., 1989). The difference between the official and the victimisation figures is largely accounted for by an increased proportion of crimes reported to the police. However, an increase in reporting together with an increase in actual crimes may disproportionately increase the recorded crime rate. Mayhew et al. (1989) examined victimisation data from 1972 to 1987 which indicated an increase of 20% in burglaries. Criminal statistics for the same period recorded an increase of 125%, but this reflects the combined effect of a much smaller real increase and an increased rate of reporting by the public.

A real increase in crime in recent decades is not in doubt, but it is likely to have been less than that recorded in official statistics. There may also have been some levelling off in the rate since the 1970s, and possibly a fall, particularly in juvenile offending (Bottomley and Pease, 1986). Social and economic factors associated with increased crime rates since the 1950s have not been clearly identified. Wilson and Herrnstein (1985) suggest that changes in society's investment in values of self-control and postponement of gratification may be significant, although the extent of such changes seems debatable. Increased opportunities and rewards for stealing presented by more self-service shopping and the wider availability of cars and other consumer goods are perhaps more likely contributors. A further factor may be change in the proportion of the population most at risk for offending. Cohen and Land (1987), for example, found that changes in American homicide and vehicle theft rates between 1946 and 1984 closely followed the pattern of changes in the percentage of the population aged 15 to 24, as well as changes in population density, unemployment rate, and imprisonment rate.

THE LEGAL PROCESSING OF OFFENDERS

In addition to problems of the official statistics as a record of criminal offences, biases in the criminal justice system may also affect the identification of convicted *offenders*. Not only do many offenders escape detection, many suspects are not convicted, and legal adjudication of a person as a criminal may be as much a function of *extra-legal* factors, such as social status, race, or sex, as of legal considerations of the seriousness or persistence of offending. At issue is not only whether known offenders are representative of offenders in general, but also whether the system fulfils the requirements of justice as equality of treatment before the law. Labelling and conflict theorists argue that it does not. Chambliss (1969), for example, contends that the decisions of judicial agents are biased against the powerless, and that class dictates who is scrutinised by the law, and the severity of sentences imposed.

From the point at which an offence becomes known to that at which a sentence is imposed, there is an interconnected network of decision-makers and decision "nodes" which mutually influence each other (Ebbesen and Konecni, 1982; Bottomley and Pease, 1986). These relate to the reporting and recording of a crime, identifying and arresting a suspect, bailing or remanding in custody, entering a plea of guilt, conviction, sentencing, and disposal. Decisions at all points are governed not simply by rules and guidelines, but also by organisational policies and pressures, and by the discretion of individual decision-makers. A suspect may exit from the system at several points in the network, and only a minority who enter as suspects end up being found guilty. Well-publicised examples of political decisions not to prosecute suspects, particularly those who are agents of the state, and the fact that white collar crimes are also less likely than "ordinary" crimes to be dealt with by formal criminal proceedings (Sutherland, 1945) indicate that biases do occur in legal decision-making, which favour the more powerful (Box, 1983). However, what remains at issue is whether there are systematic biases operating *against* the interests of the disadvantaged.

Police processing of suspects

Research on how offenders are dealt with by criminal justice agents has focused on decisions at three points: (1) the arrest of suspects; (2) the subsequent actions of the police in relation to those who are apprehended; (3) the sentencing decisions of the courts. A relatively consistent picture of factors determining arrest emerges from studies in American cities, in which observers accompanied police officers on patrol. Only a minority of incidents to which the police are called results in an arrest, and this depends on the seriousness of the crime and the wishes of the complainant, but also to some extent on the characteristics of suspects. For example, in 281 encounters between police and juveniles observed in three cities by Black and Reiss (1970), only 15% led to an arrest, seriousness of offence being the most important factor. While 21% of black suspects, but only 8% of whites were arrested, this was largely due to greater seriousness of offence among black youths, and to the insistence of complainants, who in the case of black suspects were more likely to be black themselves. These findings were replicated by Lundman, Sykes and Clark (1978).

Piliavin and Briar (1964), however, found that black youths were more likely to be stopped, and that antagonistic youths, and those with a "tough" style of dress and appearance, were more likely to be arrested. Black and Reiss (1970) and Lundman et al. (1978) found that both antagonistic and deferential youths were more likely to be arrested, but that most suspects behaved in a civil manner. However, Smith and Visher (1982) obtained further evidence that race influences arrest in a study of 24 American cities. Black suspects were more likely to be arrested, as were antagonistic suspects; but while blacks were also more likely to be antagonistic, the race difference remained after controlling for offence seriousness and complainant behaviour. The decision to arrest a suspect in a street encounter is, then, likely to be influenced by immediately perceived characteristics and by stereotypes of a delinquent "type".

Police discretion influences whether an apprehended suspect is charged, given a formal caution, or dealt with informally. Since the 1960s, British police have made increasing use of cautions, particularly for young offenders and those involved in minor property or sexual offences. This diverts offenders from court, although cautions are routinely recorded in the published statistics. The proportion of offenders cautioned for indictable offences in England and Wales rose from 10% in the early 1960s to 28% in 1988 (Home Office, 1989a), particularly for those aged 10 to 13 (from 27% to 86% for males, and from 40% to 95% for females). Age and sex are thus strongly related to the decision to caution, as is offence history and seriousness, and most first offenders are dealt with in this way (Farrington and Bennett, 1981; Tutt, 1984). There are, however, disparities between police forces in rates of cautioning, particularly for recidivists (Bottomley and Pease, 1986). While local variations in departmental procedures explain some of the disparities, offender characteristics may also play a part. Landau (1981) examined police records relating to decisions to charge a juvenile immediately or to refer to the juvenile bureau (making a caution more likely) for 1444 decisions in five London police divisions. Previous offences, age, area of offence, and race were particularly related to the decision to charge. There was, however, an interaction between type of offence and race, more black youths being charged when the offence was burglary, violence, or public disorder than when it was theft or auto-crime.

Processing in the courts

If charged by the police, offenders are subsequently exposed to others who may influence judicial outcome, such as lawyers, probation officers or social workers. In the United States, a defendant may avoid the risk of a severe sentence by agreeing with lawyers to plead guilty to a lesser charge, and this practice leads to the majority of defendants pleading guilty. Such plea-bargaining, which is not formally acknowledged in Britain, may allow some defendants to benefit according to their status. Newman (1956) did not find evidence for this, but socioeconomic status does affect the level of legal skills which can be hired, which may well determine outcome. Probation officers and social workers also influence sentencing through their recommendations to the court. In English juvenile courts, social inquiry reports are a significant determinant of custodial placement (Tutt, 1984), and such reports by their nature take account of extra-legal variables. Hagan (1975), for example, found that Canadian probation officers made less favourable recommendations to the court for more serious, antagonistic, nonwhite, and lower class offenders.

There is clear evidence of disparity between courts in rates of acquittal, the use of different sentences, and their length (Bottomley and Pease, 1986). Studies of variations in sentence severity have focused particularly on the race and socioeconomic status of offenders in both juvenile and adult courts, but results have been inconsistent. In a study of one American juvenile court, Thomas and Cage (1977) found that with offence seriousness and prior record held constant, males, blacks, school dropouts, and those from broken homes were more severely dealt with, although the association of these variables with disposition was relatively weak. On the other hand, Cohen and Kluegel (1978) found that the major determinants of severity of disposition in two American juvenile courts with contrasting judicial philosophies were offence and prior record, race and class not being significant factors. Similar results have been obtained in surveys of English courts (Crow, 1987). However, Peterson and Hagan (1984) suggest that the treatment of blacks by the courts has changed over time, and depends on the nature of the offence, victimless crimes being dealt with more leniently in recent years.

Welford (1975) concluded that there was little evidence for discrimination in law enforcement or legal punishment, and that legal factors are the major determinants of outcome. However, from data obtained in 17 studies, Liska and Tausig (1979) discerned evidence for differential effects of race, and to a lesser extent socioeconomic status, at all stages in the judicial system. The evidence to date, then, appears to indicate that extra-legal factors *can* and often do play a significant part in determining who is ultimately identified as an official delinquent or criminal. Nevertheless, offender characteristics account for only some of the variation in legal decision-making, which is also determined by social contextual factors, such as local organisational policies.

Only limited attention has been paid to the question of *how* offender attributes influence legal decisions. A common assumption is that police and judges are biased by class and racial prejudice, and this view has some support. For example, the police tend to hold negative stereotypes of criminals (Garrett and Short, 1975), and Colman and Gorman (1982) found a sample of English police officers to be more conservative and authoritarian than controls. However, psychological attributes of offenders may also contribute to police decisions. Werner et al. (1975) found that police officers expected youths to be polite, co-operative, and to answer questions in an encounter, and that training delinquent youths in relevant social skills resulted in more favourable evaluations by police. Inappropriate responses to being approached by the police were also among the social skill deficits of delinquents identified by Freedman et al. (1978).

Characteristics of judges may also be significant. Palys and Divorski (1984) established that the most likely sources of disparity in sentencing lie in the legal objectives, such as rehabilitation or protection of the public, which individual judges seek to maximise, and in the aspects of particular cases they accordingly emphasise. Since attitudes towards crime control are closely related to ideological beliefs and personality variables (Carroll et al., 1987), individual differences may account for much of this variation. However, organisational requirements are likely to limit the impact of personal characteristics of judges. Tarling (1979), for example, noted considerable consistency in the decision-making of individual English courts despite changes in magistrates. It would appear, then, that biases may emerge whenever criminal justice agents have discretion, but that this is never wholly unconstrained.

DEMOGRAPHIC CORRELATES OF CRIME

Certain characteristics of crime are well established. Crime rates are higher in urban areas and in poorer parts of towns and cities, and officially known offenders are more likely to be male, young, and in the United States, black. Most delinquents also offend in the company of others, solitary offending being characteristic of only a minority of juveniles, though a majority of adult criminals (Zimring, 1981). However, these features may not be static, and correlates of offending suggested by official statistics have not always been confirmed by alternative sources.

Considerable information about the backgrounds of offenders has accrued from longitudinal research (Farrington, Ohlin and Wilson, 1986), and the following discussion draws particularly on findings from four major studies: (1) the first Philadelphia birth cohort of 9945 boys born in 1945 (Wolfgang, Figlio and Sellins, 1972); (2) the second Philadelphia birth cohort of 13 160 boys and 14 000 girls born in 1958 (Tracy, Wolfgang and Figlio, 1986); (3) the Cambridge study of 411 London boys born in 1953 (West, 1982; Farrington and West, 1990); (4) the National Youth Survey of some 1700 American adolescents, which obtained repeated measures of self-reported delinquency from 1977 to 1980 (Elliott, Huizinga and Ageton, 1985).

Socioeconomic status

A traditional assumption in criminology is that disproportionately more of those of lower socioeconomic status (SES) engage in illegal activities. This gained support from the ecological research of Shaw and McKay (1942), who demonstrated that the geographical distribution of crime rates in Chicago coincided with residence in the poorest areas of the city. They regarded ecological variables, such as income level, unemployment rates, or proportion of families in slum housing, as the outcome of a selective segregation of the socially disadvantaged, high crime rates being mediated by social disorganisation in the form of lack of group or family ties. Disorganised areas were held to support criminal traditions through pressures on those lacking access to resources and status to resort to crime, and the community's failure to control its members.

Correlations between social characteristics of areas and aggregate crime rates overestimate correlations at the individual level (Robinson, 1950), but an inverse relation between crime rates and SES appears to be consistent with official crime data. For example, a national survey of 17 year old British boys in 1963 revealed that 13.8% of lower working class, 6.1% of upper working class, 4.2 of lower middle class, and 0.8% of upper middle class youths had a conviction for an indictable offence (Douglas et al., 1966). Longitudinal research in Denmark also suggests a negative, though small correlation between parental SES and later criminality (McGarvey et al., 1981), while in the Philadelphia cohorts, differentials of 19% (cohort 1) and 18% (cohort 2) were found between boys of low and high SES who became known delinquents (Tracy et al., 1986).

Early self-report studies indicated much weaker class differentials (e.g. Hirschi, 1969), and this apparent discrepancy fuelled suspicions of biases in the official processing of delinquents (Box, 1981). However, reviewing 35 studies, Tittle, Villemez and Smith (1978) noted that while the mean correlation between class and delinquency was stronger in official than in self-report data, the magnitude of the relationship had declined over time to near zero for both measures in the 1970s. Braithwaite (1981), on the other hand, surveyed a larger number of studies, and concluded that official data overwhelmingly support a class differential, while self-report studies do so at a lower level.

Elliott and Huizinga (1983) question the methodological adequacy of earlier self-report analyses. Using scales distinguishing kinds and categories of offence, and separating prevalence from incidence, they found marked class differences for more serious crimes against the person and property in the National Youth Survey, particularly for incidence. They suggest that earlier studies were biased by limited sampling and frequency distributions of offences. However, in a reanalysis of data based on comparable scaling methods, Weis (1987) found only weak negative correlations of class with both official and self-report data. Whether the two data sources diverge in this respect has also been questioned. Hindelang et al. (1981) observed that in studies providing simultaneous official and self-report data, correlations of delinquency with class converged, being close to zero in both cases.

A critical issue is the measurement of social class. Thornberry and Farnworth (1982) note that class is a nebulous concept, and that most research measures *family* social status, typically by occupation of the principal wage earner. They found offenders to be distinguished by lower *personal* status as adults, particularly in terms of educational attainment and job stability, but neither juvenile nor adult offending was predicted by social status of the family of origin. However, the relation between crime and family status or income level may be nonlinear, and confined to the extreme of the distribution. In the working class cohort of the Cambridge study, economic deprivation predicted early delinquency, and in a self-report study of California schoolchildren, delinquency was related to parental unemployment, though not occupational level (Hirschi, 1969). Measurement of class by unemployment and welfare status also produces more consistent correlations with official and self-report measures of violent crime (Brownfield, 1986). Any class differential in crime rates may therefore reflect the contribution of an economically deprived "underclass".

Much of the relevant research has been carried out in North America, and social status may have different meanings in other countries. However, Rutter and Giller (1983) suggest that, as in America, the available data indicate a less robust relationship between class and delinquency in Britain than previously thought. How this small correlation between crime and SES might be mediated remains unresolved. The assumptions that unequal distribution of opportunities creates pressures towards illegal behaviour, and that poor neighbourhoods foster criminal traditions are common sociological themes, while psychological theories also link delinquent behaviour to the internalisation of group and family values (Chapters 4 and 5). Yet Tittle (1983) argues that none of the major criminological theories unambiguously predicts a class differential.

Age

The attention to juvenile delinquency in criminology reflects the proportionately greater involvement in crime of young people. Cross-sectional data on arrests or convictions indicate that rates of offending are substantially higher among adolescents and young adults, and the age distribution curve consistently shows a steep rise from age 10 to a peak between 15 and 18, followed by a less steep decline after age 21. In 1988, for example, the peak age for males cautioned or found guilty of indictable offences in England and Wales was 18, the rate per 100 of the population being 7.6, compared with rates of 0.8 at age 10, and 6.2 at age 20 (Home Office, 1989a). For females, the peak was at age 15 (1.6 per 100), rates at 10 and 20 being 0.1 and 0.9, respectively. In the United States, peak age of arrest for UCR index offences was 17 for both males (5.8 per 100) and females (1.2: US Department of Justice, 1989).

However, peaks are not uniform for all offences, and while property crimes in the United States peaked at 17 for males and 16 for females, violent crimes peaked at 18 for males, and 24 for females. Earlier UCR data also indicate that while burglary, auto-theft, and vandalism are "youthful" crimes peaking in mid-adolescence, other offences such as fraud and embezzlement peak in later adult years (Steffensmeier et al., 1989). Self-reports suggest similar patterns, with an overall peak between 15 and 17, but with shoplifting and minor stealing peaking earlier than violent crime or fraud (Farrington, Ohlin and Wilson, 1986). The data appear to reflect a peak in prevalence. Few studies have examined incidence rates, which may not follow the same pattern.

Attempts to account for the age distribution invoke both biological and social factors, such as changes in physical strength or behavioural experimentation at a time of emerging self-identity, and an apparent "spontaneous remission" suggested by declining prevalence at early adulthood has led to particular attention in longitudinal research to the termination of criminal careers. However, this focus is criticised by Gottfredson and Hirschi (1990). They argue that the age distribution is invariant across time, culture, sex and race, but this reflects the distribution of crimes, not criminal propensity. They claim that the latter is stable, and that its causes are the same at all age levels. Longitudinal research will not, therefore, yield more information about causes of criminality than will cross-sectional research. This argument has been rejected on the grounds that the age distribution is not invariant either across crimes or time periods (Farrington et al., 1986; Steffensmeier et al., 1989), but the distinction between criminal acts and criminal propensity deserves further consideration in this context.

Gender

Sex differences are among the most significant features of recorded crime. In 1988, 3.7 times more males than females were arrested for index crimes in the United States, the ratios being 3.1 for property offences, and 7.7 for violent crimes (US Department of Justice, 1989). Ratios were smallest for those aged 10 to 14 (3.8) and 21 and over (3.8), and highest in the late teens (4.7 at 17 and 18). The pattern in the UK was similar, the male:female ratio for those cautioned or found guilty of indictable offences being 5.6 (Home Office, 1989a). Again, the difference was smaller for the early teens (4.8 for 10 to 13 year olds) and for adults (5. 3 for those aged 21 and over), and greatest during the late teens (7.2 for 17 to 20 year olds). At all ages, ratios are smallest for theft, and substantially higher for burglary, robbery, and violence. Theft and fraud, in fact, make up a higher proportion of female offences, accounting for about 80% at all age levels in the UK.

The sex differential may reflect biased reporting and processing of female crime rather than a real difference. It has been argued, for example, that males are more "chivalrous" when dealing with female offenders. On the other hand, juvenile females have traditionally been more liable to custodial dispositions for "moral" violations and status offences. Smaller sex differences are found in self-report delinquency measures than in official statistics, and the finding that differences are minimal for such traditional "female" delinquencies as prostitution, truancy, or running away seems to support the suspicion of bias (Cernkovich and Giordano, 1979; Canter, 1982a). The latter studies also found that although both prevalence and incidence of offending are higher among males, the *pattern* indicated by rank order of offence involvement is similar for both sexes. However, sex ratios for more serious self-reported delinquency approach official figures (Hindelang et al., 1979). Estimates of female involvement in personal crimes from victimisation data also approximate to official measures (Hindelang, 1979).

There is little consensus regarding reasons for the male predominance in crime. Since this is most pronounced for serious personal crimes, one view is that it reflects apparently universal differences between the sexes in dominance, aggression, and nurturance, and that physique or hormone balance are the critical factors. This hypothesis is difficult to falsify, but variations in female crime rates also correlate with the degree of subordination or powerlessness in the cultural role of women (Box, 1983). However, sex role differences are not arbitrary, and probably reflect a response to biological differences (Cohen and Machalek, 1989). Traditional female roles further entail less access to gangs or criminal subcultures, and more limited opportunities for crime (Steffensmeier, 1980). This opportunity hypothesis accords with the predominance of shop thefts and cheque frauds in female crime.

Female socialisation is also characterised by greater parental control and supervision, as well as greater emphasis on the "ethic of care" (Gilligan, 1982), and this may account for the greater conformity of females. Both Lombroso and Freud believed that females who do offend reject traditional feminine roles, but this was not supported in a review by Widom (1978a). She found evidence for relatively high levels of stress in the family backgrounds of female offenders, who are also more likely to show educational underachievement, lower intelligence, and marital disorganisation. Higher rates of psychopathology have also been suggested, but there have been too few comparisons of male with female offenders to determine how far the causes of female offending differ from those proposed to account for male crime. However, biological predisposition may play a greater role in female than in male deviance (Widom and Ames, 1988).

Increased female involvement in crime has led to claims that females have become more violent and antisocial. In England and Wales the male:female ratio for cautions or findings of guilt up to the age of 17 fell from 7.1 for those born in 1953 to 5.3 for those born in 1963 (Home Office, 1987). Smith and Visher (1980) also found a narrowing of the gap in American studies reported from 1940 to 1975, although a fall in the ratio of male to female delinquents in New York from 60:1 in 1902 to 8:1 in 1932 (Metfessel and Lovell, 1942) suggests that changes were already occurring early in the century. However, Steffensmeier (1980) showed that the absolute gap between male and female offenders in the United States has actually widened for most crimes, and that the relative proportion of female offenders has increased only for property crimes, such as theft, forgery, and fraud. This is borne out by a longitudinal comparison of 31 countries (Simon and Baxter, 1989). Alternative data sources are less consistent on the issue of increased female offending. Smith and Visher (1980) found that the narrowing of the gap was more pronounced for self-report than official measures up to 1975, but in a comparison of 1977 with 1967 self-report findings, Canter (1982a) found increases only in the prevalence of drug and alcohol use, which applied to both sexes. Laub (1987) also reports that victimisation surveys between 1973 and 1981 point to a decline in the number of 12 to 17 year old females committing personal crimes, and only a slight increase in the case of older groups. Increased seriousness of female offending has therefore been overstated, and changes seem primarily related to traditionally female crimes, such as shop theft and welfare benefit fraud.

It has been speculated that increased female involvement in crime is a result of femininism and greater emancipation of women (Adler, 1975). Thus, access of women to traditionally male preserves may increase illegitimate as well as legitimate opportunities. However, Figuera-McDonough (1984) found no direct relationship between femininist orientation and self-reported delinquency, and recent levels of female crime across countries correlate more with industrialisation and general economic opportunities than with female education or labour force participation (Simon and Baxter, 1989). While it is possible that the women's movement has reduced "chivalry" in legal processing, changes in the pattern and involvement of females reflect the general increase in crime, and do not appear to justify the notion of a new form of emancipated female criminal (Steffensmeier, 1980).

Race

Claims that ethnic minorities were overinvolved in crime followed the extensive immigration to the United States and the migration of blacks to its northern cities at the turn of the century. However, long term data obtained by Shaw and McKay (1942) suggested that urban areas with high crime rates retained their high rates despite changes in ethnic composition. Subsequent surveys also indicate that delinquency rates in Chicago are higher in areas where there is rapid change in racial composition, but not in those where the black population has stabilised (Bursik and Webb, 1982).

Nevertheless, official data in the United States continue to indicate an overrepresentation of blacks among offenders, which is particularly apparent in the populations of penal institutions. Currently, blacks make up some 11% of the American population, but accounted for 33% of index crimes related to property in 1988, and 47% of violent crimes (US Department of Justice, 1989). Official data from London in 1987 similarly reveal that blacks of Afro-Carribean origin are more likely to be arrested than whites, particularly for violent crimes (Home Office, 1989b). Ethnic minorities also represent 11.5% of the English prison population, compared with 5% of the general population (Home Office, 1986b).

In contrast, early self-report studies found no evidence for a racial differential (Hirschi, 1969), supporting the argument that official data were inflated by biases. However, Hindelang et al. (1979) observed that discrepancies between official and self-report data break down when offence seriousness is considered, and that self-reports demonstrated a higher prevalence of serious and violent offenders among blacks. This was confirmed by Elliott and Ageton (1980). Hindelang (1978) also found that victimisation and UCR data agreed on the higher proportion of blacks involved in rape and robbery, but not on prevalence of arrests for assault, supporting alleged official bias only in the case of the latter. The more recent American data, then, converge in indicating an overinvolvement of blacks in serious crime, although victimisation studies point to a decline of offending by black youths during the 1970s (Laub, 1987).

British data on this issue are limited. Rutter and Giller (1983) note that until 1970, the delinquency rates of black and Asian immigrants were unexceptional, but that data from the 1970s indicate higher rates for children of West Indian origin. This is confirmed in more recent data from London (Home Office, 1989b). While the resident population was 85% white, and 5% were of West Indian origin, the latter accounted for 54% of arrests for robbery. Asian children, on the other hand, have been found to have lower rates than those of indigenous whites (Mawby, McCulloch and Batta, 1979; Ouston, 1984). In the United States, some ethnic groups, notably the Japanese, have also been observed to have lower than average rates. Rushton (1990) reports a comparison of international rates of homicide, rape, and serious assault, which when grouped by predominant race of country indicate that, although there is marked intra-racial variation, Mongoloids have the lowest rates, and Negroids the highest, with Caucasoids in between.

Although biases in the legal processing of offenders cannot account wholly for the overinvolvement of blacks in crime in the United States and Britain, racial discrimination limits the economic and occupational opportunities available to ethnic minorities, and some theories predict that this, rather than race itself, will create pressures towards crime. Ouston (1984), in fact, found that racial differences disappeared when family social status was controlled for. Other factors known to correlate with crime, such as family size or parental supervision, may also be significant. However, Rushton (1990) claims that racial differences observed also correlate with variations in brain weight and IQ, rate of maturation, reproductive behaviour, and personality and temperament, which he believes supports a gene-based evolutionary origin. The reliability of these differences in offending and of their correlates is unclear. While the argument cannot be dismissed solely because of its ideological implications, the evidence appears to be indirect and circumstantial.

GENERALITY AND CONTINUITY IN CRIME AND DELINQUENCY

Theories of criminal behaviour typically aim to account for crime in general. It will be apparent, however, that the distribution of crime across demographic variables depends on the category and seriousness of offence. Moreover, popular conceptions of criminals, as well as some theories, assume that persistent offenders specialise in particular kinds of crime, and terms such as burglar or rapist do not simply denote the commission of a particular act but also imply a tendency to repeat it. This section considers how far criminals are distinguishable by types or patterns of criminal activity as well as the frequency and duration of involvement. To the extent that criminal careers vary in kind as well as degree, attempts to formulate general theories of crime are likely to be of limited utility.

Specialisation versus versatility in offending

Several multivariate statistical studies of self-reported delinquency data have attempted to determine whether there are specific factors or clusters of criminal behaviour. Hindelang and Weis (1972) described a cluster analysis of self-report delinquency items. They identified seven clusters (general deviance, traffic/truancy, aggression, theft, malicious destruction, and two drug use factors), which suggest that delinquent behaviour is multidimensional, but positive correlations between clusters pointed to an underlying general factor. Factor analyses of self-report scales usually yield a general factor to which most items contribute, additional factors accounting for little of the common variance (e.g. Gibson, 1971; Allsopp and Feldman, 1976; Hindelang et al., 1981; Emler, 1984). The behaviour of delinquents is thus likely to be versatile rather than confined to a particular kind of delinquent act.

Official data lend themselves less readily to this kind of analysis, and Klein (1984) found few significant correlations among 40 legal offences for which juvenile gang members had been apprehended. He suggests that delinquent behaviours are selected randomly, or "cafeteria style", rather than according to a specific pattern. From a survey of 33 studies, he concluded that the majority showed no evidence of patterning or specialisation in delinquent acts, and this conclusion is supported by Stattin and Magnusson (1991). In a cluster analysis of patterns of offence behaviour by individuals in a longitudinal study, they identified six patterns among adolescents, and seven among adults, but none of these suggested more than limited specialisation.

Other research suggests that the general factor of delinquent or criminal behaviour in self-reports is part of a broader dimension of *general deviance*.

In a study of high school and college students, Jessor and Jessor (1977) found significant generality among measures of problem drinking, illicit drug use, sexual precocity, and delinquent behaviour, which related to personality variables reflecting unconventionality. The hypothesis of a single common factor of unconventionality was supported for adolescents, college students, and young adults by Osgood et al. (1988) in an analysis of similar measures, and they also demonstrated longitudinal stability in these behaviours. Those who engage in one form of socially disapproved behaviour are therefore also more likely to engage in others. Further support comes from the Cambridge study. From interviews at age 18, delinquents were found to differ from nondelinquents on several characteristics reflecting "antisociality" (tattooed, hostile attitudes, unstable employment, antisocial friends, driving after drinking, heavy smoking, drinking, gambling, use of illicit drugs). Similar characteristics distinguished persistent offenders at age 32 (Farrington and West, 1990).

Further evidence favouring lack of specialisation comes from longitudinal studies which derive matrices of the conditional probabilities of one offence category being followed by another. Wolfgang, Figlio and Sellin (1972) examined arrest histories of juveniles in the first Philadelphia cohort up to age 18, dividing offences into five broad categories (injury, theft, damage, nonindex, and combination). Arrest for a particular offence category showed little association with an increased probability of offending in the same category. Bursik (1980) criticised this analysis, and showed that when account was taken of the distribution of offence types, some evidence of specialisation emerged, particularly for property offences. Rojek and Erickson (1982) also found evidence of modestly increased probabilities of offence repetition for property offences among male delinquents, and status offences among females, but concluded that versatility in offending was more striking.

However, follow-up of the second Philadelphia cohort to age 26 reveals stronger indications of specialisation, particularly for property offending by males, status offences among females, and robbery by black males (Kempf, 1986). Holland and McGarvey (1984) also found that transition probabilities for nonviolent offences were high in adult offenders, but low for violent offences, suggesting no specialisation in the latter. Mednick and Kandel (1988), in contrast, report evidence for specialisation in violence in a Danish birth cohort followed up to age 27. First-time violent offenders were nearly twice as likely to commit a further violent offence as first-time property offenders, and this applied to juvenile as well as adult offending. However, other research on violent criminal careers indicates that, although some offenders go on to repeat violence at a high rate, most do not, and relatively few violent offenders confine themselves to violent crime (Weiner, 1989). The Philadelphia studies also suggest an escalation in offense seriousness among adult recidivists (Wolfgang, 1983; Tracy, Wolfgang and Figlio, 1986), although not juveniles, but Holland and McGarvey (1984) found that a violent offence was more likely to be followed by a nonviolent crime.

Specialisation in offending, then, may be the exception rather than the rule among juveniles, but adult offenders seem somewhat more likely to specialise. However, while offenders may be disposed to violate social rules in general rather than selectively, it seems improbable that criminal acts serve interchangeable psychological functions. As Alker (1972) notes, overtly dissimilar responses may serve the same function for an individual, and equally, similar responses may serve different functions for different individuals. Undue reliance on legal offence definitions may in this respect obscure regularities in what are ostensibly versatile careers.

Continuity in offending and deviance

The age distribution of crime implies that many youthful offenders outgrow delinquency, only some going on to be adult offenders, and this is supported by longitudinal studies. Wolfgang (1983) followed up a sample of the first Philadelphia cohort to age 30. Of boys with arrest records prior to age 18, 39% went on to be arrested as adults, compared with 9% of nondelinquents. The former comprised 75% of those arrested as adults. Similarly, in the second Philadelphia cohort, 38% of male juvenile offenders, and 10% of females, were arrested as adults, and together these made up 58% of adult arrestees (Kempf, 1986). McCord (1979) described a 30-year follow-up of 200 American boys involved in the Cambridge–Somerville project of the early 1940s. She found that 47% of those convicted of serious crimes as juveniles had adult convictions, compared with 18% of nondelinquents. Of those obtaining adult convictions, 42% had juvenile records, compared with 15% of those not convicted as adults. While proportions vary according to sample and criteria of criminal record, the evidence suggests that most juvenile delinquents, particularly females, do not go on to an adult criminal career. However, while many offenders do not become criminal until adulthood, a majority of adult offenders has a record of juvenile off ending, suggesting significant continuity in criminal behaviour for some.

   Some degree of continuity is also apparent in deviant behaviour more generally (Osgood et al., 1988; Farrington, 1992). Several studies suggest that greater variety, as well as early onset, high rates, and cross-setting consistency of antisocial behaviour in childhood are associated with later antisocial behaviour (Loeber, 1982). In long term follow-ups of child guidance cases, black males, and Vietnam veterans, Robins (1978) found that adult problems of alcohol and drug abuse, violence, job difficulties, and criminal behaviour were associated with early problems of fighting, sexual misbehaviour, truancy, drinking, and childhood and adolescent arrests. Number and variety of childhood antisocial behaviours were a better predictor of adult deviance than were specific behaviours alone. Across three samples, she found that between 23% and 41% of antisocial children were subsequently identified as seriously antisocial adults, while the majority of antisocial adults (65% to 82%) had been identified as antisocial children. This again implies "spontaneous remission" for the majority, but persisting conduct problems for a sizeable minority. Robins' research has influenced recent conceptions of antisocial or psychopathic personality (Chapter 3). These findings are consistent with the view of Gottfredson and Hirschi (1990) that there is a stable disposition of criminality, related to general lack of self-control. However, Loeber (1990) suggests that there are three identifiable developmental paths in deviance. The first is an *aggressive–versatile* path progressing from early conduct problems to violent offences, with or without property crimes. Second is a *nonaggressive* path starting with nonaggressive conduct problems and progressing to property offences. *Substance abuse* is a third, independently developing path, although substance *use* is associated with the first two paths. Evidence for the differentiation of these problems in pre-adolescents is reported by Gillmore et al. (1991).

From the labelling perspective, continuity in criminal behaviour may be a *consequence* of offending, since official processing as a delinquent may produce further deviance, or "deviance amplification", through the assumption of a deviant identity by the child. Some evidence for this was found by Farrington, Osborn and West (1978), insofar as self-reported offending and hostile attitudes increased following a first conviction after age 18. However, this was not found for those first convicted prior to age 14, nor was it a persisting effect for older delinquents. Labelling effects, then, seem unlikely to account for much of the observed continuity in offending.

Varieties of criminal career

Longitudinal studies have been particularly concerned with the identification of early precursors of delinquency, the aim being to develop predictive indices to identify those at risk, as well as to establish possible "causal" influences. Those who become delinquent are more likely to have a prior history of conduct problems and poor educational performance during the early school years, and family factors—such as poverty, large family size and history of parental criminal behaviour—are also significant predictors of delinquency. The theoretical significance of these factors will be considered in later chapters, but of immediate interest is the extent to which such precursors differentiate *between* offenders with differing criminal careers or involvement in crime. Delinquency is clearly a transient phenomenon for many, but a more stable characteristic for some. In the first Philadelphia cohort, for example, of boys identified as delinquent by age 18, 46% were one-time offenders, 35% were nonchronic recidivists, while 18% were chronic recidivists (five or more offences): in the second cohort the figures were 42%, 35% and 23%, respectively (Tracy et al., 1986). In an English sample, 55% of males and 78% of females convicted up to age 28 were one-time offenders (Home Office, 1987). It is obviously of both theoretical and practical importance to differentiate the persistent or chronic offender from the more casual or less committed delinquent.

West (1982) distinguished four career patterns on the basis of onset and continuity of offending: (1) juvenile one-time offenders; (2) latecomers; (3) temporary recidivists; (4) persistent recidivists. The Cambridge study provides systematic data on differences between these. One-time juvenile offenders, for example, differed only slightly in background from nondelinquents. On the other hand, in comparison with the sample as a whole, persistent recidivists, defined by at least two juvenile and one adult conviction, were more likely to come from large, low income families with a history of parental crime, and to have been identified as less intelligent and more troublesome by teachers by the age of ten. A simple index combining high scores on teacher ratings of troublesomeness with history of criminal record in parents or siblings identified 51% of those who became persistent recidivists and 5% of the remainder of the sample as being at risk. It will be noted that 49% of the persistent offenders were not identified by this index (false negatives), and half of those predicted to be at risk did not, in fact, become recidivist (false positives). This degree of misclassification is common in delinquency prediction. However, the false positives, who were characterised by early family adversity but did not go on to become recidivists, displayed other social problems, and tended to be unemployed, socially isolated, and living in poor conditions as adults (Farrington and West, 1990).

Early onset also predicts persistent offending, and recidivists are typically found to have been arrested at an earlier age than one-time offenders (Loeber, 1982). In the Philadelphia cohorts, negative correlations approaching unity were found between number of offences and age of first police contact (Tracy et al., 1986), while in the Cambridge study, the 23 who were the most chronic offenders by the age of 25 (six or more offences) had all sustained their first conviction by the age of 15 (Blumstein, Farrington and Moitra, 1985). However, not all early delinquents became recidivists.

Blumstein, Farrington and Moitra, (1985) attempted to distinguish *persisters* from *desistors* (temporary recidivists). From offence histories obtained in four longitudinal studies, they found that the probability of a further arrest or conviction increased with each successive offence up to the sixth, stabilising thereafter at about 0.8. They argue that the increasing probabilities reflect the dropping out of desistors, and the increasing proportion of persisters in the recidivist population. Using data from the Cambridge study, they found that on an index of seven childhood measures relating to disruptive conduct, social handicap, low IQ, and poor parental child-rearing, a cut-off at four identified 65% of persisters, 20% of desistors, and 7% of nondelinquents as at risk for chronic offending. While noting the problems of false negatives and positives, they propose that such an index might be developed to identify persistent recidivists at an early age. However, Dunford and Elliott (1984) are critical of the use of official criminal records to identify career offenders. They used self-report data from the National Youth Survey to distinguish categories of career offender on the basis of offence seriousness, frequency, and duration. While their categories were significantly differentiated by arrest record, and also by measures of delinquent attitude, the more persistent and serious offenders identified by self-report were not identified as chronic offenders by official measures. While these data are not in accord with findings from the Cambridge study, they were derived from only a three year period.

Persisters and desistors have also been found to differ on later characteristics. Osborn and West (1980) interviewed persistent offenders, delinquents who had desisted by the age of 19, and nondelinquents, and compared them on social behaviour at the age of 24. Both persisters and desistors had previously shown evidence of more antisocial deviance at 18 (unstable employment, fighting, heavy drinking, smoking and gambling), compared with nondelinquents. At age 24, however, desistors were significantly less antisocial than persisters, and closer to nondelinquents, suggesting that they had changed their lifestyle. At age 32, desistors continued to drink heavily and to get in fights, but had more stable accommodation and employment than persisters (Farrington and West, 1990).

There are some recent uncontrolled studies involving interviews with desistors. Trasler (1979) and Wilson and Herrnstein (1985) propose that desistance is a response to changing reinforcement contingencies, and that it occurs when nondelinquent activities become more rewarding. Consistent with this view, changes in social networks and increased personal ties were reported by young delinquents (Mulvey and Larosa, 1986) and middle-aged chronic petty offenders (Shover, 1983) who had given up crime. However, from interviews with 17 former robbers, Cusson and Pinsonneault (1986) concluded that a major factor is a delayed deterrent effect of the negative consequences of offending. Data from these three studies suggest that desistance results from a reappraisal of personal goals together with the availability of social support for change. Apart from the limitations of uncontrolled retrospective data, a major problem in this kind of research is the identification of desistance, since offenders may "go straight" for several years and then re-offend (Osborn and West, 1980).

Less attention has been paid to *latecomers* whose first offence occurs in adulthood. As noted earlier, these are less numerous than persistent offenders, although they comprise a quarter or more of adult offenders in some samples. In the Cambridge study, comparisons of latecomers with persisters, desistors, and unconvicted men revealed that, while the latecomers were likely to have been in the low IQ group as children, they were less likely to have experienced early family adversity or to have criminal parents, being closer to the unconvicted in this respect (West, 1982). On the other hand, they were more likely than the unconvicted to have been troublesome at school, and had higher self-report delinquency scores at 14 and more antisocial attitudes at 18. At age 32, they were similar to unconvicted men in terms of domestic and employment stability, but were more prone to heavy drinking, fighting, and psychiatric problems (Farrington and West, 1990). They thus showed some of the characteristics of persisters, but appeared less committed to crime.

Chapter 3

Classification of Offenders

INTRODUCTION

Advances in any science depend on descriptive analytic schemes which identify similarities and differences between the entities comprising the universe of interest. While counts of crimes or offenders are basic to many criminological inquiries, the development of theories of crime and of methods to control or prevent it calls for such schemes. Classification in this context has two meanings. It refers first to the systems by which entities are grouped, and second to the assignment of individual entities to the classes of a particular system. The latter is commonly the goal of clinical assessment and diagnosis, but this chapter is primarily concerned with classification *systems* which attempt to distinguish classes of criminal acts or criminal actors.

Issues in taxonomy

The development of classifications raises several issues about the properties and structural arrangement of classes, most of which are illustrated by psychiatric classification. One basic issue is the objection that "typing" entails negative and stigmatising labelling, and denies individual uniqueness. However, classifying events or people is an inherent feature of language, and stigmatisation is more likely when informal and judgemental stereotyping prevails, as it often does in custodial institutions. While classifications ignore uniqueness, they do not deny it, but rather serve purposes for which commonalities are of greater importance. They are necessary in scientific and professional activities not only for communication, but also for decision-making and prediction (Blashfield and Draguns, 1976; Brennan, 1987a).

The traditional model is the Linnaean classification of plants. Attributes, events, or individuals are divided into classes on the basis of a common principle, such as variation in form or function. Classes are defined by necessary and sufficient criteria of class membership, and assumed to be homogeneous and mutually exclusive. However, cognitive research indicates that class concepts in the natural language and in science rarely meet these requirements (Rosch, 1978). Rather are classes identified by a few *prototypical* features shared by most but not all class members. For example, "feathers", "wings", and "flight" are prototypical for the class "bird"; "swims" is less prototypical, and a swallow is a better exemplar of the class than is a duck. This characteristic of classes has been increasingly recognised in psychiatric classification by the acceptance of *polythetic* classes in which members are identified by only some of the defining criteria (Cantor et al., 1980; American Psychiatric Association, 1987). Homogeneity is in these terms relative, and requires that class members be similar to each other rather than identical.

Conventional monothetic classification assigns entities to discrete *categories* on the basis of all-or-none criteria, but unlike pregnancy, few psychological attributes take an all-or-none form. Conceptual domains such as personal dispositions or deviant response tendencies, may be more appropriately defined by *dimensions*, which distinguish extremes, but do not yield discrete classes. Dimensions locate individuals along quantifiable continua of frequency or intensity, and permit greater precision and flexibility in evaluating empirical relationships (Eysenck, 1960; Hempel, 1965; Strauss, 1973). However, independent dimensions defining a domain are not the same as mutually exclusive categories, since individuals have a position on all dimensions. Classes can therefore be formed by grouping those with similar positions on several dimensions by empirical methods, such as hierarchical cluster analysis (Blashfield, 1980). This preserves naturally occurring interactions between attributes, and yields polythetic categories defined by continuous rather than dichotomous criteria. While psychiatry has resisted dimensional description because of a preference for everyday categorical thinking (Kendell, 1975), categorical classification in psychiatry frequently imposes artificial boundaries between normality and abnormality.

Classifications originate in four ways. First, classes may be formed from subjective impressions of *ideal types*, which represent the modal or prototypical features shared by group members, when an observer detects apparent covariation of attributes. Many psychiatric classes, such as Cleckley's concept of the psychopath (Cleckley, 1976), originated in this way. Second, they may be distinguished by attributes of central concern to a particular theory, as in the Freudian theory of neurosis. Third, they may be formed pragmatically by combining variables of immediate interest, as in the use of temporal variables to distinguish criminal careers in the Cambridge study (Chapter 2). Fourth, they may be generated empirically by multivariate statistical methods, an approach which has been of increasing interest in both abnormal psychology (Lorr, 1982), and criminology (Brennan, 1987a).

In each case, class concepts are theoretical terms, which must be subject to validation, and a classification is, in fact, the foundation of a theory. Whatever the nature of a classification, its adequacy depends on reliable criteria, consistency of usage, and theoretical relevance to explanation and prediction (Hempel, 1965; Blashfield and Draguns, 1976). Many systems fail to meet these requirements because they do not apply a common principle of classification. For example, psychiatric classification continues to identify some categories by observed dysfunctions (e.g. depressive disorder), others by aetiology (organic personality disorder), and others by theory (conversion hysteria). This creates classes which are not mutually exclusive, and although the reliability of psychiatric classification has recently been improved, the validity of many classes remains to be established.

CLASSIFICATION IN CRIMINOLOGY

Neither crimes nor criminals are homogeneous, and classifications are needed for three main purposes. The first is for *management* decisions in the penal system, which aims to maximise external security of the public, internal security of staff and inmates, and the smooth running of institutions by allocating prisoners to different kinds of custodial setting on the basis of age, sex, level of risk, length of sentence, or training needs. Offender characteristics similarly enter into attempts to predict future dangerousness or response to parole (Chapter 12). A second purpose is to facilitate *treatment* decisions by matching categories of offender to the kinds of setting most likely to meet the goals of supervision, training, or rehabilitation. A third use is for *theoretical understanding*, for example, in constructing causal theories for particular classes of offence or offender. A classification system is unlikely to meet all purposes equally well, and must be judged in terms of its specific purpose.

Although much theorising and research continues to address only the gross dichotomies of delinquent versus nondelinquent, or criminal versus law-abiding, most investigators recognise a need to reduce the heterogeneity of offenders. Many studies make pragmatic distinctions on the basis of implicit dimensions of offending, such as frequency (recidivist versus one-time offender), seriousness (victimless versus "victimful"), motivation (acquisitive versus aggressive), or target (property versus person). However, unless tied to theory, such classifications are of limited utility.

Some argue from a legalistic view that any typology must contain reference to criminal behaviour (Morris, 1965), and a few classifications focus on offences. A pragmatic scheme is described by Chaiken and Chaiken (1984), in which they divided criminal behaviour into eight dimensions of assault, robbery, burglary, drug deals, theft, auto theft, fraud, and forgery or credit card swindles. When each dimension was dichotomised by "yes/no" options, ten of the 256 possible configurations accounted for 59% of inmates. While this approach creates homogeneous classes, the number of possible classes depends on arbitrary decisions about the number of dimensions and their division, and legal offence descriptions may not adequately reflect the behavioural characteristics or functional significance of a crime. For example, empirical studies of homicides (Blackburn, 1971a; McGurk, 1978), and drunk drivers

(Donovan and Marlatt, 1982) indicate heterogeneity of personal attributes within these categories.

Some sociological classifications categorise offenders by reference to social patterns associated with offending. *Criminal behaviour systems* (Sutherland and Cressey, 1970; Clinard and Quinney, 1973) describe criminal acts in terms of their integration into social traditions, which unite individuals with whom the offender identifies. For example, professional theft is distinguished from "amateur" theft and other criminal systems, such as white-collar crime, by regular involvement in theft, taking the form of confidence tricks or pocketpicking, appropriate technical skills, high status among criminals, and a social network supporting criminal activities. A related concept is the *role career*, which distinguishes criminal roles according to the offence behaviour, its setting, the career of the offender, and the associated self- and role-related attitudes. Gibbons (1965) proposed nine types of role career among juvenile delinquents, and 15 among adult criminals, the latter including such types as the professional thief, the automobile joyrider, the psychopathic assaultist, and the nonviolent sex offender. Such proposals ignore the taxonomic requirements of common classificatory principles or mutually exclusive classes (Morris, 1965), and not surprisingly, attempts to apply these typologies to offenders find that few fit uniquely into a single category. Gibbons (1988) now believes that typing offenders in this way is a "barren vein", since behavioural diversity rather than career specialisation characterises most lawbreakers.

Psychological attempts to reduce the heterogeneity of offenders generally eschew the legalistic approach. Offender types are distinguished by attributes which are not unique to lawbreakers, but which are assumed to be relatively more common among offenders, and a particular concern is with differential responses of individuals to specific forms of management or treatment (Warren, 1971; Palmer, 1983; Sechrest, 1987; Andrews, Bonta and Hoge, 1990). Some criminologists view such typologies with suspicion because of their explicitly "clinical" orientation and similarities to psychiatric classification. However, treatment in this context means helping the offender, rather than eliminating a disease, and the identification of psychological types in terms of developmental, cognitive, or social characteristics does not imply any discontinuity between deviant and nondeviant behaviour.

Megargee (1977) suggested that a useful offender classification should meet seven criteria; comprehensive coverage of the offender population, unambiguous operational definitions of categories, reliable categorisation, valid distinctions between types, sensitivity to changes, treatment relevance, and economy of application. Many classifications have been proposed since the time of Lombroso, but few approach these requirements. Brennan (1987a) notes that most impressionistic or theoretical systems of the 1960s have proved to be of little utility, and that the more recent concern is with quantitative and empirically derived systems. Although all classifications rest on at least implicit theoretical assumptions (Faust and Miner, 1986), systems of current interest can be divided into those identifying categories from an explicit theory, and those which derive categories empirically.

THEORETICALLY DERIVED CLASSIFICATIONS

Psychodynamic writers distinguish classes of offender in terms of unconscious motivation and deficiencies in psychic organisation. Marshall (1983) integrated previous typologies, seeing the main delinquent types as the normal gang delinquent, the neurotic, the psychopathic, and the psychotic. While the first three are pervasive in criminal classifications, psychodynamic typologies tend to be anecdotal and unsupported by investigations of their utility.

Theories which identify sequential stages of cognitive and interpersonal development have been of increasing interest in differentiating between delinquents. Most prominent is Kohlberg's theory of moral development, which is discussed in Chapter 5. Two theoretically based schemes of more immediate relevance to classification are the *interpersonal maturity level classification* developed by Warren (1971; 1983) and Palmer (1974), and the *conceptual levels model* described by Hunt and Hardt (1965).

Interpersonal maturity level

Sullivan, Grant and Grant (1956) proposed a stage theory inspired by neo-Freudian and social psychological theories, which sees perceptual development in terms of increasing involvement with people and social institutions, accompanied by progressively more differentiated perceptions of the world, the self, and others. It posits seven stages of integration (I-levels), which in brief are: differentiation of self from nonself (I-1); differentiation of persons and objects (I-2); differentiation of simple social rules (I-3); awareness of the expectations of others (I-4); empathic understanding and the differentiation of roles (I-5); differentiation of self from social roles (I-6); a high level of empathy, and awareness of integrating processes in self and others (I-7).

Fixation at a particular level determines relative consistency in goals and expectations, and a "working philosophy" of life, the I-7 level being attained by very few. While no causal relation is proposed between maturity level and antisocial behaviour, those progressing beyond the I-4 level are assumed to be less likely to conflict with society, and most delinquents are found to fall at the I-2, I-3, or I-4 levels. However, within these levels, Warren distinguishes nine delinquent subtypes characterised by different interpersonal response styles. The three levels and their associated styles are summarised in Table 3.1. For research purposes, these are sometimes reduced to broader groups of "passive conformist" (Cfm), "power oriented" (Cfc and Mp), and "neurotic" (Na and Nx), which accounted respectively for 14%, 21% and 53% of delinquents in the California Youth Authority's Community Treatment Project (Palmer, 1974). The association of delinquency with type but not level was supported by Harris (1983), who found that while most adolescents could be assigned to I-levels, only a third could be assigned to subtypes, these tending to show more maladjustment. He also found that those in the Cfc, Mp and Nx groups were more likely to be official delinquents. On the other hand, Davis and

Table 3.1 Interpersonal maturity level system, showing characteristics of integration level (I-level) and nine subtypes (after Warren, 1983)

I-2 level. Egocentric concern with own needs; sees others as givers or withholders; unable to comprehend or predict reactions of others.

    1. *Asocial, aggressive (Aa)*. Actively demanding and aggressive when frustrated.

    2. *Asocial, passive (Ap)*. Whining, complaining and withdrawn when frustrated.

I-3 level. Some awareness of effects of behaviour on others, but limited understanding of their differences from self; sees environment as manipulable and organised along a power dimension; lacks internal values; relies on external, black and white rules.

    3. *Passive conformist (Cfm)*. Compliant to whoever has power at the moment.

    4. *Cultural conformist (Cfc)*. Conforms to specific reference group of delinquent peers

    5. *Antisocial manipulator (Mp)*. Undermines authority figures to usurp power for self.

I-4 level. Sees self in terms of expectations of others; concerned with status and respect; adopts roles observed in others, including identification with heroes; has internalised, but rigid standards which produce feelings of inadequacy, self-criticism and guilt.

    6. *Neurotic, acting out (Na)*. Acts out guilt reactions to avoid conscious anxiety or self-condemnation.

    7. *Neurotic, anxious (Nx)*. Emotionally disturbed when conflicted by feelings of inadequacy and guilt.

    8. *Situational emotional reaction (Se)*. Acts out immediate family or personal crisis.

    9. *Cultural identifier (Ci)*. Lives out delinquent beliefs in response to deviant identification.

Cropley (1976) found that nonrecidivists showed higher levels of maturity than recidivists.

Assignment to levels and subtypes is made by means of a semistructured interview, for which interrater reliabilities are satisfactory, although higher for level than type (Harris, 1988). An alternative approach uses the Jesness Inventory (Jesness, 1988), a 155-item questionnaire measuring 10 variables relevant to the assessment of delinquents (e.g. value orientation, immaturity, social anxiety), from which scales to identify I-level subtypes have been developed against criterion groups selected by the interview procedure. The most recent version shows 67% agreement with interview classification of level, but only 35% for type (Jesness and Wedge, 1984), and Jesness cautions against assuming a direct correspondence between the two procedures. The inventory measures are more economic and reliable, and their construct validity was established by Jesness and Wedge (1984), who found significant differences between subtypes across a range of demographic, social, attitudinal, and delinquency-related measures. However, there are insufficient data to judge whether the interview procedure yields more valid discriminations.

The I-level system has been used primarily as a classification for differential treatment, on the assumption that offenders at different maturity levels offend for different reasons, and require different kinds of intervention to reduce the likelihood of recidivism. Although initially employed in the treatment of court-martialled naval prisoners (Grant and Grant, 1959), the system has been most widely used with juvenile wards of the California Youth Authority, particularly in the Community Treatment Project, which ran from 1961 to 1976. This aimed to determine whether reductions in recidivism can be optimised by exposing different I-level subtypes to different treatment settings, treaters, and types of treatment, and differential outcomes were demonstrated in several instances. For example, "neurotic" delinquents did better when supervised in the community, while "power oriented" delinquents did better with initial placement in a traditional institution (Palmer, 1974). Also, I-2 and I-3 Cfc types responded more favourably to behaviour modification than to transactional analysis, the reverse being the case for I-3 Mp youths (Jesness, 1975).

These differential outcomes support the construct validity of the system, which is currently used in penal settings in several countries (Harris, 1988). However, I-level theory has yet to be subject to close research scrutiny. It remains to be shown, for example, that I-levels correspond to distinct sequential components of development, and whether they reflect change within a single or several dimensions. Also, while the theory resembles other cognitive developmental theories, its advantages are unclear. In one of the few tests of the theory, Austin (1975) found that despite the focus on social maturity, I-level measures related more closely to intelligence and moral attitudes. He questions the validity of the classification procedures. Subtype distinctions are similarly untested hypotheses, and whether they are tied to levels as proposed, or represent mutually exclusive classes, has not been addressed. While the system is a sophisticated approach to distinguishing delinquents and their needs, equally useful distinctions might be achieved by more basic cognitive and personality dimensions. For example, a correlation of about 0.3 has been found consistently between I-level and general intelligence, and Smith (1974) found that the Jesness types were significantly differentiated by Eysenck's dimensions, more particularly scales of impulsivity, psychoticism, and neuroticism.

Conceptual levels matching

The *conceptual levels model* originates in the conceptual systems theory of Harvey, Hunt and Schroder (1961), which shares a similar theoretical parentage with I-level theory. It also assumes that socialisation proceeds through stages of increasing cognitive complexity in interpersonal orientation, but proposes four levels: (1) *egocentric* (concrete thinking, "me" oriented); (2) *norm-oriented* (uncritical, acceptance-seeking); (3) *independent* (inquiring, assertive, "I" oriented); (4) *interdependent* (cognitive complexity, "we" oriented). Although there is evidence for an unorganised, primitive conceptual level (sub-1) among delinquents (Hunt and Hardt, 1965), applications of the system are less concerned with causal explanation than with differential treatment.

The model assumes that individuals function optimally when their conceptual level matches environmental characteristics, an inverse relationship being suggested between conceptual level and degree of environmental structure (i.e. rules, control, support, negotiation). Individuals at lower conceptual levels function better in environments with high structure and low ambiguity, those at higher levels profiting more from low structure and flexibility. A person–environment mismatch generates tension and disruption, and environmental programming is necessary to achieve "contemporaneous matching", which produces stability, or "developmental matching", which promotes change.

The system has been developed mainly in educational and clinical settings, but Reitsma-Street and Leschied (1988) describe recent applications to the design of correctional programmes. Individual conceptual level is assessed by a brief, semi-projective procedure, and the routines, expectations, activities and social atmospheres of residential or training environments are restructured to match offender groups of different levels. While there has not yet been any long term investigation of the effects of conceptual levels matching with offenders, its prescriptions for person–environment interactions offer an innovative focus for offender rehabilitation.

EMPIRICAL CLASSIFICATIONS

Empirical approaches rely on the identification of dimensions through factor analysis of behavioural *items* assessed across individuals, or the delineation of types through cluster analysis of *individuals* assessed across items or dimensions. An early study, however, clustered items derived from case-note descriptions of 500 "problem children" in a child guidance clinic (Hewitt and Jenkins, 1946). Four clusters were identified and described as "unsocialised aggressive behaviour" (UA), "socialised delinquency" (SD), "overinhibited" (OI), and "physical deficiency". Children in the UA group were distinguished from SD children by more aggression and destructiveness, and lack of group loyalty, and the UA group has been regarded as a childhood precursor of psychopathic personality (Jenkins, 1960). Shinohara and Jenkins (1967) supported the validity of the typology, finding that UA delinquents described themselves as more psychologically deviant than SD on the MMPI. A 10-year follow-up also found that SD delinquents were less likely to violate parole or to become adult criminals (Henn, Bardwell and Jenkins, 1980). However, the utility of the typology is limited by its derivation from case history data and crude statistical methods, and only a minority of children in the original study could be unambiguously assigned to nonoverlapping types. In applying the typology to British approved school boys, Field (1967) similarly found that few could be assigned specifically to a single type.

Quay's behaviour classification dimensions

More systematic is the work of Quay, who has identified dimensions of deviant behaviour through factor analyses of self-report, case history, and behaviour rating data obtained from delinquent populations, as well as from clinical, pre-school, and school samples (Quay, 1977a; 1987a). Although identified by differing labels, the four main dimensions emerge from other studies of child behaviour disorder. They are currently described as *unsocialised aggression* (UA), *anxiety–withdrawal–dysphoria* (AW), *attention deficit* (AD), and *socialised aggression* (SA).

The first two factors appear consistently in all measurement media, and correspond to higher-order "externalising" and "internalising" factors found ubiquitously in measures of child problems (Achenbach and Edelbrock, 1978). They also have counterparts in adult populations (Blackburn, 1979a; Quay, 1984). UA has been described variously as conduct disorder, psychopathy, aggression, or undercontrol, and its defining features are assaultive, disobedient, destructive, untrustworthy, and boisterous characteristics. AW, also described as personality problems, withdrawal, neuroticism, or overcontrol, is defined by hypersensitive, shy, socially withdrawn, and sad traits. The remaining two factors are less consistently identified. SA (socialised delinquency, subcultural) appears mainly in case history data, and reflects gang-based delinquency, as seen in a history of mixing with bad companions, group stealing, loyalty to delinquent friends, truancy, and staying out late. AD was previously described as immaturity–inadequacy, and is most prominent in observer ratings. It is defined by preoccupation, short attention span, daydreaming, sluggishness, and impulsivity, and is similar to the DSM-III category of Attention-deficit Hyperactivity Disorder.

Delinquents are grouped into categories on the basis of their highest score on a particular dimension. Factors can be measured by composite scores derived from different assessment media, but more commonly by rating scales of the Behaviour Problem Checklist (Quay, 1977a). Reliabilities are satisfactory for UA and AW, though less so for AD and SD. Evidence on validity has accumulated in several studies which demonstrate differential performance of groups in response to laboratory experiments and criminal justice interventions (Quay, 1987a).

Quay (1984) describes an extension of this approach to adult offenders. The *Adult Internal Management System* (AIMS) identifies five factors, labelled aggressive–psychopathic, manipulative, situational, inadequate–dependent, and neurotic–anxious, which are measured by a rating scale and case history checklist. This classification is currently used by several American prisons to facilitate "internal management", which aims to divide prisoners into more homogeneous and manageable subgroups (Levinson, 1988). Its use has successfully identified groups differing in response to institutional regimes, and reduced the level of serious institutional incidents.

Quay's work justifies the view that theories or interventions with little utility for unselected samples of delinquents may nonetheless be applicable to homogeneous subgroups. However, there are limitations to the classification.

First, correlations of factors across different assessment media are at best modest (Quay, 1984). Attempts to resolve this by composite, multimedia assessment are not entirely successful, since they confound personality traits (UA, AW) with symptoms of disorder (AD) and socially deviant behaviours (SA). Second, factors are not statistically independent. For example, Quay (1984) reports correlations of 0.68 between the aggressive–psychopathic and manipulative scales of AIMS, and 0.48 between the inadequate–dependent and neurotic–anxious scales, suggesting that discriminations might be achieved with fewer factors. Third, the system blurs the distinction between dimensions and persons. Individuals are classified by their highest factor score, but since all individuals can be assigned a score on all factors, this procedure produces artificial categories, which only approximate naturally occurring groups. The system could therefore be refined by the identification of multidimensional *patterns* of factor scores.

Megargee's MMPI-based classification

Multidimensional profile types are usually identified through cluster analysis, which has been applied by some investigators to differentiate homogeneous personality subgroups within specific offence categories (Blackburn, 1971a; Donovan and Marlatt, 1982). However, the most extensively investigated typology applied to unselected offenders is the *MMPI-based criminal classification system* developed by Megargee from studies of young male adult inmates of the Federal Correctional Institution (FCI) at Tallahassee in Florida (Megargee and Bohn, 1979). Hierarchical cluster analysis of samples of standard MMPI profiles identified 10 types, most of which have been found in other samples, including female and mentally disordered offenders, though the applicability of the typology to juveniles is less clear (Zager, 1988).

Applying the system to all 1214 inmates of FCI, Megargee and Bohn (1979) found that a combination of computerised classification rules and inspection of profiles reliably assigned 96% to profile classes. The classes were identified by neutral alphabetic titles (Able, Baker, Charlie, etc.), and compared on 116 variables covering demographic, educational, developmental, familial, offence, and institutional behaviour, as well as psychological interview and test data. Significant differences between the 10 types were obtained in 97% of comparisons, supporting concurrent and predictive validity, and the more distinctive features of seven of the groups have been replicated by other investigators (Zager, 1988). Table 3.2 illustrates the salient characteristics of the 10 types and the percentage of FCI inmates falling in each group. The types are listed in increasing order of deviance, as suggested by the defining MMPI profiles.

Zager (1988) summarises research on the system, which suggests that it is replicable across different institutional samples, can be reliably applied, and predicts both institutional and postrelease adjustment. While further data are needed on its sensitivity to change and its utility in predicting response to intervention, the system has been considered sufficiently promising to be adopted in several federal correctional institutions.

Table 3.2   Megargee's MMPI-based criminal classification system

Group, percentage of FCI, and MMPI scale patterns	Salient characteristics and management needs
Item (19%) No scales elevated	Stable and well adjusted; most socialised; drug and liquor law violators; middle class; easily managed; no treatment needs.
Easy (7%) Normal, but high on 4 and 3	Best adjusted; bright, but underachieving; favourable home environment; least deviant or violent; need motivating to achieve potential.
Baker (4%) 4 and 2 elevated	Poor adjustment; anxious; passive; withdrawn; alcohol problems; troublesome in prison; need psychotherapy or counselling.
Able (17%) 4 and 9 elevated	Dominant, hostile, and opportunistic; amoral; self-accepting; socially skilled; high recidivism; need structured, confrontive therapeutic approach.
George (7%) High 4 and 2	Unaggressive; drug and liquor offences; bright; deviant families; accept criminal values; high recidivism; no marked deficits, but career skills training needed.
Delta (10%) High 4	Hedonistic; egocentric; bright; poor family relations; poor prison adjustment; high recidivism; unlikely to respond to psychological treatment.
Jupiter (3%) High 9, 8, and 7	Mainly blacks; anxious; poor interpersonal adjustment; unstable families; violent in prison, but only moderate recidivism; need practical help in rehabilitation.
Foxtrot (8%) High 9, 4, and 8	Dominant; violent; least socialised; poorly educated; disorganised, deprived backgrounds; extensive criminal records; high recidivism; need firm management.
Charlie (9%) High 8, 6, 9, 4 and 7	Hostile; withdrawn; unempathic; aggressive; extensive criminal records; academic and social skill deficits; significant mental health problems; poor prognosis.
How (13%) Most scales very high	Low intelligence and achievement; anxious; passive; withdrawn; aggressive; early delinquency and interpersonal problems; recidivist; mentally disordered.

There are, however, several limitations to the utility of the system. First is its derivation from standard profiles of the MMPI, which—despite a rich sampling of adjustment problems and continued popularity among American clinicians—is psychometrically flawed. The clinical scales are highly intercorrelated, and factor analyses indicate that they measure little more than combinations of the well known neuroticism and introversion–extraversion dimensions (Kassebaum, Couch and Slater, 1959; McCrae and Costa, 1986). Differences between profile types may therefore partly reflect differences of degree rather than kind. A second, related issue is whether differentiation of 10 profile types is warranted. Several profiles overlap, and a smaller number might be equally discriminating. While Megargee and Bohn (1979) argue that the 10 types are sufficiently distinguished by nontest variables to be regarded as independent, they offer no *a priori* criteria for deciding whether the tenfold typology is optimal, other than the procedural rules of the cluster analytic method employed. A third question is whether the typology is replicable across *methods* of cluster analysis, an essential step given indeterminacies in cluster analytic procedures. Finally, the inductive approach adopted in developing this typology was atheoretical. In this respect, reliance on the standard MMPI, which does not adequately mirror any coherent personality theory, represents a significant shortcoming.

Comparisons between systems

The entities within a domain of interest can be divided in different ways, and the utility of a particular classification depends on its purpose. The classifications described above differ in the extent to which they were developed to aid in research, management, or treatment, and also in terms of theoretical underpinnings, psychological attributes given primacy, assessment methods, and offender populations in which they were developed. They cannot, then, be regarded as competing or interchangeable. At the same time, they are not mutually exclusive, and some overlap might be expected.

Warren (1971) attempted to identify convergence across 16 systems proposed in the literature, and suggested that the following six types were represented by conceptually similar categories in different systems: *asocial* (I-2, Jenkins' and Quay's UA, conceptual level sub-1, DSM-I passive–aggressive and aggressive); *conformist* (I-3 Cfm and Cfc, Jenkins' SD, Quay's immature–inadequate and socialised delinquency, conceptual level 1); *antisocial manipulator* (I-3 Mp, DSM-1 antisocial personality); *neurotic* (I-4 Na and Nx, Jenkins' OI, Quay's AW, DSM-1 sociopathic personality, conceptual level 2); *subcultural identifier* (I-4 Ci, Jenkins' and Quay's socialised delinquency, conceptual level 2); and *situational* (I-4 Se, conceptual level 2).

There are few data on which to judge the validity of these proposals or the extent of overlap between systems. Jesness and Wedge (1984) note significant correlations of I-level with other systems of cognitive developmental level, including a correlation of 0.45 with Hunt's conceptual level system. Jurkovic and Prentice (1977) also found some relation between Quay's system and Kohlberg's stages, UA (psychopathic) delinquents being at a lower moral stage than controls or delinquents classified as SA or AW. Carbonell (1983) attempted a cross-tabulation of the MMPI and Jesness I-level systems with adult inmates. Although the association was significant, this was largely due to an overlap of I-2 with the most deviant MMPI types (Charlie, Foxtrot, How), and she concluded that overall there was little overlap between the typologies.

The only multiple cross-classification reported to date is a pilot for a study of five classifications (I-level, Megargee's MMPI system, Quay's AIMS, Hunt's conceptual level, and Kohlberg's stages of moral reasoning) conducted with adult prisoners (Van Hoorhis, 1988). The results point to weak to moderate convergences. For example, the three developmental stage systems were positively correlated, highest correlation being 0.31 between the I-level and Kohlberg systems, and AIMS aggressive–psychopathic was related to both I-3 level and to MMPI Charlie and Foxtrot profile types. Both MMPI and AIMS systems predicted prison disciplinary infractions, while victimised inmates were more likely to be at the lowest conceptual and I-levels. Little correspondence was found between "neurotic" or "situational" types from different systems. Given the sample size of 52, these results are tentative, but they highlight the heterogeneity of prisoners.

PSYCHIATRIC CLASSIFICATION AND ANTISOCIAL BEHAVIOUR

Psychological classifications of offenders have developed independently of psychiatric classification, and are concerned more with patterns of strengths and deficits than the identification of disorder. Nevertheless, shared features can be expected given overlap between criminal and clinical samples. The relation of crime to the major mental disorders is examined in Chapter 10, but since antisocial behaviour is implicated in several psychiatric categories, some consideration of these is warranted here. The discussion centres on the revised third edition of the Diagnostic and Statistical Manual (DSM-III-R; American Psychiatric Association, 1987), which has achieved wider international recognition than previous editions.

DSM-III attempted to improve the reliability of psychiatric diagnosis by introducing operational criteria to define specific categories. A mental disorder is conceptualised as:

> ... a clinically significant behavioural or psychological syndrome or pattern that occurs in a person and that is associated with present distress (a painful symptom) or disability (impairment in one or more important areas of functioning) or with a significantly increased risk of suffering death, pain, disability, or an important loss of freedom.

Deviant behaviour or conflict with society which is not a symptom of personal dysfunction is ostensibly excluded. Classification is multiaxial, clinicians being required to evaluate and code a presenting problem in terms of mental disorder (Axes I and II), physical disorder (Axis III), severity of psychosocial stressors (Axis IV), and global level of functioning (Axis V). Axis I comprises the major clinical syndromes (schizophrenia, mood disorders, etc.), and Axis II developmental and personality disorders. The distinction between Axes I and II implicitly acknowledges the conceptual separation of "illness" and "personality" (Foulds, 1971), and recognises that the two are not mutually exclusive, but frequently coexist.

Axis I

Axis I includes *psychoactive substance use disorders*, which often correlate with criminal behaviour, and *sexual disorders*, some of which are associated with sexual crimes (Chapter 11). It also includes *impulse control disorders*, a residual classification used only when the behaviour is not a clear component of some other mental disorder. The essential features are: (1) failure to resist an impulse, drive, or temptation to perform an act which is harmful to the person or others; (2) increasing tension or arousal prior to the act; (3) the experience of pleasure, gratification, or release at the time of committing the act. DSM-III-R lists five specific categories (Table 3.3). Intermittent explosive disorder (previously explosive personality disorder) is similar to the "episodic dyscontrol syndrome" (Chapter 6). Other disorders are remnants of an obsolete class of "monomanias", which attributed repetitive deviant acts to a pathological "fixed idea", and which included not only dipsomania and nymphomania, but also drapetomania (the running a way of slaves!). They are hypothetical causes rather than descriptions, and reflect the limited success of DSM-III in achieving its positivist aims of theory-neutral description (Faust and Miner, 1986).

Table 3.3 Specific categories of DSM-III-R impulse control disorders

1. Intermittent explosive disorder	Discrete episodes of loss of control of aggressive impulses, resulting in serious assaultive acts or property destruction; out of proportion to stressors; no generalised aggressiveness between episodes; not due to intoxication, psychosis, organic disorder, or other personality disorder.
2. Kleptomania	Recurrent failure to resist impulses to steal objects not needed for personal use or monetary value; tension before, and relief during theft; not due to anger, vengeance, conduct disorder, or antisocial personality disorder.
3. Pathological gambling	Preoccupation with gambling; increasing bets over time; irritability if unable to gamble; "chasing" losses; interference with obligations, and sacrifice of other acts; persistence despite legal or social consequences.
4. Pyromania	Deliberate and purposeful firesetting on more than one occasion; tension prior to, and gratification or relief during firesetting; curiosity about, or attraction to fire and associated characteristics; not motivated by gain, anger, or concealment of crime.
5. Trichotillomania	Failure to resist impulses to pull out one's hair; tension prior to and gratification during hair-pulling.

DSM-III distinguishes impulse control disorders from "true" *compulsions* on the grounds that, in the former, the person derives pleasure from the act. This is somewhat arbitrary, since "release" from tension is explicit in the definition of both, and traditionally, "pathological" gambling, theft, or firesetting have been regarded as compulsive acts. They are of legal interest in view of the acceptance in some criminal jurisdictions of "irresistible impulse" as an insanity defence (Chapter 10), and the controversy over the criminal status of "compulsive crimes" (Cressey, 1969; Cunnien, 1985).

The validity of impulse control disorders as a distinct class is questionable on conceptual grounds. An "impulse" is a circular inference of cause from the behaviour it supposedly impels, and "failure to resist an impulse" is similarly inferred from the observation that an act has been performed. Moreover, these disorders are distinguished by the exclusion of acts having an immediately "obvious" motive. Thus, firesetting becomes pyromania only when it is not motivated by material gain, anger, ideology, or concealment of a crime, or is not a response to a delusion or hallucination. This, however, reduces the criteria to social judgements of "irrational" or "not intuitively understandable". As Cressey (1969) notes, labels implying "compulsion" are, in fact, applied when neither the perpetrator nor an observer can account for the behaviour in terms of motives which are current, popular, or culturally sanctioned. For example, the behaviour of the wealthy shoplifter who steals items of small value is not obviously explained by economic need, and is more likely to be attributed to "pathological" need. However, this reflects a dubious assumption that shoplifting in general is adequately explained by economic need.

Concepts such as kleptomania also imply that the behaviour is intrinsically motivated, or reinforced *sui generis*, but if extrinsic motives can be demonstrated, then the concept becomes redundant. Burt (1925) observed that kleptomania and pyromania were pseudo-scientific terms, and that thorough analysis of specific repetitive delinquencies usually revealed them to be substitute or symbolic activities related to "mental conflict". More recent writers take a similar view. Gibbens (1981), for example, found that a significant but small minority of shoplifters was depressed, and that trivial thefts in such cases appeared to serve the function of providing "a treat", expressing spite, or punishing self or others. Marshall and Barbaree (1984) also argue that these putative disorders can be understood in social learning terms. They construe kleptomania and pyromania as inappropriate forms of assertion developing in the context of deficient social skills. Jackson, Glass and Hope (1987) similarly propose an analysis of recidivist arson in which firesetting is a learned means of exerting control over the environment in the context of poor self-esteem and deficient assertion. Other theoretical analyses may be equally plausible, but compulsive harmful behaviour can clearly be accounted for without invoking fictitious "manias".

The classification of impulse control disorders, then, does not identify specific psychological disorders having distinguishable referents. Rather are these classes explanatory fictions introduced when people are unable to attribute their repeated deviant acts to an "acceptable" or "rational" cause. Repetitive aggression, shoplifting, or arson can serve a variety of functions, which may sometimes be related to personal crises, conflicts, or dysfunctions in ways which the person does not fully comprehend. While there is a case for subdividing particular forms of repetitive deviant behaviour according to categories of motive (or reinforcer), a classification which effectively rests on arbitrary distinctions between "rational" and "irrational" has no scientific utility.

Axis II: developmental disorders

Under "Disorders usually first evident in infancy, childhood, or adolescence", DSM-III-R identifies several specific disorders, such as *mental retardation*, *pervasive developmental disorders* (e.g. autism), *specific developmental disorders* (inadequate development of academic, language, speech, and motor skills), and *anxiety disorders of childhood and adolescence*. Of particular relevance to antisocial behaviour are *disruptive behaviour disorders*, which refer to "externalising" symptom patterns observed predominantly in boys, appearing often in the preschool years. The specific categories are: *attention-deficit hyperactivity disorder* (ADHD); *conduct disorder*; and *oppositional defiant disorder*.

ADHD covers developmentally inappropriate degrees of inattention, impulsiveness and hyperactivity, as shown, for example, by frequent fidgeting, distractibility, excessive talking, and difficulty in sustaining attention or remaining seated. In earlier literature, this symptom complex was described as *hyperactivity*, which emphasised motor restlessness, and which in turn has been used interchangeably with the aetiological concept of *minimal brain dysfunction* (MBD: Rutter, 1982). The current DSM concept reflects greater emphasis on attentional aspects. However, the validity of the concepts of ADHD, hyperactivity or MBD remains controversial (Henker and Whalen, 1989), and the assumption that child attentional and motoric problems are symptoms of "subclinical" brain damage has been increasingly questioned. Disagreement about the utility of these terms is reflected in international diagnostic variations, hyperactivity being diagnosed in about a half of child psychiatric referrals in North America, but in only 1% of referred cases of normal intelligence in Britain (Rutter, 1982).

Conduct disorder denotes persistent antisocial behaviour which violates the rights of others and age-appropriate societal norms, onset being usually prepubertal. Criteria include stealing, running away from home, lying, firesetting, truancy, breaking and entering, property destruction, cruelty to animals, forced sexual activity, and fighting. The category is subdivided into group, solitary, and undifferentiated types. Oppositional defiant disorder involves less serious antisocial behaviour, occurring mainly in the home, and is defined by negativistic, hostile and defiant acts, such as loss of temper, defying adult requests, being easily annoyed, and swearing.

It will be noted that conduct disorder in adolescents would amount to delinquency, and there are some parallels between the categories of ADHD and conduct disorder and Quay's attention deficit and unsocialised aggressive dimensions, respectively, although conduct disorder also subsumes socialised aggression. Nevertheless, the independence of the DSM-III-R categories continues to be debated, and there is no empirical or theoretical basis for distinguishing oppositional defiant disorder as a distinct disorder. Hyperactivity has long been linked with child conduct problems, such as aggression or stealing, but the nature of the relationship has been obscured by the inclusion of such problems among the diagnostic criteria in earlier work. Factor analytic studies have now established that hyperactivity and conduct disorder or aggression are separate factors having different correlates (Hinshaw, 1987), and hyperactivity has also been distinguished from inattentiveness (McGee, Williams and Silva, 1985). However, ratings of these factors typically correlate quite highly, and diagnoses of hyperactivity or ADHD and conduct disorder overlap substantially. The relationship between hyperactivity and delinquency is examined further in Chapter 6.

Axis II: personality disorders

Personality disorders refer to psychological problems arising from personal dispositions rather than breakdown or discontinuity in psychological functioning. Forensic psychiatric populations contain many individuals with these disorders (Tyrer, 1988; Blackburn et al., 1990), and surveys suggest that they are prevalent among prisoners (Chapter 10). Firm data are sparse, particularly since differentiation within this class has been overshadowed by a focus on the more global concept of psychopathic personality. Interest in these disorders has also been limited as a result of controversy over the utility of trait concepts, and debates within psychiatry about whether they should be regarded as mental disorders (Schwartz and Schwartz, 1976).

The inclusion of personality disorders under Axis II has renewed interest in their classification (Widiger et al., 1988). DSM-III emphasises personality *traits*, which are defined as "enduring patterns of perceiving, relating to, and thinking about the environment and oneself". Traits constitute personality disorder when they are "inflexible and maladaptive" and result in social dysfunction or subjective distress. Eleven categories of disorder are recognised, while tentative categories of sadistic and self-defeating disorder were added to an appendix in DSM-III-R. Table 3.4 shows the central features exemplifying the 13 categories, and examples of defining criteria.

Classification is polythetic, assignment to categories requiring the presence of only some of the defining criteria. It will be noted that criminal behaviour appears among the criteria for *antisocial personality disorder* (APD), which has some affinity with earlier concepts of psychopathic personality, and Hare (1983) found that 39% of prisoners in two Canadian prisons met the criteria for this disorder. It is also prevalent among substance abusers (Khantzian and Treece, 1985), and mentally disordered offenders (Barbour-McMullen, Coid and Howard, 1988; Hart and Hare, 1989). However, other categories, such as borderline and narcissistic disorders, are also prevalent in antisocial populations (Hare, 1983; Frosch, 1983; McManus et al., 1984).

Despite the provision of operational criteria for each disorder, the reliability of clinical judgements of personality disorder remains low. Mellsop et al., (1982), for example, found a mean interjudge reliability (kappa) of only 0.41, highest agreement being for APD. This low level of agreement between clinicians seriously restricts the utility of the classification. It reflects the inferential nature of many criteria, as well as problems in making dichotomous judgements about the presence of traits from restricted observations (Widiger and Frances, 1985a). Nevertheless, improved reliability has been achieved by

Table 3.4 Characteristics of DSM-III-R personality disorder categories

Category	Pervasive tendencies and representative traits
Paranoid	Interprets peoples' actions as demeaning or threatening (expects exploitation, questions trustworthiness, bears grudges).
Schizoid	Indifferent to social relations, restricted emotional experience and expression (solitary, aloof, indifferent to criticism or praise, strong emotions rare).
Schizotypal	Deficient personal relationships, peculiarities of ideation, appearance, and behaviour (social anxiety, no close friends, magical thinking, unusual perceptions, odd speech).
Antisocial	Conduct disorder before, and irresponsible and antisocial behaviour since age 15 (poor work record, illegal acts, fights, defaults on debts, impulsive, reckless, irresponsible parenting, no consistent attachments, lacks remorse).
Borderline	Instability of mood, interpersonal relations, and self-image (intense relationships, mood instability, intense anger, identity disturbance, impulsive, self-mutilation, fears abandonment).
Histrionic	Excessively emotional and attention seeking (seeks attention and approval, self-centred, inappropriately seductive, exaggerated and shallow expressions of emotion).
Narcissistic	Grandiose in fantasy or behaviour, lacks empathy, hypersensitive to evaluation (exploitative, self-important, feels entitled to admiration, preoccupied with success, upset by criticism).
Avoidant	Social discomfort, fears negative evaluation, timid (hurt by criticism, fears embarrassment, avoids involvements, socially reticent, exaggerates risks).
Dependent	Dependent and submissive (needs reassurance, lets others make decisions, fears rejection and criticism, lacks initiative).
Obsessive compulsive	Perfectionism and inflexibility (strict standards, preoccupied with detail, indecisive, insists others do things his/her way).
Passive aggressive	Passive resistance to demands for adequate social and occupational performance (procrastinates, sulky, resents suggestions, avoids obligations, obstructive, works slowly and reluctantly).
Sadistic	Cruel, demeaning, and aggressive (intimidating, humiliating, amused by suffering, fascinated by weapons and violence).
Self-defeating	Avoids pleasurable experiences or seeks relationships which produce suffering (incites rejection, self-sacrificing).

the development of questionnaires, rating scales, and structured interviews (Widiger and Frances, 1987).

The validity of the classification remains largely unexplored. Although DSM-111 drew on the theoretical classification proposed by Millon (1981), and on recent psychodynamic formulations of abnormal personality (Fromm, 1973; Kernberg, 1975), the current categories depart from these in several ways, and do not reflect a single coherent model of personality. DSM recognises overlap between categories, and recommends multiple diagnosis when a person meets criteria for more than one disorder. Nevertheless, to establish validity it needs to be shown that categories are internally consistent and distinguishable from each other. Evidence for the validity of specific categories is limited and on the whole weak (Blackburn, 1988a), and although Morey (1988) found that criteria clustered into categories which broadly resemble those proposed in DSM-III, it seems unlikely that the categories currently specified represent the optimal clustering of inflexible and maladaptive dispositions.

Dimensional classification of personality disorder

While the concept of personality disorder assumes quantitative rather than qualitatative variations from normality, the use of categorical classification in DSM-III spuriously implies a discontinuity between disorders, and between disorder and normality. Several attempts have been made to describe these disorders in dimensional terms. Marshall and Barbaree (1984), for example, see them as unskilful behaviours, and suggest that the criteria can be sorted into behavioural dimensions describing different kinds of social dysfunction, such as inappropriate assertiveness, dysfunctional social cognitions, or social anxiety.

Personality disorders are primarily deviations from the norms of interpersonal behaviour (Foulds, 1971), and an empirically established dimensional system for describing interpersonal behaviour is the *interpersonal circle* originating in the work of Leary (1957), and developed subsequently by several writers (Wiggins, 1982; Kiesler, 1983: Strong et al., 1988). The relationship between interpersonal behaviours can be represented by a circular array, or circumplex, around two orthogonal dimensions of power or control (dominant–submissive) and affiliation (hostile-friendly), different interactions being varying blends of these two. Interpersonal styles can also be identified by this system as segments of the circle around the dominance and hostility axes, and these have clear parallels in the categories of personality disorder (Widiger and Frances, 1985a). However, as these segments do not have precise boundaries, the notion of discrete categories of disorder becomes simply a convenient fiction. Such a system more realistically portrays the continuity between normal and abnormal personality.

Figure 3.1 outlines how personality disorder categories might be accommodated by this model (Blackburn, 1989). The continuous circle of interpersonal traits is marked by summary labels of hostile, withdrawn, etc. The inner circle represents the normal range, and the outer circle the more extreme inflexible styles, which reflect different combinations of hostility and dominance. Thus, avoidant personality represents hostile submission, narcissistic personality dominance and hostility. This analysis suggests that the domain of personality disorder could be represented by a smaller number of styles. The model may also provide a means of integrating some of the offender classifications described earlier. For example, Quay's unsocialised aggressive and anxious–withdrawn dimensions appear to correspond to the coercive–compliant and withdrawn–sociable axes of the circle, respectively.

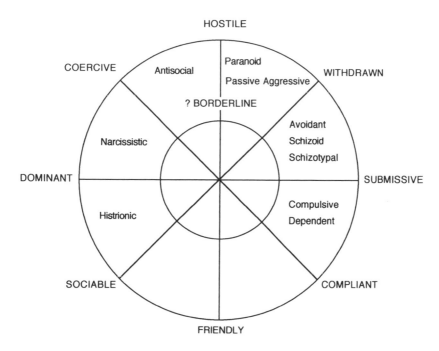

Figure 3.1 Hypothesised relation of categories of personality disorder to the interpersonal circle. From Blackburn (1989), reproduced by permission

Although there is only limited empirical research on the relation between the DSM-III classes and this scheme (Kiesler et al., 1990), it has theoretical underpinnings with implications for explanation and intervention. Interpersonal theory proposes that social exchanges generally follow a complementary pattern, i.e. social behaviours "pull" either opposite (dominant–submissive) or congruent (friendly–friendly or hostile–hostile) behaviours from other people (Carson, 1979; Kiesler, 1983; Strong et al., 1988). Carson (1979) suggests that there is a causal link between beliefs about how others are likely to react, the enactment of behaviours consistent with these expectations, and confirmatory reactions from others. A hostile person, for example, expects hostility as a result of aversive life experiences, and behaves in a way which elicits confirmation of these expectancies from the reactions of others. Inflexible interpersonal styles thus come to be maintained as self-fulfilling prophecies which impede the learning of more appropriate skilled behaviour, and invalidation of these dysfunctional beliefs is therefore a central goal of therapy (Safran, 1990). This model underlies recent attempts to account for the consistency of an aggressive disposition across the lifespan (Chapter 9).

However, while reference to interpersonal dimensions is necessary to the classification of personality disorders, it may not be sufficient. Some criteria are *intra*personal dispositions, such as self-attitudes, and other dimensional systems for describing personality may also be relevant. There is now some consensus that most traits are subsumed by "the Big Five" dimensions of extraversion, agreeableness, neuroticism, conscientiousness, and openness to experience (McCrae and Costa, 1986), the first two of which define the interpersonal circle. Wiggins and Pincus (1989) examined the relation of these five dimensions to measures of personality disorder, and found that while histrionic, narcissistic, antisocial, schizoid, and avoidant disorders projected clearly onto the interpersonal circle, reference to all five dimensions, particularly neuroticism, provided a more complete representation. This convergence across the domains of personality disorder and dimensions of personality is confirmed by Schroeder, Wormworth and Livesley (1992). The salience of the neuroticism dimension may derive from its association with self-esteem (Watson and Clark, 1984).

PSYCHOPATHIC PERSONALITY AND PERSONALITY DISORDER

Historical background

The concept of psychopathic personality has occupied a prominent place in discussions of antisocial behaviour, but it must be emphasised that the term "psychopath" is a personality construct, and is not synonymous with "criminal". Although it has come to imply a category of antisocial or *socially damaging* individuals, as it originated in German psychiatry, psychopathic personality meant literally a *psychologically damaged* person.

The term no longer appears in formal classifications, but is represented by APD in DSM-III. The concept has been controversial throughout its history, and Pichot (1978) and Millon (1981) trace disagreements over its meaning to differing uses by German and English-speaking psychiatrists. Schneider (1950) followed Kraepelin in describing a tenfold typology of psychopathic personalities. He explicitly excluded antisocial behaviour from the criteria for abnormal personality, which he construed in statistical terms as a deviation from average. Psychopathic personalities were abnormal personalities who cause suffering to themselves or others. Paradoxically, this generic concept of psychopathic personalities corresponds to the broad class of personality disorders in DSM-III.

Schneider's concept was never widely adopted in Britain, where the nineteenth century notion of *moral insanity* resulted in the statutory category of *moral imbecile* in the 1913 Mental Deficiency Act, and eventually in the category of *psychopathic disorder* of the English Mental Health Act ("a persistent disorder or disability of mind ... which results in abnormally aggressive or seriously irresponsible conduct on the part of the person concerned"). Although the term psychopathic is adopted from the German, this category bears no resemblance to Schneider's concept. The definition in fact contains no reference to personality, the only defining features being the antisocial conduct from which a "mental disability" is inferred.

A similar transformation of the term psychopathic has occurred within American psychiatry, where it has been used interchangeably with *sociopathic*, a term denoting any form of socially deviant behaviour. Karpman (1948) explicitly rejected Schneider's concept of psychopathic personalities, and indeed the notion of personality disorders. He proposed that some of Schneider's categories were *primary psychopaths*, whose antisocial behaviour reflects uninhibited instinctual expression unmodified by conscience or guilt. The remainder were *secondary psychopaths* whose antisocial behaviour results from dynamic disturbance, and who were more properly classified with neuroses or psychoses. McCord and McCord (1964) also identify a narrow category, describing the psychopath as "an asocial, aggressive, highly impulsive person, who feels little or no guilt, and is unable to form lasting bonds of affection with other human beings". However, the concepts of primary and secondary psychopath have been adopted by some researchers to distinguish nonanxious from anxious deviant personalities in antisocial populations (Lykken, 1957; Schmauk, 1970; Blackburn, 1975a).

Cleckley (1976) took a similar view to that of Karpman, seeing most categories of personality disorder as neurotic or psychotic disorders, but he proposed a "distinct clinical entity" of psychopathic personality defined by 16 criteria, such as superficial charm, unreliability, lack of remorse, egocentricity, and interpersonal unresponsiveness. Cleckley's concept has been influential in guiding psychological research (Hare, 1986), but it has also been criticised as a misleading stereotype (Vaillant, 1975).

The DSM concept of antisocial personality, however, was influenced by the research of Robins (1978), and the category is defined by detailed criteria of delinquent and socially undesirable behaviour. Reference to personality traits is limited to irritability and aggressiveness, impulsivity, and recklessness, although lack of remorse was added in DSM-III-R.

Measurement of psychopathy

Given the varying conceptualisations of psychopathy, it is perhaps not surprising that unanimity on appropriate operational definition has not been achieved, and available measures reflect differing assumptions about psychopathy and the preferences of different investigators for particular forms of measurement. Most research during the past three decades has relied on one or more of the following measures.

(1) *Cleckley's criteria.* Lykken (1957), and subsequently Hare (1986), popularised Cleckley's concept as a basis for identifying psychopaths in deviant populations. Assessment has usually entailed a global rating of the extent to which an individual's life history data meet Cleckley's 16 criteria, rather than detailed ratings of the specific criteria. Satisfactory interrater reliabilities have been achieved, but use of this measure has rested on the assumption that Cleckley's concept is valid, and his criteria internally consistent.

(2) *Psychopathy Checklist (PCL).* In an attempt to produce a more objective scale, Hare has developed a checklist from factor analyses of ratings of Cleckley's criteria and other attributes of psychopaths suggested by the literature (Hare,

1980; Hare et al., 1990). Items of the scale reflect both a history of social deviance and deficiencies in interpersonal sensitivity emphasised by Cleckley (Table 3.5), and are rated from case history data and a structured interview. The scale has satisfactory reliabilities, and correlates highly with global Cleckley ratings. Offenders scoring high and low on the scale have been shown to differ on a variety of behavioural and laboratory measures, supporting its construct and predictive validity. While the mixture of personality attributes with static antisocial life history data restricts its utility to nonclinical studies with criminal populations, recent analyses indicate that two oblique factors are distinguishable (Hare et al., 1990). One is an interpersonal dimension of selfish, callous and remorseless use of others, the other a dimension of socially deviant lifestyle.

(3) *MMPI scales*. Scale 4 of the MMPI (*Pd*: Psychopathic deviate) was developed empirically against a criterion group of psychologically disturbed delinquents, and is usually the scale on which offender samples score highest. While it has been used in some studies as a measure of psychopathic personality, its content is primarily concerned with nonconformity and conflict with family and authority, and seems more appropriately construed as social rule-breaking rather than psychopathic personality *per se* (Hawk and Peterson, 1974). A more specific criterion is the combined elevation of scales 4 and 9 (*Ma*: Hypomania), the latter relating to impulsivity or "acting out". The 4–9 profile is common among offenders, and in Megargee's MMPI classification, defines group Able, which was the second largest group in the FCI study (Megargee and Bohn, 1979). This pattern conforms to the notion of primary psychopath, since it reflects relatively low scores on scales measuring emotionality. When combined with elevations on scales assessing anxiety (7: Psychasthenia; 0: Social Introversion), moodiness (2: Depression) or deviant perceptual and interpersonal experiences (6: Paranoia; 8: Schizophrenia), it suggests traits of the secondary psychopath.

Cluster analyses of MMPI profiles of abnormal murderers (Blackburn, 1971a) and offenders in the English Mental Health Act category of psychopathic disorder (Blackburn, 1975a) identified the 4–9 profile as one of four main patterns, and Blackburn (1982) developed the SHAPS (Special Hospitals Assessment of Personality and Socialisation) to measure the main variables contributing to differentiation between these patterns. This 10-scale questionnaire is based mainly on MMPI items, but most of the variance is summarised by two factors, for which scales have been developed (Blackburn, 1987). The first (Belligerence) measures impulsivity and hostility versus conformity, the second (Withdrawal) measuring shyness and poor self-esteem versus sociability and confidence. Primary and secondary psychopaths are identified in the empirical classification by high scores on the first factor, but opposite extremes on the second.

(4) *Socialisation scale* (*So*). The 54-item *So* scale from Gough's California Psychological Inventory (Gough, 1969) measures the extent to which a person has internalised social values and considers them personally binding. It is one of the best validated self-report scales in use, having a point biserial

Table 3.5   Items of the Psychopathy Checklist (PCL)

---

 1. Glibness/superficial charm
*2. Previous diagnosis as a psychopath
 3. Egocentricity/grandiose sense of self-worth
 4. Proneness to boredom/low frustration tolerance
 5. Pathological lying and deception
 6. Conning/lack of sincerity
 7. Lack of remorse or guilt
 8. Lack of affect and emotional depth
 9. Callous/lack of empathy
10. Parasitic lifestyle
11. Short-tempered/poor behavioural controls
12. Promiscuous sexual relations
13. Early behaviour problems
14. Lack of realistic, long-term plans
15. Impulsivity
16. Irresponsible behaviour as a parent
17. Frequent marital relationships
18. Juvenile delinquency
19. Poor probation or parole risk
20. Failure to accept responsibility for own actions
21. Many types of offence
*22. Drug or alcohol not direct cause of antisocial behaviour

---

*Omitted in revised PCL

From Hare (1980). Reproduced by permission of Pergamon Press Ltd.

correlation of 0.73 with a criterion of more versus less delinquent ($N = 10296$). Gough (1948) proposed that the central feature of psychopathy is an inability to take the role of "the generalised other", and there is evidence to support the assumption that *So* indexes role-taking ability (Rosen and Schalling, 1974). Low scores have therefore been used by several investigators as a criterion of psychopathy (Schalling, 1978), while Heilbrun has employed the sum of *Pd* minus *So* for this purpose (Heilbrun, 1982; Heilbrun and Heilbrun, 1985).

(5) *Quay's behaviour dimensions*. As described earlier, a factor of unsocialised aggression, conduct disorder, or psychopathy has consistently emerged from Quay's analyses of self-report and behaviour rating items among delinquents. Scores on this factor have been used to identify psychopathic delinquents in several studies (Quay, 1987a).

Available evidence indicates that these various measures are correlated with each other, but that the correlations are not sufficiently high for them to be regarded as interchangeable. The "psychopaths" of one investigator do not, then, necessarily correspond to those of another. Hare (1985) compared scores on several of the above measures in 274 prison inmates. Intercorrelations between Cleckley ratings, PCL score, and DSM-III diagnosis of APD ranged from 0.57 to 0.80, while correlations of these three with *Pd*, *So*, and *Pd* minus *So* ranged from 0.21 to 0.44. Factor analysis clearly separated the observer measures from self-report scales, and Hare suggests that the latter are not useful in assessing psychopathy among inmates. This conclusion, however, is unwarranted, since observer ratings and self-reports tap different personal attributes (Becker, 1960), and given the measurement limitations inherent in each, adequate assessment of a personality construct ideally requires multiple measures (Widiger and Frances, 1987). Since psychopathy is a theoretical construct rather than a palpable entity, there can be no "true" measure, and the utility of different measures has to be judged against external and theoretically relevant correlates. Any assessment of personality which ignores the person's self-image and self-presentation is inevitably one-sided (Hogan and Jones, 1983).

Psychopathic personality and the classification of personality disorders

Recent notions of psychopathy have developed with little reference to personality theory or to the classification of personality disorders, and Karpman and Cleckley saw the latter as unnecessary. This view is clearly not reflected in the DSM-III classification, and the relationship between the concept of psychopathic personality and the classes of personality disorder needs to be clarified. For example, it remains unclear whether psychopathic personality is one of several "narrow-band" categories of personality disorder, as the APD category implies, or whether it is a "broad-band" or higher order construct embracing several classes. The correlation of Cleckley ratings and Hare's PCL with APD (Hare, 1983, 1985) appears to suggest that APD is equivalent to Cleckley's "distinct clinical entity". However, the traits associated by Cleckley and others with psychopathic personality are also found among DSM criteria for other personality disorders, such as histrionic, narcissistic, paranoid, sadistic, and borderline. Psychopathy may therefore be more appropriately construed as a higher order category. In a hierarchical analysis of the DSM-III items, Morey (1988) found two superordinate clusters of "anxious rumination" and "acting out". The latter includes items from APD, narcissistic and histrionic categories, and seems closer to Cleckley's concept than is the narrower APD. Hart and Hare (1989) also found that the PCL correlated with ratings of antisocial, narcissistic, and histrionic personality disorder, supporting the notion that psychopathic personality is a supraordinate construct.

A related issue is whether individuals identified as psychopathic or antisocial form a homogeneous group in terms of personality traits. Some current definitions mix classification criteria, and are unlikely to define a homogeneous class. In particular, the inclusion of antisocial behaviours among the criteria for APD is inconsistent with the aim of defining personality disorders in terms of traits. Deviant acts may or may not be a consequence of personality characteristics, but they are not in themselves traits, and belong in a different conceptual domain of *social deviance* (Blackburn, 1988b). Since personality disorder and social deviance are not mutually exclusive, a person may display either, neither, or both. Socially deviant behaviours, then, are neither necessary nor sufficient criteria of a disorder of personality, and there is no *a priori* reason for expecting those who are homogeneous in terms of social deviance to belong to a single category of personality deviation. Available data, in fact, suggest that those meeting criteria for APD are also likely to meet the criteria for other DSM categories, such as narcissistic or borderline (McManus et al., 1984).

Homogeneity is appropriately tested by cluster analysis of profiles of *persons* assessed on traits which include those purporting to define psychopathy. A few studies of this kind have been carried out. Using self-report data, Blackburn (1975a) identified four distinct personality patterns among offenders in the English Mental Health Act category of psychopathic disorder, and other analyses have identified the same patterns among murderers, violent male criminals, and violent mentally disordered offenders (Chapter 9). From their modal characteristics, these four types are described as *primary psychopaths* (impulsive, aggressive, hostile, extraverted), *secondary psychopaths* (impulsive, aggressive, hostile, socially anxious and withdrawn), *controlled* or *conforming* (defensive, sociable, unaggressive), and *inhibited* (unaggressive, withdrawn, introverted). This research therefore reveals two groups showing "psychopathic" traits rather than a single category of psychopaths. Analyses of observer ratings, however, yield conflicting results. Tyrer (1988) identified a single cluster of "sociopaths" from ratings of traits of personality disorder. Blackburn and Maybury (1985), on the other hand, found two clusters of mentally disordered offenders who were rated highly on Cleckley's criteria, one being aggressive and impulsive, the other withdrawn.

The relationship between psychopathy and the classification of personality disorders may, however, be more readily understood by reference to a dimensional rather than a categorical system. While Cleckley's designation of psychopathic personality as an "entity" implies a discrete category, this reflects a curious moral assumption that socially undesirable traits are confined to a small section of the human race. Traits such as egocentricity or callousness vary in degree, and the statistical development of Hare's PCL clearly supports a continuous dimension. Several factor analyses, in fact, identify a general dimension defined by traits which are prominent among Cleckley's criteria, such as egocentricity, irresponsibility, and lack of interpersonal warmth (e.g. Hare, 1980; Tyrer, 1988). Blackburn and Maybury (1985) demonstrated that this factor aligns closely with the hostility axis of the interpersonal circle (Figure 3.1), and Harpur, Hare and Hakstian (1989) found that the PCL also falls close to this axis. However, of the two factors identified in the PCL, the "selfish, callous" dimension was more closely related to the interpersonal circle, and corresponded to the coercive–compliant axis.

Psychopathy, then, may be construed as one dimension of the interpersonal circle. However, two dimensions are required to locate an *individual* in the interpersonal space. For example, if psychopathy is broadly equivalent to the coercive–compliant dimension, then some "psychopaths" will tend to be sociable, while others will be withdrawn (see also Figure 5.1). This is consistent with the differentiation of primary and secondary psychopaths. It also indicates how several categories of personality disorder, such as narcissistic, antisocial, borderline, and paranoid, may have similar positions on a dimension of "psychopathy", while having different interpersonal styles. This dimensional interpretation accords with the view of psychopathic personality as a superordinate construct, and can be reconciled with more specific classes of personality disorder. However, the categorical concept of psychopath is, in these terms, merely a convenient fiction, and improved classification of personality disorders will probably render it redundant.

Chapter 4

Social and Environmental
Theories of Crime

INTRODUCTION

The distinction was made in Chapter 1 between criminality as a disposition to break rules and criminal acts as specific behavioural events. Theories of crime are not always explicit about which of these they are attempting to explain, but while some recent theories are concerned with factors which facilitate or inhibit criminal acts, most theories focus on criminality rather than specific events. They vary in the extent to which this is construed as a generalised or specific tendency, whether it is the outcome of distal or proximal determinants, and whether these determinants reside in the individual or the social environment. To reiterate, the latter question is not the same as the "person–situation" issue, which is about the proximal factors influencing specific events. Rather does it concern the nature and origins of the tendency to engage in or refrain from crime which a person brings to a situation.

Most theorising and empirical research on delinquency has come from sociology, which seeks to identify causes in social structures and cultural factors. Since these can only be expressed in behaviour through psychological processes at the individual level, there is no firm dividing line between sociological and psychological explanations. However, many psychologists, as well as control theorists in sociology, assume that people are by nature self-seeking and deviant, and are hence concerned to explain conformity. Traditionally, this is accounted for by the socialisation processes which foster compliance with social rules, particularly the moral rules regulating interactions between people. Criminal behaviour is therefore construed by several theorists in terms of a more general failure of moral learning. These vary in their metatheoretical assumptions about the nature of moral standards and behaviour (Kurtines, Alvarez and Azmitia, 1990), but commonly postulate the development of an internalised mechanism of self-control or restraint which promotes *resistance to temptation*. Criminal acts are thus held to result from a deficiency or temporary breakdown of this mechanism. While the classic studies of Hartshorne and May (1928) suggested that there was no generalised propensity to resist cheating, and that immediate situational factors determined whether or not a child gave into temptation, subsequent re-analyses have suggested that a general tendency is, in fact, apparent in their data (Epstein and O'Brien, 1985). Evidence cited in Chapter 2 also indicates that criminality reflects a generalised tendency to break rules, which displays significant continuity over the lifespan.

However, while socialisation theories assume original sin, and focus on the development of restraints or inhibitions against deviance, social psychological and sociological theories more commonly assume that humans are essentially conforming, and deviate only when pressured into doing so by societal influences. This alternative emphasis on the social creation of criminal propensities perhaps explains why sociology has produced several theories of crime and delinquency, while psychological accounts of crime are usually derivatives of more general theories of development and learning.

Theories emphasising the contribution of the individual to crime will be considered in the next chapter. This chapter examines theories which address causal processes in the social environment. The division is somewhat arbitrary since socially oriented theories are often an attempt to explain how social processes produce individual differences in the tendency to violate the law, while individually oriented theories focus on the outcomes of those processes. The difference is thus one of emphasis. As social factors are the particular concern of sociology, sociological concepts of crime will first be outlined.

SOCIOLOGICAL THEORIES

Colvin and Pauly (1983) identify six main sociological theories of crime, these being learning (differential association), strain, control, labelling, conflict, and radical criminology. Conflict and radical criminology were considered briefly in Chapter 1, and the first four, which represent "mainstream" criminology, will be examined here. The interested reader will find comprehensive appraisals in sociological texts (e.g. Taylor, Walton and Young, 1973; Kornhauser, 1978; Lilly, Cullen and Ball, 1989).

Differential association

As a reaction against early psychological and psychiatric positivism, initial sociological theorising located "pathological" causes of crime in social conditions rather than individuals. Early ecological studies identified inner city areas with high delinquency rates, which correlated with poverty, high population density and turnover, and social problems (Chapter 2). Crime was therefore attributed to *social disorganisation*, in which normal controls of behaviour by social institutions had broken down. Although it is now recognised that these correlations do not establish the causes of crime, this work suggested that criminal traditions exist alongside conventional value systems, and that youthful gangs drawn from an economic underclass provide support for delinquent behaviour. Sutherland, however, preferred the concept of *differential social organisation*, which implies different subcultural traditions with potentially conflicting norms rather than a criminogenic and pathological section of society. His theory of *differential association* originated in 1939, and has subsequently been reiterated with only minor modifications (Sutherland and Cressey, 1970).

Differential association (DA) theory specifies the process by which criminogenic traditions are transmitted, and takes the form of nine propositions: (1) criminal behaviour is learned, rather than inherited or invented by individuals; (2) it is learned in social interaction, and (3) within intimate personal groups, rather than through the media; (4) what is learned includes both crime techniques and criminal motives, drives, rationalisations, and attitudes; (5) the specific direction of motives and drives is learned from definitions of the legal code as favourable or unfavourable, depending on support for the code (norms) within a subculture; (6) a person becomes delinquent because of an excess of definitions favourable to violations of law over definitions unfavourable to violation of law, as these are assimilated from the surrounding culture; (7) differential associations vary in frequency, duration, historical priority, and intensity or emotional impact; (8) the process of learning by association with criminal and anticriminal patterns involves mechanisms entailed in any other learning, and not imitation alone; (9) criminal behaviour is not explained by general needs, since the same needs and values underly criminal and noncriminal behaviour.

The theory is concerned with the *ratio* of exposure to criminal norms, rather than with criminal associations as such. It also specifies differential exposure to criminal and anticriminal *patterns of behaviour*, which include endorsement of deviant definitions by noncriminals, and not simply excessive contact with criminals. While Sutherland regarded the mass media as unimportant, Glaser (1956) argued that direct personal contact is not necessary, and that the theory could usefully incorporate *differential identification* with real or imagined reference groups whose acceptance is valued. De Fleur and Quinney (1966) suggested that the first six propositions constitute the essence of the theory, which they succinctly reformulate as: "Overt criminal behaviour has as its necessary and sufficient conditions a set of criminal motivations, attitudes, and techniques, the learning of which takes place when there is exposure to criminal norms in excess of exposure to corresponding anticriminal norms during symbolic interaction in primary groups."

The theory, nonetheless, remains vague on several points, and is considered untestable by some. It accounts only for the acquisition of criminal tendencies, and not their maintenance or performance, and it says nothing about the differential receptivity of individuals to their associations. It is particularly difficult to quantify "excess of definitions", and attempts to test the theory typically define DA in terms of acquaintance or friendship with delinquents. Several studies find that delinquents are more likely to have, and to identify with delinquent friends who report similar kinds of behaviour (Short, 1957;

Matthews, 1968), consistent with the theory, although Reiss and Rhodes (1964) found that this applied mainly to vandalism and petty theft. These correlational findings, however, may simply reflect a tendency of delinquents to select delinquent friends, and any effect of DA on crime may be indirect. Jackson, Tittle and Burke (1985), for example, found that among adults, DA with criminal acquaintances increased self-reported crime indirectly through increased motivation to engage in criminal behaviour, rather than directly or through attitude change. DA is also an incomplete theory, since it rests on vague psychological assumptions about human learning. Imitation, for example, appears to refer to mimicry. However, recent revisions of the theory draw on psychological concepts of learning to specify the mechanisms by which criminal behaviour is acquired. The theory is therefore discussed further below.

Strain and subcultural theories

Merton (1939) rejected the notion that deviance results from the breakdown of controls against basic impulses, and proposed that nonconformity reflects pressures exerted by the social structure. *Anomie* refers to a disjunction between means and ends, which arises when a culture promotes valued goals of success, but the class structure limits access to those goals. Legitimate opportunities for achieving success are more restricted for the lower classes, who therefore experience the frustration or strain of a disparity between aspirations and expectations. While the majority conform and accept the available goals and means, some adapt by rejecting the goals, the conventional means, or both, and turn to illegitimate behaviour. Anomie assumes that people perceive themselves to be *relatively* deprived, and appears to account for the paradox of high crime rates in affluent societies.

While perceived opportunity correlates negatively with self-reported delinquency (McCandless, Persons and Roberts, 1972), delinquents lack skills as well as opportunities, and some studies suggest that they are not typically motivated by frustration of high aspirations (Hirschi, 1969). Bernard (1984) challenges this evidence, and argues that strain theory finds support from research on more serious, lower class delinquents. However, some recent statements conceptualise strain more generally in terms of a discrepancy between personal goals and opportunities for realising them which is not class linked (Elliott, Huizinga and Ageton, 1985).

Subcultural, or cultural deviance theorists follow Sutherland in assuming normative conflict between class cultures or subcultures. Delinquent behaviour is considered normal for some subcultures, particularly those of male, lower class, urban adolescents. Cohen (1955) argued that working class culture fosters present-oriented, hedonistic values, which do not match up to the "middle class measuring rod" imposed by the school system. Working class boys are therefore subject to status anxiety. While some react by accepting the dominant values of achievement, those who fail in school repudiate these values through a defensive reaction formation, and flout conventional values in the context of the delinquent gang. While Cohen saw anomic frustration as relevant to older criminals, he characterised the adolescent delinquent gang as nonutilitarian, malicious, and negativistic. This was challenged by Miller (1958), who suggested that the relevant cultural influences are those of the lower class community. This, he claimed, has a number of "focal concerns" (trouble, toughness, smartness, excitement, fate, and autonomy), which are expressed in antisocial behaviour supported by the peer group. No motivation from strain is necessary, but he suggested that working class child-rearing is female dominated, and that the same sex peer group provides the first opportunity for learning the masculine role.

Cloward and Ohlin (1961), however, argued that lower class neighbour-hoods provide *differential opportunities* for illegitimate activities. Combining anomie and differential association, they suggest that a delinquent subculture presupposes not only the learning of deviant roles, but also the opportunity to perform them, which is unevenly distributed. They distinguish the *criminal* subculture, which is socially integrated and focuses on utilitarian property crimes, from the *conflict* subculture, which is more individualistic and violent, and a product of disorganised slums. Individuals who fail to succeed in either of these form a *retreatist* subculture associated with drug abuse.

However, Matza (1964) noted that subcultural theories "overpredict" crime among the working class, and the evidence for criminal subcultures is tenuous. For example, the residents of underprivileged areas are not notably more tolerant of delinquency (Maccoby, Johnson and Church, 1958), and youthful gangs are neither as prevalent nor as socially co-ordinated as assumed by subcultural theorists (Hirschi, 1969). Where they exist, only a minority of their members engage in more serious delinquency (Stott, 1982). Most offences of delinquents, in fact, occur in groups of only two or three, while violent offences are more likely to be committed by solitary delinquents (Aultman, 1980). While more recent theorists adopt a conflict perspective which denies a consensus culture, and which emphasises a diversity of countercultures emerging from the antagonism between classes (Young and Matthews, 1992), the notion of a static delinquent subculture now seems questionable.

Control theory

Where strain and subcultural theories assume people to be naturally conforming unless forced into deviance, control theories assume that conformity to a "conventional order" requires explanation. Control in this context refers to restraining factors in the individual, in the form of internalised norms comparable to the superego and ego, and the controlling influence and authority of social institutions, such as the family, school, or neighbourhood. Reckless (1961), for example, sees conformity in terms of *inner containment* through a favourable self-concept, goal orientation, frustration tolerance, and commitment to norms, and *outer containment* which comes from the availability of meaningful roles and social acceptance. Violation of these restraints involves personal costs in the form of punishment, social rejection, or loss of future opportunities. Whether a person yields to temptation therefore depends on the balance between anticipated rewards and costs (Piliavin, Hardyck and Vadum, 1968).

Most influential has been the social control theory of Hirschi (1969, 1978, 1986), which proposes that conformity depends on the *bond* between the individual and society (a "stake in conformity"), and that deviance results when this bond is weak or broken. The correlated elements of the bond are: (1) *attachment* to others in the form of conscience, internalised norms, and caring what others think; (2) *commitment* to conventional goals; (3) *involvement* in conventional pursuits incompatible with delinquent activities; and (4) *belief* in the moral validity of conventional values. No special motive to deviate is proposed, since everyone is exposed to temptation, and the theory is concerned with criminality in general rather than the commission of specific crimes.

The predicted negative correlations between bonding elements and delinquency have been found in cross-sectional self-report surveys (Hirschi, 1969), supporting the view that a stake in conformity inhibits delinquency, rather than creating strain or subcultural rebellion. However, in a longitudinal study, Agnew (1985) found that bonding elements failed to predict self-reported delinquency over time. He suggests that control variables may be significant mainly for minor delinquencies among younger adolescents.

The theory is silent about how bonds develop or break down, or how weak bonds produce deviant behaviour other than by leaving the individual "free to deviate" (Conger, 1976; Box, 1981). Several theorists maintain that weakness of the social bond can only partially account for deviant behaviour, and that individual variation in the motivation to deviate must be taken into account. This is the position taken by Elliott et al. (1985), who propose an integration of strain, control, and social learning theories (Chapter 5).

However, Hirschi and Gottfredson have recently reaffirmed the view that no special motivation is required to explain crime, which is a natural consequence of unrestrained human tendencies to seek pleasure and avoid pain (Hirschi and Gottfredson, 1988; Gottfredson and Hirschi, 1990). They emphasise the compatibility of classical choice theories of criminal acts and the positivist concept of criminality as the tendency to commit crimes, but see the latter as a function of *self control*. Criminal acts are held to be the immediate gratification of common human desires, and require little planning, effort, or skill. They depend on opportunities and temptations, and are closely related to other socially disapproved acts, such as drinking, smoking, drug-taking, illicit sex, and even accidents, all of which become more likely when people lack self control. Those having this generalised attribute "tend to be impulsive, insensitive, physical (as opposed to mental), risk-taking, short-sighted, and nonverbal". Low self control is preferred to "criminality" because of the positivist implications in the latter of positive causes, and hence differences between crimes in motives. Since the only common element in crimes and analogous acts is lack of self control, it is unnecessary to distinguish types of crime or criminal.

This general theory is held to be consistent with the stability of deviance from childhood, the versatility rather than specialisation of offenders, and the correlation of crime with other forms of social deviance. The origins of low self control are said to lie in deficient child rearing, which is itself a function of lack of self control in caretakers. Social institutions other than the family play little role, and strain, cultural deviance, and social learning theories are considered inadequate because of their failure to recognise the natural, short term hedonism common to all crimes.

Apart from emphasising that criminal acts are not simply the outcome of criminal propensities, the theory is similar to other individual level theories of socialisation (Chapter 5). However, perhaps because they retain the positivist notion of independent and unidirectional "causes", Hirschi and Gottfredson fail to apply the act-propensity distinction to the behaviour of caretakers, and allow no contribution of either social conditions or the characteristics of the child itself to parental behaviour. Moreover, while they suggest that individual differences "may have an impact on the prospects for effective socialisation", they deny that criminals have any special hedonic needs or values. Finally low self control is said to be manifest in the characteristics of the psychopath (Gough, 1948) and antisocial personality (Robins, 1978), but neither the nature of low self control nor how it is to be measured independently of the deviant acts to which it gives rise are otherwise specified. Evidence on the relation of this concept to crime is examined further in Chapter 8.

Labelling theory

The labelling perspective assumes that social reactions to norm violation may alter the course of deviance. Although there is no unanimous theory, its main concerns are with the characteristics and sources of labels such as "criminal" or "handicapped", the conditions under which they are applied, and their consequences for the recipient of the label (Plummer, 1979). One influence on this approach was the indication in the early 1960s that the overrepresentation of the lower classes in official crime statistics was not matched in self-reported delinquency. Another was the positivist failure to consider how acts achieved the status of crimes through societal definitions. Labelling theory also reflects the focus of the symbolic interactionist tradition on the social meanings of an act, and how the sense of self is socially constructed.

Three assumptions characterise this approach (Becker, 1963; Lemert, 1967). First, acts are not intrinsically deviant, and crime is a label which becomes attached to conduct for social reasons, in particular, the interests of the powerful. Second, the reactions of criminal justice agents are governed by characteristics of offenders, such as age, race, or class, rather than by characteristics of the offence. Third, being publicly labelled a criminal or delinquent results in a deviant self-image, and hence fosters a delinquent career. The interest is therefore in *secondary deviance* as an adjustment to stigmatisation from the agents of social control. The initial act of norm violation (primary deviance) is largely incidental since it is only a problem when labelled as such.

Evidence for biases in the processing of offenders was examined earlier, and the effect of labelling on the self-concept is discussed in Chapter 8. Labelling theory has been criticised for focusing on the deviance of the "underdog" rather than that of the powerful (Box, 1981), and for oversimplifying the relation between attitudes, self-concept, and behaviour (Welford, 1975). Welford further argued that offence seriousness is more important than discriminatory practice in criminal justice decision-making. Some proponents also assume a passive respondent, but Morash (1982) found that public labelling did not affect adolescents equally, having little effect on serious delinquents. Klein (1986) similarly found that involvement with the justice system had a greater effect on youths who were of higher socioeconomic status, female, white, or first-time offenders.

While concern with the criminalisation of deviance by powerful groups has been taken up by conflict theorists, evidence that labelling affects delinquent careers is not strong, and interest in this perspective has declined in recent years. Plummer (1979), nevertheless, defends its utility, arguing that its critics have focused unduly on vulgarised versions. Psychological studies of expectancy confirmation, or the self-fulfilling prophecy, also demonstrate that labels and stereotypes can bias perceptions, which are communicated to and influence those to whom they are applied (Jones, 1986). The process of labelling, then, cannot be discounted as contributory to the development of delinquency.

LEARNING THEORIES

Although learning principles have been applied to interventions with offenders for three decades, only a few psychologists have developed a comprehensive learning theory of crime. It is sometimes dogmatically claimed that the acquisition and maintenance of criminal and noncriminal behaviour are governed by the same principles, and that no special theory of crime is therefore necessary (e.g. Bandura and Walters, 1963; Ayllon and Milan, 1979). This does not, however, advance us very far. No behaviour is inherently criminal and the behaviours involved in most crimes are within the repertoire of virtually everyone. An adequate account must therefore specify not simply the processes through which behaviour is acquired, but also what is learned, or fails to be learned. In particular, it must explain how people come to enact behaviours which they *know* to be socially prohibited or morally condemned.

Learning accounts variously emphasise Pavlovian or classical conditioning, operant conditioning, or observational learning, and these have their provenance in the behaviourist tradition. However, as in other areas, there is no unitary "behavioural" approach to crime, and three distinctive schools can be identified: (1) *applied behavioural analysis*, based on radical behaviourist philosophy (Morris et al., 1987); (2) *neo-behaviourism*, drawing on both Pavlovian conditioning and the learning concepts of Mowrer, Miller, and Hull, currently represented particularly in the work of Eysenck (Chapter 5); (3) *social learning theory*, which emphasises the role of cognition in learning. At the level of intervention, these approaches are identified broadly with behaviour modification, behaviour therapy, and cognitive–behaviour therapy. However, the latter covers an amalgam of models, some of which treat cognition as "covert behaviour" (Chapter 13). Social learning theory, on the other hand, has become increasingly concerned with cognition as the structuring of experience, and is now identified as social *cognitive* theory (Bandura, 1986).

These differences are frequently overlooked, and "social learning" has been applied broadly to a variety of theories which incorporate imitation in accounting for criminal behaviour. In its basic sense, "social learning" emphasises the social context of much human learning, and not a particular principle of learning, but social learning *theory* (SLT) differs radically from models based on classical or operant conditioning (Bandura, 1974, 1986; Mischel and Mischel, 1976). Not only does it focus on cognitive learning through modelling or imitation, it also postulates that knowledge exerts control over behaviour. This is in marked contrast to the anti-mentalism of radical behaviourism. Skinner (1953; 1978), for example, regards private events, such as intentions or expectations, as simply "early stages of behaviour", and asserts that "No creative or initiating function is to be assigned to them".

SLT represents both a different theory of learning and a contrasting philosophical position, and differs from radical behaviourism on three main counts. First, symbolic processes are not simply "covert responses" with the same status as observable behaviours, but rather provide the reference mechanisms for the evaluation and regulation of behaviour. Second, reinforcing contingencies provide information about outcomes and incentives for action by creating expectations for particular outcomes, and do not function simply as automatic shapers of conduct. Third, while radical behaviourism treats living creatures as essentially passive recipients of the influences of an autonomous controlling environment, SLT sees people as activating and creating their environments, and proposes a reciprocal determinism in which thought reciprocally interacts with action and the environment. "Social learning" analyses of criminal behaviour which ignore these distinctions may acknowledge reciprocal effects between behaviour and environment, but adopt a mechanistic perspective on the role of knowledge (e.g. Feldman, 1977; Braukmann, Kirigin and Wolf, 1980; Stumphauzer, 1986).

There are two dominant themes in learning perspectives on crime. One views crime and delinquency as a failure of socialisation, while the other sees antisocial deviance as itself a learned phenomenon. Before specific theories are described, the learning processes held to be involved will first be considered.

Learning processes in socialisation and deviant behaviour

Despite the opposition of many of its proponents to psychoanalysis, neo-behaviouristic learning theory has relied substantially on translations of Freudian concepts, and considerable research efforts in the 1950s and 1960s were devoted to determining the socialisation processes entailed in the internalisation of moral prohibitions. These were guided by two main theoretical views.

Early applications drew on the Mowrer–Miller *two-process theory* which stimulated the development of behaviour therapy. In this model, cues associated with punishment, including kinesthetic cues, become conditioned stimuli which elicit an anticipatory emotional state of fear or anxiety. This functions as an aversive drive, which is reduced by instrumental escape or avoidance behaviour, such as inhibition of the punished response. Socialisation therefore depends on response inhibition based on conditioned anxiety. Failure to acquire socialised restraints may result from ineffective training on the part of parents, or from a child's relative inability to form conditioned responses. This drive reduction model of avoidance learning has been found inadequate in the light of evidence that neither anxiety nor autonomic arousal are necessary for successful avoidance learning (Bolles, 1972; Bandura, 1986), but still has some adherents.

An alternative approach reflects the emphasis of SLT on cognitive learning and mediation. Aronfreed (1968), for example, sees internalisation in terms of affective responses to cognitive representations and evaluations of one's own behaviour. These are under the control of internal and external cues established by aversive conditioning, positive reinforcement, and imitation. Bandura and Walters (1963) also make use of all recognised learning principles in accounting for social development. Reinforcement contingencies are relevant to the *performance* of behaviour. Operant shaping, however, is too slow a process to account for novel responses, and the *acquisition* of behaviour is primarily dependent on *imitation* through observation of a model's behaviour.

Imitation involves learning by contiguity at a cognitive level. In infants, it is motivated to secure interpersonal responsiveness, but subsequently by the exercise of mastery or the achievement of personal efficacy. It is not a passive process of mimicry, but rather results in the novel organisation of information and rule-governed performance. It is a source of new response patterns, as well as the inhibition or disinhibition of previously acquired behaviour, and can thus promote both prosocial and deviant behaviour. It is, however, a selective process, a model's influence being determined by status or prestige, the observed consequences of the modelled behaviour, and the observer's susceptibility to social influence. Imitation is equivalent to the psychodynamic concept of identification (Chapter 5). However, where psychoanalysts see this as a defensive process for coping with antecedent fears of loss of love or harm from the competing parent, experimental studies suggest that children are more likely to identify with and imitate a model which displays the power to control rewards, rather than one whose status is envied (Bandura and Walters, 1963).

The selective nature of modelling must be stressed, since it is one of the most overused *post hoc* explanations in the literature on antisocial behaviour. People do not simply re-enact the observed behaviour of others: they utilise what they have observed according to their goals and the situational demands.

SLT gives particular emphasis to *self-regulation*, and socialisation is seen as dependent on the acquisition of self-controlling responses. Self-regulation involves self-imposed goals or standards and self-produced consequences in the form of self-reinforcement or self-punishment. This entails the adoption of contingency rules which specify expected behaviour, performance criteria, and the consequences of achieving or failing to reach those standards. Self-control is hence largely a function of self-rewarding and self-punishing responses when self-imposed standards are met or violated. Although SLT emphasises the role of internal reactions in self-control, it dismisses the notion of a unitary internal moral agent, such as the superego, and assumes that self-regulatory capacities are selectively activated according to the dynamics of the situation. Also, self-restraining influences can be disengaged by cognitive restructuring which provides moral justification for normally disapproved actions. This may be achieved, for example, by exposure to deviant models or persuasive communications which blame or devalue the victim, minimise the consequences, or displace responsibility. These are the "techniques of neutralisation" considered significant in sociological accounts of criminal acts (Chapter 8).

Adults or peers who supply the models for self-controlling responses may also shape behaviour more directly through reinforcing contingencies. While socialisation depends on the elicitation and reinforcement of prosocial behaviours which are incompatible with an ongoing deviant pattern, more attention has been paid to aversive methods in the control of antisocial behaviour. However, the effects of *punishment* on human behaviour continue to be contentious in the psychological literature (Moffit, 1983). One problem is the lack of an agreed definition. Operant theorists define punishment as the suppression of a response contingent on the presentation of a stimulus (positive punishment), or the withdrawal of a positive reinforcer (negative punishment). Others object to the circularity of this functional definition, and define punishment in terms of aversive stimulation.

While Skinner has maintained that punishment has no more than a temporary disruptive effect in controlling behaviour, laboratory experiments demonstrate that punishment can be an effective way of establishing response inhibition, depending on parameters such as timing, intensity, punishment schedule, or the availability of alternative responses (Johnston, 1972; Zillmann, 1979). At issue is the extent to which aversive stimulation is critical in the development of resistance to deviation under natural conditions. Since two-process theory assumes the formation of a conditioned emotional response, it gives particular weight to the application and timing of punishment in socialisation. Thus, a painful stimulus applied early in a response sequence is held to generate fear which becomes conditioned to response-generated cues, and to produce response inhibition and resistance to deviation. Punishment late in the sequence generates a conditioned emotional response of "guilt", which is less effective in response inhibition. However, experimental support for this differentiation (Solomon, 1964; Aronfreed, 1968) relies on laboratory analogues employing physically noxious stimulation. Such studies are of limited generality for three reasons. First, they fail to capitalise on human symbolic processes. For example, verbal rationales or statements of rules are more effective than noxious stimuli in producing resistance to deviation in young children, and are not subject to the same constraints of timing or intensity (Parke, 1974). Second, under natural conditions, punishment is rarely timed to coincide with the deviant act. Third, punishment in its everyday application is dependent on *moral judgement* about what constitutes transgression, and its effects depend on its perceived legitimacy on the part of the recipient (Zillmann, 1979).

The use of aversive stimuli in itself may not, then, be the most effective component of socialisation. Parental disciplinary techniques, in fact, involve not only the presentation of aversive stimuli, such as physical punishment or verbal criticism, but also the withholding or withdrawal of positive reinforcers whose reinstatement is contingent on compliance or self-critical responses, and the use of reasoning. Research on parental discipline suggests that it is the interpersonal context in which punishment is applied rather than punishment itself which is critical in socialisation (Chapter 7).

Conditioning and avoidance learning in criminality

Early learning models of criminal behaviour drew on two-process theory. Lykken (1957) proposed that psychopaths do not condition anxiety responses readily, and hence fail to avoid behaviour which attracts punishment. Tong (1959), however, suggested that delinquent behaviour could arise through either excessive conditioned anxiety, leading to panic reactions in the form of aggression or sexual assault, or deficient anxiety resulting in impulsive crimes or stereotyped petty delinquency. These approaches focus on individual differences in autonomic responsiveness as critical factors in antisocial development.

Trasler (1962, 1978) provides a more comprehensive application of this paradigm to criminal behaviour, which he sees as the outcome of a failure of socialisation. He proposes that socialisation develops through the conditioning of fear to stimuli preceding a punished response, which results in response inhibition through passive avoidance learning. Most delinquent behaviour is held to reflect inefficiencies in parental training methods, which are a function of parent–child relations, and family and class differences in the form and consistency of punishment procedures employed. However, Trasler agrees with Lykken that some individuals are resistant to training because of a relative inability to acquire conditioned fear responses. This theory has some similarity to that of Eysenck, and is discussed further in Chapter 5.

Operant conditioning and social learning theories

The assumption that delinquent and criminal acts are operants acquired and maintained by their reinforcing consequences is implicit in several approaches to offender rehabilitation, but only a few theorists have offered an explicitly Skinnerian account of crime. Jeffery (1965) proposed that criminal behaviour is operant behaviour maintained by the changes it produces on the environment, property offences being positively reinforced by the acquisition of stolen items, assaultive crimes being negatively reinforced by the removal of an enemy. Criminal acts are under the control of immediate environmental reinforcing stimuli, and occur in the environment in which the actor has been reinforced for this behaviour. Sociocultural variations and the absence of immediate aversive consequences are thus the main determinants of criminal behaviour. Operant control of criminal behaviour is similarly central to the theory of Wilson and Herrnstein (1985), but since their analysis also incorporates classical conditioning mechanisms, individual differences, and sociological variables it is considered in Chapter 5.

Williams (1987) also presents a radical behaviourist perspective. He defines delinquency as a class of operants under the control of discriminative stimuli and "anticipated consequences" (sic). He proposes a typology of delinquent acts, which are distinguished according to whether the victim is present or absent (discriminative stimulus), the reinforcer is extrinsic (material gain) or intrinsic (sexual activity), and whether the response is a verbal or nonverbal operant. He suggests that this may provide a basis for identifying appropriate interventions.

More common, however, have been accounts of criminal behaviour in social learning terms. While Bandura's initial research involved studies of aggressive delinquents (Bandura and Walters, 1959), and he has subsequently developed a detailed application of SLT to aggression (Chapter 9), he offers no specific theory of crime. However, applications of SLT principles to delinquent behaviour were noted by Bandura and Walters (1963), and these form the basis of subsequent social learning approaches.

Bandura (1986) adopts a control perspective on crime. People favour their self-interest, but refrain from criminal acts through anticipatory self-condemnation (internalised moral sanctions), cognitive appraisals of risks to social position (informal sanctions), or of risks of legal punishment (formal sanctions). All three forms of sanction have been found to be inversely related to self-reported delinquency (Grasmick and Green, 1980). Additionally, the benefits of prosocial behaviour outweigh the inducements of antisocial activities. The former depend on personal competencies. However, these are not fixed characteristics, but combine in various ways according to individuals, situations, and the nature of transgressive acts.

Failure of socialisation reflects a failure to develop self-controlling responses, and is seen, for example, in the preference of delinquents for immediate rather than delayed reward (Mischel, Shoda and Rodriguez, 1989). In keeping with strain theories, failure of delay of reward may arise when valued goals are unattainable through lack of opportunity or skill, resulting in the selection of alternative and illegitimate means. These deficits are attributed to modelling influences within the family and peer group. For example, Bandura and Walters (1959) found that the fathers of aggressive delinquent boys were less socially rewarding, and less likely to be imitated than the fathers of nondelinquents. Delinquency and psychopathy are thus seen in terms of a deficient self-regulatory system, which facilitates susceptibility to deviant influences and the emergence of antisocial responses, but which is under the control of selective discriminative stimuli. In the context of a delinquent group, the performance of antisocial acts is modelled and reinforced both vicariously and directly, thereby reducing competing inhibitions. Once established, such behaviour persists because of intermittent positive reinforcement which outweighs the inhibitory effects of punishment.

Feldman (1977), however, suggested that socialisation research has overemphasised the learning of response inhibitions in childhood, and gives greater weight to learning to offend in adolescence and adulthood. Studies of transgression and aggression are taken to be analogues of offences against property and persons, respectively, and while classical conditioning is suggested as significant in the learning of aggression, vicarious and direct reinforcement are proposed as the main sources of acquisition of property offending. Performance of a criminal act is held to be dependent on the availability of transgressing models and relevant skills, as well as the incentive value of the goal, and the perceived risk of detection and punishment. Maintenance of the behaviour is a function of intermittent schedules of external and self-reinforcement. Feldman considers labelling theory to be consistent with operant principles, and a useful account of delinquent role development. He also acknowledges a role for individual differences. These, however, are seen in terms of Eysenck's personality dimensions, whose relation to imitation and reinforcement is speculative.

Braukmann, Kirigin and Wolf (1980) also see delinquent behaviour as taught directly by peer modelling and reinforcement, but note in addition that failures to acquire skills essential for obtaining rewards and for avoiding negative consequences in school may make youths more susceptible to delinquent peer influence. They suggest that inducements to engage in deviant or conventional behaviour may be a function of the "reinforcement value" of available reinforcement agents, which they relate to the attachment concept of control theory. They cite findings of an inverse relation between amount of interaction between teachers and predelinquent boys and the degree of self-reported delinquency of the latter as consistent with both concepts.

There are few direct studies of the development of delinquency, but field studies of antisocial boys in their family contexts by Patterson (1982, 1986) confirm the contribution of early family training to later deviant behaviour. This work is described in Chapter 7.

Learning theory and sociological theories of crime

Several sociologists have drawn on learning theories to expand on Sutherland's assertion that criminal behaviour is learned. Burgess and Akers (1966) and Akers (1977, 1990) reformulate DA in terms of operant conditioning and imitation. "Intimate personal groups" are those which control the individual's major source of reinforcement, including reference groups which may be imaginary or portrayed, and DA is therefore a function of the differential reinforcing value of these groups. "Definitions" are norms or meanings given to behaviour which may be directly reinforced, and which function as discriminative stimuli for other behaviours. They define deviant behaviour as permissible through association with positive reinforcement of that behaviour. Alternatively, they serve to neutralise definitions "unfavourable to law violation" through negative reinforcement of verbalisations which avoid disapproval from self or others. Deviant outcomes are determined not so much by excesses of definitions favouring deviance as by differential positive reinforcement of one set of verbalisations over another, although deviant acts may also be directly reinforced.

The reformulation thus proposes that a person participates in deviant behaviour to the extent that it has been differentially reinforced over conforming behaviour, or defined as more desirable or justified than conforming alternatives. The role of definitions as mediators of normative meanings goes beyond a strict operant interpretation, and Akers notes that the model is consistent with symbolic interactionism and with the social cognitive emphasis of Bandura. Since differential reinforcement depends on social structures, the model provides an integration of several sociological theories with psychological theory, and it is applied to a variety of criminal and noncriminal deviant behaviours.

This reformulation has been criticised by Adams (1973) for straying beyond strict operant principles, and in contrast by Halbasch (1979), for failing to do justice to Sutherland's theory. However, Akers et al. (1979) provide a test of the theory in relation to self-reported drug and alcohol use among adolescents. Imitation, definitions, differential association, and differential reinforcement were operationalised by self-report scales. Multiple regression analysis demonstrated that, both individually and in combination, these variables accounted for a major part of the variance in substance use. It is, however, questionable whether the demonstration of a correlation between self-reported substance abuse and approval and use of similar substances by friends constitutes a strong test of the model.

The only experimental tests of DA have come from Andrews (1980). He notes that the major implications of the cognitive social learning reformulation are for controlled tests of the causal and practical implications of DA. He describes a series of experimental studies examining the effects of the contingencies (exposure to criminal and anticriminal patterns) and interpersonal conditions (intimate personal groups) on criminal attitudes and behaviour in the context of interventions within prisons and probation services. For example, it was shown that anticriminal learning by prisoners was a function of differential exposure to criminal and anticriminal patterns manipulated within a group counselling programme. Also, attitude change and recidivism rate in probationers were significantly influenced by the attitudes and interpersonal skills of probation officers, while increased anticriminal attitudes were significantly associated with lower recidivism rates. These studies therefore demonstrate predictive validity of the reformulated DA theory in terms of the processes influencing attitudes and behaviour change among criminals.

The theory that criminal behaviour arises through excessive modelling and social reinforcement of criminal patterns by individuals or groups who are significant in a person's life therefore has some empirical support. However, with the exception of the research of Andrews, this support is cross-sectional, and it remains to be determined that DA provides necessary and sufficient conditions for the natural learning of criminal behaviour. Both DA theory and the differential reinforcement reformulation, for example, emphasise unidirectional environmental influences, and do not consider the interaction of these with individual factors which may determine differential receptivity or resistance to criminal influences. It is also unlikely that DA represents the only causal process in the development of delinquent behaviour. Jensen (1972) reported that with DA (delinquent definitions) held constant, parental control exerted an independent effect on delinquency. Matsueda (1982) reanalysed these data, and suggested that the effect on delinquency of attachment to parents was indirect, and mediated by DA. However, Patterson's data suggest that family processes are a significant antecedent of delinquent development (Patterson, 1986).

There have also been several proposals that SLT can be synthesised with Hirschi's control theory. Hirschi (1978, 1986) acknowledges similarities between his theory and learning accounts of socialisation, but regards the notion that criminal behaviour is learned as inconsistent with the assumption of control theory that crime is asocial. His own data appeared to contradict differential association in suggesting that, although boys with low commitment to the conventional order were likely to have delinquent friends, they were neither attached to nor influenced by them. However, Conger (1976) notes that Hirschi's data in fact reveal an interaction between commitment and number of delinquent friends in relation to delinquency. For boys with high commitment, delinquency level was low, regardless of the number of delinquent friends, but boys with low stakes in conformity showed more delinquent activities only when they had several delinquent friends. This is not predicted from control theory, which ignores the role of attachment to deviant others, but is consistent with SLT, which predicts that the relationship between attachment and delinquency will depend on the extent to which rewarding others are conventional or deviant. Conger regards control theory as incomplete in that it explains only restraints and not the facilitation of delinquency supplied by delinquent peers, and suggests that SLT provides a broader perspective on how bonds influence deviance.

Evaluation of learning theory perspectives

Although learning theorists have not produced a unitary perspective on crime, they nevertheless specify critical processes by which criminogenic influences in the environment can become translated into individual behaviour. In this respect, they have considerable potential in enhancing understanding of crime. However, as Nietzel (1979) observed, their analysis of criminal behaviour rests on the application of a few simple principles to complex phenomena. They do not, for example, readily account for the generality of delinquent behaviour, since both operant and SLT accounts assume relative specificity of learning, nor do they explain age and sex variations. There is also little consideration of the role of individual differences. While SLT emphasises that person variables are the *products* of the individual's total history, which mediate the influence of new experiences (Mischel and Mischel, 1976; Sarason, 1978), reference to individual differences is limited mainly to skill deficits which limit the person's ability to gain rewards. There is little attention to goals, expectations, or beliefs, or to social stimulus characteristics which might determine the attachments or differential associations that a person has. "Reinforcement value", for example, is not an inherent property of a reinforcing agent, but rather the outcome of an interaction between individuals. In this respect, learning theorists have continued to focus on unidirectional determinism, and the potential of SLT remains to be exploited.

Evidence for the validity of learning theory accounts also continues to be limited. While these accounts are plausible insofar as they are consistent with what is known about the influence of parents and peer groups on delinquency, supporting evidence rests largely on extrapolations from laboratory analogues and correlational self-report surveys, and naturalistic studies continue to be the exception rather than the rule.

THE RATIONAL CHOICE PERSPECTIVE

In contrast to positivist models, which do not allow a role for reasoning, the classical utilitarianism of Bentham and Beccaria saw criminal behaviour, like any other, as the outcome of rational calculation of the costs and benefits of alternative courses of action. During the past two decades, there has been a significant revival of this position marked by an interest in the cognitive and situational determinants of the decision to commit a crime. Although there is no single "rational choice" model, the common assumption is that most criminal acts are mediated by some degree of means–end deliberation, even though this may not be methodical or strictly rational in an objective sense. This includes impulsive and violent crimes which may seem "irrational" to an observer. However, while this approach makes explicitly psychological assumptions about individual behaviour, it spans several disciplines, and its recent antecedents are in situational approaches to crime.

Environmental criminology

Three overlapping approaches emerged during the 1970s which focus on crimes as events occurring within a specific physical context (Jeffery, 1976). These assume that criminals choose when to commit a crime according to environmental opportunities and situational constraints, although they do not address the decision processes involved.

First, architects and geographers concerned with urban planning argued for causal effects of factors such as building design, land use, and spatial layout on street crimes of robbery, theft, or vandalism, as a function of the amount of surveillance permitted. Newman (1972), for example, found that in New York housing estates, crime rates varied directly with the height of buildings, and particularly with the extent to which there were "semi-public" entrances or access routes which were neither the concern of private owners, nor constantly used by the general public. He proposed that *defensible space*, over which people exercise surveillance as a result of their proprietary concerns, reduces opportunities for criminal behaviour. However, the effects of design characteristics have been found to depend on social factors such as the age, family structure, and density of the resident population (Pyle, 1976; Wilson, 1980).

A second approach examines opportunities for crime in terms of the spatio-temporal location of people and property (Cohen and Felson, 1979; Felson, 1986). People satisfy basic needs through *routine activities*, such as work, childrearing, shopping, or leisure pursuits. These determine where and when people are, and what they are doing, and hence the location and vulnerability of personal and property targets. Predatory crimes directed to people and their property are events occurring at specific locations in time and space, which require the convergence of three minimal elements: (1) a motivated offender; (2) a suitable target; (3) the absence of a capable guardian. The latter two are particularly dependent on patterns of routine activities, which will therefore influence the level of crime. In support of this assumption, Cohen and Felson (1979) showed that changes in the pattern of personal and property crimes in the United States during the 1960s were significantly predicted by changes in routine activities, as reflected in such factors as the number of married women working, people living alone, out of town travel, and the size and weight of consumer items.

A third approach arose from a concern with *situational crime prevention*, which sees crime as the outcome of immediate choices and decisions, and which focuses on the proximal rather than distal influences on crimes as specific events (Clarke, 1977, 1980; Hough, Clarke and Mayhew, 1980). It reflects a disenchantment with the "dispositional bias" in criminological theory, but does not assume environmental determinism, nor that individual variations are unimportant. "Career criminals" are motivated to create opportunities for crime, while situational constraints may have little impact on impulsive or emotionally disturbed individuals. However, "...much crime is best understood as rational action performed by fairly ordinary people acting under particular pressures and exposed to specific opportunities and situational inducements" (Hough et al., 1980). "Opportunistic" crimes which are particularly susceptible to the availability of appropriate situations are likely to include shoplifting, tax evasion, or vandalism. The latter, for example, occurs in places where surveillance is minimal, such as empty buildings, or the least supervised areas of buses (Sturman, 1980). Such acts can therefore be prevented or reduced by increasing surveillance, or by "target hardening", such as substituting steel telephone coin boxes for more vulnerable aluminium boxes. This is discussed further in Chapter 14.

Criminal decision-making and the deterrence hypothesis

Prominent in the rational choice perspective is the *deterrence hypothesis*. In its general sense, deterrence refers to any process by which an act is prevented or hindered, and is entailed in any consideration of compliant behaviour. However, where traditional sociological and psychological theories see compliance as a consequence of internalised norms or moral prohibitions, deterrence emphasises external controls. In the context of criminal behaviour, it refers specifically to the process by which people are influenced to refrain from an act from fear of external sanctions, fear in this sense denoting the perception of negative consequences. While a distinction is commonly drawn between *general* deterrence (the effect of *threatened* punishment on potential offenders) and *special* deterrence (the effect of *actual* punishment on the future behaviour of an offender), similar considerations apply in each case.

Bentham argued that deterrence results when the calculated costs of punishment outweigh the subjective benefits or profits of a deviant act, the effect being dependent on the certainty, severity, and swiftness of punishment. This view persists in the criminal justice system, but has generally been dismissed by social scientists. The issue is conceptually and empirically complex (Beyleveld, 1979), and frequently entangled with ideological positions on punishment, particularly the death penalty. A common objection is that many crimes are impulsive or emotional and involve an absence of reasoning about consequences, and that people's perceptions of legal sanctions are in any case inaccurate. It is also difficult to establish that laws influence behaviour specifically through fear of punishment. For example, legal sanctions may increase compliance through other processes, such as strengthening moral commitment to norms.

However, contemporary statements of the hypothesis emphasise that deterrence is a variable process, which differentially affects both individuals and behaviour (Andenaes, 1974; Cook, 1980). It has been suggested, for example, that a deterrent effect is more likely with *instrumental* crimes such as burglary or tax evasion, which further some material end, rather than in *expressive* crimes which articulate some nonmaterial need, such as assault or sexual offences. Again, acts which are *mala prohibita* may be more susceptible to external control than those which are *mala in se*, for which internal controls may be more relevant. Current views also recognise that people vary in their willingness to take risks, and in their commitment to norms, as well as their objective circumstances which dictate what they have to gain or lose (Cook, 1980). They also allow for the likelihood that some groups of individuals, such as the young, the emotionally disturbed, or the committed criminal may be less susceptible to the threat of sanctions.

Contrary to the view that rising crime rates and high levels of recidivism among ex-prisoners contradict the existence of any general or specific deterrent effects, Andenaes (1974) points out that most first offenders who experience legal action do not re-offend. He also cites instances of police strikes in Liverpool in 1919 and Montreal in 1956, which were followed by marked increases in robbery and burglary, and which strongly suggest that the criminal justice system has an *overall* preventive effect. There have also been demonstrations that legislation *can* influence conduct. For example, the highly publicised introduction of the Road Safety Act in Britain in 1967, which made it illegal to drive with blood alcohol levels in excess of 0.08%, was followed by a reduction in deaths from road accidents of about a quarter, although this was not subsequently maintained (Ross, 1973). However, for many offences, the effects of changes in the certainty and severity of legal punishment are likely to be marginal (Cook, 1980).

The deterrence hypothesis invokes psychological processes at an individual level, but much of the empirical research focuses on crime rates at the aggregate level. Economists have been the staunchest proponents of the rational choice perspective, and view general deterrence as the principal instrument of crime control (Palmer, 1977; Ehrlich, 1981). Their analyses rest on the Benthamite assumption that criminals choose options which maximise their expected utilities. The decision to engage in a criminal act therefore depends on the balance between the benefits and costs of criminal and alternative lawful activities. The benefits of crime are pecuniary (money or goods) and/or nonpecuniary (enjoyment or psychic return). Costs include the resources needed, the nonenjoyment involved, the loss of lawful opportunities, and the material and social consequences of legal punishment. The latter is a function of the probability of arrest and conviction (certainty) and the severity of conviction. The estimation of costs is also influenced by the individual's "attitude to risk", economists assuming that decision makers generally avoid risk. The model specifies that if any one of the cost components exceeds the benefits, a crime will not be committed. However, empirical studies have focused mainly on the punishment component.

Econometric models have been employed to examine the relationship between aggregate crime rates and aggregate measures of the certainty and severity of legal punishment, such as police clear-up rates and the average sentence for a particular offence category. The results have generally been interpreted as favouring a deterrent effect of punishment for a variety of crimes, such as rape, murder, robbery, and burglary (Tullock 1974). Particularly contentious is a study of the death penalty in the United States by Ehrlich (1975), which claimed that over three decades, an additional execution each year may have resulted, on average, in seven or eight fewer murders. This conclusion has been contested (Beyleveld, 1982), and econometric studies of punishment have been criticised by sociologists for employing unreliable indices of punishment (Cook, 1980; Matsueda, Piliavin and Gartner, 1988).

Economic analyses have also been criticised for being confined to actual rather than perceived threat of punishment. Bandura (1986), for example, suggests that any deterrent effect of legal sanctions depends on beliefs about the effectiveness of the criminal justice system, and that the lawabiding typically overestimate risk. Individual level analyses of self-reported offending and perceptions of risk have been less consistent in demonstrating a deterrent effect of legal punishment. Some studies support findings of economists that certainty of punishment is more significant than severity, but also suggest that perceived personal risk of being caught is more important than perceived risk to people in general. Claster (1967), for example, found that delinquents did not differ from nondelinquents in their estimates of clear-up or conviction rates for several crimes, but judged themselves less likely to be caught, suggesting a "magical immunity" effect. Jensen, Erickson and Gibbs (1978), however, found that although perceived risk to self was most strongly related to self-reported delinquency, perceived risk in general was also significant.

Several studies have compared the influence of legal sanctions with other variables. Schwartz and Orleans (1967) reported less tax evasion by taxpayers exposed to moral arguments for compliance than by those for whom penalties were emphasised, and Tittle (1977) found that reinforcement value of rule violation and moral commitment were more potent influences on perceived likelihood of rule violation than was fear of formal sanctions. Fear of informal sanctions, such as loss of status or social respect, however, was highly significant. In a survey in Chicago, Tyrer (1990) also found that personal morality and the perceived legitimacy of legal authority had a stronger influence on compliance with laws than deterrence through external consequences. This is more consistent with traditional socialisation theory than with the self-interest assumption of deterrence theory.

Others, however, have found the effects of sanctions to be conditional, having a greater impact on those least committed to societal norms (Bishop, 1984). This was not confirmed by Piliavin et al. (1986), who found that neither formal nor informal sanctions had an effect on the self-reported offending of high-risk groups, perceived benefits of crime being the most salient factor. Previous studies may have overemphasised less serious offences, which may be more subject to informal control. Bridges and Stone (1986) also found little evidence for a special deterrent effect on incarcerated offenders, and suggest that for experienced criminals, potential benefits outweigh costs.

Psychological studies of risk perception have required subjects to judge the likelihood of choosing a crime opportunity in hypothetical situations varying in the probability of success and failure, and the magnitude of gain or loss. Rettig and Rawson (1963) found that preference of students for unethical choices was influenced by all variables, but severity of punishment accounted for half the variance. This was replicated among criminals (Rettig, 1964; Krauss et al., 1972), although Krauss et al. found that psychopaths were more sensitive to expected gains. Siegel (1978) also found that psychopaths were less sensitive to punishment in the form of monetary loss when this was uncertain, supporting a "magical immunity" effect. Carroll (1978), in contrast, found that monetary gain was the strongest influence for both offenders and nonoffenders, being twice as powerful as penalties. He also found that individuals tended to focus on only one dimension. While for half the subjects, this was magnitude of gain, a third focused on certainty of capture or severity of penalty. A strict deterrent effect would therefore be limited to this minority.

Limited rationality and criminal events

Clarke and Cornish (1985) have attempted an integration of decision-making approaches to crime, which incorporates several aspects of traditional criminological theories. They make three essential assumptions. First, offenders seek to benefit themselves by decisions which are to some degree rational. Second, the explanatory focus is on crimes rather than offenders, and is both crime-specific and situation specific. Third, criminal *events* are distinguished from criminal *involvement*. Events are criminal acts chosen in particular locations, which dictate differences in motive, method, and individual concerned. Involvement is the outcome of decisions at different points in time to begin, continue, or desist from criminal activities, and which are a function of more traditional criminological variables, such as temperament, the peer group or demographic status. While Clarke and Cornish emphasise that events and involvement entail different patterns of decision-making, they are not committed to a particular model of decision-making, noting, for example, that expected utility theory may hold for corporate crimes involving extensive planning.

The expected utility maximisation model of economics emphasises a strong form of optimal or *normative rationality*, in which the human decision-maker gathers and codes all relevant information, combining it multiplicatively. This has been criticised as an unrealistic model of human information processing, which is constrained by biological and time limitations to edit information into simple and subjective representations, and which hence exhibits bounded or *limited rationality* (Simon, 1978). This latter position is supported by the work of behaviour decision theorists, who find that subjective probabilities are governed by judgmental heuristics, such as the availability of examples in memory, and that the same decision problem yields different choices depending on how it is described or "framed" (Kahneman and Tversky, 1984).

Recent empirical studies of criminal decision-making are more consistent with the limited rationality view (Carroll, 1982; Johnson and Payne, 1986). Carroll's finding that both offenders and nonoffenders judge crime opportunities in terms of a single dimension (Carroll, 1978), for example, suggests that criminals ignore some aspects of potential crimes in judging their feasibility. However, Carroll notes that criminal decision-making may also be sequential, so that different dimensions are considered at different points in time, or at different stages of an offender's career. This was supported in a process-tracing analysis of shoplifters' verbalised thoughts during simulated shoplifting expeditions in stores (Carroll and Weaver, 1986). Expert shoplifters were sensitive to many features of opportunities for crime, but evaluated only a few at the point of decision. Their focus differed from that of novice shoplifters, who were primarily concerned with decisions about becoming a shoplifter.

Rational choice theories of crime are consistent with the cognitive trend in psychology generally, and are compatible with social learning and control theories of criminal behaviour. Hirschi (1986), for example, notes that the distinction between events and involvement is equivalent to the distinction between crimes as acts and criminality as a disposition; rational choice theories emphasise the former, and control and socialisation theories the latter. Akers (1990) goes further, and suggests that rational choice and control theories are subsumed by social learning, although this may overestimate the contribution of the latter to the analysis of cognitive processes by decision theorists.

However, recent interest in this approach has been fostered by concerns with crime control, and in focusing on situational decision-making, rational choice perspectives risk ignoring the constraints on choice imposed by personal background and the wider social context (Norrie, 1986). This encourages a legalistic conception of individual responsibility and a retributive philosophy of punishment. Although it attempts to deal with parameters of crime not addressed by more traditional theories, this perspective currently lacks a comprehensive theory of cognition, and represents as yet little more than an amalgam of utilitarian philosophy and specific theories of decision-making.

DELINQUENCY AS SELF-PRESENTATION

Role theory, in which social behaviour is seen as a function of given or expected social roles, has a long tradition in sociology, but attributes role performances primarily to situational demands. Some psychological theorists have recently suggested that delinquent behaviour is self-presentation which establishes a social identity, but see this as motivated behaviour related to cognitive structures. Gold (1978), for example, suggests that delinquent behaviour emerges in the school as a means of enhancing self esteem and avoiding the reality of incompetence in academic and social roles (see also Chapter 8).

Hogan and Jones (1983) propose a *socioanalytic theory* of criminal behaviour, which draws on evolutionary theory, depth psychology, and symbolic interactionism. The critical structures of personality are held to be: (1) self concept or identity, which is the view of the self originating in parent–child interactions, and which is also what one would like others to believe; (2) self-presentation, or the role-playing tactics employed to project one's self-image; (3) the person's reference group, which is the internalised view of the expectations of significant others; (4) interpersonal skills of sensitivity and competence, which relate to reading the expectations of others and relating them to self-image through role performance. Basic to these structures are universal human needs for attention and approval, status, and predictability.

Criminals are held to vary from the law-abiding in all of these structures. Individuals who emerge from childhood with poor interpersonal competencies and hostility to adult authority will develop an uncooperative and rebellious interpersonal style. When combined with poor educational skills and opportunities, this will lead to the adoption of a deviant role. The reference group is the immediate peer group of similar individuals, and the self-image is negotiated to maximise approval of this group. Depending on temperament, modelling experience, and social opportunities, the typical self-presentation is of an image of being tough, alienated, reckless, and exhibitionistic. Choice of criminal career is rational, though not necessarily conscious, and "for many working class men, being a criminal is their social identity". Hogan and Jones present data indicating that this is indeed the image delinquents project.

Emler (Emler, 1984; Reicher and Emler, 1986) similarly sees delinquency as a nonpathological and rational social identity chosen by young people because it makes sense to them in terms of their circumstances. Delinquency is conceptualised as a general behaviour characteristic varying among young adolescents, of which official delinquency is the extreme. This behaviour is not covert or secretive, and is communicated visibly in social interaction with peers, as well as in self-reports of delinquent acts. Self-presentation relates to the longer term goal of establishing and sustaining a *reputation* within a community of acquaintances, reputation being the means of access to desired resources. It is hence proposed that presentation of self in a way which is unfavourable to authority is not, as some suggest, a reflection of skill deficits, but is rather motivated behaviour consistently aimed at managing a reputation relevant to a particular segment or audience of the adolescent peer group.

Reicher and Emler (1986) provide evidence that delinquent behaviour conveys a clear impression to adolescents of a tough, cruel, and less cowardly disposition, which is evaluated favourably by the more delinquent. They suggest that a social identity in terms of future prospects is established during the early secondary school years, and that experiences of streaming and educational failure lead many to reject formal authority and the "social contract" ideology on which it is based. A coherent alternative identity is provided by the availability of delinquent traditions and support for such an identity within the peer group. Establishing and maintaining a place within this group is contingent on delinquent acts which achieve the appropriate reputation.

The self-presentational approach departs from traditional psychological theories in that delinquency is construed as socially meaningful behaviour motivated by non-pathological processes, rather than being "mindless" nonconformity. It makes contact with subcultural theories which identify working class "focal concerns" (Miller, 1958), and the emphasis on the lack of commitment to the established order is particularly consistent with control theory. The significance of delinquent friends and the experience of school failure also finds support in sociological research on delinquency. However, neither Hogan nor Emler account adequately for the heterogeneity of delinquents, and while Hogan explicitly includes temperament and early family experience as significant determinants of the choice of a delinquent role in adolescence, Reicher and Emler's analysis leaves unclear the extent to which the adolescent's personal attributes contribute to school failure. Finally, this approach appears to predict desistance from delinquency as the adolescent peer group breaks up. It does not clearly indicate why only some delinquents go on to become adult criminals.

Chapter 5

Individually Oriented and Integrated Theories of Crime

INTRODUCTION

The limitation of theories which posit social and cultural processes as the critical determinants of deviant behaviour is that individuals exposed to similar environments do not develop in uniform fashion. It therefore seems inescapable that individual differences emerging early in development moderate the effects of the social environment. This chapter examines three general psychological theories which focus on "internal" factors mediating deviant development, although it should be noted that none assumes that the individual develops in a social vacuum. The chapter concludes with a consideration of recent attempts to integrate theories of crime.

PSYCHOANALYSIS AND CRIME

As Lazarus (1980) has put it, the crucial Freudian contribution to abnormal psychology was the idea that people experience distress and are inept in their coping because they carry around with them childhood agenda which interfere with adult good sense. Freud, however, had little to say about crime, and although subsequent psychoanalysts have shown extensive interest, it has always been indirect and focused on the pathological processes of which criminal acts are thought to be a manifestation (Glover, 1960). There are consequently several psychoanalytic commentaries on crime (e.g. Feldman, 1964; Marshall, 1983; Kline, 1987), but no unitary psychoanalytic theory. What follows attempts to summarise the more orthodox concepts of the psychodynamic perspective.

Socialisation theory

Freud regarded humans as inherently antisocial. Individuals are held to be biologically endowed with egocentric pleasure seeking and destructive impulses which conflict with the demands of the social group. To ensure social survival, these impulses must be controlled or redirected by individuals themselves, and this is achieved in two ways. First, the primary process activity of the *id* is opposed by the emergence of the secondary process, an *ego* function guided by the reality principle. The development of reality oriented thinking and imagination thus permits delay of gratification through the employment of fantasy and planfulness, or the inhibition of overt motor discharge (Singer, 1955).

Second, in channelling id drives, the ego is guided by the *superego*, which represents the internalisation of group standards. Although originally conceived as an unconscious agency, the superego is now regarded as mainly conscious, or preconscious (Nass, 1966), and has two components. The *conscience* is concerned with moral rules, and impulses contrary to these are neutralised, or prevented from reaching consciousness through the ego's defence mechanisms. The *ego-ideal* represents standards to which the self aspires, and hence provides the ego with positive values and goals. In the psychodynamic hydraulic model, ego and superego are counterbalancing components of a psychic system in which energy generated in the id must be discharged directly, transformed, or neutralised. If strong impulses which violate superego standards break through into consciousness or action, the superego turns the aggressive energy of the id on the ego in the form of guilt experiences. The ego therefore regulates behaviour in accordance with superego standards to avoid the pain of guilt.

Superego formation depends on psychosexual and ego development through the child's relations with its parents, and is associated with the resolution of the oedipal conflict around the age of five. Prior to that, a rudimentary conscience develops as the child learns to control its impulses, but this depends primarily on external sanctions (Malmquist, 1968). Starting from a state of primary narcissism in which the child is its own ideal, and which is analogous to intrauterine equilibrium, the infant learns that it is not omnipotent, and must form relations with the "objects" on which it depends for its needs. These object relations centre on the affection and approval of parents, who are sources of both satisfaction and frustration. As the child progresses through oral, anal, and genital stages, ego development determines the control of impulses to optimise their gratification, while ensuring the continued approval of parents. Satisfying parental relations are therefore critical to early development, and impaired relationships produce fixation points to which the individual subsequently regresses at times of crisis. Conflicts at the anal stage, for example, may lead to oppositional and sadistic tendencies, which are elicited in situations involving obedience.

With the onset of the genital stage, incestuous wishes for the opposite-sexed parent and hostility to the same-sexed parent generate tension because of fears of counteraggression (castration anxiety) in the boy, and loss of love in the girl. This conflict is resolved by defensively identifying with and introjecting the attributes of the threatening parent, i.e. adopting their imagined thoughts, feelings, and behaviour. The child is therefore able to renounce oedipal strivings by abandoning investment in external objects and incorporating them into itself. Conscience at this point is consolidated by *identification with the aggressor*. Thus the boy avoids the threat of paternal punishment by internalising the father's perceived aggression toward him, utilising it against the self, and maintains the object relation with the mother as one of affection rather than possession. The ego-ideal is formed by *anaclitic identification*, through which the desirable image of the loved objects is incorporated. This restores the lost narcissism of infancy and provides an agency of wish fulfilment and self-esteem. While the early theory considered the superego to be essentially formed at this stage, later theorists see superego standards as developing throughout adolescence (Nass, 1966).

Psychoanalysts continue to disagree about the functional differentiation of superego from ego, but agree on the essential notion of an inner moral agency governing conduct whose development depends on satisfying parent–child relationships. However, recent developmental theorists have been more influenced by ego psychologists and neo-analysts such as Sullivan, and question the classical instinct model. *Attachment theory* (Sroufe and Fleeson, 1986; Ainsworth and Bowlby, 1991) is an eclectic approach grounded in psychoanalytic concepts, but drawing also on ethology, evolutionary theory, and cognitive psychology. The focus is on the quality of infant–caregiver attachment during the first year of life as a determinant of later cognitive and social development. Early attachment affects later behaviour through the internalisation of the relationship as a working model of dyadic relationships. Insecure attachment, for example, is seen in anxious-avoidant and anxious-resistant infants who come to expect that others are not available for support and cannot be trusted. Such children are subsequently likely to select and shape disordered interactions which recreate aspects of relationship systems previously experienced. This more cognitively oriented theory is seen in recent accounts of personality disorder (Carson, 1979), child abuse (Egeland, Jacobvitz and Sroufe, 1988), and sex offending (Marshall, 1989).

Applications to criminal behaviour

Inadequate superego formation and functioning are central to psychodynamic accounts of criminal behaviour, and as Glover (1960) notes, "Crime is *one* of the results of unsuccessful domestication". However, the superego is never totally absent, and its role must be seen in the total context of the dynamic system. Since behaviour depends on the balance of the psychic energy system, disturbance in any component structure produces maladaptive development. For example, superego deficiencies may be expected to correlate with deficiencies in ego control, and failure to delay gratification. Further, disturbed parental relationships are unlikely to be confined to the oedipal stage, and superego problems are hence associated with unconscious conflicts arising at all developmental stages. These conflicts motivate deviant acts in later life, when early conflict situations are reproduced. Psychoanalysts therefore propose three main sources of criminal behaviour, which relate to a harsh, weak, or deviant superego.

First, criminal acts may reflect a harsh superego, and resemble a *neurosis*. In both symptomatic and criminal neurosis, the unconscious conflict is repressed, the only difference being that in the former, it is experienced as an *autoplastic* change in the individual's functioning, while in the latter, the conflict is "acted out" in an *alloplastic* attempt to change the environment. In "compulsive" theft, for example, the act of stealing or the object stolen symbolises the conflict. One variant of this view is that the neurotic criminal has a punitive superego, and experiences extreme unconscious guilt over repressed infantile wishes. The acted-out wish invites punishment in the form of legal sanctions (Freud, 1915/1957). Alternatively, delinquency may represent substitute gratification of needs for security, acceptance, or status, which are not met in the family (Healy and Bronner, 1936). Unfulfilled unconscious wishes may be sublimated and find expression in alternative actions which provide the needed recognition or status, for example, in the context of gang delinquency. While not employing an orthodox Freudian model, Stott (1982) also sees delinquency as a solution to the frustration of emotional needs for personal effectiveness and social attachment within the family. From observations of Glasgow delinquents, he suggests that their delinquent acts were typically responses to family stress, and motivated by one or more of the following; escape from the home situation, avoidance of stress through excitement, hostility, loyalty testing, and compensatory bravado.

The effect of a weak superego has long been associated with psychopathic personality, and the notion of an egocentric, impulsive, guiltless, and unempathic individual is, in fact, a psychodynamic portrayal. Although an early formulation identified "impulse-ridden" characters, who express primitive instinctual needs unmodified by either superego or developmental fixations, most writers propose a combination of unresolved oedipal and pre-genital fixations. Glover (1960), for example, sees psychopaths as arrested at an earlier stage of superego formation involving hostile identifications with parents of either sex, and for whom "the central issue of mental life is the control of sadism". He sees the psychopath as constitutionally predisposed to aggression and the use of projection as a defence. When combined with experiences of frustrating parents who fail to satisfy the child's dependency needs, the result is narcissistic fixation, resulting in egocentricity and exploitativeness. A similar view appears in recent accounts of narcissistic personality (Akhtar and Thompson, 1982). In addition, frustrations at oral and anal stages exaggerate the psychopath's natural tendencies towards sadism, as the child introjects the hostility projected onto the frustrating parent. However, Glover suggests that the superego is not a unitary entity, but is made up of layers formed by identifications at different stages. Since poor relationships may be confined to one parent and a specific developmental stage, only parts of the superego may be deficient. The psychopath's behaviour may therefore be deviant only at times of crisis. Glover's account resembles Kernberg's description of "borderline personality organisation", which includes antisocial personality (Kernberg, 1975).

Also relevant in this context is Bowlby's hypothesis that the disruption of attachment bonds between mother and child is a significant precursor of later deviance (Bowlby, 1979). His original view of "maternal deprivation" was based on findings of a history of separation from the mother before the age of five among juvenile thieves showing "affectionless character" (Bowlby, 1944). However, these findings were not substantially replicated, and the effects of separation have been questioned on both methodological and conceptual grounds (Wootton, 1959; Rutter, 1971). Rutter's analysis pointed up ambiguities in the "maternal deprivation" concept, and his review found little to support the causal significance of separation *per se*. However, he found some indication that failure to *form* an attachment bond with the caretaker (not necessarily with the mother) was significant in later delinquency. This aspect is emphasised in recent accounts of psychopathy, which see the hostility and apparent lack of anxiety as a defence against painful feelings of dependency and powerlessness originating in early maternal rejection and inconsistency (Vaillant, 1975; Marshall, 1983).

The third source of delinquent behaviour is where superego standards develop normally, but those standards reflect *deviant identification*. This may occur when a criminal father has a good relationship with his son, who introjects his father's criminal attributes. In this case, the child's delinquent behaviour reflects an absence of guilt, but not abnormality of psychic structures. A related concept is that of "superego lacunae" (Johnson, 1959), which implies that delinquents may be adequately socialised in general, but lack prohibitions against specific forms of deviance. This is held to result when parents encourage criminal activities which serve as vicarious gratification of their own unconscious conflict. For example, a mother with concerns over her own history of shoplifting may pay undue attention to the possibility of stealing by her child, to the extent that her expectation becomes a self-fulfilling prophecy (Aldrich, 1987).

The validity of psychodynamic hypotheses of criminality

Psychoanalysis does not offer a comprehensive theory of crime, and fails to account for several features. For example, the theory would not explain the age distribution of offending. While the increase in delinquency at puberty might plausibly be linked to a resurgence of infantile conflicts at the end of the latency period, this would not account for desistance in late adolescence. Furthermore, Freud maintained that since females do not fear castration, they do not resolve the oedipal complex as completely as do males, and hence should have weaker superegos. This is not consistent with sex differences in crime, and is contrary to evidence that females show a stronger moral orientation than males at all ages (Hoffman, 1977).

The theory seems to rest on the following claims: (1) socialisation depends on the internalisation of society's rules during early childhood; (2) impaired parent–infant relationships are causally related to later criminal behaviour; (3) unconscious conflicts arising from disturbed family relationships at different stages of development, particularly the oedipal stage, are the causes of *some* criminal acts. The first assumption is not unique to psychoanalysis, and the second is also shared by other theories, although explanations of how family factors influence delinquency differ (Chapter 7). The third assumption is the most unique and hence critical to the theory.

It should be emphasised that not all crimes are held to result from unconscious conflicts. Kline (1987) notes that many acquisitive crimes, such as white collar crimes, and even some aggressive crimes, are "ego crimes", which involve rational goals and planning, and the explanatory utility of psychodynamic theories may be limited to "irrational" criminal behaviour. The available evidence also suggests that neurotic and psychopathic individuals do not make up the majority of offenders, although Stott (1982) believes that most persistent delinquents exhibit some form of maladjustment. As yet, however, the basis for the claim that some offenders offend because of unconscious conflicts rests largely on *post hoc* clinical observations, which typically avoid the risk of exposure to invalidation.

Kline (1987) points to the availability of subliminal stimulation techniques which provide tests for the presence of conflict and the use of defence mechanisms, and proposes that there are testable and falsifiable predictions which can be made using such techniques. However, the validity of these procedures is questionable (Balay and Shevrin, 1988), and the theory does not adequately predict when conflicts will be expressed as alloplastic rather than autoplastic symptoms. Neurotic conflicts may also be as much a consequence as a cause of crime, and Feldman (1964) points out that psychodynamic writers ignore the reciprocal effects of involvement in crime on personality disturbance.

Nevertheless, the psychodynamic hypotheses cannot be rejected out of hand. Psychoanalysis is the only theory which attempts to deal systematically with the phenomena of affective experience, and contrary to the somewhat overdone positivist critiques, the theory has proved to be falsifiable, and has withstood the test in several respects (Dixon and Henley, 1980). The resistance of psychologists to the notion of unconscious processes has also begun to dissipate (Meichenbaum and Gilmore, 1984), and with the cognitive "revolution", psychology has moved closer to psychoanalysis (Lazarus, 1980; Erdelyi, 1985).

EYSENCK'S THEORY OF CRIMINALITY

Eysenck's theory of personality has evolved over almost half a century, and continues to stimulate research. However, many aspects remain contentious, particularly those relating to crime. The present discussion focuses on the theory of criminality originating in 1964, but subsequently developed by Eysenck (1977) and Eysenck and Gudjonsson (1989).

Criminality is construed as a disposition to commit crimes, and as a continuously varying trait, which ranges from "altruistic behaviour through normal conduct to victimless but possibly antisocial behaviour to victimful behaviour in criminality" (Eysenck and Gudjonsson, 1989). The theory centres on "the actively antisocial, psychopathic criminal", who exemplifies the undersocialised extreme. Family murderers and "inadequate" criminals are excluded from the theory, which to this extent is not a theory of criminal behaviour in general. Rather does it seek to explain why some people fail to comply with rules.

The attributes of criminals are deduced from three sets of propositions. First, the *descriptive model of personality* relates variations in human temperament to three independent dimensions of Neuroticism–Stability (N), Psychoticism–Superego (P), and Extraversion–Introversion (E). N and E have been defined by successive questionnaires, notably the Maudsley Personality Inventory (MPI) and Eysenck Personality Inventory (EPI). The more recent Eysenck Personality Questionnaire (EPQ; H. J. Eysenck and S. B. G. Eysenck, 1975) measures N, E, and P, and contains a Lie (L) scale, which despite its name, taps traits of rigid conformity or lack of openness to experience (McCrae and Costa, 1985).

Second, Eysenck presents evidence for genetic influences on N, E, and P, which supports the *biological basis of personality*. N is held to reflect greater reactivity in the limbic and autonomic systems, resulting in stronger emotional responses to stress, and higher levels of "drive". Underlying E is the level of cortical arousal or arousability, governed by activity in cortico-reticular circuits. Extraverts have low arousal relative to introverts, and are predicted to form conditioned responses less readily, to require more intense stimulation to maintain "hedonic tone" (i.e. pleasurable states of consciousness), and to be less responsive to pain. More tentatively, P relates to circulating androgens.

Third is a control theory of *socialisation*. Like Freud, Eysenck sees people as naturally hedonistic, and socialisation involves the acquisition of restraints in the form of "conscience" or "superego". Morality or rule-compliance is a function of involuntary emotional responses to temptation, which are acquired through classical conditioning as a result of punishment of antisocial behaviour by parents and others. Resistance to temptation thus entails avoidance of punished behaviour mediated by the arousal of a conditioned anxiety response, and "conscience is indeed a conditioned reflex". Given that extraverts are less susceptible to the pain of punishment, and form conditioned responses slowly, other things being equal, they will be less well socialised than introverts.

The theory does not assert that criminality *per se* is biologically determined. Adult conduct depends on the quality of conditioning received in childhood as well as the child's degree of conditionability, but Eysenck is primarily concerned with individual differences. While acknowledging that criminals are heterogeneous, he predicts that as a group they will be more extraverted, and will exhibit lower arousal and weaker conditionability. However, from Hull's theory that drive interacts with habit strength to potentiate a prepotent response, they are also predicted to score highly on N. Extraverts who are also "neurotic" will therefore exhibit stronger antisocial tendencies. Criminals are further predicted to score highly on P. This is not derived from theory, but from findings that criminality and psychopathy are more prevalent among the relatives of psychotic patients, from which it is argued that the genetic predisposition to develop psychotic disorder is also expressed in antisocial tendencies. The traits of the high P scorer (hostile, socially insensitive, cruel) are also noted to be those attributed to psychopaths. It is therefore proposed that high P scores characterise primary psychopaths, while secondary psychopaths will be high on N and E. As a group, however, psychopaths and criminals will have higher mean scores on all three personality dimensions.

The most powerful explanatory component of the theory is clearly that linking E with low arousal and undersocialisation. This is independent of the predictions regarding N and P, which carry little explanatory power. Psychophysiological research on arousal and conditioning in offenders will be discussed in Chapter 6, and the focus here is on the evidence relating crime and antisocial behaviour to personality dimensions. However, the basic propositions are first examined more closely.

The dimensional structure of personality

The misleading concepts of "neuroticism" and "psychoticism" derive from a basic assumption that N and P are the phenotypic expressions of genetic predispositions to develop the major forms of psychiatric disorder. N and P are thus what "neurotics" and "psychotics" have "in common" (Eysenck, 1960). However, the identification of symptom patterns as "neurotic" in psychiatry reflects the psychoanalytic theory of neurosis. The term has no precise meaning outside the framework of this theory. "Neuroticism" is therefore a reification, which has obscured the identity of N with the trait anxiety dimension of American investigators (Blackburn, 1968a). In fact, N is pervasive in self-evaluative questionnaires, and measures proneness to anxiety, depression, hostility, and poor self-esteem, or *negative affectivity* (Watson and Clark, 1984). These attributes are not specific to "neurotic" patients, and characterise many "psychotics" and personality disorders. However, if N measures trait anxiety, the predicted high N of criminals is difficult to reconcile with a lack of conditioned anxiety.

Even greater uncertainty surrounds the meaning of P (Howarth, 1986). There is no evidence that the P scale measures a genetic predisposition to psychosis or precursors of psychotic disorder (Davis, 1974a; Bishop, 1977). There is also no justification for equating predisposition to psychosis with an absence of "superego", which according to the theory is a function of E. Eysenck has sometimes suggested that P may be better construed as "psychopathy", an interpretation favoured by other investigators (Zuckerman, Kuhlman and Camac, 1988).

Introversion–extraversion is also an ambiguous concept, and questions have been raised about whether it describes a single dimension. The issue centres on the relation of E to the "sociable" and "impulsive" components of extraverted behaviour. *Sociability* denotes gregariousness, talkativeness, and group involvement, as opposed to aloofness or withdrawal, although introverted preference for solitary activities is distinguished from shyness or social anxiety ("neurotic introversion"). *Impulsiveness* or impulsivity implies acting without forethought or restraint, and among trait theorists, typically refers to speedy decisions or motor responses to *external* stimulation. However, impulsivity in psychological theories more generally also refers to control of *internal* emotional "impulses" (e g. Shapiro, 1965).

In Eysenck's hierarchical model, sociability (SOC) and impulsiveness (IMP) are primary traits, which correlate with others, such as assertiveness or dominance, to yield the higher-order E dimension. This is supported in studies of the E scale of the EPI (H. J. Eysenck and S. B. G. Eysenck, 1963; McCrae and Costa, 1985), and Eysenck (1974) suggested that conditionability is related to IMP rather than to SOC, and that IMP is the more important component of extraversion in criminality. IMP items, however, are largely absent from the E scale of the later EPQ, and IMP is now considered to be a component of P (S. B. G. Eysenck and H. J. Eysenck, 1978). If IMP carries the theoretical significance attached to E (low arousal, weak conditionability, deficient conscience), and IMP is related to P, the theory of criminality is seriously undermined.

However, some writers argue that SOC and IMP represent *independent* dimensions (Carrigan, 1960; Guilford, 1977). Since P correlates with impulsivity, nonconformity and lack of restraint (Raine and Venables, 1981; Zuckerman, Kuhlman and Camac, 1988), it could also be argued that P is a component of a broader dimension of impulse control, and that the E and P dimensions of the EPQ correspond to what others have identified as independent dimensions of social extraversion and impulsivity. While Eysenck is committed to a hierarchical model, the relationship between traits such as SOC and IMP can, in fact, be represented alternatively by a two-dimensional circular array, or circumplex (Wiggins, 1982). Figure 5.1 shows such an arrangement as demonstrated in the MMPI scales by Kassebaum, Couch and Slater (1959), and replicated by Blackburn (1971b). Kassebaum et al. showed that the two main factors in the MMPI were essentially N and E, but argued that the vectors at 45 degrees (factor fusions) to the primary reference axes are important in explicating the meaning of the main axes. These vectors are defined by scales of social withdrawal versus social participation (i.e. sociability) and impulsivity versus control. In this analysis, then, SOC and IMP are independent dimensions which correlate with E (and N), but not with each other, and the Eysencks' finding of correlated clusters can be attributed to a narrow selection of items emphasising motoric aspects of IMP rather than emotional control. Many of the traits which Eysenck claims to make up P (dominance, masculinity, aggression) are, in fact, sufficiently accounted for by the circumplex arrangement (Blackburn and Maybury, 1985; Wiggins and Broughton, 1985).

If IMP and SOC are construed as an alternative rotation of the axes defining the two-dimensional space, they may represent the main lines of causal influence on individual differences. This is the essence of Gray's revision of Eysenck's theory (Gray, 1981). Although distinguishing N from *anxiety*, and labelling his rotations impulsivity and anxiety, Gray's dimensions are the impulsivity and social withdrawal (i.e. social anxiety) axes of Figure 5.1. However, applications of Gray's theory to criminality focus on anxiety/social withdrawal rather than on impulsivity (see below).

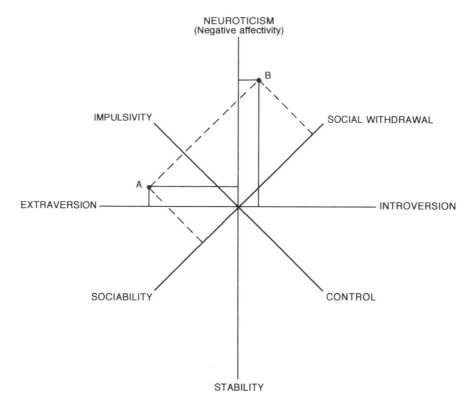

Figure 5.1   Relation of impulsivity and sociability to neuroticism and extraversion. A and B represent primary and secondary psychopaths

The biological basis of personality

The theory that the substrate of N lies in thresholds of activation in limbic structures lacks firm support, and the hypothesis linking P to androgen level has yet to be investigated. This section examines the implications of the hypothesis linking E to cortical arousal.

EEG measures, which are potentially the most direct index of cortical arousal, do not consistently discriminate introverts from extraverts (Gale and Edwards, 1983), but some predictions from the model have been supported. For example, introverts are expected to show superior conditioning under conditions of (a) partial reinforcement; (b) weak unconditioned stimulus; and (c) short interval between conditioned and unconditioned stimulus. When these conditions do not obtain, extraverts will exhibit superior conditioning, and Eysenck cites evidence demonstrating this. However, the notion of a disposition of conditionability generalised across physiological systems is open to question (Levey and Martin, 1981). Developments in conditioning theory also now emphasise informational aspects of classical conditioning, rather than a simple reflex arc model (Rescorla, 1988).

A further prediction from the arousal postulate is that extraverts require more stimulation to support positive "hedonic tone", and thus have a higher *optimal level of stimulation*. Eysenck notes that delinquent activities often appear to stem from boredom and risk taking, and Baldwin (1985) suggests that sensation seeking, which is most prominent among adolescent males, may account for both the age and sex distribution of crime. Other theorists also posit a relation between low arousal, stimulation seeking and deviant behaviour. Quay (1965, 1977b) explicitly relates "stimulus hunger" to psychopathy, while Farley (1986) proposes that delinquents more generally are likely to be underaroused and sensation seekers. In a presentation of "arousal theory", Ellis (1987) hypothesises that eight behaviour patterns are related to suboptimal arousal (resistance to punishment, impulsiveness, childhood hyperactivity, risk-taking, recreational drug use, active social interactions, broad-ranging sexual experiences, and poor academic performance), and proposes that all are associated with "criminality and/or psychopathy".

The links between extraversion, stimulation seeking, and arousal, however, are by no means clearly established. Optimal level of stimulation has commonly been measured by Zuckerman's Sensation Seeking Scales (SSS; Zuckerman, 1969), but research with these indicates that stimulation seeking is related to IMP rather than SOC (Blackburn, 1969; Farley and Farley, 1970). It also correlates with P and with undersocialisation, and together, these variables define a factor independent of extraversion as measured by EPQ E (Zuckerman et al., 1988). Stimulus seeking is not, then, a direct function of E.

The optimal level of stimulation concept itself presents difficulties. It denotes a *preferred* level or standard, departure from which is assumed to motivate stimulation seeking or avoidance. It is therefore the discrepancy between this postulated standard and the current level of input which is assumed to be motivating, not the level of arousal *per se*. The nature of this putative standard, however, remains obscure, and there is no obvious reason why a high optimal level should be related to low arousal level. There is, in fact, evidence that the aversiveness of "boredom" results from *increased* autonomic arousal (Berlyne, 1960; Zuckerman, 1969; London, Schubert and Washburn, 1972).

Optimal level of stimulation theories emphasise the nonspecific arousing effects of stimulus intensity, but research on sensory deprivation demonstrated that what is reinforcing for stimulus-deprived subjects is not stimulus intensity or variability as such, but rather the *information* contained in stimulation (Berlyne, 1960; Jones, 1969). Several theorists therefore proposed that people seek an *optimal level of information* in the form of uncertainty or incongruity (Hunt, 1965). These are not inherent properties of "raw" stimulation, but rather depend on how stimulation is appraised. While novel or complex stimulation is arousing, this effect is a consequence of information processing. If stimulus hunger represents a departure from a preferred optimum of incongruity, then sensation seeking behaviour should have more to do with mediation by central cognitive control mechanisms than with reductions in nonspecific arousal level.

Zuckerman (1984) concluded that there is *no* evidence for a relationship between optimal level of stimulation and low arousal, at least as far as sensation seeking is concerned, and recent research suggests that sensation seekers have an excitable central nervous system, being *more* aroused and arousable (Smith et al., 1989). Zuckerman now sees sensation seekers as compensating for low tonic activity in brain catecholamine systems governing release of noradrenaline. This may well relate to the control of information flow, since the noradrenaline system is involved in stimulus sampling and the filtering out of irrelevant information (Mason, 1984).

It would appear, then, that stimulus seeking is not directly related to E or to arousal level. While this does not invalidate the hypothesised link between arousal and extraversion, it compromises the theory of criminality, since Eysenck's prediction that criminal behaviour represents stimulus seeking rests on the link between extraversion and optimal level of stimulation.

Gray also minimises the role of arousal in individual differences, which are proposed to be more closely associated with specific forebrain systems (Gray, 1981). Underlying the dimension of "anxiety" is the Behavioural Inhibition System (BIS), a septo-hippocampal system responsive to conditioned stimuli for punishment or the absence of anticipated reward, which mediates passive avoidance. The BIS interacts with the Behavioural Activation System (BAS), which mediates responsiveness to conditioned stimuli for reward or nonpunishment, and underlies impulsivity, although the biological substrate for this is less clear. Psychopaths are held to be characterised by a deficiency in the reactivity of the BIS, leading them to be relatively insensitive to threat stimuli (Trasler, 1978; Fowles, 1988). Fowles proposes that this deficiency will be manifest in hyporesponsiveness of the electrodermal system. No dysfunction of the BAS is suggested, but reward seeking behaviour is held to be disinhibited in psychopaths by virtue of the failure of conditioned stimuli for punishment to inhibit approach responses.

Quay (1986), however, suggests that in childhood behaviour problems, conduct disorder is a function of an overactive BAS, attention-deficit disorder reflects an underactive BIS, and social withdrawal results from an overactive BIS. This appears to be more consistent with the personality correlates of these systems as hypothesised by Gray. It should, nevertheless, be emphasised that all individuals will have a position on both dimensions, and some may therefore be extreme with respect to both BIS and BAS functioning. In Figure 5.1, for example, A and B represent the positions of two individuals who are both highly impulsive, and hence would be predicted to have an overactive BAS. B, however, is socially withdrawn, and would be expected to have an overactive BIS, while A should have an underactive BIS. A and B, in fact, correspond to groups of primary (A) and secondary (B) psychopaths as identified empirically (Blackburn, 1986).

The theory of socialisation

The claim that socialisation is mediated through the conditioning of anxiety or fear is difficult to demonstrate. While the importance of punishment in child training is widely accepted, many argue that reinforcement of behaviour which is incompatible with socially disapproved behaviour is equally involved. Observations of parent–child interaction further suggest that deviant families positively reinforce deviant behaviour (Chapter 7), while social learning theorists emphasise the role of modelling in both prosocial and antisocial behaviour, and the development of cognitive self-regulation in socialisation. Eysenck's theory has therefore been criticised for relying on a narrow concept of human development derived from animal laboratory studies (Passingham, 1972; Trasler, 1978). The conditioning model of fear acquisition, which has always been debatable in the light of Hebb's classic studies on the role of cognitive incongruity in fear reactions (Hebb, 1946), has also been increasingly challenged in recent years (e.g. Rachman, 1977).

It was noted earlier that introverts show superior conditioning under certain conditions. Given the lack of evidence of a generalised trait of conditionability, the relevance of this to socialisation depends on acceptance of eye-blink or electrodermal conditioning as analogues of natural emotional conditioning. It is, however, doubtful that any differences in acquisition of conditioned responses between introverts and extraverts could adequately account for real-life differences. As Passingham (1972) points out, conditions favouring conditioning in introverts (weak unconditioned stimulus, short intervals between conditioned and unconditioned stimulus) are infrequent in everyday circumstances. Gray (1981) similarly argues that conditioning is relevant to socialisation only to the extent that introverts are biologically more susceptible to fear, and condition more readily with an aversive unconditioned stimulus.

Raine and Venables (1981) describe a test of the socialisation theory in normal adolescents, employing an electrodermal conditioning paradigm in which the parameters favoured introverts. Subjects were divided into more and less socialised by means of scores on a factor extracted from self-report tests of socialisation and personality, but no differences were found in conditioning. Although this failed to support Eysenck's theory, partial support was claimed from an interaction between social class and conditioning: antisocial boys from middle class families showed poorer conditioning than less antisocial boys, the reverse being the case for lower class boys. This is interpreted as consistent with Eysenck's suggestion that introverts reared in more criminogenic environments will themselves become antisocial because of their superior conditionability (although it is unclear how antisocial behaviour can be directly conditioned). However, the data do not provide a test of this prediction, since the measure of socialisation was unrelated to EPQ E.

Trasler's theory of socialisation (Trasler, 1962, 1978) is more immune to the above criticisms. While he also sees socialised behaviour as dependent on conditioned anxiety rather than aversive contingencies in the immediate environment, he relates this specifically to *passive avoidance learning*. Thus, cues associated with punishment arouse conditioned anxiety, which is reduced by inhibiting the punished response. However, this does not depend on a general conditioning process, and "aversive inhibitory conditioning" is held to be a primitive and relatively independent form of learning, which in humans capitalises on cognitive abilities in the form of instructions and reference to rules or principles. In emphasising verbal mediation, Trasler departs from Eysenck, who regards it as playing a subsidiary role in socialisation.

Trasler gives greater weight to withdrawal of approval than to physical punishment as the source of punishment, anticipation of loss of approval or nonreward being functionally equivalent to anticipated pain. Parents who utilise "approval-related" training methods, which assume a dependent parent–child relationship, will be more effective as socialising agents, and socialisation will there fore be optimal in middle class and intact homes. He thus places more emphasis on the social conditions surrounding child training. Criminality may reflect a lack of appropriate training conditions more than a deficient ability to respond to training, and Trasler doubts that personality factors related to conditionability are significant for the majority of offenders. However, psychopaths represent the "type case of deviance", being deficient in the mechanisms necessary for learning social prohibitions. This is not due to any generalised deficit in conditionability, but rather to a specific deficit in responsiveness to punishment cues. Trasler equates this with a deficit in Gray's BIS.

Personality and crime

The preceding discussion suggests a number of flaws in Eysenck's general theory, which cast doubt on its adequacy as an explanation of criminality. Nevertheless, tests of the prediction that antisocial behaviour is related to high levels of E, N, and P provide a focus for examining the relation between personality and crime. Studies employing earlier forms of Eysenck's questionnaires yielded little support for the theory. Cochrane (1974) summarised the results of 20 studies up to 1972. Only one showed delinquents to be more extraverted, while five found them to be more introverted. Subsequent studies, which rely more on the EPQ, produce more consistent results, though not always those predicted. In an acerbic review, which questioned the validity of the Eysenck questionnaires, Farrington, Biron and Le Blanc (1982) examined 16 comparisons of officially defined offenders with controls. In the majority, offenders were higher on P and N, but not consistently higher on E. In contrast, seven self-report studies indicated an association with E, while a correlation with P was suggested in a few studies including this scale. There was no clear association with N.

Farrington et al. describe a study of self-report delinquency in Montreal which also indicated an association with E and P, and a tendency for boys and girls with a combination of high N and E scores to report more delinquent behaviour. Data from the Cambridge study also revealed a significant association of E with self-report delinquency, and of N with official delinquency, while high NE combinations obtained at age 16 were related to both official and self-report delinquency in adulthood. Since these associations did not hold when juvenile self-report delinquency scores were taken into account, the authors suggest that the relation between E and self-report delinquency reflects a response bias. They also dismiss the correlation with P as an artefact of scale construction, on the grounds that items were selected to maximise the delinquent–nondelinquent discrimination, although this claim is not substantiated.

Although Farrington et al. conclude that Eysenck's theory lacks support, some consistencies in their data are also apparent in subsequent research. Rushton and Christjohn (1981), for example, found that self-report delinquency correlated consistently with E and P, and negatively with L, across seven samples of schoolchildren and students. Their finding that self-report delinquency scores had loadings on three personality factors (extraversion, toughmindedness and psychoticism) also seems to argue against any simple interpretation in terms of response bias. Goma, Perez and Torrubia (1988) summarised research in Spain which also found self-reported delinquency in nonoffender samples to be significantly related to P and E. Consistent with the review by Farrington et al., incarcerated offender samples scored highly on P and N, but not E. However, S. B. G. Eysenck and McGurk (1980) found that young offenders in a detention centre scored significantly higher than controls on P, E, and N, as well as on IMP.

Further evidence comes from studies of observed antisocial behaviour in schoolchildren. Saklofse (1977) found that the P scale significantly discriminated boys nominated by teachers as well- or badly-behaved, and Powell and Stewart (1983) similarly reported that teacher ratings of antisocial behaviour correlated with the P scale of the Junior EPQ. In a series of studies, Lane (1987) found that children with records of serious trouble in school scored higher on P and E, while P was correlated with ratings of hostility. In a five year follow-up, official delinquency was predicted by high scores on P, but also *low* scores on N, as well as L. P was additionally correlated with number and persistence of offences, and with violent offending, correlations with E and N being insignificant. In these studies, then, it is the P scale which is most consistently related to antisocial behaviour. However, Berman and Paisey (1984) found that more serious (violent) delinquents scored higher than less serious (property) offenders on P, E, and N, and lower on L.

Only limited evidence is available on Eysenck's predictions regarding psychopathy. Hare (1982) found that inmates of a medium secure prison in Canada scored close to the normative mean on all scales of the EPQ, but there was a small positive correlation between P and the Psychopathy Checklist, correlations being highest with items relating to boredom and impulsivity. However, among mentally disordered offenders, Blackburn (1987) found that contrary to Eysenck's prediction that P will characterise primary psychopaths, highest scores on the EPQ P scale were obtained by *secondary* psychopaths, who were also more introverted than primary psychopaths. Both psychopathic groups scored highly on N, but primary psychopaths scored highest on the Sensation Seeking Scales. The latter is consistent with previous research on psychopaths (Blackburn, 1978), although sensation seeking has also been found to correlate with self-report delinquency (White, Labouvie and Bates, 1985; Goma, Perez and Torrubia, 1988), official delinquency (Farley and Sewell, 1976), and with more serious antisocial behaviour among delinquents (Farley and Farley, 1972; Berman and Paisey, 1984).

The most consistent findings, then, are that P is related to both official and self-report delinquency as well as to unsocialised behaviour not amounting to formal crime. There is also some evidence that high P scores may characterise the more serious and persistent offenders, although not necessarily primary psychopaths. Although high N scores are also common among officially adjudicated offenders, at least one study finds *low* N to predict delinquency. However, while some studies have found offenders to be more extraverted than controls, this is not a robust finding, and the strongest support for an association between E and antisocial behaviour comes from self-report studies. It remains possible that this reflects a tendency of extraverted youths to exaggerate or brag about their misconduct (Gibson, 1975; Farrington, Biron and Le Blanc, 1982), and given the theoretical centrality of extraversion, the failure of E to discriminate official offenders with any consistency seriously undermines the credibility of the theory.

Eysenck advances several reasons for failures of prediction regarding E. One is the influence of age. Self-report studies typically employ samples of schoolchildren, whereas studies of offenders are more likely to employ incarcerated adults. Eysenck suggests that E is more relevant to the antisocial behaviour of young children and juveniles, N to older criminals, although he has also stated that the theory is less applicable to juvenile delinquency than to persistent offending into adulthood (Eysenck, 1974). In one study involving comparisons of prisoners and the EPQ normative sample at several age levels, P and N discriminated at all ages, but E was discriminating only for prisoners over 40 (S. B. G. Eysenck and H. J. Eysenck, 1977). This is not consistent with the view that E is significant mainly in the offending behaviour of youth. It would also appear that persistent offending relates to P rather than E or N.

Another reason given for the failure of prisoners to score highly on E is that their *sociability* scores may be depressed because of the restrictions on their social behaviour. This seems implausible, since scores on personality tests of sociability reflect *preferred* as much as *actual* behaviour, and on any motivational theory, deprivation of preferred activities is more likely to increase than reduce interest. Also, short-term prisoners are no more likely to be extraverted than longer-term, institutionalised offenders (Burgess, 1972). More plausible is the suggestion that it is the IMP rather than the SOC component of extraversion which is relevant to antisocial behaviour, and there is some evidence that IMP is related to both self-report (Silva, Martorell and Clemente, 1986) and official delinquency (S. B. G. Eysenck and McGurk, 1980). However, it has been noted that the theory now links IMP more closely to P than E, which negates its explanatory power.

One further reason for the failure of E to discriminate offenders lies in the *heterogeneity* of the offender population. Eysenck emphasises that his theory will not apply to all offenders, and in one study, it was shown that EPQ scales distinguished *between* categories of criminals with differing careers (S. B. G. Eysenck, Rust and H. J. Eysenck, 1977), although discriminations involved mainly scores on P and N. Cluster analytic studies have indeed identified patterns of personality test scores which suggest that the theory might be relevant to only some groups of offenders. In a comparison of EPQ clusters in delinquents and controls, McGurk and McDougall (1981) found that, while neurotic introvert and stable extravert clusters appeared among both groups, clusters of NE and high PNE appeared only in delinquents, these patterns being those most clearly implicated by Eysenck's theory. McEwan (1983) obtained similar results in younger delinquents, and also found that the high PE group had the most convictions. However, while this approach is promising in elucidating the relation between personality and crime, it cannot be regarded as an adequate test of Eysenck's theory, which is primarily concerned with differences *between* the antisocial and the conforming, not with differences *within* offenders. Differences between PE and NE groups of offenders, for example, are not derivable from the theory.

It must be concluded that Eysenck's theory of criminality is not well supported. While attempts to test it have produced a number of significant findings, these are not for the most part related to the central components of the theory, which is concerned with the relation between extraversion, its physiological substrate, and the process of socialisation. The evidence points to a more consistent link between antisocial behaviour and the P dimension rather than E, but given the ambiguities surrounding the meaning of P, and the lack of a theory linking P to socialisation, this association currently has little explanatory power. Moreover, cluster analytic studies reveal that high P scorers form only a small minority of the delinquent population. While it is clear that extraverts are more likely to describe themselves as prone to delinquent acts, and also that some criminals are extraverted in personality, the crucial prediction that the ranks of criminals are swelled by extraverts has not been upheld with sufficient consistency to justify confidence in the theory.

COGNITIVE-DEVELOPMENTAL THEORY

Theories of socialisation which appeal to the development of superego, conscience, or self-control view criminal behaviour as part of a more general failure of moral development. Morality in these terms entails the acquisition of conforming behaviour and beliefs through conditioning, modelling, or identification, and represents the internalisation of society's rules through the influence of parents, teachers, or peers. On this view, moral discriminations of right and wrong are primarily *affective* responses originating in biological need or in the pursuit of social reward and the avoidance of punishment. Moral action is hence *irrational* conformity to culturally relative standards (Lickona, 1976; Gibbs and Schnell, 1985).

The socialisation model of morality has been challenged by Piaget (1959) and Kohlberg (Kohlberg, 1976; Colby and Kohlberg, 1987), who see morality as motivated by cognitive needs for self-realisation and the understanding of reality. Moral development involves cognitive growth in which children actively *construct* moral judgements through experiences of social interaction, rather than passively internalise those of socialising agents. Moral principles are held to relate to the *structure* or form of the moral reasoning process, i.e.

how people think about and derive their beliefs, rather than the *content* of those beliefs.

In Piaget's structural theory, moral reasoning follows from intellectual development, which consists of sequential transformations of cognitive structures in response to internal and external pressures. Stages of moral reasoning are preset by universal stages of cognitive development. Thus, the childhood stage of concrete operational thought is associated with heteronomous reasoning, in which adult rules are seen as immutable. As children move to the formal operational stage, there is a corresponding shift to autonomous reasoning, in which rules are viewed as the products of group agreement, and justice becomes a rational principle regulating interpersonal interaction.

Kohlberg also defines the development of moral reasoning in terms of successively more advanced understanding of a universal principle of justice, the core of which is the distribution of rights and duties regulated by concepts of equality and reciprocity. However, he extends Piaget's theory by proposing three levels of moral reasoning, each having two stages (Table 5.1). These levels represent three types of relationship between the self and society's rules. The *preconventional* level is associated with concrete operational thinking, and characterises pre-adolescent children and a minority of adolescents and adults. It represents an understanding of society in terms of relationships between isolated selves. At the *conventional* level, which is reached by most adolescents and adults, the individual is able to judge relationships from the standpoint of the group or society. The *postconventional* level is reached by only a minority of adults. At this level, the individual understands society's rules in terms of the general moral principles underlying them.

The second stage of each level is a more advanced form of the general perspective. The stage 3 perspective, for example, is that of shared relationships of caring, trust, or loyalty between two or more individuals, whereas at stage 4, such relationships are seen from the viewpoint of the social system as a whole. Each stage is defined in terms of what is right, the reasons for upholding the right, and a social perspective underlying that reasoning, and represents a logically coherent structure of connected ideas. The six stages thus form a hierarchical sequence of more complex and abstract modes of moral reasoning, each presupposing the logic of the prior stage. In more recent statements, substages of moral orientation are identified within each stage, substage A being oriented to given rules of authority, substage B to fairness and personal responsibility (Kohlberg and Candee, 1984). Also, stage 6 is now considered an elaboration of the B substage of stage 5, rather than being a distinct stage.

Movement through this sequence is held to be invariant and universal. Progression to the next stage is dependent on appropriate levels of cognitive development and social perspective or role-taking, which are necessary, though not sufficient prerequisites for a shift in reasoning. Movement to a higher stage depends particularly on cognitive stimulation, social experiences of dialogue and exchange through group participation, and the experience of cognitive conflict resulting from exposure to the logic of the next higher

Table 5.1 Levels and stages of moral development in Kohlberg's theory

---

Level 1

Preconventional or premoral: Moral and self-serving values are not differentiated: rules and social expectations are external to the self.

Stage 1—Obedience and punishment orientation: Right action consists of obedience to rules backed by punishment, and administered by powerful others. Avoidance of punishment is the reason for doing right.

Stage 2—Instrumental purpose and exchange: Right action is what serves someone's immediate interest, and also what is a fair exchange. The emphasis is on meeting one's own needs while recognising those of others.

Level 2

Conventional: Moral value is defined in terms of social conformity, mutual interpersonal expectations, and interdependent relations: self has identified with, or internalised the rules and expectations of others.

Stage 3—Interpersonal accord and conformity: Right action consists of living up to one's expected roles. Behaviour is judged in terms of good intentions, trust, loyalty, and concern for others.

Stage 4—Social accord and system maintenance: Right consists of fulfilling one's agreed duties, upholding laws, and contributing to the group, society, or the institution.

Level 3

Postconventional or principled: Rules and conventions of a particular social system are distinguished from shared standards and universal moral principles: self is distinguished from the rules and expectations of others.

Stage 5—Social contract, utility, and individual rights: Right action is what upholds the values and rules relative to one's group because they are the social contract. Some nonrelative rights, such as life and liberty, are given priority.

Stage 6—Universal ethical principles: Right is defined in terms of self-chosen and universal ethical principles of justice, human rights and dignity. Laws and social agreements are supported to the extent that they derive from these principles. The reason for doing right is rational belief in, and commitment to the validity of universal moral principles.

---

stage. Thus, where learning theories see the environmental influences on moral development in terms of the availability of models of conformity and rewarding and punishing contingencies, Kohlberg emphasises *role-taking opportunities*. This assumption forms the basis for educational applications of moral development principles.

Level of moral judgement has been assessed in several ways. The Moral Judgement Interview (MJI) presents the subject with hypothetical moral dilemmas, which pose a choice between acting on the basis of sanctioned authority or human welfare needs. Responses are probed to determine reasoning about issues such as punishment, personal relationships, or conscience, and are coded in terms of dominant stage, or moral maturity scores related to the stage sequence. While earlier scoring procedures attracted criticism for their subjectivity, a standardised method with satisfactory psychometric properties is now available (Colby and Kohlberg, 1987).

Objective, self-administered procedures have also been developed, which correlate quite highly with the MJI (see Jennings, Kilkenny and Kohlberg, 1983), but these rely on comprehension and preference for moral arguments, rather than spontaneous production, and do not yield identical results.

Kohlberg's theory represents a return to the classical rationalism of Plato and Kant, which assigns primacy to the role of reason rather than external experience as the source of knowledge, and assumes that moral standards are absolute rather than historically and culturally relative (Kurtines, Alvarez and Azmitia, 1990). However, while now absorbed into mainstream psychology, it continues to be controversial on both ideological and empirical grounds. For example, the notion of a universal concept of justice is seen as an ethnocentric and specifically American ideal (Hogan, 1975). Social learning theorists also challenge a stage concept of moral development on the grounds that the level of moral reasoning varies across domains of content, and that people are selective in their use of the moral principles they understand (Bandura, 1986). Nevertheless, significant support has accumulated for the validity of the theory. For example, Snarey (1985) examined 45 cross-cultural studies to test the claim of an invariant progression towards universal ethical principles. He found significant support for the universality of stages 1 to 4, but the data suggested that, while the higher stages were not entirely ethnocentric, they required more pluralistic definition to accommodate nonwestern cultures. It is also claimed that there is a sex bias in the theory and method, which emphasises masculine ideals of rights and fairness at the expense of the "ethic of care" predominant among females (Gilligan, 1982). However, sex differences in moral judgement have not generally been found (Walker, 1986), and Nunner-Winkler (1984) argues that female preferences for relationships as opposed to task-oriented pursuits relate to ego-strength rather than moral orientation.

Moral development and delinquency

Kohlberg offers neither a theory of behaviour in general nor of delinquency in particular. Nevertheless, he regards moral reasoning as the single most important mediator of moral action, though not the only factor. Clearly, people may reason in terms of high moral principles, but fail to live up to them, and conversely, prosocial action is not the prerogative of those capable of principled moral thought. The theory acknowledges that nonmoral factors, such as attention, ego-strength, empathy-arousal, or situational factors enter into moral action, and that the effects of moral reasoning on behaviour are not only a function of judged rightness, but also of perceived personal responsibility (Jennings, Kilkenny and Kohlberg, 1983). Moral decisions have also been shown to be a function of both task characteristics and individual variation in moral value preferences (Kurtines, 1984). The relation between moral thought and action is therefore neither simple nor direct (Blasi, 1980).

The relationship of moral development to delinquency is similarly complex. Delinquency is not synonymous with immoral behaviour, and no clear relationship can be anticipated between moral stage and status offending, or between moral reasoning and crimes committed when reasoning is impaired. Thornton (1987a) observes that, although the reasoning of higher moral stages is less likely to endorse a criminal lifestyle, justifications for law violation can be found at all stages, e.g. if it involves no punishment (stage 1), if it preserves relationships (stage 3), or if it protects basic human rights (stage 5). The absence of sex differences in moral judgement also argues against a straightforward association between moral reasoning and delinquency. Jennings et al. (1983) argue that the relationship is too complex to justify any causal claims, and that at most it provides a necessary, but not sufficient, condition. It is necessary to the extent that preconventional stages limit obligations to conform with any norms, while postconventional reasoning insulates against delinquency. It is not sufficient insofar as other personal and social factors are involved.

The simplest prediction, then, is that on average, delinquents will exhibit developmental delay as shown by lower moral maturity than nondelinquents. Research to date tends to support this (Blasi, 1980; Jurkovic, 1980; Jennings et al., 1983; Arbuthnot, Gordon and Jurkovic, 1987; Thornton, 1987a). The typical finding is that with age, sex, IQ and social status controlled, delinquents obtain lower moral maturity scores on Kohlberg's MJI than nondelinquents, and in many, though not all studies, more delinquents are functioning at stage 2. Arbuthnot, Gordon and Jurkovic (1987) note that only three of 19 controlled studies using the MJI failed to find significant differences. Further support comes from a meta-analysis of 15 controlled studies of juvenile delinquents, including unpublished research by Kohlberg, which found a significant mean effect size of 0.74 (Nelson, Smith and Dodd, 1990). Thornton (1987a) also describes unpublished data showing an association between moral stage and teacher ratings of antisocial conduct. Less consistent findings are reported in studies using recognition of moral arguments rather than production of moral reasoning (Gavaghan, Arnold and Gibbs, 1983). Delinquents' understanding of conventional reasoning may therefore exceed their capacity to produce and apply it in practice.

There is also some support for the theoretical expectation that moral immaturity is a consequence of restricted role-playing opportunities in the family backgrounds of delinquent youths. More mature reasoning is found in children whose parents encourage participation and collective problem solving, and who employ inductive disciplinary techniques (Hoffman, 1971; Olejnik, 1980), and lack of these conditions may be a significant factor in the moral development of delinquents. Hudgens and Prentice (1973), for example, found that the mothers of delinquents showed significantly lower moral reasoning than mothers of nondelinquents, although this has not been a consistent finding (Jurkovic, 1980). Delinquents who experience absence of a father, or surrogate, are also particularly likely to show lower moral reasoning (Daum and Bieliauskas, 1983).

The conclusion that delinquents are more likely to demonstrate preconventional reasoning must, however, be qualified on several grounds. First, it is confined to officially identified delinquents, and no firm relation has been found between moral stage and self-report delinquency. Emler, Heather and Winton (1978), for example, found that delinquents showed less principled reasoning than matched nondelinquents, as well as scoring higher on a self-report delinquency measure, but there was no relation between the measure of principled reasoning and self-report delinquency. While Tsujimoto and Nardi (1978) found that moral judgement predicted scores on a self-report measure of avoidance of stealing, it was unrelated to a more general scale of rule compliance.

Second, delinquents are no more homogeneous in moral reasoning than they are in other respects. Many delinquents, in some cases a majority (Gibbs et al., 1984), are clearly functioning at a conventional level, and lower moral reasoning may be more characteristic of recidivists (Jennings et al., 1983). Psychopathic delinquents seem particularly likely to reason at preconventional levels (Jurkovic and Prentice, 1977; Kegan, 1986), consistent with the egocentric and hedonistic reasoning characteristic of preconventional development. There is also some evidence that older delinquents are more likely to be at stage 3, and delinquents who exhibit lower moral maturity may simply be developing at a slower rate, rather than being fixated at a preconventional level.

The relationship between moral development and offending also seems to vary with type of offence. Thornton and Reid (1982) noted that preconventional reasoning would justify crimes in which personal gain outweighed the risk of punishment (prudent crimes), while "imprudent" crimes might be less likely to relate to moral stage. Consistent with prediction, they found that recidivists convicted of prudent crimes (robbery, burglary, theft) were more likely to exhibit preconventional reasoning than controls or than recidivists convicted of imprudent offences (assault involving no material gain), who did not differ from controls. Similar differences obtained for prudent and imprudent sex offenders (Thornton, 1987a). Renwick and Emler (1984) also found differential relations between stage of moral reasoning and self-reported delinquency in students, stage 4 showing a small negative correlation, but stage 5 a small positive correlation. They argue that these stages are confounded with conservatism–radicalism.

Although few offenders appear to exhibit postconventional reasoning, the evidence that many have reached conventional levels casts doubt on the claim that higher moral development serves to insulate against delinquent involvement. Several reviewers suggest that the offences of conventional level youths may be more related to situational pressures or intrapersonal difficulties, drug addicts, for example, being more morally mature than other delinquents (Jennings et al., 1983). Jurkovic (1980) also notes that solutions to hypothetical moral dilemmas may not be directly relevant to delinquents' experiences of problem situations, and that the performance of delinquents may not match their levels of competence in reasoning, either because of situational pressures, such as the "moral atmosphere" of an institution, or deficits in other cognitive skills.

The available evidence, then, suggests a correlation between moral development and delinquency, but preconventional reasoning seems most evident in younger and in more psychopathic delinquents. What remains unclear is how moral reasoning interacts with nonmoral personality and situational factors in affecting moral action. There continues to be debate about the influence of content, and particularly the affective loading of moral beliefs, on moral conduct, and some argue that the content of values may have stronger functional ties to behaviour (Lickona, 1976). It has also been suggested that moral judgement may be more predictive of delinquency if related to moral character traits (Tsujimoto and Nardi, 1978), the bonds of attachment and commitment suggested by control theory (Jennings et al., 1983), or history of aversive conditioning (Burton, 1984). Gibbs and Schnell (1985) similarly conclude that Kohlberg's individualistic and rationalist approach must be considered complementary to more social and affect-oriented theories, rather than a sufficient account of sociomoral development. Some of these alternative approaches will be considered in Chapter 8.

INTEGRATED THEORIES

None of the traditional criminological theories has proved to be more than moderately predictive of either criminality or criminal acts, and an integration combining more promising elements of these theories may be more powerful. Akers (1977, 1990), for example, sees the process of becoming deviant in reinforcement terms. Anomie, subculture, and conflict theories identify the social conditions which determine the patterns and schedules of reinforcement, while control theory specifies the outcome of the developmental process. Labelling reflects changes in differential reinforcement surrounding later deviant behaviour.

An integration of strain, control, and social learning theories is proposed by Elliott, Huizinga and Ageton, (1985). They argue, contra Hirschi, that delinquency requires positive motivation, which is supplied by the experience of failure at school and by bonding to deviant peers (Chapter 7). This integration goes beyond the single component theories by specifying a sequential process of individual development dependent on experiences with successive socialising agencies. Colvin and Pauly (1983), however, argue that such an analysis neglects the macro-social structures emphasised by conflict and radical theories. They propose that both the form and content of socialisation experiences in the family, at school, and with peers is shaped by the control systems of the wider class structure. Thus, experiences of control by authority in the workplace determine the nature of the bonds of individuals to the conventional order, which may be negative (alienated), intermediate (calculative), or positive (moral). In turn, these control relationships will be reproduced in child-rearing, and selectively reinforced at school by teachers and by peers with similar socialisation experiences.

While incorporating psychological processes of learning, these sociological integrations are in the tradition of unidirectional environmental determinism, and pay no attention to individual differences. These, however, are central for Wilson and Herrnstein (1985) who describe a general eclectic theory combining operant and rational choice theories, but which also draws on classical conditioning, equity theory, and individual difference variables suggested by Eysenck and Kohlberg. Their concern is with criminality as a tendency to commit "predatory crimes", but their analysis centres on the criminal act as the outcome of choice when people are faced with temptation or criminal opportunity. The choice of crime depends on the ratio of reinforcing and punishing consequences of crime to those of noncrime. The net rewards of crime may include both material gains and psychological consequences, such as approval, emotional gratification, or the restoration of equity, while losses include "the bite of conscience", disapproval, or retaliation. The value of noncrime lies in the future, and includes the benefits of avoiding legal punishment, loss of social reputation, and shame. Individual differences in the ability to take account of future consequences are therefore significant, and these may have a biological origin. Wilson and Herrnstein accept Eysenck's notion of conscience as a conditioned reflex, but argue that when opportunity is strong or immediate, the outcome is determined more by the individual's calculation of risks, which is a function of operant conditioning. Impulsiveness and the discounting of time make individuals less susceptible to operant learning. Individuals additionally differ in the values assigned to crime and noncrime as a result of variations in sentiments such as sympathy and justice. However, value is also a function of social context, since the greater the total supply of reinforcers, the less the impact of a small reward on crime.

The theory is held to be consistent with traditional sociological theories, which are, however, considered incomplete. Thus, strain theory focuses on the availability of some reinforcers for noncrime, such as job opportunities, but ignores others, such as sanctions; control theories emphasise the social reinforcers associated with noncrime, but ignore individual differences in time perspective or impulsiveness which may override them; subcultural theories also emphasise the role of social reinforcers, but neglect individual variations in susceptibility to the influence of deviant and nondeviant groups.

As a psychological model, the theory falls short by attempting to incorporate cognitive mediators, such as anticipated consequences or evaluations of equity into a noncognitive operant model. Moreover, while "reward" is used interchangeably with "reinforcer", it retains its vernacular meaning of what is valued rather than the operant meaning of reinforcer as whatever consequence strengthens behaviour. The kinds of consequence which reinforce crime are not therefore clearly addressed (Gibbs, 1985). Gibbs, however, sees the theory as "a challenge" to sociological criminology, and this is taken up by Cohen and Machalek (1989). They argue that while the individual is the appropriate unit of observation, the appropriate units of analysis are *behavioural strategies*, whose selection depends on the evolution and distribution of alternative strategies within a population. Thus, the choice of a strategy which expropriates the resources of others depends as much on the social dynamics of choices adopted by others as on biological and psychological differences.

The most eclectic integration is that of Farrington (1990, 1992), who accounts for findings from the Cambridge study by drawing on Trasler's social learning, subcultural, opportunity, control, differential association, rational choice, and labelling theories. Antisocial tendency depends on a number of personality factors, such as low arousal, impulsivity, low empathy, lack of conscience, and on internalised beliefs and motives for material goods, status among intimates, and excitement. These beliefs are enhanced among working class children because of class biases towards short-term goals, while a relative lack of prosocial beliefs results from lack of supervision, and harsh, erratic punishment and modelling by parents and peers. Working class children also tend to choose illegal or disapproved methods of satisfying these motives because of greater school failure and low status employment, which is in turn a function of low intelligence resulting from unstimulating environments. Commission of a crime depends on appraisal of costs and benefits, and is influenced by social reinforcers as well as by personal characteristics such as impulsivity. Labelling may make it more difficult for the offender to achieve his aims legitimately, while successful offending will reinforce criminal beliefs. The onset of offending is particularly related to poverty, low intelligence, and poor child-rearing, while peers and deviant family members may enhance a continued criminal career. Desistance is facilitated by marriage, stable employment, and moving from criminal areas.

Such eclectic integrations treat the human actor as a passive recipient of multiple causes, and ignore critically different assumptions about the nature of human behaviour which underlie different theories (Hirschi and Gottfredson, 1988). For example, control theories assume that people are naturally hedonistic, whereas subcultural theories deny the pre-eminence of self-interest and assume that social conformity is the natural order. Similarly, the rationalism of Kohlberg and rational choice theories does not readily marry with the irrationalism of Eysenck or Freud. Attempts to integrate theories have therefore not as yet proved to be an advance over more traditional theories because of the absence of a coherent "model of man".

Chapter 6

Biological Correlates of Antisocial Behaviour

INTRODUCTION

People are biological as well as social beings, but many criminologists resist the notion that crime may be related to biological endowment. Not only is this seen to encourage a view of criminals as inherently defective, and to divert attention from criminogenic social conditions, it also seems to imply drastic solutions to crime control in the form of genetic engineering or psychosurgery. Biological approaches are therefore often portrayed as tainted with methodological individualism, the medicalisation of social problems, and right-wing political ideology (Nassi and Abramowitz, 1976; Rose, Kamin and Lewontin, 1984).

Such criticism often relies on misrepresentation, but is not entirely unfounded. Researchers who describe hereditary influences on crime as "genetic disorder" do little to dispel suspicions that they equate nonconformity with defect or ill-health, and some neurologists have made extravagant generalisations about the role of brain pathology in antisocial behaviour on the basis of rare clinical phenomena. On the other hand, the political views of biological researchers are unlikely to be homogeneous, nor can the validity of a scientific belief be judged by who holds it. Moreover, few have espoused a one-sided biological determinism. *Crime as Destiny* (Lange, 1931), which described the first twin study of criminality, is often cited as exemplifying a claim that heredity determines who becomes criminal. However, Lange merely affirmed that "...the natural tendencies one is born with, the surrounding world he grows up in, these are essentials, these are destiny." More recent investigators similarly advocate a biosocial interactionism, which views "nature" and "nurture" as interdependent (Rowe and Osgood, 1984). For example, temperament differences in activity level, social responsiveness, and emotionality are apparent soon after birth, and play a significant role in subsequent development (Chess and Thomas, 1984), but their effects depend on the opportunities and reactions of different social environments. Thus, socialisation is not a unidirectional process in which the child is a passive recipient of parental influence. Rather is the behaviour of caretakers shaped in part by the characteristics of the child (Bell, 1968; Harper, 1975; Bouchard et al., 1990).

It must also be stressed that, despite its association with positivist theories, biological research on crime does not necessitate any commitment to a reductionism which would render psychological or social analyses redundant. These are different levels of analysis involving different languages, each with its own context-dependent meanings. For example, an act is only "criminal" within a social context. We may legitimately attempt to translate one language into another, but only a limited translation is possible (Rose, 1987). However, while behaviour may be regarded as an emergent function of physical systems which cannot be described solely in terms of those systems, brain activity provides the causal (generative) mechanisms for behaviour, and constrains its form (Manicas, 1987). Biological processes are therefore as real a cause of crime as are social processes, and to deny this is to invite a one-sided sociological determinism.

While the role played by biological processes in crime is likely to be relatively modest and indirect and not equally important for all classes of deviant individual, the evidence to date is sufficient to indicate that criminology cannot ignore the relevance of a biological level of analysis. Some studies have explored the possible role of structural abnormalities of the nervous system in antisocial acts within clinical populations, but psychologists are more interested in how normal biological variation contributes to criminality as a disposition to break rules. This variation may reflect influences at the innate, congenital, or constitutional levels (Cattell, 1966). Where *innate* refers to genetic inheritance from parents, together with the effects of possible mutations, *congenital* is what is present at birth, and subsumes the additional influences of the uterine and perinatal environment. *Constitution* denotes phenotypic characteristics of the developed individual resulting from genotype–environment interaction, which are assumed to be relatively fixed, and includes not only morphology or physique, but also physiological and endocrine function. This chapter therefore examines correlates of criminal behaviour at each of these levels.

GENETICS AND CRIMINALITY

Genes are often said to set the limits on behaviour, while environments determine development within those limits. This is reflected in the attempts of behaviour geneticists to quantify the genetic contribution by "heritability" estimates. However, this assumes independent causes, and there are reasons to doubt whether the continuous and interdependent interaction of genes with environments permits such a separation (Overton, 1973). Since it seems more important to understand *how* genes might contribute to criminality, rather than *how much*, no reference will be made to such estimates.

A search for genetic influences on antisocial behaviour assumes neither a specific gene for crime, nor "preprogramming" of complex human actions.

Genotypes give initial direction to development by providing basic elements of behaviour which are incorporated into larger adaptive units through learning. They influence phenotypes through the successive intermediaries of enzymes, hormones, and neurones, and may contribute to criminality through the medium of stable neural properties associated with learning and temperament (Shah and Roth, 1974). However, some evolutionary theories propose that genes influence the motivation for criminal behaviour. Ellis (1988), for example, draws on a theoretical continuum of "r/K selection" of reproductive strategies, which are held to maximise species survival, depending on competition for resources. Species at the "r" extreme produce large numbers of offspring and devote little time to gestation and care of their young, whereas those at the "K" extreme produce few offspring and invest considerable energy in their rearing. While humans fall towards the "K" extreme, there is likely to be interindividual variation, and Ellis proposes that criminal victimisation reflects r-selection. He argues that this may account for relatively consistent findings of an association between victimful criminality and large family size, prematurity and low birth weight, early sexual activity, promiscuity, broken homes, child neglect and abuse, and shorter life expectancy, all of which he suggests are r-selected traits.

However, there is no single path from genotype to phenotype. Scarr and McCartney (1983) propose that genotypes influence phenotypes through the combination of genes and environments supplied by parents, through differential reactions from others to biologically different individuals, and through differential selection of environments by those individuals. Genetic research on criminality attempts to identify innate influences on these complex pathways through several research designs, involving studies of families, twins, adoptees, and chromosome anomalies.

Family studies

Family or pedigree studies compare the distribution of antisocial behaviour in the biological relatives of offenders and nonoffenders. A consistent finding is that criminal parents are more likely to have criminal children (Chapter 7). In the Cambridge study, for example, boys with a criminal father were twice as likely to become delinquent as those with noncriminal fathers (West, 1982). Family studies of delinquent females also suggest that they have more socially deviant relatives than other females, as well as more familial pathology than antisocial males, but that familial factors are of equal importance for the development of criminality in both sexes (Cloninger et al., 1978). However, family studies do not permit any clear differentiation of genetic and environmental influences.

Twin studies

Identical or monozygotic (MZ) twins have the same genotypes, whereas fraternal or dizygotic (DZ) twins have only half their genes in common, as do other siblings. Twin studies therefore rest on the logic that phenotypic differences between same-sex MZ and DZ twin pairs reflect genetic influences, assuming similar rearing conditions. The relevant differences are usually expressed as the percentage of criminal twins who have a criminal co-twin (pairwise concordance).

About a dozen twin studies with varying sample sizes have been reported. Lange (1931) identified 13 MZ and 17 DZ male twin pairs from several sources, and found that 77% of the MZ pairs were concordant in having convictions leading to imprisonment, compared with 12% of DZ pairs. Others have consistently found differences in the same direction, although not always to the same degree. Earlier studies, on average, found some 60% concordance for criminal history in MZ twins, and 30% for DZ twins (Christiansen, 1977a), but Gottesman, Carey and Hanson (1983) note that differences are significant only for adults. Across six studies of juveniles, concordance rates for MZ and DZ were 87% and 72%, respectively, suggesting minimal genetic influence on juvenile delinquency. However, Rowe (1983) reports a self-report delinquency study of 265 twin pairs among high school students, which found higher correlations for the delinquency measure among MZ twins (males, 0.66; females, 0.74) than among DZ twins (males, 0.48; females, 0.47). While the MZ–DZ differences favour a genetic influence, all correlations are significant, pointing to the additional influence of shared environments.

The earlier studies employed selected samples of twins, and unreliable methods of determining zygosity (Dalgaard and Kringlen, 1976). Lower concordance rates emerge from more recent Scandinavian studies, which rely on unselected samples of twins from national registers, and determine zygosity from blood samples. Christiansen (1977b) drew on a complete twin population of 3586 pairs from the Danish islands. Among males who became criminal, pairwise concordance rates were 35% (MZ) and 13% (DZ), while for females, they were 21% (MZ) and 8% (DZ). Absolute *discordance* rates are therefore high in all cases, indicating substantial nongenetic effects. However, a similar study in Norway found male concordances of only 26% (MZ) and 15% (DZ) (Dalgaard and Kringlen, 1976). The difference is not significant, and the authors conclude that the contribution of heredity to crime is "nonexistent".

However, all studies have found differences between MZ and DZ twins in the same direction, and the difference between the Norwegian and Danish findings remains unexplained. Dalgaard and Kringlen argue that phenotypic similarities of MZ twins represent more similar treatment by parents, and this remains a possible confound in studies of twins reared together. However, Scarr and Carter-Salzman (1979) found that while up to 40% of parents and twins misperceive zygosity, resemblances between co-twins on psychological tests were more related to actual than to perceived zygosity. Greater experience of environmental similarity by MZ twins may therefore be an *effect* of their genetic similarity.

The available twin data favour some genetic influence on criminality, but are inconclusive in the absence of data on twins reared apart. However, recent studies suggest that on most measures of intelligence, personality, interests, and social attitudes, MZ twins reared apart are as similar as those reared together (Bouchard et al., 1990).

Adoption studies

If children adopted shortly after birth resemble biological more than adoptive parents in some attribute, this is strong presumptive evidence for genetic influence. Research on criminality in adoptees employs two basic designs. The first identifies criminal parents who have given up their offspring for adoption, and compares their children with the adopted offspring of noncriminal biological parents. For example, Crowe (1972) found that 8 of 52 adopted offspring (probands) of incarcerated female offenders had an arrest record compared with only 2 of 52 control adoptees, while 19 and 8, respectively, had been arrested for traffic offences. Six probands, but no controls, also met criteria for antisocial personality. Cadoret (1978) similarly found that 4 of 18 adoptees with biological parents diagnosed as antisocial personalities received this diagnosis as adults, compared with none of 25 controls.

The second design is analogous to cross-fostering, and begins with a heterogeneous sample of adoptees. Criminal and noncriminal adoptees are then compared in terms of criminality in biological and adoptive parents. In a study of 143 criminal and 143 control adoptees in Denmark, for example, Hutchings and Mednick (1975) found that 36.2% of sons became criminal when both biological and adoptive fathers were criminal, compared with 21.4% when biological father only was criminal, 11.5% when adoptive father only was criminal, and 10.5% when neither father was criminal. These data are consistent with both a genetic influence on criminality and a genotype–environment interaction, but subsequent research in Stockholm points to interactions of type of crime with alcoholism. Bohman, Cloninger, Sigvardsson and von Knorring (1982) found a significant excess of criminality without alcoholism in the adopted sons of biological fathers who were criminal but not alcoholic, crimes of both fathers and sons being mainly petty and nonviolent. In contrast, criminal behaviour in alcohol abusers was more likely to be violent, and correlated with alcoholism in biological fathers. This suggests genetic involvement in petty criminality, but not violent crime. However, for some offenders, violent behaviour is associated with alcohol abuse, which may itself be genetically influenced.

A further Danish study examined criminality in 14 427 adoptees, of whom 981 males and 212 females had one or more convictions (Mednick, Gabrielli and Hutchings, 1984). When both biological and adoptive parents (mother or father) were criminal, 24.5% of sons became criminal, compared with 20.0% when a biological parent only was criminal, 14.7% when an adoptive parent only was criminal, and 13.5% when no parent was criminal. The effect is significant for biological but not adoptive parents. While there was a positive correlation between recidivism in biological parents and their sons, this was significant for property offences, but not violent crimes, consistent with the findings of Bohman et al. (1982). Nevertheless, number of crimes was more important than type of crime committed by biological parents, suggesting the transmission of a generalised rather than specific predisposition.

In these studies, only a minority of adopted children of criminal parents become criminal, and the results imply a modest genetic contribution to crime, given certain environments. However, pre-adoption influences include *perinatal complications* determined by the living conditions of the mother. Stott (1982) notes that stress during pregnancy, poor prenatal care, and prematurity all increase the risk for child handicaps, such as physical defects, developmental delays, or behaviour disorders. Such stresses are most marked in low income groups, from which the criminal mothers of illegitimate children most often come, and Stott suggests that this itself may account for the relationship between criminality in adoptees and their biological parents. This possibility gains credence from the observation of Mednick et al. (1984) that the effect was stronger for criminal biological mothers than for fathers.

However, perinatal difficulties may be significant only for more serious offenders. Lewis, Shanok and Balla (1979), for example, found a history of such difficulties in 37% of institutionalised delinquents, and a majority of a small group of violent boys, but only 8% of noninstitutionalised delinquents. Mednick and Kandel (1988) also report that minor physical anomalies, which indirectly index perinatal problems, were unrelated to property offending, but associated with violent crime when the individual was reared in an unstable family. Nevertheless, the possible contribution of perinatal environment to the greater criminality of adoptees with criminal biological parents requires attention.

Chromosome anomalies

Variations from the normal complement of 23 chromosome pairs usually arise from errors in cell division, and represent genetic factors which are innate but not inherited. These rare anomalies, as determined from the appearance of the chromosome sets (*karyotype*), have been linked with behaviour disorder, and of particular interest are sex chromosome patterns which depart from the typical configurations of 46,XY in males and 46,XX in females. Most studies focus on males showing a 47,XYY complement, or on the 47,XXY configuration (Klinefelter's Syndrome).

The XXY karyotype has long been known to be more frequent among the mentally retarded, but research in the 1960s also indicated elevated frequencies of XYY males in prisoners and mentally disordered offenders. For example, Price et al., (1966) identified 9 XYY males among 315 patients of the State Hospital in Scotland, a special hospital for mentally disordered offenders, but none among random population samples. Most were of above average height, intellectually retarded, and said to show personality disorders. However, further comparisons with control patients revealed similar intelligence, and only marginal differences on personality tests (Hope, Philip and Loughran, 1967). Subsequent research confirmed a higher prevalence of the XYY karyotype in institutionalised antisocial populations, particularly mentally disordered offenders, but also revealed an incidence in the general population of about 0.1% (Jarvik, Klodin and Matsuyama, 1973; Shah and Roth, 1974).

The initial studies appeared to illustrate a genetic determination of criminal behaviour, and were also interpreted in terms of what might be contributed to crime by the normal Y chromosome. It was suggested that the sex difference in crime reflected the masculine traits contributed by the Y chromosome, while possession of the extra Y exaggerated masculinity and highlighted the association between maleness and violence (Jarvik, Klodin and Matsuyama, 1973). However, possession of a supernumerary X chromosome also correlates with criminality, and characteristics of the XYY male have typically been inferred from small samples in institutions (Owen, 1972). In a study avoiding sampling bias, Witkin et al. (1976) karyotyped 90% of 4591 males born in Copenhagen between 1944 and 1947 who attained a height of more than 184 cm, and identified 12 XYY and 16 XXY individuals. While 41.7% of the XYYs, 18.8% of the XXYs, and 9.3% of the remainder had criminal records, confirming an association of the extra Y with criminality, the offences of the former groups were mainly petty and nonviolent. Since both XYYs and XXYs were also of lower intelligence, and the former had abnormal EEGs, the authors suggest that chromosome abnormality makes a nonspecific contribution to criminality through the medium of genetic disorganisation and developmental failure. Further research on this sample showed that, although the XYY males had higher levels of plasma testosterone, this did not mediate their criminal behaviour (Schiavi et al., 1984).

One further aspect which has attracted some attention is the length of the Y chromosome in 46,XY males, and some studies suggest that this may be longer in offenders. Kahn et al. (1976), for example, found that although chromosome length did not distinguish borstal boys from factory workers, controls with a longer Y chromosome were more likely to have a prior criminal record. However, this *post hoc* finding is not conclusive, and other studies have not produced consistent results. Dorus (1978) notes that while evidence points to gene loci on the Y chromosome which control the development of the testes, spermatogenesis, and stature, the contribution of the Y chromosome to behaviour may be small. Failure to confirm early speculations that the XYY pattern creates an antisocial "supermale" has resulted in a decline of interest in this rare phenomenon.

CONSTITUTIONAL RESEARCH

The association of deviant psychological attributes with overt physical characteristics attracts ridicule because of its connection with phrenology and physiognomy, which influenced Lombroso's "criminal anthropology". Lombroso's early claim that criminals represented a genetically primitive and inferior species rested on the high frequency of physical anomalies in, for example, the skull, ears, or face of incarcerated criminals, which he found in postmortems and anthropometric measurements. His observations were criticised as statistically unsound, but more modern research nevertheless demonstrates a correlation between *physical appearance* and antisocial behaviour. Agnew (1984), for example, found higher self-reported delinquency among schoolchildren rated as unattractive in general appearance, and Bull (1982) has also shown that stereotypes of criminal "types" held by the police and general public have some validity in terms of the judged appearance of apprehended offenders. The association may, however, reflect a self-fulfilling prophecy, in that those who are facially unattractive are judged in negative terms, and react accordingly.

Research on body build, or *somatotype*, follows a European tradition of attempting to link physique to temperament and psychiatric disorder. Sheldon (1949) assessed somatotype in terms of three embryologically derived concepts of *endomorphy* (fat, circular), *mesomorphy* (muscular, triangular), and *ectomorphy* (thin, linear). These were proposed to correspond, respectively, with temperament components of *viscerotonia* (relaxed, hedonistic), *somatotonia* (energetic, adventurous), and *cerebrotonia* (restrained, solitary). Rating the three somatotype components from photographs on scales of 1 to 7 (least to most), Sheldon found mean ratings for 200 college students of 3.2, 3.8, and 3.4, respectively (standard deviations *c.* 1.2 for each). The comparable somatotype for 200 male delinquents was 3.5-4.6-2.7, delinquents being significantly more mesomorphic and less ectomorphic. He also divided the delinquents into several types on criteria of deviance or "disappointingness" (e.g. mentally insufficient, criminal, normal). The criminal group had the most extreme somatotype of 3.4-5.4-1.8. Hartl, Monnelly and Elderkin (1982) describe a 30-year follow-up of Sheldon's delinquents, and employing a similar classification found that the most seriously criminal adults had a somatotype of 3.5-5.0-2.3. As well as being more mesomorphic than the "normal" group, criminals also had higher ratings on andromorphy, a measure of masculinity of secondary sex characteristics.

Sheldon's research was criticised by Sutherland (1951) and Cortès and Gatti (1972) for the selectiveness of his "delinquents", the unreliability of his somatotyping procedure, and the arbitrariness of his delinquent types. His "criminals" were, in fact, identified by absence of other forms of "disappointingness", rather than by delinquent history alone. After reclassifying subjects on legal criteria of delinquency, Sutherland (1951) concluded that the most delinquent did not differ in somatotype from nondelinquents. However, Cortès and Gatti (1972) showed that this re-analysis overlooked significant associations between delinquency and mesomorphy. In their own study of 100 institutionalised delinquents, they found that 57% were mesomorphic and 16% ectomorphic, compared with 19% and 33%, respectively, of controls. Gibbens (1963) also observed that endomorphic mesomorphy predominated in a sample of 56 English borstal boys, while Epps and Parnell (1952) found English female delinquents to be more muscular than students, and shorter and heavier in build. However, McCandless, Persons and Roberts (1972) found no relationship between mesomorphy and either official or self-reported delinquency among institutionalised males, and no distinctiveness of physique was found among delinquents in the Cambridge study (West, 1982).

None of these studies is free from methodological problems, such as the reliability of somatotyping, or the questionable representativeness of either delinquent or control samples, and Eysenck and Gudjonsson (1989) believe that somatotype is more appropriately assessed by height and width of body build. Nevertheless, the data provide support for the view that delinquents are likely to be muscular and less fragile in physique. However, mesomorphy is neither necessary nor sufficient for delinquency, and the significance of the relationship remains unclear. It may be mediated by associated temperament factors, such as assertiveness or activity level, since Cortès and Gatti (1972) found that mesomorphs described themselves as significantly more active, dominant, and aggressive, and ectomorphs as more socially avoidant, supporting Sheldon's hypotheses. The combination of mesomorphy and andromorphy may also reflect higher testosterone levels and greater aggressiveness (Hartl, Monnelly and Elderkin, 1982). Alternatively, delinquent peer groups may differentially reinforce toughness, while criminal justice agents may react more negatively to tough appearance.

PSYCHOPHYSIOLOGICAL AND BIOCHEMICAL STUDIES

Genetic effects are likely to be manifest in stable properties of the nervous system, and correlates of criminality have therefore been sought in peripheral recordings of cortical and autonomic activity or biochemical assays. Although early studies were descriptive and atheoretical, research since the 1960s has drawn on theories such as those of Eysenck, Trasler and Gray (see Chapter 5) which link nervous system functioning to personality, motivation, learning, and more recently, information processing. Physiological mechanisms mediating aggression, stimulation seeking, passive avoidance learning, conditionability, and emotional responsiveness have provided the main potential links with an antisocial disposition, and research therefore focuses particularly on psychopathic personality. It should, however, be noted that this research is predominantly correlational, and that psychophysiological variations may often be as much a consequence of *psychological* reactions to experimental conditions as of stable physiological differences. Autonomic reactions to "stressors", for example, may depend more on cognitive appraisals of events as stressful than on inherent properties of the individual's autonomic system. Physiological differences between people are also likely to reflect adaptations to different environmental histories as much as genetic influences.

Electrocortical correlates

The EEG (electroencephalogram) recorded from scalp electrodes is a complex waveform made up of a number of rhythms and transient changes, and indexes the activity of neuronal groups in the cortex. Its components are usually described in terms of amplitude and frequency, the rhythms being conventionally divided into four frequency bands of delta (0.5–3 Hz), theta (4–7 Hz), alpha (8–13 Hz), and beta (14–30 Hz) activity. Clinical interest has centred on the presence of abnormalities in the resting or stimulated waveform, as determined by visual inspection, but the notion of "abnormality" is somewhat arbitrary. It includes unusual focal spike discharges, but more predominantly refers to diffuse slow wave activity or excesses of theta activity in central or posterior temporal areas. These variations are interpreted variously as reflecting developmental lag, abnormalities in limbic system nuclei involved in emotional expression, or in terms of cortical arousal level, since changes from a relaxed to an alert state are typically accompanied by reduced amplitude and increased frequency of the alpha rhythms. However, their functional significance remains unclear, since they do not uniformly coincide with structural abnormalities in deeper parts of the brain. Moreover, they are found in about 15% of normal adults, and more than a quarter of young children, and basic amplitude and frequency characteristics are largely genetically determined (Bouchard et al., 1990). What are described as abnormalities may, then, often represent quantitative rather than qualitative deviations from normality.

An extensive literature on EEG correlates of behaviour disorder suggests high frequencies of abnormalities in aggressive and psychopathic samples. In an early study of psychiatrically disordered combat troops, for example, Hill and Watterson (1942) observed EEG abnormalities in 65% of aggressive psychopaths, 32% of inadequate psychopaths, 26% of neurotics, and 15% of nonpatient controls. Nevertheless, the literature contains many inconsistencies, and is generally marred by unreliability in EEG analysis and subject classification, experimenter bias, and inadequate control of such variables as age or recording conditions (Gale, 1976). Temporary situational effects may account for some findings, since slow wave activity in the alpha or theta bands increases with boredom and drowsiness under monotonous conditions. Gendreau et al. (1972), for example, demonstrated that solitary confinement of offenders results in EEG slowing.

Research employing replicable measurement of psychopathy and EEG quantification raises doubts about the extent of abnormalities among antisocial personalities. Syndulko et al. (1975) detected no differences in alpha or theta activity between psychopathic and nonpsychopathic outpatients, and Blackburn (1979b) also found that psychopathic and nonpsychopathic mentally disordered offenders were not differentiated by these variables. However, in the latter study, secondary psychopaths displayed more theta activity and lower alpha frequency at rest than primary psychopaths, and Howard (1984) similarly found a higher prevalence of slow waves in secondary psychopaths. Harpur et al. (1986) also found that prisoners with medium scores on Hare's Psychopathy Checklist showed higher alpha amplitude than those with high or low scores, but the latter did not differ from each other. EEG abnormalities, and by implication, low cortical arousal, are not, then, uniformly characteristic of psychopaths.

While evidence of abnormalities in violent adults and hyperactive children is slightly more compelling, it is not unequivocal (Gale, 1976). Williams (1969) found abnormalities in the EEGs of 65% of 206 habitually aggressive criminals compared with 24% of 127 offenders who had committed isolated acts of aggression. In contrast, Blackburn (1975b) found no differences in alpha or theta amplitude between habitually aggressive mentally disordered offenders and relatively unaggressive patients. In view of the data on psychopaths, it seems likely that EEG abnormalities will be observed most frequently in aggressive offenders who are also deviant in other aspects of personality.

Mixed findings have also been reported in unselected samples of incarcerated criminals or delinquents. However, in a prospective study of Danish boys, Mednick et al. (1981) related EEG data obtained when subjects were 10–13 years old to history of delinquency six years later. Boys arrested on two or more occasions showed significantly more slow alpha activity in their earlier EEGs than nondelinquents. This was replicated in a 12-year follow-up of a Swedish sample (Petersen et al., 1982). The delinquents in these studies were predominantly property offenders, indicating that EEG abnormalities are not specific to violent offenders. However, they are also not specific to offenders, and Hsu et al. (1985) found similar EEG abnormality in a quarter of both delinquents and adolescent psychiatric patients. High amplitude, slow waves in the EEG may therefore be associated with increased risk for social problems generally, rather than antisocial behaviour specifically.

Recent attention has focused on topographic analysis and event-related potentials not readily analysable from the raw EEG trace. Of particular interest is the possible association between idiosyncrasies of information-processing and antisocial behaviour. From a review of research on sensory *evoked potentials* in psychopaths, Raine (1989) observed that diverse methodology precluded any firm conclusions. He investigated the late P3 component, which is related to the subjective meaning or relevance of an event, in long-term prisoners, and found that in comparison with nonpsychopaths, psychopaths produced parietal P3 waves to a visual target stimulus which were of greater amplitude than those to nontarget stimuli. Psychopaths also scored higher on a "parietal index" derived from the WAIS Block Design and Object Assembly subtests, and this correlated significantly with P3 amplitude. The results supported other findings suggesting that psychopaths allocate more attentional resources to events of immediate interest. Raine suggests that psychopaths attend more proficiently to task-relevant events, and that this may be a correlate of sensation-seeking and low arousal. However, his results are open to other interpretations. His "parietal index", for example, is also a measure of field independence.

Individual differences in evoked potentials are also observed in the modulation of stimulus intensity, or *augmenting–reducing*. With increasing stimulus intensity, some individuals show an increased amplitude of the early P1–N1 component (augmenters), while others show a decrease (reducers). The concept of augmenting–reducing originates in research on kinaesthetic figural aftereffects (KFA), which suggested that those who attenuated the perceived size of an object (reducers) required more sensory input to avoid boredom

(Petrie, 1967). Thus, reducers were found to be more tolerant of pain, but intolerant of sensory deprivation, and more extraverted. Reducers on the KFA task were also found to be more prevalent among delinquent boys than among nondelinquent controls, consistent with the hypothesised greater "stimulus hunger" of offenders. However, using evoked potential criteria, Silverman, Buchsbaum and Stierlin (1973) found that male delinquents showed greater *augmenting* than either nondelinquent males or delinquent females. Sensation seeking also correlates with augmenting of the evoked potential (Zuckerman, 1984), contrary to what would be expected from Petrie's concept. Davis, Cowles and Kohn (1983) note that the apparently contradictory findings of the KFA and evoked potential measures derive from both procedural differences and semantic ambiguities. They suggest that Petrie's reducers are, in fact, evoked potential augmenters, both being characterised by less "sensitive" nervous systems.

A few studies of psychopathy have examined the *contingent negative variation* (CNV), or "expectancy wave", elicited in a forewarned reaction time experiment, but results have not been consistent. McCallum (1973) found smaller amplitude CNVs in psychopaths prior to a button pressing task, but this was not confirmed by Syndulko et al. (1975), and Fenton et al. (1978) found *higher* CNV amplitude in psychopathic than in nonpsychopathic offenders, though not controls. In contrast, Raine and Venables (1987) found no relation between CNV amplitude and socialisation in schoolboys. These inconsistencies appear to reflect both differing criteria of psychopathy and task requirements. Howard, Fenton and Fenwick (1984) showed that, in a simple button pressing task, higher CNV amplitude correlated with sociability, a characteristic of primary psychopaths. Subjects in the earlier studies of McCallum and Syndulko et al. appear to have been mainly secondary psychopaths. However, while low CNV amplitude has been found to characterise impulsive offenders and nonoffenders when the response avoids white noise, this varies with site of measurement (Brown, Fenwick and Howard, 1989). The research to date, then, has not produced any clear implications for the psychophysiology of psychopathy.

Electrodermal and cardiovascular correlates of antisocial personality

Studies of autonomic correlates of antisocial behaviour have for the most part examined electrodermal (ED) and heart rate (HR) activity in psychopathic offenders, or in nonoffenders showing psychopathic traits or undersocialisation. In experimental tasks involving avoidance learning, psychopaths do not show any deficit in active avoidance of punishment, when response contingent electric shock serves as a punishment paradigm, but their postulated deficit in *passive avoidance learning* has been found with some consistency (Lykken, 1957; Schacter and Latané, 1964). However, Schmauk (1970) found that when punishment involved loss of money, primary and secondary psychopathic offenders performed similarly to nonpsychopaths. Anticipatory ED responses paralleled avoidance responses. Psychopaths do not therefore show a generalised deficit in passive avoidance, and can learn to avoid punishment when motivated. Cognitive factors may also determine the responsiveness of psychopaths to punishment. Siegel (1978), for example, found that psychopaths were similar to nonpsychopaths in suppressing responses when punishment was certain. They displayed less suppression when it was uncertain, suggesting a belief in personal immunity.

However, Newman, Widom and Nathan (1985) have argued that passive avoidance deficits of psychopaths are confined to situations where there are competing cues of both reward and punishment. They suggest that psychopaths overfocus on reward, which interferes with attention to punishment cues. Favouring an attentional rather than a motivational explanation, they argue that it is failure to alter a dominant response set which results in deficient avoidance of punishment. In a successive go/no go discrimination task in which the same response could be rewarded with secondary reinforcers or punished by their withdrawal, psychopathic delinquents (Newman, Widom and Nathan, 1985) and adult offenders (Newman and Kosson, 1986) were more deficient in passive avoidance than nonpsychopaths. In the absence of competing goals, however, psychopaths and nonpsychopaths learned to inhibit punished responses equally well. This pattern resembles the effects of septal lesions in rats, and is interpreted as consistent with an underactive BIS in psychopaths. However, since the results do not demonstrate insensitivity to punishment cues, they seem more consistent with an overactive BAS.

Nevertheless, research on ED and HR responses of psychopaths prior to *noxious* stimulation confirms a deficiency in anticipating punishment. For example, when forewarned that shock would follow a particular stimulus in a series, psychopaths produced less anticipatory ED arousal than nonpsychopaths (Hare, 1965). However, while early studies also found weaker ED conditioning in psychopaths, a study by Hare and Quinn (1971), which involved both noxious and pleasant unconditioned stimuli, and recordings of both ED and HR responses, demonstrated that their deficient conditionability is confined to anticipatory responses to noxious stimuli, and to the ED system. These findings contradict Eysenck's hypothesis of a generalised deficit in conditionability in psychopaths, but are consistent with a deficit in the BIS, primarily manifest in ED hyporesponsiveness.

However, threatening aversive stimuli which elicit smaller ED reactions in psychopaths simultaneously produce *larger* HR responses (Hare, 1978). Hare suggests that this dissociation of HR and ED responding reflects "cortical tuning" involving cardiovascular-induced reduction of cortical arousal via baroreceptors in the carotid sinus. Psychopaths may thus have a protective mechanism which reduces the emotional impact of aversive stimuli. This model remains untested, but it is of interest that Zuckerman and Como (1983) found a relation between cardiac acceleration and evoked potential augmenting to strong stimulation.

There is no consistent evidence that psychopaths in general are hyporesponsive in their *orienting reactions* (OR) to simple, nonaversive stimuli, but this has been observed in secondary psychopaths (Blackburn, 1979b), and schizoid offenders (Raine, 1986). Some studies, however, find that psychopaths are distinguished by rate of *habituation* of the OR, which is partly independent of autonomic reactivity or conditionability, and related to higher cortical functioning. Hare (1968) found that psychopaths habituated more slowly in cardiac ORs to tones, but not in ED ORs, and related this dissociation to drowsiness and lower cortical arousal. Blackburn (1979b) also observed this uncoupling of autonomic and cortical activity when subjects became drowsy, but rapid ED habituation, and slower cardiac habituation characterised *secondary* psychopaths.

A related phenomenon is the appearance of *nonspecific fluctuations* (NSFs) in ED records when subjects are unstimulated, which is associated with vigilance and allocation of attentional resources. Lower rates of NSF have been found in secondary psychopaths (Blackburn, 1979b), and in criminals scoring low on the So scale (Schalling et al., 1973). Schalling (1978) points out that NSFs are related to cortical arousal level via a common brainstem excitatory mechanism, and suggests that low rates might reflect weak vividness of imagery, and deficient role-taking and empathy. Supporting this, weak vividness of emotional imagery has been found in secondary, but not primary psychopathic delinquents, and correlates with low scores on the *So* scale (Blackburn, 1980a).

One other ED variable of interest is *response recovery time*. Mednick (1975) suggested that slow autonomic recovery would lead to a failure of reinforcement of passive avoidance responses by fear reduction, and that slower recovery might characterise antisocial individuals. Siddle et al. (1976) found that extremely antisocial delinquents displayed slower ED recovery times, and slow recovery is also associated with low scores on *So* among criminals (Levander et al., 1980). However, the functional significance of ED recovery time remains unclear.

Psychopaths have not been found to be characterised by lower *autonomic arousal level*, but there is some evidence of lower cardiac rates in delinquents. In a prospective study, pulse rates were recorded in a large sample of English schoolchildren while they waited for a mildly stressful medical examination (Wadsworth, 1976). Those who subsequently became delinquent had a significantly lower pulse rate than nondelinquents. Raine and Venables (1984) also found lower heart rates in unsocialised schoolboys, while Maliphant, Watson and Daniels (1990) found that lower heart rates distinguished 7 to 9 year old boys rated as disruptive by their teachers. Venables and Raine (1987) cite Danish research showing children of criminal fathers to have lower heart rates than children of noncriminals, but this did not characterise children of psychopaths. These authors suggest that low tonic heart rate may be associated with low cortical arousal, and that lower arousal in general may be a correlate of petty delinquency, though not psychopathy. This may interact with social factors, in that biological influences are more significant in socialisation among those for whom social backgrounds are less criminogenic.

Research to date has produced only limited indications of psychophysiological idiosyncrasies among offenders in general, and psychopaths in particular. The most consistent finding is that psychopaths display ED hyporesponsiveness when anticipating or experiencing *aversive* stimulation. While this appears to suggest an underactive BIS, psychopaths show deficient passive avoidance only under limited conditions, and hence are not generally insensitive to punishment cues. Also, while young delinquents appear more likely to be reducers, psychopaths do not attenuate sensory input in general, nor have they been found to show lower arousal. Mawson and Mawson (1977) proposed that inconsistencies in the research data might reflect a tendency for psychopaths to oscillate from a state of low to high arousal and reactivity, but a more plausible reason for inconsistencies may be the heterogeneity of offenders identified as "psychopaths." Some evidence, for example, suggests that lower arousal and reactivity may characterise secondary psychopaths, who are socially anxious or schizoid. This raises questions about the role of the arousal of fear or anxiety in antisocial behaviour, since this group is distinguished by *higher* levels of anxiety-proneness, and might therefore be expected to have an *overactive* BIS. Fowles (1988), however, suggests that schizoid withdrawal reflects a deficiency of approach motivation resulting from an underactive BAS.

Biochemical correlates

Hormones secreted by the endocrine glands affect the central nervous system through extensive feedback loops, and may influence behaviour through their role in normal development as well as effects on temporary state. Possible correlates of criminal behaviour and related temperament variables have therefore been sought in the production and level of several hormones, particularly those secreted by the gonads (androgens and oestrogens), the adrenals (adrenaline and noradrenaline), and the pancreas (insulin).

Androgens are crucial in the genital differentiation of the foetus, and the appearance of secondary sexual characteristics at puberty, and *testosterone* level has therefore been considered as a possible factor accounting for the universal correlation of criminal behaviour with gender and age, and the greater aggressiveness of males. Ellis (1987), for example, suggests that excessive androgen levels may increase the probability of antisocial behaviour by lowering the level of arousal. Goodman (1976) attempted to relate female antisocial behaviour to excesses of male hormone. He identified seven delinquent females (from a sample of 400) with a history of aggression and hypersexuality, and found that six had been exposed to virilising hormones *in utero* or in early childhood.

Findings on the personality correlates of testosterone level, however, have not been consistent. Persky, Smith and Basu (1971) found that both rate of production and level of testosterone correlated positively with scales of the Buss–Durkee Hostility Inventory in younger, though not older nonoffenders, but several subsequent studies have failed to replicate these results. Olweus et al. (1980), for example, found associations of testosterone level with self-reported response to provocation in male adolescents, but not with rated aggression, antisocial behaviour, body build, EPQ, or the *So* scale. In contrast,

Daitzman and Zuckerman (1980) found that testosterone levels correlated with sensation seeking, EPQ Extraversion, and with low neuroticism and socialisation.

Results from offender samples are equally inconclusive. Ehrenkrantz, Bliss and Sheard (1974) found higher testosterone levels in aggressive prisoners than in unassertive prisoners, but the former did not differ from unaggressive but socially dominant prisoners. Rada, Laws and Kellner (1976) also found higher levels in a small group of extremely violent rapists than in other rapists or controls. Mattsson et al. (1980), however, found no relation between testosterone level and ratings of aggression in adolescent delinquents, although the mean level of delinquents was higher than that of controls. Moreover, drugs administered to sex offenders to lower testosterone levels do not influence nonsexual aggression (Bradford, 1985). The evidence, then, has not consistently revealed a direct relationship between testosterone level and criminality, and Mazur (1983) argues that testosterone has more to do with dominance than aggression.

However, testosterone may have an indirect effect on behaviour through the activity of brain neurotransmitters. It inhibits the activity of the enzyme *monoamine oxidase* (MAO), which metabolises several neurotransmitters, and this may allow monoamines, such as noradrenaline, to accumulate to higher levels in the brain. Blood platelet MAO activity is lower in human males than in females, and lower MAO is associated with "disinhibitory" temperament variables such as impulsivity, sensation seeking, and undersocialisation (Zuckerman, 1984; Schalling et al., 1987). Low MAO activity is also correlated with low concentrations of a serotonin metabolite, *5-hydroxyindoleacetic acid* (5-HIAA) in cerebrospinal fluid, and Virkkunen, Dejong and Bartko (1989) found significantly lower levels of 5-HIAA in impulsive and recidivist offenders. Levels of 5-HIAA have also been observed to be reduced in suicidal patients and in patients with a history of behaviour disorder and aggression, though not premeditated violence. Coccaro (1989) therefore suggests that reduced central serotonin is associated with lowered thresholds for "impulsive aggression".

Androgens have also long been thought to relate to female crime through hormonal changes occurring in the menstrual cycle, and in particular *premenstrual tension* (PMT). Although there continues to be debate about whether this constitutes a "syndrome", PMT symptoms include depressed mood, irritability, fatigue, muscular tension, and headaches, and Dalton (1961) suggested that PMT makes females more vulnerable to deviant behaviour as a consequence of their irritability or lethargy. She found that of 156 female prisoners who were menstruating regularly, and who committed their crime during the 28 days prior to interview, 49% had offended during the eight days preceding or during menstruation (paramenstruum), compared with a chance expectancy of 29%. This peaking was most marked for theft (56%), and among those experiencing PMT (63%), and it was also found in 54% of prisoners disciplined for violations of prison rules. Hands, Herbert and Tennent (1974) similarly observed that disturbed females in a security hospital were more likely to be secluded for behaviour problems in the premenstrual week. Similar results have been obtained in American studies, and in Britain, PMT syndrome has been successfully used in diminished responsibility pleas (see Widom and Ames, 1988). However, while d'Orban and Dalton (1980) found that female crimes of violence were also more likely to be committed during the paramenstruum, they found no significant association with PMT. The apparent peaking of antisocial behaviour during the paramenstruum is therefore not specific to violent behaviour. Also, since severe PMT symptoms occur in 20% to 40% of women, they are obviously neither necessary nor sufficient to account for female offending. Widom and Ames (1988) point out that since the research to date has relied on retrospective studies of selected female samples, the extent of an association between crime and the menstrual cycle must remain questionable.

Criminal acts have been reported to occur in states of *hypoglycaemia*, which is related to increased insulin secretion. This may follow from starvation, excessive carbohydrate diet, and alcohol ingestion in particular, and consequences include impaired cerebral functioning manifested in loss of concentration and irritability. Dietary habits have been suggested to contribute to antisocial behaviour, and there are some controversial data suggesting that reduced sugar intake reduces misconduct in institutionalised delinquents (Schoenthaler, 1983). Research also indicates an association of violence with dysfunction in glucose metabolism. Susceptibility to hypoglycaemia can be measured by the fall in blood sugar following oral administration of glucose to fasting subjects (glucose tolerance test). Yaryura-Tobias and Neziroglu (1975) found that aggressive behaviour in psychiatric patients was associated with glucose dysfunction and EEG abnormalities, and Virkkunen (1988) similarly reports slower recovery from hypoglycaemia in habitually violent adult offenders. He also observed lower cholesterol levels following fasting in homicidal offenders whose violence was associated with alcohol, and notes that prolonged drinking without food preceded criminal acts in many cases. He suggests that such individuals are particularly susceptible to enhanced insulin secretion under such conditions. However, how the hormonal changes trigger a violent act remains unclear, and while hypoglycaemia-proneness may reflect endocrine pathology in some cases, it varies within the general population. For example, reactive hypoglycemia correlates with self-reported aggressiveness in students (Benton, Kumari and Brain, 1982).

Secretion of the catecholamines *adrenaline* and *noradrenaline* has been of interest because of earlier hypotheses linking adrenaline (A) increase with fear, and noradrenaline (NA) increase with aggression. These hypotheses are now seen as too simple, but a few studies have examined urinary catecholamine in relation to antisocial behaviour, guided by the view that antisocial individuals may be less responsive in anticipating stress. Among offenders awaiting trial, for example, psychopaths showed less increase in A immediately prior to trial, suggesting less stress responsiveness or less involvement in the situation (Lidberg et al., 1976). More recent Scandinavian studies also suggest that antisocial individuals secrete less adrenaline under stress. While Olweus et al. (1980) found that testosterone level correlated with provocation to threat in male adolescents, Olweus (1986) reports that urinary

A levels under mild stress were lower in nonanxious extraverts and in those rated as liable to *unprovoked* aggression. He also found lower A in persistent bullies. However, Olweus considers adrenaline increase to be related more to cortical alertness than specifically to stress, and suggests that unprovoked aggression reflects stimulus seeking in individuals who are characteristically underaroused. Magnusson (1988) makes a similar suggestion to account for the lesser increase in adrenaline in response to mild stress shown by hyperactive boys. He also found lower adrenaline secretion at age 13 among those who later obtained criminal convictions at ages 18 to 26.

Biochemical studies have so far examined relatively isolated endocrine responses in disparate samples, but Venables (1988) attempts to integrate the hormonal and psychophysiological data in terms of the concepts of ergotropic and trophotropic balance, or sympathetic versus parasympathetic tuning. He notes that insulin secretion is normally opposed by adrenomedullary hormones, while testosterone increases catecholamine output by lowering MAO. Low cortical arousal, lower heart rate, hypoglycaemia-proneness, and low adrenaline output, which characterise more antisocial individuals in some studies, would all be consistent with vago-insulin dominance, or parasympathetic balance. However, the difficulty with this interpretation is that these are more pronounced in nonviolent delinquents, whereas hypoglycaemia is associated with violence.

BRAIN DYSFUNCTION AND ANTISOCIAL BEHAVIOUR

Damage to the brain may result from perinatal complications, head injuries, tumours, infections, or exposure to toxic substances, such as atmospheric lead, but such conditions do not invariably lead to structural damage. As Rutter (1982) notes, brain damage has to be severe before significant psychological disturbance ensues, and unsocialised behaviour is not a necessary consequence. For example, Virkkunen, Nuutila and Huusko (1976) found that fewer than 6% of 507 veterans who sustained head wounds received a criminal conviction leading to imprisonment in the 30 years following injury. In the absence of known cerebral insult, brain pathology remains difficult to detect. Most research relies on indirect signs, such as medical history, "soft" neurological signs, EEG records, or neuropsychological tests, which detect brain *dysfunction*, but not necessarily tissue *damage*.

Even if firm evidence of a correlation between brain lesions and antisocial behaviour is obtained, any causal implications are likely to be obscured by interactions of brain dysfunction with socioeconomic conditions or temperament. Research in this area has also rested on implicit assumptions of brain–behaviour relations. In the traditional hierarchical concept of brain organisation, the cerebral cortex is assumed to control more primitive subcortical areas. In these terms, impulsive and aggressive acts may be *positive symptoms* of brain disorganisation, representing a release of subcortical activity from inhibitory control. The persisting influence of this view is seen in the concept of the "dyscontrol syndrome", and in current references to conduct disorder, hyperactivity, and antisocial personality as "disinhibitory psychopathology". Alternatively, antisocial behaviour may be a *negative symptom* of brain pathology, in that cerebral impairment results in an absence or deficiency of functions necessary to support cognitive development and socialisation.

Epilepsy and dyscontrol

Epilepsy, or recurrent seizures, is a symptom of electrical disorganisation within the brain. In many cases, the source of seizure activity is unknown (idiopathic epilepsy), but in others, a specific abnormal focus may be identified, and because of connections between the temporal lobes and limbic nuclei thought to be involved in aggression, there has been particular interest in abnormalities in this area. While most sufferers from epilepsy are psychologically adjusted, about a third show psychological problems (Parsons and Hart, 1984). However, this is not necessarily a direct biological effect, and often reflects the experience of stigma resulting from societal reactions or the reduced sense of personal control. Epilepsy also correlates with socioeconomic status, being more prevalent in disadvantaged groups. A correlation of epilepsy with crime is not, therefore, unequivocal evidence for a causal influence of brain abnormality on antisocial behaviour.

British and American estimates suggest that some 0.5% of the population suffer from epilepsy. There is evidence of higher rates among offenders, at least in incarcerated samples. Gunn and Bonn (1971) found a prevalence of 0.71% among English prisoners, which they considered an underestimate. While a more recent survey found only 0.5% (Gunn, Maden and Swinton, 1991), Whitman et al. (1984) found that 2.4% of males admitted to an American prison had a definite history of seizures. Lewis et al. (1982), however, found that 18% of institutionalised delinquents had a definite or probable history of seizures, although their criteria have been criticised (Whitman et al., 1984). Attention has focused on the questions of whether people with epilepsy may commit crimes automatically and without awareness (automatism), and whether temporal lobe epilepsy (TLE) increases the likelihood of violence. Automatism is of legal interest, since it can negate the *actus reus* requirement, but appears to account very rarely for the offences of criminals with epilepsy (Goldstein, 1974; Fenwick, 1990). For example, Gunn and Fenton (1971) found that only 13 of 187 offenders with epilepsy had committed their offences near to the time of a seizure, and in only three cases was there any suggestion of automatic behaviour. Although Mark and Ervin (1970) claimed that rage reactions are frequently associated with psychomotor seizures, Rodin (1973) was unable to identify any instance of aggression in photographs of induced seizures in 150 patients. Delgado-Escueta et al. (1981) televised seizures of 13 patients selected from a large sample because of suspected aggression during epileptic attacks. They observed incipient aggression in seven, but in all cases the behaviour was brief, unsustained, and lacked purpose. They suggest that criminal behaviour which goes beyond the fragmentary character of automatisms is unlikely to reflect a seizure. The rare instances in which a crime is associated with a seizure are therefore most likely to reflect post-ictal confusion (Fenwick, 1990).

The assumed relation between TLE and violence has also been challenged (Goldstein, 1974; Stevens and Hermann, 1981). Rage reactions or aggressive outbursts have been reported in more than a third of adult and child patients with TLE (Ounstead, 1969), but these may reflect referral biases, and true prevalence rates are unclear. Rodin (1973) found a history of assaultive behaviour in only 4.8% of 700 referrals to an epilepsy clinic, and these were not differentiated from unaggressive patients by the nature of their seizures. Mungas (1983) similarly found that violent and nonviolent neurological outpatients were not distinguished by temporal lobe abnormalities. While Herzberg and Fenwick (1988) also found that aggressive and unaggressive patients with TLE were not differentiated by EEG, CT scan or neuropsychological measures, their aggressive patients had a significantly earlier onset of epilepsy, more childhood behaviour problems, and lower levels of educational and occupational attainment. They suggest that the aggression of these patients is only partially attributable to brain damage.

In two studies comparing prisoners with and without epilepsy, those with epilepsy were no more likely to have committed violent crimes (Gunn and Bonn, 1971; Whitman et al., 1984), and Gunn and Bonn found that violent crimes were more common among those with idiopathic epilepsy than those with TLE. In contrast, Lewis et al. (1982) obtained a correlation of 0.38 between ratings of violent history and symptoms of psychomotor epilepsy among 97 delinquents. They also identified at least one epileptic symptom in 78% of the sample. However, their criteria of both violence and epilepsy are very broad.

Also controversial is the concept of the *dyscontrol syndrome*, which assumes that lesions in the temporal lobe and limbic system cause violence, even though observable seizures are absent. "Epileptoid" dyscontrol is proposed by Monroe (1978) to be characterised by intermittent, explosive outbursts of violence on minimal provocation, with evidence of adequate adjustment between episodes. A broader concept of dyscontrol was advanced by Mark and Ervin (1970), who identified physical assault, violence during alcohol intoxication, impulsive sexual behaviour, and serious traffic violations as the cardinal symptoms.

Dyscontrol is held to reflect epileptic-like discharges from sites of focal abnormality in the limbic system. Evidence for these, however, rests on indirect indicators such as EEG abnormalities, perinatal trauma, head injury, hyperactivity, learning disabilities, or soft neurological signs, which also form the basis for inferring minimal brain dysfunction (see below). Clinical studies suggest that these are common in patients referred for neurological or psychiatric evaluation following recurring episodes of unprovoked rage or assault (Bach-y-Rita et al., 1971; Elliott, 1982), and Monroe (1978) reports that 30% of violent prisoners showed such signs. However, dyscontrol simply describes a correlation between a vaguely defined behavioural syndrome and signs of brain pathology whose validity are not clearly established, and Bach-y-Rita et al. (1971) noted that childhood deprivation and family violence or disruption could equally account for the violence of their dyscontrolled patients.

Specific neural triggers for aggression have not been identified (Valenstein, 1976), and a study by Mungas (1983) suggests that the involvement of brain dysfunction in violence is indirect and nonspecific. He analysed episodes of violence in neurological outpatients in terms of frequency, severity, provocation and organisation, and identified five homogeneous subgroups through cluster analysis. Two groups showed dyscontrol characteristics in terms of histories of frequent, severe, relatively unprovoked and disorganised acts of violence, but while they were more susceptible to seizures, they were not differentiated from nonviolent patients by other neurological disorders, including temporal lobe disorders. Mungas suggests that violence proneness is dependent on prior personal history, and that the role of brain dysfunction may be to weaken control in predisposed individuals. Cerebral impairment may also be associated with violence as a consequence of lowered alcohol tolerance (Häfner and Böker, 1982).

Hyperactivity

Many child behaviour disorders are assumed to be symptomatic of brain dysfunction resulting from cerebral trauma sustained in the perinatal period or early infancy, and adverse medical histories appear to be relatively more frequent among delinquents. Analyses of hospital records, for example, indicate that although perinatal problems are significant only in the histories of institutionalised and violent delinquents, male and female delinquents in general are more likely to have sustained head and facial injuries in infancy (Lewis et al., 1979; Shanok and Lewis, 1981). Such histories have suggested a relationship of delinquency to minimal brain dysfunction (MBD) and *hyperactivity* (attention deficit hyperactivity disorder). Diagnoses of MBD and hyperactivity also overlap with the educational identification of learning disabilities (Chapter 8).

As was noted in Chapter 3, there is some overlap between diagnoses of hyperactivity and child conduct disorder. However, children displaying hyperactive behaviour are not uniformly antisocial, and antisocial character- istics are most pronounced when hyperactivity is combined with conduct disorder (Walker et al., 1987). Childhood hyperactivity is nevertheless thought to predispose to antisocial behaviour in later adolescence and adulthood. Follow-up studies of clinical samples suggest that although motoric and attentional problems tend to decline in intensity with age, many, if not a majority, of those diagnosed as hyperactive show persisting problems of restlessness and distractibility, which are accompanied by poorer academic achievement, lower self-esteem, and antisocial behaviour (Weiss et al., 1985; Lambert, 1988). Satterfield, Hoppe and Schell (1982) compared arrests for serious crimes in hyperactive and control adolescents eight years after referral to a child clinic. Subjects were divided according to low, middle, or high socioeconomic status, and 58%, 36% and 52% of the hyperactive children in these categories subsequently had an arrest record, compared with 11%, 9%, and 2%, respectively, of controls. In addition, 25% of the hyperactive children, but only 1% of controls, had been committed to penal institutions. Several studies also find that hyperactive children are more likely to meet criteria for antisocial personality disorder in later life (Satterfield, 1978). Weiss et al. (1985), for example, found that at a 15 year follow-up, 23% of hyperactive children, but only 2.4% of controls met these criteria, and this was the only diagnosis distinguishing the two groups as adults.

However, it appears to be the interaction of hyperactivity with other characteristics which contributes to deviant behaviour. Lambert (1988), for example, found that while pervasive aggression or pervasive hyperactivity in childhood both predicted later conduct disorder at age 17, only the combination predicted adjudicated delinquency. A prospective study by Mannuzza et al. (1989) also suggests an indirect role for hyperactivity. At follow-up in young adulthood, significantly more hyperactive children than controls had been arrested (39% vs 20%), convicted (28% vs 11%), and incarcerated (9% vs 1%). However, the relationship was almost entirely accounted for by the presence of antisocial conduct disorder in young adulthood, and although more of the hyperactive group showed such disorder, hyperactivity alone did not contribute to later criminal behaviour.

A significant minority of children who are hyperactive, then, show later antisocial behaviour, but apart from the obvious problems of social training presented by a child who is restless and unable to sustain attention, the nature of the contribution of hyperactivity to criminality remains unclear. Earlier attributions of hyperactivity to MBD are now seen as simplistic, since firm evidence that hyperactivity is symptomatic of brain damage has not been forthcoming, and MBD as an inferred cause rests on the dubious assumption that brain damage has uniform behavioural consequences. Nevertheless, hyperactivity continues to be seen in biological terms. Satterfield (1978), for example, suggested that restlessness reflects stimulation seeking consequent on low arousability. However, Lambert (1988) found that delinquent outcomes in hyperactive children were related to both early biological aspects, and to later familial and social characteristics. Other factors, including the reaction of parents and others, are therefore important in the antisocial development of hyperactive children.

Neuropsychological dysfunctions

Neuropsychological tests are employed to make inferences about cerebral dysfunction because of their ability to discriminate populations having known brain damage. However, their utility in localising lesions in nonclinical populations is questionable, and when used in this way, they probably overdiagnose brain damage. Such tests tap complex cognitive functions which depend on the co-ordination of multiple brain systems, and while cognitive deficits imply brain dysfunction, to attribute them to structural damage in the absence of other evidence is a speculative inference.

Performance of offenders on neuropsychological tests has been cited as evidence for brain dysfunction in a number of studies (see Miller, 1988). Early evidence of deficits came largely from findings with intelligence tests, notably the WAIS or WISC (Chapter 8), and particularly the dominance of performance IQ (PIQ) over verbal IQ (VIQ) in delinquents. VIQ and PIQ are assumed to have some association with the differential functions of the left (linguistic processing, sequential analysis) and right (spatial and qualitative analysis) cerebral hemispheres, respectively. The PIQ dominance in delinquents has therefore been interpreted in terms of reduced left hemispheric lateralisation. This was supported by Gabrielli and Mednick (1980), who found higher lateralisation scores indicating right hemisphere dominance in 12 year old boys who subsequently became delinquent.

Berman and Siegal (1976) compared adjudicated delinquents and nondelinquent adolescents of similar age and socioeconomic status on the Halstead–Reitan neuropsychological test battery (HRB). Delinquents produced not only a larger PIQ > VIQ sign, but also poorer scores on five of seven tests comprising the HRB impairment index. The pattern of deficits shown by delinquents suggested only minimal dysfunction in motor and attentional skills or gross sensory functioning, but significant deficiencies in problem-solving abilities requiring verbal, perceptual, and nonverbal conceptual skills. Moffitt (1988) reports similar findings from a study of self-reported delinquency in New Zealand. A composite measure was used to select the most antisocial males and females from a sample of 850 thirteen year olds, who completed a battery of tests assessing memory, language-based, and "executive" (frontal lobe) functions. Male delinquents showed significant deficits on VIQ, PIQ, language-based tests, and memory tests, but not on tests measuring nonlinguistic or frontal lobe functions. In contrast, female delinquents were deficient mainly on the latter two measures.

Other studies, however, suggest that lateralised deficits in the left or dominant hemisphere are more characteristic of violent and psychopathic offenders. Yeudall and Fromm-Auch (1979) summarised research with the HRB indicating abnormal test profiles in 89% of violent offenders, which implicated mainly left hemispheric and anterior cortical dysfunctions. Similar results were obtained in 60% of psychopaths. However, among nonpsychopathic criminals exhibiting personality and affective disorders, test deficits suggested mainly anterior and right hemisphere dysfunction. This was also the predominant pattern in 99 persistent delinquents, 84% of whom showed abnormal HRB profiles in contrast to 11% of nondelinquent controls (Yeudall, Fromm-Auch and Davies, 1982). Violent delinquents in this study did not, however, differ from the nonviolent, although the number of the former was small.

Research with other test batteries also points to significant neuropsychological dysfunction in both juvenile and adult violent offenders, deficits suggesting most commonly an involvement of anterior cortex and/or the left hemisphere. Krynicki (1978), for example, found that assaultive delinquents and organically impaired adolescents were distinguished from less assaultive delinquents, but not from each other, on laterality tests suggesting left hemispheric dysfunction. Bryant et al. (1984) also found that violent prisoners were distinguished from nonviolent inmates on all scales of the Luria–Nebraska neuropsychological battery. Seventy-three percent of prisoners diagnosed as brain damaged by test criteria fell in the violent group, compared with 28% of the non-brain damaged, and from CT scan observations the authors infer that fronto-temporal areas were primarily implicated. However, Tarter et al. (1983) suggest that neuropsychological impairments are confined to only a small section of the offender population. They compared nonincarcerated violent, nonviolent, and sex offenders who had no known neurological abnormalities on an extensive test battery, but found no significant differences between groups. In a later study, they were also unable to detect any relation between the PIQ > VIQ sign and history of violence in delinquents (Tarter et al., 1987).

The proposal that psychopaths may be characterised by frontal and left hemispheric dysfunction has received qualified support. Frontal lobe damage has long been associated with impulsive, disinhibited, and poorly planned behaviour, and the frontal lobes are now believed to be involved in the integration, regulation, and direction of voluntary behaviour. Fronto-limbic connections are also part of Gray's BIS. Gorenstein (1982) hypothesised that disinhibitory syndromes, including psychopathy, entail deficits similar to those produced by frontal damage, and compared psychopathic and nonpsychopathic patients on several measures thought to be sensitive to frontal dysfunction. The hypothesis was supported by the performance of psychopaths, which suggested significant impairment in the modulation of response sets. Hare (1984), however, was unable to replicate these results in psychopathic prisoners selected by the Psychopathy Checklist.

Using a tachistoscopic word recognition task, Hare (1979) also failed to confirm the hypothesis that psychopaths have weaker left hemispheric lateralisation. However, subsequent studies involving more complex semantic processing suggest that psychopaths may be characterised by less specialised lateralisation of language functions (Hare, Harpur and Williamson, 1988). Hare proposes that the cerebral organisation of language in psychopaths may be marked by poorer integration of affective and other components linking cognition and behaviour. He speculates that this involves genetic "hard-wiring" rather than structural brain damage.

Neuropsychological studies of offenders have so far been limited by methodological problems such as small samples, lack of controls, and an overemphasis on institutionalised populations (Moffitt, 1988). Nevertheless, Miller (1988) suggests that impairment of language-related skills and regulative functions controlled by the frontal lobes have been found with some consistency in antisocial populations. He regards this as indicative of developmental failure rather than neurological damage, and proposes that delinquents, more particularly those identified as violent and impulsive, may have a relative inability to use inner speech to modulate attention, affect, thought, and behaviour under conditions of stress.

Chapter 7

Familial and Social Correlates of Crime

INTRODUCTION

Work reviewed in the last chapter suggests that individual attributes with a genetic origin play some role in the development of criminal behaviour. The child is not simply a *tabula rasa* whose characteristics are shaped by an all-controlling environment, but rather contributes to its own development by influencing the reactions of others. However, individual variations in temperament and problem-solving which emerge early in life appear to rest on rather fundamental parameters of physiological activity, and their differentiation into complex psychological functions emerges only through reciprocal interaction with the social environment.

This chapter examines social influences on the development of criminality. Studies of the correlates of conduct disorder and aggression are also considered, since not only are these significant precursors of later social deviance (e.g. Robins, 1978; Farrington, 1989), they also appear to have similar antecedents to those of criminality. Psychologists traditionally focus on the family as the primary agent of socialisation, the influence of the neighbourhood, school, workplace, and marriage being considered more the province of the sociologist, and this is reflected in the following pages. Nevertheless, socialisation entails not only the transmission of cultural mores through parents, but also the assimilation of values and standards associated with changing social roles throughout the lifespan. The effects on criminality of social influences beyond the family will therefore be discussed.

FAMILY PATTERNS AND INTERACTIONS

Comparisons of the family environments of delinquents and nondelinquents indicate adverse conditions with some regularity. Many of the findings to be summarised were anticipated in the early work of Healy and the Gluecks, but have since been replicated in longitudinal studies such as the Cambridge study (Farrington and West, 1990) and the long-term follow-up of boys in the Cambridge–Somerville study in Massachusetts (McCord, 1979, 1986), as well as in a number of cross-sectional comparisons (for reviews, see Hetherington and Martin, 1979; Loeber and Stouthamer-Loeber, 1986; Snyder and Patterson, 1987). Until the 1950s, most research on family correlates of crime was influenced by psychoanalytic conceptions of the significance for later development of the first five years of life, and a continued interest in early relationships is seen in attachment theory. More recent research, however, focuses on parent–child interactions up to and beyond adolescence, and has been guided more by social learning and social control perspectives. This has entailed not only changes in methodology to include direct observation as well as interviews and retrospective reports, but also a shift of emphasis from the emotional needs of children to the effectiveness of caretakers in shaping and transmitting skills and performance standards. While the variables receiving most attention overlap, they can be divided into *functional* aspects, or interpersonal processes which have a direct effect on behaviour, and *structural* aspects, such as family size, whose influences are less direct. These aspects are examined here under the headings of child rearing practices, family relationships, family disruption, parental deviation, family size, and socioeconomic deprivation.

Child rearing practices

Child rearing practices include the range of parental behaviours which may inculcate prosocial development, but this section focuses on disciplinary techniques. Although not always distinguishable from other daily encounters, such techniques are relatively consistent styles of interaction engaged in by parents to terminate, prevent and modify a child's undesirable behaviours. They have often been studied in isolation, and there continues to be a lack of an agreed theoretical framework for guiding observations of family functioning. As a result, this area suffers from a profusion of loose terminology. For example, disciplinary practices within the families of delinquent or aggressive children are frequently described as harsh, punitive, lax, and erratic, and as displaying "poor" mothering ability (Glueck and Glueck, 1950; Cortés and Gatti, 1972; Feldhusen, Thurston and Benning, 1973; West, 1982; Kolvin et al., 1988). However, these global and value-laden descriptions do not clearly identify the parameters of rearing techniques most conducive to antisocial development.

Attempts to organise the data focus variously on the content, style, and consistency of disciplinary encounters. One approach identifies patterns of reward and punishment dispensed in disciplinary confrontations, distinctions being made between *power assertion* (physical punishment, criticism and threats, and material deprivation), *love withdrawal* (nonphysical expression of disapproval, and the withholding of affection), and *induction* (reasoning and focus on the consequences of the child's action for others: see Hoffman,

1977). Among normal children, moral development is associated positively with greater parental use of induction, and negatively with the use of power assertion, but not consistently with love withdrawal (Hoffman and Saltzstein, 1967). The relative ineffectiveness of power assertion in socialisation is attributed to its dependence on the presence and fear of the punisher, and to its provision of a model for hostile behaviour. Withdrawal of affection is also limited in its effects to relationships which are already affectionate. Induction, on the other hand, is more likely to teach contingency rules, to elicit responses incompatible with ongoing deviant activity, and to capitalise on the child's capacity for empathy (Hoffman, 1977).

Several studies suggest that delinquent families are more likely to employ power assertive techniques. Bandura and Walters (1959) observed that parents of delinquents made frequent use of ridicule and physical punishment, whereas parents of nondelinquents relied more on induction and love withdrawal. Mothers of young conduct disordered children also tend to follow both deviant and nondeviant behaviours of the child with higher rates of commands and criticisms than other mothers (Lobitz and Johnson, 1975; Patterson, 1982). McCord (1979), however, found that parental aggression against the child was a significant precursor of later crimes against the person, but not of property crimes.

However, the content of disciplinary encounters is not independent of the style of interaction. Maternal behaviours towards a child can be summarised by a circumplex model in which differing forms of interaction are arrayed around two independent dimensions of *affection* (acceptance and warmth versus rejection and hostility) and *control* (demanding and restrictive versus undemanding and permissive; see Maccoby and Martin, 1983). This reconciles the description of parental styles of delinquent families as harsh but lax, since these represent extremes of different dimensions. Combinations of these dimensions give rise to four distinct parenting styles: *authoritative* (accepting–demanding); *indulgent* (accepting–undemanding): *authoritarian* (rejecting–demanding); and *neglecting* (rejecting–undemanding). Authoritative discipline is more likely to promote self-control and self-confidence. The authoritarian style is associated with the use of power assertion, and is particularly likely to have a negative impact on the child in terms of lower moral development, higher aggression, and lower self-esteem. However, deficient socialisation may also result from indulgent and neglectful styles, and the literature implicates both authoritarian and neglecting styles in delinquency.

The consequences of disciplinary styles will also vary with the intensity, frequency and consistency with which they are applied. Erratic or inconsistent practices may denote a lack of consistency in techniques between parents, or on the part of one parent, and both of these have been observed in delinquent families. A combination of maternal laxness and paternal restrictiveness, for example, is frequently reported (Hetherington and Martin, 1979). However, inconsistency in the form of *noncontingent* consequences is emphasised in behavioural approaches. This perspective is exemplified in the work of Patterson (1982, 1986), whose pragmatic research programme has evolved with the aim of constructing a social learning theory of *coercive family process* to account for antisocial behaviour in the preschool and preadolescent child.

Patterson has observed that innocuous aversive child behaviour in the form of yelling, whining, teasing, and ignoring, is common in all families. However, the rate of such behaviour declines with the use of effective, nonphysical punishment practices entailing time out from reinforcement, withdrawal of privileges, and assignment to chores, coupled with the teaching of competing prosocial behaviours through specifications of rules. These contingencies appear to relate to patterns of induction and an authoritative style of parenting described by other investigators. Aversive behaviour tends to persist in antisocial children, and deviant families are distinguished by the use of high rates of punishment in the form of humiliation and threats which are not followed up. Microsocial observations of sequential interactions indicate high frequencies of reciprocal coercive exchange between parent and child in such families. The mother is more likely to attend to and interact with the child following deviant behaviour, and reacts to transgressions with "nattering" involving threats which are not carried out. She may also engage in prolonged coercive exchanges with the child which sometimes escalate to physical abuse. Aggressive behaviour in the child is positively reinforced by the attainment or reinstatement of parental attention and interaction, or negatively reinforced when parental punishment is terminated by counterattack from the child. As well as modelling aggression, the parent reinforces a coercive style of behaviour in the child which generalises to other situations inside and outside the home.

Patterson therefore emphasises that it is the use of severe but inconsistent punishment, rather than punishment itself, which characterises deviant families. However, he distinguishes two kinds of disciplinary style in families with antisocial children, linked to differing forms of child deviance (Patterson, 1982; Snyder and Patterson, 1987). *Social aggressors* tease and hit sibs, and have frequent tantrums, while *stealers* show a pattern of lying, overactivity, firesetting, and stealing. Parents of social aggressors are more likely to display an enmeshed style in which trivial misbehaviours elicit irritability and a high rate of commands and criticisms, and coercive interactions are particularly likely to develop in such families. Parents of stealers tend to be uninvolved with the child, showing a lax style in which few antisocial behaviours are punished. When punishment is used, it is not administered contingently. Both styles are ineffective in modifying the child's deviant behaviour.

Lax and enmeshed styles seem equivalent to the neglecting and authoritarian styles described by Maccoby and Martin (1983). However, the lax style is most clearly associated with later delinquency. Of those who were stealers at age 8, 84% had a police contact by age 14, compared with 24% of social aggressors, and 21% of normals, and two thirds had already become chronic offenders (Moore, Chamberlain and Mukai, 1979). The low delinquency rate of the social aggressors seems somewhat surprising, but the classification relates to behaviour in the home only, and Loeber and Stouthamer-Loeber (1986) note that the most coercive families produce children displaying both patterns.

The lax style is particularly associated with inadequate *supervision* or monitoring of the child's behaviour. This refers to parental awareness of the child's whereabouts, associates, and free time activities outside the home, and the child's independence of rules about coming home, and it has been found to be a significant correlate of both official and self-reported delinquency in several studies (Hirschi, 1969; McCord, 1979; Wilson, 1980; Patterson and Stouthamer-Loeber, 1984; Cernkovich and Giordano, 1987). Inadequate supervision also characterises the histories of aggressive boys (Feldhusen, Thurston and Benning, 1973; Loeber and Dishion, 1984). In Wilson's studies of boys from a deprived inner city area (Wilson, 1980, 1987), poor maternal supervision was more important than either social handicap or parental criminality in distinguishing delinquents from nondelinquents.

However, despite the obvious practical relevance of supervision for child discipline, the term has little explanatory power. Patterson regards monitoring as a significant component of maternal skill, and it correlates with effectiveness in handling confrontations and the use of social reinforcement (Patterson and Stouthamer-Loeber, 1984). He considers it central to delinquent development since many deviant behaviours go unpunished. Hirschi and Gottfredson (1988), however, suggest that it is more relevant to the commission of crimes than to the development of criminality, which is likely to appear earlier. Apparently consistent with this is the finding that parental monitoring is more closely associated with delinquency in older adolescents than in preadolescent children (Snyder, Dishion and Patterson, 1986; Weintraub and Gold, 1991).

Family interaction

Extremes of rejection and indifference found in disciplinary styles appear to extend to interactions in delinquent families more generally. Conflict between parents in the form of disagreements, quarrelling, hostile attitudes, and marital instability or breakup has been found to be prominent in the early lives of delinquents in longitudinal studies (McCord, 1979, 1986; West, 1982; Kolvin et al., 1988). Marital discord also correlates with conduct disorder in boys, though not girls (Emery and O'Leary, 1982), and with generalisation of boys' aggression outside the home (Loeber and Dishion, 1984).

Parents of delinquents are also more likely to show negative attitudes towards their children, although it is not entirely clear whether negative interactions with the father or mother are more significant. Glueck and Glueck (1950) found that both mothers and fathers of delinquents showed less affection for their children compared with parents of nondelinquents, but Bandura and Walters (1959) observed that relationships between father and son were more likely to be impaired than those between mother and son, fathers of delinquents showing less warmth and spending less time with their sons than fathers of nondelinquents. Hanson et al. (1984) also found that conflictful father-son relationships predicted a child's involvement in crime. In McCord's longitudinal study, on the other hand, lack of affection by the mother when the child was between age 5 and 13 was significantly related to later property crimes by the son, but not to crimes against the person. The latter were associated with parental conflict and aggression to the child. Differing findings may reflect the changing influence of fathers relative to mothers as boys reach adolescence, although there may also be a cumulative effect in that rejection by both parents has a stronger effect on subsequent delinquency than rejection by only one (Rutter, 1971; McCord, 1986).

Delinquents also describe negative perceptions of their families. Bhagat and Fraser (1970) found that delinquents evaluated their mothers on a semantic differential less favourably than did nondelinquents, and rated their fathers as less like their ideal self. Recidivist delinquents also describe their families as less cohesive and expressive on Moos' Family Environment Scale, and as less oriented to achievement or recreation compared with nondelinquents (Leflore, 1988). Self-reported delinquency is also related to lack of involvement with parents (Hirschi, 1969), and to adolescent reports of high parent–child conflict, low parental trust, and less intimate communication (Cernkovich and Giordano, 1987). Canter (1982b), however, found that lack of family attachment was more strongly related to delinquency in boys than in girls.

Lack of involvement is also reflected in findings that delinquent families share fewer leisure activities (Bandura and Walters, 1959; Cortès and Gatti, 1972), and Farringon and West (1990) report that having a father who rarely joined in his son's activities at the age of 12 significantly predicted persistence into crime beyond the age of 20. When they do interact, their exchanges are more likely to reveal disharmony. Hetherington, Stouwie and Ridberg (1971), for example, observed that during structured interactions, delinquent families displayed less warmth and more hostility, more negative expectations of each other, and were less likely to reach agreement than families of nondelinquents. Similar findings have been obtained in observations of mother–son interactions in father-absent families, which reveal less positive communication and affect in delinquent families (Blaske et al., 1989).

In some families, discord extends to physical abuse of children by parents. Family violence is discussed in Chapter 9, but of relevance here is the view that the experience of physical abuse is a precursor of delinquency in general, and violent crime in particular. Widom (1989a) reviews evidence on the relation of physical abuse in childhood to later antisocial behaviour, and notes that only tentative conclusions about a causal relationship are justified. Most abused children are not subsequently antisocial, and some studies suggest that physical abuse may not be a significant factor in delinquent development. McCord's follow-up, for example, suggests that the experience of parental rejection rather than abuse itself is significant, since serious juvenile crimes were committed by 50% of children who had been rejected, but by only 20% of abused and neglected children, and 11% of those who were loved (McCord, 1986). A study of adolescents by Brown (1984) also found an association of self-reported delinquency with reported neglect and emotional abuse, but not with physical abuse. Widom (1989b), however, describes a 20-year follow-up of children who had been officially identified as abused or neglected, in which she found that they were more likely to have acquired a criminal record by adulthood. Among males, 42% became criminal, compared with

33% of controls, figures for females being 16% and 9%, respectively. Abuse was also significantly associated with later violent crimes, although for males only. Inconsistencies in research in this area probably reflect varying criteria of abuse.

Family disruption

Offenders have long been observed to be more likely to come from homes "broken" by the absence of one or both natural parents. For example, in a survey of court-referred children in Florida, Chilton and Markle (1972) found that 28% of white male delinquents came from single parent families, compared with a national rate among whites of 13%, figures among black males being 59% and 43%, respectively. Highest rates are typically reported for institutionalised offenders (e.g. Cortès and Gatti, 1972; Hollander and Turner, 1985). However, since the absence of an intact home may itself influence the decision to incarcerate a delinquent, such findings probably overestimate the relationship, and in the Cambridge–Somerville study, father absence in childhood did not predict later juvenile or adult crime (McCord, 1979). Community surveys also suggest a relatively weak association, and Hirschi (1969) found no consistent relation between father-absence and self-reported delinquency. While others report such a relationship (Canter, 1982b), Rankin (1983) found that absence of at least one biological parent was associated with only some forms of delinquency, notably status offences such as truancy or running away.

Overall, there seems to be a modest effect of absence of a biological parent on delinquency, and boys from father-absent homes also show more aggression and lower levels of moral development (Hoffman, 1971; Santrock, 1975). However, few studies adequately control for reasons for, or duration of parental loss, and inconsistent findings may also reflect sampling variations. For example, the association tends to be stronger among boys than among girls (Canter, 1982b), among older rather than younger children, and among white rather than black youths (Chilton and Markle, 1972). Moreover, the "broken home" concept is ambiguous, and the "intact" versus "broken" home dichotomy an oversimplification, which typically relies on a physical rather than a functional concept of family life (Wells and Rankin, 1986).

Attention to the reasons for parental absence reveals that the association is most apparent when the break occurs through divorce, desertion, or parental separation rather than through death (Gibson, 1969; Rutter, 1971). Similarly, students identified as poorly socialised report a higher rate of parental divorce, but not death, in comparison with their more socialised counterparts (Megargee, Parker and Levine, 1971). McCord, McCord and Thurber (1962) observed that although more boys from father-absent homes had convictions than those from intact homes, they did not differ in this respect from boys from intact but conflictful homes. It has therefore been concluded that the effect of broken homes on delinquency is primarily a result of the family discord which precedes or follows divorce or separation (Rutter, 1971; Loeber and Stouthamer-Loeber, 1986). This may also apply to conduct disorder in the children of divorced families. Lahey et al. (1988) found that among clinic children, conduct disorder was significantly related to antisocial personality disorder in parents, but not to divorce, suggesting that the relation between divorce and conduct disorder results from the greater tendency of antisocial parents to divorce.

However, the stress of divorce or separation on the remaining parent, usually the mother, may exacerbate conflict between parent and child. Mothers in single parent families tend to experience problems arising from reduced social supports, financial difficulties, and lack of relief from household tasks, and there is evidence of a deterioration in parenting practices during the first year following divorce (Hetherington and Martin, 1979). This may depend on characteristics of the mother, since McCord et al. (1962) found that the likelihood of delinquency in father-absent homes was reduced when the mother was warm and nondeviant. The finding that broken homes increase the likelihood of self-reported status offences more than other forms of delinquency (Rankin, 1983), particularly for boys (Canter, 1982b), also supports this view, since truancy and running away are most likely when the mother is neglectful and uncaring.

A related hypothesis is that added burdens on the mother reduce opportunities for supervision. Patterson and Stouthamer-Loeber (1984) cite an unpublished study by McCord showing differing probabilities of adequate supervision according to family status. This was 0.70 for intact homes, 0.50 for homes where the parents were in conflict, and 0.20 in broken homes with an unaffectionate mother. Lack of supervision may also account for the finding of Steinberg (1986) that "latch key" children whose working mothers are not at home when they finish school were more susceptible to peer pressure to engage in antisocial behaviour. However, this varied with the mother's disciplinary style.

An alternative hypothesis is that father-absence itself is critical, since the child lacks a model of masculine behaviour. A cross-cultural study of preliterate societies by Bacon, Child and Barry (1963) supports this. They found that rates of both property and personal crimes were significantly higher in societies in which fathers are uninvolved in child-rearing, which they attribute to inadequate opportunities for masculine identification, and subsequent concerns with masculinity. This would account for the greater impact of broken homes on boys, and for the greater influence of the peer group on delinquency in father-absent homes (Hanson et al., 1984). However, it is not sufficient to explain the apparently greater effects on delinquency of discordant homes compared with homes broken by death.

One sociological perspective sees the family not so much as an agency of socialisation and control, but rather as the source of a person's position in the wider social structure (Wells and Rankin, 1986). In these terms, the broken home may cause delinquency by altering the social relationships of the family, for example, by creating stereotypes of children from homes broken by divorce as deviant, which become a self-fulfilling prophecy. The stronger relationship of broken homes to official than to self-reported delinquency is consistent with such a view. On the other hand, this would account for secondary deviance, but not for the primary deviance arising from discordant relationships in both broken and intact homes.

Parental deviation

Criminals are more likely than noncriminals to have criminal parents (Glueck and Glueck, 1950; Robins, West and Herjanic, 1975; McCord, 1979; Offord, 1982; West, 1982). In the Cambridge study, for example, 37.9% of boys who became delinquent had a parent with a criminal record by the time the child was age 10, compared with 14.6% of nondelinquents. Family criminality also predicted persistent criminality after the age of 20, as well as convictions for violence (Farrington and West, 1990). Conversely, delinquents are more likely to produce delinquent children (Robins et al., 1975), and similar intergenerational transmission has been found for aggression (Huesman et al., 1984). This also appears to hold for conduct disorder, since Lahey et al. (1988) found that 50% of clinic referred children showing conduct disorder had a parent (mainly father) with antisocial personality disorder, compared with 11% of children with other disorders.

Several possible explanations have been advanced. One is that the association reflects genetic factors common to parent and child, although this is more plausible for persisting offending than for short-lived delinquency. A second is that it involves modelling of antisocial behaviour by parents. In the Cambridge study, the association was strongest when parental criminality continued into the period of child rearing, and was not found for those who first offended after the age of 18 (West, 1982). However, West and Farrington found no evidence that criminal parents directly modelled or involved their sons in criminal activities. While they consider greater surveillance of criminal families by the police to be a possibility, they regard ineffective child rearing practices as a more plausible factor, since after controlling for other variables, the most prominent feature of criminal parents was poor supervision of their children. Parental criminality was also associated with lax discipline of children living on poor housing estates in Birmingham (Wilson, 1980).

However, parental criminality correlates with irregular employment and reliance on welfare, which may add to family stress and disruption (West, 1982), and parents of delinquents have also been found to be deviant in other ways. McCord (1986) found that paternal deviance had its strongest effect when combined with parental aggressiveness and conflict, while the effect was relatively weak when the father showed respect for the mother and affection for the child. Kolvin et al. (1988) also observed that parents of boys who later became offenders were more likely to have been described as aggressive or "ineffective". Failure of deviant parents to provide models of normative and prosocial behaviour is therefore a further possible explanation for the effects of parental criminality.

Family size and sibling relationships

Large family size is another established correlate of delinquency (Fischer, 1984). In the Cambridge study, delinquents were more likely to come from families with four or more children (West, 1982), and Hirschi (1969) found a similar relationship for self-reported delinquency. Recidivists also come from larger families (Buikhuisen and Hoekstra, 1974), although family size does not appear to be significant for female delinquents (Offord, 1982).

As with parental criminality, explanations are complicated by the association of size with other family variables. Large families are more likely to live in poor and overcrowded homes, and those with a delinquent child are more often headed by criminal parents. Greater stress and family disorganisation are therefore possible factors, but the relationship remains after family income, socioeconomic status, and parental criminality are partialled out (Fischer, 1984). Large families are also more difficult to discipline, and individual children may receive less supervision, but in Hirschi's study, the effect of family size remained after controlling for supervision. A further possibility is that children in such families are less likely to receive parental attention and affection, and are hence restricted in the development of prosocial skills. Only children are less likely to be delinquent (Hirschi, 1969; West, 1982), and there is a tendency for delinquents to be middle children (Hirschi, 1969; Leflore, 1988). However, Hirschi found that the effect of size remained after controlling for affectional ties and amount of interaction with parents. In contrast, in a comparison of male and female delinquents with their near-age, nondelinquent siblings, Reitsma-Street, Offord and Finch (1985) found that delinquents reported less positive interactions with their parents early in life. It therefore remains possible that children in large families who become delinquent are treated differently by parents.

The most potent factor may be exposure to delinquent siblings. Glueck and Glueck (1950) noted that 65% of their delinquent sample had a delinquent sibling, compared with 26% of nondelinquents. Since this holds for both small and large families (Robins et al., 1975), it may be more important than size itself. Moreover, the effect of size depends on the number of brothers rather than sisters in the family, suggesting a "contagion" effect (Offord, 1982). The association with large family size may therefore reflect a tendency for the children to rely more on their siblings as models and sources of social training.

Socioeconomic deprivation

Although delinquency is now thought to be only weakly related to social class, it is commonly assumed that delinquents tend to come from family backgrounds which are "deprived" through material disadvantage such as poverty, poor housing, overcrowding, and dependence on welfare. The association of these with delinquency is well established. In the predominantly working class sample of the Cambridge study, low family income was a relatively independent predictor of later delinquency (West, 1982), and the greater dependence of delinquent families on welfare has been observed in several studies (e.g. Offord, 1982; Ouston, 1984). Hirschi (1969) also found a relation between self-reported delinquency and father's unemployment, though not with social class.

The psychological effects of such conditions are again obscured by their association with other variables, such as parental criminality and supervision. However, it is unlikely that they exert a direct effect on criminal behaviour, since deprivation is defined in relative rather than absolute terms, and delinquents do not often steal solely because they lack food or clothing. Moreover, not all poor families produce delinquents. Wilson (1980), for example, found that within deprived areas, social handicap was associated with lax supervision, but not with serious self-reported delinquency.

Strain and subcultural theories see the effects as mediated by the norms acquired by children growing up under such conditions, but these theories have not fared well (Chapter 5). However, the living conditions of socially disadvantaged families may foster values and standards which exemplify the child rearing characteristics attributed to the working class more generally. These include more frequent use of power assertive discipline, which may in turn be associated with a greater emphasis on externally imposed rules rather than self-direction, the use of a "restricted" as opposed to an "elaborated" linguistic style of communication, and orientation to the present rather than the future (Gecas, 1979). A further possibility is that economic hardship is a source of stress, which impairs parenting skills (Patterson, 1982). However, the available evidence does not permit a choice between these alternatives.

Differences between delinquents

Most research on family variables has focused on nonspecific effects on delinquency as a global outcome, and only limited attention has been paid to possible associations with specific forms of deviant behaviour. There are, however, a few relevant findings. From multiple regression analyses, McCord (1979) identified differing patterns of family predictors of personal and property crimes. The former were associated with family conflict, and lack of maternal affection and supervision, while the latter were related primarily to lack of maternal affection and supervision. It was also noted earlier that stealers in Patterson's research came mainly from lax homes, aggressors from more enmeshed and coercive families, while children displaying both patterns came from the most coercive families.

Hewitt and Jenkins (1946) also found that socialised aggressive delinquents more often came from homes characterised by neglect and permissiveness, while unsocialised aggressive children commonly showed a history of parental rejection, and anxious–withdrawn children a history of parental overcontrol. Jenkins (1960) compared psychopathic and neurotic veterans, and found that the former described significantly more parental conflict and rejection by the father, but more negative attitudes to the mother. Fodor (1973) also found that in contrast to nonpsychopathic delinquents, psychopaths described their fathers as less nurturant and rewarding, and their mothers as demanding less achievement.

Hetherington, Stouwie and Ridberg (1971) compared the families of nondelinquents with those of psychopathic, neurotic and subcultural delinquents, as defined by Quay's dimensions, on a behavioural interaction measure and a parent questionnaire. Parents of subcultural delinquents showed less marital conflict, and less rejection of their children, but were more permissive. Parents of neurotic subjects were more rejecting and likely to use power assertive discipline. Families of psychopathic delinquents were similar to the latter, but encouraged sons to be aggressive outside the home. There were also differences in dominance relationships, the father tending to be dominant in the home of subcultural delinquents, and to a lesser extent in the families of psychopaths, mothers being more dominant in the homes of neurotic delinquents. Less clear differences were apparent among the families of female delinquents.

There are some suggestive trends in these data, in particular the apparently greater parental conflict, paternal rejection, and use of coercive discipline in families of aggressive and psychopathic delinquents, and the greater laxity and neglect in families of subcultural delinquents and those who steal. However, these conclusions must be tentative.

Overview of the family and delinquency

Family variables have been shown to differentiate delinquents in both cross-sectional and longitudinal research designs, and in the case of both official and self-report criteria of delinquency. Similar relationships hold for child conduct disorder and aggression, and probably also for other forms of deviance, such as drug and alcohol abuse (Loeber and Stouthamer-Loeber, 1986). The role of the family is also emphasised by findings that a small minority of families account for a large proportion of offences. For example, by the time boys in the Cambridge study had reached adulthood, 4.6% of families accounted for 48% of all convictions (West, 1982). However, the theoretical significance of the association between family variables and current or later delinquency remains conjectural, for several reasons.

First, the strength of the association tends to be modest. In the Cambridge study, most family variables ceased to correlate with self-reported delinquency when official delinquency was partialled out, suggesting that the contribution of the family to delinquency may be exaggerated by police attention to known deviant families. It is unlikely that this accounts for the association between delinquency and interaction within the family, which is also found in the case of conduct disorder in younger children (Rutter and Giller, 1983), but it emphasises the relatively small amount of variance explained by family factors.

Second, the relative importance and independence of different variables remains unclear. In their meta-analysis, Loeber and Stouthamer-Loeber (1986) found variations in relative predictive power according to whether studies were concurrent or longitudinal, but functional variables such as supervision, parental rejection, and parent–child involvement were consistently stronger predictors than structural variables. However, family variables are not independent. McCord (1979) found correlations of up to 0.40 between parental deviance, supervision, conflict, and attitudes to the child, while Patterson and Stouthamer-Loeber (1984) report correlations from 0.14 to 0.73 between supervision, effectiveness of discipline, use of social reinforcement, and problem solving.

This interdependence remains to be unravelled, but combinations of variables tend to correlate more strongly with delinquency than do single variables. For example, delinquency and conduct disorder are more likely when both parents are rejecting rather than one (Rutter, 1971), and supervision is more strongly related to delinquency in the context of parental criminality (Wilson, 1980; West, 1982) or maternal rejection (Patterson and Stouthamer-Loeber, 1984) than when these other factors are absent. Whether these represent additive or multiplicative effects is unclear, but several investigators have employed combinations of variables in attempts to predict delinquency. The Glueck prediction index comprising maternal affection, paternal affection, maternal supervision, paternal discipline, and family cohesiveness (Glueck and Glueck, 1950, 1964), for example, predicts later delinquency well beyond chance levels (Loeber and Stouthamer-Loeber, 1986). In the Cambridge study, low family income, large family size, unsatisfactory child-rearing, low IQ, and parental criminality were relatively independent predictors of delinquency. Of 63 boys who were "vulnerable" in showing three or more of these, 46 (73%) had convictions by age 32 compared with 30.7% of the remainder (Farrington, 1990). However, while the association is highly significant, more than two thirds of delinquents did not come from the high risk group, which constitutes a high false positive rate. Similarly, Kolvin et al. (1988) found that of those who experienced one or more forms of deprivation (marital instability, parental illness, poor child care, social dependency, overcrowding, poor mothering skills), more than half subsequently had a criminal record, but more than two thirds of the offenders in the sample had not been subject to deprivation. This again emphasises the modest contribution of family variables. A third point is that in no case has the relationship been shown to be causal, and the correlation of family factors with delinquency may reflect the influence of a third factor, for example, genetic factors or the child's temperament. Alternatively, poor parental practices may be the result of stress created by structural factors such as poverty and poor housing, or by the delinquency of the child itself. The process by which family interaction may promote deviant tendencies therefore remains unclear.

Learning theorists see the critical factor as the degree of efficiency and effectiveness of parental discipline (Trasler, 1978; Patterson, 1982, 1986). Patterson considers inept parental management skills to be the major causal factor. These relate to deficiencies in monitoring the child's behaviour, stating the rules, contingent punishment of transgressions, reinforcing conformity, and negotiating disagreements, as a result of which the child learns deviant ways of meeting its needs. Similarly, in the absence of sharing and communication, parents fail to transmit normative values and problem solving skills to their children (Snyder and Patterson, 1987). The antisocial child is not only aversive to peers and teachers on entry to school, but also lacks skills of self-help, intimacy, and academic related work behaviour. These characteristics result in poor school performance, further rejection by family as well as peers, and low self-esteem, accelerating a drift to delinquency. This emphasis on parental skills is consistent with control theory, since the family fails to establish the child's bonds to the social order.

Another factor may be the opportunities for the child to develop deviant styles of behaviour through the modelling of parental or sibling deviance. However, both social learning and attachment theories would predict that disruption in dependency relations results not only in hostility in the child, but also in *reduced* motivation to identify with or imitate the parent. Male delinquents have, in fact, been noted to be less likely to accept their parents as role models (Bandura and Walters, 1959; Canter, 1982b).

A further possibility is that it is the absence of parental affection which is most significant, and parental rejection of the child seems to be one of the stronger predictors of delinquency. This would be predicted by both psychodynamic and control theories, but it is also consistent with both the parental skill deficit and modelling assumptions. Skills are not applied mechanically, but rather depend on the motivation to exercise them. Parents who find their children aversive are less likely to interact positively with them or to attend to their social training. Conversely, children are less likely to imitate parents who are cold or hostile towards them. They are also more likely to be susceptible to influences outside the family.

SCHOOL AND PEER GROUP INFLUENCES

The prevalence of delinquency peaks during and immediately following the later years of compulsory education, and academic failure at this time is associated with increased risks of delinquency, as measured by both official and self-report criteria (Hirschi, 1969; Elliott and Voss, 1974). Adult offenders are also more likely to have a history of low educational attainment (Thornberry and Farnworth, 1982). However, the causal role of the school remains unclear. Some theorists maintain that the educational system contributes to delinquency by imposing middle class standards on working class youth who are unwilling to accept them (Cohen, 1955). Critical criminologists further argue that universal education was created to ensure the socialisation of the majority into the obedience and willingness to do routine tasks required by industry: those who are disruptive and become delinquent are rebelling against the demand to engage in alienated labour (Liazos, 1978).

While there is evidence that those who fail in school become alienated and hostile to the school system, and are more likely to truant and leave school early, some theorists implicate characteristics of failing pupils, such as limited intellectual ability (Hirschi and Hindelang, 1977), or lack of the social skills necessary to meet classroom demands and to form peer relations (Patterson, 1986; Patterson, DeBarshye and Reynolds, 1989; Dishion et al., 1991) more than the school system itself. The relationship of intellectual and other attributes to delinquency is examined in Chapter 8. It is sufficient to note here that these analyses assume school factors to be relatively constant, and do not see schools themselves as playing an active role. However, schools vary in educational philosophies and social organisation, and may also differ in the extent to which they facilitate or inhibit delinquency.

Delinquent schools

It is well established that schools vary widely in the rates of delinquency exhibited by their pupils, but it is less clear that this is due to processes within the schools or what these might be. In a study of 20 inner London secondary schools, Power et al. (1967) found that annual delinquency rates (court appearances) ranged from less than 1% to 19%, and these were consistent over a six year period. These variations were not related to the delinquency rates of the school's catchment area, suggesting that factors within the school were responsible. Reynolds (1976) similarly observed varying delinquency rates between nine secondary schools in Wales, which were not due to the social class or ability levels of the schools' intake population, again implicating within-school processes. Findings from the Cambridge study, however, challenge this view (Farrington, 1972). The six primary schools from which the cohort was drawn did not differ in the subsequent delinquency rates of their pupils, but there was marked variability in the rates of the 13 secondary schools to which most boys went. However, high delinquency schools admitted a greater proportion of boys rated as "troublesome" by teachers at age 8 and by peers at age 10. This variable strongly predicted later delinquency, 44.6% of the most troublesome boys becoming delinquent, compared with 3.5% of the least troublesome. Since the continuity between troublesomeness and delinquency was largely unaffected by the kind of secondary school a boy attended, Farrington argued that the schools themselves had little effect on delinquency. He attributed the higher delinquency rates of some schools to characteristics of the boys they admitted, possibly reflecting parental choice of schools with better reputations, or school selection of better behaved boys.

Farrington's general conclusion is supported by Rutter et al. (1979), who studied 12 inner London comprehensive schools. They examined relationships between a number of school process variables, such as teaching skills, use of rewards and punishments, and pupil participation, and four outcome measures (absenteeism, behaviour in school, academic attainment, and delinquency), while controlling for intake characteristics of parental occupation and academic attainment. School delinquency rate was primarily related to intake, higher delinquency schools having a significantly lower intake of high ability pupils. The remaining outcome measures were relatively unaffected by intake, but all four outcome variables were significantly correlated at the aggregate (i.e. school) level, and despite being most strongly predicted by intake, delinquency was significantly associated with the following process variables: high autonomy of teachers in planning their courses, tendency of teachers to teach only their own subject, varying rather than group-based disciplinary standards, frequent use of "lines" and extra work as punishment, infrequent use of praise for pupils' work, lack of expectations that pupils will look after their own resources, and low stability of pupil peer groups.

This study has been criticised for its atheoretical selection of process variables (see Graham, 1988), and the findings do not point to any immediately obvious social psychological implications. Nevertheless, it would appear that while the delinquency-proneness of a school's intake influences its delinquency rate, some school features may affect the progression to delinquency. Findings from other studies are also suggestive. For example, from participant observation in a single secondary school, Hargreaves (1980) hypothesised that some forms of streaming facilitated the formation of a delinquency-prone subculture. Also, Reynolds (1976) noted that high delinquency schools tended to be coercive and rigid in their discipline, while low delinquency schools were more likely to negotiate a "truce", in which certain rules, such as those against smoking or out of school behaviour, were not rigidly enforced.

Hargreaves (1980) integrates these various findings in an attempt to outline the salient features of the high delinquency school. He notes that there is a complex interaction in which the ethos or climate of a school, its social organisation, and interactions at classroom level influence each other, and that a school's delinquency level may be the unintended outcome of policy decisions attempting to deal with academic reputation and school order. The "typical" high delinquency school, he suggests, is located in a relatively disadvantaged neighbourhood. While school selection or parental choice may result in the "creaming off" of more able pupils, more important is the *belief* of staff that pupils are of low ability, the effect being low staff commitment and high staff turnover.

Against this background, the critical policy decisions relate to streaming of both pupils and staff, and the way in which the school enforces its authority. First, a flexible system of streaming in which pupils are regularly promoted or demoted according to academic attainment increasingly segregates the most and least able. In contrast to a stable streaming system, which creates a relatively heterogeneous peer group, a flexible system more readily produces a polarisation between a delinquency-prone subculture in the lower stream and an academic subculture ("snobs" and "swots") in the upper stream. It also more obviously labels some pupils as failures and deviants. Second, this polarisation is exacerbated when staff are streamed so that "poorer" quality teachers are assigned to lower streams. Such staff are more likely to have negative expectations of their pupils, and when allowed to impose rules, are likely to be "deviance provocative", or coercive in attempts to control the class. Strict enforcement of rules which pupils do not recognise as legitimate, such as those against choice of dress, enhances the "status deprivation" of lower stream youths by denying them the adult status to which they aspire, thus increasing their opposition to the school.

Hargreaves acknowledges that this process is speculative, and evidence in support remains fragmentary (Graham, 1988). There are however some relevant findings on the effects of streaming, labelling, and teacher disciplinary practices which Hargreaves identifies as critical. First, streaming is not consistently associated with delinquency. Finlayson and Loughran (1976) found that pupils in higher streams were more oriented towards educational goals in both high and low delinquency schools, but delinquents predominated in the lower streams only in the low delinquency schools. While some American research points to a facilitating effect of academic streaming, or tracking, on delinquency, Wiatrowski et al. (1982) were unable to confirm this in a longitudinal study of self-reported delinquency.

There is also some evidence that the labelling of pupils as deviant is associated with delinquency. In a longitudinal study of American high school students, Elliott and Voss (1974) found higher levels of self-reported delinquency in those who subsequently dropped out of school, but the delinquency of dropouts declined after they left, suggesting that antisocial behaviour was influenced by the "failure role" imposed by the school. They proposed that a combination of educational failure and response of the school to it determines antisocial outcomes. This view receives support from Menard and Morse (1984), who found that perceived negative labelling in school and association with delinquent peers accounted for substantially more of the variance in the self-reported delinquency of 13 year olds than IQ and academic performance. School performance has also been found to be related to teacher expectancies, indicating that differential treatment of those of low ability can have significant effects on behaviour (Jussim, 1986).

Teacher disciplinary practices have received more attention in the context of classroom behaviour than of delinquency, but given the correlation between disruptive behaviour in school and delinquency outside it, such practices may have an indirect effect on delinquency (Graham, 1988). More coercive discipline in high delinquency schools is suggested by the finding that pupils in such schools perceived their teachers to be more authoritarian in their use of power (Finlayson and Loughran, 1976). Studies of behaviour modification in the classroom also highlight the role of teacher management skills in promoting or controlling disruptive behaviour. Graham (1988), for example, notes evidence that effective rule enforcement involves a punishment regime in which sanctions are systematic, predictable, and immediately and consistently applied by caring teachers, a pattern resembling an authoritative parental style. Again, teacher expectancies may be critical. Teachers readily form expectations of the future competence of their pupils, and treat them differently depending on whether they expect high or low attainment (Jussim, 1986). Pupils for whom teachers form low expectations are particularly likely to be criticised for failure, praised less for success, and given less emotional support.

There is, then, suggestive evidence that school processes which "marginalise" certain pupils can facilitate a drift to delinquency. Conversely, some school processes may inhibit this progression. This undoubtedly reflects complex interactions of school processes with the attributes of pupils themselves. However, how much difference schools make to the risk of delinquency compared with earlier predisposing factors in the person and the family remains unknown. The psychological mechanisms mediating the effects of school on delinquency are also unclear. Hargreaves' analysis would suggest that delinquency is engendered by hostility to the school's frustration of adult status, which gains support from an anti-school culture. Others propose that school failure lowers self-esteem, which is restored by gaining the approval of a deviant peer group (see Chapter 8). It is also likely that much disruptive behaviour in school is motivated by stimulation seeking in the face of academic demands which are increasingly irrelevant and boring to certain pupils (Graham, 1988).

The peer group

Whatever the nature of the aversion to school, peer support is assumed to be a critical determinant of delinquent outcomes. Numerous studies find that one of the strongest predictors of delinquency among adolescents is the delinquency of close friends, and delinquent acts among juveniles are typically committed in groups. In a study of court appearances in Maryland, for example, Aultman (1980) found that about two thirds of offences had been committed with others, mainly in small groups of two or three. However, group offending was more pronounced for nonviolent than for violent crimes (65% versus 43%), and solitary offending predominates among adult offenders (Zimring, 1981). In the Cambridge study, offending with others, including brothers, was also more common among younger delinquents, and co-offenders tended to live close to each other and to the location of offences (Farrington and West, 1990). This association of delinquency with group processes is held to reflect a more general shift of influence from parents to peers with the onset of adolescence. However, as with family and school correlates, a causal effect is not firmly established. Not only is there uncertainty about how delinquent groups are formed, there is also disagreement about how far such groups affect the propensities of their members to engage in criminal acts.

Subcultural theories propose that the delinquent peer group directly causes delinquency. The formation of delinquent friendships is seen as an outcome of the availability of delinquent subcultures in the neighbourhood, this being the dominant influence on friendships for many adolescents. Hargreaves' analysis of school influences is a variant of this view (Hargreaves, 1980), although the evidence for anti-school, delinquency-prone subcultures is equivocal (Graham, 1988). Hargreaves also echoes strain theory in suggesting that "status-deprivation" provides both the motivation for an anti-school orientation and a focus for group formation, but different processes are proposed by other investigators. Gold (1978), for example, suggests that the discrepancy between scholastic aspirations and achievement is associated with rejection by the school and lowered self-esteem. Antisocial behaviour is self-presentation conveying a message of defiance, which is rewarded by peers with similar problems.

Patterson (1986), however, argues that peer rejection of aggressive and socially unskilled youths provides an impetus for the latter to affiliate with peers of similar status, and association with deviant peers has been found to be significantly correlated with social skill deficits (Snyder, Dishion and Patterson, 1986), and with peer rejection and academic failure in preadolescent and early adolescent boys (Dishion et al., 1991). Also consistent are findings that children rejected by their peers in school are more aggressive and disruptive, and both rejected and aggressive children are more likely to have later adjustment problems, including criminal involvement (Parker and Asher, 1987).

However, if aggressive children are socially isolated and unskilled, their peer group relations would be expected to be tenuous, which seems inconsistent with the assumed role of the peer group in delinquency. A self-report study of friendship and delinquency by Giordano, Cernkovich and Pugh (1986) questions whether delinquents are unskilled in forming friendships. They found that the most delinquent were not social isolates, and appeared to be capable of establishing and maintaining friendships, while the more conforming youths tended to be least attached to their friends. Others find that although aggressive children are less popular with their peers, they are not social isolates, and tend to form friendships with other aggressive children (Cairns et al., 1988). Hodgins and McCoy (1989) also observed that rejected but nonaggressive children were more deficient in their social interactions than those who were rejected but aggressive. The relationships of rejection, aggression, and interactional skills to delinquent group formation therefore require further clarification.

Social learning analyses do not assume a delinquent subculture, but nevertheless propose that the peer group facilitates the acquisition, initiation, and maintenance of delinquent behaviour through modelling and reinforcement by peer approval. A delinquent outcome therefore depends on the extent to which deviant peers control the adolescent's sources of reinforcement, relative to parents or conforming peers. This differential control is implied by findings that delinquents have delinquent friends, spend more time with them, and engage in more peer oriented leisure activities such as dating, hanging around the streets, or riding in cars (Hirschi, 1969; Agnew and Peterson, 1989). Some studies also find that delinquents report observing deviant behaviour by liked peers, who provide social approval for such behaviour (Akers et al., 1979; see also Chapter 4). The finding that specific kinds of delinquent behaviour reported by delinquents are closely correlated with similar behaviour reported by delinquent friends is also consistent with direct modelling effects (Conger, 1976).

However, where subcultural theories assume that adolescents are passively recruited into delinquent groups, which then socialise them into delinquency, social learning theory proposes active selection of similar companions on the basis of personal attributes. Thus, those who select unsocialised companions are already likely to be unsocialised as a result of earlier training (Bandura and

Walters, 1963; Patterson, 1986; Dishion et al., 1991). This is consistent with the traditional view that interpersonal attraction depends on perceived similarities in attitudes and behaviour. Evidence that delinquent groups are both selected by individuals and socialise their members into deviant behaviour is provided by a longitudinal study of Kandel (1978), who examined the degree of similarity in self-reported marijuana use, political orientation, educational aspirations, and delinquency in adolescent friendship dyads. Prior similarity as a determinant of interpersonal attraction was indicated by the finding that friendship pairs which subsequently dissolved were less similar than pairs who later formed friendships. Friendship pairs which were stable tended to increase their similarity over time, suggesting a further process of mutual influence.

Some investigators, however, argue that the peer group makes little difference to delinquency-proneness, which is already established prior to group formation. Glueck and Glueck (1950) suggested that delinquent peer groups were the result of the association of "birds of a feather", and in his original formulation of control theory, Hirschi (1969) also proposed that deviant peers were relatively incidental to delinquency. The critical factors were weak bonds of attachment and commitment to family, school and peers, which left the adolescent "free to deviate", whether alone or with others. However, Hirschi found that having delinquent peers increased the level of delinquency, even in those with strong bonds to the family, and he acknowledged that control theory underestimated the influence of the peer group.

The denial of peer group influence by control theory reflects the assumption that it is unnecessary to explain the motivation for delinquency, since the strength of the bonds to the conventional order is the primary predictor of deviance. Linden and Hackler (1973), however, demonstrated that an interaction between conventional bonds and those to deviant peers determined the level of self-reported delinquency. Highest levels of delinquency were shown by those with weak attachments to parents and conventional peers, and strong attachments to deviant peers, those with strong bonds to parents and conventional peers and weak bonds to deviant peers reporting the lowest levels. These results are more consistent with a social learning analysis, which proposes that the motivation for delinquency is not inherent or constant, but rather depends on which group provides social reinforcement (Conger, 1976; Elliott, Huizinga and Ageton, 1985).

In their integration of strain, control, and social learning theories, Elliott et al. (1985) argue that the development of strong bonds to deviant peers is the most direct and proximate cause of delinquent behaviour and its maintenance. This is facilitated by weak bonding to conventional others, which is in turn influenced by conditions of strain, inadequate socialisation, and social disorganisation. Their longitudinal study of self-reported delinquency supports the model, indicating that the effects of strain and control variables are indirect, and mediated by their influence on the formation of deviant peer attachments. Their results are therefore consistent with previous evidence that deviant peers influence delinquent behaviour, but that some adolescents are more susceptible to recruitment to delinquent groups as a result of inadequate socialisation, and frustrations experienced in the family and at school.

However, while this study appears to clarify the role of the peer group in delinquency, two questions remain unanswered. The first is how far the peer group is uniformly necessary or sufficient in promoting adolescent delinquency. As was noted earlier, a substantial minority of delinquents are solitary offenders, and Elliott et al. (1985) found that their model accounted for less of the variance in serious offending and hard drug use than in general delinquency and marijuana use. While the peer group may therefore provide the most frequent avenue to delinquency, it may not be the major influence for all offences or all offenders. Second, if those who participate in delinquent groups are already delinquency-prone, how far does the peer group contribute anything to the *learning* of delinquency, as opposed to merely facilitating the *performance* of delinquent acts? As Gottfredson and Hirschi (1990) suggest, the peer group may facilitate the commission of *crimes*, but a criminal propensity is already likely to be established by the time of adolescence.

EMPLOYMENT AND MARRIAGE

The fall in the crime rate following the secondary school years correlates with the transition from adolescence to adulthood. It is commonly suggested that this is a period of maturational "reform" for delinquents, facilitated by changing relationships. Thus, entry into the labour force and marriage may not only reduce influence from the earlier peer group, but also increase commitment to the conventional order. Conversely, failure to find work may perpetuate criminogenic influences, while loss of employment may create financial pressures facilitating criminal behaviour.

Unemployment rates are typically highest among groups with the highest rates of delinquency, such as school leavers and those living in urban slums, but the causal influence of unemployment on criminal behaviour remains disputed. Psychological effects of unemployment include depression, anxiety and apathy, perhaps because of reduced self-esteem or loss of perceived control over outcomes, but these depend on age and position in the workforce. Jackson and Warr (1984), for example, found that unemployed men had higher scores than the employed on the General Health Questionnaire, a measure of psychological dysfunction. However, the impact was less for those who had only recently left school, and greater for those with strong commitment to work. Financial stress was also a significant, though less potent mediator.

Whether such effects facilitate criminal behaviour among the unemployed is unclear, but a link between employment and crime is anticipated by traditional criminological theories. Strain theory predicts that lack of job opportunities produces frustration, and increases the attraction of criminal pursuits, while control theory sees regular employment as necessary to strengthen the social bond by increasing the "stakes" in conformity. As well as affecting the propensity for criminal behaviour at the individual level, labour market conditions may also have an indirect effect on the crime rate through affecting community controls. In this way, high unemployment may increase criminal activities both among the employed and among those out of work (Allan and Steffensmeier, 1989). Economic analyses employing a rational choice model also assume that low availability of conventional employment is a "market" factor which will increase crime as an alternative source of material gain (Palmer, 1977).

However, evidence for an association of unemployment with crime rates at the aggregate level is inconclusive. Allan and Steffensmeier (1989) suggest that there are other critical features of the labour market in addition to the level of employment, and that these will not affect all age groups or all types of crime equally. They analysed relationships of UCR arrest rates for four property crimes to several indices of labour market conditions for juveniles and young adults. Higher arrest rates were associated with job *availability* (level of unemployment) only among juveniles. For young adults, the significant factor affecting arrest rates was the *quality* of employment (low pay, fewer full time jobs). For those leaving school, then, lack of work itself may increase the attractiveness of criminal alternatives, while for young adults, work with poor rewards and prospects reduces the stakes in conformity.

Evidence for a direct effect of unemployment on criminal behaviour at the individual level is also equivocal. Elliott and Voss (1974) found a slight reduction in self-reported delinquency among school dropouts who obtained regular work and married, and in the Cambridge study, boys between age 15 and 18 committed more offences, primarily involving financial gain, during periods of unemployment than when employed (West, 1982). There is also some evidence that unemployment payments to released prisoners reduce recidivism (Dale, 1976; Rauma and Berk, 1987). However, while these findings suggest that the experience of unemployment may increase criminal motivation, or weaken controls, unemployment may arise through choice or personal characteristics. For example, delinquents are not only likely to leave school with fewer skills, but also to be hedonistic and less interested in stable employment (Gottfredson and Hirschi 1990). Delinquents in the Cambridge study were, in fact, more likely to have a history of job instability by the age of 18. At age 32, those with convictions tended to be in lower paid jobs, and to have had long periods of unemployment, the most persistent offenders having the least satisfactory employment records (Farrington and West, 1990). Thornberry and Farnworth (1982) also found that among young adults, both official and self-reported delinquency were related to job instability, but not to occupational level or income. Unemployment, then, may influence the commission of crimes, but may itself be influenced by criminal propensity.

Data from the Cambridge study also suggest that a simple unidirectional effect of marriage on criminal behaviour is unlikely. Knight, Osborn and West (1977) found no differences in official or self-reported delinquency at age 21 between those who married and those who stayed single. However, the marriages of delinquents were more likely to have been precipitated by pregnancy, and most of those who were cohabiting rather than married had a delinquent history. Subsequent interviews at age 24 revealed that the effects of marriage were offset by the tendency of delinquents to marry delinquent females, and those who did so were more likely to obtain further convictions (West, 1982). By the time the sample was aged 32, more of those with criminal records had been divorced or separated, or had a history of conflict with their spouse or cohabitee (Farrington and West, 1990). A stable marriage may therefore have some effect on criminal behaviour, whether by reducing contacts with delinquent peers or opportunities for crime, or by increasing conformity. However, the stability of a marriage appears to be influenced by the criminality of the partners.

PROTECTIVE FACTORS

Conditions correlating with delinquency are regarded as risk variables insofar as exposure to them appears to increase the likelihood of criminality. Since many individuals exposed to poverty, family discord, delinquent schools, or whatever, do not become delinquent, there is some interest in identifying what distinguishes those who are *resilient* in the face of adverse circumstances from those who are also vulnerable but succumb. Protection from risk may come from personal dispositions, relationships, social support systems, or events, which interact with risk variables to make a delinquent outcome less likely (Rutter, 1987; Werner, 1989). Female gender, for example, is clearly protective in this sense, while stable employment may protect against the continuation of criminal career in young adults who are delinquency-prone.

Only a few studies have so far attempted to identify factors which counteract or reduce the risk of delinquency among individuals growing up in discordant families with criminal members or in high delinquency neighbourhoods. Dispositional variables which may be protective include intellectual abilities, strong achievement motivation, and favourable self-esteem (see Chapter 8), and temperament factors may also be relevant. In the Cambridge study, those at risk for delinquency but who remained unconvicted were more likely to have few or no friends at age 8, and subsequently tended to remain solitary (Farrington et al., 1988). The protective processes are unclear, but seem likely to include less frequent exposure to delinquent peers or opportunities, since these isolated individuals rarely went out in the evenings.

Supportive relationships may also reduce the impact of risk factors by restricting opportunities for contact with delinquents, and by reinforcing commitment to conformity. In discordant families, for example, maternal affection reduces the criminogenic effects of parental aggression, permissiveness, and disciplinary inconsistency (McCord, 1986), and positive evaluation by the mother of the child at age 10 also distinguished the more socially successful vulnerable children in the Cambridge study (Farrington et al., 1988). Again, in families with a delinquent child, nondelinquents have greater involvement than their sibs with adults, clubs, and Sunday school (Reitsma-Street et al., 1985). The protective influence of a significant adult was also identified by Ross and Glaser (1973). They compared black and Mexican-

American adults from ghetto areas who were in steady employment and had avoided trouble with the law with those from the same neighbourhood who were unsuccessful in these respects. They identified differences between the groups in terms of allegiance to two contrasting subcultures, one emphasising values of achievement, work, and mainstream society, the other a street culture of toughness, violence and absence of long-term goals. Interview data suggested that the significant determinant of membership in the former subculture was an effective parent, or in some cases an adult outside the home. Similar relationship factors differentiate mothers at risk for child abuse who do not abuse their children from those who do (Egeland, Jacovitz and Sroufe, 1988).

Rutter (1987) notes that many protective processes involve key "turning points" in people's lives which open up new opportunities, such as the effect of moving home. Buikhuisen and Hoekstra (1973), for example, found that delinquents released from prison had lower recidivism rates if they moved away from their original home area. Similarly, boys in the Cambridge study who moved away from inner London subsequently had fewer convictions than those who remained, and also reduced their self-reported delinquency (West, 1982). The environmental changes may have removed the boys from the influence of delinquent peers, although they may also have reduced the opportunities for criminal acts.

However, whether such events constitute a significant turning point in a person's life trajectory is likely to depend on the reciprocal influence of personal attributes and social variables supporting the development of a particular life path (Bandura, 1982). Bidirectional influences of this kind are indicated in Werner's longitudinal study of children on the Hawaiian island of Kauai who became competent adults despite exposure to high risk early family environments (Werner and Smith, 1982; Werner, 1989). Compared with those who became delinquent by age 18, the more resilient children were more often first born, active and socially responsive as infants, and already appeared more confident and independent by the age of two. They tended to have greater affection and support from parents, but this partly depended on their capacity to elicit positive responses from their social environment. They also tended to have complementary role models, fathers being modelling influences for girls, and the resilient children were more likely to display androgynous sex role-taking. As adults, they were more achievement oriented, displayed an internal locus of control, and were more likely to be in skilled employment. It was also found that delinquents who did not go on to be adult criminals had been identified as less troublesome at school, consistent with findings from the Cambridge study, and were more likely to be from an intact family unit.

While studies of protective factors shed some light on the developmental processes contributing to optimal adjustment, they have yet to further understanding of the development of criminality, and the search for them reflects the positivist concern with independent "causes". Rutter (1987) and Werner (1989) emphasise that what is important is the *interaction* between the protective factor and risk variables, but the research to date has not been guided by any clear theoretical framework from which either protective factors or interactive processes might be selected from the large number of possibilities. Thus, McCord (1986) reports interactions between family variables correlating with criminality which showed that some risk variables have little effect when other risk factors are absent. For example, lack of maternal affection has less impact when the mother is self-confident and consistent in discipline, but maternal affection reduces the effects of inconsistent discipline. Since the factors identified as protective are simply the opposite of risk, the demonstration of such interactions does little to advance explanation.

The notions of "protection" and "risk", which reflect a disease metaphor, are also misleading, since they imply that different psychological processes govern socially undesirable and socially valued outcomes. We do not, for example, inquire about what "protects" against the "risk" of career success. In fact, the question of what causes some individuals from an apparently criminogenic background to become lawabiding is simply part of the more general question of what factors influence people's life paths. As Bandura (1982) notes, these may often be chance encounters which are not predictable in advance.

Chapter 8

Personal Attributes of Offenders

INTRODUCTION

The performance of criminal acts clearly depends on their proximal antecedents and the situational contexts in which they occur, but must also be understood in terms of the personal attributes which the actor brings to the situation. This chapter is concerned with individual characteristics which might contribute to criminality as a disposition or readiness to perform such acts. These characteristics include the social and temperament traits of traditional personality research, but person variables also encompass competencies, values, beliefs, and goals emerging from the individual's history, which mediate the effects of new experiences (Alston, 1975; Mischel and Mischel, 1976).

Research on the personality of criminals has employed more than a hundred psychological tests (Waldo and Dinitz, 1967; Arbuthnot, Gordon and Jurkovic, 1987), but while most studies comparing criminal samples with controls on standardised measures have identified significant differences, these have not always been replicated. Some reviewers therefore remain sceptical about whether differences found shed any light on the personal antecedents of crime, and conceptual and methodological shortcomings pervade much of this area of research.

First, many studies have been method-driven, the selection of measurement instruments being dictated more by their availability than by a clear theoretical rationale of what personality variables relate to crime. The MMPI, for example, has been widely used in this context, but while it has some empirical utility in distinguishing offenders (Gearing, 1979), it emphasises psychopathology rather than personality traits, and was not standardised for use with criminals (Dietrich and Berger, 1978). A second problem is the selection of subjects, and the definition of "criminal". There has been an overemphasis on incarcerated criminals, who may not be representative of offenders generally, or on groups selected by type of offence, which does not always reliably index a disposition to engage in that kind of behaviour. A single crime of extreme violence, for example, does not necessarily indicate a persisting violent tendency (Chapter 9), and Holland, Holt and Beckett (1982) suggest that only property offending shows a "career" pattern for which dispositional correlates might be identified. Again, discretionary influences in the criminal justice system undermine the reliability of "recidivism" as an index of persistent offending (Repucci and Clingempeel, 1978; Hollin and Henderson, 1984).

A further problem is the implicit assumption in many studies that offenders are homogeneous. Despite the debate about specialisation among criminals, and the persisting interest in antisocial personality, the evidence indicates that offenders are heterogeneous in personality (Chapter 3). The assumption of a distinct "criminal personality" is therefore questionable, and comparison of unselected offenders with nonoffenders is likely to be a strategy with limited payoffs. It is also unlikely that specific traits in isolation are significant mediators of offending, but investigations of interactions between person variables remain the exception rather than the rule.

Research on some of the more theoretically significant personal attributes was discussed in Chapter 5, but individual correlates of crime continue to be sought in the context of less systematic or more specific theories, or through the use of multi-trait inventories, notably the MMPI (Gearing, 1979) and CPI (Laufer, Skoog and Day, 1982). This chapter presents a selective review, focusing on concepts of relatively enduring or recent interest.

INTELLIGENCE, ATTAINMENT AND COGNITIVE FUNCTIONING

Intellectual functioning

Intellectual ability has been of continuing interest in psychological criminology since the early studies of Goddard (1914), and is considered a critical factor in development in cognitive–developmental and social learning theories. IQ tests do not capture the full range of cognitive skills, but political debate surrounding their use in educational selection has tended to obscure issues of their validity. The available evidence indicates that they measure significant aspects of problem-solving skills, which are relatively stable, though not entirely immutable individual characteristics (Weinberg, 1989).

Surveys in the early part of the century suggested that a third or more of offenders were feebleminded, according to test criteria, and it was assumed that low intelligence contributed directly to antisocial behaviour through its effects on the learning and understanding of moral rules. This figure shrank with improvements in test standardisation, and applying a criterion of IQ 70 to Binet data collected in a large number of studies, Zeleny (1933) estimated that the ratio of feebleminded offenders to feebleminded nonoffenders was 1.8:1.

More recent estimates of the proportion of offenders who are mentally retarded continue to indicate that they are an overrepresented minority, although figures vary markedly. Coid (1984), for example, cites figures from surveys of sentenced prisoners ranging from 2% to 45%. However, prevalence estimates from penal populations must be treated with caution, since they reflect not only local and national policies for diverting mentally retarded offenders to the mental health system, but also variations in criteria and methods of assessment. In a study in Florida, for example, Spruill and May (1988) found that 4% of the prison population obtained IQs of less than 70 on a group intelligence test (Revised Beta) administered to inmates on entry to prison. Subsequent individual testing with the WAIS suggested that only 1% met this criterion of mental retardation, and that group testing of inmates at the time of admission yielded inflated estimates because of temporary anxiety or failure to co-operate.

While offenders with serious mental handicaps pose significant problems of rehabilitation, the conventional but arbitrary cutoff of IQ 70 is of little theoretical relevance in assessing the contribution of intelligence to crime. More significant is the much larger proportion of offenders whose abilities are below average, and although criminologists have tended to dismiss lower scores of delinquents as artefacts of sampling bias or social disadvantage, research consistently indicates a small but significant negative correlation between intellectual level and delinquency. For example, Caplan and Siebert (1964) reviewed IQ data obtained on delinquents dealt with in Cleveland, Ohio, between 1929 and 1963. Mean IQ increased from 80 to 92 following the replacement of the earlier Stanford–Binet by other tests, notably the Wechsler scales, but the latter figure was relatively stable. The authors estimated that almost a half of the delinquents dealt with had an IQ below 90. The Cambridge study also found a disproportionate number of offenders to be of low intelligence. Of those who subsequently became delinquent, 39% had an IQ of less than 90 at age 8, compared with 22% of nondelinquents, while 57% of the recidivists were of below average IQ (West, 1982). Recent studies further suggest that *higher* intelligence is a protective factor against criminal development in those who are at risk for criminality, either through having a criminal father (Kandel et al., 1988), or through child conduct disorder (White, Moffitt and Silva, 1989).

From a comprehensive review of studies comparing delinquents with nondelinquents, Hirschi and Hindelang (1977) concluded that the mean IQ of unselected delinquent samples was about 92, and that the association held when social class and race were statistically controlled. Moffitt et al. (1981) also found a significant negative correlation of 0.2 to 0.3 between intelligence and number of offences in two birth cohorts in Denmark, which remained when social class was partialled out. The suggestion that the lower intelligence of officially adjudicated delinquents simply reflects failure of the less able delinquent to avoid detection and apprehension is contradicted by the finding of a comparable relationship with self-reported delinquency (West, 1982). This holds up whether or not high scorers have been officially detected (Moffitt and Silva, 1988).

Although low scores on global measures of IQ commonly distinguish delinquents, their scores on measures of verbal (V) ability tend to be most discriminating. Since the introduction of the Wechsler scales, it has been a common finding that delinquent males (though not females) produce discrepancies between performance (P) IQ and VIQ in favour of the former, and since PIQ means tend to be only marginally lower than those of nondelinquent samples, the PIQ > VIQ sign has generally been interpreted in terms of deficient verbal skills rather than superior nonverbal abilities. Studies using the WISC-R find sample mean VIQs of delinquents which are typically almost a standard deviation (10 to 12 points) below the general population mean, and suggest that about two thirds of delinquents have some deficiency in verbal ability (Quay, 1987b). A minority of delinquents, however, shows an imbalance in the direction of VIQ > PIQ. Walsh, Petee and Beyer (1987) found that 37% of a male delinquent sample produced a PIQ > VIQ of 9 or more points, and 11% a VIQ > PIQ of similar magnitude. These compared with 26% and 23%, respectively, of a nondelinquent sample. While the underrepresentation of the VIQ > PIQ group in the delinquents suggests that a verbal dominance protects against delinquency, Walsh et al. found that both imbalaced groups had a more frequent involvement in delinquency than delinquents not showing this imbalance.

Some studies suggest that the PIQ > VIQ sign may be particularly discriminating within delinquent populations. Haynes and Bensch (1981), for example, found that 70% of recidivists showed a PIQ dominance on the WISC-R, compared with 42% of nonrecidivist delinquents. Hubble and Groff (1982) also found that delinquents identified as psychopathic or neurotic by Quay's system produced a larger performance dominance than those classified as subcultural. However, the PIQ > VIQ sign has a relatively high base rate in the general population, and has little diagnostic utility in the individual case. A longitudinal survey of a large New Zealand birth cohort by Moffitt and Silva (1987) also revealed that WISC-R VIQ–PIQ discrepancies were only moderately stable between the ages of 7 and 11, and were not associated with factors indicative of brain dysfunction. On the other hand, a large performance dominance was consistently associated with poor academic achievement.

How low intelligence contributes to criminality remains unclear. Quay (1987b) suggests that low verbal ability may contribute directly to antisocial behaviour through limiting the development of higher order cognitive functions, such as verbal self-regulation and social problem solving. A more common view is that the effect is indirect, and dependent on school performance (see below). Intelligence probably also interacts with other personal attributes. Heilbrun (1982), for example, showed that among adult prisoners, history of violent crime was influenced by the interaction of intellectual level with psychopathy. Less intelligent psychopaths were more likely to have a history of impulsive violence, and also lower degrees of empathy, than more intelligent psychopaths or less intelligent nonpsychopaths. It must also be noted that a significant minority of offenders is of above average intelligence. Caplan and Siebert (1964), for example, estimated that 9% of delinquents in their survey had IQs higher than 110. The more "gifted" offender has received relatively little attention in research, although there is some evidence that both male delinquents (Tennent and

Gath, 1975) and female delinquents (Cowie, Cowie and Slater, 1968) of high intelligence are more likely to show psychological abnormalities.

Learning disabilities and educational attainment

In North America, considerable attention has been paid in recent decades to the relation between delinquency and *learning disabilities*. This term is less favoured in Britain, where the notion of learning *difficulties* has come to replace the concept of mental retardation or handicap. Learning disability (LD) refers to a discrepancy between what is expected of a child on the basis of established ability, and actual educational achievements, and it includes cognitive and perceptual-motor problems such as dyslexia, aphasia, or attentional deficits. LDs are widely believed to have a constitutional basis.

Although retrospective prevalence estimates of LDs among delinquents have ranged from 26% to 73% (Zimmerman et al., 1981), a causal link cannot be assumed. In a review of the earlier literature, Murray (1976) observed that although learning *problems* are probably common among delinquents, the prevalence of specific LDs remained unclear as a result of varying definitions of LDs and inadequate sampling of the delinquent population. Zimmerman et al. (1981) assessed discrepancies between measured intelligence and achievement in large and heterogeneous samples of schoolboys and delinquents of both sexes. They found that 18% of the former and 33% of the latter met criteria for LDs, the prevalence being higher in male than in female delinquents. However, LD subjects were not distinguished from those without LDs on self-report delinquency measures, indicating an absence of a direct relationship between LDs and antisocial behaviour.

Recent work emphasises that LD subsumes heterogeneous disorders which are unlikely to have a single aetiology. Rourke (1988), for example, has shown that there are varying forms of LD which are differentially related to both academic achievement and social disturbance. LDs involving nonverbal deficits are more clearly associated with problems of social adjustment than LDs involving primarily psycholinguistic skills. Meltzer, Roditi and Fenton (1986) also showed that a fine-grained analysis of LDs can identify different patterns of educational and cognitive functioning, which are not uniformly shown by delinquents. In a comparison of delinquents, LD adolescents, and normally functioning schoolchildren, which examined learning styles and error patterns across several educational skills, they found that 14% of delinquents had a profile similar to that of the LD group, while a third were similar to controls. Some forms of LD may therefore be associated with antisocial development in some delinquents.

Educational underattainment correlates with antisocial behaviour in the early school years as well as with later delinquency in several studies (Elliott and Voss, 1974; Feshbach and Price, 1984; Dishion et al., 1984), and it has generally been assumed that the influence of both intelligence and LDs is an indirect one mediated by poor school performance (Murray, 1976; Rutter and

Giller, 1983). A common view is that the experience of school failure leads to negative self-esteem or hostile attitudes to school, which in turn leads to association with other "problem" children, and hence greater opportunity for delinquent behaviour. Control theory, for example, sees educational failure as promoting negative attitudes to school, and hence weaker attachment to the societal values represented by the school (Hirschi and Hindelang, 1977). Consistent with this is the finding of Austin (1978) that the relation between intelligence and self-reported stealing largely depended on negative attitudes to teachers.

There are, nevertheless, other explanations for the association of intellectual functioning with delinquency. It may, for example, reflect the influence of a third factor, such as class, family, or temperament characteristics. However, Hirschi and Hindelang (1977) found that the effect of IQ remains after controlling for social class and race. Similarly, McGarvey et al. (1981) found that, although social class of parents contributed indirectly to criminality through its influence on educational performance, intelligence exerted an independent effect. The same appears to apply to family influences. Offord (1982), for example, found that there was no difference in IQ or school performance between delinquents and their nondelinquent sibs, and that delinquents failing at school were more likely to come from disorganised families. He suggests that both antisocial behaviour and poor school performance are a consequence of family disorganisation. Others, however, find that delinquents are less intelligent than their sibs (Healy and Bronner, 1936), and in the Cambridge study the effect of intelligence on later delinquency was independent of family factors (West, 1982).

In the Cambridge study, however, the effect of intelligence disappeared when "troublesomeness" at age 8 to 10 was taken into account, suggesting that both later failure at school and delinquency may be attributed primarily to deviant temperament, and several studies support this. Stattin and Magnusson (1989), for example, found that after partialling out intelligence and socioeconomic status, teacher ratings of aggression in 10 year olds remained significantly correlated with later delinquency. Patterson's work also suggests a direction of effect from antisocial behaviour to school failure and delinquency (Patterson et al., 1989). A recent longitudinal study by Tremblay et al. (1992) not only emphasises the influence of deviant personal attributes, but also raises some doubts about the significance of school performance. They found that disruptive behaviour of boys at age 7 was associated with both poorer academic achievement at age 10 and self-reported delinquency at age 14, but path analysis indicated that academic achievement was incidental to later delinquency. Academic achievement, however, mediated the relation between disruptive behaviour at age 7 and personality traits associated with delinquency at age 14.

While IQ was not measured in the latter study, the findings are consistent with the suggestion that its effects on later delinquency may be mediated by temperament factors, and this is supported by the 22-year follow-up study of Huesmann, Eron and Yarmel (1987). They found that IQ was related to peer nominations of aggression at age 8, but adult intellectual achievement was more strongly predicted by childhood aggression than was adult aggression (including criminal behaviour) by childhood IQ. Huesmann et al. suggest that low intellectual ability may contribute to child aggression by impairing the development of social problem-solving skills, but that aggressiveness subsequently has a continuing effect on academic achievement. This does not exclude later additional effects of educational achievement on delinquency, nor the role of differential treatment of some children by the school system (Menard and Morse, 1984; see also Chapter 7). It does, however, emphasise that the relation of IQ and school performance to delinquency is dependent on earlier developmental factors.

SELF CONTROL AND IMPULSIVITY

The ability to delay or inhibit a response is of concern in all analyses of development and learning, and has been examined variously under the headings of impulse control, self control, delay of gratification, or tolerance for frustration. Since criminal acts frequently involve the satisfaction of immediate needs at the risk of longer term aversive consequences, criminals are commonly assumed to be deficient in control or delay functions (Wilson and Herrnstein, 1985; Gottfredson and Hirschi, 1990). Impulsivity is also central to clinical concepts of psychopathic personality, and features of the "antisocial lifestyle" found to be associated with both official and self-reported delinquency—such as heavy drinking, smoking, gambling, sexual precocity, and drug abuse (Chapter 2)—can be construed in similar terms (Farrington, 1992). The childhood disruptive and aggressive behaviour which precedes later delinquency can also be understood as a manifestation of lack of impulse control.

Impulse control refers to both a psychological *process* and a generalised style or *trait* of impulsivity, but the concept is only loosely tied to observable behaviour. Since it implies that there is an impulse to be controlled, an act said to manifest lack of control may simply be the expression of a strong impulse. An "impulse", however, is merely a circular inference of the presumed inner cause of some behaviour, and as Skinner (1953) observed, the notion of "self control" begs the question of "who is controlling what?" Moreover, everyday descriptions of an act, or person, as impulsive depend on prior history and social context. Someone's crime, for example, may be said to have been "impulsive" simply because they were previously of "good character".

In psychological and psychiatric use, impulse control is similarly a vaguely defined term, which is highly dependent on theoretical presuppositions (Pulkinnen, 1986). In psychodynamic theory, delay of gratification is a function of ego control, in which instinctual impulses are restrained through fantasy and planning (Singer, 1955). Inadequate control may be manifest both in primary process thinking and unrestrained motor discharge of tension. It may take the form of specific symptoms, such as pyromania or kleptomania, or a generalised impulsive disposition of character disorder. Shapiro (1965), however, rejects the instinct model, and sees impulsivity as a style of speedy and unplanned responding, which is related to cortical processing, and which is expressed in cognition, affect, and overt behaviour.

Learning theorists, however, regard self regulation as acquired behaviour which is context-specific. Skinner (1953) analyses self control in terms of behaviour emitted by the individual which arranges the contingencies governing another response. The controlling response is itself under the control of environmental contingencies, and for behaviourists, self control is ultimately situational control (Stuart, 1972). For social learning theorists, on the other hand, self regulation is also under the control of attentional processes, standards of self reinforcement, and outcome expectancies (Lopatto and Williams, 1976; Kanfer, 1980). Kanfer, for example, defines self control as a case of self management under conditions of response conflict. The person engages in behaviour that previously had a lower probability than that of a more tempting behaviour, consequent on a commitment or intention to select the delayed alternative. A further approach to impulse control comes from cognitive–behavioural therapists who draw on Russian concepts of the verbal regulation of behaviour through "inner speech" (Meichenbaum, 1977; Kendall, 1984).

The focus here is on evidence for an impulsive disposition in criminals, but it should be apparent that this is a multifaceted concept. A large number of tests has been developed to measure lack of impulse control as a trait or style (see Pulkinnen, 1986). These variously assess psychomotor speed and accuracy, delay of reinforcement, or choice decision time, and impulsivity appears in different guises in most multi-trait personality inventories. Psychodynamic influences are apparent in some measures which emphasise control over the arousal and expression of anger and aggression. More commonly, however, trait measures assess personal tempo, or the tendency to react to events with speedy decision or action, and without deliberation of future consequences, as exemplified by the inventory question; "Do you often act on the spur of the moment without stopping to think?" As S. B. G. Eysenck and H. J. Eysenck (1978) note, this describes a narrow trait, and they suggest that a broader conception should include traits such as risk-taking and liveliness. However, this does not necessarily encompass emotional arousal and expression. These conceptual ambiguities are reflected in disagreement about whether impulsivity is a primary trait or a higher-order dimension (Chapter 5).

Self-report inventories

The *Ma* (Hypomania) scale of the MMPI is commonly interpreted as an index of impulsivity or "acting out", and many items of the SC (Self Control) scale of Gough's CPI come from the MMPI. An MMPI impulsivity (IM) scale was also derived by Blackburn (1971b) from factor analysis of these scales, the content reflecting lack of moral restraint, easily aroused anger, and need for excitement. Comparisons of offenders with nonoffenders generally show that the only MMPI scale which discriminates significantly is *Pd*, which contains few items related to impulse control. As was noted earlier, however (Chapter 3), the combined elevation of scales 4 (*Pd*) and 9 (*Ma*) is associated with primary psychopathy, and offender samples are generally found to obtain their highest mean scores on these scales and on scale 8 (Schizophrenia), which taps deviant thinking. Two large scale prospective studies showed that adolescents with this pattern of scores were subsequently more likely than those with other score combinations to become official delinquents (Monachesi and Hathaway, 1969). All three scales also correlate with self-reported delinquency, particularly measures of theft, use of soft drugs, and property destruction (Rathus and Siegel, 1980). Impulsivity as measured by *Ma*, then, appears to increase the likelihood of criminality, but only when combined with high scores on *Pd*. The latter may tap the attachment bonds of control theory.

Impulsivity has occupied a significant, though contentious place in Eysenck's theory of criminality (Chapter 5). While Gillan (1965) found no difference between female delinquents and controls on an early impulsiveness scale, S. B. G. Eysenck and McGurk (1980) found that male delinquents scored higher than controls on a recently developed scale of impulsiveness. This scale also correlates with self-reported delinquency in both male and female Spanish adolescents (Silva, Martorell and Clemente, 1986).

The F (Surgency) scale of Cattell's 16PF (Cattell, Eber and Tatsuoka, 1970) is also regarded as a measure of impulsivity. In a longitudinal study, Kelly and Veldman (1964) compared children who became school dropouts or delinquents with nondeviant children on F scores obtained four years earlier. Both deviant groups had higher F scores. However, delinquents were not differentiated on this scale by Cattell et al. (1970). Saunders, Repucci and Sarata (1973) also found no differences between delinquents and schoolboys on Barratt's Impulsivity scale, or on the Matching Familiar Figures Test, which is held to measure a cognitive style of "reflection–impulsivity".

Impulsivity may contribute to variations in frequency or type of offending. and there are some indications that recidivists are more likely to be impulsive. Gough, Wenk and Rozynko (1965), for example, compared parole-violating and nonviolating delinquents on the MMPI, CPI, and a base expectancy table derived from prior history. The latter yielded the best discrimination, but the *Ma* and CPI SC and *So* scales also discriminated between the two groups. Como (1977) also found that recidivists scored higher on Blackburn's IM than first offenders, and this scale correlated with reoffending by mentally disordered offenders (Black and Spinks, 1985), and with self-reported delinquency within a sample of official delinquents (Renwick and Emler, 1991). Mack (1969), in contrast, obtained no MMPI differences between recidivist and nonrecidivist delinquents, and while Gendreau et al. (1979) found that *So* contributed to the prediction of recidivism, *Ma* was not significant in this respect.

Differences between offenders categorised by offence type have proved elusive. Panton (1958) observed no MMPI differences between six offence categories, although he noted that they all deviated from the normative mean. While Laufer, Johnson and Hogan (1981) found that drug related offenders were more impulsive than murderers on Block's Ego Control scale, which measures psychodynamic concepts of delay and impulse expression, other studies indicate that murderers are heterogeneous on MMPI impulsivity scales (Blackburn, 1971a; McGurk, 1978).

Delay of gratification

One paradigm for the study of self-control is *self-imposed delay of reward*, in which a reward available at some future point in time is preferred to a smaller but immediately available reward. Studies of delay in children indicate that it is a cognitive skill involving the ability to deploy attention to minimise the arousing properties of the desirable reward, and which tends to be optimal by the age of 9 to 10 (Mischel, Shoda and Rodriguez, 1989). Delay also depends on the formation of contingency rules specifying the conditions under which self-reinforcement is appropriate, and therefore exhibits variability within individuals and between situations. However, it also shows significant generality and stability over time (Mischel, 1984), and Mischel sees delay and impulsivity as contrasting trait patterns. More consistent delay is associated with sustained attention, higher intelligence and cognitive development, and resistance to temptation, and it is more typical of middle class and achievement oriented groups. Conversely, preference for immediate reward is related to a present-oriented time focus, lower socioeconomic status, and membership in groups in which achievement needs are low.

Mischel suggests that preference for immediate reward contributes to delinquency and psychopathy, and this was supported in a study of delinquents in Trinidad (Mischel, 1961). Reformatory school boys more frequently opted for immediate reward than did secondary school boys, although almost half the delinquents chose delayed reward. Variations in preference for delay of reward within delinquents were noted by Roberts et al. (1974), who found that recidivists were more likely than nonrecidivists to have chosen immediate reward when tested prior to release.

Psychomotor impulsivity

Impulse control is often measured by the degree of care or accuracy during task performance, or motor inhibition. For example, Kelly and Veldman (1964) found that future delinquent and dropout schoolchildren were more speedy and inaccurate on simple tasks of motor production. Most widely used has been the Porteus Mazes (Porteus, 1959). This paper-and-pencil test requires the solution of a series of visual mazes, and yields a Test Quotient (TQ) and a Qualitative error (Q) score. TQ correlates moderately with spatial skill, and is held to measure foresight and planning ability. Q reflects carelessness and rule-breaking within the test, and has hence been construed as a measure of impulsivity.

Porteus summarised studies revealing highly significant differences on Q between workers exhibiting disciplinary problems and those considered "satisfactory", delinquents and nondelinquents, and adult criminals and noncriminals. TQ was less discriminating. These findings on offenders have been replicated in a number of studies (Riddle and Roberts, 1977). O'Keefe (1975), however, criticised this research for failing to control for institutionalisation. He found no differences between young institutionalised delinquents and boys in a children's home, and no relationship of Q score to staff ratings of impulsiveness.

On the other hand, Q score distinguishes within delinquent populations in several studies. Roberts et al. (1974) found that Q significantly predicted recidivism in delinquents, and also correlated with verbal and behavioural measures of delay of reward. Schalling and Rosen (1968) also found that psychopathic offenders, defined by Cleckley's criteria, attained higher Q scores than nonpsychopaths. Negative findings have nevertheless been reported in some studies. Q scores were found to be unrelated to either institutional rule infraction or MMPI impulsivity scores among Borstal boys (Gibbens, 1963) or mentally disordered offenders (Davis, 1974b). Psychopathic criminals, as identified by MMPI patterns, were also found to score *lower* on Q than nonpsychopaths by Sutker, Moan and Swanson (1972).

Gibson (1964) criticised the derivation of the Q score, and devised a Spiral Maze (SM) to measure more homogeneous errors of motor execution. Scores derived are (a) total time to traverse the maze, and (b) errors of touching the sides of the maze or obstacles. With time scores partialled out, errors correlate moderately with Q scores. Gibson regards the test as a measure of risk taking. He found that both delinquents and schoolboys rated as "naughty" by teachers performed the task more quickly and carelessly. Davis (1974b) also found that error scores were significantly related to ratings of institutional nonconformity, but Gillan (1965) observed no differences between female delinquents and controls. Neither of the latter studies found any relation between SM performance and self-report trait measures of impulsivity.

A task resembling the above tests is the Arrow–Dot (AD) subtest of the IES (Impulse, Ego, Superego) test of Dombrose and Slobin (1958), which attempts to operationalise psychodynamic structural concepts. The AD test requires the subject to draw a line to a dot, avoiding various "barriers", and performance is held to symbolise impulse strength, ego control, and superego inhibition. Rankin and Wickoff (1964) found that second offender motor thieves obtained higher impulse scores than college students, but generalisation from this comparison is questionable. Other studies using the AD test have failed to identify any difference between more and less compliant institutionalised delinquents (Saunders et al., 1973).

Time orientation

Delay of gratification is presumed to involve consideration of future consequences, and the experience of time has been examined as an index of impulse control in a number of studies. Impulsive individuals are expected to be more concerned with immediate than with future events, and hence to have a restricted future time perspective. They are also assumed to have a faster "internal clock", and to overestimate the passage of time.

Studies of time estimation in offenders have produced moderately consistent results. Siegman (1966) found that delinquents showed evidence of a faster internal clock than army recruits, as shown by underestimates of the lapse of short periods of time and overestimates of the length of time intervals. Although this contradicted his earlier results, it is consistent with findings on sociopathic patients (Getsinger, 1976).

Delinquents have also been found to have a shorter future time perspective than nondelinquents, as indicated by story completion tasks, or estimates of the closeness in time of significant events, such as getting married or becoming a grandfather (e.g. Stein, Sarbin and Kulik, 1968). This characterises recidivist delinquents in particular (Roberts et al., 1974). However, Landau (1976) suggested that previous research had failed to control for the effects of institutionalisation on time orientation. He found that institutionalisation (imprisonment, military service) had the effect of shortening future time perspective in both delinquents and soldiers, but that future orientation increased with the approach of release.

Despite some negative findings, impulsivity has been found to contribute to delinquent tendencies in several studies, but two problems continue to confound research in this area. The first is the heterogeneity of criminals, and while impulsivity as a temperament trait, preference for immediate reward, careless psychomotor performance, or restricted future time perspective may be significant factors in some groups of offenders, not all criminals display these characteristics. Those rated as "psychopathic" are likely to score highly on inventory measures (Cattell, Eber and Tatsvoka, 1970; Kipnis, 1971), but profile analyses of test data of offenders clearly establish that there are also subgroups who obtain low scores on impulsivity scales (Blackburn, 1975a; 1986; McGurk and McGurk, 1979; Megargee and Bohn, 1979). The second problem is that relationships between different measures of impulse control are in some cases negligible, and factor analytic results suggest that impulsivity does not describe a unitary domain of behaviour (Twain, 1957; Gillan, 1965). This is a reflection of the ambiguities in the concept of impulse control, which has sometimes been observed to be an explanation in need of a phenomenon. More attention seems necessary to the theoretical contexts in which different measures of impulsivity are embedded, and to distinctions between the cognitive, affective, and motivational aspects of this global construct.

ATTITUDES, VALUES, AND BELIEFS

The developing area of *social cognition* represents converging interests of social psychologists and those investigating higher cognitive functioning, and reflects the assumption that social behaviour is the outcome of reciprocal interactions between the individual's cognitive structures and processes and the reactions of others. This approach has also influenced research and intervention with deviant populations, and investigations of social cognition are described in the following sections. Although a somewhat arbitrary division, this section focuses on the content of socially relevant cognitions in offenders. The following section examines sociocognitive processes and skills.

The self concept

While relegated by behaviourism to the status of an epiphenomenon, the self as the subjective experience of a separate "I" or "me" is regarded in several theories as a unifying factor determining both protective and goal seeking behaviour (Wylie, 1968). When used to denote "the total personality", a global and undefined concept of "self" or "ego" can be justifiably criticised as a mystical homunculus, but social cognitive theorists have revived a view of self as an active information-processing structure, or cognitive schema (Greenwald and Pratkanis, 1984; Bandura, 1989). Epstein (1973), for example, uses the metaphor of a scientific theory in describing the *self concept* as a self-theory, whose postulates are continuously validated in the appraisal and seeking out of relevant information. Self concept therefore refers to knowledge and beliefs about oneself, including attitudes of affective regard or *self esteem*. Since the self is generally believed to derive from and mediate social interaction, a deviant self concept may also mediate antisocial behaviour (Wells, 1978).

Self attitudes are held to supply organisation and direction to behaviour, but there remains disagreement about the motivational processes involved. One view is that people seek consistency between their beliefs and the information received from their environmental exchanges. Dishonest behaviour, for example, may be more likely to occur when it does not violate the self image, and there is evidence that those whose self esteem is low are more likely to take advantage of opportunities to cheat (Eisen, 1972). An alternative view is that people are motivated to maintain or enhance their self esteem. This may be achieved by deviant behaviour, since the anticipated approval of a deviant reference group is esteem enhancing. However, the maintenance of cognitive consistency seems more relevant to the content of the self concept, which is not necessarily related to the direction of evaluation or self esteem. Howells (1978), for example, describes a repertory grid study of a poisoner, whose self concept was that of a famous, successful person. This was an unusual case, but it indicates that a person may have a self concept which is deviant from society's viewpoint, without experiencing self derogation.

Low self esteem is, nevertheless, associated with nonconformity in adolescents (Richman, Brown and Clark, 1984), and characterises delinquents in several studies. Early research established higher levels of worry and emotionality in delinquents (Metfessels and Lovell, 1942), and "neuroticism" is higher in officially defined offenders, although less clearly related to self-reported delinquency (Chapter 5). Since the neuroticism dimension is closely related to self esteem (Watson and Clark, 1984), these findings imply a more negative self image.

More direct measurement of the self concept tends to confirm this. Bhagat and Fraser (1970), for example, found that compared with nondelinquents, delinquents evaluated "real self" less favourably, and lower levels of self esteem as measured by the Tennessee Self Concept Scale have been observed in both American and British samples of delinquents (Lund and Salary, 1980; Eyo, 1981). However, there are variations in self concept among offenders. Eyo (1981), for example, found that while delinquents as a group scored lower than controls on moral, personal, social, and family components of the self concept, Borstal boys showed a greater emphasis on physical aspects, and also had a more rigidly defended self image than boys on remand.

These studies are correlational, and do not establish a causal relation between self concept and criminality, but there are three theoretical approaches implicating the self concept in deviant behaviour. First, Reckless (1961) proposed that the promotion of conformity and self-control through inner *containment* is a function of a favourable self concept, goal orientation, frustration tolerance, and commitment to norms. A "good" self concept in this context is an *insulator* against deviant influences, a need for cognitive consistency being assumed. Reckless and Dinitz (1967) described research showing that boys nominated by teachers as "good" or "bad" differed on self-report measures of socialisation and self concept, and on subsequent delinquent outcome. The self concept scale correlated with both teacher nominations and socialisation, and it was argued that boys exposed to adverse family and socioeconomic conditions were less vulnerable to delinquency when they had a favourable self concept. Orcutt (1970), however, criticised this research for biased selection of "good" and "bad" boys, and inadequate conceptualisation of self concept, and concluded that Reckless' argument was not established. Although interest in containment theory has waned, partial support was obtained in a factor analytic study by Thompson and Dodder (1986), who found that self-reported delinquency was related to self concept in white boys, though not among white girls or black boys and girls. However, studies of those from ethnic minorities who avoid trouble with the law, despite high risk backgrounds, lend support to the notion of self concept as a factor which protects against delinquency. Interview observations suggest that such "resilient" individuals have higher self esteem, which they derive from personal achievement (Ross and Glaser, 1973; Werner, 1989).

A second approach sees negative self attitudes as an outcome of labelling. According to labelling theory, a deviant self image is a consequence of the stigmatisation accompanying legal processing, and mediates subsequent secondary deviance. While this again assumes needs for consistency, the focus is on lowered self esteem as a *reflected appraisal* of the negative reactions of others. The evidence of a correlation between official delinquency and low self esteem from cross-sectional studies can be interpreted in this light, and a longitudinal study by Ageton and Elliott (1974) supports the hypothesis. Among boys with no prior police contact, those who subsequently experienced such contact also adopted a more delinquent self orientation than those who remained free of legal apprehension. Other studies, however, produce inconsistent findings. Gibbs (1974), for example, found that although motor thieves had a more delinquent self image than controls following police apprehension and subsequent court appearance, both their self concept and self esteem moved closer to that of controls following appearance in court. In view of the evidence for the weak effects of labelling on subsequent delinquency, the case for a motivating influence of reflected appraisal is correspondingly weakened. Indeed, it might be anticipated that labelling effects depend on *prior* self concept.

The most comprehensive model relates delinquency to esteem enhancement (Wells, 1978; Gold, 1978; Kaplan, 1980). In Kaplan's analysis, self esteem derives from competence and confidence in achievements, and acceptance in social relationships. Failures in these areas lead to self derogation, which motivates alternatives to conventional behaviour. Delinquency is one alternative, since the delinquent reference group enhances self esteem by providing acceptance and approval. Self esteem is thus a mediator of the relation between academic and social failure and delinquency, and not an ultimate cause or effect. This model predicts an initial negative relation between self esteem and delinquency, but a subsequent positive relation as delinquency restores self esteem. Tests of the model therefore require longitudinal analysis.

Kaplan (1980) reports several studies of the relationship of self esteem to delinquency at different points in time, which are consistent with the developmental features of the model, but does not examine the continuous causal sequence. Three other studies have examined self esteem and self reported delinquency at repeated waves of the Youth in Transition survey. From cross-lagged correlations between self esteem and delinquency at the first two waves, almost two years apart, Rosenberg and Rosenberg (1978) concluded that self esteem predicted later delinquency, although the effect was stronger for lower class youth. Brynner, O'Malley and Bachman (1981) criticised this analysis, and extending the study to a later wave, found little effect of self esteem on subsequent delinquency. However, they found a modest positive effect of delinquency on later self esteem, consistent with the enhancement model. A further analysis, in contrast, failed to demonstrate either a motivating effect of lowered self esteem on delinquency, or an enhancement effect of delinquency on subsequent self esteem (Wells and Rankin, 1983).

The research to date, then, has not established any consistent causal relationship between self concept and delinquency, and it remains to be demonstrated whether the negative correlation observed in several studies represents anything more than a coincidental effect of other factors on these two variables. However, this research suffers from several limitations, not the least being a lack of an adequate theory of self concept. Self concept and self esteem are not always clearly differentiated, and are commonly measured globally, rather than in relation to specific areas of achievement, or components of the self. Greenwald and Pratkanis (1984), for example, suggest that public, private and collective aspects of the self need to be distinguished. Also, little attention has been paid to the "trait–state" distinction. The longitudinal data suggest that self concept is relatively stable over time, but it is probable that temporary changes in self esteem are more relevant to specific deviant acts. Longitudinal surveys may not, then, be sensitive to any reciprocal effects between self esteem and delinquent behaviour.

Values and beliefs

Willingness to comply with social rules is often regarded as a function of *moral values* or the affective strength of attitudes or beliefs. *Moral knowledge* is related to general intelligence, and insofar as most people probably know the basic rules of "right" and "wrong", it is unlikely to be a major source of variation in noncompliant behaviour (Hogan, 1973). However, several theories suggest that delinquents are committed to deviant values which the majority of society do not accept. Subcultural theorists, for example, propose that delinquents value toughness, aggression, and excitement, and reject routine work. Matza (1964), on the other hand, argued that these are "subterranean" values which permeate society, and that delinquents share conventional values. They "drift" into crime through "episodic release from moral constraint".

Matza's proposal is not unequivocally supported. Heather (1979) reported two repertory grid studies of delinquents and nondelinquents. The same factors of conventional and subterranean values emerged in both groups, but the subterranean factor accounted for more of the variance among delinquents, suggesting that it was a more dominant component. Cochrane (1971), however, found differences in value priorities between adult prisoners and controls, males endorsing valued goals of more immediate personal relevance, females having a more masculine value system. There are thus some indications that delinquents are characterised by deviant values.

An inverse relationship has generally been assumed between delinquency and *religiosity*. Although early studies found a small negative relation between delinquency and religious attendance, inconsistent findings have been reported. Elifson, Peterson and Hadaway (1983) employed several indices of religiosity and self-reported delinquency, and confirmed the negative correlation. However, strongest correlations were obtained for victimless crimes, such as using marijuana, and religiosity had no predictive power which was independent of other variables. It was suggested that the influence of religion on delinquency is most likely to be mediated via the type of family and friends it dictates.

Values are related to needs or *goals*. Values of excitement or toughness, for example, imply preferences for certain experiences or outcomes. There has, however, been only limited exploration of motivational factors in criminality. This may reflect the influence of control theories which assume that crime expresses common human needs, although strain, subcultural and social learning theories imply that delinquents have strong needs for status and approval of the peer group. Some studies find that delinquents tend to lack aspirations for achievement or career success (Tutt, 1973), and Jessor and Jessor (1977) found that deviant behaviour in adolescence was associated with a greater concern for independence relative to academic achievement. It was also, however, related to needs for affectional ties with peers.

Neutralisation and attributional processes

If offenders do have conventional values, one reason why these fail to inhibit deviant conduct may be that they are neutralised by a temporary excuse or rationalisation. Sykes and Matza (1957) proposed five *techniques of neutralisation*: (1) denial of responsibility (one's actions are a consequence of external factors, such as poverty, broken home, or drunkenness); (2) denial of injury (little harm is entailed); (3) denial of the victim (the victim deserves it); (4) condemnation of the condemners (attention is shifted to those who condemn the act, such as criminal justice agents); (5) appeal to higher loyalties (needs of others, such as peers, take precedence). This assumes cognitive consistency between attitudes and behaviour. It also assumes that neutralisations are temporary excuses invoked by a specific situation, rather than persisting negative attitudes towards deviance (although Agnew and Peters (1986) see "acceptance of neutralisations" as a predisposing factor). An illustration of neutralisations is provided by the beliefs that shoplifters described as associated with their thefts, such as "merchants deserve it", "everybody does it", and "it's not a major crime" (Soloman and Ray, 1984).

The hypothesis that neutralisations are causally prior to an offence is clearly difficult to test directly, but some studies attempt to identify neutralising effects retrospectively. Minor (1980) noted that earlier studies yielded inconsistent results. He was unable to find differences between prisoners convicted of assault, robbery, or burglary in either the types of neutralisation they preferred, or in the excuses they favoured for offences similar to their own. He considered this unfavourable to the hypothesis. However, Matza (1964) suggested a modification to the personal neutralisation hypothesis, proposing that verbal excuses conform with expected, but misperceived neutralising attitudes of peers rather than with personally accepted neutralisations. Hindelang (1974b) failed to support this, finding that delinquent act-committers believed their friends to be equally or less approving of their acts than they were themselves, but Ball (1983) obtained results consistent with Matza's hypothesis. "Attributed" neutralisation (i.e. how others perceive the deviant act) was more closely related to self-reported delinquency among sixth-graders than was personal neutralisation, although the latter was more important in ninth-graders. However, these correlational data throw little light on the question of whether neutralisations are *post hoc* accommodations following deviant acts, or whether they are antecedent.

The concept of neutralisation has a clear parallel in the notion of disengagement from self-restraining influences suggested by social learning theorists to account for situational influences on moral conduct. It can also be seen within the context of attribution theory, which examines how unexpected or unwelcome events are explained in everyday thinking through the ascription of cause, responsibility, and blame. Matza's "denial of responsibility", for example, clearly reflects the attribution of one's behaviour to external causes, which may be stable (poverty) or unstable (drunkenness). Whether or not they mediate criminal acts, offenders' explanations for their acts may be particularly relevant to the reactions of the criminal justice system to them, and to their ways of coping with penal sanctions.

Saulnier and Perlman (1981) confirmed several predictions from attribution theory regarding the causal assignment of inmates for their offences. For example, stable and internal causes were more likely when the offence was consistent with previous record, while—consistent with the "actor–observer" bias—staff tended to attribute crimes to internal causes, inmates to external factors. Similar results were obtained from interviews with violent offenders by Henderson and Hewstone (1984), who examined attributions of both cause and responsibility. The latter was defined by the use of excuses (denial of responsibility, and attribution to external factors) as opposed to justifications (acceptance of responsibility, but with justifying reasons). Offenders' explanations for their offences were not only predominantly external, but were also more likely to be justifications than excuses. However, excuses were used more often when the victim died. The findings of these latter studies were predicted from research on attributional processes in general, and do not imply deviant thinking on the part of offenders in this respect. Nevertheless, dispositional biases to attribute cause or responsibility to others may contribute to criminality, and work suggesting such an attributional bias among aggressive individuals is discussed in Chapter 9.

Another variable which has been linked to delinquency, and which is related indirectly to attributions of causality, is *locus of control*. The dimension of internal versus external (I–E) locus of control reflects generalised beliefs that outcomes are controlled by one's own actions as opposed to external factors, such as chance or powerful others (Rotter, 1975). Since delinquents often experience external barriers to legitimate achievement, it has been suggested that they are more likely to display expectancies that events are not under their personal control. While some studies find that offenders indeed have a more external orientation on Rotter's I–E scale (Parrott and Strongman, 1984), others have not confirmed this (Valliant, Asu and Howitt, 1983). An alternative suggestion that offenders from ethnic minorities are particularly likely to have an external locus also has inconsistent support (Valliant et al., 1983). The predictive power of Rotter's I–E scale has proved to be weak in several areas of research, partly because it fails to distinguish positive from negative outcomes, and the relevance of this dimension to the explanation of criminality remains obscure. Nevertheless, internality has been identified as a significant protective factor among those at risk for criminality (Werner, 1989).

Yochelson and Samenow's "Criminal Personality"

Yochelson and Samenow (1976) emphasise cognitions in their analysis of *the criminal personality*, which is based on extensive interviews with 240 male offenders. Their sample includes young offenders seen in community clinics, but is made up predominantly of adult "hard core" offenders committed to St Elizabeth's Hospital in Washington, DC for psychiatric evaluation, or as "not guilty by reason of insanity". Yochelson and Samenow describe their disenchantment with psychoanalytic, psychological and sociological explanations of crime, and their adoption of a "phenomenologic" approach. This focuses on the thinking of criminals, who are seen to be in control of their lives, despite attempts to disown responsibility. The authors contend that what turns a person into a criminal is "a series of choices" made from an early age. However, while acknowledging reciprocal influences of parent and child on individual development, they offer no explanation for the origins of the choices a person makes.

"Criminality" is conceptualised very broadly as a continuum encompassing a wide range of thinking processes as well as criminal acts. The noncriminal end of the continuum is defined by "responsible thinking and action", responsible people being those who are basically moral, fulfil their obligations, and function within the law. At the other extreme are criminals who have a system of erroneous thinking patterns. Over 40 "thinking errors" are described, these being grouped into three kinds.

First, there are criminal thinking patterns which overlap with "character traits" identified by others. For example, thought is characterised by pervasive fearfulness, particularly of a "zero state" in which the individual feels worthless, while a central pattern is "the power thrust", relating to a need for power and control. Other patterns include "fragmentation" (inconsistencies in thinking), sentimentality, perfectionism, an indiscriminate need for sexual excitement, and lying. Second, there are automatic errors of thinking, which include "the closed channel", or a secretive style of communication, the victim stance, failure to put oneself in another's position, failure to assume obligations, lack of trust, and poor decision-making. Third are errors associated more directly with criminal acts. They include extensive fantasies of antisocial behaviour, a "corrosion" of internal and external deterrents, an opinion of oneself as good, and superoptimism. It is contended that criminals are not impulsive, since no matter how opportunist a crime may seem, it has typically been preceded by fantasies and premeditation. These various thinking patterns are manifest during attempts at evaluation or change, and may take the form of tactics aimed at defeating the examiner or therapist.

The emphasis placed by Yochelson and Samenow on thinking processes as determinants of deviant behaviour is clearly consistent with the "rational criminal" perspective, and with the increased attention paid to the role of cognitive dysfunction in deviant behaviour. Their observations also coincide with the view that offenders neutralise inhibitions against deviance. However, their account is open to serious criticism on several grounds. First, their definition of "criminality" is value-laden and subjective, and no attempt is made to demonstrate that "criminal errors of thinking" are absent in "responsible" citizens. Second, they generalise from an unrepresentative sample, while offering no supporting evidence other than clinical observations. The formulation is therefore at best a series of hypotheses, rather than a test of a theory. Third, their "thinking errors" make no contact with any systematic theory of cognitive functioning, and are an arbitrary list of needs and irrational beliefs. Wulach (1988) notes that despite the rejection of psychoanalytic theory, many of these "thinking errors", such as "the power thrust", "fragmentation", or "the victim stance", correspond to the defence mechanisms attributed by recent psychodynamic writers to narcissistic and borderline disorders. He suggests that the characteristics of the criminal personality described by Yochelson and Samenow coincide with the DSM-III-R criteria for antisocial, narcissistic, histrionic, and borderline personality disorders, and also Cleckley's concept of the psychopath, and do not define a unique personality type.

SOCIOCOGNITIVE AND INTERPERSONAL SKILLS

Role-taking, empathy, and guilt

Role-taking is a critical concept in cognitive–developmental theory. Piaget proposed that through interpersonal contact, pre-adolescent children gradually shift from an egocentric perception of the world to a comprehension of the perspective of others. Role-theory originating in symbolic interactionism similarly sees socialisation as dependent on the ability to take the role of "the generalised other", and Gough (1948) hypothesised that a deficit in role-taking ability accounts for the undersocialisation of psychopaths. For Kohlberg, the development of role-taking ability is a prequisite to shifts in moral reasoning, and Selman has proposed a stage theory of role-taking which parallels Kohlberg's stages (Gurucharri, Phelps and Selman, 1984). Role-taking links the cognitive with the moral since it entails understanding the feelings of others, as well as their reasons and intentions, and developmental delays in the acquisition of role-taking skills are associated with failure to respect the rights of others (Chandler, 1973). Persisting egocentrism is therefore likely to be significant in social deviance.

   Gurucharri et al. (1984) found that pre-adolescent children showing conduct problems were at a lower level than normal controls on Selman's interpersonal stages, although they tended to catch up in later adolescence. Chandler (1973) found particularly striking differences in egocentrism between 11 to 13 year old children, who were already chronic delinquents, and age-matched nondelinquents. While Kaplan and Arbuthnot (1985) were unable to replicate this in older delinquents, Lee and Prentice (1988) obtained significant differences between delinquents and nondelinquents on other role-taking tasks. Short and Simeonsson (1986) also found that institutionalised delinquents judged aggressive by their peers were significantly more egocentric on Chandler's measure than unaggressive delinquents. Hickey (1972), on the other hand, observed that some late adolescent delinquents had acquired a relatively mature level of social role-taking, which significantly exceeded their level of moral maturity. This finding emphasises that while failure to develop role-taking skills may impede socialisation, their acquisition does not guarantee socialised behaviour. Role-taking may, for example, be involved in manipulative as well as co-operative behaviour.

A related concept is that of *empathy*, which involves not only understanding the perspective of others, but also the ability to respond to their feelings. This is of potential significance to delinquency since the ability to imagine the distress of another may inhibit harmful behaviour, and lack of empathy is prominent in descriptions of psychopathic personality. It might also account in part for sex differences in delinquent behaviour, since cultural stereotypes dictate that females are more empathic than males.

There is, however, longstanding disagreement about how to conceptualise and measure empathy, and how to distinguish it from role-taking on the one hand, and sympathy on the other. While empathy is generally construed as an affective response, some use the term to denote the vicarious matching of another's emotional experience, while others emphasise the cognitive awareness of another's feelings without the requirement of emotional matching. Where sex differences have been found, they depend on the method of assessment, and the assumed advantage of females in empathy is confined largely to measures entailing verbal reports of feelings (Eisenberg and Lennon, 1983). It is less evident in more cognitively oriented measures of perspective taking.

Hogan (1969) developed a self-report trait measure of empathy (*Em*) to assess "the imaginative apprehension of another's condition or state of mind". This emphasises cognitive rather than affective aspects, and *Em* correlates with both spatial ability and social acuity. In Hogan's theory of moral character (Hogan, 1973), moral maturity is held to result from the development of socialisation, empathy, and autonomy. Empathy in these terms is a dispositional skill which allows one to take "the moral point of view", and compensates for deficient socialisation in inhibiting antisocial behaviour.

Consistent with this proposal, Hogan (1969) found that prison inmates and young delinquents, who achieved low scores on Gough's *So* scale, also achieved the lowest scores among several groups on *Em*. College students whose *So* scores matched those of delinquents were distinguished from delinquents by higher *Em* scores, supporting the compensation hypothesis (Kurtines and Hogan, 1972). Ellis (1982) also found that *Em* significantly discriminated delinquents from nondelinquents, and aggressive delinquents from nonaggressive delinquents. Neurotic delinquents also scored lower than psychopathic delinquents, who in turn scored lower than subcultural delinquents and controls. However, Kendall, Deardorff and Finch (1977) found that while first offenders, recidivists, and nonoffenders were distinguished by scores on *So*, they did not differ on *Em*. Using other scales of empathy, Lee and Prentice (1988) were also unable to differentiate between delinquents and nondelinquents, or between subgroups defined by Quay's dimensions. However, their empathy measures were unrelated to measures of sociocognitive development, and they question the validity of self-report scales of empathy.

Other studies yield inconsistent results which vary with the measures employed. Rotenberg (1974) distinguished cognitive from affective role-taking, although calling them empathy and sympathy, respectively, and defined them by response to experimental tasks. Delinquents displayed lower affective role-taking than schoolboys, but did not differ in cognitive role-taking. Kaplan and Arbuthnot (1985) also obtained only limited support for the expectation of deficient empathy in delinquents. Cognitive role-taking was defined by a Piagetian task, and affective empathy by means of both a trait measure and a specific unstructured task involving self-description. Although delinquents performed marginally lower than nondelinquents on all measures, they differed significantly only on the unstructured task.

There is clearly a need for greater clarity in the conceptualisation of empathy, which may not be a unidimensional ability. The most systematic model is that of Hoffman (1982), who sees empathy as a universal affective response to the distress of another, which changes with the child's progress through socio-cognitive stages. He distinguishes *guilt* as a special case of empathic distress aroused by the causal attribution of responsibility for another's plight to the self, which is a relatively late developmental acquisition. Guilt is therefore an interpersonal "hot cognition", rather than conditioned anxiety or symbolic fear of parental punishment, and is an outcome of the parent's use of inductive discipline. Social deviance associated with developmental delays in perspective taking may, then, be accompanied by deficiencies in guilt, as well as empathy. Studies employing the Mosher Guilt Scale indicate that although delinquents as a group do not differ from nondelinquents in expecting guilt reactions to their own behaviour (Persons, 1970), delinquents whose moral reasoning is at a conventional level are more likely to report guilt-proneness than those at lower stages (Ruma and Mosher, 1967). Some delinquents are therefore deficient in perspective-taking skills and affective interpersonal reactions held to be dependent on them, but whether these are the more recalcitrant or persistent offenders remains to be determined.

Interpersonal problem solving

Deficiencies in interpersonal problem solving may be causally related to socially ineffective or maladaptive behaviour (Tisdelle and Lawrence, 1986). Work in this area receives much of its impetus from the conceptualisation of problem solving advanced by D'Zurilla and Goldfried (1971), who view it as a cognitive–behavioural process which (1) makes available response alternatives for dealing with problem situations, such as interpersonal conflict or loss of reinforcers, and (2) increases the probability of selecting the most effective response from those alternatives. The focus is on the "discovery" of solutions through a sequence which involves recognition of the problem, formulation of goals, generation of alternative solutions, decisions on an optimal strategy, and testing out the outcome. Impersonal problem solving is dependent on IQ, but interpersonal problem solving is more a function of acquired skills (Spivack, Platt and Shure, 1976).

Hains and Ryan (1983) compared delinquent and nondelinquent boys at two age levels on several tasks involving social cognitive processes. Delinquency was unrelated to moral judgement or to deficits in knowledge of social problem solving strategies. However, on a social problem solving task, delinquents were less exhaustive in considering certain dimensions, such as the antecedents of problem situations, suggesting a tendency to initiate social behaviour on the basis of incomplete or inaccurate inferences.

Other studies are confined to differences within delinquent populations. A commonly used measure of interpersonal problem solving is the MEPS (Means–Ends Problem Solving test), which presents the beginning and end of hypothetical problem situations, and requires the subject to generate means by which the solution is reached. Platt, Scura and Hannon (1973) compared addict and nonaddict reformatory inmates on the MEPS, and found that the addicts showed a significant deficit in the ability to conceptualise means of reaching goals in problem situations. Parole failures among young offenders were also found to be deficient in means–end thinking and alternative thinking in an unpublished study cited by Platt and Prout (1987). Higgins and Thiess (1981) used the same measure to compare institutionalised delinquents who were adjusting well to the institution, with those who were a disciplinary problem, and those rated by both staff and inmates as misfits. The misfits showed the most marked deficits in generating means. They also produced less relevant solutions than the other two groups, while those who were disciplinary problems produced fewer means than the more adjusted delinquents. Several recent studies suggest that problem solving deficits are particularly prominent in aggressive children (Chapter 9).

Social skills

Sarason (1968) was among the first to suggest that delinquents are deficient in socially acceptable and adaptive behaviour, and social skills training has become a popular technique in the treatment of offenders (Chapter 13). However, evidence relevant to the assumed social skill deficits of offenders is limited. One problem is the lack of a generally agreed definition of "social skills" and the paucity of valid measures (Bellak, 1983). The extent to which overt social skill deficits can be separated from dysfunctional cognitions or problem solving skills is also unclear.

Freedman et al. (1978) developed the API (Adolescent Problems Inventory), which requires the subject to indicate how he would (or should) respond to a number of verbally presented problem situations. They found that delinquents' responses indicated less competent strategies than those of "good citizens" or "leaders". Although the API correlated significantly with IQ, the differences remained among IQ-matched subgroups. The API also distinguished the more disruptive delinquents. Veneziano and Veneziano (1988) found the mean score of a large delinquent sample on the API to be lower than that of both the delinquents and nondelinquents in the study of Freedman et al. Dishion et al. (1984) further found that the API was related to both official and self-reported delinquency, although they comment that social incompetence has not been shown to cause delinquency. Howells (1986) also emphasises that any correlation between social skill deficits and criminal behaviour may be incidental.

Although the API does not distinguish between delinquents in terms of number or type of offences (Hunter and Kelley, 1986), Veneziano and Veneziano (1988) demonstrated the convergent and discriminative validity of the scale. They divided institutionalised delinquents into socially incompetent, moderately competent, and competent groups on the basis of API scores, and found that the incompetent group differed on a number of variables. Not only were they less intelligent, they also showed more disciplinary problems and family disturbance, and described themselves as more impulsive, hostile, aggressive, and as having an external locus of control. Female delinquents have also been shown to be less socially skilled than their nondelinquent counterparts on a similar inventory developed for girls (Gaffney, 1984). This scale is also related to both official and self-reported delinquency (Ward and McFall, 1986).

The API, however, measures only limited aspects of social performance. Observations of nonverbal behaviour produce less clear findings. Spence (1981) examined both molecular and global components of social interaction derived from a brief interview with institutionalised delinquent boys and noninstitutionalised schoolboys. Delinquents differed on several molecular components, showing more fidgeting and fiddling, and lesser eye contact, head movements and speech. They were also rated as less socially skilled or employable, and as more anxious, though not less friendly. Collingwood and Genther (1980) also report that delinquents show deficits in basic interaction skills, such as attending and listening, and that among adolescents completing a skills training program, recidivists had lower skill levels than nonrecidivists, both before and after training. Renwick and Emler (1991), in contrast, reported that mean scores of a delinquent sample on both ratings of social skill and self-reported social difficulties were similar to those obtained by nondelinquents in other studies. Neither set of measures correlated with self-reported delinquency. However, generic social skills may be less relevant to antisocial behaviour than specific skills for dealing with particular situations, such as peer pressure, conflict or encounters with authority figures (Spence, 1982; Howells, 1986).

It is probable that delinquents are heterogeneous in social competence (Veneziano and Veneziano, 1988), and studies of responses to social cues also point in this direction. It has often been suggested that delinquents are unresponsive to social cues as a result of the failure of disorganised families to supply adequate discrimination training. Verbal conditioning experiments appear to support this insofar as delinquents show less change in behaviour with social "reinforcement" (Johnson, 1976). However, Stewart (1972) demonstrated that not only were delinquents heterogeneous in this respect, they were not insensitive to social cues. During verbal conditioning trials, neurotic delinquents increased their verbal responses, indicating a social reinforcement effect. Psychopaths, in contrast, significantly *decreased* their responding relative to baseline operant level. They were therefore sensitive to the social cues provided by the experimenter, but appeared to find them aversive.

These latter findings also highlight the ambiguity inherent in attempting to identify social "skills" from the standpoint of the observer. Trower (1984) argues that social skills cannot be defined or understood outside the context of the intentions of the actor and the social meanings conveyed by behaviour. A study of institutionalised boys by Rimé et al. (1978) illustrates this. Psychopathic and nonpsychopathic adolescents were observed during a brief interview. The psychopaths showed significantly *more* eye contact, less smiling, more hand gestures, and more forward leaning. Although the authors interpret this pattern as intrusive behaviour consequent on insensitivity to interpersonal cues, they also found that the interviewers spoke less when interacting with psychopaths. Moreover, there was greater correspondence between the nonverbal behaviours of the interviewers and interviewees during interactions with psychopaths than with nonpsychopaths. An alternative interpretation is that the psychopathic boys intended to intimidate or dominate the interviewers. In these terms, far from being insensitive, they were actually competent in achieving their goals. This is consistent with the proposal of self-presentation theorists that offenders adopt an interpersonal style in which a "tough" image is presented. Such a style can only be regarded as "unskilled" to the extent that alternative behaviours for coping with the situation are lacking in the person's repertoire.

Research on sociocognitive functioning has so far parallelled earlier studies of personality and cognitive variables. Not only is there a continuing focus on younger and institutionalised populations, there is also continuing evidence of the heterogeneity of offenders, and as Ross and Fabiano (1985) emphasise, sociocognitive deficits are apparent in only some offenders. There also remain considerable theoretical problems in linking sociocognitive skill deficits to deviant behaviour. Nevertheless, the available data are sufficient to suggest that many offenders become involved in antisocial behaviour because of an egocentric level of cognitive development, deficiencies in considering the social consequences of their actions, and in their skills for dealing with interpersonal problem situations. While more data are needed on adult offenders, this line of research has significantly influenced recent developments in offender rehabilitation (Chapter 13).

Chapter 9

Aggression and Violent Crime

INTRODUCTION

Reports of apparently "mindless" brutality not only fuel moral outrage, but also unsettle the predictability of the environment. Violence therefore monopolises public disquiet about "law and order", and a recent opinion poll in Britain revealed a widespread belief that 50% of offences dealt with by the courts were violent. However, less than 9% of males and 4% of females before the courts in England and Wales in 1988 were found guilty of crimes against the person (Home Office, 1989), and victimisation surveys show that public fears of violence are disproportionate to the actual risks. Nevertheless, in terms of immediate harmful effects and longer term social and psychological consequences for victims and their families, violence represents a public health problem.

Violent crime constitutes only a small part of the phenomenon of human aggression, which, despite its negative connotations, is neither statistically abnormal, nor, for the most part, illegal. This chapter focuses on individual violence within the context of aggression as everyday behaviour.

DEFINING VIOLENCE AND AGGRESSION

Violence denotes the forceful infliction of physical injury. Criminal violence is the illegitimate use of force, and includes criminal homicide, assault, robbery, rape, and other sexual assaults. Homicide is the killing of another human being. Killing in self- defence may be justifiable in law, but the concern here is with criminal homicide, which covers murder (intentional unlawful killing) and manslaughter (unlawful killing under provocation, without intention, or through negligence). Assaults are acts causing bodily injury, but common or simple assaults are threats or attempts to harm in which no injury ensues, while robbery refers to theft involving the threat or use of force. Although rape is seen as primarily a violent offence, it is discussed with sexual crimes in Chapter 11. Crimes such as arson, criminal damage, and violations of industrial safety legislation, may also entail serious physical harm, but these are not generally included under the heading of violence.

Aggression describes the intentional infliction of harm, including psychological discomfort as well as injury, although it is sometimes loosely equated with vigour in competitive situations. However, what is construed as harmful depends on values and social context, and socially legitimised punishment or self-defence is less likely to be identified as aggression. Aggression therefore refers to harm-doing which is *unjustified* from the observer's perspective, and the concept cannot be divested of its moral significance (Van Eyken, 1987). Only limited parallels to human aggression can therefore be found in the behaviour of other animals.

Given this dependence of the identification of aggression or violence on the attributions and values of the observer, a consensual definition is, not surprisingly, lacking. Definitions used by social scientists do not always embrace the same range of events. Some focus on injurious *effects*, others on the *form* of behaviour, such as threats or attempts to harm. Some ignore intent and social meaning, and hence categorise behaviours with disparate *goals* as equivalent. Behaviourists, for example, often define aggression "objectively" as "a response that delivers noxious stimuli to another organism" (Buss, 1961). This would include the behaviour of dentists, magistrates, and careless drivers! However, despite behaviourist aversions to unmeasured inferential terms, intent is implicit in both vernacular and research use. For example, "hit" describes an intentional action, not merely an observed movement.

Most psychologists now explicitly include intent in the definition of aggression, and delimit the term to actions which aim to inflict injury or harm on a person who is motivated to avoid it (Zillmann, 1979). This covers legitimate as well as illegal behaviour, but distinguishes malevolently intended harm from benevolently intended injury, such as surgery, and from injury infliction which is sought masochistically by the victim. It therefore co-ordinates with the notion of criminal violence as intentional injury of an unwilling victim. Within this definition, aggressive behaviour may take the form of the infliction of physical injury, verbal derogation, or passive obstruction, and its effects may range from loss of life to wounded pride.

To subsume such diverse phenomena under a single rubric implies that they serve broadly equivalent functions. However, *angry* or *annoyance-motivated* aggression, in which harm or injury to the victim reduces an aversive emotional state, is commonly distinguished from *instrumental* or *incentive-motivated* aggression, in which injury facilitates the attainment of nonaggressive goals (Buss, 1961; Zillmann, 1979). As this distinction implies, the emotional state of *anger*, which has physiological, cognitive, and expressive components, is not a necessary accompaniment of aggressive behaviour. Criminologists similarly distinguish instrumental from hostile or expressive violence. Robbery therefore represents instrumental aggression, but most unplanned or impulsive violence is probably mediated by anger (Berkowitz, 1986).

A related term is *hostility*, which Buss (1961) confined to negative evaluations or attitudes of resentment, mistrust, or hate. Some authors use hostility and aggression interchangeably, while Zillmann (1979) differentiates aggression as the infliction of injury from hostility as the infliction of nonphysical harm. However, the tendency to hold negative beliefs about others needs to be distinguished from the tendency to attack others when angry (Blackburn, 1972), and Buss's use is followed here.

Tedeschi (1983) regards all definitions of aggression as value-laden and inadequate, and proposes the alternative notion of *coercive power*, a form of social influence involving the use of threats or punishments to gain compliance. This implies that what is labelled aggression is reinforced by power and control, but Berkowitz and Donnerstein (1982) maintain that injury infliction is the primary reinforcer of angry aggression. However, the attainment of injury infliction and control are not readily distinguishable in practice, and Tedeschi's conception has the advantage of emphasising the interpersonal context of aggression. It also clarifies the distinctions between aggression, dominance, and assertion, which often prove troublesome. All involve influence through the exercise of power, but entail varying degrees of hostility. This is reflected in the Leary interpersonal circle, in which coercion represents a combination of dominance and hostility (Chapter 3).

The main *operational definitions* of aggression are summarised by Bertilson (1983) under the headings of case studies and surveys, interviews, personality measures, direct behavioural observations, field experiments, and laboratory procedures. These encompass self-reported aggression and observations of mild retaliations, as well as involvement in legally defined violence. However, laboratory studies have been criticised for failure to articulate operational with conceptual definitions, their artificiality and neglect of social meaning, and their questionable external validity (Tedeschi, 1983). For example, a widely used experimental paradigm is the Buss "aggression machine", in which subjects press a button to deliver noxious stimulation to a "learner". One criticism is that subjects may actually be acting altruistically rather than with malevolent intent.

Replying to these criticisms, Berkowitz and Donnerstein (1982) argue that experimental settings and subjects need not be representative to have external validity, and that the artificiality of the laboratory is its strength in testing causal hypotheses. They cite examples of external correlates of laboratory procedures, such as the "aggression machine". They also argue that generalisability depends on the meanings assigned by subjects to their situation, and that aggression experiments elicit intentionally injurious behaviour. Nevertheless, it remains the case that many experiments on aggression do not establish the meanings assigned by their subjects, and typically examine aggression which is legitimised by the setting. They may in this respect throw more light on the behaviour of judge and jury than on that of the prisoner in the dock.

PATTERNS OF VIOLENCE

Criminal violence

Homicide has a high police clearance rate, and considerable information has accumulated on its distribution, and the characteristics of victims and offenders. Most homicides occur in large cities, but national rates vary widely, and correlate with violence in a society generally. Table 9.1 shows comparative rates for several countries, although these must be treated with caution because of differences in recording procedures. Highest rates are found in central America, while those for Britain are among the lowest. The United States has the highest rate among industrialised nations, but rates vary considerably between southern and north-eastern states. It is of interest to note by comparison that Given (1977) estimates the homicide rate for thirteenth century England as 15 per 100 000. All countries have recorded substantial increases in homicide since the late 1960s, although in the United States at least, this partly reflects the exceptionally low rates of violence during the 1950s (Block, 1977). In England and Wales, the average number of homicides recorded annually by the police increased from some 300 in the 1960s to over 600 in the late 1980s. Homicide nevertheless remains a rare crime.

Table 9.1   National homicide rates per 100 000 population, *c.* 1984

Country	Rate	Country	Rate
Colombia	37.4	Poland	1.6
Mexico	17.9	Austria	1.4
Brazil	13.4	Israel	1.4
Venezuela	12.9	France	1.3
USA	8.5	Scotlad	1.3
Ecuador	7.1	New Zealand	1.2
Argentina	3.8	FDR	1.2
Hungary	2.7	Spain	1.0
Canada	2.3	Greece	0.9
Italy	2.1	England and Wales	0.7
Australia	1.9	Egypt	0.5

Source: United Nations (1988). *Demographic Yearbook*. New York: United Nations Publishing Division.

Wolfgang (1958) analysed 588 homicides committed in Philadelphia between 1948 and 1952. Two thirds of the crimes occurred between 8.00 p.m. on Friday and Sunday, and both offenders and victims were most likely to be black, male, and under thirty. Victims and offenders were acquainted or related in 59% of male killings, and 84% of female deaths, and whereas men killed and were killed more of ten outside the home, women were most commonly killed in the home, 41% of them by their partner. In contrast, only 11% of male victims were killed by their wives. While stabbing was the most frequent method of killing, a third of offences involved shooting, and recorded antecedents were vague altercations, domestic quarrels, jealousy, or arguments over money. Less than 3% of offenders were declared insane, but 4% committed suicide following the homicide.

Subsequent studies in Houston (Pokorny, 1965) and Chicago (Block, 1977) produce similar findings, although Block found an increase in shootings and killings of strangers, related to an increase in robbery-murders. Similar patterns have been reported in other countries, but there are variations. In Britain, the racial element has been less apparent, and fewer homicides involve shootings or robbery-murders, while a greater proportion of victims are females or males who are acquainted (Gibson, 1975). About 30% of offenders are regularly judged to be mentally disordered, and until the 1960s, some 30% of killers in Britain committed suicide. This figure has recently fallen to about 8%.

Most homicides are "crimes of passion" involving an interaction between acquaintances. Multiple-victim homicides (multicide) other than family killings are rare, and usually involve strangers. In *mass murders*, several victims are killed on one occasion, while in *serial murders*, killings are repeated over an extended period. In view of their infrequency, they have received little systematic scrutiny, except from journalists. However, Holmes and De Burgher (1988) estimate that there may be 350 serial murderers at large in the United States, responsible for 3,500 unsolved homicides. Jenkins (1988), in contrast, suggests that 35 killers of about 400 victims are more likely figures. He identified only 12 serial murderers in England between 1940 and 1985.

Serious assaults are demographically and spatially similar to homicide. Pittman and Handy (1964) found that aggravated assaults were again more frequent at weekends and predominantly intra-racial, but occurred more in public than in private places, and a much higher proportion involved knives than in homicides. Data obtained by Pokorny (1965) and Block (1977) suggest that most homicides are assaults which go further than intended, the outcome depending on the victim–offender interaction and the weapon used.

Robbery is more commonly directed to male strangers "on the streets". It is again a large city crime, offenders being mainly adolescent and young adult males. Although weapons may be used to threaten compliance, most robberies do not result in injury to the victim. For example, Block (1977) found that robbery-murders in Chicago accounted for 20% of murders, but only 1% of all robberies. Studies of robberies in London (McLintock and Gibson, 1961) and Philadelphia (Normandeau, 1969) revealed that 75% fell into one of two categories. The first involves robbery of those in charge of money as part of their employment, such as taxi drivers or shop assistants, and is typically planned. The second consists of unplanned and opportunistic acts, such as handbag snatching or mugging in public places. Offenders are likely to be young, and their victims selected as less likely to resist.

Family violence

Violence between family members is clearly not new, yet child abuse became an acknowledged social problem only during the 1960s, and wife abuse only during the following decade. Domestic violence has traditionally been tacitly accepted as "normal", and rights of chastisement remain enshrined in laws which accord unequal rights of husbands over wives, and of parents over children. While most western countries now have statutes requiring the reporting of child neglect, abuse, or cruelty, and it has been increasingly accepted that assaults on family members merit criminal justice intervention, considerable tolerance for family violence remains within society. For example, American surveys indicate that over 90% of parents inflict physical pain on their children at some time during disciplinary encounters (Straus, Gelles and Steinmetz, 1980).

Given this ambivalence about family violence, the definition of "abuse" is as problematic as that of "aggression", and an objective definition which is independent of community norms has proved elusive (Parke, 1977; Emery, 1989). The term is often a catch-all covering physical aggression, neglect of a child's material needs, sexual exploitation, and emotional mistreatment; but some distinguish abuse as an act of commission resulting in harm, from neglect as an act of omission with negative consequences, and this use is followed here. Within these categories, definitions focus variously on the intent of the perpetrator, the form, frequency, and severity of the act, or the consequences to the victim, with the result that investigators using the same term may be describing different behaviour patterns. For example, acts of pushing may represent intentional physical abuse, but may not have injurious consequences.

Reliable prevalence estimates are hence difficult to obtain, particularly since victims are often unwilling, or unable to complain. Official reports of child abuse and neglect in the United States rose to over a million during the 1980s, which probably represents a gross underestimate, but some of the more visible consequences indicate that family violence is a major source of criminal violence. For example, a fifth of all homicides in the United States and more than a third in Britain are family murders. As Wolfgang (1958) found, women are more likely to be murdered in the home, and are also more likely to be the victims of spouse or boyfriend than of strangers. Again, 1200 children in the United States died of physical abuse or neglect in 1986 (Widom, 1989a).

Self-report data were obtained in a National Survey of Family Violence in the United States in 1975 (Straus, Gelles and Steinmetz, 1980), and again in 1985 (Straus and Gelles, 1988). The more recent survey entailed telephone interviews with 3232 couples with a child of age 17 or under, and inquired about incidents of family violence defined as acts carried out with the intention of hurting another. Overall, 16.1% of couples had experienced an incident of violence, including slapping or pushing, while 6.3% had experienced severe violence during the previous year. Acts making up the severe violence index included being kicked, bitten, punched, hit with an object, beaten up, choked, threatened with a knife or gun, and using a knife or gun. Severe violence was directed by husbands to 3.4% of wives, and by wives to 4.8% of husbands, yielding national estimates of 1.8 and 2.0 million, respectively. Almost all children of age 3 and under, and about a third of those over 14, had been hit by their parents, while 11.0% of all children had experienced an act of severe violence. Severe violence had also been directed by 53% of children towards a sibling, and by 9% against a parent.

These figures indicate that intrafamilial aggression occurs frequently, but they must be treated with caution, for several reasons. First, the authors suggest that they may be underestimates because of social desirability responding. On the other hand, violence was defined in terms of intent rather than outcome, which may not have been severe in many cases. Second, the figures cannot be generalised to other countries, and those for wife assault, for example, are more than three times higher than comparable data from New Zealand (Fergusson et al., 1986). Third, data on violence by wives against husbands are controversial, since they contradict the view that spouse violence involves predominantly attacks by husbands on wives. Straus and Gelles (1988) note that male violence typically has more injurious consequences, and that violence by wives may be more commonly self-defensive. However, the latter is not borne out by research on married couples in which females report initiating aggression at a relatively high rate (O'Leary et al., 1989).

Child neglect is more than six times as prevalent as physical abuse in official data, but evidence on the extent of other forms of maltreatment is more limited. Violence occurs in courtship, and in one study, 32% of dating students had experienced violence from their partner, while 25% had been abusers (Murphy, 1988). Abuse of the elderly is also thought to be common, although much of this probably falls in the category of spouse abuse. The extent to which these differing forms of abuse overlap is not known, but some findings suggest that it may be considerable. In one study, for example, battered women reported that 80% of their batterers were also violent to other targets, including children and parents (Walker, 1988).

THEORIES OF AGGRESSION

Theories rest on different assumptions about the nature of aggression, and hence vary in their emphasis on unlearned or learned components, internal or external determinants, and affective or cognitive processes. They therefore differ in how they address the critical questions of how aggressive tendencies are acquired, maintained, and regulated, and how acts of aggression are "triggered" or provoked. Representative theories will be summarised with respect to how they deal with these issues. For convenience, they are grouped into biological, psychodynamic, social learning, and social psychological perspectives.

Biological Perspectives

Humans clearly have a greater capacity than other species for learning different ways of achieving the same injurious goals. However, like any co-ordinated activity, aggressive behaviour depends on inborn structural properties of brain and musculature. Biological approaches assume that this co-ordination is under the control of innate and specific neurochemical systems, and emphasise similarities rather than differences between humans and other animals.

Ethological studies of lower vertebrates led Lorenz (1966) to propose a *universal instinct* of aggression, which ensures population control, selection of the strongest animals for reproduction, brood defence, and social organisation. Instinct relates to a spontaneously generated energy source in the nervous system which discharges through fixed action patterns in response to specific releasing stimuli. Lorenz therefore postulates that a constant need to discharge aggressive energy governs human behaviour, and sees parallels between human militaristic displays or competitive sports and aggressive activities in other animals. There is, however, no physiological evidence to support this hydraulic model, even in lower animals, and despite speculations, universal releasers have not been demonstrated in humans. Lorenz has therefore been criticised for anthropomorphic extrapolation and for neglecting the role of learning.

A more sophisticated conception comes from sociobiologists such as Wilson (1978), who sees social behaviour in evolutionary terms. Emotions, self-understanding, and overt behaviour are postulated to be under the control of genetic predispositions, which evolved to enhance reproduction of the species, survival of the individual, and altruism. Aggression expresses a universal emotional predisposition, but is subject to cultural adaptation and individual learning. All humans possess this predisposition, but aggressive behaviour is an adaptive reaction to threats to survival, rather than an eruption of spontaneous energy.

Phylogenetic continuity of behaviour is also envisaged by Moyer (1981), who draws on research on electrical brain stimulation and surgical lesions in animals and in patients with organic pathology. He categorises aggression as predatory, inter-male, fear-induced, irritable, territorial, maternal, sex-related, and instrumental. Except for instrumental aggression, which requires no specific physiological basis, these behaviours are said to be controlled by *organised neural circuits* which are sensitised by hormones and blood constituents. When fired in the presence of a relevant target, these systems produce integrated attacking behaviour, although human learning can influence the selection of targets and the inhibition of behaviour. Mark and Ervin (1970) and Monroe (1978) similarly argue for a definable system in the human brain which organises directed attacking behaviour. They focus on the "dyscontrol syndrome" shown by violent people, in which limbic system mechanisms normally inhibiting aggressive behaviour are held to be damaged (see Chapter 6).

These theorists therefore assume an evolutionary origin for human aggression. While some allow for individual learning, all attribute overt aggression to internal physiological mechanisms which can override voluntary control. These views are now rejected by many biological and social scientists (American Psychological Association, 1990), and are subject to three criticisms. First, they typically employ a broad concept of aggression, which treats status conflicts, "ritualised" territorial protection, and reactions to danger as equivalent, and rely on superficial analogies between human and animal behaviour (van Eyken, 1987). Much animal aggression, however, has little relevance to human behaviour. Reis (1974) notes that Moyer's classes of animal aggression can be categorised as either *affective* or *predatory*. Affective or defensive aggression, which involves autonomic arousal and "rage" reactions to threat, is universal among vertebrates, and appears equivalent to human angry aggression. Predatory aggression, in contrast, involves food-seeking behaviour, and is species-specific.

Conversely, instrumental aggression is confined to humans, and since it requires no specific physiological system, its origins must lie in cultural evolution and individual development. Similarly, the capacity to delay revenge is uniquely human. Sociobiologists concede this, but argue that human aggression has itself evolved because of genetic advantages, and note the ubiquity of intergroup conflict and aggression. However, archaeological evidence suggests that prehistoric humans were quite peaceable, and that organised intergroup aggression has appeared only in the last 10 000 years (Turner, Turner and Fix, 1976). This seems insufficient time for genetic evolution.

A second criticism concerns the evidence for physiological systems specific to aggression. Brain stimulation and ablation research has not produced unequivocal evidence for such systems in lower animals, still less in humans (Goldstein, 1974; Valenstein, 1976). While some studies have elicited components of attacking behaviour from hypothalamic or limbic stimulation in animals, the interpretation of such findings is ambiguous with respect to a specific physiological system. Behavioural effects may, for example, result from changes in general excitability level which interfere with perceptual functions (Karli, 1981). Studies of neurological patients also suggest that prior aggressiveness determines the relation between organic disorder and violence (Mungas, 1983).

A biological basis for anger is more plausible. The role of the sympathetic-adrenal system in mobilising "fight or flight" reactions, and the central integration of emotional arousal and expression by hypothalamic–limbic circuits, are well established. Although the same system subserves different aroused states, anger seems to be associated with a relatively specific physiological pattern of noradrenaline increase, which can be elicited simply by imagining provocation (Roberts and Weerts, 1982). Many developmental theorists therefore assume that there are primitive innate connections between anger and aggression, which become modified by experience. Averill (1982), however, argues that biological components of emotional expression are not the crucial elements, and that anger is a socially constructed emotion.

A third criticism focuses on the implied inevitability of human aggression. Karli (1981) notes that evolutionary development determines adaptive *strategies* for coping with different classes of events rather than specific *behavioural outcomes*, and that biological theorists overemphasise the latter. Genetic programming may have created a state of *readiness* to aggress under certain conditions, such as anger arousal, but whether this readiness translates into directed action is likely to depend more on ontogeny than phylogeny.

The social and cultural modifiability of aggression is also a key issue in accounting for *sex differences*. Gender role differences clearly depend on the learning of cultural stereotypes, but the apparent ubiquity of greater aggressiveness in males of all species is often cited as evidence for the phylogenetic origin of aggression. Animal, anthropological, cross-cultural, and child development research all points in this direction (White, 1983), but there are exceptions, even in other animals. Averill (1982) found few sex differences in the experience and expression of anger, and socialisation studies in humans indicate that gender differences in aggression are not inevitable (White, 1983). Innate preparedness therefore accounts for only part of the variance, and biological differences between the sexes probably interact with cultural sex-role prescriptions by dictating differential reinforcement of particular behaviours by males and females (Cohen and Machalek, 1989).

Attempts to account for sex differences in aggression, and for male criminal violence, in terms of genetic and hormonal factors have not yielded consistent findings (Chapter 6). Although twin studies support a genetic contribution to individual differences in aggression (Rushton et al., 1986), it remains unclear whether this involves the transmission of specific mechanisms, such as testosterone production, or nonspecific factors, such as activity level, which facilitate the learning of aggression.

Psychodynamic Perspectives

There is no single psychodynamic theory of aggression, but an aggressive instinct or drive is generally assumed (Kutash, 1978). Theories focus on how aggressive drive is channelled and controlled in the course of individual development, and how it is accommodated and regulated by the internal mechanisms of the ego and superego.

Freud initially saw aggression as a reaction to frustration and pain. He later introduced the notion of a death instinct (Thanatos), a tendency to self-destruction which is diverted by the self-preserving libidinal instinct (Eros) to objects in the external world which threaten vital interests (Freud, 1920/1955). Many psychoanalysts reject this notion, but accept an instinct of aggression. Instinctual manifestations include not only destructive behaviour, but also fantasy aggression, intergroup hostility, and suicide, and aggressive drive undergoes the same developmental vicissitudes as the libido. It is therefore manifest in biting (oral sadism), or faeces retention (anal sadism), and through fixation, these reactions may become lasting aggressive character traits. While aggression may be provoked by external events, such as rivalry with siblings, aggressive impulses are constantly generated, and may erupt as irrational violence in those lacking superego control. Aggressive energy may also be displaced to other targets, and a key assumption in the instinct model is the notion of *catharsis*, i.e. the "purging" of aggressive tension by means of direct or substitute expression. This underlies the popular view that suppression of anger is unhealthy, and that vigorous competition dissipates aggressive feelings.

Ego psychologists have elaborated on the development of "aggression in the service of the ego". In addition to redirection by displacement, and modification of destructive aims by sublimation, aggressive energy may be *neutralised*, enabling the ego to fulfil self-assertive and constructive goals (Hartmann, Kris and Lowenstein, 1949). Superego development permits internalisation of aggressive energy through guilt, but instinctual energy is still generated, and continuous sublimation or neutralisation is needed to cope with conflicting demands of the libido, superego, or reality. In the healthy individual, ego control modifies aggressive drive, and prevents violence. In personality disorders, ego weakness results in the repression of aggression and its expression in fantasy or symbolic acts, or "acting out" in impulsive violence (Kutash, 1978).

The psychodynamic instinct model is similar to that of Lorenz. The shortcomings of an hydraulic concept of instinct have already been noted, and the assumption of cathartic dissipation of aggression has little empirical support (Geen and Quanty, 1977). Also, the proposal that nonaggressive behaviours, such as constructive self-assertion, are manifestations of transformed destructive energy allows virtually any activity to be construed as aggressive.

Non-Freudian psychoanalysts criticise the instinct concept, and argue for sociocultural origins of aggression. Fromm (1973) distinguishes defensive or *benign aggression*, a biologically programmed reaction to threat, from destructive or *malignant aggression*, which is a specifically human phenomenon arising when socioeconomic conditions prevent the fulfilment of existential needs for interpersonal ties or personal effectiveness. Malignant aggression is not derived from benign aggression, and is distinct from instrumental aggression. It is seen in cruelty and torture, and typifies *sadistic characters*, who need to control others. Fromm's concept influenced the inclusion of sadistic personality disorder in DSM-III-R. However, it is arguable whether malignant aggression can be separated from either benign (angry) aggression or instrumental aggression, and sadism as a means of interpersonal control is clearly encompassed by the notion of coercive power.

Learning and social cognitive perspectives

Learning approaches apply operant and modelling paradigms, and see human aggression as acquired and maintained according to the individual's history of direct and vicarious reinforcement and punishment. While rejecting the instinct notion, most learning theorists retain an energising concept in the form of drive or arousal, but differ in their accounts of the relation between arousal and cognition.

The assumption that aggression becomes more likely following the experience of successful aggression or observation of aggressive models is now well established by experimental and observational studies. Patterson (1982), for example, demonstrates how coercive behaviour in families is increased and maintained by its consequences in the form of terminating aversive treatment or gaining attention. However, what constitutes a reinforcer for aggression remains unclear (Zillmann, 1979). Instrumental aggression is, by definition, *positively reinforced* by the attainment of rewards, such as material goods, status, or approval. Angry aggression, on the other hand, is assumed to be *negatively reinforced* by the alleviation of anger or the removal of aversive treatment. Some accounts, however, suggest that it may be positively reinforced by the attainment of injury, and that signs of damage are inherently reinforcing. This assumption has not received unequivocal experimental support, and signs of pain or injury are more likely to inhibit aggression (Zillmann, 1979). Nevertheless, it is a moot point whether an aggressive act, such as a robbery, attains a reinforcer (money) or removes an aversion (poverty). Similar ambiguities surround the effects of punishment on aggression, since punishment can be regarded as counteraggression.

Of particular concern have been the antecedents of aggression and the factors mediating between these and an aggressive outcome. Dollard et al. (1939) drew on early Freudian theory in formulating the *frustration–aggression hypothesis*, which asserted that frustration in the form of thwarting of goal-directed activity is the critical antecedent of aggression. Frustration instigates attempts to injure the source of frustration, but if punishment is anticipated, the response is inhibited unless displaced to an alternative target.

Although influential, the original theory has not been widely accepted, since frustration instigates responses other than aggression, and aggression is equally provoked by insult or attack, threats to self-esteem, or pain (Buss, 1961). Berkowitz, however, has long defended the theory, arguing that there are elements of frustration in such antecedents. He sees instigation as a reactive drive state of anger, which inclines the individual towards injury of the target, but learned cues such as weapons are necessary to release aggressive responding. The theory therefore applies to angry rather than instrumental aggression. Although punishment may inhibit instrumental aggression, it constitutes frustration, and increases angry aggression. In his recent *cognitive–neoassociationist* formulation, Berkowitz (1989) argues that the frustration–aggression relation is a special case of a more general relation between aversive stimulation and aggressive inclinations. Noting that aggression is heightened by physical discomfort and negative mood, as well as by thwarting or insult, he suggests that negative affect is the basic source of angry aggression. Thus, events perceived as unpleasant elicit negative affect which is connected by associative networks to memories and expressive motor reactions related to both escape and aggression. Anger-related thoughts primed by this linkage will lead to aggression depending on cognitive appraisals of the situation. However, cognitive appraisals have a secondary rather than a primary role.

Other theorists give more weight to cognitive mediation, and replace the notion of a specific aggressive drive with a concept of nonspecific arousal. Experimental studies demonstrate that anger increases attempts to injure (Rule and Nesdale, 1976), and Averill (1982) similarly found that everyday anger arousal increases thoughts of harming the target. He also found that frustration was a common antecedent of anger. However, the notion of a specific drive to injure is questioned by studies which show that tension produced by frustration can be reduced by nonaggressive behaviour which removes aversion, as well as by direct aggression (Hokanson, 1970). The effects of frustration and punishment have also been shown to depend on whether the recipient perceives them as justified (Zillmann, 1979; Averill, 1982). This clearly entails normative judgements and cognitive appraisals about the intent of a frustrator.

The most comprehensive cognitive theory of aggression is that of Bandura (1983). Reinforcing contingencies provide information about the effects of behaviour, but such information is most readily acquired through observational learning, through which people develop expectations about the likely outcomes of different behaviours in meeting their goals. These, however, include consequences for the self, and behaviour is adjusted to meet personal and social standards through self-regulatory processes of self-reward and punishment. Standards may nevertheless be overridden or neutralised by cognitive distortions such as blaming or dehumanising the victim.

Bandura rejects the notion of a specific aggressive drive, and regards the distinction between angry and instrumental aggression as unnecessary, on the grounds that all aggression is instrumental in gaining a desired end. He proposes that both aversive experiences and positive incentives produce a general increase in emotional arousal. This energises whatever relevant responses are strongest in the behavioural repertoire. In coping with aversive experiences, aggression is only one of several possible strategies, which might include avoidance or constructive problem-solving, depending on the individual's skills. In these terms, persistent aggression may result not only from reinforcement for such behaviour, but also from failure to learn nonaggressive ways of coping with aversive events or obtaining desired rewards.

Although Bandura gives no special treatment to *anger*, this is a recent focus of interest for social cognitive theorists (Averill, 1982; Novaco, 1978; Novaco and Welsh, 1989; Levey and Howells, 1990). The tendency to experience frequent and intense anger is a stress reaction which impairs social functioning and physical health. While the equation of anger with aggressive drive is questionable, it has been noted that anger has a distinct physiological pattern, and that anger arousal motivates attempts to harm the source. However, inflicting harm is only one means of alleviating anger, and the more basic function of anger may be to regulate relationships. As Averill (1982) puts it, "people are known by the things that make them angry". From reports of daily monitoring of anger, he found that it is a frequently experienced emotion aroused primarily in intimate relationships, and that although often unpleasant, its communication and expression typically have constructive consequences. To the extent that violent crime entails angry aggression, aggressive criminals may have problems in both the experience and expression of anger (below).

The conditions which arouse anger remain controversial. One influential view has it that the nature of emotional experience depends on the cognitive label applied to a nonspecific state of arousal (Schachter, 1964). Consistent with this, Zillmann (1979) found that when subjects were provoked to anger, further arousal from extraneous sources, such as exercise, heat, or erotica, was misattributed and intensified aggression. However, these effects were obtained under laboratory conditions in which sources of arousal were ambiguous, which is probably infrequent in the natural environment. A contrary view comes from Lazarus (1991), who has long argued that the nature of emotional arousal is itself determined cognitively by processes of *appraisal* operating at both schematic and conscious levels. Beck (1976) draws on this theory, and sees specific emotions as the consequence of specific cognitive appraisals. Thus, anxiety results from the appraisal of danger, while anger follows the appraisal of an *unwarranted violation* of one's domain, which includes self concept and values, as well as personal relationships and possessions. Novaco similarly sees anger as a consequence of the appraisal of physical attack, verbal threat or insult, reductions in anticipated reinforcers, and inequity, and like Beck, specifies sources of bias in the content and operations of cognitive schemata which promote dysfunctional anger.

At a more general level, attribution theorists propose that anger results from specific causal attributions (Ferguson and Rule, 1983; Weiner, 1986). Ferguson and Rule, for example, suggest that anger is aroused not simply by the degree of perceived aversive treatment by others, but also by judgements of whether the aversion is intentional, malevolent, foreseeable, and unjustified. Such inferences derive from what the individual construes *ought* to be the case, and therefore reflect what is important in terms of personal values, rights, and self-esteem. In these terms, there is a significant moral dimension in anger.

While few now question the mediating role of cognitive attributions in anger arousal, their primary causal role is disputed. Berkowitz (1990) proposes that the primary appraisal initiating emotional arousal is confined to the perception of *unpleasantness*. Causal attributions influence behaviour only after anger has been primed by associative networks. He therefore denies that emotion is a consequence of the appraised personal *meaning* of an event. However, the relation between emotional arousal and cognition seems likely to be reciprocal. Prior mood state can clearly affect the threshold of anger arousal, and Zillmann's research suggests that people *can* misattribute the source of their arousal under certain conditions.

Social psychological perspectives

Recent social cognitive approaches incorporate social influences on aggression, but give primacy to individual factors. Several social psychologists argue that aggression can only be understood by reference to the social context and meaning of the aggressive act. Felson (1978), for example, proposes that aggression is a means of impression management, which restores one's threatened identity. Others emphasise the wider influence of social structures and cultural norms. Three approaches will be summarised by way of illustration.

Tedeschi (1983) emphasises social causes of the use of *coercive power*. Drawing on exchange theory, he notes that coercion is often a last resort when other tactics of social influence are unsuccessful. Coercive power is reflected in the communication of threats that punishment will follow noncompliance, or in the delivery of punishment. It becomes salient in situations of conflict over rewards, threats to power or status, or when harm is threatened or experienced, and may be dictated by normative standards or by individual characteristics. The offensive use of coercive power is usually proscribed or antinormative, but coercion is commonly defensive or retaliatory, and prescribed by social norms. Norms of reciprocity call for harm to a harm-doer in proportion to the harm done. These are widespread in society, and encourage interpersonal and intergroup violence. Norms of equity create perceptions of relative deprivation and injustice, which may motivate illegitimate access to resources (cf. anomie theory). The decision to employ coercive power depends on the value and probability of success and costs, and is enhanced by the need to preserve self-image or maintain authority, and by fear. It is also more likely when the individual lacks self-esteem and feels powerless to influence events, or when people misperceive costs through distorted time perspectives, egocentricity, or intoxication. Several of these causes of the use of coercion are compatible with social cognitive theories, and Tedeschi's approach differs mainly in specifying interpersonal compliance as the goal or reinforcer of interpersonal harm.

In the tradition of class-based theories, Wolfgang and Ferracutti (1967) proposed a *subculture of violence*, which dictates a norm to be violent. This is part of a "machismo" pattern of attitudes favouring excitement, status, honour, and masculinity, threats to which demand combative reactions. Since the highest homicide rates are found in young, male, nonwhite, and lower class groups, it was suggested, with acknowledged circular reasoning, that these groups support violent subcultural values which conflict with those of the dominant culture. However, attempts to test this have not yielded favourable results. Ball-Rokeach (1973) was unable to demonstrate a pattern of "machismo" value preferences among violent males, regardless of education or income level. While finding that poor, black, and younger males were more likely to report fighting, Erlanger (1974) also failed to support the prediction that males who fight should feel more accepted by their group. He suggests a "subculture of masculinity", in which violence is simply one of many outlets. Although still popular, the subculture of violence hypothesis remains unsupported. Some suggest that it is the dominant culture itself which supports norms of violence.

Marsh (1985; Marsh, Rosser and Harré, 1978) adopts a more phenomenological approach to youth subculture, and has investigated how social rules govern the aggressive behaviour of British football fans. This work draws on Harré's ethogenic social psychology, and aims to uncover the rules which people ascribe to their behaviour through an analysis of their *accounts* of intentions and emotions. Although British soccer fans have achieved notoriety for violent clashes with rival supporters, Marsh's observations suggest that extreme violence is exceptional, and that most football "hooliganism" is ritualised violence taking the form of taunting and gestures. This is governed by mutually understood rules which prescribe hostile postures and a "rhetoric of violence", but group rules minimise physical contact. The football terraces are important for urban working class males because they provide not only a sense of belonging and worth, but also an opportunity for excitement lacking from their routine lives. Ritualised contests therefore serve a constructive function, and contain aggression. Marsh notes analogies in lower vertebrates, and hence comes close to sociobiology. However, the notion of ritualisation presumes aggressive functions of intergroup rivalry, which may not be the salient factor. Nevertheless, Marsh's work indicates that the occurrence of violence may be governed by shared conceptual schemata which specify when it is appropriate.

These approaches assume that aggression is rational, and not abnormal when seen in its social context, but do not distinguish instrumental from angry aggression. Some argue that they are of limited relevance to the latter or to individual acts of criminal violence. Berkowitz (1986), for example, concludes from interviews with violent offenders that their offences were largely impulsive acts of angry aggression, which were neither governed by social norms nor motivated by needs to project a particular self image. Zillmann (1979) also suggests that the cognitive control of aggression is determined by the level of physiological arousal. At high or low levels, cognitive mediation is minimised, and aggression is likely to be impulsive and under immediate stimulus control. However, violent acts which deviate from social norms (which is implicit in the label of "impulsive") may nonetheless be rule-governed, albeit by idiosyncratic *personal* rules.

ANTECEDENTS OF AGGRESSION

The distinction between dispositions and acts is particularly important in understanding violence, since the antecedents of a *tendency* to behave aggressively are likely to be distal, such as early childhood experiences. The antecedents of an *act* of aggression, on the other hand, include proximal factors such as recent life events or situational factors preceding an assault. The nature of aggression as a disposition is considered in the next section. The concern here is primarily with social and other environmental antecedents of acts of aggression, whether or not the participants are disposed to behave in that way.

Situational antecedents of violent acts

There have been several attempts to identify regularities in the sequence of events leading to a violent crime. Wolfgang (1957) suggested that many homicides were *victim-precipitated*, in that the victim was the first to resort to violence. A quarter of the Philadelphia homicides were of this kind, and in several respects, victims in such cases were more like offenders in nonvictimprecipitated homicides. Wolfgang's notion has been extended to include other provocations, and Amir (1971) estimated that 19% of his rape cases were victim-precipitated. Curtis (1974), however, found evidence for this in only 4% of rapes, although he found signs of victim precipitation in 22% of homicides, 14% of aggravated assaults, and 11% of robberies.

While some regard the notion of victim-precipitation as "blaming the victim", it coincides with a symbolic interactionist view of violent encounters as "situated transactions" in which participants engage in "character contests". Analyses of event sequences in reports of homicide and assault indicate that reciprocal retaliation is a significant factor (Toch, 1969; Luckenbill, 1977; Felson and Steadman, 1983). Retaliation may be either an attempt to save face or a strategic form of self protection. Incidents typically begin with an attack on the antagonist's identity by insult, followed by attempts and failures to influence the other, threats, and escalation of verbal conflict to physical attack. A violent outcome is thus more the result of events causing a conflict to escalate than the characteristics or initial goals of the participants.

From his interviews with assaultive offenders in a Scottish prison, Berkowitz (1986) concluded that although face-saving may instigate an aggressive exchange, its intensification is mainly the result of impulsive attempts to hurt the victim. However, it seems likely that interactions culminating in violence will vary according to the context and the interpersonal styles and skills the participants bring to the situation.

Media influences on aggression

Given the uses of mass communication media to change attitudes and behaviour, the view that portrayals of violence in films and television (TV) may increase aggression in viewers seems unremarkable. Empirical evidence was obtained in the 1930s (Wober, 1989), but concerns about the exposure of children to high frequencies of violent incidents on TV have generated extensive research in recent decades, especially in the United States.

The current consensus is that filmed violence has a small but significant effect on subsequent aggression among viewers (Geen, 1983; Friedrich-Cofer and Huston, 1986), although violence depicted as justified has a greater effect, and not all viewers are affected equally. Eron and Huesmann (1986) cite evidence that children between the ages of 8 and 12 are particularly susceptible, but contrary to earlier findings, girls are influenced as much as, if not more than boys. Personal attributes, such as low educational achievement and unpopularity, are also associated with stronger effects, and although not consistently found, there is some evidence that TV violence exerts a stronger influence on aggressive than on nonaggressive children (Wober, 1989). Effects also depend on the extent to which a child watches TV, sees TV as realistic, and identifies with aggressive TV characters (Eron and Huesmann, 1986).

Much research focuses on short-term increases in minor acts of aggression, but some studies have examined effects on criminal violence. Hennigan et al. (1982), for example, compared crime rates in American cities with and without TV between 1949 and 1952. They found that the introduction of TV did not increase the rates of homicide, aggravated assault, burglary or auto theft, although there was an increase in larceny, which they attributed to increased awareness of relative deprivation among the poor. Phillips (1983), on the other hand, claimed that "mass media violence *does* provoke aggression in the real world" on the basis of findings of increased daily homicide rates in the United States following the showing of championship boxing matches. A peak increase of 12.5% was observed on day 3 following the fight, and since race of victims changed to match that of the loser, Phillips argued for a modelling effect. However, victim changes did not coincide with the overall peak on day 3, which itself requires explanation, and such a strong conclusion from these aggregate data seems premature.

There is some evidence that viewing of TV violence has long-term as well as immediate influences on antisocial aggression. Eron (1987) reports that childhood viewing of violence was significantly associated with the level of aggression 22 years later, including criminal violence, suggesting that TV violence may strengthen an aggressive disposition. However, a retrospective study of violent offenders by Heath, Kruttschnitt and Ward (1986) found that heavy TV viewing was related to later violence only when combined with experience of parental abuse.

Some reviewers challenge the causal relationship. Freedman (1984) questioned the external validity of laboratory research in this area, and argued that field experiments have not produced findings consistent with a causal effect. While accepting the consistent demonstration of a correlation of about 0.2 between amount of TV violence viewing and measures of aggressiveness, he argues that this reflects the influence of other variables, or the selection of violent programmes by aggressively disposed viewers. However, Friedrich-Cofer and Huston (1986) note that the correlation is relatively unchanged when IQ, achievement, class, family factors, and level of prior aggressiveness are held constant, and that the convergence of evidence from different sources justifies the causal assumption. Nevertheless, the effects are now seen as *bidirectional*. Thus, those with aggressive propensities are more likely to prefer and select violent TV viewing, which then influences the level of aggression further.

The processes by which violent TV viewing influences aggression are clearly complex. It is generally assumed that effects depend on modelling of aggressive solutions to conflict, although this is not an indiscriminate process, and there is little to suggest imitation of specific violent acts. Short-term effects may involve increased arousal, which activates aggressive responses when these are prepotent. Repeated exposure to TV violence may also have a desensitising effect, weakening inhibitions against aggression (Thomas et al., 1977). However, violent TV programmes are produced in a social context, and are as much a product as a shaper of prevailing reality and norms. The effects of TV violence viewing cannot therefore be determined in isolation from other social influences on aggression.

Alcohol, drugs, and violence

Mythologies about alcohol and drug use have fostered the belief that they are prominent causes of criminal acts, particularly violence. However, research indicates that delinquency and substance use are part of a deviant lifestyle originating in a variety of factors, and any association may be incidental (Osgood et al., 1988). Nevertheless, Goldstein (1989) distinguishes three ways in which substance use and abuse may be causally involved in violence. In *psychopharmacological violence*, effects of the drug itself facilitate violent acts. In *economically compulsive violence*, the need to support drug use motivates instrumental crimes such as robbery. In *systemic violence*, the system of drug distribution and dealing creates conflicts resolved by violence, as seen, for example, during Prohibition in the United States, and more recently over cocaine distribution in Miami.

Concerns about alcohol focus on psychopharmacological violence. In his analysis of homicide, Wolfgang (1958) found that 55% of offenders and 53% of victims had been drinking, and many studies obtain similar findings. Alcohol has also been implicated in other violent crimes. Shupe (1954) analysed urinary alcohol concentrations in 882 offenders following arrest. Levels indicating intoxication were present in 88% of those charged with cutting, 67% of murderers, and 45% of those charged with rape. Also, in incidents of violence reported in the 1988 British crime survey, the offender was drunk in over 60% of non job-related offences. For job-related incidents, the offender was drunk in 83% of assaults on males, though only 16% of those on females (Mayhew, Elliott and Dowds, 1989).

Such findings do not establish a causal relationship. Data on drinking levels in comparable groups who have not offended have not been reported, and most research draws on police reports or retrospective accounts of offenders, of uncertain reliability. Offender reports may be biased, since claiming intoxication is a common form of "deviance disavowal" (McCaghy, 1968). Some studies also indicate that high proportions of nonviolent offenders have been drinking prior to offending (Collins, 1989), suggesting that drinking is associated with criminal behaviour in general, or perhaps a failure to avoid detection. Moreover, aggression is not the most common effect of alcohol. From interviews with a Canadian community sample and observations in bars, Pernanen (1991) noted that indiscriminate positive affect and "harmless folly" are the most frequent accompaniments of drinking, and that dangerous acts are rare. However, the balance of evidence favours a special link between alcohol and aggressive crimes, and the facilitative effect of alcohol on aggression has also been demonstrated in laboratory studies (Bushman and Cooper, 1990).

There is, nevertheless, no simple relation between alcohol ingestion and aggression. Small doses of ethanol may increase autonomic arousal, while larger doses produce cortical de-arousal, but neuronal effects are not stable (Brain, 1986). Impairment of psychomotor skills, reaction time, and complex cognitive processing are well established consequences of alcohol intake, but psychological effects vary not only according to the type and amount of drink, but also with individual differences in body build, metabolism, and acquired tolerance. Moreover, the effects on mood and social behaviour are highly dependent on social and cultural context. Several possible explanations for the link between alcohol and aggression have therefore been advanced.

Graham (1980) identified four categories of theory, which differ according to the role ascribed to alcohol itself. A *direct cause* is explicit in "disinhibition" theories, which assume that alcohol acts on brain mechanisms inhibiting aggression. This notion derives from a moral view of drunkenness (Critchlow, 1986), and has been sustained by instinct theories of aggression, as witnessed in the jocular definition of the superego as "that which is soluble in alcohol". However, this view is undermined by the lack of evidence for brain centres of aggression, and by the variable effects of alcohol. Moreover, given the high frequency of occasions on which alcohol is consumed with nonaggressive consequences, the disinhibition hypothesis is clearly simplistic. Theories arguing for an *indirect cause* assume that effects of alcohol are mediated by changes in arousal and cognition. Taylor and Leonard (1983) propose that alcohol reduces ability to attend to multiple cues and switch attention, with the result that the intoxicated person is more stimulus-bound, less guided by inhibitory cues or anticipated future consequences, and takes more risks. Pernanen (1991) similarly suggests that alcohol affects cognition, narrowing the perceptual field, and makes behaviour more situationally determined. A third approach emphasises the *motive for drinking*, which may be the attainment of anxiety reduction or feelings of power, which then interact with other effects of alcohol. For example, reduced ambiguities of situational cues may enhance feelings of control, which are potentiated in those with power concerns, leading to overestimated prowess.

A fourth set of theories sees the alcohol–aggression correlation as reflecting *predispositional or situational factors*. Personality factors may lead people both to drink and to behave aggressively. Buikhuisen, Van Der Plas-Korenhoff and Bontekoe (1988), for example, found that students who reported becoming aggressive after drinking were distinguished from unaggressive drinkers by more self-reported delinquency, hostility, dominance, impulsivity, and inconsistent upbringing, as well as by increased skin conductance recovery time after drinking. Expectations about the effects of alcohol, and the culturally permitted "time out" from social rules allowed for drinkers, may also encourage deviant behaviour after drinking (Critchlow, 1986). Finally, some drinking situations themselves are more conducive to aggression. For example, Graham et al. (1980) found that the most aggression-prone bars in Vancouver were more physically unattractive, unfriendly, run-down, tense in atmosphere, and imposed few limits on acceptable behaviour.

These theories overlap rather than compete, but a meta-analysis of experimental studies on alcohol and aggression suggests that they are not all equally plausible. Bushman and Cooper (1990) found significant effects of alcohol on aggression in comparison with placebo and control conditions, indicating that alcohol itself has a facilitating effect. However, placebo (expect alcohol but do not receive it) and antiplacebo (do not expect alcohol but receive it) conditions failed to produce significant effects, suggesting that neither pharmacological nor psychological factors alone are the important determinants. Whether alcohol ingestion leads to aggression therefore seems to depend on an interaction between the characteristics of the drinker, the psychological effects of alcohol, and provoking and constraining factors in the situation.

Those who are acutely intoxicated when offending are not necessarily chronic drinkers, but it is well known that drink-related problems are common among prisoners. Prevalence estimates vary with the criteria for alcohol dependence, alcohol abuse, or problem drinking, but several studies suggest that a third or more of prisoners have serious drink problems. Using a symptom criterion, Edwards, Hensman and Peto (1971) estimated that 34% of a sample of long-term English prisoners, 55% of short-term prisoners, and 86% of those convicted for drunkenness showed moderate to severe alcohol dependency. Some recent studies employ quantitative criteria which permit comparisons with normative data. Violent and nonviolent prisoners in a Scottish study (Myers, 1982) reported an average weekly consumption of 70 units, while 47% drank more than 80 units a week (one unit = a half pint of beer or one ounce of spirits). Among young English prisoners, McMurran and Hollin (1989) found a weekly average of 58 units, and 43% drank more than 50 units. In comparison, 18 to 24 year old male drinkers in a Scottish community survey reported a weekly average of 26 units, while 8% of the sample consumed more than 50 units (Saunders and Kershaw, 1976).

Prolonged elevations of blood alcohol level impair information processing and judgement, and may make aggressive interactions more likely. High alcohol consumption in discharged prisoners also impedes rehabilitation, and may encourage economically compulsive crimes. However, it is probable that only a minority of alcoholics become criminal, and not all of these are violent offenders. For example, alcohol dependence was found to be more prevalent among petty than among serious offenders by Edwards, Hensman and Peto, (1971). Coid (1982) suggests that alcoholism is probably not related to violence, but that personality disorder in a subgroup of alcoholics predisposes them to both drinking and violence.

Fewer research findings are available on the relationship of illicit drug use to violence, partly since the involvement of drugs in a crime is often not revealed, and partly because of an assumption that only a small amount of crime is due to drugs. The evidence suggests that marijuana, opiates, and tranquillisers do not facilitate aggression, and may actually be inhibitory (Goldstein, 1989). Amphetamine and barbiturates are more likely to facilitate violence, but as with alcohol, the outcome seems to depend on predispositional and situational factors. On the other hand, delusional states produced by toxic substances increase the likelihood of impulsive violence, and heightened irritability may accompany withdrawal from opiates or marijuana (Goldstein, 1989). However, drug-related offending remains part of the "dark figure" of unrecorded crime. Nurco et al. (1985) report that many narcotic addicts engage in high rates of crime, of which fewer than 1% result in arrest. Most of this consists of theft and dealing to support addiction rather than violence, and it has been thought that opiate addicts are not unusually prone to violence. However, Goldstein (1989) cites recent American studies which have found illegal drugs, particularly cocaine, in the urine of between one and two thirds of those arrested for violent crimes, and estimates that 10% of homicides in America may now be the result of drug use. How much of this is pharmacological rather than economically compulsive or systemic violence remains unclear.

Physical and social environmental changes

Environmental changes affecting biological, psychological, or social func-tioning may be experienced as aversive or frustrating. A possible influence on aggression would therefore be consistent with several theories, and considerable data have been amassed suggesting a relationship between human aggression and environmental factors such as noise levels and climate (Mueller, 1983). Some studies have also tested the folklore of a lunar influence on deviant behaviour. Lieber and Sherrin (1972) speculated that lunar gravitational forces might affect emotional functioning, and obtained data indicating periodicity in homicidal rates in two American counties, peaks coinciding with a full moon and following a new moon. Forbes and Lebo (1977), however, were unable to identify such an effect on rates of arrest for violence.

There is firmer evidence for the effects of temperature. Anderson (1989) reviewed field and laboratory research, and found that although data from the latter were not entirely consistent, field studies uniformly showed that hotter regions, and hotter years, seasons, months, and days, were associated with increased rates of murder, rape, assault, riot, and wife-beating. Similar effects have been found for air-pollution, as indexed by ozone levels (Rotton and Frey, 1985). While the effects of weather changes may be partly mediated by changes in social contact and opportunities for aggression, Anderson (1989) suggests that the evidence is consistent with effects at the individual level, such as increased negative affect, or misattribution of arousal. Mueller (1983) similarly proposes that changes in the physical environment (noise, heat, air pollution) and interpersonal environment (territorial invasion, personal space violations, high population density) function as stressors, and make aggression more likely through the facilitation of dominant responses, impaired information processing, or perceived loss of control. However, such stressors do not have uniform effects, and are not themselves sufficient for aggression.

A variable of interest in this context is the maintenance of *personal space* (proxemic behaviour). O'Neal et al. (1979) showed that anger arousal increases preferred interpersonal distance, and there is evidence that the latter may characterise violent offenders. Kinzel (1970) found that violent inmates displayed a larger personal space than nonviolent prisoners, and that this was most pronounced for approaches from the rear. He suggested that this reflects homosexual anxiety. This latter finding has not been replicated, but several studies confirm the larger preferred interpersonal distance of violent offenders (e.g. Booraem et al., 1977), and among nonoffenders, preferred distance correlates with a quarrelsome and aloof interpersonal style (Gifford and O'Connor, 1987). Methodological variations, including reliance on a single offence to indicate a violent disposition, may account for failures of replication (e.g. Eastwood, 1985). However, although personal space is often equated with territoriality in other animals, its functional significance remains obscure. Preferred space may not be a stable characteristic, since Kinzel (1970) found that it declined with repeated measurement. Its association with an aggressive disposition may therefore represent a hypervigilance for interpersonal threat which becomes marked in the presence of strangers.

A further factor which may be particularly relevant to group violence is the level of anonymity. Zimbardo (1970) proposed that certain conditions, such as anonymity, involvement in group activity, diffusion of responsibility across group members, and accompanying changes in arousal, produce a state of *deindividuation*. This consists of the feeling that one does not stand out as an individual, reduced self-awareness, and decreased concern for negative consequences, which facilitates impulsive harmful behaviour. Experimental support for this phenomenon is rather weak (Diener, 1977), but Prentice-Dunn and Rogers (1983) find support for the view that the critical feature of deindividuation is reduced *private* self-awareness, in which there is decreased reliance on internal standards and reduced cognitive control, making the person more responsive to aggressive cues. Critical antecedents are immersion in group activities and other conditions which lead to an external focus of attention. However, deindividuation remains a contentious concept. Bandura (1986), for example, notes that diffusion of responsibility can disinhibit aggression through cognitive restructuring and neutralising beliefs rather than through loss of control.

PERSONALITY AND AGGRESSION

Acts of aggression may sometimes be committed by people who are not habitually aggressive. This distinction between act and disposition is ignored by studies which identify "violent offenders" by reference to the most recent conviction alone. Since situational factors and a person's temporary state clearly contribute to violent incidents, involvement in a single act of violence is not a reliable index of a violent disposition. However, some people are more ready than others to engage in acts of aggression, and the concern of this section is with what contributes to such a tendency.

The consistency of aggression

Several longitudinal studies have established the temporal stability of aggression as a trait. Olweus (1979) reviewed evidence on the stability of aggression in males as measured by observer ratings, peer nominations, and direct observation, and identified twelve investigations in which assessments had been made on at least two occasions, which ranged from 6 months to 21 years apart. The average corrected correlation between the two assessments was 0.79. He therefore concluded that there is substantial stability in aggression which cannot be attributed to situational constancy. In a subsequent review (Olweus, 1981), he found only slightly lower levels of stability among females.

Subsequent studies are consistent with Olweus' findings. For example, Huesmann et al. (1984) found that peer nominations of aggression made at age 8 correlated significantly with self- and spouse-reported aggression and also criminal record 22 years later. Structural models yielded estimated stability coefficients for aggression of 0.50 for males, and 0.35 for females. Similarly in the Cambridge study, ratings of aggression at age 8 to 10 correlated significantly with self-reported aggression in adolescence and adulthood (Farrington, 1989). Since these studies involve reassessment of aggression by different methods and in different contexts, they suggest cross-situational as well as temporal consistency. Cross-situational consistency was demonstrated more directly by Feshbach and Price (1984), who found that among schoolchildren rated for aggression over two years, correlations between ratings made at home and at school ranged from 0.39 to 0.59. Aggressive tendencies are, then, relatively enduring attributes which differentiate between people from early in life.

Criminal violence appears to be a function of such a disposition. Farrington (1989) found that 22.4% of those rated as highly aggressive by teachers at age 12 to 14 subsequently had a conviction for violence, compared with 7.2% of less aggressive boys, and the former accounted for 60% of the violent offenders. Similar data were obtained by Stattin and Magnusson (1989). Robins (1978) also found that fighting in childhood consistently predicts violent behaviour in adults, and in all of these studies, early aggression was associated with later social deviance in general. This justifies the notion of a "syndrome" of antisocial behaviour, of which aggression is a prominent feature.

All of these studies, however, have a high false positive rate, and although a majority of those who exhibit violence in adulthood have been identified as aggressive in childhood, only a minority of aggressive children go on to be seriously aggressive. Many of the remainder may continue to be aggressive in less obvious ways, but it must be emphasised that stability is only relative in this context. Thus, early manifestations of aggressiveness as a trait make later violence more likely, but whether a criminal outcome ensues depends on other personal and environmental factors.

Origins of consistency in aggression

Aggression may be influenced by genetic factors, and a twin study by Rushton et al. (1986) found evidence for substantial heritability for self-reported aggressiveness. This is not inconsistent with learning analyses, but suggests that the child may be an active contributor to the learning of aggression. Buss (1961), for example, proposed that temperament traits of impulsivity, activity level, intensity of emotional reactions, and independence would all contribute to the learning of aggression, partly by creating more opportunities for aversive exchanges with caretakers or siblings.

Current views assume that persistent aggression originates primarily in family modelling and reinforcement. Longitudinal studies show that family histories of aggressive children and delinquents are characterised by higher rates of parental deviance, marital conflict, parental indifference and lack of supervision, and violent adults frequently report a history of witnessing violence and experiencing physical abuse in childhood (Chapter 7). Cross-sectional studies produce comparable data. Busch et al. (1990) found that 58% of 71 adolescents who had killed had a criminally violent family member compared with 20% of demographically matched nonviolent delinquents. These findings are consistent with the social learning view that the family provides a learning environment where violent behaviours are modelled, rehearsed, and reinforced. Such families are more likely to be economically deprived and embedded in a wider context of social disorganisation. While the relation of violence to social class has been questioned, Brownfield (1986) found that both self-reported and official violent delinquency were related to a measure of underclass defined by family unemployment and welfare dependency, although only weakly to more traditional measures of class, such as parental occupation.

Family variables nevertheless account for only a small part of the variance in later violence. In an uncontrolled study of violent delinquents, Fagan and Wexler (1987) found some association of self-reported violence with criminality and violence in the family, but violence correlated more strongly with delinquent peer friendships. Blaske et al. (1989) also found that among father-absent boys, violent delinquents showed more rigid and disengaged relationships with their mothers and greater association with deviant peers, in comparison with sex-offenders and nonviolent subjects. Similarly, of the adolescent homicides studied by Busch et al. (1990), 41% were involved with gangs, compared with 14% of nonviolent delinquents. These latter studies are consistent with the integrated theory of Elliott et al. (1985), and suggest that violent offending is the outcome of deficient family bonding and the learning of aggression in families, together with strong bonding to deviant peers.

However, exposure to such conditions is not sufficient to account for the perpetuation of an aggressive style of interaction across the life course. Social learning and cognitive analyses provide the basis for recent attempts to account for consistency. Caspi, Bem and Elder (1989) identify two forms of person–environment interaction which promote consistency. *Cumulative continuity* arises when a person's disposition leads to the selection of environments which sustain the disposition. For example, dropping out of school because of poorly controlled temper may restrict career options to frustrating occupational roles which evoke further patterns of ill-tempered behaviour. In *interactional continuity* the immediate and recurring consequences of coercive exchanges short-circuit the learning of more controlled forms of interaction. Caspi et al. found that children who exhibited explosive tempers in childhood were judged more undercontrolled and irritable 20 years later, and had shown a life course pattern of educational, occupational and marital failure consistent with a recurring maladaptive coercive style.

Interactional continuity can be understood in terms of expectancy confirmation processes. Expectancies are rules about future stimulus and response outcomes (Bandura, 1986). Once established as relatively general rules, expectancies may override the objective contingencies in a situation, and become self-fulfilling prophecies (Carson, 1979). For example, a hostile person expects others to be hostile, and behaves in ways which elicit the expected reaction. A related concept is the *script* (Abelson, 1981). Scripts are cognitive schemata by which sequences of events are anticipated, and like other schemata, they permit rapid identification of meaningful events, but at the cost of distortions in everyday interaction. Huesmann and Eron (1984) suggest that scripts control aggressive strategies, but that their persistence and stability depends on the encoding of the original behaviour, cognitive rehearsal, and retrieval by cues associated with encoding. They propose that encoding is strengthened when a child fails to foresee inappropriate consequences of aggression, or to rehearse alternative strategies. This may account for the association of childhood aggression with low intelligence (Huesmann et al., 1987). Similarly, aggressive strategies will be strengthened by fantasy rehearsal. Consistent with this, aggressive children reported more fantasy aggression, more violent TV viewing, and identified more with TV characters. Aggressive scripts may thus be amplified and perpetuated into adult life by a cycle of rehearsal, expectancy confirmation and environmental selection. They provide a basis for the selective and hostile appraisal of diverse situations as equivalent, and for reacting automatically with coercive behaviour sequences.

Failure to discriminate between present and past events is, however, commonly regarded as dysfunctional, and greater consistency of aggression may therefore be more characteristic of maladjusted individuals. For example, Raush (1965) found that while hyperaggressive and normal boys were similar in following an unfriendly antecedent with an unfriendly response, the aggressive boys were more likely to follow a friendly antecedent with an unfriendly response. They were thus less able to differentiate between events, responding to friendly events as if they had a hostile meaning. Similarly, when asked to describe their responses to thwarting or provoking situations, mentally disordered offenders showed greater consistency and less discrimination between situations than did students (Blackburn, 1984). Recent work by Wright and Mischel (1987) also suggests that consistency in aggression is a function of maladjustment or skill deficits. Among problem boys, cross-situational consistency of rated aggression was significant, though modest, when the boys' skills matched those required by the situations, but was substantially higher when the competence requirements of the situations exceeded those possessed by the boys. The authors interpret these findings as indicating that lack of "construction competencies" with which to cope with a situation is stressful, and leads to indiscriminate responding.

Individual differences and aggression

Although aggressiveness is a relatively stable disposition, its consistency and expression depend on personal attributes which determine what is aversive or anger arousing and on what other coping strategies are available to the person in conflict situations. A traditional assumption is that violent individuals lack internalised controls. Thus, psychodynamic and early learning theorists saw individual differences as residing in the acquisition of emotional inhibitions restraining harmful behaviour, such as anxiety, guilt, empathic concern, and tolerance for frustration. However, where traditional approaches focus on affective aspects, current theories emphasise the role of cognitive appraisals and inferences, and recent research pays more attention to factors which facilitate aggression, such as anger arousal, and to the cognitive processes which mediate facilitation or inhibition.

Carney (1978) described violent offenders as unable to trust because of role-playing deficits, unable to feel as manifest in acting out to defend against pain, unable to fantasise as shown in impulsivity and lack of empathy, and unable to learn as shown by failure to generalise from experience. This represents the psychodynamic view, and also the traditional concept of psychopathic personality. The association of aggression with psychopathy is supported by Hare and McPherson (1984), who found that most prisoners meeting Cleckley's criteria had a history of serious violent crimes, and were more likely to be aggressive in prison. Serin (1991) similarly found that high scores on Hare's Psychopathy Checklist among prisoners were associated with more frequent violent offending, as well as with self-reported aggressiveness and impulsiveness. Correlational studies also indicate that aggressiveness is associated with a broad personality dimension of unsocialised aggression or psychopathy, which includes impulsivity and extrapunitive hostility (Blackburn, 1972, 1979a; Quay, 1987a).

A propensity for criminal violence is also associated with a disposition to experience *anger*. Selby (1984) found that violent inmates scored higher than nonviolent criminals on scales of anger and hostility, and Blackburn and Lee-Evans (1985) similarly found that psychopathic offenders anticipated greater anger and aggression in situations of frustration and provocation. Related to this may be the level of *self-esteem*. Threats to masculine self-image and self-image promotion or defending were significantly associated with violence in Toch's observations of violent encounters between police and delinquents (Toch, 1969). Armstrong (1980) also found that anger in delinquent males was predicted by a combination of low self-esteem and stereotyped masculine role. However, it appears to be an unstable, fluctuating self-esteem, rather than low self-esteem itself which is most strongly related to anger arousal (Kernis, Grannemann and Barclay, 1989).

Tedeschi (1983) suggests that low self-esteem makes a person vulnerable to threat, but people with low self-esteem may also adopt coercive means of influence because they lack noncoercive skills with which to achieve power and status. There is some evidence that aggression is associated with deficiencies in *social skills*. For example, Kirchner, Kennedy and Draguns (1979) observed that in role-played responses to conflict situations, offenders were more aggressive than nonoffenders but lacked nonaggressive assertive skills. However, not all aggressive offenders show social skill deficits (Henderson, 1982).

Intellectual deficits have also been implicated in violence. Neuropsychological studies suggest that reduced left hemispheric lateralisation may be particularly characteristic of delinquents showing psychopathic traits and a history of violence, and this may reflect a relative inability to modulate control by means of inner speech (Chapter 6). Several studies also indicate a significant association of aggression with low intelligence. Huesmann et al. (1987), for example, found a consistent negative correlation of aggression with IQ and attainment over 22 years, but suggest that intelligence exerts an effect on aggression primarily in childhood. However, a relation of intellectual ability to type of offending is suggested by the finding that less intelligent psychopaths had a history of impulsive violence, whereas the offences of intelligent psychopaths were more likely to be sadistic (Heilbrun, 1982).

Although intelligence may influence early *social cognitive development*, current theories suggest that individual differences in ease of anger arousal relate more broadly to expectancies and judgemental processes which bias appraisals of interpersonal events. Several recent studies have examined these aspects in children who are aggressive in school, and rejected by their peers. Since such children are at risk for becoming delinquent (Chapter 7), this work casts some light on the factors which may mediate later antisocial aggression.

Research on social cognitive *processes* follows two directions. First, aggressive boys have been shown to be less accurate in interpreting peers' intentions in unambiguous situations, and to have a bias to perceive hostile intent in ambiguous interpersonal situations having a negative outcome (Dodge, 1986). This reflects quick responding to minimal information, and selective attention to social cues, suggesting a biased expectancy to perceive malevolent intent. Although replicated in several studies, this effect is not entirely consistent, and attention has focused primarily on its correlation with observed aggressiveness, rather than anger arousal. However, Dodge and Somberg (1987) demonstrated that attributional bias is more apparent under conditions of mild threat, which may prime hostile expectancies. Social problem solving skills are a second area of interest, and it has been found that rejected–aggressive boys generate fewer solutions to interpersonal problem situations (Richard and Dodge, 1982), and also produce more aggressive and less effective solutions (Asarnow and Callan, 1985). Dodge (1986) integrates these findings in a sequential model. He proposes that effective problem solving proceeds through stages of encoding, interpretation, response search, response selection, and response enactment. Aggressive children display deficits in the first four stages.

Less attention has been paid to the *content* of social cognition, but some recent studies examine beliefs associated with aggression from a social learning standpoint. Perry, Perry and Rasmussen (1986) found that preadolescent aggressive children had stronger self efficacy beliefs about their ability to enact aggressive responses, relative to their less aggressive peers, and also showed outcome expectancies for aggression which emphasised gaining tangible rewards and reducing aversive treatment, but not gaining peer approval. Slaby and Guerra (1988) replicated these findings and those of Dodge, and extended them to violent delinquents. They compared incarcerated violent delinquents

scents rated as aggressive or unaggressive in school on problem
ills and beliefs about aggression. Both delinquents and aggressive
ts showed problem solving deficits, such as generating fewer
and selecting less information, and also endorsed more positive and
neutralising beliefs about the consequences of aggression, such as self-esteem
enhancement, and minimal suffering to the victim. Males consistently showed
more deficits and aggressive beliefs than females, suggesting a more restricted
consideration of interpersonal outcomes.

Personality types and violence

It has been stressed that the occurrence of a single act of violence does not itself
indicate an aggressive disposition, and inconsistent findings on personality
correlates of violent offending may reflect the heterogeneity of those who
have committed violent crimes. Several attempts have therefore been made to
distinguish different types of personality among violent criminals.

From interviews with violent prisoners, Toch (1969) discerned two
broad interpersonal orientations, which were associated with ten types of
motivational concerns. Common to all of these is a tendency to see human
relations as governed by the exercise of power. One group feels vulnerable
to manipulation, and employs violence as a self-preserving strategy. Within
this group, Toch identifies six orientations, which involve the defence of
reputation, enforcement of norms, self-image defending, self-image promotion,
self-defending, and removing pressures by violence because of limited social
skills. The second group sees other people as objects to meet their needs, and
employs violence manipulatively. Four categories are distinguished according
to whether violence takes the form of bullying, exploitation, self-indulgent
coercion, or cathartic discharge. While Toch presents data supporting the
reliability of this typology, it does not appear to have been cross-validated
with other samples.

Generalised inhibitions against aggression are central to the concept
of the *overcontrolled* assaultive offender. Megargee (1966) proposed that
undercontrolled offenders, who are likely to be identified as psychopathic
personalities, have weak inhibitions, and respond aggressively with some
regularity. Overcontrolled offenders, in contrast, have strong inhibitions,
and aggress only when instigation (anger arousal) is sufficiently intense to
overcome inhibitions. They are therefore expected to attack others rarely,
but with extreme intensity if they do so, and should hence be found more
commonly among those who have been extremely assaultive or homicidal.
Supporting this hypothesis, Megargee found that boys with a record of
extreme assault were rated as more controlled and unaggressive, and showed
greater control and conventionality on personality tests than moderately
assaultive and nonviolent delinquents. Further support was obtained in a
study of mentally disordered offenders (Blackburn, 1968a). Extreme assaultives
were significantly more controlled, inhibited and defensive on psychological
tests than moderate assaultives, and were significantly less likely to have a

prior criminal record or to be diagnosed as psychopathic personality. In a subsequent study of 56 murderers, almost half showed such characteristics (Blackburn, 1971a). Additional support comes from a study by Lang et al. (1987), who found that murderers differed from assaulters in having a less criminal prior history, and scored lower on measures of hostility and the EPQ P scale. Consistent with the theory, they were also more defensive, as indicated by the EPQ Lie scale, but the authors construe this narrowly in terms of situational dissimulation. Since high Lie scores are associated with conforming behaviour (Chapter 5), a dispositional interpretation is warranted.

Megargee developed a scale of overcontrolled hostility (OH), and Lane and Kling (1979) found that OH differentiated male forensic patients with a history of infrequent but intense violence. They considered that high scores on OH reflected rigidity, excessive control, repression of conflicts, and a reluctance to admit to psychiatric symptoms. Walters and Greene (1982) also found that psychiatric outpatients scoring high on OH were more likely to be described by their therapists as prone to chronic, but rigidly suppressed, anger and hostility. Murderers scoring highly on OH have also been found to be characterised by lack of assertiveness in role-plays, and by less anger expression in response to provocation (Quinsey, Maguire and Varney, 1983). However, some studies fail to support the validity of OH (Truscott, 1990).

The overcontrol hypothesis sheds some light on why typically *unaggressive* individuals are found among violent offenders, but rests on an energy model, in which anger arousal accumulates with repeated provocation. Current theorising would predict that anger is most likely to be maintained by the cognitive rehearsal of grievances, resulting in a bias to respond more readily to subsequent provocation (Zillmann, 1979). The model does not, however, clarify whether it is anger arousal, its expression, or the lack of aggressive habits which is problematic for overcontrolled individuals. There is evidence for two overcontrolled types (Blackburn, 1971a, 1986). One denies angry or hostile tendencies, and describe themselves as sociable, nonanxious, and conforming. This group comes closest to Megargee's original concept. The second group describes relatively strong anger experiences, social avoidance, and poor self-esteem, and is more likely to display social skill deficits (Henderson, 1982). Both groups appear to have acquired nonaggressive, avoidant ways of coping with conflict situations, but the problems of the first group relate to denial and avoidance at a cognitive level. For the second group, it appears to be the expression of anger which is problematic.

However, two undercontrolled patterns are also apparent. Blackburn (1971a) found four distinct personality patterns in a cluster analysis of MMPI data obtained from 56 mentally disordered murderers, and these were subsequently shown to be the main patterns among violent mentally disordered offenders more generally (Blackburn, 1975a, 1986). These same types have been identified among "normal" murderers (McGurk, 1978) and violent male criminals (Henderson, 1982), although one MMPI study of murderers undergoing pretrial evaluation produced somewhat different types (Holcomb, Adams and Ponder, 1985). These four types have been described as primary psychopaths, secondary psychopaths, controlled or conforming, and inhibited (Chapter 3). The former two groups are similar in showing relatively strong impulsive and aggressive tendencies, and resemble Toch's manipulative and self-preserving groups, respectively. The latter two groups represent the two forms of overcontrol described above. Consistent with the overcontrol hypothesis, 52% of primary psychopaths, but only 8% of the inhibited group, were found to have a history of repeated violence (Blackburn, 1984).

These four groups represent combinations of extremes on two dimensions labelled *psychopathy* (PY) and *social withdrawal* (SW: Blackburn, 1986). SW appears to moderate the relationship between aggressive tendencies (PY) and observed aggressive behaviour, probably because SW is related to inhibitory tendencies and lack of assertiveness. It may also contribute to hostility, since hostility tends to be maintained when there are barriers to interpersonal communication. The violence of the socially withdrawn psychopath may therefore be less predictable and more impulsive, and Heilbrun and Heilbrun (1985) found that the combination of psychopathy, low IQ, and high SW was associated with the highest level of violence within a prison.

However, these types also emerge from taxonomic studies of unselected prisoners (Holland and Holt, 1975; Widom, 1978a; McGurk and McGurk, 1979), only the inhibited group being prominent among more extremely violent offenders. The clusters of attributes identified in these studies are not, then, unique to violence, but may rather represent patterns of personality deviation which contribute to socially deviant behaviour more generally. It must be reiterated that personality variables are not in themselves sufficient to account for violence. Hostile attitudes or low self-esteem may bias people to perceived malevolent intent more readily, while an aggressive disposition and limited cognitive and social skills make attempts to resolve conflict by coercive means more likely. However, while certain dispositions may increase the likelihood of criminal violence, these do not inevitably lead to violent acts. It is probable that the majority of aggressive personalities do not exhibit flagrant antisocial behaviour, even though they may be prone to conflict with those around them (Millon, 1981).

THE CYCLE OF VIOLENCE

As introduced by Kempe et al. (1962) the "battered child" described "a clinical condition in young children who have received serious physical abuse, generally from a parent or foster parent". A focus on nonaccidental injury also accompanied the later concept of "battered wife". However, attention has subsequently shifted from the physical aspects of abuse and the characteristics of perpetrators, to the psychological consequences for the victim. Since children and women who are victims are at risk of becoming abusers themselves, the present discussion considers both causes and effects of child and wife abuse. Sexual abuse is examined in Chapter 11.

Child abuse

Although extreme violence towards children is extensively publicised, many incidents of child physical abuse involve minor injury, and are impulsive acts occurring during unsuccessful attempts at discipline (Wolfe, 1987). These typically reflect the progressive development of aversive parent–child exchanges. For example, inconsistent punishment of a child will result in greater resistance to suppression of deviant behaviour, and a reduction in the parent's capacity to control behaviour through positive reinforcement. Under such conditions, attempts at discipline involve punitive tactics of accelerating intensity, and an increased likelihood of escalation to violence (Parke, 1977; Patterson, 1982). Possible causal factors in abuse therefore include characteristics of parent and child, the history of their interaction, adverse family conditions exacerbating aversive interactions, and social and cultural factors supporting punitive discipline.

A child's characteristics may increase the risk of abuse by imposing stress on the parent, or by eliciting parental rejection, and unskilled mothers can be "trained" by their children to use aversive discipline (Patterson, 1982). A review by Friedrich and Boriskin (1976) indicated a greater incidence of prematurity, mental retardation, physical handicaps, and temperament difficulties among abused children, and a tendency of abusive parents to perceive their children as different. Reciprocal parent–child influences may therefore contribute to abuse, although some of these factors, such as mental retardation, may be as much a consequence as a cause.

Attention has focused particularly on mothers who perpetrate abuses, although probably more physical abuse is perpetrated by males, and neglect by females (Wolfe, 1987). Low parental intelligence has been implicated, but this is more likely in cases of neglect, and there is a consensus that only 5% to 10% of abusive parents exhibit severe mental disorder. However, personality disturbance was thought to characterise most abusers in early studies, and Spinetta and Rigler (1972) noted that clinicians generally attributed abuse to a defect in the control of aggressive impulses. This was held to result from emotional deprivation in the childhood of abusers, which produced frustrated dependency needs, inability to empathise, and misunderstanding of the requirements of child-rearing. At times of stress, these mothers looked to the child for satisfaction of emotional needs, projecting aggression to the child when this was not forthcoming. Abusing parents were thus thought to show deviant attitudes, expectations and child-rearing techniques.

Subsequent research lends some support to the notion of deviant parental dispositions, although these are seen increasingly in terms of skill deficits. Abusing parents are more likely to have experienced abuse themselves, and deficiencies in self-control and appropriate anger expression are common findings. Rohrbeck and Twentyman (1986), for example, found that abusive mothers were more impulsive on cognitive and motor tests than neglecting and nonabusing mothers. Abusive parents are also likely to be depressed (Lahey et al., 1984), and show distorted expectations, attributing the child's misbehaviour to intentional annoyance (Larrance and Twentyman, 1983). There is, moreover, consistent evidence of deficient child-rearing skills, in the form of ineffectual discipline and proportionately more negative than positive interactions with the child (Lahey et al., 1984). These deficits are associated with insensitivity to cues and signals from the child, poor monitoring, and difficult social relationships outside the family, suggesting more generalised social incompetence manifested in a coercive interpersonal style. Burgess and Youngblade (1988) propose that such a style emerges from modelling and reinforcement of aggression in the early lives of the parents, which may be central to the intergenerational transmission of abuse. However, some abusive acts may result from stress-produced arousal rather than learning *per se* (Emery, 1989).

Although recent evidence continues to implicate parental characteristics in abuse, there is no distinctive personality "profile", and abusers are not homogeneous (Wolfe, 1987). Moreover, child abuse has multiple determinants. Self-report studies support a correlation of abuse with poverty and unemployment (Straus, Gelles and Steinmetz, 1980; Browne, 1984), and abusive families often lack external social support, being less involved with their local community. Gelles (1973) saw these social factors as stressors, which interact with parent characteristics and marital and child-produced stress to lead to abuse. Cultural factors are also relevant. Parkes (1977) notes that levels of family violence correlate with levels of violence in a society more generally. He suggests that consistent exposure to punitive discipline serves to sanction such behaviour as normative, and that parents are socialised into child abuse through the interaction of cultural, community, and family influences. However, the processes of interaction remain unclear.

Psychological research on child abuse has drawn on psychodynamic and social learning models, and these approaches have also guided attempts to identify effects of abuse on the victims. Martin and Rodeheffer (1976) noted that negative psychological effects could result from both physical abuse (e.g. brain damage) and ongoing disturbance in parent–child relationships. They suggested that the more prominent effects were interpersonal ambivalence and hypervigilance regarding the behaviour of others, disturbed self-concept and superego development, and delays in the development of speech, language, and motor functions. While these are common findings, no uniform pattern of psychological problems has been identified (Wolfe, 1987; Emery, 1989). Abused children have been found to perform lower on intelligence tests, to be deficient in empathic concern and social cognitive development, to be depressed, and to show difficulties in interactions with peers as well as families (Conaway and Hansen, 1989; Emery, 1989). However, effects vary according to the type and severity of maltreatment, and the age at which abuse occurs. Moreover, not all abused children suffer lasting harmful effects. A moderating factor appears to be whether the child attributes abuse to parental malevolence or to stress (Herzberger, Potts and Dillon, 1981). Negative effects may also be ameliorated by a supportive relationship with another adult (Egeland, Jacobvitz and Sroufe, 1988).

Abused children are consistently found to be aggressive with their peers (Hoffman-Plotkin and Twentyman, 1984), and since abusing parents frequently report a history of experiencing abuse, there is a common belief in a "cycle of violence", in which abused children reproduce aggression towards their own children and others. However, many abusers do not have a history of being abused, while only about 30% of abused children are likely to become abusers themselves (Kaufman and Zigler, 1987). Widom (1989a) reviewed the relation of child abuse to later criminal violence, and similarly concluded that the majority of abused children do not go on to become violent offenders. Her own prospective study revealed that 19% of abused males later committed violent crimes, compared with 14% of controls (Widom, 1989b). She found no significant effect in the case of females, nor for sex abuse. There is thus only modest support for the "cycle of violence" hypothesis, and many mediating factors determine whether or not an abused child becomes an abuser or a violent delinquent (see Chapter 7).

While intergenerational transmission of abusive behaviour is consistent with social learning theory, the psychological mediators remain unclear. Child abuse has "internalising" consequences such as depression and lowered self-esteem, as well as "externalising" effects in the form of aggression, and this may be more adequately accounted for in terms of attachment theory (Emery, 1989). An alternative possibility is that aggression may be enhanced in abused children by chronic post-traumatic stress disorder (Collins and Bailey, 1990a). The aspects of the abused child's environment which are psychologically most damaging are also uncertain. While it is assumed that major effects result from maltreatment by a caretaker on whom the child depends and looks to as a model, other significant sources of impaired child development include witnessing violence between family members (Wolfe et al., 1985), and the social consequences of the labelling of a family as abusive.

Wife abuse

Physical abuse of women by marital partners or cohabitees often occurs concurrently with child abuse, and the majority of battered women have also been subject to marital rape (Walker, 1988). Interviews with battered women indicate that abuse typically occurs against a background of increasing coercion in the relationship, and that abusive acts involve a rapid escalation from verbal argument to physical assault over a few minutes (Dobash and Dobash, 1984). Arguments focus mainly on possessiveness or jealousy, domestic work demands, or money, and most acts occur between 10 p.m. and 2 a.m. at weekends. They occur predominantly in the home, often in the presence of children or relatives, and the most frequent injuries are bruises from slapping, punching or kicking, which may involve repeated blows. Violent acts may initially be followed by contrition and reconciliation, but this diminishes as the violence is repeated.

Given the unpalatable nature of wife abuse, it is perhaps inevitable that explanations are entangled with political, moral, and interdisciplinary issues.

Feminists were prominent in drawing attention to wife abuse, and some challenge individual level explanations which appear to "blame the victim", giving primacy to cultural prescriptions of gender roles and unequal power between the sexes. Some sociologists adopt a similar stance. Ptacek (1988), for example, finds it "disturbing" that causes should be sought in psychological abnormality of the batterer, since this implies that "...violence lies outside the realm of choice". Dobash and Dobash (198 4) similarly object to suggestions of victim-precipitation of violence, and argue that wife assaults are "...deeply embedded in the existing intentions of male aggressors", which are in turn shaped by the cultural context of patriarchal domination. Whatever the merits of this rational choice perspective, such polemics substitute the attribution of moral blame for explanation. Cultural factors do not account for *variations* in abusiveness between individuals, and as with child abuse, it is necessary to consider multiple determinants at both the social and individual level.

Psychological research on wife abuse has so far been limited, and much of the available information comes from battered women themselves. There is, nevertheless, consistent evidence that abusers are likely to be deviant in a number of ways. Both clinical surveys and controlled studies indicate that the majority of abusers have experienced violence in childhood or witnessed parental violence, and are also likely to show alcohol problems (Gayford, 1975: Straus et al., 1980: Rosenbaum and O'Leary, 1981; Fitch and Papantoniu, 1983). Fitch and Papantonio (1983), for example, found that 71% of their sample had witnessed parental violence, and 59% had abused alcohol. However, while they also observed an above average level of unemployment in their sample, a strong relationship with socioeconomic status has not generally been found, and many abusers come from high income groups (Johnson, 1988). Abusers are also more likely to have a criminal record, and to exhibit violence more generally (Walker, 1988). These observations are consistent with the "cycle of violence" hypothesis, and with the view that abuse is role-modelled behaviour passed on through social learning. They also suggest a coercive and externalising style of problem resolution. Ulbrich and Huber (1981), for example, found that in a national sample of American adults, males who had witnessed parental violence were more accepting of wife-hitting as a solution to domestic conflict. However, witnessing parental violence appears to produce "internalised" problems as well as externalising behaviours (Wolfe et al., 1985), and not all abusers have been exposed to such violence. Spouse abuse therefore reflects more than the learning of aggressive solutions to conflict. It also appears to entail distorted expectations of relationships which make conflict more likely.

Several observers point to rigid stereotypes of the female role held by abusers, which may in turn have been transmitted by their fathers. Rosenbaum and O'Leary (1981) found that abusers showed more conservative attitudes to women than did nonabusing husbands, and were also more conservative than their wives. Johnston (1988), in contrast, found no differences in attitudes to women between abusers and nonabusers. Other possible cognitive distortions include expectations that females will protect them from harm, and unrealistic expectations of intimacy (Walker, 1988). Dutton and Browning (1988) propose that abusers have an exaggerated need for power, combined with fears of intimacy, so that changes in the level of intimacy in their relationships are perceived as threats to their control, which instigate anger. In support of this, they found that physically abusive males reacted more strongly than controls to videotaped scenarios portraying abandonment by the female as an outcome of male–female conflict.

A further hypothesis is that abusing males have low self-esteem, and that their violence compensates for feelings of inadequacy, and proves their masculinity. This was supported by Johnson (1988), who found lower self-esteem in abusers, which correlated significantly with experience of abuse as a child. Margolin (1988), however, found no variations in self-concept associated with wife abuse in a volunteer sample. The mechanisms by which abuse is mediated therefore remain unclear, although the evidence to date suggests that deviant psychological characteristics of the abuser contribute significantly to marital violence. However, it seems unlikely that abusers are homogeneous.

Abused women themselves may contribute to the development of an abusive relationship. This is suggested by observations that female victims have often been subject to abuse in childhood, although revictimisation appears to be more likely when childhood abuse was sexual as well as physical (Shields and Hanneke, 1988). Revictimisation in adulthood might be mediated by an expectancy for victimisation and its association with a dependent relationship, and a helpless, compliant response to violence which reinforces the abuser's aggression, or, alternatively, refusal to accept a traditional gender role, which provokes anger in some men (Walker, 1988). Evidence, however, is largely impressionistic. Hanks and Rosenbaum (1977), for example, discerned three types of family background in the partners of abusing males, two of which were particularly associated with violence. They suggest that abused women helped to "ignite" violence by seeking out relationships similar to those of their mothers, but offer no test of this hypothesis.

Psychological effects of wife abuse on victims are less well documented than those of child abuse, but appear to be substantial. Walker (1988) suggests that abused women are frequently vulnerable to learned helplessness as a result of childhood victimisation, and that they exhibit cognitive and affective dysfunctions comparable to post-traumatic stress disorder. She also notes their susceptibility to aggression and criminal acts. Not only are battered women likely to batter their own children while living with a wife abuser, between 50% and 80% of incarcerated women report having been abused by their partner. Their crimes include property and drug offences, but also child abuse and homicide, most commonly while under duress from a violent partner.

Chapter 10

Crime and Mental Disorder

INTRODUCTION

Interest in the relationship between mental disorder and crime reflects changing interactions between criminal justice and mental health systems as much as scientific concern. Indeed, the relationship is not a simple objective one between two distinct sets of variables, since the same social processes influence the "construction" of these terms (Menzies and Webster, 1989). Sociologists see psychiatry and law as alternative systems for controlling the socially deviant (Foucault, 1978; Bean, 1985), while some psychiatrists have also maintained that criminality is a disease (e.g. Karpman, 1949). Few, if any, currently take this position, but Menzies and Webster (1989) observe that DSM-III broadened the definition of mental disorders to include more antisocial deviance, particularly in the case of child disorders and antisocial personality disorder. Concerns about this "psychiatrisation" of crime, however, have been paralleled by concerns over the "criminalisation" of mental disorder, reflected in claims that the deinstitutionalisation of mentally ill people has led to more of them being processed by the criminal justice system. Scientific questions in this area cannot therefore be divorced from issues of social policy and professional power.

Concepts of "mental illness" or "mental health" continue to elude precise definition (Scott, 1958; Kendell, 1975; Gorenstein, 1984), and many offenders clearly have personal problems and psychological disabilities beyond the bounds of psychiatric disorder (West, 1980; Chapter 8). However, the focus of this chapter is on psychological abnormalities defined in psychiatric terms as mental disorders. It should be noted that mental *disorder* is currently the preferred generic term in psychiatry (American Psychiatric Association, 1987), mental illness tending to denote more severe disorders, but these terms will be used interchangeably in the following discussion.

MENTAL DISORDER AND THE MEDICAL MODEL

With the development of psychological and sociological theories of deviant behaviour, the "medical model" of mental illness was challenged from the

1960s onwards both from within and without psychiatry, but while alternative perspectives are now reflected in the range of mental health services, they have had insufficient impact on the major psychiatric disorders to displace the "illness" notion. The latter therefore remains the dominant paradigm, but many critical issues are unresolved. Indeed, the retention of separate terms for *mental* illness or disorder points to continued doubts about the assertion that "mental illness is an illness like any other", which is central to the medical model. These issues impinge particularly on the area of mental disorder and the law, and it is therefore pertinent to examine them here.

Critiques of the medical model

The "symptoms" of mental illness are abnormalities of behaviour and experience, but there is no single criterion which is necessary and sufficient to define abnormality. A behaviour may be labelled abnormal if it is statistically rare or unusual, socially inappropriate or undesirable, subjectively distressing, deviates from optimal social or psychological functioning, or fails to meet some ideal of "health". Each of these is problematic, and while the conjoint use of several criteria would encompass many phenomena currently identified under the rubric of mental disorder, no combination covers all forms. This is recognised in DSM-III (American Psychiatric Association, 1987), which notes that there are no sharp boundaries between normality and abnormality, and conceptualises mental disorders as behavioural or psychological syndromes defined by criteria of distress or disability. Nevertheless, the notions of "symptom" and "syndrome" clearly retain the medical implications of a disease.

Price (1978) distinguishes between a *model* and a *metaphor* in science. A model is an analogy guiding research which attempts to understand the unfamiliar by treating it *as if* it were like some familiar event or process. The medical model is therefore an attempt to understand abnormal behaviour as analogous to physical illness or disease. However, while a model is tentative, Price suggests that differing perspectives on psychological abnormality are closer to metaphors, which may begin as analogies, but which transform the original concept so that it is applied literally, and becomes a more dogmatic assertion of identity.

Despite frequent criticism of the medical model, there is no unanimity as to what it is, and critiques frequently entangle questions of scientific explanation with disputes about professional power. The Kraepelinian classification of mental disorders assumed a finite number of disease entities, each with its distinct cause, psychological form, outcome, and cerebral pathology (Kendell, 1975). It is this model which has been attacked as a "myth" by Szasz (1960) and others (e.g. Sarbin, 1967). The issues are complex, and the critics are not themselves unanimous. Szasz, for example, objects to the determinism of the disease concept from an antipositivist view, while others champion the claims of alternative deterministic models. However, a basic objection centres on the problem of how a "mind" can be "diseased". If disease is a somatic process, then "mind" can be diseased only by analogy, and mental "illness" is mythic when it assumes brain disease which has not been demonstrated. It also sees the sufferer as a *patient* to whom things have happened, rather than a purposeful *agent*. Additionally, it locates the causes of disorder "inside" the person. However, it should be noted that it is not an appeal to "inner" variables which distinguishes the traditional medical model, but rather an appeal to physical rather than psychological causes (Sarason and Ganzer, 1968).

This critique, then, assumes that the medical model relies on notions of disease entities. However, while the concept of disease as bodily abnormality might appear to present few problems, it lacks an agreed meaning in medicine. The notion prevailing since the nineteenth century has been that of "disease as lesion", the assumption being that illness always involves structural damage or pathology, and is qualitatively different from health (Kendell, 1975). A disease entity is thus a specific alteration of part of the body causing a distinct symptom pattern. However, conditions without a known physical cause are thereby excluded from the category of disease, which is why those of unknown aetiology are described as "disorders", and the lesion concept has been further undermined by the recognition that many illnesses do not have a single cause.

Several attempts have therefore been made to reformulate the disease concept to cover not only known physical disorders, but also mental disorders. Ausubel (1961), for example, proposed that disease included any marked deviation from normally desirable standards of structural and functional integrity, whether physical, mental, or behavioural. This, however, is a normative definition which extends the disease concept well beyond its present uncertain boundaries. More conservatively, Engel (1977) suggested that disease encompasses *biopsychosocial* functioning, in which a biochemical defect is a necessary but not sufficient condition. While these arguments would broaden the concept, Kendell (1975) proposes that it be confined to statistical abnormalities which confer "biological disadvantage" in terms of increased mortality and reduced fertility. On these criteria, the psychoses, some sexual deviations, drug dependence, and possibly some neuroses and personality disorders qualify as diseases. However, this disqualifies common conditions, such as tooth decay, and also disorders which have an immunising effect.

An alternative analysis is offered by Boorse (1975, 1976), who argues that disease is defined by functional rather than structural abnormality, and that the analogy of a mental disease is legitimate. He distinguishes *disease* as an interference in natural functioning, which applies equally to physical and mental processes, from *illness* as a serious form of disease which entails incapacitation. In this functional approach, what is unhealthy must be determined empirically, and relates to what contributes causally to goals pursued by individuals as part of their natural biological design (e.g. survival and reproduction). While accepting a materialist view of mind, and hence the position that a mental disease is ultimately a physical state, Boorse argues that this does not imply a physical disease of the brain. The defining property of mental disease is that mental events (beliefs, feelings, experiences) causally impair natural mental functioning. Mental illness is not therefore necessarily a consequence of bodily disease.

The functional concept provides a defence of the mental illness analogy which avoids reductionism. It also plausibly counters the claim made by critics such as Bean (1983) that psychiatry, and by implication clinical psychology, are simply normative disciplines governed by social values, rather than objective sciences. Wakefield (1992), however, argues that the concept of disease or disorder necessarily entails values, since it is confined to conditions which are harmful to the person according to prevailing cultural standards. He notes, for example, that albinism, reversal of heart position, and fused toes are not considered disorders, even though they are the result of breakdown of natural functioning. He proposes that what defines mental disorder is *harmful dysfunction*, i.e. conditions depriving a person of some socially valued benefit which result from the inability of some mental mechanism to perform its natural function.

The disease-as-lesion model nevertheless persists in psychiatry, as shown by priority for the funding of biomedical research into the nature and treatment of mental disorder. The view of many psychiatrists that personality disorders are outside their purview (Schwarz and Schwarz, 1976; Lewis and Appleby, 1988) also rests on the belief that some mental disorders but not others are physical diseases.

The preceding discussion centres on the utility of the disease analogy as an aetiological explanation of psychological abnormality. Other critiques focus on its implications for the boundaries of medicine (Sarason and Ganzer, 1968; Kendell, 1975). The objection here is to the treatment of aberrant behaviour as "a facsimile of medicine" (Bean, 1983), and challenges the appropriateness of medicine to be the arbiter of all interventions in mental disorder. It therefore relates to issues of professional power and the control of care delivery services. One aspect is rivalry within the mental health professions, particularly in the United States, where clinical psychology and psychiatry now compete in the marketplace of health care. While the issues raised by the medical model are clearly much wider than a squabble between an aspiring and an established profession, they are nevertheless inevitably coloured by it, since any concession on the status of the mental illness concept has implications for the vested interests of the professions involved.

Disputes over the medical model therefore continue to simmer unresolved, partly because the model has undergone some retrenchment, partly because it retains some utility in practice, and partly because no single model of intervention has proved consistently viable across the range of mental disorders. Protagonists now recognise the appropriateness of nonmedical interventions for some forms of mental disorder, while antagonists for the most part accept that somatic treatments may be necessary for psychoses, and have a place in emotional disorders. As Gorenstein (1984) suggests, the source of continuing disputes lies less in the status of the abstraction "mental illness", about which there may be some measure of agreement, than in the ethical, legal, and professional consequences of authorising medical care for those judged mentally disordered.

Criminal behaviour and the medical model

The popular notion that criminals are "sick" implies a disease analogy, and it is commonly argued that the medical model has been pervasive in the criminal justice system. However, few now suggest that all, or even a majority of criminals are mentally ill, and critiques of the medical model when applied to crime have somewhat diffuse and confused targets.

It is *de rigueur* for psychologists to distance themselves from the medical model because of the implication that criminal behaviour is symptomatic of some underlying psychopathology requiring "cure" through "therapy" (e.g. Izzo and Ross, 1990). Medical in this context is often a proxy for "psychodynamic", but correcting the deviant attitudes or cognitive deficits of delinquents seems equally to imply that deviant behaviour is symptomatic of an "underlying" problem. Moreover, most psychological interventions in antisocial behaviour implicitly follow a medical analogy of infectious disease insofar as the temporary application of "treatment" is expected to lead to permanent "cure" (Kazdin, 1987).

For sociological critics, the main target is individualism. They object to theories which assume that criminogenic factors can be located within the person, and which hence divert attention from the creation of deviance by societal labelling (Balch, 1975). MacNamara (1977) goes further, seeing the medical model as competing with classical doctrines of free moral agency and individual responsibility. The objection is thus to most psychological theorising, and not simply psychiatric conceptualisations.

At the level of intervention, the target is individualised treatment, which follows from the assumption that crime is the product of individual defects to be corrected. This is part of the wider attack on rehabilitation, and since this includes psychological, educational, vocational, and welfare interventions, as well as psychiatric treatment, the notion of "medical model" in this context is again something of a catchall. Allen (1959) foreshadowed most of the later arguments by suggesting that rehabilitation was a humane ideal which had become debased. Not only have institutions become oppressive and failed to provide the therapy promised by this ideal, rehabilitation has been used as an excuse for more severe legal punishment, particularly in the form of indeterminate sentencing, which serves incapacitative rather than rehabilitative functions. In addition, the goals of rehabilitation give discretionary powers not only to the judiciary and parole boards, but also to psychiatrists and probation officers, who have frequently abused them to deprive people of their liberty. Professionals have thus exceeded their levels of competence, and strayed into the realms of legal and moral decision making. This claim has been widespread in recent years, and has come not only from social scientists and lawyers (Bazelon, 1978; Morris, 1983; Bean, 1985), but also from mental health professionals themselves (Nietzel and Moss, 1972; Szasz, 1979; Halleck, 1987). These issues underlie much of the continuing controversy surrounding the relation of psychiatry and law.

West (1980) has defended this broad notion of a medical model by redescribing it as *clinical criminology*. He argues that many offenders have psychological problems which are not necessarily causes of their offending, and which go beyond the bounds of psychiatric illness. There is therefore a need for individualised treatment of disturbed or deviant psychological states by mental health professionals, which should be part of rehabilitation. Gendreau (1985), however, regards clinical criminology as a weak re-affirmation of the rehabilitative ideal, because it overemphasises individual disorder at the expense of system variables which affect the outcome of therapeutic programmes.

THE LAW AND MENTAL DISORDER

State intervention in the lives of individuals is traditionally justified by appeal to the principles of police power and *parens patriae*, the former in the interests of public protection, the latter to provide care and protection of those unable to care for themselves (Chapter 1). While the *parens patriae* principle underlies legislation for the civil commitment of the mentally disordered, mental health law also deals with criminal commitment of mentally disordered individuals charged with a crime, who may be diverted to special mental health facilities. However, it is doubtful whether the justifying principles are ever clearly separable in mental health legislation, and whatever the original humane intentions, the asylums of nineteenth century Europe and America became custodial institutions emphasising public protection rather than medical care.

   This blurring of powers directed to public protection and individual care is particularly apparent in the control of mentally disordered offenders, where protection of others becomes the major criterion of confinement, and the psychiatrist is forced to compromise the traditional medical role of helper and patient's agent by becoming policeman and opponent (Stone, 1984; Arboleda-Flórez, 1990). As a result of changes in psychiatric treatment and the closure of traditional mental hospitals, the dispositions available to the courts for dealing with mentally disordered offenders, and the facilities available, have been the subject of increasing attention from both lawyers and mental health professionals during the past three decades.

Mentally disordered offenders

The courts have long sought to distinguish the "sane" from the "insane", but it should be noted that insanity is a legal concept which has no formal psychiatric meaning. The statutory requirements for establishing mental disorder vary according to the social and legal context. For example, different tests are used in relation to making a will or contract, being held responsible for a crime, and being compulsorily admitted to hospital. From the standpoint of the criminal justice system, there are five critical points at which evidence of mental disorder affects legal action (Halleck, 1987). First, most states make provisions for the police and public officials to exercise discretion in charging someone causing a public nuisance or suspected of a crime who may be mentally disordered, and to remove them to hospital without prosecution. Second, at the time of trial, a defendant may be found incompetent or "unfit to plead", and detained in a mental hospital without a conviction being recorded. Third, insanity may be pleaded as a defence, resulting, if successful, in the "special verdict" of "not guilty by reason of insanity". Fourth, a defendant may be found guilty, but evidence of mental disorder may mitigate the severity of sentence, and the court is empowered to order "treatment" rather than "punishment". Finally, convicted prisoners who become mentally disordered while in prison may be transferred to the mental health system. Laws relating to these provisions vary from jurisdiction to jurisdiction.

Those formally designated *mentally disordered offenders* therefore comprise a diverse group whose mental disorder must be recognised as sufficiently disabling to justify substantially different treatment from that of other offenders. While many other offenders may have psychological problems, and the dividing line is somewhat arbitrary, mentally disordered offenders make up only a small minority of either those receiving psychiatric treatment on the one hand, or those convicted of a crime on the other. However, they invite disproportionate attention because of the issues they raise about the nature of crime and punishment. In particular, they serve a symbolic function, since the holding of the majority of offenders as "sane" and hence responsible and punishable is thereby justified (Stone, 1984).

Such offenders are found mainly in secure facilities outside the prison system, but also in prisons, ordinary mental hospitals, and in the community under the joint supervision of probation and mental health services. Surveys in the United States in 1978 (Steadman et al., 1982) and 1982 (Kerr and Roth, 1986) revealed a range of facilities run mainly by state mental health departments, but including psychiatric units in prisons. These varied from small "forensic" units in state hospitals to large maximum security hospitals with 500 or more residents. Steadman et al. estimated that some 20 000 patients were admitted annually to these facilities, and that the daily resident population was about 14 000. About 5% were female, and a similar proportion juveniles. Overall, they made up 3.2% of institutionalised offenders, and 7.3% of the institutionalised mentally disordered population.

Other western countries make similar provisions, but there are significant variations owing to different mental health statutes. In Britain, only a small proportion is found incompetent or not guilty by reason of insanity, and the British courts have more liberal powers than their American counterparts to hospitalise offenders under the Mental Health Act. The more serious offenders are detained in "special hospitals" (Broadmoor, Rampton, and Ashworth in England, and the State Hospital in Scotland). These are maximum security establishments which house some 2000 patients, about a fifth of them female. However, this represents only a minority of mentally disordered offenders dealt with by the courts. Many are dealt with as patients of the National Health Service, in open psychiatric hospitals or as outpatients on probation orders. During the past decade, these services have centred increasingly on Regional Secure Units (RSUs), which are small psychiatric facilities offering medium levels of secure confinement.

Despite provisions for transferring mentally disordered prisoners to the special hospitals and other parts of the mental health system, many continue to remain in prison. A treatment prison was established at Grendon Underwood, near Oxford, in 1962, and a minority of disordered prisoners also receive treatment from the prison medical and psychological services, or from visiting psychotherapists. Nevertheless, recent estimates suggest that out of an adult prison population of some 50 000 in England and Wales, some 2% exhibit serious mental disorders which would be more appropriately dealt with in the mental health system (Gunn, Maden and Swinton, 1991).

The basis for current provision lies in the Mental Health Act for England and Wales of 1959, and its subsequent revision in 1983. (Scotland and Northern Ireland have separate, though broadly similar legislation.) The 1959 Act liberalised policies for the compulsory detention and treatment of the mentally disordered generally, and mentally disordered offenders in particular. It defines mental disorder as "mental illness, arrested or incomplete development of mind, psychopathic disorder and any other disorder or disability of mind". In the 1983 revision, *mental illness* is not defined, but generally covers the most serious mental disorders, such as schizophrenia or affective psychosis, and the majority of patients in special hospitals and RSUs fall in this category. *Mental impairment* refers to "a state of arrested or incomplete development of mind (not amounting to severe mental impairment) which includes significant impairment of intelligence and social functioning and is associated with abnormally aggressive or seriously irresponsible conduct on the part of the person concerned". *Severe mental impairment* is defined in similar terms, except that impairment is "severe" rather than "significant". *Psychopathic disorder* is "a persistent disorder or disability of mind, whether or not including significant impairment of intelligence, which results in abnormally aggressive or seriously irresponsible conduct on the part of the person concerned". It must be stressed that these are legal categories, not clinical diagnostic terms. Problems arise particularly with the category of psychopathic disorder (Chapter 3), which has always been contentious because of the doubts of many psychiatrists that "psychopaths" are treatable (Dell and Robertson, 1988). In practice, the category includes the more serious violent and sexual offenders who additionally show personality disorder. They make up about a quarter of patients in the special hospitals.

The Act provides comprehensively for both compulsory civil and criminal commitment. It empowers the courts to remand accused persons to hospital for assessment or treatment, and where a mentally disordered offender has been convicted of an offence punishable with imprisonment (other than murder, which carries a mandatory life sentence), the court may authorise guardianship by the social services, or detention in hospital when the mental disorder "is of a nature or degree which makes it appropriate for him to be detained in hospital". The hospital may be any prepared to admit the patient, but those constituting a grave and immediate danger to the public are likely to be admitted to a special hospital. In addition to the hospital order, the court may impose a restriction order, which may be for an unlimited time, when it is "necessary for the protection of the public from serious harm", release being dependent on the decision of the Home Secretary or a Mental Health Review Tribunal. These powers are an alternative to the powers of the court to imprison, fine, or make a probation order.

Historical background to legal provision

While some Roman writers regarded madness as divine punishment, and suggested that the mad should be excused from punishment because they had been punished enough, insanity as a legal excuse was not widely accepted until the thirteenth century (Dreher, 1967; Walker, 1985). Prior to the Conquest, the various Anglo-Saxon legal codes were governed by the theory of *absolute liability*, the commission of a wrongful act being sufficient to entitle the injured party to take action in redress without intervention by the state, no account being taken of mitigating circumstances. In contrast, the Canon Law of the English Church distinguished offending acts on the basis of moral guilt, or *mens rea*, and on the grounds of their inability to form a guilty intention, infants and lunatics were not held to be criminally culpable.

This principle was popularised by Bracton, a prominent thirteenth century English judge and ecclesiastic, but it was not until the sixteenth century that the recognition of "furious madness" as an excuse led to an acquittal. Although the insanity defence rarely succeeded, Walker (1985) notes that it was offered in over 100 cases at the Old Bailey during the latter half of the eighteenth century, and was successful in about half. Those acquitted under the defence were entitled to release, and ceased to be subject to the criminal law. However, if necessary, they could be confined as dangerous lunatics through a civil commitment under the Vagrancy Act of 1744. No specific provision was made for their detention, which could be in gaols, houses of correction, or private madhouses, along with other lunatics detained under the Poor Laws (Parker, 1985).

The trial of James Hadfield in 1800 was a significant landmark (Moran, 1985). Hadfield, a former soldier who had received head wounds, shot at George III, and his counsel argued successfully that Hadfield's offence was due to a paranoid delusion. This led to a verdict of not guilty, "he being under the influence of insanity at the time the act was committed". Hadfield was remanded to prison, but because of concern that the criminal law had no immediate power over him, the government passed the 1800 Act for the Safe Custody of Insane Persons Charged with Offences. This empowered the court to order the confinement of an insanity acquittee until "His Majesty's Pleasure be Known". The 1800 Act similarly established powers for the court to order the detention of those indicted for a criminal offence found to be insane on arraignment. This Act, then, laid the foundation for all subsequent legislation permitting the preventive and indeterminate detention of mentally disordered offenders.

The new Act made no provision for places of detention, but facilities were made available at Bethlem Hospital (Bedlam) in London in 1816. The first asylum for criminal lunatics in Britain was established at Dundrum, near

Dublin, in 1852, to be followed by the opening of Broadmoor, near London, in 1863. A second state asylum was opened at Rampton, near Nottingham, in 1912. However, after an administrative structure for dealing with mental defectives was established by the Mental Deficiency Act of 1913, Rampton became a state institution for dangerous mental defectives in 1921, along with Moss Side Institution, near Liverpool. In 1948, all three institutions came under the Ministry of Health, and under the 1959 Mental Health Act, they became "special hospitals" providing for patients who "require treatment under conditions of special security on account of their dangerous, violent or criminal propensities". A fourth special hospital was completed at Park Lane, near Liverpool, in 1984, but was subsequently amalgamated with Moss Side to form Ashworth Hospital.

Although the powers provided by hospital orders are in advance of those available in the United States, where more emphasis has been placed on probation orders and confinement in psychiatric sections of prisons, American laws relating to mentally disordered offenders tended to follow a similar pattern to those in England until the 1950s (Morris, 1983). Thus, legislation for "defective delinquents" or "sexual psychopaths" allowed for diversion of offenders to criminal lunatic asylums or special units in state hospitals. From 1938, for example, 25 states and the District of Columbia enacted "sexual psychopath" statutes allowing for the indeterminate detention of sex offenders in asylums. These laws were typically a panic response to highly publicised sexual crimes, and were invariably passed without regard for the problems of defining, identifying, or treating "sexual psychopaths" (Sutherland, 1950). Most have now been repealed.

The 1959 English Mental Health Act represented the victory of treatment philosophies over legalism (Bean, 1985). Where legalism demands protection of individual liberty through judicial constraint on nonlegal experts, the Act gave considerable discretionary powers to psychiatrists. As has been noted, the treatment philosophy in the criminal justice system has been the target of attack. Stone (1984) traces the shift towards legalism in the United States during the 1960s and 1970s to the uncovering of abuses and punitive practices in the institutions created by defective delinquent and sexual psychopath statutes. There was also concern over the arbitrariness of decisions leading to the indeterminate detention of those found incompetent to stand trial. Exposures of the "quasi-criminal" institutions led to legal decisions on the right to treatment rather than confinement alone, the right to refuse treatment which was coercive, and the right to detention in the least restrictive setting. This swing to legalism extended to psychiatry generally, as marked by radical reforms of the laws of civil commitment, and the moves to deinstitutionalise the mentally disordered. However, the effect was to focus on dangerousness as a requirement of confining the mentally ill, with the result that patient populations of mental hospitals have become more like those of the earlier quasi-criminal institutions.

While more muted in Britain, legalistic concerns about the discretionary powers created by the Mental Health Act were also voiced (Gostin, 1977). Some psychiatrists also felt that too much was expected of the ability of hospitals to cope with mentally disordered offenders (Rollin, 1969). At the same time, the "open door" policy of psychiatric hospitals led to a decline in facilities for disruptive patients requiring a moderate degree of secure containment, and the reluctance of many hospitals to admit offenders resulted in overcrowding in the special hospitals, and the accumulation of mentally disordered offenders in prisons. The powers of the Home Secretary in relation to indefinite restriction orders were also challenged by the European Commission on Human Rights.

One consequence of the increased scrutiny of mentally disordered offenders was the setting up of the Butler Committee to review legal provision (Home Office/Department of Health and Social Security, 1975). The Committee's report exposed many problems in the law, and although only some of its recommendations have been implemented, it has remained a significant influence on approaches to mentally disordered offenders. A related development was the revision of the Mental Health Act in 1983. This introduced requirements for consent to treatment, treatability criteria for the admission to hospital of patients in the psychopathic and mental impairment categories, a Mental Health Act Commission to oversee the interests of detained patients, and increased powers of Mental Health Review Tribunals to order the discharge of restricted patients. The revised Act thus marked a significant return to legalism.

The insanity defence

While Hadfield's case was a landmark in determining the legal detention of mentally disordered offenders, the plea of "partial insanity" in the form of delusions did not establish a firm legal precedent. Of major significance in this respect was the trial of Daniel McNaughtan at the Old Bailey in 1843. McNaughtan attempted to assassinate the prime minister, Sir Robert Peel, but mistakenly shot and killed Edward Drummond, Peel's private secretary. It was agreed that McNaughtan suffered from persecutory delusions related to the Tories (although Moran (1985) suspects that his beliefs were not entirely unfounded), and a defence of "partial insanity" was again offered. The judge directed a verdict of not guilty "on the ground of insanity", but as a result of public indignation, including that of Queen Victoria, the common law judges were required to clarify the insanity defence to the House of Lords. Their opinions, now known as the McNaughtan rules, included the requirement that for the defence to succeed, it had to be proven that "at the time of the committing of the act, the party accused was labouring under such a defect of reason, from disease of the mind, as not to know the nature and quality of the act he was doing; or if he did know it, that he did not know he was doing what was wrong". McNaughtan was subsequently among the first patients transferred to Broadmoor, where he died in 1865.

The McNaughtan rules survive in Anglo-American law, but they provide a very strict standard, which McNaughtan himself would not have satisfied, and have been a continual source of controversy. They focus on the assumed cognitive effects of "disease of the mind", a legal concept which assumes defects arising from "internal" disease, and not external factors such as voluntary ingestion of alcohol or drugs. It must also be established that "defect of reason" is a result of the "disease". By "nature and quality of the act "is meant the physical nature of the act (e.g. squeezing someone's throat rather than a lemon), while not knowing that it was wrong means legally, and not morally, wrong. An early criticism was that few people lack the capacity to distinguish right from wrong, and this cognitive test of insanity excluded mentally disordered people who know what they are doing, but are unable to control it, for example, in "kleptomania". A test of volitional control in the form of an "irresistible impulse" criterion was adopted in Alabama in 1887, and subsequently in several other American states. Although controversial, this standard was also accepted in some British courts, and may now form part of a diminished responsibility plea (below). However, the problem with the "irresistible impulse" notion is that it is never logically possible to distinguish inability to resist an "impulse" from simple unwillingness, and it may lead to the commission of an incomprehensible crime being adduced as evidence of insanity (Wootton, 1959).

A further test, introduced in New Hampshire in 1870, but adopted more widely after *Durham v US* in 1954, rejected both the cognitive and volitional aspects, requiring instead that the act was "the product of mental illness". This reflected the influence of the medical model, and gave free rein to psychiatric testimony. However, this led to problems of establishing a causal link between crime and mental illness, and the use of medical terminology in court. The effect was for expert witnesses to pronounce on nonmedical "ultimate issues" about legal responsibility, a criticism made by Judge Bazelon (1978), who framed the Durham rule. This rule was rejected in *US v Brawner* in 1972.

The special verdict of "not guilty by reason of insanity" (NGRI) is technically an acquittal, but it leads to detention in secure psychiatric facilities. However, from 1883 to 1964, the verdict in England was changed to "guilty but insane", and some American states have recently introduced a "guilty but mentally ill" verdict which mandates the provision of treatment in prison or hospital for a determinate period, in an attempt to reduce the use of the NGRI verdict. This has been criticised for not in practice allowing any mitigation for the mentally disordered (Halleck, 1987). A more widely adopted test in the United States has been that proposed by the American Law Institute (ALI), which by 1980 was used in federal courts and over half of the state jurisdictions. This states that "a person is not responsible for criminal conduct if at the time of such conduct as a result of mental disease or defect he lacks substantial capacity to appreciate the criminality of his conduct or to conform his conduct to the requirements of law". It therefore incorporates both cognitive and volitional tests, while in substituting "appreciate" for "know", implies an affective response to knowledge. The ALI test formed the basis for the defence of John Hinckley, who shot at President Reagan in 1982, and who despite disagreement between psychiatric witnesses, received a NGRI verdict. As in the earlier cases of Hadfield and McNaughton, the verdict provoked a public demand for reform, which was directed to the insanity defence, but which was also an attack on psychiatric involvement in major trials (Stone, 1984). As a result, there have been several further attempts in the United States to revise the insanity defence.

A widely accepted alternative has been the Bonnie rule, which proposes that a defendant should be found NGRI if "as a result of mental disease or defect he was unable to appreciate the wrongfulness of his conduct at the time of the offence". This was recommended in a position statement of the American Psychiatric Association (1983), which argued that it was scientifically more feasible for psychiatrists to establish reliable judgements of cognitive than of volitional defects. It added that the "mental disease" recognised in the defence should be restricted to "serious" mental disorders of the severity of the psychoses, and should hence exclude personality disorders. The American Psychological Association (1984) was critical of the hasty attempts to change the insanity defence, noting that they were not based on any empirical evidence about the utility of the defence to the law, and Rogers (1987) provides evidence that the reliability of the judgements of forensic psychiatrists and psychologists of volitional control is as high as those of cognitive appreciation. However, the Bonnie rule was adopted in federal courts in 1984.

Empirical research on the insanity defence

Demands for reform of the insanity defence reflect assumptions about its abuse and the "psychiatrisation" of crime, but the available empirical data indicate that these rest on public misconceptions (Steadman, 1985; Pasewark, 1986). Rates of use and success of the NGRI plea appear to be substantially overestimated. In one study in Wyoming, for example, legislators believed that it was used in 8% of all felony charges, but the actual figure for the state was 0.46% (Pasewark and Pantle, 1979). Steadman (1985) estimated that there were 5180 NGRI pleas across the United States in 1978, which amounted to 0.2% of all felony arrests. Of these, about a third succeeded, and NGRI detainees amounted to about 2% of all hospitalised psychiatric patients. In England, the plea is now considered to be almost obsolete, but Mackay (1990) identified 49 successful NGRI pleas between 1975 and 1988, suggesting that it is less rare than imagined.

The view that NGRI is a defence of the rich is contradicted by findings that most acquittees are poorly educated and occupationally unskilled. They also tend to be unmarried, and women are overrepresented by comparison with the prison population (Steadman, 1985). This was found in Mackay's English study, in which 11 of the 49 acquittees were female. The main factor distinguishing successful from unsuccessful pleas appears to be history of frequent hospitalisation (Steadman, 1985), but acquittees are not uniformly psychotic. Pasewark, Pantle and Steadman (1982) found that, in a sample of 50 NGRI acquittees in New York state, a diagnosis of schizophrenia was made in 26, but personality disorder in 14. Similarly, Mackay (1990) found that 25 of his 49 acquittees were diagnosed as schizophrenic, but four as depressed, four as epileptic, and three as personality disordered. Moreover, both American and English studies find that although NGRI acquittees are more likely to have been charged with violent offences, relatively minor crimes such as deception or burglary are not uncommon. This contradicts the view that the defence is used mainly by murderers to evade legal punishment.

On the other hand, the public view that the detention of NGRI acquittees is relatively short and the legalistic concern that it is prolonged both receive some support. Pasewark, Pantle and Steadman (1982) compared NGRI detainees with prisoners charged with similar crimes, and found that after care of the NGRIs passed from the Department of Corrections to the mental health system, they tended to be detained for shorter periods than matched convicted prisoners. Mackay (1990) also found that over half of his sample were detained in RSUs rather than special hospitals, and that many of these were released in less than a year. However, although length of stay has been found to be variable, it tends to be related to offence seriousness, suggesting that punitive retribution rather than remission of disorder is a deciding factor (Pasewark, 1986).

Follow-up studies suggest relatively high, though variable re-arrest rates, ranging from 13% to over 50%, although Pasewark et al. (1982) found that NGRIs and matched felons had similar re-arrest rates of 15% and 18%, respectively, mainly for minor crimes. Steadman (1985) notes that data from New York state indicate that NGRIs have higher re-arrest rates than former mental hospital patients generally, though lower rates than those found incompetent, but the generality of this remains to be determined.

Incompetence to stand trial

The determination of competence to stand trial follows from the need to ensure the guilt of those who are punished. In England, "unfit to plead" is the common expression, although the Criminal Procedures (Insanity) Act of 1964 refers to "under disability such that it would constitute a bar to his being tried". In Scotland, the equivalent is "insane in bar of trial", while in the United States, "unfit to stand trial" is the common description (Morris, 1983).

In England, the criteria for competence are usually whether a defendant is able to understand the trial proceedings, so as to make a proper defence, to challenge a juror, and to understand the substance of the evidence (Home Office/Department of Health and Social Security, 1975). American jurisdictions emphasise fitness to understand charges and court proceedings, and to co-operate with the defence attorney (Halleck, 1987). These were commended by the Butler Committee. It is generally assumed that disability arises from serious mental disorder (deaf-mutism may also be accepted, but amnesia is not), and in some jurisdictions the court allows the psychiatrist or psychologist to state a conclusion as to competence, usually on the basis of psychosis. However, the criteria relate to specific cognitive and communication skills, and call for more than a conventional clinical examination (Roesch and Golding, 1987).

The plea is used more frequently than the insanity defence. Halleck (1987) notes an estimated 25 000 competency evaluations in the United States in 1978, although the courts found only a minority of these incompetent. In their survey of American facilities for disordered offenders, Kerr and Roth (1986) found that 11% of residents had been adjudicated unfit to stand trial, while a further 6 % were undergoing competency evaluations. In England, fewer than 2% of mentally disordered offenders have been dealt with in this way in recent years, and Grubin (1991) noted a mean annual number of 22.7 findings of unfit to plead between 1976 and 1988. It is, how ever, used much more frequently in Scotland (Chiswick, 1978). Chiswick found that incompetent patients resident in the State Hospital were older than controls, more likely to have been charged with homicide, more were diagnosed as psychotic and fewer as personality disordered or subnormal, and they had been detained for significantly longer periods.

Although such patients have not been found guilty of a crime, they are subject to indeterminate detention, usually in a secure hospital. Procedural changes have therefore been recommended in both England (Home office/Department of Health and Social Security, 1975) and America (Morris, 1983), which would result in adjournment of the trial for up to six months to allow for possible recovery, and hence a normal trial. In the case of the "unrestorable incompetent", a special trial of the facts is proposed to allow for a possible "not guilty" verdict, with judicial discretion on disposal when such a verdict could not be reached. However, the number of "unrestorables" is probably small, and in the United States, programmes aimed at restoring competence through clinical treatment and training in court-related skills have proved highly successful (Pendleton, 1980).

Diminished responsibility

The insanity defence in England has dwindled since 1960, partly following the introduction of hospital orders in the Mental Health Act, but in particular as a result of the Homicide Act of 1957, and the subsequent abolition of capital punishment in 1965. The Homicide Act introduced the defence of *diminished responsibility*, following practice in Scotland, which if accepted leads to a conviction of manslaughter. This does not carry the mandatory life sentence of a conviction for murder, and the court may then impose sentences other than life imprisonment, although the latter is not ruled out.

Section 2 of the act requires that for the defendant to "suffer from" diminished responsibility, he must display "such abnormality of mind (whether arising from a condition of arrested or retarded development of mind or any inherent causes or induced by disease or injury) as substantially impaired his mental responsibility for his acts or omissions". This goes beyond the "defect of reason" of the McNaughtan rules, "substantial impairment" meaning impairment falling short of total. Griew (1986) observes that the wording of Section 2 is "elliptical almost to the point of nonsense", and it has not been improved by judicial interpretations. In the case of *R v Byrne* in 1960, Lord Parker ruled that "abnormality of mind" means "a state of mind so different from that of ordinary human beings that the reasonable man would deem it abnormal". He also judged that "mental responsibility" referred to "the extent to which the accused's mind is answerable for his physical acts", an interpretation which Griew (1986) considers "somewhat worse than the original". The Butler Committee noted that the "mental" responsibility referred to is "either a concept of law or a concept of morality; it is not a clinical fact relating to the defendant". Rather is the issue one of a person's responsibility *for* his or her acts, and the extent to which legal liability is diminished as a result of "substantial impairment".

The ambiguous implication that what is "diminished" is a psychological faculty of "responsibility" has again resulted in psychiatrists pronouncing on "ultimate issues", and public antipathy to the role of psychiatrists in murder trials surfaced in the case of Peter Sutcliffe, the so-called "Yorkshire Ripper", who killed thirteen women (Prins, 1986). Although defence and prosecution psychiatrists agreed that Sutcliffe suffered from paranoid schizophrenia, the trial, like that of Hinckley, became a "media event" focusing critically on the psychiatric evidence. In this case, however, the jury rejected the plea of diminished responsibility, finding Sutcliffe guilty of murder. Nevertheless, Sutcliffe's mental disorder became apparent in prison, and he was subsequently transferred to a special hospital.

Diminished responsibility has been accepted in a range of cases, including reactive depression, premenstrual tension, and psychopathic personality as well as psychosis. It does not, however, necessarily lead to more lenient disposal, and only about a third of males found guilty of manslaughter under Section 2 have received a hospital order in recent years, possibly reflecting an increased tendency of psychiatrists to argue that psychopaths are untreatable (Dell and Smith, 1983). The verdict has nonetheless displaced findings of unfit to plead and the special verdict. Between 1900 and 1949, these accounted for 14% and 26%, respectively, of those committed to trial for murder, excluding infanticides (Hart, 1968). Since the Homicide Act, these categories account for less than 3%, while manslaughter verdicts have accounted for 37% (Morris, 1983).

The Butler Committee recommended that the special verdict be changed to "not guilty on evidence of mental disorder", mental disorder being defined more stringently than in the Mental Health Act. Indefinite hospitalisation would not be automatic, and judges would have discretion on disposals. This would make the special verdict more attractive than that of diminished responsibility, and the Committee recommended abolition of this and the mandatory life sentence for murder. Although these proposals have not been adopted, they have influenced recent recommendations of the Law Commission (Mackay, 1990).

Mental disorder and criminal responsibility

One reason for the continued controversy surrounding the insanity defence has been a lack of attention to the question of *why* mental disorder should affect criminal responsibility, and some of the recent arguments in legal philosophy will be touched on here. They represent attempts to identify the basis for the common moral "intuition" that the mentally disordered should be excused blame and punishment.

The traditional criteria for exculpating an act are ignorance (mistake), compulsion, and involuntariness. The latter relates strictly to movements rather than actions (e.g. automatisms), and hence the first two are the essential basis of excuses (Radden, 1985). They have their parallels in the cognitive and volitional components of insanity tests, respectively. One interpretation of the insanity defence is that it negates *mens rea* since insanity reflects absence of criminal intent. Fingarette and Hasse (1979), however, dispute this, arguing that *mens rea* elements such as malice or intent are frequently present in insane criminals, and that it is not the absence of criminal intent which exculpates, but rather the origins of the intent in a mental disability.

Another view is that it is the presence of a "mental disease" which exculpates, since we do not blame people for getting a physical disease (i.e. they are patients rather than agents). Radden (1985), however, argues that it does not follow that we withhold blame from actions resulting from a disease, and that where we do, it is on the basis of the traditional excuses of ignorance or compulsion. Disease may mitigate blame on the basis of sympathy and mercy, but is not itself an excuse for action. There is, in fact, strong resistance to the idea that any form of mental disorder identified in the psychiatric nosology is sufficient to exculpate, notably in the view that those with personality disorders should be held criminally responsible (American Psychiatric Association, 1983; Rachlin, Halpern and Portnow, 1984). The Durham rule came close to accepting the presence of mental disorder itself as the basis for a defence, and the Butler Committee seems to accept that legal conceptions of insanity should move closer to psychiatric conceptions. However, they equivocate on this by limiting their recommended verdict of "not guilty on evidence of mental disorder" to *severe* mental illness or subnormality.

The Butler Committee also took the view that the weakness of the McNaughtan rules lay in "the now obsolete belief in the pre-eminent role of reason in controlling social behaviour", and went on to assert: "Contemporary psychiatry and psychology emphasise that man's social behaviour is determined more by how he has learned to behave than by what he knows or understands." Insofar as this seems to mean that the behavioural sciences take an empiricist rather than a rationalist view of behaviour, it would now be difficult to sustain in the face of "the cognitive revolution" in psychology. Several legal philosophers also argue that our intuitions to exculpate the insane are grounded less in the traditional excuses than in the impairment of powers to engage in conduct governed by *reason*. Fingarette and Hasse (1979), for example, propose that an irrational condition of mind underlies the various insanity tests, although their concept of rationality goes beyond the cognitive to include emotional responsiveness to the significance of "crime ". Offenders described as psychopaths might be regarded as irrational in this respect. However, Radden (1985) regards this notion of irrational as too diffuse. She proposes a concept of *exculpating unreason* as a pervasive inability to hold and act on sufficient reasons and to avoid holding inconsistent beliefs and desires as the basis for excusing the insane. She sees parallels between the unreason of the insane and the prerational thinking held by Piaget to characterise young children, i.e. an inability to reason logically, think reflectively, communicate fully, and act voluntarily.

Radden suggests that rationality is a necessary condition for personal agency and hence for ascribing praise or blame, and a similar position is developed by Moore (1984). He notes: "We hold people retrospectively responsible in law or morals only if they are accountable agents who negligently or intentionally and without justification or excuse perform actions that cause some state of affairs they were obligated not to bring about." Each condition of responsibility, he suggests, presupposes that people are *practical reasoners*, and that autonomy and rationality are essential to holding people accountable. Animals, infants, corporations, and the mentally ill are excused because they lack the status of person conferred by these attributes. It is thus a general incapacity for rational action which forms the basis for exculpating the insane.

The view that it is the ability to reason which underlies the ascription of responsibility to human agents reaffirms classicism, and has affinities with rational choice theories. Norrie (1986), however, criticises Moore's view of practical reasoning, since like the legal concept of a rational agent, it relies on an abstract notion of reasoning ability. He argues that from the standpoint of critical realism, which Moore purports to adopt, human agency arises from *situated reasoning* in which actions depend not simply on reasoning capacity or form, but also on the personal and social context which supplies the premises of reasoning. He notes that the basis for accepting compulsion as an excuse is not that reasoning as an abstract ability is impaired, but rather that choice is constrained by fear. As this is in principle no different from choice constrained by adverse social conditions or one's character, it is an inconsistency in Moore's argument, and "a chink in the law's armour" to maintain that interference in abstract reasoning grounds the withholding of responsibility.

Moral philosophers are concerned with what *ought* to be the case, and the question of *how* people attribute responsibility is an empirical psychological issue which is not considered in this debate. It may well be the case, for example, that there is no single universal principle of excuse which is applied on a context-free basis. Nevertheless, in the light of these disagreements, attempts to reform the insanity defence inevitably continue to be controversial. Those who see impaired reasoning ability as the rationale for excusing conditions favour maintaining the defence, while drawing the line of responsibility on criteria of such disability. Moore, for example, argues that legal insanity should be defined in terms of irrationality, not by whether a person is mentally ill in psychiatric terms. Norrie's claim that choice is always constrained, in contrast, challenges any attempt to establish criteria for criminal responsibility, and the case against considering mental disorder in criminal trials has been made by several writers. Szasz (1979) accepts the justice model, seeing punishment as morally legitimate, but believes that psychiatry should play no part in determining who is responsible and punishable. While also equating responsibility with punishability, Wootton (1959, 1980) argues that dispensing with the former would remove the need to attempt artificial distinctions between "sick" and "healthy" criminals. She proposes dispensing with *mens rea* requirements in trials by extending strict liability. The question of mental disorder would only arise at the sentencing stage, which would entail pragmatic consideration of the needs of the offender and society. The distinction between penal and health systems would thus disappear. This position was favoured by the British Psychological Society (Black et al., 1973).

However, Hart (1968) has pointed out that considerations of moral responsibility are not tied to a justice model, but enter into any legal intervention to prevent crime (see also Chapter 1). To apply any form of punishment without considering a person's capacity and opportunity violates basic principles of fairness to individuals. He proposes that *mens rea* should be retained as a necessary condition of liability, but that mental disorder should only be raised at the sentencing stage. This would entail eliminating insanity or diminished responsibility as a defence and extending the use of the Mental Health Act. However, Fingarette and Hasse (1979) note that if *mens rea* is retained, mental disorder must be considered because it is relevant to beliefs and intent. They argue for a "disability of mind" defence based on criteria of irrationality.

The recommendations of the Butler Committee for a verdict of "not guilty on evidence of mental disorder" are perhaps closest to the latter position. The line for criminal responsibility, however, is drawn at psychiatric concepts of severe subnormality and severe mental illness, the latter being defined by five criteria: lasting impairment of intellectual functions, lasting alteration of mood producing delusional appraisal, delusional beliefs, abnormal perceptions associated with delusional misinterpretation, and thinking so disordered as to prevent reasonable appraisal of the patient's situation. These proposals are considered coherent by most psychiatrists and by the Law Commission, but their basic rationale remains obscure. However, whether they rest on the view that it is mental illness itself or deranged thinking which constitutes an excuse, it is arbitrary to draw the line at what amount to criteria of psychosis. These criteria are particularly strained by theoretical developments which point to the determining role of cognitive dysfunction in neurotic and personality disorders (Beck, 1976, 1990). If, for example, personality disordered offenders are no more responsible for holding their irrational belief systems than are paranoid schizophrenic offenders for their delusions, why should they be held more culpable for acting on them?

MENTAL DISORDER AND CRIME

This section considers attempts to examine the relation between mental disorder and criminal behaviour in general. Violence is considered in the following section. It was noted earlier that the relationship between mental disorder and crime is not a simple objective one, and all research in this area suffers from significant methodological problems which preclude more than tentative conclusions. In particular, the diagnostic framework for identifying mental disorders remains subject to the clinical orientation of researchers, who have often employed idiosyncratic schemes of uncertain reliability and validity. Moreover, studies have typically relied on samples whose representativeness is questionable (Wessely and Taylor, 1991). Whether these problems are "insuperable", as Menzies and Webster (1989) suggest, remains to be seen.

The problem of representativeness is highlighted by Monahan and Steadman (1983), who draw the epidemiological distinction between *true* and *treated* prevalence. Those identified as patients by the receipt of health care services provide only "treated" rates of mental disorder, which substantially underestimate the "true" prevalence of mental disorder in the community at large. Convicted offenders similarly represent the "treated" minority of those committing criminal offences. Ideally, true prevalence rates of both and the relation between them should be determined from random community samples through interviews or self-reports, but data of this kind have only recently become available (Monahan, 1992).

Teplin (1984, 1985) describes an observational study of 1382 police–citizen encounters, in which evidence of severe mental illness was assessed by a brief symptom checklist. Of 506 persons suspected of a crime, 30 showed signs of mental illness, and significantly more of these were arrested than other suspects (47% vs 28%). However, contact between the police and the mentally ill was not determined primarily by suspicion of a crime, since although the mentally ill were marginally more likely to be suspects, they were also more often the objects of concern or assistance. Also, patterns of crime for which they were suspected were not significantly different from those of other suspects. The results therefore indicate a bias towards arrest of the mentally ill, either because of "disrespectful" behaviour or because of limited alternative dispositions. However, they do not indicate greater proneness to criminal behaviour on the part of the mentally ill.

This study provides a closer approximation to the ascertainment of true crime prevalence among the "untreated" mentally ill than most other research. Other studies to be considered have been primarily concerned with arrest rates in treated mentally disordered samples, or with true rates of mental disorder in treated (i.e. legally processed) offenders.

Criminal behaviour in psychiatric patients

Studies in this area have examined the subsequent arrest rates of patients discharged from mental hospitals and compared them with general population rates. Such research clearly rests on several assumptions about current psychiatric status, demographic comparability of patients with the general population, and absence of bias in liability to arrest. In the light of Teplin's findings, the latter is questionable.

In a review of American studies, Rabkin (1979) found that research prior to 1965 consistently showed former patients to be *less* likely to be arrested after release from hospital than members of the general population. Studies reported subsequently indicated that patients were *more* likely to be arrested, and for more serious crimes. However, the best predictor of later arrest was previous arrest, and comparisons between earlier and later studies suggested that the difference was largely due to the admission to hospital of increased numbers of patients with previous arrest histories, these accounting for most of the post-discharge offending. The later data are therefore attributed to changes in mental health and criminal justice policies, with hospitalisation being increasingly restricted to those who are more socially disruptive or dangerous.

Representative of the later research is a 19-month follow-up of patients discharged from hospital in New York State in 1968 and 1975 by Steadman, Cocozza and Melick (1978). Of the two samples, 6.9% and 9.4% were subsequently arrested, their rates being about three times higher than the general population rate, although the arrests were not confined to any particular category of crime. Subsequent arrest was related to prior arrests, age, and diagnosis of personality disorder or alcohol abuse, although these diagnoses were largely dependent on age. For patients with no prior arrests, subsequent arrest rates were actually lower than those of the general population, and comparison with an earlier study indicated that the critical difference lay in an increase in the proportion of patients with prior arrest histories from 15% to 40% over a 30-year period. Consistent with the suggestion that serious mental disorder does not increase the risk of crime is a 15-year follow-up of all schizophrenic patients discharged from hospital in Stockholm in 1971 (Lindqvist and Allebeck, 1990). Offence rates for males were only marginally higher than the general population rate. However, females offended at twice the expected rate.

Sosowsky (1980), in contrast, reported that patients released from a state hospital in California who had no previous arrest history nevertheless had post-discharge arrest rates more than five times higher than that of a local county. However, Monahan and Steadman (1983) question the appropriateness of the comparison, and note that like Steadman et al. (1978), Sosowsky found prior arrest and age to be more important predictors of subsequent arrest than psychiatric diagnosis. In agreement with Rabkin (1979), they conclude that offending among psychiatric patients is associated more with the same demographic factors of age, gender, social class and ethnicity which predict crime in general than with psychiatric status itself.

The implication seems to be that the criminal acts of patients depend on criminal disposition rather than disorder. However, it must be noted that these studies are concerned with patients discharged from hospital, whose current psychiatric status is unclear. While there appears to be no firm evidence on the extent of offending by psychiatric patients when acutely disordered, Toch and Adams (1989) found that the previous offences of disordered prisoners tended to have occurred during periods of greater psychiatric disturbance. A recent longitudinal study of an unselected community sample in Sweden also found that those who develop serious mental disorder, or are intellectually handicapped, are also more likely to commit a crime than those not identified as disordered or handicapped (Hodgins, 1992).

Mental disorder in criminals

Studies of the prevalence of mental disorder among convicted offenders are plagued by the lack of consistent diagnostic criteria across studies and over time, as well as by the filtering out of many disordered offenders at an early stage in criminal justice processing. Brodsky (1972) summarised nine American studies of court or prison samples from 1918 to 1970 which suggested rates of psychiatric disorder ranging from 16% to 95%, the higher figures being obtained from more recent studies. Rates of psychosis ranged from 1% to 4%, while the highest rates were for personality disorder or "behaviour disorders". The vague criteria for these latter disorders accounts for much of the variation in overall rates. Studies of court samples, which may be somewhat more representative of the offender population than incarcerated offenders, have been rare. Coid (1984) identified only two, which were conducted in America prior to and shortly after the Second World War. These indicated low rates of disorder, although there was an increase in the proportion of personality disorders from 6.9% in the earlier study to 24.9% in the later survey, reflecting changing criteria.

More recent studies are confined to imprisoned samples. While there has been greater concern with diagnostic reliability, there appears to be no study of a random sample employing DSM-III criteria. Guze (1976) interviewed 223 male and 66 female felons in Missouri prior to release from prison, using research diagnostic criteria. All of the females and 90% of the males received a psychiatric diagnosis. Rates of psychosis and mental retardation were low, but 78% of males and 65% of females received a diagnosis of sociopathy. The latter, however, must be treated with scepticism, since this category was defined by criteria of previous social deviance, such as trouble with the police or school delinquency, and in the case of females included prostitution. Like the more detailed DSM-III criteria for antisocial personality disorder, they say little about the attributes of the subjects, and merely reaffirm the criminological truism of an association between imprisonment and past social deviance.

Somewhat lower figures are reported from British surveys of prison samples, and Gunn (1977) notes estimated rates of between 27% and 46%. Gunn et al. (1978) found that 31% of randomly selected prisoners in south east England met psychiatric case criteria, most receiving diagnoses of personality disorder or alcoholism. More recently, Gunn, Maden and Swinton (1991) assessed a random sample of 1365 adult males and 404 young males from 16 English prisons, deriving ICD diagnoses by means of a semi-structured interview and file information. Overall, 37% received a primary diagnosis. Main diagnoses were substance abuse (23%), personality disorder (10%), neurosis (6%), psychosis (2%), and organic disorders (0.8%).

While there are inconsistencies in the patterns of disorder found in different samples, which may, of course, reflect real differences, it would appear that a third or more of prisoners show some form of mental disorder, but that this is mainly a reflection of high rates of alcohol and drug abuse and personality disorder. It will be noted that these are the disorders whose status as mental illnesses is contentious within psychiatry. It is unclear whether the rates of disorder in prisoners are significantly different from general population rates. Monahan and Steadman (1983) cite estimates from American community surveys yielding a range overall of 16% to 25%. Median prevalence rates were 1.7% for psychosis, 15.1% for neurosis, and 7.0% for personality disorder, although the rates for lower socioeconomic groups, from which prisoners are more likely to be drawn, are higher. Robins et al. (1984) have also found lifetime prevalence rates of substance abuse in American samples of from 15% to 18%. Taking account of social class, most surveys of prisoners yield rates of disorder which may not be significantly different from these rates, suggesting that mental disorders in general do not carry an increased risk of offending. However, this can be only a tentative conclusion. Coid (1984) notes that symptoms of stress are frequent among prisoners, but many may not be recognised by a formal diagnosis of neurosis.

While the causal implications of these findings are uncertain, they nevertheless carry policy implications for services to offenders. They are also relevant to the "criminalisation" hypothesis. From findings of an inverse relation between psychiatric bed provision and prison populations in European countries, Penrose (1939) proposed that a change in the population of one institutional system forces an inverse change in the population of another. Weller and Weller (1988) found a correlation of 0.94 between the falling numbers in psychiatric hospital in England since 1950 and the increasing numbers in prison, apparently consistent with Penrose's "hydraulic" hypothesis, and suggest that it reflects a greater tendency for former patients who offend to be sent to prison. However, Lurigio and Lewis (1987) found little evidence of this in an American study of discharged patients, and the figures obtained by Gunn et al. (1978) and Gunn et al. (1991) also suggest that there has been no substantial change in the proportion of English prisoners with serious mental disorders during the last decade.

Mental disorder and specific offences

While crime and mental disorder may vary independently, their distributions will nonetheless overlap. Given that the cumulative lifetime prevalence of offending is over 40% in males and 14% in females (Farrington, 1981), and that more than 10% of the population receives psychiatric treatment, the two will frequently co-occur even in the absence of a causal relationship. However, an apparent lack of a relationship at the aggregate level does not preclude significant relationships at the individual level, and in view of the heterogeneity of the mentally disordered and offenders, there may well be relationships between some forms of disorder and some forms of crime (Wessely and Taylor, 1991).

Most attention has been paid to violent crime, which is examined below. Evidence on other offence categories is piecemeal, but there are a few suggestive findings. Shoplifting, for example, is not associated with mental disorder to a significant extent, but among the disordered minority, depression is overrepresented (Gibbens, 1981). Gunn (1977) notes that offenders convicted of personal violence, sexual offences, and criminal damage are disproportionately likely to be identified as mentally disordered in terms of receiving hospital orders in English courts. This may reflect biases in legal processing, but an association of mental disorder with property destruction is supported by findings of Taylor and Gunn (1984) that over 60% of remand prisoners charged with or convicted of arson or criminal damage showed signs of disorder, half of them psychosis.

MENTAL DISORDER AND VIOLENCE

The public view of the mentally ill as dangerous is claimed by Foucault (1978) to have been fostered by nineteenth century psychiatrists, who introduced the explanatory fiction of "homicidal monomania", a mental illness manifested only in the crime, to account for serious crimes not having an obvious reason. Although this gave way to concepts of moral insanity and sexual perversions, the notion that many crimes are symptoms of mental disorder was extended by the suggestion of other "monomanias" (Chapter 3). Case studies of mental illness in serious criminals also encouraged a belief among psychiatrists in a high risk of violence among the mentally ill, and there continue to be debates about whether the sudden appearance of violence in young adults may signify incipient psychosis (Häfner and Böker, 1982). Research now questions the assumption of an inherent connection between mental disorders and violence (Howells, 1982; Taylor, 1982; Krakowsky, Volavka and Brizer, 1986; Monahan, 1992), but serious crimes are clearly sometimes committed by mentally disordered people. While the relation between the true prevalence of mental disorder and violence is likely to remain elusive, evidence from several sources suggests that some disorders may increase the risk.

Homicide and mental disorder

While not necessarily representative of violence in general, high police clearance rates for homicide allow for firmer generalisations. However, data are confounded by national variations in the recording of homicide and the legal recognition of mental disorder, and in the possible contaminating effect of violence on the diagnosis in some cases.

The most systematic epidemiological study is that of Häfner and Böker (1982). They surveyed all 533 cases of murder, attempted murder, and manslaughter in the Federal Republic of Germany between 1955 and

1964, who were excused legal responsibility because of serious mental disorder (schizophrenic or affective psychosis, organic brain disorder, mental retardation). Although there were problems in deriving strictly comparable official crime data, the authors estimated that the mentally disordered accounted for 2.9% of convictions for serious violence, and for 5.6% of murder victims. Psychiatric assessments of 2000 persons arrested for murder in St Louis between 1964 and 1973 yield congruent findings: Schizophrenia was diagnosed in 0.98% of cases, affective disorder in 0.4%, and organic brain disorder in 0.5% (Henn, Herjanic and Vanderpearl, 1976).

In Britain, however, mental disorder has been recognised in between 30% and 40% of homicides for much of this century, and during the 1980s, about a fifth of those convicted of homicide were deemed to be suffering from diminished responsibility. Additionally, in some 7% of recorded homicides, the suspect committed suicide following the crime (Home Office, 1989a). The latter figure represents a reduction from about a quarter in earlier decades. Among 107 remand prisoners in London charged with or convicted of homicide, Taylor and Gunn (1984) found that more than a third showed symptoms of disorder (schizophrenia, 9.3%; affective psychosis, 1.9%; mixed disorders, 26%). Taylor (1986) also found that among life sentenced prisoners in London, most of them murderers, 9% had been reported to show symptoms of schizophrenia, while 13% were depressed, and 33% personality disordered. While these figures are not inconsistent with the rates of abnormality found among homicides in Britain, they suggest higher rates of psychosis than usually found.

However, in view of variations in national homicide rates, proportions who are mentally disordered may be misleading. In a cross-cultural comparison of mentally disordered murderers and those who commit suicide following the offence, Coid (1983) found an inverse correlation between national homicide rates and proportions of disordered homicides. The rate of mentally disordered homicides per head of population appeared to be relatively constant across countries and over time, at about 0.10 per 100 000. Fluctuations in homicide rates are therefore likely to reflect social factors which influence "nonpathological" murder. This finding would also account for the decline of the proportion of abnormal homicides and murder–suicides in Britain as the overall murder rate has risen. The more pertinent question is therefore whether particular kinds of disorder increase the risk of homicide and other forms of violence.

Violence and specific types of psychiatric disorder

Häfner and Böker (1982) found that in comparison with nonoffender patients, schizophrenia was overrepresented, and affective psychosis underrepresented in their violent mentally disordered group, although this was related to sex differences. However, they estimated that the risk of serious violence in schizophrenia was 0.05% (i.e. 5 of every 10 000 schizophrenics are likely to become violent), while in affective disorders and mental retardation it was 0.006%. While emphasising the very low rates of violence in these disorders, this suggests that schizophrenia is the disorder with the greater risk. In their follow-up of discharged schizophrenic patients, Lindqvist and Allebeck (1990) also found that violent offending was four times more frequent than expected, although this was confined to only 7% of the sample. However, the more extreme violence of schizophrenics is typically directed to family members or acquaintances, and bizarre self-mutilation, such as enucleation, is more likely than mutilatory murders (Taylor, 1982). There are, of course, exceptions, such as the serial murderer Peter Sutcliffe (Prins, 1986).

Studies of violence in psychiatric hospitals are relevant in this context, although there are many inconsistencies in the data (Haller and Deluty, 1988; Monahan, 1988). Evidence from Britain (Noble and Rogers, 1989) and Canada (Harris and Varney, 1986) suggests that violence in hospitals has increased since the 1970s, apparently as a result of changing admission policies, although this seems to relate to an increased concentration of younger, but chronic and "unmanageable" patients than to those with histories of criminal violence. However, while violent incidents in hospitals are frequent, they are typically minor, and few lead to serious injuries (Fottrell, 1980; Noble and Rogers, 1989). They are also perpetrated by a small minority, Harris and Varney (1986), for example, finding that fewer than 5% of residents in a maximum security hospital were responsible for 74% of incidents. However, it is less clear that schizophrenic patients are more likely to be responsible. Some surveys suggest so (Fottrell, 1980; Pearson, Wilmot and Padi, 1986; Noble and Rogers, 1989), but this was not found by Harris and Varney (1986) or James et al. (1990). It is possible that there are qualitative differences between violent offences and the minor incidents observed in hospitals, since some studies report that the latter are perpetrated more by females. Quinsey and Maguire (1986) also found that assaultive behaviour in a maximum security hospital did not predict subsequent violent crime in the community, suggesting that it is as much a product of institutional milieu as of patient pathology. This view is supported by findings that factors in the social environment contribute to hospital violence (Drinkwater and Gudjonsson, 1989; James et al., 1990).

Schizophrenic patients, however, are not homogeneous, and violent behaviour seems more likely in the presence of particular symptoms. As Krakowsky, Volavka and Brizer (1986) note, planned, successful violence assumes a degree of intact functioning not compatible with severe impairment or disorganisation, and violent acts by schizophrenic patients are more likely during the acute, active phase of disorder (Planansky and Johnson, 1977; Häfner and Böker, 1982). The presence of delusions appears to be the most frequent correlate of violence in psychotic patients. Planansky and Johnson (1977) found that of 59 schizophrenics who made threats or assaults, nine complained of urges to kill, seven claimed hallucinatory instructions, and six catatonic patients attacked suddenly and in a frenzy, but 39% of incidents involved delusional misperceptions. Mowat (1966) found that delusions of infidelity (morbid jealousy) were prominent in 12% of male and 3% of female murderers admitted to Broadmoor. However, while these were associated with schizophrenia in a third of cases, they were also associated with depression and with alcoholism, and in some cases were the only symptom.

The extent to which psychotic symptoms explain violence, however, remains problematic. Krakowsy et al. (1986) assert that "violence in psychiatric patients is closely related to the psychopathology underlying it", but not all violent acts by patients can be attributed to their disorder. Violent incidents in hospital, for example, more often relate to provocations or disputes over personal space or food than to psychotic symptoms (Harris and Varney, 1986; Pearson, Wilmot and Padi, 1986). Taylor (1985), however, estimated that 20% of the offences of schizophrenic prisoners were definitely motivated by delusional or hallucinatory symptoms, and a further 26% probably so. However, while abnormal beliefs or perceptions may be necessary to explain the violence in such cases, they are rarely, if ever, sufficient, since those with such experiences rarely act on them. Even though psychotic beliefs remain in need of explanation, accounting for the violence in the context of those beliefs requires reference to general models of aggressive behaviour, and to the personal, social, and situational factors associated with violence in the population generally (Taylor, 1982). Personality has received little attention in this context, but Blackburn (1968c) found that differences in aggression between paranoid and nonparanoid schizophrenics were related to personality traits. Howells (1982) also notes that the attributional processes associated with the violence of deluded patients are those associated with aggression more generally. Similarly, Convit et al., (1988) found that the variables predicting assaultive behaviour among young schizophrenic male patients were those predicting violence in other populations, such as deviant family background or prior violent history.

It was noted earlier that *affective psychosis* may carry a lesser risk of violence than does schizophrenia, but the evidence is far from consistent. Depression has been associated with serious violence, particularly homicide, but primarily among females, and in the context of "extended suicide", in which the killing of associates is linked to the killing of oneself (Häfner and Böker, 1982). This has been considered significant in murder followed by suicide. Häfner and Böker (1982) suggest that in males, depression may actually decrease the risk of violence. However, Yesavage (1983) and Binder and McNeil (1988) found that male patients with bipolar disorder who were manic, but not depressed, were more likely to be assaultive in an inpatient setting. Collins and Bailey (1990b), on the other hand, found that after controlling for demographic and problem drinking variables, mood disorders in recently incarcerated male prisoners were not consistently associated with expressive violence (homicide, rape, assault), but depressive symptoms were associated with a history of adult fighting. No clear conclusions can be drawn from the available findings.

Risk of violence seems to be associated with *mental retardation*, but again in only a small proportion of cases (Hodgins, 1992). In Häfner and Böker's sample, the mentally retarded offenders were most like the "normal" violent group in demographic variables, and were also more likely than nonoffender patients to have a history of family disturbance and antisocial behaviour, suggesting that mental retardation itself was not a cause of violence. Although mental retardation is not consistently overrepresented in prison samples (Chapter 8), mentally retarded offenders who are compulsorily detained also show a disproportionate rate of sexual offences both prior to hospitalisation and following release (Gibbens and Robertson, 1983; Coid, 1984). Since diagnosis of mental retardation relies on signs of social ineptitude as well as low intelligence, higher rate of sexual offending probably reflect deficient interpersonal skills in this group rather than intellectual deficit itself.

Some recent studies implicate *post-traumatic stress disorder* (PTSD) in violence. Although aggression is not among the criteria for PTSD in DSM-III-R, it is noted that irritability may be an accompaniment, and that the disorder is sometimes associated with "unpredictable explosions of aggressive behavior" (American Psychiatric Association, 1987). Solursh (1989) describes a pattern of "combat addiction" among Vietnam veterans with chronic PTSD who had experienced repeated exposure to combat. A central feature is the recurrence of flashbacks or nightmares which are experienced as exciting or as a "high", which oscillate with periods of depressed moods. This pattern was present in 94% of a PTSD sample of 100 veterans, of whom 97% were also explosive and irritable, 87% were socially avoidant, and 72% were substance abusers. While 81% were also reported to engage in combat-related habits, such as keeping a loaded gun and hunting, it is unclear how many had a history of assaulting people. However, Collins and Bailey (1990a) report a relationship between violent crime and PTSD not related to combat experience in a prison sample of 1140 males. After controlling for demographic factors, problem drinking, and antisocial personality disorder, the 2.3% of the sample meeting PTSD criteria were significantly more likely to have been arrested or incarcerated for an act of expressive violence. A similar pattern held for those showing one or more PTSD symptoms, which in the majority of cases preceded the offence.

The category most often associated with violence in clinical lore is *personality disorder*. However, there is very little evidence to permit any generalisation about the relationship. One problem is the tendency to identify social deviance *as* personality disorder, which negates any possibility of evaluating the contribution of personality deviation itself (Blackburn, 1988b). A related problem is the tendency to diagnose personality disorder as a global category, ignoring heterogeneity, and there do not appear to be any comparisons of criminal violence in different categories of personality disorder as defined in DSM-III. It seems unlikely, for example, that dependent or avoidant disorders are associated with violence to the same extent as antisocial or borderline disorders.

Several studies have examined reoffending in mentally disordered offenders (Murray, 1989). Since these samples have already been identified as violent, this research is only indirectly relevant to the question of the differential susceptibility to violence of particular psychiatric disorders, and as it has been mainly concerned with the clinical prediction of dangerousness, it is discussed further in Chapter 12. However, some findings suggest that personality disorder carries a greater risk of violence than does psychosis. Quinsey et al. (1975), for example, found higher rates of violent recidivism in released maximum security patients with a diagnosis of personality disorder than in those with a diagnosis of psychosis, although within the former group, extent of prior violence predicted later violence. In a later study of patients from the same institution, in contrast, diagnosis did not predict subsequent serious offending (Quinsey and Varney, 1986). Patients admitted to English special hospitals in the legal category of psychopathic disorder also tend to commit more violent offences following release than those categorised as mentally ill (Tennent and Way, 1984; Black and Spinks, 1985), but the difference may reflect other factors. Black and Spinks (1985), for example, found that psychopathic disorder did not predict violent recidivism when previous offending was taken into account. These findings are also ambiguous given the heterogeneity of the category, and the influence of previous criminal behaviour on classification. Nevertheless, a few studies based on stricter criteria of psychopathy support an association with violence, both in prisoners and mentally disordered offenders (Chapter 9), and Hare, McPherson and Forth (1988) report higher recidivism rates for most crimes, including violence, among psychopathic prisoners than among nonpsychopaths. Supporting the view that psychopaths "burn out" with age, the criminal activities of psychopaths declined after age 40.

In summary, with the possible exception of some forms of personality disorder, none of the major categories recognised by psychiatry seems strongly associated with a propensity for violence. Although there appears to be an increased risk in schizophrenia, particularly in paranoid schizophrenia, it must be reiterated that only a small minority of patients in this category are violent, and that the disorder itself is rarely sufficient to account for violent acts in instances where they do occur. It will probably be more fruitful for research to focus on specific symptoms or states than on global diagnostic categories, and to determine how these interact with personal and social factors. There is also a need for long-term prospective studies of unselected community samples of the mentally disordered who have not come to the attention of the criminal justice system.

IMPRISONMENT AND MENTAL HEALTH

Interest in mental disorder among prisoners is dictated partly by the theoretical question of the causal relation of mental disorder to crime, and partly by concerns about mental health services for offenders. A further question is how far long-term imprisonment affects the psychological wellbeing of inmates. However, research on the effects of imprisonment is complicated by the heterogeneity of penal institutions and their inmates, and any generalisations must therefore be tempered by considerations of interactions between types of offender and types of regime (Bukstel and Kilmann, 1980).

The pains of imprisonment

There is little disagreement that penal institutions are uncongenial environments. Not only are physical conditions often squalid and inadequate, social conditions commonly impose boredom, humiliation, exploitation, and exposure to violence from other inmates and sometimes staff. Newton (1980) cites several American studies demonstrating that incarceration is inhumane and has "devastating" effects on the health and wellbeing of inmates. For example, a 1973 survey of adult state and federal prisons found that homicides occurred in about a third, the rate being 74.4 per 100 000 compared with 9.4 for the United States population. Homosexual rape is also reported to be common, although Walker (1983) suggests that this occurs infrequently in British prisons.

Those most at risk for violence are prisoners who have molested or ill-treated children, are informers ("grasses"), have convictions for fraud, or who fail to pay debts incurred in prison (Walker, 1983). This reflects the existence of an inmate culture with its own "code". Sociologists have been particularly concerned with the process of *prisonisation*, which Clemmer (1958) defined as "the taking on in greater or lesser degree of the folkways, mores, customs, and general culture of the penitentiary". This informal subculture is generally seen as opposed to the formal organisation of the prison and its goals, and as characterised by norms of toughness, inmate solidarity, and manipulative relations with staff. One view is that such a system arises as a means of coping with, or neutralising, the "pains of imprisonment", which are a consequence of the deprivation of liberty, goods and services, heterosexual relationships, autonomy, and personal security (Sykes, 1966). Reported increases in assaults, collective disturbances, and hostage-taking during the last two decades suggest that the personal security of inmates in particular has deteriorated (Bartollas, 1990).

Prisonisation has usually been defined in terms of degree of rejection of staff norms, but research has not produced consistent findings. Clemmer (1958) believed that prisonisation increased over time, but in a cross-sectional study of a state reformatory, Wheeler (1961) found that conformity to staff norms varied with length of time *remaining* to be served. Those in the early and late phases of their sentence were more conforming than those in the middle phase. However, while obtaining some evidence of this U-pattern, Garabedian (1963) found that patterns varied with the adoption of different prisoner roles, as identified by prison argot. For example, "right guys", who were most obviously resistant to prison staff, showed a U-pattern of conformity, whereas "outlaws", who were isolated from both staff and inmates, showed a linear pattern of prisonisation. The prison culture therefore had a differential impact on inmates.

There are alternative models of the origins of the prison culture (Thomas, 1977). Where the deprivation model sees it as a reaction to the negative effects of prison organisation, the importation model argues for the influence of pre-prison socialisation experiences. For example, some American prisons have experienced gang conflict based on rival racial grouping, which is imported directly from urban areas from which the prison draws its inmates (Bartollas, 1990). However, Thomas (1977) found that both within-prison and pre-prison experiences influenced prisonisation, the former accounting for more of the variance.

However, the prisonisation concept has been criticised, and Zamble and Porporino (1988) argue that it may most usefully be seen as an attitudinal factor which combines with other variables in determining adaptation to prison. It also neglects individual differences in reactions to imprisonment. For example, it is assumed that prisonisation impairs adjustment and socialisation following release, but Goodstein (1979) noted that "institutionalisation" represents an alternative adaptation involving conformity to the formal prison culture, which is equally likely to lead to problems on release. She found that the most institutionalised inmates had the most problems during the first two months following release, as reported by parole officers, while the most prisonised adjusted the most easily. These differences disappeared by the third month, suggesting the influence of the more immediate environment.

Some of the deprivations of imprisonment are an inevitable consequence of incarceration, but they can clearly be eased or exacerbated by the nature of the custodial regime. Management style appears to influence inmate behaviour. Davies and Burgess (1988), for example, found that rates of disciplinary reports at an English prison varied significantly with the characteristics of the governor. Cooke (1991) notes evidence that inmate violence varies with regime factors, such as staff–inmate communication, staff training, access to visitors, and level of stimulation. Such factors may account for the successful reduction of the violence of recalcitrant prisoners in the Barlinnie Special Unit in a Scottish prison, which is run on therapeutic community lines (Cooke, 1989).

In Europe and America, the prison population has more than doubled in the past three decades, owing to a combination of increased numbers sent to prison and increases in the lengths of sentences for some crimes. This has not been matched by an increase in new prisons, and particular attention has been paid to *overcrowding* as a source of stress and deviant behaviour (Gaes, 1985). Cox, Paulus and McCain (1984) summarise studies of several American prisons showing associations of population variations with rates of illness, mortality, disciplinary infractions, self-mutilations, and suicide attempts. They propose that the effects are due to increased social interactional demands, mediated by fear, frustration and cognitive overload, social density (number of individuals) being more critical than spatial density (space per individual). However, Gaes (1985) criticises the reliance on aggregate level correlations, and suggests that only a few consistent findings emerge from prison crowding research. These relate mainly to the effects of dormitory accommodation on physiological functioning, illness complaints, and assaults. Bonta (1986) also notes that it may be the concomitants of overcrowding, such as more strangers and noise, or higher temperatures, which produce negative effects.

It remains unclear which features of the prison environment most significantly affect inmate behaviour. Attempts have been made to capture organisational properties with the concept of *social climate*, the most popular measure being the Correctional Institutions Environment Scale (CIES: Moos, 1975). This assesses staff and inmate perceptions of three postulated dimensions of relationships, personal development, and system maintenance, each having three components. However, the CIES has been criticised for reflecting individual variation more than organisational properties (Thornton, 1987b), and Wright (1985) notes the lack of evidence for its validity. Wright proposed that prison social climate is reflected in eight global concerns which are perceived and experienced universally by inmates (privacy, safety, structure, support, emotional feedback, social stimulation, activity, freedom). He constructed an inventory whose structure supported the validity of these factors, and which was only moderately influenced by individual variation. Thornton (1987b), however, questions the assumption that environments have uniform and unidirectional effects on inmates. He argues for the assessment of inmate–regime interactions in evaluating regimes, and describes the validation of the Custodial Adjustment Questionnaire. This measures attitudes to staff, attitudes to inmates, institutional deviance, and emotional distress, which are related to both personal and regime characteristics.

Aspects of the prison environment identified as problematic by researchers may not necessarily be those perceived by inmates themselves as most salient. In a study of long- and short-term prisoners in England, Richards (1978) found that of 20 potential problem areas, those ranked amongst the most severe were "missing somebody", "feeling that your life is being wasted", and "missing social life". These were ranked higher than, for example, "being bored" or "wishing you had more privacy". Zamble and Porporino (1988) also found that "missing family and friends" was the problem most frequently identified by Canadian prisoners. Loss of external relationships therefore seems to be among the most severe deprivations of prison life. There is also some evidence that maintenance of family ties during imprisonment reduces recidivism (Homer, 1979). While it is commonly assumed that imprisonment leads to the breakup of family relationships, this appears to occur primarily with long sentences, despite the economic and emotional hardships entailed for the families of most prisoners (Walker, 1983).

Effects on psychological functioning

Findings on the psychological effects of imprisonment permit only limited generalisations. Apart from methodological problems and a paucity of controlled longitudinal studies (Bukstel and Kilmann, 1980; Zamble and Porporino, 1988), much of the research has been atheoretical, failing to specify which aspects of imprisonment are likely to have particular effects on which individuals. For example, apart from the privations of confinement itself, potential debilitation might arise from reductions in perceived control over the environment, the stigma of being a prisoner, or the uncertainties of an indeterminate sentence. The effects of such variables will depend on individual circumstances, making uniform effects of imprisonment unlikely.

Effects on mental health seem particularly likely to reflect person–situation interactions, although there is little evidence on factors influencing vulnerability. Anecdotal reports have long drawn attention to acute psychotic reactions in prisoners ("prison psychosis"), and Heather (1977) found that a fifth of a sample of life-sentenced prisoners in Scotland reported psychotic symptoms on the Delusions–Symptoms–States Inventory. Clinically significant symptoms were described by 59%. Taylor (1986) also found a high incidence of psychiatric disorder, including psychosis, reported in the records of life-sentenced prisoners in London. Rasch (1981), however, identified no psychotic symptoms in a similar sample in Berlin, although he noted that a half were "disturbed" on psychological tests. How far severe disorders reflect situational effects is unclear, but Arboleda-Flórez (1980) describes four cases of homicides who developed symptoms related to their crime, such as visions of the victim, flashbacks, and depression. He suggests that these are instances of psychogenic psychosis, although they would probably now be identified as symptoms of post-traumatic stress disorder (Kruppa, 1991).

While cross-sectional surveys of prisoners have not generally found a high prevalence of psychotic disorder, a relatively consistent finding is a higher level of anxiety and depression. However, this is typically higher in the early stages of a sentence. Heather (1977), for example, found a negative correlation between symptoms and length of imprisonment, and suggests that this reflects an initial impact of imprisonment. Mackenzie and Goodstein (1985) also found that long-term offenders in the early stage of their sentence had lower self-esteem, as well as being more anxious and depressed than those in later stages, although findings on self-esteem have not been consistent (Bukstel and Kilmann, 1980). In their 16-month longitudinal study of Canadian prisoners, Zamble and Porporino (1988) similarly found that while levels of self-reported anxiety, depression, and hopelessness were initially between those of normals and psychiatric patients, these declined significantly over time. Although it is sometimes assumed that these reactions reflect the impact of long-term incarceration, they may equally reflect responses to confinement itself. For example, Thornton (1987b) observed higher levels of emotional distress in junior detention centre trainees during their first two weeks than subsequently. Since anxiety level has also been observed to increase with the approach of release (Bukstel and Kilmann, 1980), there are parallels with the U-pattern found in prisonisation studies.

Risk of suicide also increases during the early stage of imprisonment. Suicide rates have been reported to be 50% higher among American prisoners than in the general population (Newton, 1980), and four times higher in Britain (Dooley, 1990). A national survey of American local jails in 1979 revealed a rate 16 times higher than that of urban populations (Hayes, 1983). These comparisons must be treated with caution, since prisoners are not demographically comparable to the population at large. Nevertheless, Dooley (1990) notes that prison suicide rates almost doubled between 1972 and 1987. Highest rates were among those on remand, homicides, and those on life-sentences, a majority occurring within the first year of sentence. Hayes (1983) found that jail inmates were particularly vulnerable during the first 24 hours after confinement, those most at risk being young, single males arrested for public intoxication. Over 90% of successful prison or jail suicides are by hanging. Self-mutilation may sometimes represent a suicide attempt, but such behaviour appears to be endemic in prison populations. Newton (1980) cites a study of a Canadian training school for female delinquents, in which 86% of inmates had engaged in "carving", apparently as a means of identifying with the inmate culture. However, self-mutilation may serve a variety of functions, such as tension relief or stimulation seeking, and is also among the criteria for borderline personality disorder.

The apparent disequilibrium occurring with initial incarceration may also be associated with personal reappraisal, since motivation for change and self-improvement is maximal in newly admitted long-term prisoners (Sapsford, 1983; Zamble and Porporino, 1988). However, this is not generally sustained. Zamble and Porporino (1988) also found some evidence that reduced motivation for change was related to greater likelihood of recidivism. They suggest that rehabilitation programmes should capitalise on the initial motivation, rather than waiting until prisoners have settled into the institutional regime.

Cross-sectional comparisons of long-term prisoners at different stages of sentence have found minimal evidence for psychological deterioration. Banister et al. (1973) found some decline in perceptual-motor speed, which was not a function of age, but intelligence test performance was unaffected. The latter was confirmed by Rasch (1981). However, some personality changes have been reported, notably an increase in self-directed hostility (Banister et al., 1973), and increased introversion (Banister et al., 1973; Sapsford, 1983; Zamble and Porporino, 1988). Sapsford (1983) suggests that changes are most likely to be found in motivation and attitudes. He found that interest in the outside world remained undiminished, but involvement declined. While some prisoners became more institutionalised, there was no general increase in apathy. Future time perspective, however, decreased, although in a study of shorter term institutionalisation, Landau (1976) found that this changed with the approach of release.

The evidence therefore suggests that imprisonment tends to have an initial debilitating effect on emotional wellbeing, but this is transitory. Most long-term prisoners appear to adopt coping strategies which enable them to reperceive or reshape their environment, and any dysfunctional effects on motivation or social behaviour seem to be limited to the prison situation rather than being permanent (Sapsford, 1983). However, while harmful effects may be confined to extremely depriving environments or vulnerable individuals, information is lacking on inmate–environment interactions. Moreover, no study identifies positive changes. Zamble and Porporino (1988) found that the histories reported by most prisoners indicated an inadequate repertoire of coping skills prior to imprisonment, and that low-level coping resources were related to an unstructured lifestyle and greater criminality. Coping in prison was a continuation of this, and although coping efficacy was rated higher during imprisonment, this reflected the more structured environment rather than change. For most inmates, their coping patterns were merely "frozen" until release.

Chapter 11

Sexual Deviation and Sexual Offending

INTRODUCTION

Sexual practices have varied across time and culture, but the role of the family as social unit dictates a norm of heterosexual behaviour between married couples which both organised religion and the law have sought to enforce. The global category of "sexual offences" therefore covers not only coercion and exploitation of unwilling victims but also victimless crimes, including in some states acts between willing married partners. However, this chapter is concerned primarily with victimful sexual behaviour, such as rape and child molestation.

Until the 1960s, criminology paid only sporadic attention to sex crimes. Gagnon (1974) observed that these lent themselves less readily than delinquency to subcultural theories or the sociology of deviance, and that sociologists focused on collective forms of deviation, such as homosexual communities or prostitution. Crimes involving victims were more the concern of psychologists and psychiatrists. Since then, there has been a surge of interest due particularly to feminist views that rape is a cultural product, and a violent rather than a sexual crime. However, psychological research on victimful sexual behaviour has also accelerated, largely as a result of interest in intervention methods. Before this is examined, sexual deviation needs to be distinguished from sexual offending.

SEXUAL DEVIATION

What is identified as sexual crime or as sexually deviant depends on changing societal standards. The decriminalising of homosexual behaviour during the 1960s, and its subsequent "depathologising" by psychiatry, clearly illustrate this dependence, and as Christie-Brown (1983) notes, the fluctuating boundaries of what constitutes "abnormal" sexual behaviour indicate a social rather than a medical basis for defining sexual deviance. Nevertheless, some sexual interests are considered psychologically as well as socially dysfunctional.

Paraphilias

Sexual deviations have traditionally been described in terms of the object, mode, frequency, or context of sexual gratification, deviation being seen as departure from the norm of genital intercourse between mature, opposite sex partners. Nineteenth century psychiatry redescribed "unnatural" sexual acts as "perversions", but in DSM-III-R (American Psychiatric Association, 1987), the term *paraphilia* is preferred to emphasise that the deviation (para) lies in that to which the person is attracted (philia). Paraphilias are distinguished from sexual dysfunctions, and are seen as recurrent intense sexual urges and arousing fantasies involving nonhuman objects, the suffering or humiliation of oneself or one's partner, or children or other nonconsenting persons. Paraphilia is diagnosed when the urges or fantasies have been experienced for at least six months, and the person has acted on them, or is distressed by them. The main forms are summarised in Table 11.1, but additional examples are telephone scatologia (lewdness), necrophilia (corpses), zoophilia (animals), coprophilia (faeces), and klismaphilia (enemas). Rape is not identified as a paraphilia, but sexual sadism includes paraphilic rape (raptophilia or biastophilia) and lust murder (erotophonophilia; Money, 1990). Abel and Rouleau (1990) also argue that rape more generally should be included, since rapists frequently report cycles of compulsive urges and rape fantasies which they act on.

As noted in DSM-III-R, the large commercial market in paraphilic pornography and paraphernalia suggests that some paraphilias are widespread, and they may be a part of "sexual games" between consenting couples (Gosselin and Wilson, 1980). Reports of sexual fantasies by volunteer samples of females (Hariton and Singer, 1974) and males (Crepault and Couture, 1980) also indicate that fantasies are used widely during sexual activity, including many which if acted on would qualify as paraphilias. Their association with general fantasy ability and positive attitudes towards sex suggests that "deviant" fantasies are not in themselves a symptom of psychopathology (Hariton and Singer, 1974). Dysfunction lies rather in the emotional and social consequences of acting on them for nonconsenting victims and often the perpetrators themselves. It is therefore doubtful if many would accept the uncompromising reductionism of Money (1990), who asserts that all paraphilias are "brain diseases".

The DSM-III-R classification provides a standardised nomenclature, but it derives from a misleading concept of discrete syndromes. Surveys indicate that multiple paraphilias may be the rule rather than the exception, and Abel and Rouleau (1990) suggest that paraphilias may reflect a generalised deficit of control over deviant sexual behaviour rather than specific dysfunctions.

Table 11.1   The paraphilias (from DSM-III-R)

Category	Characteristics
Exhibitionism	Exposure of one's genitals to a stranger, sometimes while masturbating; further sexual involvement is not attempted
Fetishism	Use of nonliving objects, such as female underwear or boots, frequently involving masturbation while holding, rubbing or smelling the object, or sometimes the wearing of the object by a sexual partner
Frotteurism	Touching and rubbing against a nonconsenting person, usually in a crowded place, excitement being derived from the contact
Paedophilia	Sexual activity with a prepubertal child by a person of 16 years or older, and at least 5 years older than the child: activity may be limited to touching or fondling, but may involve fellatio, cunnilingus, and vaginal or anal penetration
Sexual masochism	The act of being humiliated, beaten, bound, or otherwise made to suffer by a partner, or the self-infliction of pain for sexual excitement
Sexual sadism	Acts in which psychological or physical suffering of the victim is sexually exciting, including domination or torture
Transvestic fetishm	Cross-dressing in female clothes, often entirely as a woman, although basic preferences are heterosexual; distinguished from *transsexualism*, in which the person wishes to acquire opposite sex characteristics, and is not sexually excited by the cross-dressing
Voyeurism	Observing unsuspecting people who are naked, disrobing, or engaged in sexual activity

Assessment of sexual arousal

Sexual arousal is a broad psychological construct denoting the subjective and physiological changes preparatory to a sexual act (Dekker and Everaerd, 1989). Clinical assessment of sex offenders is discussed in Chapter 13, but the assessment of sexual arousal is prominent in behavioural research on deviant sexual behaviour, and is described here. Several self-report measures have been developed for assessing sexual deviation (Laws, 1984), but many clinicians are wary of accepting an offender's account of his deviant behaviour, which may be distorted because of denial, reluctance to disclose events with implications for criminal conviction or continued incarceration, or inability to discriminate critical factors controlling the behaviour. More objective assessment of deviant sexual arousal has therefore been developed (Laws and Osborn, 1983).

While self-ratings of experienced sexual excitement provide one index of arousal, the most widely used measure is *penile plethysmography* (PPG), which is a recording of genital tumescence to relevant sexual stimuli obtained under laboratory conditions. The rationale for this assessment is: (1) sexual arousal is a critical component in the chain leading to sexual behaviour; (2) penile erection is the most reliable and specific index of male sexual arousal; (3) stronger arousal to a particular category of person or activity relative to others indicates sexual *preference* for that category. Much of the early development of PPG was due to Freund (e.g. Freund, 1967; Freund et al., 1972), who utilised a glass cylinder sealed with a sponge rubber ring into which the penis was inserted, erectile response being recorded as volumetric change in cylinder air. This device is probably the most accurate, but more common is the measurement of penile circumference change by means of a strain gauge, either a metal caliper-like device or a mercury-filled rubber tube which encircles the penis (Laws and Osborn, 1983). This records changes in resistance to a weak electric current as the penis expands from flaccidity to full erection, the output being amplified as a continuous polygraph record.

Sexual stimuli may be slides, for example of nudes varying in age and gender in the assessment of paedophilia, or short videotaped sequences of mutually consenting sexual intercourse, rape, and nonsexual violence in the case of sexual aggression. While filmed material evokes the strongest reactions, problems in obtaining relevant pornographic depictions (and ethical concerns about the exploitation involved in their production) have led many clinicians to rely on audiotaped descriptions, which are easily made, and can be tailored to be relevant to the individual client. Responses are usually recorded as percentage of full erection, although some workers advocate other transformations (see Barbaree, 1990). Problems arise in assessment because some males do not achieve tumescence under laboratory conditions, and erectile response is partly under voluntary control (Laws and Rubin, 1969). Some clients may therefore attempt to inhibit responses to deviant stimuli through attentional shifts or imaginal manouvres. However, this is often utilised to evaluate self-control, by instructing the client to attempt to suppress erection.

While PPG correlates highly with known deviant interests, it assesses one component of sexual arousal, and not sexual behaviour itself, and is probably most useful in identifying and monitoring targets of change in well motivated clients. Its use as a "sexual lie detector", or to forecast dangerousness, is not warranted, since its predictive utility has not been unequivocally demonstrated, and there are recent debates about the limits of its utility (Hall, 1990; Simon and Schouten, 1991). Evidence for its ability to discriminate rapists is now questioned (Blader and Marshall, 1989), although it is thought to be a valid measure of paedophilic interest. While Hall, Proctor and Nelson (1988) found that PPG responses to paedophilic stimuli did not discriminate sex offenders who had assaulted adults from those who offended against minors, Quinsey and Laws (1990) argue that this is an idiosyncratic finding which may reflect problems with the stimulus material. Nevertheless, a review by Simon and Schouten (1991) emphasises that there remain a number of theoretical and technical issues to be resolved before the validity and clinical utility of PPG assessments can be considered to be firmly established.

SEXUAL OFFENCES AND SEX OFFENDERS

Sexual offences are defined mainly by the use of force, disparities in age, violations of close relationships, and violations of public order, but their relationship to clinical concepts of sexual deviation is indirect. Not all paraphilic acts are illegal, and not all sexual offences are paraphilias. Child molestation or sexual abuse, for example, describe antisocial acts which are not necessarily signs of paedophilia, while "sexual assault" is used broadly to cover acts involving unwilling victims rather than a particular deviation. Moreover, some sexual offences may not appear under this heading in official statistics (Table 11.2). Making "obscene" telephone calls (telephone scatologia), for example, may be charged under telecommunications statutes, or as theft (of electricity !). Indecent exposure (exhibitionism) may be dealt with under the Vagrancy Act, or bylaws against offending public decency, while "peeping Tom" activities (voyeurism) may be charged as a breach of the peace. While the more serious acts involving victims are specifically sexual offences, the effects of offences not involving contact are not always trivial. Obscene telephone calls, for example, which may entail silence ("heavy breathing") or verbal abuse and threats, may provoke extreme distress in the recipient.

Table 11.2   Notifiable sex offences recorded by the police in England and Wales in 1979 and 1988

Offence category	Offences in 1979	Offences in 1988	Percentage change
Buggery	632	951	+50.5
Indecent assault on a male	2 385	2 512	+5.3
Indecency between males	1 333	1 306	−2.0
Rape	1 170	2 855	+144.0
Indecent assault on a female	11 834	14 112	+19.0
Unlawful sexual intercourse with a girl under 13	248	283	+14.1
Unlawful sexual intercourse with a girl under 16	3 558	2 552	−28.3
Incest	334	516	+54.5
Procuration	107	201	+87.9
Abduction	91	277	+204.4
Bigamy	151	93	−38.4
Gross indecency with a child	(not available)	871	−
Total	21 843	26 529	+21.5

Source: This information is based on data which appears in *Criminal Statistics England and Wales 1988* (Home Office, 1989), and is adapted with the permission of the controller of Her Majesty's Stationery Office, London.

Legal definitions of sex offences vary between jurisdi
changed considerably during the last century. Rape, for exa
defined as "carnal knowledge of a woman forcibly and a\$
some states include sexual acts in addition to vaginal inte
United States and Canada, there have been moves to bring u.
assault under a single legal heading. Chappell (1989) notes that ..
notions of rape were often interpreted to emphasise lack of consent rather tha.
the use of force, which placed the onus on the prosecution to demonstrate
victim resistance. This has been a target of feminist criticism. Rape within
marriage has also only recently been legally recognised as an offence in Britain.

Incidence and prevalence

Sexual offences constitute only a small proportion of officially recorded crimes.
In 1988, they represented 0.7% of notifiable offences in England and Wales,
and fewer than 2% of offenders convicted (Home Office, 1989a). Although
these offences have risen in all countries during the past three decades, the
rate of increase has been less than that of crime in general, with the notable
exception of rape. Sexual offences in England rose in the 1960s, then decreased
during the 1970s, so that the 1983 total was actually lower than that of 1963
(Bottomley and Pease, 1986). Table 11.2 indicates that the total in 1988 was
some 22% higher than that of a decade previously, but this compares with
a 43% increase for all crimes. However, apart from the doubling of recorded
abductions, which remain small, the most notable change is the increase in
rape, which represents an almost sixfold increase from the 1963 figure of 422.

Official statistics of sex crimes, however, underestimate the true prevalence
to a greater extent than those of other crimes, since victims are less likely
to report sex offences. In some cases, this may reflect the trivial nature of
the offence, but serious assaults may not be reported because the victim is
too young, is intimidated by the offender, the perpetrator is a relative, or
because of the added stress of reporting the offence to criminal justice agents
who may "blame the victim". Increases in the rape statistics in England are
probably due partly to changes in police procedures for dealing with rape
victims in 1985, which have encouraged more victims to come forward. Even
so, the 1988 British Crime Survey estimated that less than a fifth of rapes and
indecent assaults were recorded by the police (Mayhew, Elliott and Dowds,
1989), while only some 10% of sexual offences known to the police result in a
conviction (Lloyd and Walmsley, 1989).

Victimisation surveys may also underestimate since they exclude young
children, and differing samples, survey methods and definitions of sex offences
result in widely varying prevalence estimates. Proportions of American adult
females reporting experience of rape or attempted rape range from 9%
(Kilpatrick et al., 1985) to 44% (Russell, 1984), while 28% of a national sample
of American female students reported such experiences (Koss, Gidycz and
Wisniewski, 1987). Figures for experience of child sex abuse are equally
variable. Finkelhor (1986) notes North American estimates of between 6% and

62% for women, and 3% to 31% for men. Other crimes receive less attention, but Pease (1985) estimated from 1982 British Crime Survey data that 10% of women with a private telephone had received obscene calls.

Self-report data also point to higher rates of victimising than suggested by official data. In the student sample of Koss et al. (1987), 8% of males admitted to rape or attempted rape, while in an anonymous survey, incarcerated rapists and child molesters admitted to between two and five times more crimes than those for which they had been apprehended (Groth, Longo and McFadin, 1982). Abel and Rouleau (1990) found that a volunteer clinic sample of 561 sexual deviants admitted to a total of 291 737 paraphilic acts involving 195 407 victims. While the bulk of these involved exhibitionism, frottage, or voyeurism, 126 rapists reported a total of 907 rapes.

A substantial amount of victimisation, then, does not come to official attention. The representativeness of convicted samples, on which much research is based, is therefore unknown, and generalisations about the demographic characteristics of sex offenders are tentative. Amir (1971) found that the majority of 646 rapists arrested in Philadelphia in 1958 and 1960 were young, black, unmarried, and came from inner city areas of low socioeconomic status. The volunteers examined by Abel and Rouleau (1990), however, were described as similar to the general population in socioeconomic status, ethnicity, and education. While these are unlikely to be a random sample, Alder (1985) also found that self-reported sexual aggression in a community sample was unrelated to family class, educational attainment, or prestige of occupation.

Official data emphasise that sex offenders are predominantly male, females representing less than 2% of those convicted. In offences of females involving a victim, this is most commonly a child, and in many cases the woman is charged with aiding and abetting a male (O'Connor, 1987). In comparison with property offenders, proportionately more sex offenders are in the over-21 age group. However, more than half of sex offender careers are likely to begin in adolescence, and adolescents may be responsible for over a third of child sex abuse (Groth, 1977; Davis and Lietenberg, 1987; Perkins, 1987). More attention is therefore being given to offenders in this age group (Sapp and Vaughn, 1990).

Recidivism and criminality

Early studies suggested a relatively low rate of further sex offences among convicted sex offenders. Soothill and Gibbens (1978) questioned this, noting that follow-up periods of 3–5 years were too short. In a long-term follow-up of sex offenders in England, they found that many subsequently reoffended after several years, and almost a quarter had reoffended by the end of the twenty second year at risk. A 9- to 13-year follow-up of sex offenders in Norway found that about a fifth committed a further sex offence (Grunfeld and Noreik, 1986). This was highest for rapists (22%) and lowest for child molesters (10%). However, a recent review found wide variability in reports of sex offender recidivism (Furby, Weinrott and Blackshaw, 1989). Although there is some evidence that homosexual paedophiles are more likely to recidivate than incest offenders, generalisations are not currently warranted.

Given evidence for multiple paraphilias, it is possible that sex offenders are "generalists" who commit a range of sex crimes. However, the evidence seems to favour specialisation. In a clinical study of adult and adolescent offenders, Groth (1977) detected continuity in type of victim and crime, and Grunfeld and Noreik (1986) observed a tendency for further offences to be similar to the original. Hall and Proctor (1989) also found evidence for specialisation. Among "sexual psychopaths" released from a state hospital, prior arrests for sex offences against adults predicted later offences of a similar kind, while arrests for child offences predicted later child offences.

Sex offending, however, may be correlated with a propensity to offend more generally. Soothill, Way and Gibbens (1980) compared the criminal careers of those convicted and acquitted for rape offences in England in 1961. The two groups were very similar. More than half had both previous and subsequent criminal convictions, sex and violent offences being prominent. Grunefeld and Noreik (1986) similarly observed that half of the rapists in their sample had previous convictions. Hall and Proctor (1989) also found that previous sex offences against adults among their incarcerated sample predicted later nonsexual offences, including violence, but this was not so for previous offences against children. It would appear, then, that for rapists in particular, their offences are often related to general criminality.

THEORIES OF SEXUAL DEVIANCE

Explanations of deviant sexual behaviour must account not only for the origins and persistence of deviant interests, but also the conditions under which people act on these interests. Since sexual deviance takes several forms, no single theory may be adequate to account for all aspects, but four broad approaches underlie current concepts.

Biological perspectives

One popular belief is that sexually deviant behaviour reflects a "high sex drive". However, while some components of arousal and orgasm are controlled by hormones and physiological reflexes, the notion of sexual "drive" or "libido" as a biological force is a misleading fiction. Circulating hormones are necessary for the establishment of sexual behaviour in male animals (Heim and Hursch, 1979), but not for its maintenance, and there is general agreement that human sexual arousal, sexual performance, and gender identity are highly dependent on learning and situational factors.

Nevertheless, given the central evolutionary role of reproduction, genetic constraints on learning are plausible. Quinsey (1984, 1986) suggests that some sexual stimulus and response categories are more "prepared" for learning by their evolutionary significance. Youthful appearance, for example, is associated with reproductively viable females, and adult males respond sexually to female characteristics along an age gradient, showing some response to pre-pubescent girls (Freund et al., 1972). Under certain conditions, children may therefore become a focus of sexual interest because of their prepared learning status.

Quinsey (1984) also points to animal studies suggesting a close link between neural centres for aggression and sexual activity, and suggests that sexual violence might be more easily acquired because of genetic advantages of forced mating in evolutionary history. Marshall and Barbaree (1990a), on the other hand, draw on the same evidence to suggest that there is a natural propensity for sexual aggression in males, which young males must learn to inhibit. However, this ignores the distinction between angry and instrumental aggression, and the latter requires no specific neural mechanism. Moreover, while the autonomic response patterns of anger and sexual arousal overlap, erection and orgasm are under parasympathetic control, and are likely to be incompatible with intense states of anger.

Psychodynamic concepts

Freud initially saw sexual deviations as unmodified continuations of childhood sexuality, but subsequently emphasised their defensive function in avoiding castration anxiety (see Rada, 1978; Howells, 1981; Kline, 1987). Psychodynamic approaches therefore construe sexual deviance in terms of unresolved oedipal conflicts and regression to earlier fixation points. Failure to identify with the father may result because of the dominance of the mother, and the boy may identify with her. However, incestuous wishes are not necessarily abandoned, and persisting castration anxiety may restrict normal heterosexual interactions. Homosexual paedophilia represents inverted narcissism, the offender seeking out immature sexual partners whom he sees as like himself, treating them as he wishes his mother had treated him. Rapists who displace their hostility to women are held to be ambivalent towards their mother, and show anal-sadistic regression under stress. Again, in sexual sadism, degradation of a woman implies a reaction formation against incestuous wishes, and anal fixation may account for the association of buggery with sadistic assaults (Kline, 1987).

More recent accounts focus on ego functions and interpersonal goals. Deviant fantasies, for example, are seen as defensive cognitive structures which represent an attempt to master childhood trauma by re-enactment or identification with the aggressor, and which may involve symbolic revenge. Groth and Burgess (1977a) emphasise nonsexual motives in deviant sexual behaviour, seeing rape, for example, as a function of anger and needs for power and control.

Learning theories

Learning theorists also emphasise the role of fantasy and avoidance of heterosexual anxiety, but give weight to the attachment of sexual arousal to inappropriate stimuli and failures to acquire heterosocial and heterosexual skills. Gagnon (1974) outlines a cognitive social learning view, noting that learning of the means to achieve the conventional heterosexual endpoint is left largely to chance, which allows for ambiguities and opportunities for error. He also emphasises that sexual interaction depends on many nonsexual social rules, seeing sexual misbehaviour in terms of sexual scripts which come to contain nonsexual elements. While this stresses the role of cognition, most learning accounts invoke "s–r" mediation rather than cognitive structures.

McGuire, Carlisle and Young (1965) proposed a classical conditioning model of sexual deviations. They suggest that an initial arousing experience subsequently supplies fantasy for masturbation, and particular cues achieve a sexual valence through being paired with sexual arousal and orgasm. This, however, would not explain why only some stimuli achieve paraphilic status. Laws and Marshall (1990) elaborate on this theory by proposing that certain stimuli are more *prepared* to become conditioned stimuli for sexual arousal through their evolutionary relevance, and that fantasied acts progress to deviant behaviour through processes of differential reinforcement and punishment, and the availability of observed and symbolic deviant models.

There is some evidence that sexual arousal can be conditioned (Dekker and Everaerd, 1989), but although conditioning mechanisms may plausibly account for the strengthening of deviant interests, they do not explain their origins. The model implies that the initial experience of any prepared stimulus and its use as masturbatory fantasy is adventitious, and that people are equally likely to acquire deviant conditioned arousal. This, however, fails to explain the choice of deviant fantasies. Social learning theory, for example, would predict that these would tend to be deterred by self-punishment. Additionally, the model does not adequately address the translation of fantasy into overt behaviour.

Interest in nonsexual aspects has centred on heterosocial skills (Abel, Blanchard and Becker, 1978). Since these are necessary to gain access to peer-aged partners and to establish relationships, deficits in these skills may result in the negative reinforcement of deviant attractions, which may be less anxiety provoking, and which will also be positively reinforced if unpunished. Howells (1981) also notes the relevance of social cognitions to deviant interests, but attempts to relate deviant sexual interests to a broader social cognitive model have only recently been made (Segal and Stermac, 1990). However, it seems unlikely that the acquisition of sexual interests, skills, and beliefs, which accelerates at puberty, can be understood in isolation from the developing social expectations and self-regulatory skills established earlier in childhood. This view is developed by Marshall, who sees sex offenders as more vulnerable to deviant sexual reactions as a result of skill deficits arising from rejecting or violent parental interactions (Marshall, 1989; Marshall and Barbaree, 1990a). He emphasises failures to develop attachment bonds and intimacy skills, which may prime some males to seek intimacy in inappropriate sexual interactions. This might also be seen in terms of Hirschi's control theory, insofar as those who act on deviant interests by victimising others are likely to lack the constraints of a wider social bond.

Sociocultural theories

Historical and anthropological studies reveal wide cross-cultural variability in the prevalence of forcible sex and sex between adults and children (Quinsey, 1984, 1986), suggesting that cultural factors play a significant role in promoting such behaviour. This view has been developed by sociologists and social psychologists during the past two decades. The focus has been on rape, and has been inspired by feminist views that rape is an expression of the power relationships between men and women in society (Brownmiller, 1975; Russell, 1984; Herman, 1990). As stated most forcibly by Brownmiller, rape is "nothing more or less than a conscious process of intimidation by which *all* men keep *all* women in a state of fear". From this perspective, rape is a crime of violence, which arises from a traditional association of masculinity with power, dominance and superiority, and which is tacitly, if not overtly, legitimised as a means of keeping women in a subordinate role.

As with family violence, this view has led to a highly politicised debate, often accompanied by "sloppy and emotional rhetoric" (Chappell, 1989), and statements such as "...all men keep all women in a state of fear" (Brownmiller, 1975), or "normal male socialisation is sufficient" for sexual aggression (Herman, 1990) must be seen as hyperbole. Nevertheless, the proposition that rape is fostered by culturally supported attitudes has some empirical support, which is examined below.

EXHIBITIONISM

Exposure of the male genitals under socially inappropriate conditions is one of the commonest sex offences, but remains poorly understood. It is typically a behaviour of males in the presence of females of varying ages, although some may expose only to children. The exposer may have an erection and masturbate while exposing himself, but this is not invariable, and sexual satisfaction may be derived from fantasies following the act. Whether the immediate intent is to shock or invite attention is unclear, but it is typically a noncontact act which is unlikely to be a prelude to an assault.

Some clinicians have nevertheless suggested that exposers progress to assaultive sexual crimes. Rooth (1973) found no evidence for this in the histories of exhibitionists who had been exposing for at least two years, but others report that up to a quarter of exhibitionists may have engaged in rape (Freund, 1990). Freund also reports a substantial co-occurrence of exhibitionism with other deviations, and almost a third of exhibitionists admitted to voyeurism or frottage. Similar findings were noted by Rooth

(1973), who suggested a particular association with paedophilia. Myers and Berah (1983) examined this possibility by comparing exhibitionists and paedophiles. The former differed significantly in having better parental relationships, more ,stable and successful educational and work histories, and a relative absence of alcohol in their offending. The authors concluded that the two groups were distinct. In contrast, Flor-Henry et al. (1991) report that both exhibitionists and paedophiles show similar EEG anomalies involving instability of the dominant hemisphere and dysregulation of interhemispheric relations. They suggest that this may be a basic component of sexual deviation related to the probability of abnormal ideation being associated with orgasmic response.

In a review of the available literature, Blair and Lanyon (1981) found few comparisons of exhibitionists with nondeviant controls. They tentatively concluded that onset is associated with stress in early adulthood, that there was little evidence of educational deficits, and that most adult exhibitionists were married, though rarely having a satisfying sexual relationship. Comparisons with other sex offenders, such as assaulters and rapists (Rader, 1977), or paedophiles (Myrah and Berah, 1983), also suggest that exhibitionists have less diffuse psychological or social problems. However, Blair and Lanyon (1981) found relatively consistent evidence of timidity and lack of social skills, and also a tendency for exhibitionists to have convictions for nonsexual offences.

There is no satisfactory theory for the aetiology of exhibitionism. Psychodynamic writers see it as a denial of castration anxiety, and a "magical" gesture which holds forbidden urges towards the mother at bay. Some behavioural theorists suggest that the behaviour may originate in parental reinforcement of genital exposure in childhood, and that it is facilitated by the development of heterosexual anxiety and avoidance, and hence negative reinforcement of the deviant act. Data are lacking to support any theory, but Blair and Lanyon (1981) note that fantasy plays a significant role in maintaining the behaviour, and that this needs to be a target of treatment.

SEXUAL AGGRESSION

Most sexual assaults entail brief attempts to touch or interfere with the victim, but sexual aggression denotes the use of threats or force to gain compliance in sexual acts, or aggressive behaviour in the context of sexual arousal. Rapes vary in both the social context and the degree of violence involved. In about half, the victim is a stranger, but many involve acquaintance or "date" rapes (Dietz, 1978). A further distinction found to have some utility is between "blitz" rape involving a sudden attack, usually by a stranger, and "confidence" rape by someone who uses deceit to gain access to the victim (Silverman et al., 1988).

A substantial proportion of rapes is perpetrated by pairs or groups. In Amir's study of rapes in Philadelphia, for example, 43% involved two or more offenders (Amir, 1971). Wright and West (1981) examined all rapes and attempted rapes reported in six English counties from 1972 to 1976, and found that 13% involved two or more assailants. Both solitary and group offenders had previous criminal records to a similar extent, and in both cases, a third had been drinking heavily prior to the offence. Group offenders, however, were more likely to be under the age of 21 (65% vs 27%), and had fewer previous convictions for sex crimes or psychiatric histories. Fewer of the victims of group rapes were strangers, but more were under 21, had been drinking, and received some injury (50% vs 32 %). The group assault appeared to be more a function of the dynamics of gang delinquency than of individual pathology. Similar findings are reported from other countries (Dietz, 1978). However, a study of rape convictions in England in 1985 reveals a greater proportion of solitary rapes than in 1972 (Lloyd and Walmsley, 1989). The more recent figures indicate proportionately fewer offenders and victims under age 21, more offenders with long criminal records, and more who are acquainted with the victim.

Some rapes involve threats to which the victim passively succumbs, but many involve violence in excess of that required to obtain victim compliance. Rape–murder is relatively infrequent, being more likely to result from attempts to quieten the victim or conceal the crime than from sadistic injury infliction, and the luridly named "lust murder" is rare. Wright and West (1981) found that 6% of rape victims sustained serious physical injury, and 66% none. However, the immediate and long-term adverse psychological consequences are more significant. Kilpatrick et al. (1985), for example, found that 19% of rape victims reported suicide attempts, compared with 2% of nonvictimised women.

Research on rape has developed around two theoretical issues. The first is whether rape is a sexual deviation. Some conceptualise rape as a *preference* for forced sex, and hence as a paraphilia, while others see it as primarily motivated by needs for power and control. The latter view has been promoted by feminists, who see it as a violent rather than a sexual offence. Herman (1990), however, disagrees, seeing rape as a sexual addiction. A second issue is whether rapists are psychologically deviant. Psychodynamic writers see rape as a symptom of psychopathology, while behaviour therapists emphasise interpersonal deficits. Feminists, however, reject these views, arguing that rape expresses normal male socialisation. Insofar as this means that all men have the capacity to rape, it no more accounts for rape than does the capacity of all humans to kill other humans account for murder. However, it directs attention to the role of social factors in explaining why a minority of men exercise this capacity.

Typologies of rapists

Rapists are not a homogeneous group, and differences in the social dynamics of date, gang, and stranger rapes may be parallelled by psychological differences between offenders. Attempts to identify homogeneous subgroups focus on motivational variations (Prentky, Cohen and Seghorn, 1985). Groth

(Groth and Burgess, 1977a; Groth, Burgess and Holmstrom, 1977) sees sexual assault as sexual behaviour in the service of nonsexual needs, and emphasises the motives of power and anger. Rape is a "pseudosexual" act involving both motives, but there is a relative dominance of one or the other. In *power rape*, the offender seeks power or control, either to express virility and dominance (power–assertive) or to resolve doubts about masculinity (power–reassurance). *Anger rape* expresses rage, contempt and hate for women, and entails excessive force. This may be motivated by revenge for perceived wrongs (anger–retaliation), or by sadistic excitement from the suffering of the victim (anger–excitation). This typology subordinates the role of sexual motivation in rape, and Groth and Burgess (1977a) cite observations that 75% of an incarcerated sample described sexual failure or dysfunction during the rape. They estimated that power rape was predominant in two thirds, with only 6% falling in the sadistic category.

Cohen, Seghorn and Calmas (1969), however, saw sexual and aggressive motives as combining in rape, and identified four groups. In *displaced aggression*, the rapist is hostile to women, and the rape is a hostile act instigated by an altercation with a female, sexual excitation being minimal. In *compensatory rape*, aggression is minimal, sexual gratification being sought in the context of feelings of sexual inadequacy. In *sex–aggression diffusion*, aggression is eroticised, resulting in sexual sadism. Finally, the *impulsive* rapist has minimal aggressive or sexual intent, and the rape is an opportunistic act, often during the course of some other predatory crime. Prentky, Cohen and Seghorn (1985) and Knight and Prentky (1990) describe attempts to develop the Cohen et al. scheme further through a series of empirical analyses. The most recent identifies four superordinate types (opportunistic, pervasively angry, sexual, vindictive), the sexual type being divided into sadistic and nonsadistic subgroups. Further subdivisions across these groups in level of social competence yield nine subtypes.

Similar variations between rapists have been identified by sociologists, who do not, however, see rape in terms of individual pathology. Scully and Marolla (1985) interviewed 114 convicted rapists to assess the offenders' views of the rewards gained from the act. Anger, power, and opportunity again emerged as significant, the main rewards discerned being revenge and punishment, an "added bonus" to a predatory crime, sexual access to normally inaccessible women, gaining power through impersonal sex, and participation in gang rape as recreation.

Typologies of rapists are essentially hypotheses which have only recently been subject to empirical testing (Prentky et al., 1985), and it remains unclear whether rapists are consistent across their criminal career. They nevertheless suggest that rape is multidimensional, and that nonsexual as well as sexual goals need to be taken into account.

Cultural factors

The feminist view that rape is encouraged by prevailing norms of power relationships predicts that rape will be associated with attitudes and beliefs about women and relations between the sexes, and this is supported by several lines of research. First, contrary to the view that rape represents a biologically programmed male propensity for aggression, anthropological studies reveal that it is not a prominent feature of all societies, and that its frequency depends on cultural organisation. Otterbein (1979), for example, found that in preliterate societies, the presence of male power groups who resort to aggression to defend their members was a moderate predictor of rape frequency, but it interacted with punishment to suppress its effects. In a study of 156 tribal groups, Sanday (1981) similarly observed that rape prone societies were characterised by greater sex segregation and the low power and status of females, and supported ideologies favouring interpersonal violence and male toughness.

Second, attitude surveys suggest wide acceptance of rape myths (e.g. "Many women have an unconscious wish to be raped"; "Women who get raped while hitch-hiking get what they deserve"). Burt (1980) found that these were frequently endorsed by a random American sample of males and females, and were related to sex role stereotyping, adversarial sexual beliefs, and attitudes supporting interpersonal violence in intimate relations. Costin and Schwarz (1987) also found correlations between acceptance of rape myths and beliefs in restricted social roles and rights for women in student samples across four countries, as well as in community samples. In a series of studies, Malamuth (1984) found that a third of students scored 2 or more on a 5-point scale measuring perceived likelihood of raping if they could get away with it (1= not at all likely, 5= very likely), while 20% scored 3 or more. Likelihood of raping was associated with more callous attitudes to rape and belief in rape myths.

Some studies of rapists also support the feminist view. Amir (1971) found that 71% of rapes were planned, which appears to contradict psychiatric concepts of rape as an impulsive crime of individuals lacking control. The majority of offenders also came from poor inner city areas with high crime rates, consistent with the "subculture of violence" thesis, although the validity of this concept is disputed (Chapter 9). Feild (1978) compared convicted rapists with rape counsellors, police, and citizens, and found that they differed on several attitude dimensions indicating acceptance of rape myths and attributions of responsibility for rape to women. However, while pro-feminist attitudes to women correlated with anti-rape attitudes, this was not so within the rapist sample. Some recent studies also fail to confirm that incarcerated rapists are distinguished by acceptance of rape myths (Overholser and Beck, 1986) or negative attitudes to women (Stermac and Quinsey, 1986).

Feminist researchers argue that convicted rapists are not representative of sexually aggressive males, but self-report studies of nonoffenders also yield inconsistent results. Koss and Leonard (1984) report that self-reported sexual aggressors were more accepting of rape myths and more likely to attribute responsibility to women, but scored lower on a scale of negative attitudes to women. Others find no direct relationship of self-reported sexual aggression with sex role beliefs, while finding a relationship with acceptance of interpersonal violence and adversarial sexual beliefs (Rapaport and Burkhart,

1984), and beliefs legitimising the sexual victimisation of women (Alder, 1985). Malamuth (1986), however, found that both acceptance of interpersonal violence and hostility to women were associated with self-reported sexual aggression.

Inconsistencies may partly reflect the differing attitude scales employed in these studies, and on the whole, there is some support for feminist arguments that tolerance for rape is associated with at least some aspects of negative attitudes to women. However, while the strongest support comes from self-report studies of sexual aggression, these are likely to reflect date or acquaintance rape, rather than stranger rape (Koss and Leonard, 1984). Moreover, the data are correlational, and the correlations generally modest.

Environmental and situational factors

Retrospective clinical studies suggest that rapists have similar family backgrounds to those of aggressive delinquents, and that cruelty by either parent is common. Van Ness (1984), for example, observed court findings of family violence or neglect in the histories of 41% of adolescent rapists, compared with 15% of nonsex offenders. Rada (1978), on the other hand, found a history of family violence in less than a quarter of rapists, and longitudinal studies are lacking. While sexual abuse in childhood has been thought to be significant, Carter et al. (1987) report that 57% of incarcerated child molesters but only 23% of rapists had such a history. However, given the association of sexual aggression with acceptance of interpersonal violence, exposure to spouse abuse in the family might be anticipated.

More proximal influences on acts of rape include situational factors affecting the sexual arousal and aggression of the offender. Amir (1971) found that a fifth of rapes in Philadelphia were "victim precipitated", but this has not been replicated (Chapter 9), and feminists object that this notion blames the victim. Alcohol is a commonly cited factor, but reports of offenders are suspect, since claiming intoxication is a form of "deviance disavowal" which insulates the offender from acknowledging that he has any problems other than drinking (McCaghy, 1968). Independent reports nevertheless point to relatively high rates of drinking prior to rape. Rada (1978) notes that 50% of the rapists he examined had been drinking at the time of the offence, while a third were problem drinkers. Amir (1971) also found that both offender and victim had been drinking in over 60% of cases, although Wright and West (1981) detected lower rates in their English sample. Experimental studies suggest that alcohol expectancy (placebo), though not alcohol itself, increases sexual arousal to erotic films, and also increases interest in erotic violence (George and Marlatt, 1986). However, findings in this area are inconsistent (Quinsey, 1984). Some studies find that alcohol abuse is associated with greater violence in rapes, but this was not confirmed by Langevin, Paitich and Russon (1985). It seems unlikely that alcohol ingestion itself has a more direct role in rape than in other violent acts. Any effects in facilitating rape are probably mediated by other situational and personal factors, such as misperception of social cues, increased feelings of power, or expectations that deviant behaviour is more permissible.

The view that rapes are often an expression of anger has been noted, and anger arousal is another commonly reported antecedent. Van Ness (1984), for example, found that 86% of a sample of adolescent rapists reported an altercation with someone between two and six hours prior to the offence, and laboratory research suggests that anger may have an effect on sexual arousal. Yates, Barbaree and Marshall (1984) examined PPG effects of descriptions of mutually consenting sex and rape in normal subjects, some of whom had been angered by the experimenters' female confederate. Prior testing showed less sexual arousal to rape than to consenting stories, but this differential subsequently disappeared for angered subjects, anger both attenuating arousal to consenting sex and enhancing arousal to rape. This latter pattern is similar to that found in some studies of incarcerated rapists (below). Yates et al. (1984) suggest that anger may disrupt empathy, or alternatively may redirect attention. However, intense anger involves heightened autonomic arousal, which under normal conditions may interfere with sexual arousal. This may be pertinent to observations that many rapes are accompanied by sexual dysfunction (Groth and Burgess, 1977a).

Effects of pornography

The possibility that sexual stimulation itself increases the likelihood of sexual aggression underlies the debate over pornography. Feminists see pornography as encouraging rape by dehumanising women (Brownmiller, 1975), but national commissions in America and Britain in the 1970s concluded that pornographic materials did not contribute to sexually offensive behaviour. A more recent commission in the United States in 1986 reached the opposite conclusion, but this has been criticised for overgeneralising (Linz, Donnerstein and Penrod, 1987). A critical consideration is the meaning of *pornography*. Some distinguish erotic portrayals of sexually explicit interactions involving mutual pleasure and freedom from power inequalities, from portrayals of women as sexual objects subject to domination, coercion, and sometimes sadism. The terms nonaggressive and aggressive pornography are used here to make this distinction.

Studies in Denmark following the liberalisation of obscenity laws in the 1960s suggested no increase in sex offending, and an actual decrease in minor offences. Court (1984) argues that more account must be taken of the increased availability of aggressive pornography in western countries since the early 1970s, although the evidence for such an increase has been questioned (Linz et al., 1987). Court proposes that "porno-violence" has a "ripple effect" on attitudes to women and sexual behaviour, and demonstrates a relationship between changes in legislation affecting the availability of pornography and changes in official statistics for rape across several countries. These aggregate level data do not establish a direct causal influence, but are consistent with the argument of a contributory effect of pornography on sexual aggression.

Experimental research also supports such an effect. Malamuth (1984) summarises several studies of the cognitive effects of exposure to aggressive sexual portrayals. For example, in one study, rape depictions increased aggressive sexual fantasy content in males, while in another, subjects who heard rape descriptions in which there was a "positive" outcome (woman becoming involuntarily aroused) subsequently rated a rape victim as having suffered less than did those exposed to rape with a "negative" outcome (woman showing disgust), or consenting sex. Malamuth also describes a field study in which males who watched movies depicting positive consequences of sexual aggression were subsequently more accepting of interpersonal violence to women than controls, and marginally more accepting of rape myths.

The effects of pornography on aggression have also been examined in laboratory studies. Experiments demonstrate that exposure to nonaggressive pornography does not itself enhance aggression to females, but does so in males who have been angered (Donnerstein, 1984). On the other hand, some studies find that the effect is stronger when the target is a male, suggesting a general arousal or disinhibitory effect rather than a specific sexual arousal effect. However, in one experiment, aggressive pornography portraying a "positive" ending for the woman increased subsequent aggression to a female in nonangered males, but depiction of a "negative" ending did not. For angered males, both depictions enhanced aggression. Donnerstein suggests that the positive ending justifies aggression and reduces inhibitions, while the negative ending produces vicarious pain cues, which reinforce subsequent aggression in angered males. In another study (Donnerstein, 1983), males were angered by a male or female confederate, and prior to the opportunity to aggress, watched either a neutral, a nonaggressive pornographic, an aggressive, or an aggressive pornographic film. When the target was a male, only the nonaggressive pornographic film increased aggression. When the target was a female, aggression was not enhanced by nonaggressive pornography, but was increased maximally by the aggressive pornographic film, and to a lesser extent by the aggression film. A subsequent study also found that portrayal of nonsexual aggression to a woman increased acceptance of rape myths and rape related attitudes (Donnerstein, 1984). It would thus seem that it is aggressive imagery and the depiction of a woman as victim in aggressive pornography which facilitate aggression to a woman more than the sexual arousal.

Although these studies suggest that pornography *can* create negative behaviour and attitudes to women, depending on the observer's emotional state and the "message" conveyed about the woman's responses, they do not establish an unequivocal causal role for aggressive pornography, which is only one of the many potential influences on sexual aggression. They are subject to the limited external validity of laboratory definitions of "aggression", and are primarily concerned with short-term and probably short-lived effects. As yet, there are no prospective longitudinal studies of the effects on sexual behaviour. Sex offenders are known to be heavy users of pornography, but Carter et al. (1987) found that child molesters were more likely than rapists to use pornography prior to and during their offences. However, sex offenders have also been found to have had less exposure to pornography than nonoffenders during adolescence (Quinsey, 1984). The contribution of pornography to the development of deviant sexual behaviour is thus unclear. Malamuth (1984) suggests that any effects are likely to be bidirectional, as with media violence more generally, and that aggressive pornography may enhance negative reactions to women in those who are already disposed towards sexual aggression.

Characteristics of sexual aggressors

Several studies have attempted to determine whether rapists are distinguishable by particular personal, sexual or social dispositions. An association with psychosis is rare, and controlled studies do not find rapists to be distinguished by intellectual characteristics (Quinsey, 1984). Rapists who have mental health contact are likely to be identified as personality disordered, but comparisons of rapists with other offenders on personality tests have not yielded consistent discriminations, suggesting that rapists may be characterised by criminality, but not by more specific personality characteristics (Rada, 1978; Koss and Leonard, 1984). The role of antisocial propensity is reinforced by findings of moderate correlations of self-reported sexual aggression with the MMPI *Pd* scale (Koss and Leonard, 1984), Gough's Socialisation and Responsibility scales (Rapaport and Burkhart, 1984), and the P scale of the EPQ (Malamuth, 1986). Malamuth and Check (1983) also found that self-reported arousal to rape descriptions was associated with reported likelihood of raping, EPQ P, and sexual power motivation, and suggest that rape proclivity is related to an aggressive disposition more generally. However, neither convicted rapists nor self-reported sexual aggressors score consistently highly on the Buss–Durkee Hostility Inventory (Koss and Leonard, 1984; Overholser and Beck, 1986).

On the other hand, MMPI studies of incarcerated rapists indicate that they are closer to violent offenders more generally than to other sex offenders (Rader, 1977; Langevin, Paitich and Russon, 1985), and that they tend to score highly on the *Sc* (Schizophrenia) scale as well as *Pd*. This pattern has been interpreted in terms of hostility, irritability, impulsivity, avoidance of close involvements, poor social judgement, and conflict with authority (Armentrout and Hauer, 1978). While the most consistent finding is therefore that rapists are poorly socialised, the MMPI data suggest that they are among the more personally deviant criminals, and more likely to be secondary psychopaths.

Another variable suggested to distinguish rapists is the level of testosterone, the assumption being that this will affect the degree of both sexual arousability and aggressiveness. Rada, Laws and Kellner (1976) found that high testosterone level did not characterise rapists as a group, but distinguished a small subgroup of highly aggressive rapists. However, Langevin et al. (1985) found no differences in testosterone level between rapists and nonviolent sexoffenders, or between sadistic and nonsadistic rapists.

Behavioural approaches have assumed that rapists have a deviant preference for forced sex, and this should be apparent in differential PPG responses to depictions of mutually consenting sex and sexual aggression. Abel et al. (1977)

presented audiotaped descriptions of mutually consenting intercourse and rape to 13 rapists and seven nonviolent sexual deviants. Nonrapists produced smaller PPG responses to rape than to consenting sex, while rapists responded similarly to both. A "rape index" (ratio of PPG responding to rape compared to consenting sex) was directly related to both the frequency of rape offences and the degree of injury caused. Responses to rape also correlated with responses to nonsexual violence to a woman, although the latter was at a lower level. While not indicating a preference for forced over consenting sex, the results suggest that rape may be motivated by deviant attraction to cues of nonconsent or the use of force. Barbaree, Marshall and Lanthier (1979) replicated these results in a comparison of rapists and nonoffenders, but suggested that rapists are not necessarily aroused by the use of force or the victim's cues, but rather fail to inhibit erection, perhaps because of less empathy. Quinsey, Chaplin and Upfold (1984), however, found that rapists responded less than controls to consenting sexual portrayals, and more to rape. Rapists also responded more to nonsexual violence to a female, though not to a male, suggesting the importance of heterosexual context. While the authors see failure of rapists to be inhibited by the victim's pain as a critical factor, their results also favour the deviant sexual preference hypothesis. In contrast, other studies find that rapists respond less to rape than to consenting sex (Langevin et al., 1985; Baxter, Barbaree and Marshall, 1986).

There are two possible reasons for these inconsistent findings. Barbaree (1990) argues that portrayals of sexual aggression contain both arousing and inhibitory stimulus elements, and that discrepant results may therefore reflect the use of different stimulus patterns by different investigators. Alternatively, there may be subject differences. Blader and Marshall (1989) note that the rapist subjects of Quinsey et al. (1984) were among the most dangerous and sadistic, and suggest that the rape index is a reliable discriminator only for the latter. They further argue that sexual arousal as assessed in the laboratory is not an antecedent of sexual assaults, which usually begin as an attempt to obtain consenting sex, and that the data imply that apart from sadists, rapists do not have a deviant interest in forced sex. It is the failure of coercive *responding* to inhibit sexual arousal which may distinguish the rapist.

However, the question remains of what reinforces the use of coercion. The limited evidence for unique characteristics of rapists is sometimes interpreted as an indication that most are undersocialised men who "steal" sex, by force if necessary, but it remains possible that rapists are motivated by some elements of nonconsenting sex. For example, Marques (1981) varied the endings of rape descriptions, and found that rapists showed enhanced erection to depictions of the victim's pleas for sympathy, but not to assertive refusal, or to establishing a relationship, or lack of resistance, suggesting the relevance of power motivation. Moreover, the rape index does have some validity in predicting self-reported sexual aggression, particularly in combination with dominance as a motive for sexual acts, hostility to women, and acceptance of interpersonal violence (Malamuth, 1986).

A further focus of interest has been the heterosocial and assertive skills of rapists. The available evidence, however, suggests that rapists do not differ markedly from other offenders in this respect. Stermac and Quinsey (1986), for example, compared rapists with nonsex offenders and community controls on conversations, role plays, and self-report measures of social interaction and skill. Both offender groups were rated as less skilled, rapists differing only in rating themselves as less assertive. The latter was not replicated by Segal and Marshall (1985), who nevertheless confirmed the similarity of rapists to nonsex offenders in other respects. Child molesters showed more obvious skill deficits, and similar results were obtained by Overholser and Beck (1986). However, Lipton, McDonel and McFall (1987) found rapists to be less accurate than other offenders in detecting affective cues of females portrayed in first-date interactions, suggesting a processing deficit in decoding information in these situations.

Since many rapists are married or have regular sexual outlets (Rada, 1978; Langevin, Paitich and Russon, 1985), deficits in basic heterosocial approach skills may have been overestimated, and deficits in forming and maintaining intimate relationships may be more important (Marshall, 1989). Given the role ascribed to beliefs about women in the genesis of rape, more attention also seems necessary to the expectations which mediate the interactions of rapists with their victims.

Research on the social and personal characteristics of rapists has yielded a number of inconsistent findings, leading some to suggest that, apart from poor socialisation, rapists are not particularly different from criminals in general. However, Marshall and Barbaree (1990a) draw on the more suggestive findings in proposing an integrated theory which incorporates biological development, childhood socialisation, and the influence of cultural and situational factors. They suggest that given a close link between the neural and hormonal substrates of sex and aggression, the pubescent boy has to learn to inhibit an inherent capacity for sexual aggression. As a result of adverse child experiences, such as exposure to unskilled parenting and violence, some boys fail to acquire appropriate empathic and social skills which would allow them to learn this inhibition and to develop satisfying heterosexual and social interactions. Their inability to form intimate relationships also promotes aggression. Such boys are more vulnerable to cultural influences such as rape myths, as expressed, for example, in pornography, and are more readily disinhibited by transitory factors, such as alcohol intoxication or anger. Once such a youth has progressed to forced sex, further assaults become more likely, particularly when punishment is not contingent. However, as noted earlier, the assumption that the central task for an adolescent is to learn to inhibit a natural propensity for sexual aggression is questionable.

Sexual sadism

One likely reason for inconsistent research findings is the motivational heterogeneity of rapists. However, attempts have been made to distinguish the characteristics of sadistic rapists. Brittain (1970) provided a prototypical description of the sadistic murderer based on his experience as both forensic psychiatrist and pathologist. Although narcissistic and egocentric, the sadist is not accurately described as a psychopath. He is introspective, solitary, and timid, as well as prudish and often religious, feeling inferior, especially sexually, and finding it difficult to relate to women. A desire for power over others is an essential feature, and the subjection of violence to power is more important than the infliction of pain. He has a rich fantasy life, which dwells on cruelty and atrocities, and seeks jobs where his desire for power can be acted out. His interests are likely to include sadistic literature and the collection of weapons. He also has a range of paraphilias, such as voyeurism and transvestism, but often no criminal record. Offending is likely to follow loss of self-esteem or denial of his masculinity, planning the offence making him feel superior. The murder involves excessive force as sexual drive and desire for power take over, and he is excited by the victim's fear and suffering. However, neither intercourse nor orgasm is a necessary component, and he may masturbate over the body or use a substitute phalus. The crime results in reduced tension, after which he behaves normally.

Although this is a composite picture, the available evidence supports several features. MacCulloch et al. (1983) proposed that sadistic fantasising and rehearsal of the crime were critical. In 13 of 16 patients in a special hospital who had committed sadistic murders or nonfatal sadistic assaults, there was evidence of recurrent sadistic masturbatory fantasies involving control and sexual violence. The offence was the culmination of the fantasy sequence, and prior try-outs in the form of stalking the victim appeared to maintain the fantasy as a source of arousal. All patients had a history of difficulties in social relationships and in approaching women. MacCulloch et al. (1983) suggest that fantasy of power is an operant that is negatively reinforced by relief from the experience of failure, sexual arousal becoming attached to it through classical conditioning. Prentky et al. (1989) suggest that the development of sadistic fantasy may be particularly important in repetitive (serial) sexual murders, and compared 25 serial with 17 single-occasion sexual homicides. Prior fantasies of rape and murder were recorded in the cases of 86% of serial murderers, compared with 23% of single murderers. There was also evidence of more premeditation in the first crimes of the serial killers than in those of the single murderers.

In their study of sexual aggression, Langevin et al. (1985) compared sadistic and nonsadistic aggressors with property offender controls. While sample sizes precluded firm conclusions, and some findings, such as a lower rape index for sadists, were contrary to expectation, some suggestive differences emerged. For example, there were trends indicating that sadists had a more feminine or ambivalent gender identity, were more likely to feel sexually inadequate, found it difficult to talk to women, who made them angry, had more conservative sex role attitudes, showed more paraphilias, and were less likely to have abused alcohol or drugs. They also scored highest on the MMPI Schizophrenia scale, suggesting more confused or distorted thinking. One significant finding was that 56% of sadists, but 0% of nonsadists and 11% of controls, showed evidence of right temporal horn dilation in CT scans, and these differences were maintained in an enlarged sample by Hucker et al.

(1988). The causal significance of this is obscure, but a few case histories in the literature have suggested an association of temporal lobe abnormalities with paraphilias. Money (1990) argues that in sexual sadism, the brain becomes pathologically activated to transmit simultaneous messages of attack and sexual arousal, this being an episodic dysfunction similar to an epileptic seizure. However, the evidence for premeditation and planning in sadistic murder (MacCulloch et al., 1983; Prentky et al., 1989) indicates that sadistic assaults are cognitively mediated and under voluntary control. Pathological brain discharge is therefore neither necessary nor sufficient to explain the behaviour.

A comprehensive account of sadistic sexual assault is offered by Burgess et al. (1986), who propose a motivational model in which sadistic fantasies and cognitive structures supporting the act of sexual murder are central. Five interacting developmental phases are hypothesised: (1) ineffective social environments in early life which impair attachment bonds; (2) formative traumatic events, such as deviant role models and the experience of abuse, which generate fantasies of control and aggression as coping devices; (3) patterned responses such as social isolation, autoeroticism, and rebelliousness which limit corrective interpersonal experiences, and the development of cognitive structures promoting a self-justifying, antisocial view of the world and the self; (4) actions towards others, such as cruelty to children and animals, through which violence is reinforced, and empathy development retarded; (5) a feedback filter which sustains deviant thinking patterns. This model is similar to sociocognitive models of aggressive delinquency.

The role of early sexual abuse is supported by Ressler et al. (1986), who found that sexual murderers with such a history were more likely to have exhibited cruelty in childhood, showed more sexual conflicts and paraphilias, and had begun fantasising at an earlier age, in comparison with nonabused murderers. They were also marginally more likely to mutilate the victim after the killing. However, as Finkelhor (1986) notes, theories which attribute male sex offending to the experience of childhood abuse must explain why females, who are predominantly the victims of abuse, do not become sexual abusers. Cruelty and pain infliction in nonsexual contexts are held to characterise sadistic personality disorder, which according to DSM-III-R is only rarely associated with sexual sadism, but the clinical observations of Brittain (1970) and Burgess et al. (1986) suggest that sadistic traits may be common in sadistic murderers. Sadistic sexual fantasies are also common in the general population (Crepault and Couture, 1980), as is their acting out in sadistic "sex games" (Gosselin and Wilson, 1980), and sadism at this level seems to be associated with a more general need for interpersonal control (Breslow, 1987). It is therefore likely that sadistic sexual assaults are the extreme of a continuum.

SEXUAL OFFENCES AGAINST CHILDREN

Sexual offences against children more commonly entail genital fondling than vaginal or anal penetration, but involve the use of excessive force in a substantial minority of cases (Abel et al., 1981). The terms *paedophilia*, *child molestation*, and *child sexual abuse* are often used interchangeably in describing these offences, but paedophilia in this respect means more than the DSM-III-R notion of a paraphilia, since some offenders appear to retain a primary sexual interest in adults. Sexual preference for children is more likely in men who offend exclusively against boys (homosexual paedophiles), who make up about a quarter of known offenders, and in the small minority who choose both male and female victims. It has been suggested to be less likely in incest offenders (Howells, 1981; Quinsey, 1986). However, some studies indicate that a third or more of the latter molest children outside the family (Williams and Finkelhor, 1990). Those who commit sexual offences against children are therefore a heterogeneous group, who vary in terms of the age and gender of preferred victims, their relationship to the victim, the extent of sexual contact involved, and the degree of force used in their offence.

Child sexual abuse

Since most sexual abuse remains unreported, knowledge comes mainly from victimisation surveys and clinical studies. Variable prevalence rates reflect not only differing survey methodologies, but also the lack of a precise definition of child sexual abuse. While this is generally understood as an unwanted sexual experience with an adult during childhood, some surveys include noncontact experiences, such as indecent exposure or verbal propositions, and define childhood as extending up to age 18 (Finkelhor, 1986). However, surveys using stringent criteria suggest that 10% to 15% of females experience sexual abuse in childhood (Mullen, 1990). In about half, this involves a single experience, although for some it is protracted. The ratio of females to males reporting abuse is about 2.5:1. For females, the abuser is more likely to be a family member or acquaintance, more males than females being abused by strangers.

Finkelhor (1986) reviews evidence on the risk factors for abuse in girls. Vulnerability tends to be higher for those aged 10 to 12, and girls who are victimised are more likely to have lived without their natural fathers, and with stepfathers, to have had mothers employed outside the home, or who were ill or disabled, to have witnessed parental conflict, and to have a poor relationship with one of their parents. Females who are black or who come from lower social strata do not report higher rates. Finkelhor notes the possible relation of these factors to poor parental supervision, and to emotional vulnerability or inability to resist on the part of the child. However, he emphasises that the preconditions for sexual abuse are an offender who is motivated to abuse, and who must overcome internalised inhibitions, external obstacles, and child resistance.

While many paedophiles do not see their behaviour as aberrant, a central issue is that children are not generally able to give informed consent, and sex between an adult and a child is the exploitation of an unequal power relationship (Abel, Becker and Cunningham-Rathner, 1984). Psychologically harmful consequences for victims have also been documented, both in the immediate aftermath of abusive experience and in the long term. Initial effects include emotional reactions of fear, guilt, hostility, and intrusive thinking comparable to post-traumatic stress disorder in more than a half of victims, and behaviour problems such as school difficulties, eating disorders, running away, prostitution, and delinquency in a minority (Finkelhor, 1986). Long-term effects include anxiety, depression, poor self-esteem, self-destructive behaviour, revictimisation, lack of interpersonal trust, and impaired sexual adjustment (Finkelhor, 1986; Mullen, 1990).

However, long-term effects are not inevitable, serious psychopathology being experienced by about a fifth of victims. A direct causal effect is therefore difficult to demonstrate, and sexual abuse probably interacts with other factors, such as family disorganisation and other forms of abuse. Some clinicians suggest that effects are greatest when the child recognises the act as inappropriate, the abuse is sustained, involves penetration and force, the abuser is a close relative, and the family is unsupportive (e.g. Abel et al., 1984). There is some evidence in support, though data are sparse (Finkelhor, 1986).

Typologies of child molesters

Attempts have been made to reduce the heterogeneity of child molesters by means of typologies comparable to those proposed for rapists. Groth and Burgess (1977b) again emphasise the role of nonsexual motives, and divide child molesters into two broad groups on the basis of the degree of force in the offence. The *sex-pressure* offence is distinguished by a relative lack of physical force. The offender feels safer with children, and desires the child as a love object. However, offenders in this group are subdivided into those who use *enticement* or persuasion, and those who use *entrapment* in the form of bribes. The *sex-force* offender uses coercion or physical force, and is either *exploitive*, using the child for sexual relief without any further relationship, and as a means of exercising power, or *sadistic*, deriving pleasure from hurting and humiliating the child. This typology represents a hypothesis based on clinical observations, and has not been validated.

An alternative approach divides offenders into *fixated*, *regressed*, and *aggressive* groups (Cohen, Seghorn and Calmas, 1969). The fixated offender prefers and feels more comfortable with children, and seeks out those who are known. The regressed offender has some adult heterosexual interest, but has feelings of inadequacy, and reacts sexually to a child following a threat to masculinity. The aggressive type engages in sadistic acts, usually with boys. Howells (1981) makes a more pragmatic distinction between the *preference* and the *situational* molester, which parallels the fixated–regressed distinction. Quinsey (1986) similarly distinguishes molesters who have a sexual preference for children from those who turn to children as surrogates when adult partners are unavailable. This is held to distinguish incest and non-incest child abusers.

Knight and Prentky (1990) describe an empirically based development of the Cohen et al. (1969) typology, which uses a hierarchical decision tree along two axes. The first axis divides offenders by the degree of fixation, and then by the degree of social competence, yielding four groups. The second axis divides them by the amount of contact with children, those with high contact being divided into interpersonal and narcissistic types, those with low contact into high or low physical injury. The latter two are further divided into sadistic and nonsadistic types. While this system is based on five variables, the use of dichotomous assignments yields 24 types, although the authors suggest that most child molesters will fall into one of 11 of these. Although this approach seems promising, most research to date has relied on simple dichotomies, or treats child molesters as a homogeneous group.

Characteristics of child molesters

Research on child molesters has been reviewed by Howells (1981), Finkelhor (1986), Quinsey (1986), and Lanyon (1986a), and on incestuous fathers by Williams and Finkelhor (1990). Finkelhor (1986) suggests that most studies have been guided by single factor theories, but are directed to one or more of four complementary questions. These address: (1) the emotional congruence of sexual relations with a child; (2) sexual arousal by a child; (3) blockage to socially approved relationships; (4) disinhibitions against sex with a child. These provide a convenient framework for summarising recent research.

The issue of *emotional congruence* is why sexual relations with a child are gratifying or congruent with a person's needs. Several motivational sources are suggested by psychodynamic theories. In particular, the fixation of many child molesters implies developmental immaturity and feelings of inadequacy. Child sexual relations are therefore less threatening than those with adults, and make them feel more powerful and in control. An extension of this is the suggestion that the attraction of the paedophile to children is narcissistic, reflecting involvement with his own likeness as a child. The latter has not been tested, but there is some support for the proposition that paedophiles find children less threatening. Howells (1979) compared the repertory grids of heterosexual paedophiles and nonsex offenders, and found that paedophiles construed adult relationships more strongly in terms of dominance–submission. Adults were more likely to be seen as imposing on them, while children were nondominant, suggesting that the pedophiles lacked skills for controlling their environment.

There is also some suggestive evidence that child molesters are "immature" and lack self-esteem or a sense of adequacy. Studies of social skills indicate that many child molesters lack self-confidence (below), and personality test data point in this direction. Wilson and Cox (1983) administered questionnaires, including the EPQ, to members of a paedophile club in England, who emerged as introverted, shy, sensitive, lonely, depressed, and humourless. Panton (1979a) compared incarcerated child molesters and incest offenders on the MMPI. Both groups scored highly on scales suggesting self-alienation, anxiety, feelings of inadequacy and insecurity, and inhibition of aggression. Incest offenders differed only in being more socially introverted. On the other hand,

Hall et al. (1986) found no distinctive patterns in the MMPIs of a large sample of incarcerated child molesters, and no discriminations related to incest, rape, or the use of force. They conclude that child molesters are heterogeneous in personality. However, only 7% of their sample had a profile entirely within normal limits, and significant elevations were attained by two thirds on the *Pd* scale, and by over half on *Sc*, suggesting that poor socialisation, alienation, and confused thinking are common in this population.

One further psychodynamic hypothesis is that child victimisation is an attempt to master the trauma of personal childhood abuse, a theme also found in explanations for sexual sadism. Finkelhor (1986) points out that the "cycle of abuse" hypothesis predicts that abuse by females should predominate. However, Carter et al. (1987) note that 57% of child molesters reported sexual abuse in childhood, compared with 23% of rapists. On the other hand, incestuous fathers do not report high frequencies of childhood sexual abuse, physical maltreatment and paternal rejection being more prevalent (Williams and Finkelhor, 1990).

The question of why some males show *sexual arousal* to children has generally been answered in terms of conditioning through masturbatory fantasies, but direct evidence on the learning of sexual arousal is lacking. Evidence for the less frequent exposure of paedophiles to pornography in childhood suggests that this is not a significant source of learning (Quinsey, 1986). However, in addition to the possible influence of traumatic experiences of childhood sexual abuse, there is some evidence that sex offenders tend to have initial experiences of consenting sex with adults at an earlier age than the average adolescent male (Longo, 1982). It is conceivable that through reinforcement and modelling, this leads to earlier sexual experimentation with peers, although in itself, this would not explain why children become more sexually arousing than adults.

Some research has focused on the stimulus characteristics which elicit sexual arousal in child molesters (Freund, 1967). One assumption has been that incest offenders will show less preference for children. Abel et al. (1981) compared PPG responses of small samples of incest offenders, heterosexual paedophiles, and mixed sexual deviants to audiotaped descriptions involving differing degrees of consent and physical coercion in child sexual interactions, physical aggression to a child, and consenting sex with an adult female. On a "paedophile index", incest offenders scored higher than paedophiles, who in turn scored higher than controls. Paedophiles, however, scored higher on an "aggression index". Avery-Clark and Laws (1984) also found that a similar aggression index discriminated between more and less dangerous child molesters. However, Barbaree (1990) describes PPG assessments of incest and nonfamilial child molesters and nonoffender controls, who were shown slides of naked females varying in age from 3 to 24. Five profile patterns were identified (child, child–adult, nondiscriminating, teen–adult, and adult), which were differentially distributed across the three groups. None of the incest group responded exclusively to children, most producing adult or nondiscriminating profiles. Child molesters were more likely to respond to children, but a third produced adult or teen–adult profiles. These findings, which are based on larger samples than those of Abel et al. (1981), therefore support the view that some child molesters, and incest offenders in particular, do not have a sexual preference for children.

It is possible that the learning of sexual preferences is influenced by physiological variables, such as hormone levels, but Rada, Laws and Kellner (1976) found that child molesters were not distinguished from rapists or controls on plasma testosterone level. There is, however, some evidence of cortical dysfunction in paedophiles. Hucker et al. (1986) found that hetero- and homosexual paedophiles had higher frequencies of abnormalities in the left temporal area than nonsex offenders on both CT scans and neuropsychological tests. This is consistent with the findings of Flor-Henry et al. (1991) of EEG anomalies in the dominant hemispheres of paedophiles and exhibitionists, and suggests that mechanisms for learning sexual preferences are impaired in sexual deviants. This would not, however, explain the specificity of paedophilic interests.

The *blockage* factor refers to the assumption that child molesters are blocked or inhibited in forming adult heterosexual relationships, and hence seek out less frustrating interactions. This notion is seen in both the psychodynamic notion of castration anxiety and the learning theory assumption that sex offenders are deficient in heterosocial skills. It is applied particularly to incest, which is suggested to be the choice of a surrogate partner in the face of marital stress or dissatisfaction. Unlike the emotional congruence factor, this hypothesis assumes that child molesters are "pushed" towards sexual contact with a child, rather than "pulled" by an explicit attraction.

Evidence for heterosexual anxiety in child molesters has been found in clinical and projective test studies (Finkelhor, 1986), and empirical support has been forthcoming from controlled observations comparing the heterosocial performance of child molesters, rapists, nonsex offenders, and nonoffenders. Segal and Marshall (1985), for example, found that child molesters were rated as more inept in interactions with a female, and also rated themselves as more anxious and less assertive. While Overholser and Beck (1986) found that the rated social skills of rapists and child molesters were similarly deficient, the latter reported greater fears of negative evaluation, and also described themselves as less assertive. Incestuous fathers have also been found to have social skill deficits and relatively weak masculine identification (Williams and Finkelhor, 1990). However, family isolation and disorganisation appears to be more significant in such offenders than marital dissatisfaction.

The fourth factor, *disinhibition*, is concerned with the absence or loss of conventional inhibitions against sex with children. Both dispositional and situational factors have been suggested. The stereotype that child molesters are either senile or mentally retarded receives no confirmation, nor is there evidence for an association with serious mental disorder (Quinsey, 1986). Consistent findings of high scores on the MMPI *Pd* scale in incarcerated samples suggest that deficient socialisation may be significant, although this is shared with offenders more generally. Studies of incestuous fathers, however, indicate that more specific factors in the relationship, such as poor bonding or empathy with the child, may play a role (Williams and Finkelhor, 1990). The greater risk of molestation for girls living with stepfathers also suggests that factors in the relationship itself are contributory.

Alcohol is also sometimes cited as a possible factor in child molestation, but whether its influence is any more specific than in other offenders seems doubtful. On the other hand, alcohol is particularly likely to be used as an excuse by child molesters (McCaghy, 1968), who are in addition prone to distorted justifications. From clinical observations, Abel et al. (1984) identified several cognitive distortions in child molesters, such as beliefs that lack of resistance by a child implies willingness, the child does not perceive genital fondling as an assault, the experience teaches the child about sex, and society will come to accept adult–child sexual relations. These observations receive support from a comparison of child molesters with rapists and several nonoffender control groups on evaluations of descriptions of adult–child sexual contact, and responses to a questionnaire (Stermac and Segal, 1989). Child molesters attributed greater benefits to a child, saw greater complicity on the part of the child in initiating sexual contact, and attributed less responsibility to adults. They also endorsed more permissive beliefs about adult–child contact. Whether such beliefs are *post hoc* rationalisations, or whether they serve to neutralise inhibitions in those attracted to children, is uncertain.

Evidence on the causes of child molestation therefore remains fragmentary, but as this brief overview indicates, there is support for a potential role for each of these four factors. As with criminal acts more generally, the decision to molest a child is likely to be the culmination of multiple influences on a person's development and cues from the current situation.

Chapter 12

Forensic Psychology and the Offender

INTRODUCTION

The concern of experimental psychology with perception and memory fostered an early interest in eyewitness testimony, and at the turn of the century a number of psychologists in Europe presented their findings in criminal and civil trials (Bartol and Bartol, 1987). In America, Munsterberg (1908) argued for the benefits to crime detection and courtroom proceedings which would accrue from attention to psychological research, but lawyers and many of his colleagues regarded his claims as extravagant. It was not until the 1950s that the law began to use social science findings in individual judgements or policy-making, but despite the recent growth of psycholegal research, this use remains uneven and selective (Webster, 1984). There has, nevertheless, been a recent increase in the use of psychological evidence in the individual case, which is the focus of this chapter.

Forensic psychology

The term *forensic psychology* is sometimes loosely equated with the application of psychology to the law in general. Connolly and McKellar (1963), for example, defined it as the application of psychology to *procedures* of courts of law, police investigations, and related matters, thus emphasising the *study* of behaviour in legal contexts. Bartol and Bartol (1987) also view forensic psychology as both *research* on behaviour related to legal processes, including criminal behaviour, and *professional practice* within the legal system. However, research relevant to law has usually been undertaken either to test psychological theories, or because behaviour in legal settings is of psychological interest (Monahan and Loftus, 1982), and is distinguished by its context of application, not by its theory or methodology. Similarly, much professional practice in the criminal justice system, such as clinical services to offenders, requires no unique techniques.

"Forensic", however, means relevant to a legal *forum*, i.e. a judicial body or court (Haward, 1981; Grisso, 1987), and in a joint statement of the American Psychology-Law Society and Division 41 of the American Psychological Association, forensic psychology is defined as

> . . .all forms of professional psychological conduct when acting, with definable foreknowledge, as a psychological expert on explicitly psycholegal issues, in direct assistance to courts, parties to legal proceedings, correctional and forensic mental health facilities, and administrative, judicial, and legislative agencies acting in an adjudicative capacity (Committee on Ethical Guidelines for Forensic Psychologists, 1991)

While this includes presenting findings from research as well as individual assessment, the focus is on evidence in particular cases, whether civil or criminal, and the only concern with convicted offenders may be with gathering evidence for appeal, parole, or tribunal hearings. In this respect, forensic psychologists exercise a specialised *function*, which departs from that of researcher or clinician in three ways. First, the production and communication of evidence calls for skills beyond those required by research or clinical practice. Second, the information is communicated specifically for use *by* legal decision makers, not by the scientific community or mental health personnel. Third, the psychologist is the agent of legal officials requesting the evidence, and not primarily a defendant. The ethical constraints thus differ from those applying when the defendant is a patient (Fersch, 1980).

Forensic psychologists may be experimental or applied psychologists, but most are clinicians who offer evidence based on individual assessments (Gudjonsson, 1985; Grisso, 1987). Their role is not confined to criminal matters, and many are increasingly involved in civil cases of child custody and compensation claims arising from personal injury or trauma. However, the emphasis here is on psychological evidence in criminal cases.

PSYCHOLOGISTS AND POLICE INVESTIGATIONS

Direct psychological services to the police have been relatively limited in Britain (Bull, 1984), but applications to police work have a long history in the United States, and include selection and training, clinical services for police officers, training in crisis intervention, and various consultancy services (Bartol and Bartol, 1987). Police practices in identifying and interrogating suspects have also been the target of research. However, most of this falls outside the scope of forensic psychology as defined above, and attention will be limited to consultancy services in the investigation of specific incidents. Two particular areas to which psychologists have contributed are offender profiling and the interrogation of suspects.

Offender Profiling

Psychological "profiling", or "crime scene analysis", aims to assist in the detection of offenders by extrapolating their personal attributes from information available in crimes (Holmes, 1989). While its forebears can be found in the deductive inferences of fictional detectives, and in psychodynamic "portraits" of politicians, current interest dates from the late 1970s, when police departments invited first psychiatrists and then psychologists to give clinical interpretations of the actions of unknown offenders. Subsequent profiling methods developed by the Behavioural Sciences Unit of the FBI Academy have resulted in a more empirical approach to the links between offences and offender characteristics (Ressler et al., 1989).

What constitutes an offender profile is not clearly agreed, but the process of profiling draws on both physical and nonphysical information. This includes the layout of the crime scene in terms of disposition of the victim and the presence or absence of significant items, evidence on what was done to the victim and the sequence of events, and the perpetrator's behaviour before and after the crime. From these data, inferences are drawn about the possible meaning and motivation of particular acts. For example, tying up a victim suggests a need for control, while stabbing the victim before sexual intercourse may imply a need for arousal from pain or blood. Characteristics of the victim, location of the crime, use of a vehicle, and relation to previous crimes may also suggest social and demographic features of the offender, such as age, race, or occupation.

Turco (1990) sees profile development as similar to clinical use of the Rorschach, a comparison which many psychologists would consider damning! Dietz (1985), however, views it as the generation of hypotheses through logical reasoning. From observations of the FBI Behavioural Sciences Unit, he detects a progression through stages of assimilation of the crime data, reconstruction of the crime as a behavioural event, formulation of motivational hypotheses, typological hypotheses about the kind of person committing the crime, and the attribution of particular characteristics to the perpetrator.

The goal is to narrow the field of investigation, basic assumptions being that an offender's behaviour at the crime scene reflects consistencies in personality and method of committing a crime (Holmes, 1989). The focus has therefore been on serial crimes and sexual assaults, and 90% of profiling attempts involve murder or rape. Holmes suggests that profiling is most useful when the crime scene reflects psychopathology, such as sadistic assaults, rapes or satanic and cult killings. However, there have been instances of its use in arson, obscene telephone calls, and bank robbery. The emphasis on pathology appears to reflect an assumption that clinical expertise may shed light on "the mind of the murderer" in bizarre or apparently motiveless crimes, and accounts for the influence of psychodynamic approaches on early profiling. This influence is seen in attempts to relate offences to typologies of sex offenders developed for clinical purposes (Chapter 11). However, reliable profiling calls for empirically established correlates of offences which can be tested out against the data available to the crime scene analyst (Dietz, 1985; Canter, 1989). Clinical typologies are of limited value to the investigator in this respect.

Some attempts have been made to develop typologies of direct relevance to profiling. FBI profilers, for example, utilise a dichotomy of *organised* versus *disorganised* crime scenes and murderers. Organised crimes show evidence of planning and control, while disorganised crime scenes suggest haphazard behaviour. Distinctive types of perpetrator are thus hypothesised. Evidence on the validity of the distinction was obtained by Ressler et al. (1986), who drew on FBI archival data on 36 sexual murderers, 24 described as organised and 12 as disorganised. During the crime, organised killers were more likely to use restraints, have sex with the victim before death, display control over the victim, and use a vehicle. In terms of personal characteristics, disorganised murderers were less intelligent or occupationally skilled, and more sexually inhibited. They were also more likely to know the victim, live alone, offend close to home, and to be frightened and confused during the assault. However, the groups overlapped on most variables. Another typology divides serial murderers on the basis of motive into visionary, mission-oriented, hedonistic, and power-control types (Holmes, 1989). These categories, however, are not mutually exclusive, and are simply anecdotal *post hoc* descriptions.

Canter (1989) proposes that actions performed during a crime are direct reflections of the interpersonal transactions an offender has with other people. For example, murderers who kill without prior victim interaction are likely to lead a solitary existence more generally. Similarly, location and spatial pattern of crimes over time may relate to more general features of an offender's lifestyle. Canter argues that models of offence behaviour are a necessary first step in establishing the relation of crime scene data to offender characteristics, and Canter and Heritage (1990) describe an exploratory study of offence variables identified from victim statements in 66 sexual assaults. Using a nonmetric form of multidimensional scaling, they identified a two-dimensional, radex structure in the data. In the centre of the space were the most frequent activities, such as vaginal intercourse, absence of reactions to the victim, use of impersonal language, and surprise attack, suggesting that the use of a woman as a sexual object is at the core of most sexual assaults. However, grouping of variables around the two-dimensional space provided support for theories which variously relate sexual assault to attempted intimacy, sexual gratification, aggression, impersonal interaction, and criminality (Chapter 11). It is suggested that there will be different combinations of these for different offenders.

It is frequently asserted that profiling is more art than science, and evidence for its validity is limited. Holmes (1989) reports 1981 FBI data indicating that in 192 cases of profile generation, arrests were made in 88, but in only 17% of these did the profile contribute to arrest. Canter and Heritage (1990) cite more recent FBI claims of 80% accuracy, although this has been disputed. As Canter (1989) notes, if psychological profiling is to achieve a firmer basis than astrology or spiritualism in aiding the police, psychologists need not only to establish the predictive validity of the process, but also why it works.

Police interrogations

Interrogations of suspects aim to elicit a confession, and American police in particular receive training in techniques which appear to be relatively effective for this purpose. These methods have, however, been of concern because of the potential for coercion, and the eliciting of false confessions in some well publicised cases. Irving and Hilgendorf (1980) describe interrogation as a process of manipulating a suspect's decision making by influencing the costs and benefits of confessing. For example, the interviewer may stress the consequences of being honest for subsequent treatment by the court, interviewer approval, or self-esteem. The effectiveness of these tactics is potentiated by the custodial environment and the relative powerlessness of the suspect.

Many suspects are highly anxious when interviewed, and some may be intoxicated, mentally ill or mentally handicapped. Some are therefore overly susceptible to techniques of persuasion to confess because of dispositional or temporary state factors, mentally handicapped suspects being particularly suggestible. Gudjonsson (1984, 1988) developed a Suggestibility Scale, which measures the extent to which a person's responses are affected by messages communicated during formal questioning. He proposes that it assesses coping strategies for dealing with the uncertainty of the interrogation situation. The scale correlates negatively with IQ and assertiveness, and positively with state anxiety and fear of negative evaluations (Gudjonsson, 1988), and discriminates false confessors from suspects who consistently deny offences (Gudjonsson, 1984). While not all those who retract confessions in court are suggestible, Gudjonsson has employed the scale to identify those whose confessions may be "unreliable".

While many suspects confess under interrogation, police manuals devote attention to detecting deception. It is assumed, for example, that lying is associated with overt behavioural cues, such as changes in eye contact, voice pitch, or gestures, although experimental evidence offers little support for the reliability of such cues (Bull, 1984). However, American police rely particularly on polygraph recordings of autonomic responses during questioning to detect deception. The validity of the polygraph as a psychophysiological research instrument (Chapter 6) is not in doubt, but the utility of "the polygraph test" as a *lie detector* is disputed.

The polygraph test was introduced by a Harvard psychologist in 1917, but rejected as evidence in court in the landmark decision of *Frye v United States* in 1923 (Blau, 1985). Nevertheless, it was subsequently developed by American police departments, and is now used in criminal investigations in several countries (British Psychological Society, 1986; Iacono and Patrick, 1987). It is also now admissible in the courts of many American states, but not in Canada, Britain, or most European countries. However, forensic applications are exceeded by its use in screening employees for "honesty" in commercial organisations and government departments, and an estimated two million tests are administered annually in the United States. Proposals by the British Government to introduce the test for security vetting elicited considerable controversy, and criticism from psychologists (British Psychological Society, 1986; Gale, 1988).

As there is no pattern of physiological responding unique to lying, the polygraph does not detect "lies", but rather changes in arousal during interrogation. Channels recorded are usually skin resistance, respiration, heart rate, and blood pressure, and while some polygraphers employ a numerical scoring system, most rely on global inspection of the trace (Iacono and Patrick, 1987). The original method compared responses to "relevant" questions (Did you commit the crime?) and irrelevant questions (Is today Tuesday?). This approach is still used, but is generally considered naive, since subjects may react strongly to relevant questions for reasons other than guilt, such as anger or embarrassment. A more common variant in employment screening is the "Relevant–Relevant" questions technique, in which relevant questions cover several issues. This has not been subject to research, and even proponents of polygraph testing doubt its validity (Raskin, 1988). However, some defend the test because it often elicits confessions of deception, and may deter dishonest employees.

Most frequently used in investigating specific incidents is the Control Question Test (CQT), in which responses to relevant questions are compared with others concerned with past behaviour (e.g. Have you ever hurt someone?). The rationale, challenged by critics, is that the guilty are more concerned with relevant questions, innocent subjects with control questions, since only on the latter are they likely to be caught lying. Another technique is the Guilty Knowledge Test (GKT), introduced by Lykken, who stresses that it is a measure of recognition rather than a lie detector (Lykken, 1988). The subject is asked multiple choice questions about the crime, for which answers to particular alternatives could only be known to the perpetrator (e.g. the weapon used, colour of garments). Since the probability of chance responding to several such questions is small, the GKT is claimed to protect the innocent.

Although a few American psychologists are involved in forensic use of the polygraph test, most polygraphers are not psychophysiologists, many being policemen who undergo a brief training. Some psychologists, notably Lykken (1988), are highly critical of its use, arguing that claims to accuracy lack a scientific basis. Others, such as Raskin (1988), suggest that it is a useful investigative tool for adequately trained personnel. Efforts to establish the validity of the CQT have not produced agreed findings. Laboratory studies permit manipulation of truth and deception, but lack external validity, since subjects are not emotionally involved in the outcome. However, Iacono and Patrick (1987) report an experiment manipulating realistic involvement, in which the CQT correctly identified 87% of deceptive subjects, but only 56% of the truthful. They suggest that the identification of many innocent subjects as liars is a typical finding.

Field studies of actual cases are limited by the lack of an independent criterion of deception, and rely on either confessions or the judgements of an expert legal panel. However, there is disagreement about what constitutes an adequate test of accuracy. Raskin (1988), for example, insists that what must be validated is the total examination conducted by a trained investigator. In contrast, critics argue that the crucial question is whether "blind" interpretation of the polygraph adds anything to the conditions of interrogation, since polygraphers may base their decisions on behavioural rather than physiological responses (Carroll, 1988; Lykken, 1988). Opposing sides in the debate therefore rely on different studies. Raskin (1988) suggests that with careful use in criminal investigations, accuracy of the CQT is likely to be about 95% for guilty subjects, and 85% for the innocent, permitting confident screening out of those who pass the test. Lykken (1988), on the other hand, concludes that the CQT is in error in a third or more of cases, and notes that the test can be beaten by countermeasures, such as biting the tongue during control questions. He argues that the GKT avoids these problems. However, the latter is not widely used, and Raskin regards it as impracticable for most investigations.

The issues raised by lie detection methods go beyond scientific questions of validity, since their use involves deceit, stress induction, and invasions of privacy, which may contravene the professional ethics of psychologists (British Psychological Society, 1986). It is therefore unlikely that the controversy surrounding them will be readily resolved by future empirical research. It is nonetheless worth noting that error rates reported in studies of lie detection are less than those obtained in clinical predictions of dangerousness (below).

PSYCHOLOGISTS AND THE CRIMINAL COURTS

A central psychological issue in criminal cases is the mental state of a defendant, and the courts have traditionally turned to psychiatrists for testimony on mental illness. However, the independent contribution of psychological methods was recognised in *Jenkins v United States* in 1962, when the Court of Appeals for the District of Columbia sanctioned the use of clinical psychologists as experts on mental disorder (Bartol and Bartol, 1987). In the 1970s, a "boom" in forensic psychology followed reforms of the commitment laws (Stone, 1984), and the American Board of Forensic Psychology was created to certify professional expertise in courtroom matters. During the past decade, at least a dozen texts on forensic psychology have appeared (e.g. Haward, 1981; Nietzel and Dillehay, 1986; Melton et al., 1987; Weiner and Hess, 1987), and many clinical psychologists in the United States and Canada now specialise in this area (Grisso, 1987; Heilbrun and Annis, 1988). Some are employed in forensic facilities, others are attached to court clinics, while many provide services from the private sector. While the exact number involved is uncertain, Grisso (1987) suggests that it is large enough to represent psychology's most pervasive source of influence on the legal system.

The courts in Britain have been more restrictive in recognising psychologists in criminal cases, but lawyers have observed an increasing contribution (Fitzgerald, 1987). A survey for the British Psychological Society in 1985 identified 185 psychologists who had given evidence in court or in Mental Health Review Tribunals, which are quasi-courts, during the previous five years (Gudjonsson, 1985). Of these, 71% were clinical psychologists, and 22% educational psychologists, and about half had appeared in criminal cases. However, only a minority appeared in court on a regular basis, and for every 10 reports submitted, psychologists were likely to give oral testimony only once or twice. The same applies in North America, and the production of evidence for legal use is a more widespread practice than its presentation on the witness stand.

Psychologists as expert witnesses

Anglo-American courts rely on an adversarial system, in contrast to the inquisitorial system of European states, the concern being not to establish truth, but rather to discover whether the prosecution's case can be proved beyond all reasonable doubt (Haward, 1981; Cooke, 1990). In this system, defence and prosecution present the best case and challenge that of their opponent, and expert testimony may be used to strengthen a case, or to undermine it. The sequence of evidence begins with examination-in-chief, or direct examination, in which the advocate calling the witness attempts to support the case of his or her client. The witness is then cross-examined by opposing counsel, who tests the quality of the expert's testimony, and may challenge its credibility. In re-direct examination, the advocate retaining the expert seeks to nullify any effects of the cross-examination, although no new material may be presented.

The nature of the evidence is governed by judicial rules. For example, the hearsay rule protects a defendant from unfair or unsafe evidence by excluding testimony not directly obtained by the witness, on the grounds that the person obtaining the evidence cannot be cross-examined. A psychologist should not therefore present the findings of an assistant, nor should a psychiatrist's report incorporate a psychologist's test results. The hearsay rule is not applied consistently, but has been invoked to exclude experimental psychological findings, on the grounds that subjects were not present to testify! (Haward, 1987).

Rules also govern the definition and role of an expert witness, although the judge decides on the admissibility of expert testimony. An ordinary witness states what was observed at the time of an offence, the "facts" being determined by the *triers of fact*, i.e. the judge and jury. An expert witness does not present "facts", but is someone qualified by relevant study and experience to draw conclusions in some specialised branch of knowledge, and to form an opinion which is a reasonable probability (Haward, 1981; Blau, 1985). While criteria for the admissibility of expert testimony vary according to jurisdiction and kind of evidence, Greene, Schooler and Loftus (1985) identify four traditional requirements: (1) the subject matter must be beyond the common understanding of the average juror; (2) the expert must be sufficiently qualified so that his or her opinion will aid the jury; (3) the evidence about which the expert testifies must be scientifically reliable and generally accepted within the scientific community; (4) the probative value of the evidence must outweigh its prejudicial effects. Each of these criteria has raised controversy.

First, it is generally accepted that medical disorders are beyond the ken of jurors, and the admissibility of clinical psychologists is often seen to be hindered by their lack of medical qualifications. For example, Hill and Griffiths (1982) noted that in *R v McKinney* in 1981, the English Court of Appeal ruled that a psychologist (actually a social psychologist) was not an appropriate expert to testify on the reliability of a witness, since this was *medical evidence*. They therefore suggested that the future of forensic psychology lay more in investigation than in direct testimony. However, medical qualifications are not a prerequisite for being a medical witness (Haward, 1987), and in practice, the courts have generally been amenable to psychological testimony on mental disorder, particularly in cases of mental retardation, brain injury, sexual deviation, and, at least in the case of Mental Health Review Tribunals, psychopathic personality (Gudjonsson, 1986; Fitzgerald, 1987). As in the United States, then, clinical psychologists in Britain have gained increasing access to the courtroom in criminal cases under the borrowed cloak of the psychiatrist.

It is, however, on the issue of "normal" behaviour that the courts remain restrictive. For example, they generally admit evidence on the effects of stress or particular situations on a mentally ill or handicapped person, but not on someone free from a mental disorder. The legal ruling is that "matters of human nature and behaviour within the limits of normality are not outside the experience and knowledge of the judge and jury" (Fitzgerald, 1987). For this reason, evidence regarding experimental findings on eyewitness testimony is not admissible in Britain, although it has been allowed in American courts when the identification of a defendant is at issue. While psychologists may feel indignant at the reduction of their subject to "common sense", a similar argument is advanced from within their ranks. McCloskey and Egeth (1983), for example, challenge the rationale of expert testimony on witness reliability, arguing that there is insufficient evidence that jurors either overbelieve eyewitnesses, or make better discriminations when presented with expert testimony. This has been vigorously contested by Loftus and her colleagues (Greene, Schooler and Loftus, 1985; Goodman and Loftus, 1988). However, Pachella (1988) goes further, and argues for the exclusion of expert psychological testimony from all criminal proceedings on the grounds that it is not outside the realm of common experience. He suggests that psychological knowledge differs from that of the layperson in being more articulated and explanatory, but not necessarily more extensive.

The criterion concerning the qualifications of an expert witness seems to be less contentious. However, lawyers are not generally aware of distinctions in training between different branches of psychology, and have sometimes called psychologists who are not appropriately qualified on a particular issue (Haward, 1987). Professional ethics would oblige them to decline to testify.

The third criterion requires that psychological methods should have general scientific acceptability, but this is problematic for a discipline which lacks a universally accepted theory. In the United States, this principle has been guided by the *Frye* decision of 1923, which excluded lie detector findings, and which specified that scientific evidence must have gained general acceptance within the particular field (Blau, 1985). One implication is that psychological evidence must draw on tests and methods which are "customary and usual practice", and produce opinions which other experts in the field would reach. Adherence to this view in Britain is reflected in the emphasis given to evidence on cognitive functioning based on traditional intelligence and neuropsychological tests (Gudjonsson, 1985). However, lack of consensual agreement has been noted by critics of expert psychological testimony (McCloskey and Egeth, 1983; Pachella, 1988). Faust and Ziskin (1988) also argue that clinicians who testify on diagnostic issues, or the future behaviour of an offender, misrepresent the reliability of clinical judgement, and go beyond what is scientifically accepted.

Finally, it has also been questioned whether psychological testimony is more probative than prejudicial. It is conceivable, for example, that jurors might be influenced by evidence on eyewitness testimony to the point of being oversceptical about reliable witnesses (McCloskey and Egeth, 1983). Despite these controversies, however, most psychological evidence seems to be favourably received by the courts (Gudjonsson, 1985).

The preparation of psychological evidence

Contributions of psychologists to court proceedings go beyond testimony about the mental state of defendants, and evidence may also be sought about the behaviour of witnesses or victims. Defence lawyers are the most frequent source of referral, and the kinds of question addressed depend partly on their familiarity with psychology, but also on the inventiveness of psychologists in translating forensic issues into psychological questions. Haward (1981), who has been prominent in the development of forensic psychology in Britain, describes a variety of contributions, for example, recreating the mental state of an alleged shoplifter under a combination of a specified dose of barbiturates and alcohol, establishing the road-using skills of a mentally handicapped youth, showing the sexual motivation of a taking and driving away offence, and demonstrating the effects of perceptual set or situational conditions on police evidence.

Haward (1981) suggests that in producing pertinent evidence, forensic psychologists adopt one of four functions. As an *experimenter*, the psychologist may summarise research findings obtained in experiments or surveys, or conduct a laboratory or field study to demonstrate the likelihood of some effect. As a *clinician*, the psychologist employs clinical assessment methods, usually to establish some aspect of psychological ability, capacity, or treatability. As an *actuary*, the psychologist utilises published data to establish the probability of some occurrence, such as the lighting conditions under which a witness claims to have observed an event. Finally as an *adviser*, the psychologist may assist counsel, for example, by making observations on the psychological characteristics of a witness, without appearing as a witness. In the United States, some psychologists similarly act as consultants in jury deselection, or *voir dire* (Nietzel and Dillehay, 1986).

The function most commonly called for is that of clinician, but clinical knowledge and assessment skills are not sufficient, since the conditions and purpose of assessment differ from standard clinical practice. For example, establishing a therapeutic relationship or securing appropriate treatment are not typically the tasks of the psychologist functioning as a forensic expert. Also, the psychologist's opinions are sought by legal officials to answer legal questions in a legal setting, and the kind of report prepared for other mental health professionals or for presentation at a case conference is unlikely to assist the court (Grisso, 1987; Weiner, 1987).

A preliminary step in preparing evidence is to ascertain the precise referral question, and its amenability to psychological evaluation (Weiner, 1987). Although some psychologists rely on behavioural assessments or interviews, evidence generally rests on test data, which in Britain are most commonly derived from intelligence and neuropsychological tests (Gudjonsson, 1985). The selection of particular tests may need to be defended. However, there is a conflict between criteria for expert testimony, such as the *Frye* standard, which dictates a conservative selection of established instruments (Blau, 1984), and the need for psychologists to use new procedures responsive to forensic issues (Lanyon, 1986b: Grisso, 1987). A few measures have been developed in this context, such as Gudjonsson's Suggestibility Scale (Gudjonsson, 1984). Other examples applicable mainly in North America are the Rogers Criminal Responsibility Assessment Scales, which quantify psychological variables relevant to the ALI standard for the insanity defence (Rogers, 1987), and the Interdisciplinary Fitness Interview for assessing competency, which can be completed jointly by a lawyer and a psychologist (Roesch and Golding, 1987). Whatever the procedures, psychologists need to be well versed in the background of the tests they use. Matarazzo (1990) notes that some lawyers have become sophisticated in obtaining psychometric guidance, and may grill a witness about issues such as test reliability, standard errors of measurement, or the meaning of subtest intercorrelations.

Since psychological testimony usually takes the form of a written report, on which cross-examination will be based if the psychologist appears in person, the report is a key feature of the evidence. Petrella and Poythress (1983) found that lawyers rated the quality of clinical psychologists' reports more highly than those of psychiatrists and social workers, but in this instance, all mental health professionals were drawn from a forensic centre which trained its staff, and the standard of all reports was judged favourably. More commonly, forensic psychological reports are criticised as neither forensic nor psychological (Grisso, 1987). Weiner (1987) offers guidelines on the structure of court reports, suggesting that the crucial features are clarity, relevance, and information value. They should contain first a statement of qualifications, including relevant experience, which tends to impress lawyers more than academic degrees. They should also detail documentary and other sources of information consulted, and how the examinee was evaluated. Descriptions of test findings should avoid jargon, and it is appropriate to explain the meaning of technical terms, such as standard score or the nature of psychological functions measured. It may also be appropriate to summarise relevant research. Finally, conclusions drawn should be stated as opinions, and listed.

Psychological testimony in court

The role of psychological evidence at different stages of a criminal trial varies within Anglo-American legal systems, but it is generally presented at three points (Fersch, 1980; Gudjonsson, 1986). At the *pre-trial* stage, the main issue is fitness to plead, or competence, which requires evaluation of a defendant's current abilities. As noted in Chapter 10, this is now infrequent in England, and depends on psychiatric evidence, but in North America, assessment of competence is a common task of forensic psychologists (Lanyon, 1986b: Roesch and Golding, 1987). Pendleton (1980) described a clinical extension of this role in a California hospital, in which skills training used in conjunction with psychiatric treatment permitted the restoration of competence to stand trial in over 90% of those initially found unfit.

At the *trial stage*, evidence may be presented relevant to either the *actus reus* or *mens rea* requirements. The concern in the *actus reus* component is with whether the alleged offence occurred, and the defendant's involvement in it, and experimental data have been presented in a number of cases relating to such issues as the reliability of evidence, perceptual distortions in witnesses, and retracted confessions (Haward, 1981; Gudjonsson, 1986). In establishing the mental state of a defendant to rebut *mens rea* or support diminished responsibility or mitigation, the concern is with functioning at the time of the offence, and the psychologist's evidence invariably supplements and complements that of a psychiatrist. Again, the insanity defence is more applicable in North America, but psychologists in Britain have contributed evidence on "abnormality of mind", usually focusing on intellectual functioning.

While psychologists have traditionally appeared for the defence, Gudjonsson (1985) found that a fifth of psychologists had appeared in cases in which a psychologist was called by opposing counsel. This is an inevitable consequence of the adversarial system, and many find it distasteful. Another consequence is that the psychologist as expert witness must expect hostile cross-examination, which may seek to discredit not only the assessment procedures, but also the professional competence of the psychologist, and even the scientific credibility of the discipline. Indeed, in the United States, some psychologists have trained lawyers in destructive questioning of clinical witnesses (Faust and Ziskin, 1988). Carson (1984) notes that advocates are expected to develop examination skills to undermine experts. For example, the advocate may cut short the witness who replies "No, but...", having elicited the damning "No" without the qualifying information. It is therefore necessary for an expert witness to learn skills to counter these techniques (Carson, 1984; Cooke, 1990).

Following a conviction, disposal options are considered at the *sentencing* stage. Treatment via a hospital order depends on psychiatric recommendations, but the courts have increasingly accepted psychological recommendations for treatment in the community under a psychiatric probation order, or a deferred or suspended sentence, for example in cases of nonviolent sex offenders or psychologically disturbed shoplifters (Brown,

1985). In such cases, a treatment plan is usually requested by defence counsel or a probation officer. Where patients are detained under the Mental Health Act, psychologists are also now involved in providing evidence to Mental Health Review Tribunals. While only psychiatric reports are mandatory, psychological evidence has been increasingly sought regarding intellectual functioning, personality disorder, sexual deviation, or violence, particularly in relation to the continued detention and treatability of patients in the categories of psychopathic disorder and mental impairment.

Problems for psychologists as expert witnesses

The role of expert witness raises a number of professional and ethical problems for psychologists. First, the majority, who appear in court only occasionally, typically lack the requisite skills of presenting written and oral forensic evidence. Brodsky and Robey (1972) contrasted the extremes of the "courtroom-oriented" and "courtroom-unfamiliar" psychologist. The courtroom-unfamiliar witness fails to communicate with attorneys beforehand, prepares a report as if for a case conference rather than a lay audience, does not understand the advocacy system or the nature of expert testimony, and is fearful, overtechnical, and muddled on the witness stand. Such a psychologist subsequently gives talks on the unbridgeable gap between psychology and law! While many psychologists in North America now appear to have joined the ranks of the courtroom-oriented, and several graduate courses provide forensic training (Heilbrun and Annis, 1988), unfamiliarity remains a problem in Britain, where courtroom demands are not as yet sufficiently regular to motivate the acquisition of the relevant skills.

A related problem is the inadequate scientific base for the practice of forensic psychology. Most publications on the subject are nonempirical (Moore and Finn, 1986), but Grisso (1987) argues that a research base is crucial to the development of standards. He identifies needs for new conceptual models to guide the forensic assessment process, for tying forensic assessments more closely to psychological theory, and for new assessment instruments. While noting some relevant advances, he expresses concerns that too few researchers are attracted to the area because of suspicions of compromise in the "market" of the legal forum, and that too few practitioners see the value of research. He proposes that psychology should acknowledge the logic of marketplace dynamics of legal settings by providing incentives for researchers, instituting professional quality control, and educating legal consumers.

However, psychologists are divided on the ethics of their involvement in the criminal courts. The adversarial system, with its emphasis on partiality, is alien to the traditions of psychology as science and as helping profession, and concerns are often voiced about its more destructive aspects (Tunstall et al., 1982). It is not uncommon, for example, for test data to be misused in court, and for confidential details of test scoring and interpretation to be elicited, contrary to professional obligations to protect such material

(Haward, 1987). Fersch (1980) has suggested that in participating in court proceedings, psychologists may not be able to adhere strictly to their agreed ethical standards. Psychologists who treat offenders under coercion, or who predict dangerousness, for example, may be misrepresenting their professional competence. In giving expert testimony, they face conflicts of allegiance which may make them the adversary rather than the advocate of the defendant, since the client is the court official requesting services. They may not, therefore, be acting in the best interests of those they have assessed. Fersch follows Szasz, and argues that psychologists should not assess or treat involuntary clients. While this position is probably a minority view, it is nevertheless allied with other critiques of the role of psychologist as expert witness. However, increased sensitivity to these issues is reflected in the recent publication of guidelines for psychologists who exercise a forensic role, whether regularly or occasionally (Committee on Ethical Guidelines for Forensic Psychologists, 1991).

PREDICTION IN CRIMINOLOGY

Forensic psychologists are often required to forecast or predict the likelihood of future offending by an individual. The clinical prediction of dangerousness is particularly controversial, and is examined in the next section. However, criminologists have long been interested in deriving empirical predictors of criminal behaviour (Simon, 1971; Farrington and Tarling, 1985; Glaser, 1987). and more general issues of prediction in criminology will be considered first.

Prediction research has generally been undertaken for three purposes. One is to identify high risk groups from the early antecedents of later criminal behaviour, with a view to providing preventive services. A second is to construct aetiological theories, since in the positivist view of science, antecedent correlates of subsequent behaviour may be identified as "causes" (Chapter 1). Longitudinal studies of delinquent careers discussed earlier relate to both of these aims. However, the concern here is with a third purpose, which is to derive predictive information for use in criminal justice decision making, for example in placement or release decisions.

A particular aim is the derivation of statistical or *actuarial* predictive indices, which objectively indicate an optimal decision. This is usually contrasted with *clinical* prediction, which involves a subjective evaluation of risk (Meehl, 1954, 1986). This oversimplifies the decision task, which depends not only on the extent to which data are combined clinically or statistically, but also on the nature of the data which are combined (Sawyer, 1966). Clinical judgements, for example, may be quantified and form part of a statistical predictor, while the latter may be one element in clinical decision making. However, the following discussion focuses on the statistical combination of "objective" data, such as biographical details or a psychological test score.

Factors determining the utility of prediction

A predictive decision requires information in the form of a *predictor*, which is associated with a *criterion* of interest, such as future violation of parole. Prediction studies seek to identify risk factors which maximise the accuracy of predicting the criterion in terms of reducing errors, but accuracy, or validity, depends on reliability in both predictor and criterion. Criminal justice predictors are often case history data whose reliability is limited by poor quality records. The reliability of criteria in the form of arrest or reconviction is also attenuated by discretionary factors determining official records. Moreover, it is unlikely that a single act, such as a further offence, can reliably index "success" or "failure". Single acts depend on situational and chance factors as well as individual dispositions (Chapter 1), but as will be noted below, prediction research has neglected the issue of what criteria are reliably predictable.

The relation between a predictor and a criterion can be seen in a 2×2 table in which the two are dichotomised (Figure 12.1 (a)). Suppose that the predictor is a factor whose presence (+) correlates with a criterion of violent recidivism (+), and whose absence (−) correlates with nonrecidivism, or the absence of the criterion (−). The decision may be to detain those who show the predictor, and to release those who do not. A *true positive* decision results when the predictor correctly predicts the outcome (*a* in Figure 12.1 (a)), while a *false positive* arises when despite the presence of the predictor, the offender does not recidivate (*b* in Figure 12.1 (a)). Similarly, a *true negative* arises when absence of the predictor coincides with the absence of recidivism, and a *false negative* is the erroneous identification of recidivists as nonrecidivists. Overall accuracy of the predictor is given by $a+d/N$, and a desirable predictor is one which maximises the correct "hits" (*a* and *d*) and minimises the errors or "misses" (*b* and *c*). However, while false positives and false negatives are equally undesirable in scientific terms, they do not have equal social consequences. A high false negative rate ($c/c+d$) is undesirable from society's viewpoint, since use of the predictor leads to the release of many who are unsafe. In contrast, a high false positive rate ($b/a+b$) is undesirable from a civil liberties perspective, since the predictor results in the continued detention of many who are "safe". Overconcern with either error therefore reflects social value judgements about whose interests are best served.

The *efficiency* of a predictor is the extent to which it predicts beyond chance. This depends not only on its correlation with the criterion, but also on the *base rate*, which is the frequency of the criterion in the population of interest (Meehl and Rosen, 1955). Suppose that an investigator identifies a predictor which is present in 40 of 50 recidivists and absent in 40 of 50 nonrecidivists (Figure 12.1 (b)). The base rate of recidivism in this sample is 50%, and the overall accuracy of the predictor is 80% (40+40/100). The false positive rate is 20% (10/40+10), while the false negative rate is also 20%. The probability of recidivism given the presence of the predictor is therefore 0.8, and the probability of nonrecidivism in the absence of the predictor is similarly 0.8.

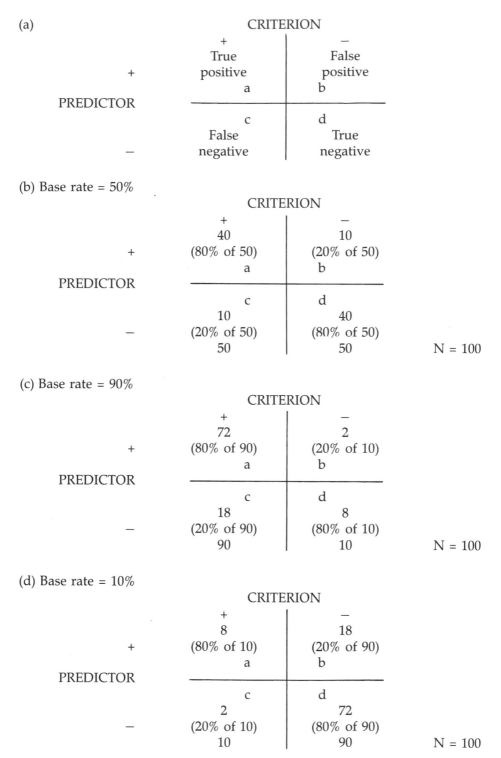

Figure 12.1 Base rates and predictive efficiency (see text)

The predictor is relatively efficient, since it correctly identifies 30% more of the population than would be identified by chance alone, i.e. the base rate of 50%. However, this does not apply with samples having different base rates. If the base rate in a new sample is 90% (Figure 12.1 (c)), the false positive rate is reduced to 2.7% (2/72+2), but the false negative rate is now 69% (18/18+8). The presence of the predictor therefore leads to a confident decision, but its absence produces more incorrect than correct decisions. Moreover, although overall accuracy remains 80%, this actually produces more errors than would be made if prediction relied solely on the base rate of 90%, and all members of the sample were predicted to be recidivists.

A similar problem is seen when the base rate is only 10% (Figure 12.1 (d)). In this case, the false negative rate is only 2.7%, but the false positive rate is now 69%. More than two thirds of those predicted to recidivate will not in fact do so. Also, the overall accuracy of 80% is again less than attained by a blanket prediction from the base rate that all of the sample are nonrecidivists. These problems arise whenever the base rate is low, as it usually is for violent reoffending. As Curtis (1971) demonstrates, "beating" a low base rate calls for predictors whose association with the criterion is greater than is typically the case in either clinical or actuarial prediction. Efficiency may therefore depend on predicting for subgroups whose base rate is close to 50%.

One further limitation on predictive efficiency is the *selection ratio*, which is the proportion selected as positive by the predictor. Optimal efficiency requires a selection ratio equal to the base rate, but the selection ratio can be changed to alter the false positive or false negative rate. For example, if the predictor is a continuous score, the cutting point may be raised to yield fewer positive predictions. However, while this will reduce the number of false positives, it also reduces the true positive rate.

Actuarial prediction in criminal justice decision making

Prediction tables were first constructed by American criminologists in the 1920s. Since they focus on background criminal and demographic variables, they are sometimes known as experience, or base expectancy tables. During the 1950s, sociologist–actuaries were employed by Illinois prisons to assist decisions on the parole of prisoners before expiry of sentence, but prediction tables have otherwise been used to only a limited extent (Glaser, 1987). They are, however, available to national parole boards in England and North America, and there are recent examples of their use to guide decisions on bail, prosecution, and sentencing (Glaser, 1987), and for assigning prisoners to institutions differing in security level (Brennan, 1987b). A further use is as a statistical control in research on the outcome of penal interventions. For example, when random allocation to different programmes is not feasible, predicted recidivism rates can be used in comparing programme effects for different risk groups, or actual with expected outcomes.

A prediction table assigns a probability of future criminal behaviour to groups (not individuals) defined by a combination of attributes. While studies may examine many variables, prediction does not improve beyond a few because of interactions between them, and usually a small number is combined to yield a prediction score. The combination may be a simple addition of unweighted points for each predictor (Burgess method). More often, it is a linear weighted total, weights being derived by multiple regression, although more sophisticated models have been used in a few studies (Gottfredson, 1987). Scores may be grouped into classes varying in risk level, or a probability of reoffending may be derived. For example, the Reconviction Prediction Score made available to the English Parole Board, and which builds on the earlier research of Mannheim and Wilkins (1955), is the sum of weighted scores on 16 variables, such as age on first conviction, offence for which imprisoned, and time in last job, the total being converted to a percentile probability of further conviction (Ward, 1987). Another approach is to use a decision tree. An example is the Assaultive Risk Screening Sheet developed by the Michigan Department of Corrections (Monahan, 1981). "Yes–No" choices to six variables (e.g. crime description fits robbery, sex assault or murder; first arrest before 15th birthday) yield a fivefold classification of risk of further arrest for a violent crime.

Variables utilised as predictors are most commonly personal history data. Pritchard (1979) summarised findings from 71 studies relating biographical data to recidivism, in which the most regularly discriminating items were type of crime, first arrest before age 18, prior convictions, stable employment, living arrangements, current income, and history of opiate use and alcohol abuse. This kind of information is used in many actuarial studies of recidivism, and also in attempts to predict institutional misconduct (Brennan, 1987b). However, the strength of any predictor–criterion relationship depends on sample and setting characteristics, and is likely to vary over time. Tables cannot therefore be assumed to generalise beyond local conditions. The Reconviction Prediction Score, for example, is limited to males serving a prison sentence of two years or more, and predicts risk of reconviction within two years. It has remained robust for this purpose on samples separated by almost a decade (Ward, 1987).

While the most usual criterion is a further offence, some attempts have been made to predict future violent offences. These have met with limited success, particularly because of the problem of low base rates. Wenk, Robison and Smith (1972) describe three attempts to predict violence among parolees in the California Youth Authority, all of which yielded high false positives. In one study, for example, 100 background variables, including prior violent history, psychiatric diagnoses, and psychological test scores were obtained for over 4000 prisoners. The base rate of violent reoffending during a 15-month follow-up was 2.5%, and the best statistical predictor would have identified 50% of the violent parolees, but with a false positive rate of almost 90%. The authors consider attempts to predict *reported* violence to be futile because of the unreliability of the criterion. Holland, Holt and Beckett (1982) reached a similar conclusion following their finding that violent recidivism was not predicted by prior violent record.

Attempts to predict future violence of psychiatric patients in the community encounter similar problems of high false positives (Cocozza and Steadman, 1974), even with base rates of 25% (Klassen and O'Connor, 1989). Recent studies have therefore focused on the prediction of assaultive behaviour in the short term, and within hospital environments. Convit et al. (1988) developed a prediction score derived from conviction for a violent crime, history of violent suicidal attempts, neurological abnormalities, and deviant family environment. While the predictor differentiated assaultive from nonassaultive patients, the optimal cutting score yielded false positive and false negative rates of about 60% and 20%, respectively. The authors summarise related studies producing comparable results. Palmstierna and Wistedt (1990) found that background variables commonly cited as predictors of violence were even less successful in predicting inpatient assaults, during either the first 8 or 28 days following admission. However, a limitation of these studies is the attempt to predict assaults within environments which aim to minimise violence by medication and social controls.

Reliance on static biographical data as predictors has been criticised for neglecting the effects on further antisocial behaviour of custody or treatment and the environment to which an offender returns (Sutherland and Cressey, 1970; Simon, 1971; Clarke, 1985). However, Bonta and Motiuk (1985) describe a standardised interview schedule, the Level of Supervision Inventory (LSI), which combines biographical data with nonstatic variables such as current employment, family problems, and attitudes to crime. The LSI predicts recidivism in probationers and also success in half-way houses. Personality variables have also been examined in some studies (Chapter 8). Diagnosis of psychopathy predicts recidivism (Ganzer and Sarason, 1973; Black and Spinks, 1985; Hare, McPherson and Forth, 1988), and psychomotor tests may have some utility (Roberts et al., 1974). However, research using questionnaires, such as the MMPI or CPI, has not produced consistent findings, and suggests at best a modest contribution to the prediction of future criminal behaviour. Gough, Wenk and Rozynko (1965) found that the best predictor of parole violation was a combination of a base expectancy table and CPI scales, notably *So*, but the base expectancy table was the best single predictor. The utility of *So* has generally been confirmed, but the standard MMPI clinical scales have been found to be poor predictors of recidivism (Mack, 1969; Gendreau et al., 1979). However, a theoretical rationale linking MMPI clinical scales to reoffending is lacking.

The ability of personality variables to predict violence in institutions or following release has also been investigated. Megargee (1970) reviewed validity studies of structured personality inventories and projective test measures of aggression. Positive associations were reported, but these were generally of a low order, and most studies were "postdictive" rather than predictive. However, a modest contribution of personality measures to prediction has been found in some subsequent studies. Structured rating scales can predict institutional misconduct (Davis, 1974b; Quay, 1984), and Panton (1979b) has developed scales from MMPI items to predict several aspects of prison behaviour. An adjustment to prison scale (*Ap*) had an overall accuracy of 74% in identifying those committing major rule infractions over a three year period, false positive and negative rates each being 25%. In this case, the base rate was 50%. A measure of escape proneness (*Ec*), however, had a higher false positive rate, and is unlikely to have much predictive power because of the low base rate of such behaviour.

Specific scales may have more utility when combined with other variables (Gearing, 1979). Heilbrun and Heilbrun (1985), for example, found that a combination of psychopathy (*Pd* minus *So*), low IQ, and social withdrawal predicted prison dangerousness, and when a current offence of violence was added, the combination also predicted assaultiveness during parole. In a 5-year follow-up of mentally disordered offenders discharged from an English special hospital, Black and Spinks (1985) also found that specific MMPI scales (the standard *F* and *Pd* scales, and scales of extraversion and impulsivity) correlated with both subsequent violence and recidivism generally, and added significantly to offence history in predicting post-release behaviour. Hall (1988) further reports that some MMPI scales contributed to the prediction of sex offender recidivism.

The limited use of predictive devices by criminal justice decision makers is in part a reflection of the mistrust of statistical prediction, despite consistent evidence that it outperforms clinical prediction (Meehl, 1954, 1986; Sawyer, 1966). However, it also reflects the relatively low power of actuarial indices in predicting future offending, and correlations with criterion measures rarely exceed 0.4 (Simon, 1971). Clarke (1985) suggests that prediction research assumed a dispositional origin of crime which it failed to confirm. However, the consistent finding that past criminal behaviour is the best predictor of future offending is a *prima facie* demonstration that criminality is a relatively stable disposition. As Simon (1971) notes, predictive devices are relatively effective at the extremes of the score distribution, as anticipated from a dispositional concept of criminality, but for the majority in the middle range, there are limits on predicting future behaviour from knowledge of past history. This is particularly the case when the criterion is unreliable.

Nevertheless, to the extent that prediction methods yield improvements over chance or over traditional clinical prediction, their use can be justified, and Glaser (1987) sees this as likely to increase. Improvements may result from better measurement of both predictors and criteria (Gottfredson, 1987). Selection of predictors, for example, needs to be guided by theory rather than "shotgun empiricism", while multiple measures of "success" may be more predictable than simple dichotomies of whether or not an offender is rearrested or reconvicted.

THE CLINICAL PREDICTION OF DANGEROUSNESS

The possibility that a person may harm others can lead to preventive confinement in the criminal justice or mental health systems. Points at which future dangerousness is considered include bail, sentencing, parole, the involuntary commitment or release of the mentally ill, the release of mentally disordered offenders, and even the carrying out of the death penalty (Shah, 1978; Hall, 1987). Legal decision makers frequently rely on the judgements of mental health professionals, but evidence accumulating during the 1970s suggested that their predictions of dangerousness were highly inaccurate (Ennis and Litwack, 1974; Monahan, 1981). While professional prediction in many areas is probably also not very accurate, inaccuracies in predicting violence have greater practical as well as moral and political implications (Monahan, 1981). Questions are raised, for example, about how much risk justifies detention, or how many false positives can be tolerated in protecting society. Evidence on predictive inaccuracy therefore resulted in calls from civil libertarians that the involvement of clinicians in legal decisions about preventive detention should cease, a view endorsed by many clinicians (Stone, 1984; Bowden, 1985).

Paradoxically, legalist concerns to restrict criteria for commitment of the mentally disordered to imminent dangerousness to self or others led to increased reliance on clinicians to identify the dangerous, and in the United States, this has extended to clinical practice more generally. For example, in 1976, the client of a psychologist in California killed Tatiana Tarasoff, for whom he had a pathological attachment, some two months after the therapist reported to the police that he was at risk of doing so. In *Tarasoff v Regents of the University of California*, the Supreme Court subsequently ruled that clinicians had a legal duty to warn third parties to whom their clients were a danger. This decision has had a significant impact on mental health practice, forcing clinicians to detain patients to avoid liability for any subsequent violence (Wettstein, 1984; Appelbaum, 1988). While many object that this police function compromises the role of professional helper, Monahan (1981, 1984) argues that balancing the interests of clients and the community is an inevitable component of many human service professions.

Dangerousness predictions therefore continue to be required, but the predictive ability of clinicians remains contentious. A major issue is the question of *what* is being predicted. "Danger" denotes the risk of harmful consequences, and "dangerousness" may be a property of acts, situations, or persons. In legal settings, it is the dangerousness of a person which is usually considered, but what is harmful depends on values. One problem in describing a person as "dangerous" is that, without specifying the nature of the dangerous acts to which the person is disposed, or the conditions under which the person will engage in those acts, the adjective is merely a vague judgement. Some writers circumvent this problem by focusing on "dangerous behaviour", and specifically violence (Megargee, 1976; Shah, 1978; Monahan, 1981). However, violence, dangerous behaviour, and dangerousness are distinct constructs (Mulvey and Lidz, 1984). Violent acts are usually considered dangerous, but not all dangerous acts are violent, for example drunken driving. Discussions of dangerousness nevertheless focus on violence.

Mulvey and Lidz (1984) suggest that the prediction of dangerousness is a twofold judgement in which both an act and a person's likelihood of committing such an act are evaluated. However, it is by no means clear that this is always the case in practice. "Dangerousness", like other dispositional concepts, implies an "if. . .then" probability, the "if" being the conditions under which the disposition will be realised as a dangerous act. The probability of these occurring is not the same as the probability that the person has such a disposition. It is, for example, one thing to identify a substance as "soluble in water", but quite another to predict the likelihood of its getting wet. While research in this area assumes that clinicians are forecasting an outcome, they may in practice be judging only the probability or strength of a person's tendencies (Gordon, 1977). The implications of this are considered below.

Outcome studies of predictions of dangerousness

The "first generation" of research on clinical predictions of dangerousness came from naturalistic studies of mentally disordered offenders released from institutions by court orders, contrary to psychiatric judgements that they were dangerous. In 1966, the United States Supreme Court held that Johnny Baxtrom had been wrongfully detained in a prison hospital for the criminally insane, and this resulted in the transfer of 969 patients to civil mental hospitals. A four-year follow-up of a quarter of the "Baxstrom patients" revealed that a half were still in civil hospitals, 27% had returned to the community, 14% were dead, 2.2% had been returned to maximum security, and 0.8% to prison (Steadman and Keveles, 1972). While 17% had been arrested at some time, only nine individuals had been convicted, mostly for nonviolent offences. In terms of predicted dangerousness, then, over 80% were false positives. Similar rulings leading to the release of smaller samples in Massachusetts (McGarry and Parker, 1974), and Pennsylvania (Thornberry and Jacoby, 1979), had comparable outcomes, only a small minority being subsequently convicted for serious crimes.

   Other studies compared offender patients released after receiving treatment with patients identified as dangerous, but nonetheless released by the court. Kozol, Boucher and Garofalo (1972) reported a five-year follow-up of sex offenders, of whom 386 were released as nondangerous following treatment, and 49 released against advice. Eight percent of the former and 35% of the latter committed further serious offences, suggesting that treatment had some effect in reducing dangerousness. Nevertheless, the 65% false positive rate for those judged dangerous suggests inaccuracies in the clinical predictions. More controversial have been findings from Patuxent in Maryland, which until 1977 was a prison hospital for "defective delinquents". Hodges (1971) reported that reconviction rates (any offence) at three-year follow-up were 37% for those completing treatment, and 71% for those partially treated and released against advice. However, the former figure excludes those recalled from parole without a further conviction being recorded. A later study by Steadman (1977) indicated that 31% of treated patients and 33% of partially treated but released patients were subsequently *arrested* for a violent crime, while for "defective delinquents" not receiving treatment the figure was 41%.

These data do not offer strong support for the validity of clinical predictions.

Also relevant are studies of pre-trial adjudications. Cocozza and Steadman (1978) describe a three-year follow-up of 257 patients incompetent to stand trial in New York State, of whom 154 were declared dangerous by psychiatrists, and 103 nondangerous. Although the two groups differed in terms of subsequent treatment, they were institutionalised for similar periods, and at follow-up, 14% of the former and 16% of the latter had been arrested for a violent crime. Low predictive accuracy was also found in a Canadian study by Sepejak, Webster and Menzies (1984). Mean correlations of pre-trial ratings of predicted dangerousness with ratings of dangerous behaviour during the next two years were 0.20 for psychiatrists, 0.17 for psychologists, and 0.12 for correctional officers, all of which were significant, while nonsignificant correlations of 0.08 and 0.03 were obtained for nurses and social workers, respectively. However individual correlations ranged from -0.48 to +0.47, indicating considerable variability in accuracy between individuals and across disciplines.

Monahan (1981) points to the consistent findings of overprediction of dangerousness by psychiatrists and psychologists, and concludes that they are accurate in no more than one of three predictions. However, these studies cannot be regarded as conclusive, for several reasons (Gordon, 1977; Blackburn, 1984; Litwack and Schlesinger, 1987). First, some of the samples may not be representative of detained mentally disordered offenders. The Baxstrom patients, for example, had a mean age of 47, and those who reoffended were significantly younger. It must also be questioned whether patients judged dangerous but released by the court (Kozol et al., 1972) are typical, since the courts usually accept psychiatric judgements, as Cocozza and Steadman (1978) observed. Second, the reliability of predictors is unclear. In the Baxstrom-type studies, it was not certain that all patients were predicted to be dangerous at the time of release. It is, for example, common for many patients in security hospitals to be detained after staff pronounce them "safe" because of problems of finding alternative accommodation.

A third issue is the reliability of the criteria. Reliance on official arrest or reconviction data may underestimate actual violence, and many false positives may be undetected true positives. Hall (1987), for example, notes that arrest rates for violence reflect only one in five actual occurrences, and in a self-report study, he found that only two of 94 incidents of arrestable violence revealed by a group of soldiers were known to the police. Moreover, it is questionable whether the occurrence of a further violent crime is a valid test of a clinical prediction of dangerousness. As Gordon (1977) notes, several studies assume that clinicians fail to distinguish "innocent" people from the truly dangerous. However, if clinicians are simply identifying a dangerous disposition, rather than predicting a specific outcome, the false positives may be correctly identified as dangerous. The fact that this disposition does not eventuate in a violent act may reflect chance factors. Monahan (1981) objects that "this makes the accuracy of prediction impossible to test". However, this reflects the positivist assumption that all events are predictable. From a critical realist perspective, the conditions which permit the realisation of a person's tendencies cannot be reliably predicted in an open system. If clinicians are predicting the strength of a disposition, the appropriate test is an aggregated multiple act criterion (Wiggins, 1981), not a single act of violence. Even then, it is probably unrealistic to expect validities higher than 0.3 to 0.5 (Gordon, 1977).

A further issue is the generalisability of these findings to other settings in which dangerousness predictions are made. What is tested in these studies is apparently prediction from one environment to future community settings, but this involves large temporal and situational gaps. Monahan (1981, 1984) suggests that prediction may prove more accurate in short-term or emergency situations. This "second generation" approach argues more cautiously that we know little about dangerousness predictions, and that they may be improved (Hall, 1987; Litwack and Schlesinger, 1987). More recent studies have therefore focused on prediction within particular settings and over shorter time periods.

Werner, Rose and Yesavage (1983) presented 15 psychiatrists and 15 psychologists with staff ratings on the Brief Psychiatric Rating Scale (BPRS) for 40 patients, together with information on pre-admission violence, and examined the relation of these to predicted and actual violence over the first seven days following admission to an acute psychiatric unit. Only modest reliabilities were found for either group, although pooled ratings for the whole group had a reliability of 0.88. Nevertheless, the accuracy of prediction was uniformly low for individuals and for the composite predictor. Average validity in terms of correlation of predicted with actual violence was 0.12, and only two judges produced better than chance correlations. Cooper and Werner (1990) similarly found that when predicting violence in prison over a six month period from pre-admission criminal and demographic data, only one of 21 psychologists and case managers predicted above chance level. Short-term studies of emergency civil commitment also suggest that predictions are of low accuracy, and yield high false positive rates (Wettstein, 1984). In contrast, McNeil and Binder (1987) claim predictive validity of clinical judgements of dangerousness in short-term commitments. They found that 72% of patients involuntarily committed as dangerous to others exhibited at least one assault-related behaviour (physical assault, seclusion, use of restraint, verbal threats or abuse) during the first 72 hours following admission, compared with 30% of involuntary patients committed for other reasons. However, the difference is due mainly to verbal aggression. Also, in studies of this kind, inhibitory effects of the environment on patient behaviour make it difficult to determine predictive accuracy.

The appropriate conclusion, then, seems to be that predictive accuracy remains to be demonstrated, even in the short term, but the available research cannot be regarded as definitive because of methodological shortcomings. Monahan (1988) argues that the research remains clouded by reliance on impoverished predictor variables, weak criteria, constricted validation samples, and unsynchronised research efforts. It is also likely that ethical constraints may preclude definitive studies being carried out, since those predicted to be violent are usually subject to interventions which prevent the testing out of the prediction. It therefore remains possible that predictions are valid under some conditions (Litwack and Schlesinger, 1987).

The process of clinical prediction

In judging the dangerousness of an offender, the clinician must consider a broad array of factors related to the person, the situation, and their interaction (Megargee, 1976; Mulvey and Lidz, 1984), and seeks out information based on prior experience of similar cases, clinical lore, and knowledge of the literature. This will clearly be a selective process. Where the outcome research addresses questions of the validity of prediction, other studies have examined factors in the process of prediction which may attenuate validity, such as low reliability or attention to inappropriate cues.

Evidence on reliability was obtained by Quinsey and Abtman (1979), who presented vignettes of offenders to four forensic psychiatrists and nine schoolteachers, and obtained ratings on several predictive scales. Inter-rater agreement on the likelihood of an assaultive offence was generally low, though higher for teachers (0.24 to 0.57) than for psychiatrists (0.19 to 0.48). Multiple regression analyses indicated that both groups combined data in similar ways, suggesting that there was nothing distinctive about the judgement of psychiatrists. Motandon and Harding (1984) similarly found that psychiatrists exhibited no higher agreement in rating dangerousness than did other professionals or lay people.

Several studies have attempted to determine what information is considered in predicting dangerousness, and a few factors seem to be attended to regularly (Mulvey and Lidz, 1984). Menzies, Webster and Butler (1981), for example, found that forensic psychiatrists reported considering current offence, cues during the interview, criminal record, childhood pathology, and social and family circumstances. Studies of dangerousness decisions generally confirm that offence related behaviour, particularly prior violence, is strongly weighted in predictions of dangerousness (Quinsey and Abtman, 1979; Werner, Rose and Yesavage, 1983; Cooper and Werner, 1990). However, previous violence is not a consistent predictor of future violent offending (Wenk et al., 1972; Holland et al., 1982).

Attention to distal factors such as childhood pathology is also questionable. Much attention has been paid to childhood history of enuresis, firesetting, and cruelty to animals since Hellman and Blackman (1966) found that 74% of delinquents with a conviction for violence displayed this "triad", compared with 28% of nonviolent delinquents. However, several subsequent studies have failed to find that the complete triad distinguishes violent offenders (Justice, Justice and Kraft, 1974), although cruelty to animals in childhood may itself be of some predictive significance (Felthous and Kellert, 1987). Threatened violence also seems to be an unreliable cue. In a six-year follow-up of 77 patients who had made threats to kill, MacDonald (1967) found that only three had committed homicide, although a further four had committed suicide. Werner et al. (1983) also found that although most acute inpatients who were assaultive also made threatening statements, the majority of those making threats were not actually violent.

Some studies have used Brunswik's cue-utilisation or lens model, which compares the way in which people use cues in prediction and how these relate to actual outcome. The general finding is that clinicians weight cues which are empirically unrelated to actual violence (Werner, Rose and Yesavage, 1983; Quinsey and Maguire, 1986; Cooper and Werner, 1990). Quinsey and Maguire (1986), for example, found that dangerousness ratings by psychiatrists and psychologists were strongly influenced by institutional assaultiveness, but this was unrelated to serious reoffending in discharged patients. Clinicians also emphasised prior homicide, but this correlated with a nondangerous outcome. The latter was also found by Black and Spinks (1985).

The problem in prediction remains not so much how to weight variables, but rather which variables to include for consideration (Faust, 1986). There is some evidence that biases in the selection of cues by clinicians may arise from personal characteristics such as cultural background and values (Ennis and Litwack, 1974) or training and education (Williams and Miller, 1977). Accuracy in judging dangerousness is also likely to be attenuated by the cognitive biases inherent in human decision-making, such as simplifying heuristics which ignore basic rules of probability (Tversky and Kahneman, 1974). More than a dozen biasing phenomena have now been identified, which include ignoring base rates, reliance on illusory correlations, and seeking out confirmatory rather than disconfirmatory evidence (Faust, 1986). Hall (1987) points to twelve common errors made by forensic mental health professionals in predictions of dangerousness: (1) failure to perceive the relevance of dangerousness prediction as a specific focus of inquiry; (2) lack of an adequate forensic data base; (3) failure to account for retrospective and current distortion by the predictee; (4) predicting dangerousness in the absence of previous dangerousness; (5) falling prey to illusory correlations; (6) predicting from clinical diagnosis; (7) failure to take account of triggering stimuli; (8) failure to consider opportunity variables; (9) failure to take into account inhibitory variables such as age or education; (10) ignoring relevant base rates; (11) use of limited outcome measures; (12) failure to offer circumscribed conclusions. Hall offers a decision tree to ensure attention to these factors.

Can dangerousness predictions be improved?

While understanding of clinical decision making remains limited, enough is known to indicate that it is highly fallible, and can be improved. Reliability, for example, can be increased by averaging over judges (Werner, Rose and Yesavage, 1983). This is equivalent to enhancing test reliability by increasing the number of items, and argues for collaborative decision making. The base rate problem may be overcome by focusing on homogeneous groups defined by particular kinds of dangerous behaviour with relatively high base rates (Quinsey and Maguire, 1986), and by using criteria broader than official criminal records. Cognitive biases may also be reduced by training (Faust, 1986; Kleinmuntz, 1990).

Faust (1986) suggests that psychologists must learn not to rely on intuitive judgements. The superiority of actuarial over clinical prediction has been consistently demonstrated, and continues to be found in studies of recidivism

(Hall, 1988). However, while research using the lens model paradigm suggests that empirical predictors may be found which outperform clinicians, actuarial prediction of violent reoffending has not so far been very impressive. Clinicians have proved resistant to the notion of statistical predictors, and a shift to the use of actuarial methods is unlikely for several reasons, not the least being that in many settings they are not available (Wiggins, 1981; Kleinmuntz, 1990). However, the use of decision aids which make the process of decision making more explicit is a step in this direction (Kroll and MacKenzie, 1983; Hall, 1987). As Sawyer (1966) demonstrated, the most effective combination of actuarial and clinical methods is not the incorporation of statistical data into clinical judgements, but rather the objective reporting of clinical judgements which can be used statistically.

These proposals would improve the reliability of clinical predictions, but it is arguable whether they would lead to more than modest increases in predictive validity. Monahan (1981) suggested that one of the errors of clinicians is to focus on dispositional variables, and that attention to situational variables would improve prediction. However, while situations are necessary to the explanation of violence, they are not predictable in advance. This is not to say that general environmental characteristics, such as peer group influence or stressors, are irrelevant to violent behaviour, but the coming together of conditions which give rise to a violent event may be fortuitous to the point of randomness (Gordon, 1977; Holland et al., 1982).

The problems of predicting dangerousness probably lie less in the elusiveness of the concept of dangerousness than in the unrealistic faith of positivism in the ability of science to predict specific events in the open world. Pollock, McBain and Webster (1989) suggest that rather than continue to search for empirical predictors of violence, it is more appropriate to focus on theoretically based decision making procedures for arriving at defensible clinical decisions about dangerousness. This is in agreement with the conclusion of Mulvey and Lidz (1984) that the best that can be hoped for is an informed judgement.

Chapter 13

Psychological Interventions with Offenders

INTRODUCTION

It is generally taken for granted that crime is undesirable and that society must take active steps to control and prevent it, but how this is to be achieved depends on assumptions about the causes of crime. Many criminologists argue that only changes in social structures will have a meaningful impact, since the roots of crime lie in social inequities and the disproportionate power of controlling groups to define crime. In these terms, interventions with individuals or families merely tinker with the problem, and blame the victim. However, as previous chapters have shown, there is no single cause of crime, and offenders are not homogeneous. Many exhibit personal problems or deficits which may be amenable to psychological help, even though the distal causes of these often lie in adverse socioeconomic conditions. Overcoming these problems may therefore be the best strategy for rehabilitating the individual and preventing further offending.

Nevertheless, preventing recidivism among apprehended offenders will clearly not prevent the crimes of first offenders or those not apprehended, and psychological concern with the individual offender can be criticised as parochial and as neglecting the wider issues of crime control. However, the crime prevention problem has parallels in the notions of primary, secondary, and tertiary prevention which have guided community mental health. Primary prevention aims to prevent the onset of disorder by promoting positive barriers to its development, while secondary prevention is intervention at an early stage, and aims to prevent a developing disorder from becoming severe or chronic. Tertiary prevention is concerned with ameliorating disability and preventing its recurrence, and represents the traditional focus on treatment and rehabilitation. While there are limitations to this analogy in the case of crime, psychological interventions have been directed at each of these levels. Primary and secondary prevention is discussed in Chapter 15, but this chapter examines the tertiary level of individual intervention, at which most psychological efforts have been directed.

Rehabilitation in the penal system has been criticised for the past two decades on the grounds that "nothing works" in preventing offending. This argument is examined in Chapter 15. However, it has also been suggested from an economic perspective that rehabilitation cannot affect the crime rate, since it is not directed to unapprehended offenders, and market forces will replace those who drop out of crime (Ehrlich, 1981; Van den Haag, 1982; Wilkins, 1985). This view lacks an empirical basis, and since a small number of offenders is responsible for a majority of crimes, it is equally plausible that rehabilitation of a proportion of high risk offenders could have a significant impact on the overall crime rate (Andrews, 1983). The case for rehabilitating individual offenders, however, does not rest simply on solving the crime problem. Whether or not it is construed as individual salvation, or "fundamentalist criminology" (Wilkins, 1985), the justification for offender rehabilitation is as much humanitarian as utilitarian. The goal in this respect is to *enable* the individual to avoid crime by increasing his personal effectiveness. Van den Haag (1982) dismisses this moral aim of rehabilitation as irrelevant to what he sees as the main goals of sentencing, which are justice and deterrence, but offers no argument to justify the moral superiority of "just deserts" over that of "saving souls".

Rehabilitation and psychological intervention

Psychological "treatment" is an ambiguous term, since psychological therapies aim to go beyond treatment in the medical sense by providing personal growth or coping skills rather than simply eliminating symptoms. Rehabilitation is an even more ambiguous concept, and debates about the utility of offender rehabilitation are clouded by the lack of an agreed definition. In clinical contexts, rehabilitation means restoring, or compensating for, impaired functions to facilitate the social reintegration of a disabled person. Most mental health professionals probably view offender rehabilitation in similar terms, the only difference being that reintegration includes the avoidance of further crime. Services are therefore directed to individual need, and the service provider is as much the agent of the offender as of society.

A narrower interpretation is that the primary goal is to prevent reoffending. Palmer (1983), for example, suggests that the "ultimate" goal is the protection of society, and that offender centred goals are simply a means to this end. However, the goal of special deterrence is also to prevent reoffending, the means being intimidation. As Halleck (1987) notes, this goal can also be accomplished by psychosurgery, drug administration, electronic "tagging", or the cutting off of an offender's hands. While Palmer (1983) distinguishes between "positive" and "drastic" rehabilitation methods, he acknowledges that this is arbitrary. The Panel on Research in Rehabilitative Techniques (Sechrest, White and Brown, 1979; Martin, Sechrest and Redner, 1981) also encountered this problem. They defined rehabilitation as "the result of any planned intervention that reduces an offender's further criminal activity, whether that reduction is mediated by personality, behaviour, abilities, attitudes, values or other factors". Since "planned intervention" is broader than individual services, the exclusion of special deterrence is difficult to sustain.

Wilson (1980) argues that the distinction between rehabilitation and special deterrence is scientifically indefensible, and should be abandoned. This assumes a value-free science, but what is done to offenders is not immune to moral criteria of what is humane. The rehabilitation "ideal" is not, in fact, based on what is "nice", as Wilson suggests, but rather on a commitment to individual welfare rather than simply social utility. While some interventions may serve both purposes, and there are inevitable conflicts in attempting to be the agent of both offender and society, the distinction between interventions which are enabling and those which are merely restrictive seems nevertheless worth retaining. The unemployed, socially isolated, alcoholic ex-offender who refrains from further crime, for example, may well be described as deterred. He can scarcely be said to be rehabilitated. The distinction implies that recidivism is a necessary but not sufficient criterion for the effectiveness of a rehabilitation programme. It also implies that the outcome of many criminal justice interventions, such as cautioning or suspended sentences, is not directly relevant to the question of whether the provision of rehabilitative services "works".

This is not to suggest that the interest of behavioural science is limited to rehabilitative interventions, since interventions with deterrent aims also make psychological assumptions, although they are often inspired by political motives. An example in Britain is the introduction in 1979 of regimes at detention centres emphasising discipline, drill and parades, which were intended to be "a short, sharp shock" for young offenders (Thornton et al., 1984). In the United States, juvenile awareness programmes have had a similar aim. These briefly expose delinquents to the negative aspects of imprisonment through visits to prisons and confrontational sessions with inmates, the assumption being that the delinquents will be "scared straight" (Lewis, 1983). The theoretical rationale for such procedures is weak, since they emphasise the severity rather than the certainty of punishment, and they have not fared well from evaluations (Gendreau and Ross, 1987). The short, sharp shock regimes were not actually experienced as aversive by inmates, and had no impact on recidivism (Thornton et al., 1984), while Lewis (1983) found that high risk delinquents in one "scared straight" programme tended to get worse.

Other interventions which are not obviously psychological also make psychological assumptions. For example, outward bound, or wilderness programmes, which are popular in North America, expose delinquent youths to tough outdoor conditions for up to three months. These can be seen in terms of deterrence, but they may also improve sense of mastery over the external environment (Garrett, 1985). Another example is restitution through victim recompense schemes or symbolic recompense through community service orders. The latter have been available in England since 1972, though have not been widely used. Restitution is a component of "overcorrection" in behaviour modification, but in criminal justice terms it is justified in terms of economy, as well as from retributive and deterrent perspectives. It can also be seen in terms of reform. While the outcomes of such preventive methods are of psychological interest, this chapter focuses on therapeutic methods aiming to prevent reoffending which utilise some form of psychological change procedure.

PSYCHOLOGICAL SERVICES TO OFFENDERS

Psychologists provide a variety of services to the criminal justice system. Some of these involve advising the courts and law enforcement agencies (Chapter 12), but a central function has been to assist the penal system in its management of convicted offenders. In the United States, psychologists were employed in diagnostic and reception centres set up after the First World War, and correctional psychology is now an established specialty with its own professional standards (American Association of Correctional Psychologists, 1980). England and Wales (though not Scotland or Northern Ireland) have also had their own prison psychological service since 1946. However, only a minority of offenders is imprisoned, and the kinds of service provided by psychologists for offenders vary according to their work setting and the legal procedures through which they receive their clients. Some offenders on probation may receive clinical psychological services in the community, and such services are also available to mentally disordered offenders diverted to the health care system. Juvenile offenders in the care of social services may also be referred to educational psychologists or child clinical psychologists.

In practice, psychological services available to those coming before the courts has always been limited, and given the large numbers processed by the criminal justice system, the selection of those who receive attention often depends on chance factors. Services tend to be concentrated in institutions such as prisons, young offender establishments, and psychiatric security hospitals. Roles and functions vary with the employing agency, but the traditional emphasis has been on mental health services; and in the United States psychologists who practice therapy with offenders are usually required to obtain licensure as clinical psychologists. However, not all psychologists working with offenders are clinicians. There were some 200 psychologists working regularly with offenders in Britain in 1991, about half of them being clinical psychologists employed in maximum security hospitals or regional forensic psychiatric services, the rest being employed in the English prison psychological service. While the latter contribute significantly to the rehabilitation of offenders, their number is small relative to the prison population, and their overall functions tend to be organisational as much as clinical.

The traditional functions of psychologists in the penal system are assessment, treatment and rehabilitation, and research (Nietzel and Moss, 1972; Brodsky, 1980; Milan and Evans, 1987). These parallel the functions of clinical psychologists, and psychologists in security hospitals have similar functions. The general mission of psychologists in prisons is to provide services which evaluate, prevent, and treat inmate problems, and contribute to a safe and humane environment (Milan and Evans, 1987). Mental health problems in this context, however, must be seen in broader terms than those of psychiatric disability, and include cognitive, interpersonal, and coping skills deficits relevant not only to offending behaviour, but also to the inmate's adjustment to imprisonment.

Assessment

Assessment is the process of gathering information necessary for making informed decisions about a client, and involves the testing of hypotheses leading to the formation of a model of the client's problems. Psychological assessment is usually distinguished by its reliance on objective methods of data collection and hypothesis testing in the form of tests, ratings, or structured observations. In a penal context, assessment is undertaken primarily for purposes of classification and treatment planning or evaluations for parole, and there is now a wide range of procedures of specific relevance to offenders (Brodsky and Smitherman, 1983; see also Chapter 3). The more distinctive features of assessment in this context are a focus on particular problems, such as antisocial beliefs, sexual deviation, or level of risk, but in general, assessment of offenders draws on the range of procedures used in mental health settings.

An early function of prison psychologists was to contribute to classification and allocation of new inmates through routine psychometric assessment with standardised tests of intelligence, attainment, personality, and psychopathology. This role is now rejected on the grounds that such assessments have little practical impact on the allocation process (McEwan and McGurk, 1981; McMurran and Shapland, 1989). However, the limited utility of assessment has often reflected the uncritical use of tests selected for their availability rather than their relevance to the problems of inmates, and the tendency to treat and report testing as an end in itself rather than as a means to understanding or a functional analysis. Psychometric principles of reliability and validity remain the foundations of applied psychology, and in the absence of sound assessment skills and procedures for identifying problems and evaluating outcomes of interventions, psychologists risk losing their claims to professional uniqueness.

Competent assessment is also an integral part of psychological treatment, and assessment continues to be needed for two purposes. The first is the identification of inmates who require services. The American Association of Correctional Psychologists (1980) recommends brief screening of all inmates with sentences of more than a year, covering prior history and emotional and intellectual abnormalities. These should be followed up with more intensive evaluations when indicated, provided they serve a useful therapeutic or dispositional function.

A second purpose is for classification relevant to rehabilitation through matching or differential treatment (Chapter 15). Existing classifications are criticised by Sechrest (1987) on the grounds that none has yet established its utility for treatment decisions. Others, however, take a more favourable view (Andrews, 1983; Andrews, Bonta and Hoge, 1990). Andrews notes that measures of attitudes, values, and beliefs supportive of crime have a firm basis as appropriate intermediate targets, and that these need to be monitored in assessing outcomes. He also argues that treatment planning requires assessment of individual characteristics which influence response to treatment, such as interpersonal maturity level (Chapter 3), cognitive skills, psychopathy, and motivation for change (Andrews et al., 1990).

Treatment of offenders

Treatment is a longstanding function of correctional psychologists (Corsini and Miller, 1954), although interventions in prison remain sparse because of limited numbers of trained personnel. Treatment services are desirable to alleviate psychological distress in offenders, whether or not it is causally related to their crimes, but such services have most frequently been developed with rehabilitative goals. It is therefore important to distinguish clinical targets, which are incidental to offending, from factors which mediate criminal behaviour. The latter are emphasised here. Interventions vary with the orientation of the psychologist, which may be behavioural, psychodynamic, or cognitive, but cognitive–behavioural approaches have dominated recent developments. These are examined later in this chapter.

Psychological treatment of offenders is more analogous to remedial education than to medical treatment, and the most realistic goal is to enable the offender to manage his problems without reoffending. The appropriate targets of intervention are therefore values which provide the "ties to crime" (Andrews, 1983), emotional problems, skills deficits, and inappropriate social behaviour which is functionally related to offending. Although psychological clinics for specific categories of offender—such as drunk drivers, minor sex offenders, or shoplifters—are now common in north America, offending behaviour is only indirectly the target of psychological treatment. Such behaviour is of low frequency and not usually directly observable, and it is the *disposition* to repeat criminal acts which is the target of change. For example, intervention with a murderer is concerned less with the prior act of killing than with the personal and social factors which may support future violence. It is these mediating variables which need to be identified and targeted.

The history of psychological treatment of offenders parallels that of the psychotherapies more generally, the early dominance of psychodynamic approaches having been replaced by a diversification of methods since the 1960s. At least 400 therapeutic techniques have been identified (Kazdin, 1986), many of which are based on home-spun theories of disorder lacking any grounding in coherent scientific propositions (leading Parloff (1984) to describe California as host to the "Silicon Valley" of technology and the "Silly Con Valley" of psychotherapy!). The problem is compounded in offender rehabilitation, where therapeutic methods have typically been transferred from mental health practice with scant regard for their theoretical connection with the problems of criminals or their relation to theories of criminal behaviour.

Developing roles

Whether or not rehabilitation is a primary goal of psychological services, it is not the only one. Prisons as social organisations impose unusual demands on those who reside and work in them, and many prison psychologists see their contribution more in terms of applying social and organisational psychology to improving the living environment than in providing direct services to inmates. Limited staff resources also inevitably limit the impact of interventions at the individual level, and Milan and Evans (1987) suggest that the mental health role has been overemphasised by both managers and psychologists. Drawing on the community mental health model, they argue for a greater emphasis on the secondary and primary levels of prevention. This entails a focus on consultancy, training, and programme design and evaluation. These roles enable the psychologist to be a wider resource to the organisation and both its staff and inmates.

McMurran and Shapland (1989) describe the development of these roles in the English prison system. Consultancy services are provided to managers in the form of information about the characteristics of the prison population, advice on problems of inmates in general, and strategies for dealing with particular problem groups, such as suicide risks or those rejected by their peers. These services also include guidance on crisis management, such as negotiation in hostage-taking situations. Staff training programmes range from instruction in basic interaction processes to the provision of skills in counselling for drug and alcohol problems or in behavioural skills training methods. Staff support, for example through stress management groups, is also provided. Programme design and development includes not only novel psychological interventions, but also institution-wide recreational, vocational, and educational activities. Finally, programme evaluation emphasises the research role, and may be directed to in-house individual and group programmes as well as to longer-term outcome studies with policy implications (e.g. Thornton et al., 1984).

PSYCHODYNAMIC AND HUMANISTIC INTERVENTIONS

Individual and group therapy

Psychoanalytic theories see antisocial behaviour in terms of either neurotic conflicts or failure of superego development (Chapter 5), but classical psychoanalysis as a treatment method focuses on the former, the crucial elements being the probing of the past, transference, interpretation by the therapist, and the working through of conflicts to achieve insight or self-knowledge. The classical form is rare in penal settings, but psychodynamically oriented methods have been used in both individual and group form with offenders, often under the vague heading of "counselling". This may denote a more superficial discussion of personal problems under the supervision of relatively untrained staff. Casework employed by probation officers or social workers is similarly often a mild form of psychodynamic therapy involving reflective discussion and emotional support. However, counselling psychology has developed as a distinct specialty, often guided by humanistic rather than psychodynamic principles, and focusing on the problems of relatively nondeviant people, particularly academic and job issues. Given this variety of meanings, and the fact that reports in the literature typically fail to specify the goals and content of "group therapy", the dismissal of psychodynamic therapy with offenders on the basis of failures of "counselling" (e.g. Feldman, 1977; Rutter and Giller, 1983) seems premature closure.

Nevertheless, evidence supporting its utility with offenders is sparse. The literature is replete with case studies and anecdotal prescriptions for dealing with patient resistance or counter-transference reactions, but evaluations of outcome are few. In a review of reports of group psychotherapy and counselling over a 25-year period, Slaikeu (1973) found only 23 which attempted evaluation, of which only two reported post-institutional adjustment, and few met sufficient criteria of methodological adequacy to permit definitive conclusions. Frequently cited as evidence of the failure of counselling with offenders is a study by Kassebaum, Ward and Wilner (1971) in which inmates in a California prison were randomly assigned to voluntary or mandatory group counselling or to control groups, and followed up for three years. No significant differences were found in parole outcome. However, Quay (1977c) argues that programme *integrity* must be considered in addition to adequacy of design and outcome. He suggests that the program described by Kassebaum et al. (1971) was based on a vague concept of counselling, and was inadequately implemented by personnel who were largely untrained and disinterested.

A few successful outcomes have been reported. Persons (1967) matched boys in a reformatory on demographic and criminal history variables, and assigned pair members randomly to an intensive programme of group and individual therapy (80 hours over 20 weeks) or an untreated control group. Group therapy was "eclectic", focusing on the development of a warm but firm relationship with the therapist, interpretation, role play, positive reinforcement for appropriate behaviour, and induction of anxiety about antisocial behaviour. Of 41 pairs, 30 of the treated and 12 controls showed reduced pathology on psychological tests, and at one-year follow-up, 13 treated and 25 control boys had been re-institutionalised. Treated boys also had significantly fewer parole violations, and more were in employment. Some success with more specifically psychoanalytic group therapy is also reported by Jew, Clanon and Mattocks (1972). Patients in a prison hospital who had at least one year of therapy focusing on insight into their antisocial behaviour were matched with untreated controls on a base expectancy table, race, and offence characteristics, and followed-up for four years. Significantly more of the treated group remained on parole after the first year, but differences diminished thereafter. This is a common finding in long-term follow-ups. However, a problem with this evaluation is that controls do not appear to have been deemed in need of treatment.

Evidence for the effects of casework with offenders has not generally been favourable, but a study in two English prisons suggests that it can influence reoffending (Sinclair, Shaw and Troop, 1974). Prisoners nearing discharge were randomly allocated to regular (monthly) sessions with a prison welfare officer or to a control group having the more usual infrequent contact. Over a follow-up of up to two years, more of the control group had been reconvicted (69% vs 48%). There was some evidence that the effect was mediated by a more personal relationship with welfare officers, although introverted prisoners benefited most.

Counselling or casework in the community does not appear to have much long-term impact on delinquency. This has been investigated particularly in relation to prevention studies, including the Cambridge–Somerville study, which is discussed in Chapter 15. However, a successful community intervention is described by Shore and Massimo (1979). Twenty boys with a history of antisocial behaviour who had dropped out of school or been suspended were randomly allocated to a treatment group or a no-treatment control. Treatment was described as a comprehensive psychotherapeutic approach combining remedial education and intensive individual therapy oriented around job placement over a 10-month period. The experimental group showed greater gains in academic achievement, improvements in self-image and control of aggression on psychological tests, more stable subsequent work history; and at 15-year follow-up only three of them, compared with nine controls, had ever been arrested. Whether success reflected the "in depth" psychotherapy or improved skills is unclear.

Some psychotherapists consider group therapy to be the treatment of choice for psychologically disturbed offenders, and it is usually a component of therapeutic communities. These are discussed in the next chapter.

Humanistic approaches

Although not always readily distinguished, some "counselling" programmes with offenders draw on humanistic principles. These also focus on self awareness through a therapeutic relationship, but the emphasis is on the present and on personal growth through the exercise of choice and personal responsibility. While this is exemplified by Rogers' client-centred therapy, a similar approach is employed by some "newer" therapies, such as reality therapy and transactional analysis, which have achieved some popularity in American correctional settings.

Reality therapy aims to develop realistic and responsible ways of fulfilling one's needs under the guidance of a warm, directive therapist who encourages plans for behaviour change (Glasser, 1975). Glasser describes its use with delinquent girls, and this approach has also been used to achieve employment planning and placement for offenders leaving prison (Bennight, 1975). However, neither of these reports describes longer-term effects.

A more interpersonally oriented approach used in several American prisons is transactional analysis (Nicholson, 1970). This usually relies on a group context in which deviant transactions are examined with the aim of moving to more healthy interactions adopting an "I'm OK–you're OK" posture. Delinquents are assumed to operate at immature levels of development, avoiding real issues by relying on social "games", group exposure of these being expected to promote personal growth and independence. While few studies have evaluated its effectiveness, Jesness (1975) carried out a comparative analysis of the effects on adolescent offenders of residence in one of two experimental institutions in California, Close and Holton. Close offered transactional analysis, treatment consisting of regular group meetings and individualised contracts related to socially desirable goals, while treatment at Holton centred on a token economy, in which points were earned for convenience behaviours (i.e. institutional requirements), academic performance, and correction of critical behaviour deficits. Close tended to produce greater changes in attitude and affect, Holton in overt behaviour, and at one-year follow-up youths from both programmes had similar rates of parole violation (33%). These were significantly lower by some 10% than those of two conventional institutions. Positive regard by inmates for counsellors accounted for a significant part of the outcome variance in both programmes.

Therapist characteristics are critical in Carkhuff's Human Resources Development (HRD) model (Holder, 1978). It is assumed that some of the variance in therapy outcome is accounted for by attributes such as empathy, positive regard, and genuineness, and that those having such attributes will more effectively teach the living, learning, and work skills likely to be deficient in delinquents. The HRD model involves selection of highly functioning counsellors, who are taught relationship, problem-solving, programme development, career development, and teaching skills. These provide the basis for systematic programmes of training offenders through the use of modelling, reinforcement and practice. The model has been used in several American state and federal institutions, as well as diversion schemes, and Holder (1978) summarises follow-ups indicating an average recidivism of 10%, compared with a two-year base rate for discharged offenders of 50%. The emphasis on skills training links this approach to behavioural and cognitive interventions with offenders.

APPLIED BEHAVIOUR ANALYSIS

While prominent in theories of criminality, classical conditioning or two process models have had more application to asocial than to antisocial behaviour, and have a place mainly in the treatment of sex offender problems, which is discussed later. Until a decade ago, applied behaviour analysis was the dominant behavioural approach to offenders (Burchard and Lane, 1982). Although often called "social learning" because of the incorporation of modelling and cognitive "events" (e.g. Stumphauzer, 1986), this approach assumes that behaviour is controlled by its environmental antecedents and consequences, and it should not be confused with the Bandura's social cognitive theory, which emphasises reciprocal determinism (Chapter 4). Methods centre on the rearrangement of environmental contingencies relevant to particular responses or response classes. Aversive consequences in the form of negative reinforcement, punishment, time out, and response cost, are often built into planned interventions, but have been used in isolation only infrequently. More commonly they are an adjunct to positive reinforcers, such as approval, money, or desired activities, or token reinforcers which provide access to such activities. Skills training by means of modelling, role-play, and feedback has also been widely used. The emphasis is on increasing the frequency of socially desirable behaviours, such as academic performance, job related skills, or appropriate social interaction, on the assumption that these are incompatible with antisocial behaviours. While in practice interventions may often be directed to individual offenders, most reports concern the consequation of behaviours of all individuals in a class room, work, or living unit, for example in token economy systems, or reciprocal consequation through contingency contracts between delinquent child and parent, or probationer and probation officer.

Institutional programmes

Contingency management methods in institutions most commonly take the form of token economies. These have been shown to have direct, short-term effects on the behaviours targeted, usually self-care, institutional maintenance tasks, rule compliance, and educational and work-related behaviour (Johnson, 1977; Nietzel, 1979; Burchard and Lane, 1982; Milan, 1987). For example, in a study with young delinquents, Hobbs and Holt (1976) recorded the effects of introducing a token economy across three institution cottages, a fourth serving as control. Tokens were contingent on rule compliance, completing chores, social interaction, and line behaviour, backup reinforcers being soft drinks, sweets, cigarettes (sic), recreation, passes home, and final release. A multiple base-line design demonstrated that introduction of the token economy to each cottage was reliably followed by an increased mean percentage in targeted behaviours. Other studies show the efficacy of token reinforcement in controlling behaviours of adult prisoners (Ayllon and Milan, 1979) and forensic psychiatric patients (Boren and Colman, 1970). However, Ross and Mackay (1976) reported deterioration in the behaviour of delinquent girls following the introduction of a token economy. Such reports are rare, although there are several accounts of the problems encountered in setting up institutional token economies as a result of lack of support from administrators, or failure of programme directors to have adequate control over staffing and other resources (Laws, 1974).

A large number of token economies was set up in correctional institutions in the 1960s and 1970s, although their use with offenders in Britain has been limited (Yule and Brown, 1987). Reid (1982) describes the development of Glenthorne Youth Treatment Centre, a secure institution for youths considered too disturbed or dangerous for community placement. At entry, youths were exposed to a points economy, but individualised targets and the development of social and self management skills were increasingly emphasised as they progressed from greater to lesser security and contact with the outside world. A similar programme for disturbed delinquents is described by Hoghughi (1979).

However, only a few programmes have been evaluated in terms of the maintenance and generalisation of positive changes following release. Evidence for longer-term effects of token economies on recidivism is weak, and considered negative by most reviewers. However, the evidence suggests that offenders exposed to such programmes return to crime less quickly. A comparison of boys completing CASE II (Contingencies Applicable to Special Education) with boys from the regular institutional programme found lower recidivism at up to two years post-release, but not at the third year (Cohen and Filipcjak, 1971). Similar results were obtained by Jesness (1975), and an evaluation of a token economy in an English private hospital for young behaviourally disordered males and females with a criminal history also suggests partial success (Moyes, Tennent and Bedford, 1985). In comparison with a group offered places but not taking them up, patients who spent at least six months in the programme had fewer contacts with the police after one year, but not after two. However, only one of these evaluations involved random assignment, and the relation of programme components to outcome remains to be established. One long-term follow-up of a token economy in a maximum security hospital failed to find any relation of performance within the programme to subsequent criminal behaviour (Rice, Quinsey and Houghton, 1990).

It appears, then, that token economies can influence the management of incarcerated offenders but that their justification as a vehicle of rehabilitation is weak. They have also been seriously criticised on several counts. First, the relevance to offending of the institutional behaviours typically targeted has not been demonstrated, and Emery and Marholin (1977) argue that contingency management in corrections has not been based on a functional analysis of criminal behaviour either in general, or at the individual level. Second, the common targets of rule compliance and convenience behaviours serve the goals of institutional management rather than inmates. Opton (1975) suggests that such programmes not only maintain a power imbalance in favour of administrators, but are also often punitive. For example, the START (Special Treatment Rehabilitation Training Program) token economy for hard-to-manage prisoners in a federal prison relied mainly on negative reinforcement to shape compliance, and gave no emphasis to new skills (Nietzel, 1979), and concerns about violation of civil rights led to its closure in 1974. Similarly there have been ethical and legal objections to the use as backup reinforcers of amenities which should be noncontingently available as rights. Finally, Ross and Price (1976) question the theoretical adequacy of the operant model in relying on extrinsic rather than intrinsic motivation, arguing that offenders need to feel responsible for their treatment rather than having it imposed. While Milan (1987) defends institutional token economies on the grounds that they make the prison environment more humane and have the potential for providing survival skills, he notes a sharp decline of interest in them since 1980.

Community interventions

Community-based behaviour modification is considered more promising since new skills are more likely to generalise when training and living environments are similar. It can also capitalise on the influence of nondeviant models and change agents who control the contingencies in an offender's natural environment. However, implementation usually requires the co-operation of other agencies, and raises a number of practical issues. Ostapiuk (1982) illustrates these in describing the development of Shape, a hostel and community housing based programme in Birmingham, which aimed to provide ex-offenders with community "survival" skills. In addition to training of staff, programme organisers were faced with such tasks as fund-raising, finding premises, establishing links with resources such as the police and local university departments, and gaining acceptance by the local community.

In an early demonstration of contingency management with offenders, Schwitzgebel (1967) contacted delinquents directly in their natural "streetcorner" environment, and invited them to participate in tape-recorded interviews, during which they were differentially reinforced for prosocial statements. However, most work has been with young offenders referred by welfare or criminal justice agencies, and focuses on academic and interpersonal skills considered likely to counteract delinquent behaviour. While antisocial behaviours, such as disciplinary problems at home or school, are also often targets, attempts to modify illegal behaviours directly have been few. Interventions usually involve working through others, such as parents or probation officers, the main applications being in residential settings, with the families of delinquents, in schools, and in probation departments.

In the United States, group homes provide supervised accommodation for up to a dozen youths, who may attend normal school or community jobs, and visit their homes at weekends. These are the setting for the *teaching family* model, originating with Achievement Place in Kansas in the late 1960s (Braukmann and Wolf, 1987). The model posits a structured family-style environment, in which trained supervisors, usually a married couple, differentially teach and support prosocial skills basic to social and family living. The programme begins with a token economy, in which privileges are contingent on points earnings, and progresses through a "merit" system and a "homeward bound" stage. A large number of studies at Achievement Place using within-subject applied behaviour analytic designs has demonstrated the contingent control of a variety of target behaviours, for example, room care, appropriate meal-time behaviour, nonaggressive speech (Phillips, 1968), group decision making (Fixsen, Phillips and Wolf, 1973), negotiating skills (Kifer et al., 1974), dealing with police encounters (Werner et al., 1975), and interactions with adults (Braukmann, Kirigin and Wolf, 1980). Attempts are also made to influence school and family behaviour through the use of remote consequences, and particular attention has been paid to training staff to teach social interaction skills (Braukmann and Wolf, 1987).

By the early 1980s, the teaching family model was employed in some 200 group homes across 20 states (Braukmann and Wolf, 1987), and it has also had some influence in Britain. Brown (1985b), for example, describes a unit at Orchard Lodge in London, which incorporated several features. However, follow-up evaluations have proved disappointing. Kirigin et al. (1982) compared the original Achievement Place and 12 similar group homes with nine conventional community homes. Teaching family programmes significantly reduced police and court contacts during residence, but not following exit from the programme. A subsequent evaluation using self-report data obtained similar results (Braukmann and Wolf, 1987). Braukmann and Wolf suggest that transitional programmes are necessary to ensure that environments to which treated youths return support prosocial skills.

More direct *family treatment* is based on findings that parents and siblings of delinquents model, reinforce and shape deviant behaviour, and that family interaction is frequently dysfunctional. Restructuring family relations may therefore serve both rehabilitative and preventive goals. The general strategy in behavioural family interventions is to teach problem-solving. For example, Kifer et al. (1974) taught negotiation skills for conflict resolution to three parent–child pairs by means of behaviour rehearsal and social reinforcement. Appropriate skills were developed, and generalised to conflicts at home. Serna et al. (1986) also showed that youths on probation were more likely to maintain communication skills following training if reciprocal skills (e.g. giving and accepting positive or negative feedback) were taught to parents. Rated interactions also improved when parents were involved in training, although longer-term effects were not examined.

A commonly used technique is contingency contracting which schedules the exchange of reinforcers between two or more parties and makes norms of reciprocity explicit (Stuart, 1971). Stuart, Jayaratne and Tripodi (1976) found that parent–child and teacher–child contracts had only modest effects on school behaviour and maternal relationships of predelinquent children, and note that contracting is most useful as part of a multicomponent programme. Stumphauser (1976), for example, successfully eliminated stealing in a 12 year old girl by a combination of contracts emphasising parental attention for nonstealing and self-control techniques (self-monitoring, self-reinforcement, and self-evaluation). However, the utility of contracting depends on therapist skills (Stuart et al., 1976) and the extent of family dysfunction. Weathers and Liberman (1975), for example, attempted to train 28 delinquent families in contracting and communication skills, but 22 dropped out, and training had little impact on those remaining. It was suggested that contracting is ineffective with families who have lost control over the reinforcers for adolescents.

The major strategies are *parent management training* and *systems behavioural family therapy*. There is now an extensive literature on parent management training aimed at improving child rearing practices (Gordon and Arbuthnot, 1987; Kazdin, 1987), but most developed is the approach of Patterson. Following from demonstrations that coercive interactions shape the antisocial behaviour of conduct problem children (Chapter 7), Patterson focuses on training parents to discriminate deviant behaviour and to differentially reward nondeviant behaviour by means of teaching social learning principles, training parents to be behaviour modifiers through modelling and role play, and training them to use time out and negotiate contracts (Patterson, 1974, 1982; Patterson, Chamberlain and Reid, 1982). Rates of deviant behaviour have been reduced to the normal range and maintained at one-year follow-up, and the programme has also been shown to have beneficial effects on sibling behaviour and maternal psychopathology. Bernal, Klinnert and Schulz (1980) failed to demonstrate the superiority of behavioural parent training over client-centred therapy, but Kazdin (1987) concludes that the utility of this approach for improving child behaviour is now established. However, effects on later delinquency are largely unknown. Patterson's approach aims to reduce coercive behaviour, and may have less effect on other antisocial activities. Moore, Chamberlain and Mukai (1979), for example, found that among children involved in Patterson's programme, a majority of stealers subsequently committed offences, but aggressors did not differ from normal adolescents. More recent applications with adolescents who have already offended have reduced delinquent behaviour during treatment, but not in the longer term (Gordon and Arbuthnot, 1987), and it may be optimally effective with younger children.

Alexander's behavioural systems family therapy, or *functional family therapy* (Alexander and Parsons, 1973; Barton and Alexander, 1981; Klein, Alexander and Parsons, 1977) is based on family systems theory in which adolescent problem behaviour is viewed as a result rather than cause of dysfunctional family communications. The focus is on family interactional styles, the goal being to make delinquent families more effective problem solvers by approximating their communication patterns to those shown empirically to distinguish nondelinquent from delinquent families. Therapists modify defensive and ambiguous interactions by modelling, prompting, and reinforcing clear and consistent communications. Relationships are also structured through contracts, and the approach now incorporates cognitive techniques of "reframing" or "relabelling" problems (Alexander, Waldron and Barton, 1989). In an early evaluation, Alexander and Parsons (1973) compared functional family therapy with client-centred, eclectic–dynamic, and no-treatment conditions. At 6- to 18-month follow-up, 26% of the delinquents in the behavioural treatment were recidivists (referred for further status offence) compared with 47% to 73% of those in other treatment conditions, although recidivism for criminal offences was not significantly different. The programme also had a significant impact on the delinquency of siblings (Klein et al., 1977). Working with more serious delinquents in a training school, Barton et al. (1985) found that at 15-month follow-up, 60% of treated delinquents had been charged with a further offence, compared with 93% of those treated by alternative methods. Gordon et al. (1988) also describe an independent replication involving more intensive home-based treatment. Only 11% of delinquents in 27 families treated by functional family therapy had a further adjudication at 2- to $2\frac{1}{2}$-year follow-up, compared with 67% of delinquents receiving probation only.

The teaching family model and family therapy illustrate a common strategy in community intervention of working through other agents, and appropriately trained paraprofessionals can be as effective as professionals (Gordon and Arbuthnot, 1988). This strategy reflects the influence of the "triadic model" (Thorne, Tharp and Wetzel, 1967) in which the psychologist functions as a consultant who trains a mediator, who in turn manipulates the contingencies controlling the behaviour of the target individual. For example, Fo and O'Donnell (1975) recruited adult volunteers as "buddies", and trained them to reinforce prosocial behaviours. Delinquents were randomly assigned to a buddy (N =264) or a non-participating control group (N =178), and arrest records evaluated during the year of the project. Outcome depended on previous record. Among those with a prior history of major offences, fewer experimental than control subjects were arrested for a major offence (38% vs 64%), but among those with minor offence histories, significantly more of the experimental group committed a major offence (16% vs 7%). It was suggested that the programme increased the exposure of the latter to other delinquents.

The triadic model is considered particularly relevant to *probation*. Nietzel and Himelein (1987) note that the efficacy of traditional probation remains equivocal, its justification resting more on economic than rehabilitative grounds, and that the combined demands of helping and surveillance produce an emphasis on aversive control. Training probation officers in methods emphasising goal setting and positive reinforcement of specific behavioural targets may therefore enhance their effectiveness (Thorne et al., 1967; Nietzel and Himelein, 1987; Remington and Remington, 1987).

Although there are several reports of behavioural training for probation officers, this approach has yet to achieve a major impact, and from their review, Remington and Remington (1987) conclude that research findings are "indicative rather than definitive". Some studies show that officers are receptive to a behavioural approach, and that their skills in behaviour analysis and contingency management can be effectively increased by short training courses. However, training is not consistently implemented in practice. While recent developments include teaching probation officers functional family therapy (Gordon and Arbuthnot, 1988) and cognitive–behavioural techniques (Ross, Fabiano and Ewles, 1988), available evaluations are limited mainly to the use of contingency contracting with juvenile probationers.

The major study is that of Jesness et al. (1975), who trained the supervisors of 90 probation officers in applied behaviour analysis and contingency contracting. The latter then worked with 412 young probationers. Implementation of contracts was sporadic, partly as a result of lack of reinforcement from senior administrators, and only a third of the officers wrote adequate contracts. Of contracted targets, 59% remitted, compared with

43% of comparable problems among controls, although significant effects were confined to noncriminal targets, such as truancy and school misconduct, and were not found for illegal activities, aggression, drinking, or associating with delinquents. At six-month follow-up, no significant differences were found in reconvictions between probationers with whom contracts were negotiated and controls (14% vs 20%). However, more positive results obtained when contracts were adequate, and this combined additively with "regard" by the officer for the probationer to yield the lowest recidivism. This project therefore demonstrated some positive outcomes, but these depended on the support and accommodation of the service more generally, and on continued supervision by the original trainers. These issues have received increased attention in programmes using paraprofessionals to deliver services (Gordon and Arbuthnot, 1988).

Academic and vocational skills have been a significant target of behavioural programmes with delinquents in both institutional and community interventions. School-based interventions usually deal with "predelinquents", i.e. youths who are at risk of progressing to serious delinquency because of academic failure and social problems, such as school misconduct or police contacts, and as these programmes aim at prevention as much as tertiary intervention, they are discussed in Chapter 15.

Job interview skills are frequently included in behavioural programmes, and a few employment programs have been reported for serious young offenders. Twentyman, Jensen and Kloss (1978) found that the interview performance of probationers with a history of psychiatric referral and chronic unemployment was rated as unskilled relative to that of unemployed controls both by vocational counsellors and the probationers themselves. A subgroup was assigned to training in finding and applying for jobs, and interview performance, including dealing with "tough" questions, by means of discussion, films, role plays, and videotaped feedback. Training improved rated interview behaviours, such as eye contact, attentiveness, and overall skill, and accuracy of completing job applications, relative to untreated controls; and at a two-week follow-up, four of five experimental subjects, compared with none of six controls, had obtained jobs. Longer-term generalisation was examined by Mills and Walter (1979) in a study of job training of 53 youths on probation, which also involved employers. At a one-year follow-up, all experimental subjects had subsequently found jobs, compared with 39% of 23 controls, and more had remained in employment (34% vs 0%). Moreover, 91% of the experimental group, but only 30% of controls avoided further arrests.

Despite theoretical allegiance to environmental determinism, community behaviour modification has tended to emphasise changing individual delinquents, and apart from functional family therapy, few approaches attempt to change the wider system. Yet, as Goldstein et al. (1989) note, community intervention needs to be more than intervention *in* the community, and needs to modify the behaviour not only of those who control the immediate contingencies in a delinquent's environment, but also of those who control resources generally. Stumphauzer, Veloz and Aiken (1981) outline how a functional analysis might be applied to a community unit, such as a delinquent neighbourhood, but the effects of such an approach do not appear to have been reported.

Overview of behavioural applications

Behavioural interventions have demonstrated short-term improvements in prosocial behaviours of young offenders in a variety of settings. However, generalisation of improvements beyond the treatment setting is not a typical finding, and only a few programmes have shown a longer-term impact on recidivism. Moreover, despite the potential for greater flexibility in manipulating environmental contingencies, community interventions have not been notably more successful than those in institutions. The promise of behaviour modification with offenders therefore continues to remain a promise (Blakely and Davidson, 1984).

Gottschalk et al. (1987) describe a meta-analysis of 30 behavioural studies of the treatment of young offenders reported between 1967 and 1983. On a qualitative rating, the majority produced positive results, but on criteria of effect sizes, the null hypothesis of no effect could not be rejected. The authors conclude that for a variety of outcomes, including recidivism, there is no substantial evidence for the efficacy of behavioural techniques in altering antisocial behaviour. One reason may be the quality of outcome research. Gottschalk et al. (1987) found some association of effect size with treatment intensity (duration) and adequacy of study design, and Blasta and Davidson (1988) note that methodological adequacy remains insufficient to permit firm conclusions. Kazdin (1987) draws a similar conclusion about the treatment of antisocial children. Behavioural interventions with offenders are often weak in intensity, consisting of the application of a limited set of techniques over a short time period to behaviours whose relation to crime is not examined. Moreover, several reports indicate that outcomes depend not only on intervention techniques, but also on behaviours targeted, setting, and characteristics of therapists and clients, but there has been little attention to the way in which these interact to determine optimal effects (Burchard and Lane, 1982; Blasta and Davidson, 1988). For example, the effects of family interventions appear to depend on both skills of trainers and degree of family dysfunction, and they may be most effective with younger, less committed delinquents from intact families.

A central concern is the apparent failure of maintenance and generalisation. As Gottschalk et al. (1987) note, generalisation is not strictly required as a criterion of the success of applied behaviour analysis, since the assumption of environmental control implies transfer of behaviour across environments only when there are common stimulus elements. Nevertheless, the credibility of behaviour modification depends on the demonstration of some impact on recidivism. At one level, this is a technical problem, since generalisation can be achieved by appropriate programming (Stokes and Baer, 1977). However, what this achieves is *stimulus* generalisation, not the generalisation of one response to another (Hollin and Henderson, 1984). It is assumed that changes in the behaviour of delinquents will alter the reactions of their social environment, making further criminal involvement less likely. However, perhaps because of the dogma that "behaviour is behaviour", only minimal attention has been paid to criminological theory, and the targets of behavioural programmes have most commonly been academic or social skills whose functional relationship to delinquency is not established (Emery and Marholin, 1977).

It is also assumed that a newly trained skill will be maintained by natural contingencies once it is established by appropriate intervention. However, this implicitly follows an acute disorder model in which "cure" is permanently established by "treatment" (Kazdin, 1987; Kendall, 1989). Given evidence that antisocial behaviour is a chronic condition, it may require continued intervention.

COGNITIVE–BEHAVIOUR MODIFICATION

Cognitive–behaviour modification includes diverse approaches which share a common view that cognitions affect behaviour, and which employ both behavioural and linguistic procedures to alter cognitive processes (Mahoney, 1974; Mahoney and Arnkoff, 1978; Brewin, 1989). However, they lack a unitary theoretical framework, and reflect an uneasy alliance of disparate philosophies. Three kinds of mediational model have been distinguished (Mahoney, 1974). In the *covert conditioning* model, cognitions are viewed as covert forms of overt phenomena which are subject to established "laws of learning". The metaphor of cognitions as "behaviours" is found in early neobehaviourist learning theories (Davison, 1980) and in radical behaviourist analyses of private events (Skinner, 1953), and provides the rationale for procedures such as self control and covert sensitisation. Skinner saw private events as no more than a weak link in a causal chain, and behaviourists differ over the utility of this model. However, some accord a significant controlling function to covert verbal behaviours (Lowe and Higson, 1980).

In the *information processing* model, cognitions are more explicitly the central mediators of behaviour, and are the processes and structures through which information from the environment is acquired, stored, and retrieved (Turk and Salovey, 1985). This view assumes a reciprocal determinism in which humans are active seekers and creators of information, responding to their own mediational rendition of the world. Although therapeutic methods have not emerged directly from this approach, it is influential in theoretical accounts of social competence (McCall, 1982) and therapeutic change (Brewin, 1989).

The *cognitive learning* model is a more molar view, which owes as much to rationalist as to empiricist philosophies. While it attempts to integrate learning theory and information processing models, it is primarily concerned with how experience is structured, reinforcement schedules being of peripheral concern (Davison, 1980). This model underlies Bandura's social cognitive theory, and is represented in Ellis's Rational Emotive Therapy, Beck's Cognitive Therapy, and problem solving and coping skills methods. However, recent statements are critical of information processing concepts drawn from computer analogies, and emphasise that knowledge is actively *constructed* rather then being simply a preserved replica of the past (Arnkoff, 1980; Guidano and Liotti, 1985; Bandura, 1986). This constructivist view permits a rapprochement with the cognitive developmental theories of Piaget and Kohlberg.

The theoretical and empirical justification for many cognitive–behavioural procedures is currently tenuous, and positivist critics argue that such methods are simply behaviour therapy directed at "a subclass of behaviours" (Beidel and Turner, 1986). However, given the lack of a unitary perspective, such critiques attack a straw man. While it has been argued that there are no differences in outcome between cognitive–behavioural and traditional behavioural methods (Latimer and Sweet, 1984), such comparisons are possible for only a narrow range of clinical problems and do not establish that cognitions are excess therapeutic baggage. They equally give substance to the claim that all successful therapy works through cognitive change (Mahoney, 1974).

Interest in applications of cognitive–behavioural methods to offender problems has grown in the past decade, although evidence on their long-term effects is so far limited (Hollin, 1990). The most comprehensive development of the cognitive learning perspective comes from Ross and Fabiano (1985), who review evidence that many delinquents have deficits in social cognitions relating to an egocentric level of cognitive development (Chapter 8). From an analysis of offender rehabilitation programmes, they concluded that the most effective were those specifically incorporating a cognitive component (although this includes behavioural procedures, such as modelling and role play, which some applied behaviour analysts argue do not *require* a cognitive interpretation). This is supported by a subsequent meta-analysis indicating a significant relation of effect size with inclusion of a cognitive component (Izzo and Ross, 1990). Ross and Fabiano (1985) therefore propose that both thinking ability and content should be prime targets of rehabilitation programmes, and that the following targets are particularly relevant: social skills; interpersonal problem solving; cognitive style; social perspective taking; critical reasoning; values; metacognition; self control. A wide range of techniques may influence these targets, but only the main strategies employed with offenders are summarised here.

Social skills training

Many behavioural programmes aim to improve the competence of offenders in dealing with social interactions, and *social skills training* (SST) more generally has been popular in both institutional and community settings (Spence, 1982; Hollin and Henderson, 1984; McGuire and Priestley, 1985; Henderson and Hollin, 1986; Howells, 1986). SST has a number of variants, such as Structured Learning Training (Goldstein, 1986), and is a component of the Human Resources Development model (Holder, 1978), common elements being the combined use of techniques such as modelling, instructions, role play and rehearsal, feedback, social reinforcement, and homework to teach interactional skills. Although firmly based on behavioural methods, and often not including specific cognitive skills training, SST has commonly been seen in information processing terms (Sarason, 1978; McFall, 1982).

There is no uniform definition of social skills nor of the essential components of training. Some programmes focus on specific skills, such as communication with particular categories of person (e.g. Golden et al., 1980; Serna et al., 1986), while others employ generic packages progressing from training in nonverbal micro-skills, such as eye contact and gestures, to more molar skills of initiating and maintaining a conversation, and specific skills of assertion, negotiation, or heterosocial interaction (Ollendick and Hersen, 1979; Spence, 1982; Hollin et al., 1986). The precise objectives of SST with offenders are not always clear, but the usual assumption is that enhancing basic or specific skills will help the offender to avoid further offending.

Most reports focus on the efficacy of training in promoting the particular skills, and from a review of 30 studies with delinquent or aggressive adolescents, Goldstein (1986) concluded that there was consistent evidence for skill acquisition at programme termination. For example, in controlled studies with institutionalised young offenders, Ollendick and Hersen (1979) and Spence and Marzillier (1981) found improved performance following SST in micro-skills such as eye contact, head movements, and speech content, although some skills, such as attention feedback, were less amenable to change. Golden et al. (1980) also successfully taught skills of justifying actions and making petitions to an authority figure (probation officer) to offenders on probation, while Serna et al. (1986) demonstrated increases in each of seven specific communication skills following SST with probationers. Maintenance of skills following training, however, has been less consistently shown. Spence and Marzillier (1981) found that basic skills were maintained at 3-month follow-up, but not at 6 months. Findings on generalisation are also variable. Goldstein et al. (1989) note that, on average, only 15–20% of individuals in skills training programmes transfer their skills outside training. In their structured learning training, they were able to increase this to 50% by ensuring the provision of general learning principles, overlearning of new skills, varying training stimuli, and programming natural reinforcement.

Trainees commonly report fewer social problems at the end of training, and some studies have found more general personality change, such as a shift to a more internal locus of control (Sarason, 1968, 1978; Ollendick and Hersen, 1979; Spence and Marzillier, 1981), or improved self-esteem (Spence and Marzillier, 1981). However, Hollin et al. (1986) were unable to replicate previous findings of changes in locus of control, and in Spence's programme, self-esteem enhancement was also shown by an attention–placebo control group. It was not maintained at 6-month follow-up.

A few institutional studies find that SST results in greater conformity as rated by staff (Sarason, 1968; Ollendick and Hersen, 1979), but others do not (Spence and Marzillier, 1981; Hollin et al., 1986). Hollin et al. (1986) found that institution discipline reports improved, but this applied to attention–placebo as well as SST groups.

Longer-term effects on offending are similarly mixed, although they have been examined in only a few studies. Spence and Marzillier (1981) found no significant effects of SST on official delinquency at 6-month follow-up, and SST trainees recorded higher self-reported offending. A few other studies report positive but inconclusive effects. In an early study of SST involving discussion of delinquent acts and role play of alternatives, Ostrom et al. (1971) found that probationers who participated were less likely to be rearrested during the first five months of follow-up, but not during the next five. However, Sarason (1978) describes a 5-year follow-up of a relatively brief institutional programme which used modelling and role play of problem situations commonly encountered by offenders following release, such as resisting pressure from peers or taking a problem to a probation officer. At follow-up, recidivism was halved in SST trainees compared with untreated controls (15% vs 31%), although SST was no more successful than discussion of the same problems. While this suggests an "attention", or nonspecific effect, discussion in this context was seen as symbolic modelling. However, Hollin (Hollin and Henderson, 1984; Hollin, 1990) is critical of the use of recidivism as an outcome criterion of SST on the grounds that it assumes a generalisation of response which cannot be justified by either behavioural or criminological theory. He notes that apart from the issue of whether social skills deficits have anything to do with offending, several programmes failed to determine whether their trainees were actually deficient in the skills selected for training.

The effects of SST with offenders, then, seem comparable to those found with clinical populations. Short-term changes in social behaviour can be achieved, but their durability and generalisation is limited. Some of the limited results may reflect the failure of penal environments to support change (Hollin et al., 1986; Howells, 1986), but there may have been unrealistic expectations of the impact of SST on offenders, perhaps because social skill is equated in popular discourse with optimal adjustment, and SST is reinforcing to trainers (Hollin et al., 1986). However, the available evidence does not warrant the routine use of SST in correctional settings. There are unresolved theoretical issues surrounding SST in general, particularly its relation to cognitive and motivational factors (Trower, 1984; Howells, 1986), as well as the relation of social skill deficits to criminal behaviour (Chapter 8). There are also procedural issues relating to frequency and duration of training sessions, the characteristics of models and trainers, and the effective components of training. While SST can be justified as a clinical procedure for helping offenders with manifest social difficulties, it needs to be used cautiously as an adjunct to other measures.

Self control

Procedures which train clients to manage their own behaviour have been derived from several theoretical perspectives. In behavioural self control, clients manipulate the antecedents and consequences of the response to be controlled by means of self monitoring, changing the controlling stimuli, and self-administration of reinforcement or punishment. Antecedents and consequences include covert events, and cognitions may also be the target responses to be controlled. Despite the frequent use of these methods to control undesirable activities such as overeating or smoking, applications to antisocial behaviour are confined to a few case reports. As described earlier, for example, Stumphauser (1976) combined self control methods and contracting to eliminate stealing in a 12-year old girl. Thought stopping, in which a self-instruction to "stop" is used to disrupt a cognitive–behavioural sequence, was also combined with other methods as a self control technique to reduce violent outbursts in a schoolboy (McCullough, Huntsinger and Nay, 1977). However, neither of these cases involved adjudicated offenders.

Self-instructional training (SIT) as an approach to self regulation is more closely linked to the cognitive learning model than to covert conditioning, although some conceptualise it in terms of the latter (Davison, 1980; Lowe and Higson, 1980). It derives from the research of Russian developmental psychologists on the role of covert speech or "self-talk" in controlling overt behaviour (Meichenbaum, 1977). Verbal instructions to guide behaviour are modelled by the therapist, and rehearsed by the client, first overtly, then gradually as covert self-statements. SIT is considered a promising method for increasing impulse control, but most demonstrations have been with preadolescent children showing problem behaviour in the classroom. Kendall (1984) summarises several studies with this group in which modelling, response cost, and social and self-reinforcement were used to teach self-instructions in coping and problem-solving. Effects were found for impulsivity as measured by the Matching Familiar Figures Test (MFFT), and in some instances for teacher-rated self control, although findings on generalisation to other classroom behaviours and long-term maintenance are mixed. Bell, Mundy and Quay (1982) applied similar SIT procedures in an analogue study with institutionalised conduct-disordered boys. Training in problem solving on a number of cognitive tasks reduced impulsive responding for the experimental group relative to controls, as assessed by Porteus Maze Q score, though not the MFFT. Kendall's procedures have recently been extended to conduct disordered children in a day hospital (Kendall et al., 1990). In a cross-over design, children were assigned to a standard individual psychodynamic treatment or to the cognitive programme, which consisted of SIT in coping and interpersonal problem-solving, including perspective taking. Significant improvements favouring the cognitive–behavioural programme were found on teacher ratings of self control and prosocial behaviours, and also self-reported scholastic competence and social acceptance, but no differential effects emerged on disruptive (externalising) behaviour or on the MFFT.

Snyder and White (1979) examined the effects of SIT on the behaviour of 15 delinquent and behaviour disordered adolescents who were not responding to an institutional token economy, and who were randomly assigned to six sessions of SIT or contingency awareness (discussion), or a no-treatment group. At a two-week follow-up, the SIT group showed greater improvements in school attendance, impulsive (antisocial) behaviours, and completion of required social and self-care tasks, all of which were maintained at two months follow-up. Bowman and Auerbach (1982) employed a multimodal programme with a similar group of 10 institutionalised delinquents, who were assigned to treatment or attention–placebo groups. Treatment consisted of 10 sessions of relaxation training, training in problem-solving, self-statement modification, and behaviour rehearsal. On a variety of dependent measures, differences favouring treated youths were confined to reduced errors on the MFFT at two-week follow-up and fewer tickets for rule infractions after two months. No effects were found for staff or peer ratings of impulsivity, or for measures of abstract reasoning, problem solving, or locus of control. There is, then, no more than suggestive evidence to date that SIT can promote generalised strategies of self control among antisocial individuals.

Self-statement modification as a means of controlling affective reactions is also central to *stress inoculation training*, which utilises self-monitoring of negative thoughts, rehearsal of positive statements, and self reinforcement for coping to develop coping skills. This has been applied to the management of anger, and is discussed in the next chapter.

Cognitive restructuring

SIT has commonalities with rational–emotive therapy (RET: Ellis, 1977) and Beck's cognitive therapy (CT: Beck, 1976). All assume that maladaptive feelings and behaviour are often a consequence of dysfunctional thought patterns, and aim to supplant these with more adaptive thinking through instruction, debate, and performance assignments. However, there are theoretical and procedural differences between these approaches. RET is the most didactic. Certain core irrational beliefs are assumed to create unrealistic demands, which when unmet produce negative emotional states. Cognitive restructuring is achieved first by detecting these beliefs through questioning, challenging and debating, and then disputing them by discriminating wants from needs and redefining overgeneralisations by means of confrontation and homework assignments.

RET has been employed with offenders showing impulse control problems. These are seen as the outcome of irrational beliefs which equate wants with needs, and see thwarting as intolerable. Therapy therefore aims to substitute more discriminating, rational cognitions. Watkins (1977) describes this use of RET with a group of individuals with impulse control problems, who included an impulsive buyer, a paedophile, an autothief, an obscene phone caller, and a voyeur, but effects on antisocial behaviour are not reported. Soloman and Ray (1984) conceptualised shoplifting in similar terms, and showed that specific irrational beliefs relating to shoplifting were common among 94 shoplifters (e.g. "Everybody does it"; "Merchants deserve it"). These beliefs were challenged in RET groups, and at one-year follow-up, only one of the sample had reoffended.

RET has been criticised for failure to attend to positive skill development, and for a lack of clear outcome data (Mahoney and Arnkoff, 1978). Beck's CT differs in several ways, being more individualised, and emphasising personal discovery of dysfunctional thoughts. It also relies on a less confrontational socratic dialogue, involving hypothesis testing, decentring (reduced personalisation), distancing (objective thinking), reattribution, and the use of behavioural assignments as "personal experiments". Although Beck (1976) elaborated the applicability of his methods to anger, most attention has focused on depression and anxiety, and the only reported use with offenders as yet appears to be in challenging the cognitive distortions of sex offenders (Murphy, 1990). However, Beck and Freeman (1990) have recently extended CT procedures to personality disorders (Chapter 14).

One other related approach is that of Yochelson and Samenow (1976) who developed procedures to change the thinking processes of "the criminal personality". Their approach is intensive, involving daily individual and subsequently small group sessions during confinement and for at least a year following release. The offender monitors his thinking in a daily diary, which is the basis for confrontation during therapy, during which distortions and errors in thinking are examined and alternative patterns indicated. The aim is not only to develop self-understanding, but also self-disgust, a target which Ross and Fabiano (1985) believe is inappropriate to an educational process. Yochelson and Samenow report that 13 of 30 criminals treated by this approach were subsequently functioning responsibly following completion of therapy, but present only limited data to support this. However, a few programmes for young offenders seem to have adopted this approach (Agee, 1986).

Interpersonal problem solving training

Problem-solving training has been incorporated into several self-regulatory training packages which focus on *im*personal problems (e.g. Kendall, 1984), but there are no firm grounds for expecting these to generalise to *inter*personal problems (Ross and Fabiano, 1985). Interpersonal cognitive problem-solving training (ICPS) employs skills training techniques of instruction, modelling, discussion, and feedback to teach cognitive components of resolving social problems with the aim of developing generalisable skills. Several variations have been reported (Tisdelle and Lawrence, 1986), but most developed are the procedures developed by Spivack and his colleagues (Spivack, Platt and Shure, 1976; Platt and Prout, 1987). These entail first the training of prerequisite skills, such as imitation, group discussion, and "thinking aloud". Problem-solving training proper focuses on: (1) problem recognition; (2) alternative thinking; (3) means–end thinking; (4) perspective taking; (5) causal thinking; (6) considering consequences.

There are some reports of the successful use of ICPS with adult psychiatric patients (Tisdelle and Lawrence, 1986), but most applications have so far been with children. Spivack et al. (1976) showed that their cognitive training could prevent poorly controlled behaviour in preschool children, but several attempts at replication have failed to find that ICPS affects later adjustment (Durlak, 1985). However, a treatment study by Kazdin et al. (1987) supports the utility of this approach. They examined ICPS for seriously antisocial, hospitalised children, comparing it with nondirective relationship therapy and a treatment contact control. Significant reductions in aggressive and externalising behaviour and increases in social adjustment were found at both home and school following ICPS, but not the relationship therapy or control conditions, and these differences were maintained at one-year follow-up. Most children who improved nevertheless remained outside normal limits on the rating scales used, indicating a need to enhance treatment strength.

Only a few applications have been reported with offenders. Hains and Hains (1987) trained five institutionalised delinquents, all diagnosed as conduct disordered, in cognitive strategies for resolving hypothetical social dilemmas, by means of instruction, modelling, and rehearsal. All improved on the training task, and for three youths, this generalised to untrained dilemmas and was maintained at three-week follow-up. The same youths also reported improved personal problem-solving, suggesting generalisation beyond training. Training was less effective for the remaining two youths, although uncontrolled observations suggested that all youths responded more positively to the institution behavioural programme. Longer-term effects were not examined. Platt and Prout (1987) have also demonstrated that ICPS results in the learning and maintenance of problem-solving skills among institutionalised heroin addicts. While they report a reduction in subsequent offending by trainees, ICPS was a component of a broader composite programme.

Problem-solving training appears to be a promising intervention since these skills are linked to cognitive maturation and relate to other variables associated with antisocial behaviour, such as child-rearing practices (Kazdin, 1987). However, their efficacy in preventing or reducing delinquency has yet to be established. Apart from a number of theoretical and procedural issues surrounding the use of ICPS (Tisdelle and Lawrence, 1986), the extent of deficits in interpersonal problem-solving skills among offenders remains largely unknown (Chapter 8). However, ICPS may be particularly relevant to interventions with aggressive offenders (Chapter 14).

Moral reasoning and perspective taking

As was noted in Chapter 8, an egocentric level of cognitive development is associated with deficits in empathy and moral reasoning, and there are suggestive findings that this characterises many delinquents. While training in empathic skills has received only limited attention because of continued problems of conceptualisation and measurement, some attempts have been made to improve perspective-taking and moral development among delinquents.

Following his demonstration of greater egocentricity in chronic young delinquents, Chandler (1973) trained them in perspective-taking by means of involvement in making videofilms, in which all participants played dramatised roles. Those in the role-taking group subsequently showed significantly greater reductions in egocentricity than delinquents in a placebo group, who simply made films, and a no-training control group. At 18-months follow-up, the offence rate of the experimental group was almost halved, compared with prior records, while that of the two control groups was virtually unchanged. Despite the common use of role-play in behavioural training programmes, there do not appear to be any other reports of its being used in this way.

Role-taking skills are held to be a necessary but not sufficient condition for advances in moral reasoning, which result from cognitive dissonance experienced through the adaptation and assimilation of new data. Acceleration from the preconventional level that is thought to characterise many delinquents therefore requires that they participate in moral debate while being exposed to conventional level reasoning. Jennings, Kilkenny and Kohlberg (1983) identify the optimal conditions for cognitive growth as moral discussion, a focus of discussion on issues of what is good, bad, and fair, role-taking opportunities, stage-adjacent reasoning, and mutual decision making.

Such conditions are most likely to be met in an appropriately structured environment, and this is the basis for the Just Community model adopted in some prisons, as well as educational settings. This model prescribes a democratic living environment aimed at creating a morally responsive atmosphere which stimulates ideas of social justice, and has some similarities to a therapeutic community. Staff–inmate inequalities are minimised, decisions shared, and the moral aspects of social situations are examined at regular community meetings. Outcome data are limited, but Scharf and Hickey (1976) evaluated the effects of a Just Community programme in a women's prison. Inmates showed a significant progression averaging a third of a stage on Kohlberg's Moral Judgment Interview, differing from controls from outside the programme, as well as from male prisoners exposed to moral discussion alone. Preliminary two-year follow-up data also indicated a recidivism rate of 15%, compared with 35% for the rest of the institution (Jennings et al., 1983).

Just Community programmes have foundered because they depend on an appropriate mix of inmates at preconventional and conventional stages, and because their democratic philosophy conflicts with the bureaucratic demands of prison administration. A less radical programme, in which moral reasoning development is embedded in an educational course, was developed by the University of Victoria within prisons in British Columbia (Duguid, 1981). The multifaceted programme focuses on cognitive restructuring through socratic debate, moral development, and problem-solving, which are integrated with degree courses in the humanities. Outcome data, however, are mixed. Early evaluations indicated a recidivism rate of 15% over a three year period for chronic offenders who volunteered for the programme (Duguid, 1981), but subsequent studies suggest no advantage (Gendreau and Ross, 1987). However, conditions of implementation varied between prisons examined.

The more common approach relies on guided group discussions of hypothetical moral dilemmas, and Gordon and Arbuthnot (1987) suggest that weekly sessions of 45 minutes over 10 to 20 sessions will typically result in upward movement of one quarter to one half of a stage for one quarter to a half of participants. Moral discussion groups in institutions may be limited by the prevailing atmosphere, which is likely to reflect preconventional level thinking (Duguid, 1981), and such programmes have produced equivocal effects. Hickey (1972), for example, found that a 36-session programme in a prison produced significant changes in moral reasoning in about half of those participating, but Copeland and Parish (1979) failed to influence moral reasoning in a military prison. Gibbs et al. (1984), however, describe a successful intervention with institutionalised delinquents. After eight 40-minute sessions of dilemma discussion, 88% of those at stage two shifted to stage three, compared with only 14% of a no-treatment control group. Whether moral discussion groups significantly influence recidivism has yet to be clearly demonstrated, but Arbuthnot and Gordon (1986) found that 16 to 20 weekly sessions of moral discussion focusing on perspective taking, problem-solving, and listening skills significantly improved the behaviour of high risk adolescents, compared with no-treatment controls. Group participants increased almost half a stage of moral maturity, and although not differing on teacher ratings or absenteeism, showed a decline in disciplinary referrals and tardiness, improved school grades, and reduced police and court contacts. These improvements were maintained after one year.

While Arbuthnot and Gordon (1986) note a need for an attention–placebo control, and for further investigation of the contribution of training in nonmoral cognitive skills, their results reinforce the credibility of moral development training as a potential means of promoting anticriminal decision making. They have also established that moral training programmes can be delivered by paraprofessionals, providing certain conditions are met, such as commitment of trainers, continuing supervision, and organisational support (Arbuthnot and Gordon, 1988). However, not all delinquents are deficient in moral development, and some may lack the prerequisites for response to training, such as role-taking skills and some degree of formal operational thinking. Moral reasoning training may therefore be most effective as part of a multimodal programme which includes training in other cognitive and social skills (Gordon and Arbuthnot, 1987; Thornton, 1987a; Goldstein et al., 1989).

Overview of cognitive–behavioural interventions

The popularity of cognitive–behavioural methods among practitioners rests partly on their theoretical and philosophical appeal. While remaining rooted in empirical behavioural science, they represent not only a move away from the unidirectional determinism and passive organism strictures of behaviourism, but also a rapprochement with nonempiricist intellectual traditions in psychology. However, outcome studies also provide an empirical justification for the application of these procedures in offender rehabilitation (Ross and Fabiano, 1985; Izzo and Ross, 1990). Cognitive–behavioural interventions with offenders are therefore clearly here to stay.

Nevertheless, their use raises similar issues to those presented by earlier behavioural interventions. For example, interactions of technique with characteristics of client, setting, and change agent have received little attention, and the functional relationship of cognitive deficits to criminal behaviour remains unclear. The selection of particular targets, such as interpersonal problem solving or moral reasoning, and the expectation that their remediation will have a generalised anticriminal effect therefore rest on tenuous assumptions. The contribution of specific techniques also remains problematic. Cognitive–behavioural interventions commonly combine techniques such as modelling, role-play, rehearsal, and verbal instructions. While it is assumed that behavioural procedures are the most powerful means of changing cognitive processes (Mahoney and Arnkoff, 1978), only a few attempts have been made to determine which are necessary and sufficient. For example, Kendall (1984) reports that a combined cognitive–behavioural package was superior to behavioural training alone in self-control training, but Hollin et al. (1986) found that the addition of SIT to social skills training made no apparent difference to outcome. Again, Sarason (1978) found that modelling and role-play of social problem situations achieved similar effects on recidivism to discussion of the same situations alone.

Given these uncertainties about the relevance of specific targets and techniques, and the evidence that criminality is associated with multiple dysfunctions, one solution is to direct interventions to multiple targets using multiple treatment modalities. Goldstein et al. (1989) propose that interventions should focus on interpersonal, cognitive, and affect-related skills necessary for community adjustment, and their *aggression replacement training* (ART) combines (1) structured learning training, to teach social skills, (2) anger control training, and (3) training in moral reasoning. Training consists of up to 30 small group sessions of modelling, role-play, feedback, and discussion. In initial controlled outcome studies with institutionalised delinquents, ART increased skills and reduced impulsiveness during the course of the programme and produced superior community adjustment at a 4-month follow-up. A subsequent community application in New York compared ART with released youths, parallel ART with youths and with their families, and a no-treatment control. At 6 months from entry to the programme, arrest rates for both ART groups were 15%, compared with 43% for controls, although results fell short of significance when supervised youths were excluded from the analysis. The authors propose going beyond the basic competence enhancement of ART to include other skills, such as stress management and empathy training.

The multimodal Reasoning and Rehabilitation Project developed in Canada by Ross, Fabiano and Ewles (1988) follows from their earlier demonstration of the importance of thinking skills in rehabilitation programmes (Ross and Fabiano, 1985). It combines several social cognitive skills training techniques to teach offenders to stop and think before acting, consider the consequences of their behaviour, particularly for others, and to conceptualise alternative ways of responding to interpersonal problems. The relevant techniques (structured learning therapy, lateral thinking, critical thinking, values education, assertiveness training, negotiation skills training, interpersonal problem-solving, social perspective-training, role-playing, and modelling) were taught to probation officers, who applied them with groups of 4–6 adult probationers in an intensive 80-hour programme of demanding exercises. After 9 months from entry to the programme, high risk probationers randomly assigned to a regular probation control group, an attention-control life skills training group, or to the cognitive programme had reconviction rates, respectively, of 70%, 48%, and 18%, demonstrating considerable effectiveness for the cognitive package.

One other multimodal programme of note is the family–ecological systems approach (Henggeler, 1989), which takes account of the multidimensional and bidirectional influences on delinquency to include family and school interactions, as well as individual cognitive and personal dysfunctions. Treatment draws on social learning, cognitive–behavioural, and family therapy techniques, and is tailored to individual need. Evaluations of this approach with chronic delinquents in the Memphis-Metro Youth Diversion Project have demonstrated that compared with conventional individual counselling, it not only ameliorates child behaviour problems and improves peer and family relationships, but also reduces both self-reported delinquency and arrest rates (17% versus 40%).

Multifaceted treatment is perhaps an ideal for clinical practice, given the heterogeneity of offenders. However, Kazdin (1987) cautions that broadbased treatments often haphazardly agglomerate techniques selected for their intuitive appeal and face validity, and the extent to which multimodal programmes produce more powerful effects than those of single component interventions has yet to be determined. Until the necessary components of change are identified, such approaches risk the charge of shotgun empiricism.

Chapter 14

Treatment of Dangerous Offenders

INTRODUCTION

Offenders who commit serious crimes against the person are likely to display multiple psychological dysfunctions. This chapter focuses on psychological interventions in three overlapping areas of sexual deviation, violence, and personality disorder. While only a minority of offenders presumed to be dangerous is treated in special units, and some may receive mental health services within the penal system, psychological treatment for dangerous offenders is most frequently carried out in forensic psychiatric facilities. Some of the issues raised by services for mentally disordered offenders are therefore examined first.

TREATMENT ISSUES IN FORENSIC PSYCHIATRIC POPULATIONS

Mentally disordered offenders are a heterogeneous group whose composition depends on statutory definitions, and not simply psychiatric diagnosis (Chapter 10). For example, they include "sexual psychopaths" in some American states, but sex offending itself is not recognised as a mental disorder by the Mental Health Acts in Britain. Again, psychopathic disorder is identified as a mental disorder in the Mental Health Act for England and Wales, but not in the comparable legislation for Scotland. These variations reflect continuing disputes about which offenders should be candidates for psychiatric attention, and not all dangerous offenders are perceived as mentally disordered. Conversely, not all mentally disordered offenders are dangerous, and many are treated in the community. Cooke (1991b), for example, describes outpatient treatment of minor offenders with problems of depression, anxiety, and alcohol abuse who were referred through a Scottish court diversion scheme. However, the major issues arise in the treatment of offenders detained in forensic psychiatric hospitals.

The justification for the diversion of mentally disordered offenders from the penal system is the presence of mental disorder, and clinicians are ethically obliged to provide treatment of distress or disability, whether or not this is a cause of offending. Clinical services for this group overlap with those in the mental health system generally. While pharmacological treatment is frequently the best strategy for treating acute psychotic disorders, psychological interventions are a more durable alternative for emotional problems such as depression or anxiety, and are critical in rehabilitation. Mentally ill and mentally handicapped offenders, for example, present problems of motivational and social deficits typical of long-stay patients, and often exhibit socially unacceptable behaviour which impedes their return to less restricted environments. Rehabilitative goals are therefore to provide the necessary coping and interpersonal skills which will enable them to survive in their optimal environment, whether an open hospital, hostel, or their own home.

Nevertheless, the quality of services in secure psychiatric institutions has been repeatedly criticised, and as Quinsey (1988) notes, treatment programmes have frequently been noteworthy primarily by their absence, poor implementation, unevaluated status, lack of conceptual sophistication, and incomplete description. There have been several follow-up studies of discharged mentally disordered offenders, which suggest that about half reoffend, while about 20% commit further violent crimes (Murray, 1989). However, these studies primarily address the question of predicting dangerousness, and little attention has been paid to the relation of treatment programmes to outcome.

Efficacy of treatment, however, is fundamental to any attempt to predict dangerousness of the mentally disordered, and *treatability* decisions are central to practice (Heilbrun et al., 1988; Quinsey, 1988). In Britain, hospital orders for offenders do not require a causal relation between mental illness and offence behaviour, but this is assumed for psychopathic disorder and mental impairment, and since 1983, hospital orders for offenders in these categories require justification in terms of treatability. The available evidence, however, suggests that clinical agreement about treatability is even less than that for dangerousness (Quinsey, 1988), and two problems in particular limit the accuracy of treatability decisions. First is uncertainty about treatment goals and outcome criteria. While clinicians emphasise the alleviation of distress or disability, involvement of the criminal justice system in release decisions reflects expectations that treatment of mentally disordered offenders will also reduce the likelihood of future offending. These two goals are not necessarily related. For example, neuroleptic medication for psychotic disorders predominates in forensic psychiatric settings, but the causes of antisocial behaviour in psychotic offenders are often the same as those in the nondisordered. Heilbrun et al. (1988) suggest that clinical goals of "psychological improvement" and criminal targets need to be addressed separately. Robertson (1989), on the other hand, argues against recidivism as an outcome criterion, suggesting that treatment in the form of hospitalisation contributes only a small part of the variance in reoffending. However, this prejudges the empirical question of outcome effects, and seems to rest on a medical conception of treatment as symptom removal, rather than a psychological conception of intervention as the provision of skills for avoiding offending.

A second problem is that treatability decisions parallel dangerousness evaluations in blurring the distinction between assessment and prediction (Heilbrun et al., 1988). The evaluation of treatability requires a distinction between the prediction of a treatment outcome and the assessment of amenability to treatment as a constellation of personal and situational characteristics. The former demands empirical data on treatment efficacy. The latter requires a reliable measure which takes account of (1) the appropriate fit between treatment goals and patient deficits; (2) history of the patient's response to treatment; (3) motivation; (4) contraindications. It must also consider the availability of treatment and environmental resources. Heilbrun et al. (1988) describe preliminary attempts to construct such a measure, which, however, foundered on the quality of available information.

Psychological interventions with mentally disordered offenders are in principle no different from those dealing with offenders generally. Reduced recidivism is a necessary but not sufficient outcome criterion, the primary need being to identify and target the mediators of antisocial behaviour, and to establish which treatments influence these mediators. However, treatment is often constrained by organisational and bureaucratic factors. For example, conflicts between therapy and custody pervade maximum security hospitals, leading some to suggest that they are inherently antitherapeutic (Pilgrim and Eisenberg, 1984).

TREATMENT OF SEX OFFENDERS

Many sex offenders either deny their offence or do not see it as a sexual problem, and do not readily become engaged in therapy. Their treatment therefore poses a number of practical and ethical problems. Groth (1983) suggests that in institutional contexts, inducements in the form of privileges are necessary. Laws and Osborn (1983) and Perkins (1987), in contrast, believe that informed consent is essential, although Perkins notes that as a treatment programme develops, both therapist and offenders become subject to pressures from courts and other agencies. However, one investigator reports that court-referred and voluntary clients in an outpatient clinic did not differ on either outcome or compliance measures (Maletzky, 1991). Nevertheless, high attrition is common, even among volunteers, and a third or more of clients may drop out of treatment before completion (Freeman-Longo and Wall, 1986; Perkins, 1987). A further issue is that closed, all-male institutions are not an optimal environment in which to develop heterosocial skills or nonsexist attitudes, and institution-based programmes need access to community facilities both for follow-up support and as an alternative base.

Despite the disappearance of sexual psychopath laws, there are now over 300 sex offender programmes in North America (Blader and Marshall, 1989), and both clinical and prison psychologists in Britain have become increasingly involved in this area. In view of the multidimensional nature of sex offending (Chapter 11), treatment goals are wide ranging, and many programmes incorporate more than one therapeutic approach. Therapy is typically directive, requiring offenders to acknowledge responsibility for offending and for change, and since programmes are often multidisciplinary and multiagency, conventional guarantees of absolute confidentiality are usually explicitly waived (Salter, 1988). While some psychologists work with victims and families, the focus here is on the offender.

Assessment

Sex offenders typically have both sexual and nonsexual problems (Crawford, 1979; Howells, 1981; Marshall and Barbaree, 1990a), and a comprehensive assessment needs to cover social, cognitive, affective, and physiological levels of functioning. Initial interviews entail analysis of the events preceding, during, and following the offence, such as the roles of mood, planning, and alcohol, the nature of the assault, and the offender's feelings about the victim and his behaviour. Interviews also cover sexual and social development, including early family relationships, frequency of deviant and nondeviant sexual activities and fantasies, and the offender's sexual behaviour with consenting partners. Lifestyle factors conducive to deviant acts, such as interpersonal style, recreations, and substance use, should also be investigated. Most clinicians advocate caution in accepting an offender's account of deviant behaviour (Laws and Osborn, 1983; Salter, 1988; Maletzky, 1991), and as well as information from independent sources, such as family members, victims, and court records, more objective assessment is necessary to provide an adequate functional analysis and to identify relevant targets.

Behaviour therapists consider assessment of sexual arousal patterns to be necessary, and while not all sex offenders will have deviant preferences, penile plethysmography (PPG; Chapter 11) remains the most reliable means of detecting these. Marshall and Barbaree (1990b) recommend that PPG responses to deviant stimuli of more than 20% of full erection indicate a need for arousal reduction, while responses to appropriate stimuli of less than 30% point to arousal enhancement as a target. Several self-report measures of sexual deviation are also available, such as the Clarke Sex History Questionnaire (Langevin, 1985), which assesses the frequency of a wide range of sexual anomalies. Salter (1988) and Maletzky (1991) detail other verbal methods, such as card sorts. Assessment of the subjective meaning of deviant interests is also advocated by Howells (1979; 1981), who used the Repertory Grid in this context.

Personality tests, such as the MMPI, have proved of limited value in distinguishing between sexual deviants, or between sex offenders and other criminals (Chapter 11), but as Hall (1990) notes, they were not developed for this purpose. Their utility lies in identifying dispositional factors such as socialisation, hostility, empathy, self esteem, or social anxiety, which are relevant to victimising behaviour.

Areas of social competence likely to be relevant include deficits not only in overt social skills, but also in social problem solving, anger control, relationship skills, and life management skills. While some information can be derived at interview, these are more readily identified through self-ratings and standardised self-report measures, and through self-monitoring and role plays during individual and group treatment. Since distorted beliefs appear to play a significant role in sex offending, these need to be assessed, and several scales for evaluating acceptance of rape myths or cognitive distortions about child–adult sex are now available (see Salter, 1988). Increased attention to cognitive processing as a target of change also calls for the evaluation of the appraisals, attributions, and self-efficacy beliefs of sex offenders in their social interactions (Segal and Stermac, 1990).

Organic treatments

Organic treatments include neurosurgery, surgical castration, and antiandrogen medication (Freund, 1980; Bradford, 1985). Their use rests on the reductionist assumption that sexual deviance is a function of sexual "drive", which Freund (1980) sees as the internal motivation of sexual behaviour or imagery arising from sex hormones. Interest centres on reducing the level of circulating testosterone. However, while testosterone influences sexual arousability and activity, there is no firm evidence linking it to deviant sexual arousal (Hucker and Bain, 1990).

Surgical destruction of hypothalamic nuclei thought to control sexual drive has been reported in a few case studies, but there is insufficient research to justify its clinical use (Freund, 1980). Legalised castration has been employed as an option for sex offenders in some European countries, and Heim and Hursch (1979) reviewed four large-scale follow-up studies which indicated recidivism rates of between 1% and 7%. However, they argue that these were methodologically flawed because of biased sampling and inappropriate controls. They also note the varied effects of castration on sexual behaviour, and conclude that it is essentially an ideologically based punishment, which lacks a scientific rationale. Freund (1980) and Bradford (1985) disagree. However, the argument is not simply an empirical one, given current ethical objections in most western countries to castration as "treatment".

Reversible changes in testosterone levels can be achieved through administration of the synthetic antiandrogen cyproterone acetate (CPA: Androcur), and the hormonal agent medroxyprogesterone acetate (MPA: Provera). CPA has been used in Europe and Canada, and MPA in the United States. They have different modes of action, but both are reported to reduce erectile responding and the frequency of sexual fantasies and acts. However, demonstrations of effects on sexual offending are limited mainly to case studies and uncontrolled follow-ups. MPA reduces sexual behaviour as long as the patient takes the drug, but Bradford (1985) suggests that CPA has longer-term effects, and may influence deviant arousal. Others are less convinced of their utility, but some workers believe that these agents may sometimes have a place when combined with methods for developing prosocial sexual behaviour.

Psychotherapy

Classical individual psychoanalysis is rarely an option for apprehended sex offenders, and current psychodynamic approaches are more likely to focus on the "history-laden present" in a small group context (Cox, 1980). Cox sees the problems of sex offenders in a special hospital in terms of primitive defences against trusting relationships, and therapy aims to enhance self-esteem and reduce defences through disclosure of anxieties arising from early traumatic relationships. Group dynamics facilitate disclosure. However, the goal is to provide insight to help the patient tolerate the "unfinished business" of early trauma, and Cox acknowledges that this is unlikely to stop the patient offending.

Groth (1983) describes a broader group programme in a maximum security prison in Connecticut. The basic premise is again that sex offending is the outcome of early maltreatment, and that deficits in self-esteem, trust, and the management of aggression are critical problems. Programme goals are that the offender should recognise he has a problem, accept responsibility for his actions, re-evaluate his attitudes to sex and aggression, and realise that sexual assault is a compulsive act over which he must gain control. The group is a vehicle for mutual aid and self-help, and the programme deals with nine specific areas under three headings. First, re-education provides sex education, understanding of sexual assault, and its impact on victims. Second, resocialisation focuses on interpersonal relationships, management of aggression, and parenting skills. Finally, counselling groups deal with warning signs surrounding the offence, personal experience of victimisation, and ways of combating sexual assault.

Groth provides a preliminary evaluation of the first four years of the programme. Of those who participated and were subsequently released, 19% committed a further offence, and 8% a further sex offence, figures for nonparticipating sex offenders being 36% and 16%, respectively. The comparability of the two groups is unclear, but the data appear to support the programme's cost effectiveness.

Cognitive–behavioural therapies

In contrast to the psychodynamic view of the sex offence as a symptom of intrapsychic problems, early behavioural treatments for sexual deviation focused on changing sexual preferences and on strengthening heterosocial skills. While some continue to see treatment goals in these terms (Lanyon,

1986a), many behavioural programmes now incorporate cognitive methods and targets, and overlap with those of psychotherapists. The general goal is to promote self-control, targets being sexual behaviours, social competence, and cognitive distortions.

Changing deviant sexual preference remains a major target in many programmes. Techniques for *reducing deviant arousal* are mainly aversive procedures. Early aversion therapies using brief electric shock to a limb or nausea-inducing chemicals assumed a classical conditioning model, the aversive stimulus (unconditioned stimulus) being noncontingently paired with the deviant fantasy or visual stimulus (conditioned stimulus) eliciting the deviant arousal (conditioned response). Alternatively, an operant (punishment) paradigm is assumed when the aversive stimulus is contingent on the deviant response (erection). Electric aversion has been successful in suppressing deviant arousal to paedophilic and forced sex stimuli (Quinsey and Earls, 1990), but now raises ethical concerns. The objections appear to be aesthetic, since the experience of discomfort or distress is integral to many psychological therapies.

Nevertheless, the use of electrical aversion has declined in recent years. More popular is covert sensitisation, in which the client imagines the sequence of deviant activity culminating in aversive consequences involving physical or psychological distress. This is conceptualised as a covert punishment procedure, and covert reinforcement can be introduced by having the client imagine rewarding consequences of controlling deviant urges. Imaginal material may be presented on audiotapes, or may be self-administered by the client. Hayes, Brownell and Barlow (1978) describe the successful use of the latter in an offender with a history of exhibitionism and sadistic fantasies. In "assisted" covert sensitisation, deviant arousal to imagery, as monitored by PPG, is paired with both an imagined aversive event and an aversive odour, such as valeric acid gas or putrifying tissue (Maletzky, 1991). Maletzky (1980) used this procedure with 38 homosexual paedophiles and 62 exhibitionists, who imagined three deviant scenes per weekly session for 24 weeks, followed by periodic booster sessions for three years. Deviant fantasies and arousal were significantly reduced, and only eight clients reoffended. Although covert sensitisation appears to be successful with a range of paraphilias, and exhibitionism in particular (Blair and Lanyon, 1981), it lacks a firm theoretical justification, and is dependent on the client's ability to achieve vivid imagery. Laws, Meyer and Holmen (1978) report the successful treatment of a sexual sadist by means of a simpler aversive procedure involving only the pairing of slides with olfactory aversion.

In "shame" aversion therapy, the client performs the deviant behaviour, such as exposing himself, before an audience, while verbalising his thoughts, and this may be recorded on videotape for subsequent viewing. Serber (1971) found that five of eight paraphilics exposed to this procedure were free of deviant behaviour at six-month follow-up, but its use has been reported infrequently. More commonly used is satiation (Marshall, 1979), in which the client masturbates to orgasm using a nondeviant fantasy, and then continues to masturbate while verbalising deviant fantasies, which may also be recorded.

Verbal satiation alone has been found to have comparable effects (Laws and Osborn, 1983), and satiation methods are now included in many programmes under the heading of "boredom tapes".

The most popular technique for *increasing nondeviant arousal* is masturbatory or orgasmic reconditioning (ORC). This was among the earliest behaviour therapy methods, and involves the client masturbating to his preferred deviant fantasy, but switching to a nondeviant fantasy at the point of orgasmic inevitability. The nondeviant fantasy is subsequently moved progressively forward in time towards the start of masturbation. ORC rests on a classical conditioning rationale, but entails backward conditioning, which is inefficient (Keller and Goldstein, 1978). Conrad and Wincze (1976) were unable to demonstrate changes from ORC in PPG or behavioural measures in four self-referred homosexuals, despite client reports of changed fantasies and interests. Laws and Osborn (1983), however, report that alternating weekly blocks of masturbation to deviant and nondeviant fantasy successfully reduced paedophilic arousal. Masturbation to nondeviant fantasy alone was also found sufficient to increase the arousal of a paedophile to adult female slides, while simultaneously reducing deviant arousal (Kremsdorf, Holmen and Laws, 1980). The mechanism of change was suggested to be cognitive, the client redefining his sexual identity as a result of perceived change in the source of arousal.

Two further methods reported in the earlier literature are shaping and fading. Shaping employs operant principles to achieve gradual approximations to appropriate arousal by reinforcing erectile responses to slides (Quinn, Harbison and McAllister, 1970). Fading (Barlow and Agras, 1973) attempts to transfer arousal from a deviant visual stimulus by superimposing a nondeviant stimulus. The latter is "faded in", and the deviant stimulus faded out, contingent on the maintenance of erection. Effects of these techniques with sex offenders do not appear to have been investigated, although biofeedback of erectile response has been used with modest success (Quinsey and Earls, 1990).

These laboratory methods for eliminating or instating arousal have proved effective with a variety of deviations, but there is insufficient empirical research to permit a choice between them. There are several unanswered questions about their use. For example, it is assumed that suppression of deviant arousal and enhancement of nondeviant arousal are functionally distinct, and not simply reciprocal, but Kremsdorf, Holmen and Laws (1980) found that suppression of deviant interest followed from increasing nondeviant arousal alone. The assumption that deviant preference predicts reoffending also remains largely untested (Hall, 1990). It is, nevertheless, agreed that other aspects of sexual behaviour require attention. Anxiety about heterosexual interaction has been dealt with by systematic desensitisation, and sex education focusing on sexual norms and relationships may eliminate sexual myths and reduce prudishness. While some workers argue against attention to knowledge about basic anatomy and physiology, Crawford and Howells (1982) found that a short course of sex education for young offenders in a special hospital successfully reduced anxiety about sexual intercourse.

Attempts to improve *social competence* rely on skills training methods employing modelling and instruction, role-play, feedback, and rehearsal. Early programmes assumed deficits in conversational, dating, and assertive skills, and focused on micro-skills of gesture, eye-contact, and verbal fluency (Abel, Blanchard and Becker, 1978; Crawford and Allen, 1979). While these are part of the staple diet of sex offender programmes (Sapp and Vaughn, 1990), they neglect cognitive components of interaction, and more subtle skills of forming and maintaining intimate relationships. Nonsexual dysfunctions are also common precursors of sexual assaults, and many programmes therefore now target not only heterosocial skills, but also social problem solving, anger management, victim empathy, leisure skills, and self-esteem. These are generally dealt with in group formats emphasising experiential learning through modelling and rehearsal (Marshall and Barbaree, 1990b).

Training in social competence therefore entails attention to sociocognitive processes, and *cognitive distortions* are also a target in many programmes. These include beliefs about sex roles, rape myths, the acceptability of child–adult sex, and the minimisation of harmful effects of sexual assault. Cognitive therapy techniques which challenge these beliefs have been utilised in individual and group settings. Murphy (1990), for example, describes cognitive restructuring procedures for combating distortions by means of information on the effects of abuse, including victim confrontation, challenging assumptions implicit in distorted beliefs, role reversal in which the offender counters these beliefs, and by examining verbalised fantasy material derived from "boredom tapes".

Most behaviourally oriented sex offender programmes combine a number of these procedures (Perkins, 1987), and Freeman-Longo and Wall (1986) describe an inpatient programme in Oregon which includes not only most of the procedures noted above, but also drug and alcohol education, group psychotherapy, and organic treatments. As yet, there has been little attempt to "unpack" these complex programmes to determine which processes are more effective.

It is also difficult to compare programme outcomes given variations not only in content, but also in the risk levels of clients, institutional or community locations, and duration, which may be from a few months to five or more years. Particular problems arise in identifying appropriate control groups, since random allocation to a no-treatment group is not usually feasible or ethically desirable (Marshall and Barbaree, 1990b). Furby, Weinrott and Blackshaw (1989) suggest that in this light, we know little about the effects of current programmes on sex offender recidivism. Others, however, take a more optimistic view. Maletzky (1991), for example, reports 1 to 17 year follow-up data on 5000 sex offenders treated by behavioural methods at an outpatient sex abuse clinic in Portland, Oregon, which found an overall success rate of 91% on stringent clinical and criminal outcome criteria. Failure rates were lowest for heterosexual paedophiles (5%) and exhibitionists (7%), but higher for homosexual paedophiles (14%) and rapists (26%). While data from untreated groups are not available, Marshall and Barbaree (1990b) describe outcome data from their outpatient programme, indicating that for treated groups, recidivism rates were 18% for heterosexual paedophiles, 13% for homosexual paedophiles, and 48% for exhibitionists. For untreated offenders in these categories, rates were 43%, 43%, and 67%, respectively. The available evidence therefore suggests a relatively favourable outcome of treatment for child molesters (Becker and Hunter, 1992). Outcomes for exhibitionists are more variable, and rapists also appear to do less well, although controlled comparisons are lacking. Nevertheless, as Perkins (1987) notes, even a moderate prevention of reoffending is likely to be cost-effective in terms of benefits to the criminal justice system, potential victims, and the offender himself.

Relapse prevention

Many workers see deviant sexual behaviour as analogous to an addiction, and have adopted procedures for preventing relapse from the addictions field (Laws, 1989). This approach assumes that initial change and the maintenance of change are governed by different processes (Brownell et al., 1986). Whether a *lapse* (a single event involving the re-emergence of a previous habit) leads to *relapse* (a return to the previous state) depends on several individual and situational factors. In Marlatt's cognitive–behavioural model (Brownell et al., 1986), a high risk situation for which the person lacks a coping response produces decreased self-efficacy beliefs, lapse, and the *abstinence violation effect*, a cognitive phenomenon involving changed perceptions of self-control, which increases the probability of relapse. Treatment programmes therefore aim to develop self-management skills enabling the person to avoid lapses, or to prevent their progression to relapse.

Pithers (1990) describes a relapse prevention programme for rapists and child molesters. A lapse, such as the recurrence of a deviant fantasy, may follow exposure to a high risk situation, such as driving around in a state of anger in the case of a rapist, or being asked to baby-sit in the case of a paedophile. The abstinence violation effect may entail attribution of the lapse to treatment failure, and expectations that relapse is inevitable. If the lapse is expected, however, it may be seen as an opportunity for refining self-management skills. The initial step of the programme is therefore to eliminate unrealistic expectations of irreversible "cure", and to encourage active problem-solving.

Relapse prevention is introduced into treatment after victim empathy has developed. Therapist and client identify precursors and facilitators of sexual deviant acts, high-risk situations, and self-efficacy beliefs about coping in those situations. Treatment focuses first on avoidance of lapses. The client is taught to recognise relapse precursors through self-monitoring, and to avoid situational factors controlling deviant acts, such as alcohol, pornography, or particular relationships. He is also taught a problem-solving approach to high risk situations to develop strategies for coping or escape, and to counter deviant urges by focusing on negative consequences. Techniques are then developed for preventing unanticipated lapses from becoming relapses. Through cognitive restructuring, a lapse is reinterpreted as a slip or mistake to be learned from, rather than an irreversible loss of self-control, and this is facilitated by a "reminder card". A contract is also agreed specifying the limits and consequences of a lapse. These procedures constitute internal self-management. However, since offenders released from residential programmes do not always report lapses, an external supervisory dimension has been incorporated, in which specific precursors of risk and lapses are monitored by collaboration between therapist, probation officer, and significant others in the client's social network. While relapse prevention procedures are at an early stage of development, Pithers (1990) reports a 4% relapse rate in a five-year follow-up of 167 offenders, most of them paedophiles.

INTERVENTIONS WITH AGGRESSIVE OFFENDERS

Aggressive offenders have received less attention than sex offenders from clinicians. Although assaultive incidents may appear in the records of "chronic" or "serious" delinquents, criminals who specialise in violence are rare, and few psychologists have chosen to specialise in dealing with aggressive offending. Also, except where mental disorder is identified or aggression disrupts institutional life, aggressive offenders are less likely to be seen as in need of treatment, since male aggression receives support from cultural norms. However, recent attention to adolescent aggression and violence in the family has led to the development of specialised programmes in which psychological interventions play a major role, although evaluations of efficacy are as yet limited.

Like sex offenders, aggressive individuals rarely volunteer for treatment, and present similar issues of denial, victim blame, and failure to accept responsibility. The primary clinical task, however, is not to deal with a past violent act, but rather with the offender's potential for carrying out similar acts in future. Whether conceived as a response tendency or a personality trait, habitual aggression is a disposition which depends on other personal attributes, and has to be seen in the context of a person's lifestyle. Attention to a single problem area is therefore rarely sufficient to support long-term change.

Violent offenders are also heterogeneous (Chapter 9) and dictate a variety of goals. For example, those who use aggression instrumentally present different problems from those whose aggression is primarily anger-mediated. For the former, the strategy may be to manipulate the environmental contingencies, or in social learning terms, to change the beliefs or outcome expectancies supporting the use of aggression. For the latter, emotional control and self-regulation are more appropriate targets. Again, treatment goals for the overcontrolled individual who has committed an isolated act of extreme violence differ from those of the undercontrolled offender who gets into fights when intoxicated. These conceptual distinctions are as yet inconspicuous in the treatment literature, but they underscore the need for individualised assessment similar to that undertaken with sex offenders.

Psychopharmacological treatment

Although evidence for a specific physiological substrate for human aggression is lacking, pharmacological agents which affect mood, emotional arousability, or information transmission in the brain can influence the performance of violent acts. Administration of drugs for nonmedical purposes nevertheless arouses social concerns, and Tupin (1986) emphasises that for clinicians, pharmacological interventions are justified only when violence has a medical–psychiatric origin. The use of drugs to inhibit violence therefore occurs mainly in psychiatric settings, although its use with prisoners is not unknown.

Major and minor tranquillisers are often administered in emergency situations, and PRN (Pro re nata) medication is a common way of managing violent incidents in psychiatric hospitals (Drinkwater and Gudjonsson, 1989). The rationale is the nonspecific one of calming or sedating the patient, which can be justified when the safety of others is threatened. However, the use of a "chemical straitjacket" raises ethical issues because of the potential for punitive use, the neglect of environmental causes of violence, and the sometimes harmful side effects. In some cases, neuroleptics and minor tranquillisers have also escalated rather than inhibited violence (Drinkwater and Gudjonsson, 1989).

The rationale for longer-term drug administration is that it ameliorates or controls the disorder which mediates violence. Tupin (1986) notes that paranoid psychosis, schizophrenia, mania, organic brain syndromes, psychotic depression, and explosive personality disorder are sometimes found in individuals who have behaved violently, and that this justifies the use of psychoactive agents. While this implies that treatment targets are psychiatric symptoms rather than aggression itself, such drugs have been used with aggressive individuals not showing major psychiatric disorder. Stimulants such as methylphenidate and dextramphetamine have been found to reduce aggression in hyperactive children and delinquents (Satterfield, 1978) and antisocial personalities (Stringer and Josef, 1983), and anticonvulsants have been advocated for the "dyscontrol" syndrome (Monroe, 1978). Lithium, originally used to treat mania, has also been found to reduce serious institutional rule infractions among aggressive prisoners (Sheard et al., 1976). O'Callaghan (1988), however, notes that the quality of evidence supporting the pharmacological control of violence is poor, and suggests that while controlled studies with psychiatric patients support the use of major tranquillisers, the effects of stimulants, anticonvulsants, beta blockers, and lithium are merely suggestive.

The case for using drugs to control violence is largely the pragmatic one that they sometimes enable disturbed patients to function more effectively, but theoretical and empirical justifications remain weak. Diagnosis is rarely sufficient to explain violence, and while psychophysiological and biochemical models continue to be proposed (Chapter 6), the effects of drugs on aggressive behaviour appear to be largely nonspecific. Moreover, voluntary acceptability of psychoactive agents is limited by their unpleasant side effects. Sheard et al. (1976), for example, found that over 40% of prisoners taking lithium dropped out of their trial within two months, mainly because of side effects such as tremors, dry mouth, polyuria, and nausea. Finally, where control of violent acts has been demonstrated, it is limited to the duration of drug administration, and does not produce learning of nonaggressive coping skills. O'Callaghan (1988), however, suggests combining pharmacological with behavioural methods, since drug effects depend on the environment, and the learning of alternative skills may be facilitated when symptoms are quiescent. Evidence that cognitive guidance of aggression is reduced at low and high levels of arousal (Zillmann, 1979) might also justify such a combination.

Psychodynamic interventions

Psychodynamically oriented therapists see problems of violence in terms of personality development, and aggressive offenders are often identified as psychopathic personalities. Treatment issues therefore overlap with those described below for psychopaths. Therapy may be individual or group based, and as with sex offenders, aims to promote self awareness, empathy, self control, and social responsibility by means of the therapeutic relationship.

Although there is no uniform approach, psychotherapists working with aggressive offenders identify similar goals, strategies, and problems (Vaillant, 1975; Carney, 1977, 1978; Madden, 1986). A core issue is to establish trust, which is both a prerequisite for therapy and a target of change for individuals who are likely to view relationships as dangerous. This requires the therapist to show acceptance of the patient, though not his deeds, while at the same time setting limits and external controls. Getting the patient to accept responsibility for his situation and for change is a particular focus. Therapy entails establishing awareness of feelings by overcoming defences against fears of intimacy and low self-esteem, and this is achieved by encouraging verbalisations of destructive fantasies, tolerating expressions of uncomfortable feelings, and reflecting these. Therapists are less distant than is traditional in psychotherapy, not only using their authority to set limits, but also providing direction. They should also provide a role model of coping with normal fears and hates.

Two issues recur in discussions of therapy with this group. First is the problem of patient motivation and capacity for change. Violent patients usually enter therapy only under pressure from families or the courts, and even among involuntarily detained patients, attendance may be erratic and dropout rates high. Group therapy is considered less threatening, and hence a more appropriate medium, and erratic attendance may be tolerated as long as the patient becomes engaged in therapy at some point. However, aggressive offenders may be passively resistant to therapeutic involvement, or may "con" the therapist with superficial gestures of self awareness. Failure of the patient to express strong emotion is prognostically unfavourable, and Lion (1978) believes that change is unlikely without the development of a depressive reaction, signifying emerging guilt. Nevertheless, the extent of change is limited by the patient's ego strength, and a "symptom oriented solution" may be the most realistic goal (Carney, 1977).

A second issue is the demands made on the therapist. Treatment requires regular sessions extending over a year or more, and continued therapist support may be necessary for much longer. While the development of a trusting relationship requires honest acceptance from the therapist, the focus on the patient's violence may generate an intense countertransference, often taking the form of fear of the patient. Therapists therefore need to explore and verbalise their own feelings, preferably with other therapists.

As with psychotherapy with offenders more generally, there are few evaluations of its effectiveness with aggressive offenders, but Carney (1977) describes an uncontrolled follow-up of group therapy in an outpatient clinic. Offenders attended as a condition of probation, and after an average of 13 months treatment, were followed up for an average of 9 months. Significant improvements were found in ratings of community adjustment, and recidivism rate was 28%. However, no changes were found on psychological tests. Carney suggests that while therapy did not change personality, it achieved control over violent behaviour.

Behavioural and cognitive approaches

Although a reduction in disruptive behaviour is a common target in token economies, investigations of the effects of behavioural methods on aggressive offending have been few. Most reports are concerned with the aggressive behaviour of young children, or the management of violent patients in psychiatric institutions, and while these have generated widely used techniques, the quality of evidence regarding durability of effects remains poor (Bornstein, Hamilton and McFall, 1981; O'Callaghan, 1988).

Bornstein et al. (1981) reviewed the application of behavioural approaches to adult aggression. Operant techniques were prominent in early reports. These entailed combinations of extinction, time out, differential reinforcement of nonaggressive behaviour, and overcorrection involving either rehearsal of incompatible behaviours or making restitutions. While the results demonstrate that aggression can be brought under environmental control by such methods, operant studies have been predominantly concerned with linguistically impoverished individuals, such as institutionalised mentally handicapped or chronically disabled psychiatric patients, who may be more susceptible to external control. Moreover, Bornstein et al. (1981) found only one report which examined maintenance effects.

The early literature also contains a few reports of the use of systematic desensitisation, but these were mainly poorly evaluated case studies, and its utility is not clearly established. Some more recent studies, however, lend support to the use of relaxation. Deffenbacher, Demm and Brandon (1986), for example, found that anxiety management involving relaxation and coping skills training had a significant long-term effect on both state and trait measures of anger and self-reported responses to frustration in angry students.

Social skills training has also been used to deal with problems of aggression in delinquents and aggressive adolescents (Goldstein, 1986). This is justified by the finding that aggressive offenders may lack nonaggressive assertive skills (Kirchner, Kennedy and Draguns, 1979). However, evidence that aggressive prisoners are not uniformly deficient in social skills (Henderson, 1982) highlights the need for individualised assessment.

Cognitive–behavioural techniques have predominated in recent work. As noted earlier, training in self-instruction and problem-solving have been used to teach self-control to children, and some interventions have been aimed particularly at aggressive children. Camp et al. (1977) used SIT focusing on problem-solving with young hyperaggressive children, and found that relative to untreated controls, trained children improved and became more similar to nonaggressive children on several aspects of cognitive functioning. They also showed improved prosocial behaviour in the classroom, but not reduced aggression. In another study with preadolescent boys, Lochman et al. (1984) compared problem-solving training to cope with anger with goal setting, a combination of the two, and no treatment. Both groups receiving problem-solving training showed reduced ratings of aggression and disruptiveness, and increased self-esteem. There was also evidence for generalisation from school to home behaviour, but only limited effects were found on the perceptions of teachers or peers of the boys' behaviour.

In one of the few studies of adjudicated delinquents, Guerra and Slaby (1990) included problem-solving in a cognitive mediational training programme in a maximum security facility for violent offenders. Training consisted of 12 weekly sessions of social problem-solving training together with attitude change procedures designed to challenge beliefs legitimating aggression, and this was compared with an attention and a no-treatment control. Cognitive training had a significant effect on social problem-solving skills, beliefs about aggression, and institutional ratings of aggression, impulsivity, and inflexible behaviour. However, while one- to two-year follow-up also revealed lower recidivism for the cognitive group, differences were not significant.

Anger is now commonly regarded as a significant mediator of antisocial aggression, and a target for cognitive–behavioural intervention (Levey and Howells, 1990). The most widely used approach is Novaco's anger management programme (Novaco, 1978), which involves cognitive restructuring and coping skills training, and is an adaptation of Meichenbaum's stress inoculation package. The three stages in the programme are:

1. *Cognitive preparation*: the client is introduced to the nature and functions of anger, and begins a diary of anger experiences both to facilitate awareness of the relation between anger and self-statements and to monitor progress; conditions eliciting anger are reviewed, and training given in discriminating justified from unjustified anger.
2. *Skill acquisition*: the client is taught how to reappraise anger eliciting events, and to employ self-instructions to guide coping attempts and as self-reinforcement; relaxation training is given as a further self-control skill,

and skills of communication and assertion are taught using modelling and role play.
3. *Application practice*: developing skills are applied and tested in graded simulated anger situations. This package can be used on an individual or group basis.

Novaco (1978) evaluated the procedure with volunteer adults, finding the full package to be more effective in reducing the frequency and intensity of anger reactions than cognitive or relaxation components in isolation. He has also successfully taught these procedures to police and probation officers. Modified versions of Novaco's package have effectively reduced angry reactions in married couples in conflict (Margolin, 1979) and child-abusing parents (Nomellini and Katz, 1983). They also produced long-term reduction of the violent behaviour of an institutionalised female patient with epilepsy (Bistline and Frieden, 1984).

However, reports of use with offenders have been few. Schlicter and Horan (1981) compared a similar stress inoculation package for institutionalised delinquents with an attenuated programme involving therapist contact but relaxation alone, and a no-treatment control. Both treatments produced significant effects on self-reported anger and aggression, and stress inoculation also enhanced role-played coping with provocation, but no effects were found on institutional behaviour ratings at two weeks follow-up. Fiendler, Marriott and Iwata (1984) employed a similar anger control package, which includes self-monitoring, self-instructional training, self-evaluation, problem-solving and arousal reduction. Delinquent schoolchildren in a school token economy showed improvements in problem-solving and teacher-rated self control, and at five-week follow-up were receiving fewer fines for misbehaviour, including aggression, within the token economy. Anger management training in an English Youth Custody centre also produced fewer disciplinary reports for some participants over a three-month follow-up (McDougall et al., 1987).

Some studies therefore indicate that training in anger management reduces aggressive behaviour in the short-term, and its utility in managing disruptive behaviour in institutions seems established (Levey and Howells, 1990). However, its effects with violent offenders and its longer-term impact on aggressive offending remain to be investigated. There are also unresolved questions about the comparative effectiveness of different procedures. For example, in a study with angry students, Moon and Eisler (1983) compared Novaco's method with social skills training in assertion and problem-solving training. All methods improved anger management, but social skills and problem-solving training had the advantage of improving assertion. The utility of other methods of cognitive restructuring with problems of anger and aggression has yet to be examined, and in view of the role of perceived inequity or moral violation in anger arousal, the combination of anger management and moral reasoning training advocated by Goldstein et al. (1989) also merits closer scrutiny.

Despite lack of firm evidence that psychological treatments produce durable changes in aggressive dispositions, it is clear that several available methods demonstrate a significant potential, and many avenues remain unexplored. Recent studies (e.g. Guerra and Slaby, 1990) have begun to fill the theoretical vacuum in which early behavioural interventions were carried out, but issues such as offender heterogeneity, effective treatment components, and treatment intensity have yet to be addressed. It is remarkable that some projects report generalised behaviour change after training in circumscribed skills extending over only a few weeks. In practice, however, interventions with habitually aggressive offenders are likely to require treatment of greater intensity.

Psychological interventions also continue to be person-centred. This is likely to be insufficient when aggression is supported by subcultural norms, which may happen in institutional contexts as well as high delinquency neighbourhoods. Toch (1975) argues that attempts to deal with violence of both prison inmates and of criminal justice agents, such as overzealous police officers or prison staff, must address the norms of the peer group. He describes work in a police department in which a police officer review panel dealt with problems of violence by officers through counselling, pressure where necessary, and reinforcement of alternative peer group norms. A positive peer culture is also advocated as a primary vehicle of change among institutionalised aggressive delinquents by Agee (1986).

TREATMENT OF PSYCHOPATHY AND PERSONALITY DISORDER

Personality disorders shade into normality, but are the most frequently identified psychiatric disorders among offenders, and are commonly associated with problems of aggression, sexual offending, and substance abuse. These disorders are particularly prevalent in forensic psychiatric populations, often accompanying more serious psychiatric disorders. Studies of special hospital samples in England, for example, indicate that, although the majority of patients are identified as mentally ill, more than two thirds meet criteria for one or more personality disorder (Tyrer, 1988; Blackburn et al., 1990). These include schizoid, avoidant and passive–aggressive disorders, and are not confined to the category of antisocial personality disorder (APD).

Clinical interest nevertheless traditionally centres on psychopathic personality, whose treatability is viewed pessimistically. However, this view rests more on anecdote than firm evidence, and the treatment literature is plagued by two major problems. First is the inconsistent use of the term "psychopath", which refers variously to personality disorder in general, a persistently socially deviant individual, or a narrow, more specific class of offender characterised by lack of guilt and empathy, impulsivity, and intolerance of frustration (Chapter 3). Populations examined in the clinical literature are therefore rarely homogeneous. For example, Blackburn (1975a) found that only a quarter of diagnosed "psychopaths" admitted to a special hospital showed characteristics approximating to the more specific category of primary psychopath, and similar findings are reported for "psychopaths" admitted to the Henderson unit (Copas et al., 1984). Harris, Rice and Cormier (1989) also note that although two thirds of patients admitted to a Canadian maximum security hospital were diagnosed as "antisocial personality", less than a quarter met DSM-III-R criteria for APD. While clinical discussions typically centre on the treatment problems presented by "classical" psychopaths, such individuals are probably a minority among the "psychopaths" or "character disorders" examined in treatment studies, and the focus on this specific category has obscured the association of persistent antisocial behaviour with other forms of personality disorder. Carney (1978) argues that differentiation of personality disorders within antisocial populations is unnecessary, since there are sufficient commonalities to make them all amenable to the same therapeutic approach. However, this "uniformity myth" is contradicted by findings in several studies that personality characteristics predict differential responsiveness to particular treatment methods (e.g. Copas et al., 1984; Harris, Rice and Cormier, 1989; Ogloff, Wong and Greenwood, 1990). Differentiation of personality disorders is therefore necessary not only to identify amenability to different treatment methods, but also to identify individual treatment targets.

A second problem is that the theoretical link between treatment technique and outcome is usually obscure. While a reduction in socially deviant behaviour is typically the goal of an intervention, the relevance of personality disorder is the extent to which such behaviour is mediated by inflexible and maladaptive traits. Demonstration of treatment efficacy in this context requires not only that treatment be shown to reduce recidivism, but also that this is a consequence of changes in mediating personality variables. Few studies, however, clearly specify targets other than antisocial behaviour. Psychodynamic programmes, for example, tend to identify vague goals, such as improved social responsibility, self awareness, or self control, but provide no reliable means of determining their attainment. At the other extreme, behavioural programmes are often concerned with concrete targets such as institutional compliance, grooming habits, or skills whose relevance to either antisocial behaviour or personality disorder is unclear. Failure to identify treatment goals appears to be widespread in clinical practice. Dell and Robertson (1988), for example, found that psychiatrists admitting "psychopaths" to a special hospital had specified a purpose or form of treatment for less than a quarter.

Personality disorders are not diseases, since they represent learned dysfunctional behaviour patterns. Personal change rather than "cure" is therefore the appropriate goal, although the provision of specific coping skills may often be the most attainable target. However, systematic outcome research on the treatment of different forms of personality disorder has yet to appear, reflecting the lack of clinical interest in personality disorders other than psychopathy prior to the advent of DSM-III (Widiger and Frances, 1985b; Beck and Freeman, 1990). This discussion will of necessity focus on the clinical literature dealing with "antisocial personalities", but it must be emphasised that conclusions about the treatability of the "classical" psychopath rest mainly on studies of poor methodology conducted with vaguely defined samples.

It is a common finding that diagnosis of psychopathic personality or personality disorder among imprisoned offenders is associated with greater risk of recidivism in general, and violent recidivism in particular, although this may often reflect the influence of entrenched criminality on the diagnosis (Chapter 10). However, evidence on the impact of treatment interventions is meagre. From a search of 295 reports on antisocial personality, Levine and Bornstein (1972) were able to identify only ten studies which approached methodological requirements (homogeneous samples, untreated controls, follow-up, and specific outcome criteria), most of which concerned juvenile offenders treated in penal settings. Eight described significant effects on antisocial behaviour, and the authors note that this limited evidence does not support the view that antisocial personalities are unamenable to change. However, none of these studies employed a reproducible criterion of antisocial personality, and it is doubtful whether any dealt with homogeneous samples. For example, almost 60% of the "character and behaviour disorders" of one study (Colman and Baker, 1969) had primary diagnoses of schizophrenia or neurosis.

This problem is emphasised by Suedfeld and Landon (1978), who reviewed the literature on individual and group therapy, milieu therapy, somatic treatment, and behaviour modification with "psychopaths" reported up to 1975. Most reports concerned the treatment of delinquents and adult criminals, and consistently inadequate criteria of psychopathy precluded anything more than the following tentative conclusions: therapy should be conducted with firm rules and non-gullible supportiveness, drugs may enable the psychopath to achieve rapport with therapists, a therapeutic community may be helpful, and psychopaths may "burn out" with age. Only a handful of relevant studies has appeared since these reviews.

Psychopharmacological treatment

Conditions requiring pharmacological treatment, such as epilepsy or mood disorders, sometimes co-occur with personality disorders, and Widiger and Frances (1985b) suggest that there may be some potential for the use of drugs as an adjunct to psychological treatment in view of the evidence for biological influences on personality. However, apart from controlling aggression, there is currently little rationale for drug treatment of these disorders, and drugs are not used widely in clinical practice. For example, Dell and Robertson (1988) found that only 14% of legally defined psychopaths had been prescribed medication.

There is a scattered clinical literature on pharmacological attempts to improve compliance in personality disorders, but findings are generally inconclusive (Suedfeld and Landon, 1978; Kellner, 1978). Kellner found little evidence for the effectiveness of neuroleptics or minor tranquillisers, but suggests that some drugs might benefit sociopaths showing uncontrollable aggression, impulsiveness, or mood lability. He notes the potential of lithium in this respect.

There is, however, a longstanding interest in the possible utility of stimulants in facilitating compliance and new learning in view of relatively consistent evidence that these agents reduce impulsive antisocial behaviour in hyperactive children. Satterfield (1978) suggests that this effect is achieved via an increase in cortical arousal, which reduces motor restlessness and improves concentration. He proposes that adult psychopaths are also underaroused, and that pharmacologically increased arousal may be a necessary adjunct to educational and other therapeutic efforts. However, the arousal hypothesis has not fared well (Chapter 6), and evidence for effects of stimulants on antisocial adults is limited to uncontrolled case studies. Hill (1947) followed up eight patients who had briefly received amphetamine, and concluded that it was of little value for inadequate, passive, hysterical, or neurasthenic personalities, but that there were beneficial effects for aggressive characters capable of warm interpersonal relationships. This does not, however, describe the "classical" psychopath. Stringer and Josef (1983) also reported the use of methylphenidate with two patients diagnosed APD who had a childhood history of attention deficit disorder. Both were more co-operative and less aggressive while receiving the drug, but this did not outlast treatment.

Individual and group psychotherapy

Psychodynamic therapies focus explicitly on personality structure, and case reports of the treatment of personality disorders appear frequently in the psychoanalytic literature. However, the few available outcome studies are confined to treatment of antisocial populations. The traditional psychoanalytic view is that the psychopath is untreatable because of the absence of neurotic conflicts, and there seems general agreement that the psychopath's resistance to treatment, manipulativeness and use of primitive defences, difficulties in forming a therapeutic alliance, and strong countertransference reactions pose significant obstacles to the attainment of insight or self awareness through the transference relationship. However, some psychotherapists do not draw a firm line between psychopaths and acting-out neurotics, believing that psychopaths have some trace of anxiety or depression (e.g. Schmideberg, 1961; Vaillant, 1975). Psychopaths may therefore be treatable under certain conditions.

In a forerunner to cognitive therapy, Thorne (1959) saw "sociopathic reactions" in Adlerian terms as an offensive–defensive life style protected by egocentric attitudes and blame-avoidance. Individual therapy emphasised limit setting, acceptance of responsibility for negative consequences, insight into self-defeating behaviour, reality testing, and the discovery that "honesty is the best policy". No outcome data were presented, but Thorne claimed that this approach was successful in all of seven patients treated, although treatment lasted up to 12 years in some cases. Vaillant (1975) is also relatively optimistic about treatment prospects. He questions Cleckley's claim that psychopaths lack anxiety and motivation for change, seeing this is a stereotype of "a patient fleeing therapy". He suggests that the behaviour of antisocial personalities represents immature defences against fears of dependency and intimacy, and describes four case studies in which inpatient containment, firm behavioural control, confrontation rather than interpretation, and peer group support were apparently successful in achieving personality change. Woody et al. (1985), however, are more pessimistic. Among outpatient drug abusers undergoing cognitive or supportive expressive psychotherapy, APD patients showed little change on a variety of psychiatric and psychological measures in comparison with APD patients who were also depressed. The authors suggest that difficulties in forming a relationship with the therapist militate against successful treatment in APD. Nevertheless, some moderate improvements in the areas of employment and illegal behaviour were found for this group.

Most psychotherapists see individual and outpatient treatment as inappropriate for antisocial personalities, and regard structured group therapy in a residential setting as the treatment of choice (Carney, 1978; Frosch, 1983). Jew, Clanon and Mattocks (1972) found that personality disordered offenders in group therapy had a significantly better parole success rate following release from prison hospital than untreated offenders during the first year (74% vs 67%), but this modest difference subsequently disappeared. The authors point to a lack of parole support facilities. Apparently supporting this, Carney (1978) reports low rates of recidivism for "defective delinquents" treated at Patuxent by a combination of individual and group therapy followed by three years of supervised parole. For those completing treatment, only 7% reoffended, in comparison with 37% for the institution as a whole. However, as noted in Chapter 12, the outcome data from Patuxent have been challenged.

Therapeutic communities

The concept of *therapeutic community* (TC) emerged in Britain in the 1940s and in California in the 1950s, and is now a generic term for several kinds of therapeutic organisation (Kennard, 1983). For present purposes, the most pertinent are the democratic–analytic and the concept-based TCs. The former, which is more common in Britain, is usually a small community of adolescents or young adults with neurotic problems or personality disorders, which aims to resolve inner conflicts and promote responsible social behaviour through exposure to a combination of democratic power sharing, permissiveness, communalism, and reality confrontation. The best known example is the Henderson Hospital, associated with the work of Maxwell Jones (1963), but these principles are also utilised by Grendon Underwood prison (Gunn et al,. 1978) and the Barlinnie unit in a Scottish prison (Cooke, 1989).

Concept-based TCs are more common in America, and are hierarchically organised communities originating in self-help philosophies. They are mainly concerned with rehabilitating alcohol or drug abusers, and are based on the Synanon and Phoenix House model, staff members usually being ex-addicts. This kind of TC has been established in several prisons (Wexler, Falkin and Lipton, 1990), and juvenile correctional facilities (Agee, 1986). Kennard (1983) suggests that despite the differing models, TCs share the following basic features: (1) an informal atmosphere; (2) regular community meetings; (3) sharing the work of running the community; (4) recognition of residents as auxiliary therapists. The general assumption is that the delegation of responsibility to residents in a "living and learning" environment which encourages open expression of feelings and exploration of relationships will facilitate self-control.

There is some evidence that TCs can benefit psychological adjustment in the short-term by reducing anxiety and depression (Gunn et al., 1978) and increasing self-esteem and self-perceived conformity and independence (Norris, 1983). Their impact in resocialising offenders is more equivocal. Craft, Stephenson and Granger (1964) randomly allocated young psychopaths to a TC or a traditional authoritarian ward. After one year, there were few differences on a range of psychological tests, but those in the authoritarian unit showed a greater increase in IQ. They had also reoffended less at 14-month follow-up, and only a quarter were in need of continued care, compared with half of those from the TC. A controlled evaluation at an English approved school by Cornish and Clarke (1975) similarly failed to demonstrate any benefits of a TC. "Suitable" boys were randomly assigned to either a TC or a traditional unit, while "unsuitable" boys also went to a traditional unit. At a two-year follow-up, reconviction rates for the three units were indistinguishable, ranging from 68% to 70%. A 10-year follow-up of prisoners discharged from Grendon Underwood also found no reduction in recidivism, 92% of the TC prisoners having a further conviction compared with 85% of a comparison group (Robertson and Gunn, 1987), and follow-up of "psychopaths" admitted to the Henderson Hospital again suggests a high failure rate. Using a criterion of no further hospitalisations or criminal offences within three to five years as indicating success, Copas et al. (1984) found that 36% of those admitted were successful compared with 19% of a group not admitted for various reasons, although success rates increased with length of stay.

Copas et al. (1984) also found that secondary psychopaths derived the least benefit, and that the more successful patients already possessed an adequate repertoire of interpersonal skills and were the least unsocialised to begin with. Similar findings are reported from Canada. Harris, Rice and Cormier (1989) carried out a 10-year follow-up of violent recidivism among offenders who had been patients for at least two years in a TC in a maximum security hospital. They found that 77% of those scoring highly on Hare's Psychopathy Checklist were violent recidivists compared with 24% of those scoring low. Ogloff, Wong and Greenwood (1990) also found that offender patients in a TC who had high scores on the Psychopathy Checklist stayed in treatment for a shorter time than those with medium or low scores, and were rated as lower in motivation and improvement.

One implication of these findings, however, is that some forms of personality disorder respond favourably, and a few studies suggest more positive benefits of the TC on offenders. Prosocial peer modelling was emphasised in a unit for habitually violent prisoners in an Indian prison, where the majority of inmates were conforming and "provided a good example" (Sandhu, 1970). Of 18 psychopaths who stayed for an average of nine months, 13 were said to be successful, but the criteria are unclear. Agee (1986) also notes an apparently low recidivism rate of 33% for a TC for chronically violent youths, although control data are lacking. A preliminary evaluation of the Barlinnie unit provides suggestive evidence of reduced violence following admission and a lower than expected recidivism rate at follow-up (Cooke, 1989), but numbers are small and again a comparison group is lacking. McCord (1983) also reports significantly reduced recidivism among preadolescent "psychopaths" exposed to milieu therapy emphasising "disciplined love". However, continued support seems to have been available after institutional release for treated delinquents, but not for controls. More definitive is a large scale study of a concept-based prison TC for drug abusers in New York State (Wexler, Falkin and Lipton, 1990). Over a follow-up period of some three years, rearrest rates for males were 27% for those completing the programme, 35% for those in a less structured milieu programme, and 41% of prisoners volunteering for the TC but not participating. Wexler et al. believe that their hierarchical TC contains the ingredients now considered necessary for successful rehabilitation, such as a social learning model (although this is not immediately obvious), a high degree of structure, and prosocial modelling. Agee (1986) also suggests that an effective institutional TC will emphasise a positive peer culture, a positive staff culture, a structure which includes effective discipline, focus on relationships, victim awareness, security, and adequate time for treatment. Her programme also includes staff–inmate matching. Whether these ingredients were lacking in the less successful TC programmes merits attention.

Despite the limited evidence for its success, the TC continues to have vocal supporters. The humane, democratic, treatment-oriented approach contrasts with the authoritarian, punitive, and degrading features of many custodial institutions, and in this respect the TC commends itself as "a paradigm of prison management" (Robertson and Gunn, 1987). Nevertheless, its ideological and aesthetic appeal may overshadow issues of rehabilitative effectiveness. There is no evidence, for example, that the TC is superior to other therapeutic modalities in promoting psychological adjustment, and the evidence suggests that most TCs do not affect criminality. Robertson and Gunn (1987) argue that reoffending has more to do with problems of marital adjustment, accommodation, or employment faced by the offender after release than with what happens in treatment. However, such problems may reflect skill deficits as much as opportunities, and Harris, Rice and Cormier (1989) note that the TC they investigated gave no emphasis to skills training or to the learning of anticriminal attitudes. One problem shared with other psychodynamic methods is the lack of specificity inherent in the goals of "insight" or "responsibility", and Kennard (1983) suggests that TCs might benefit from addressing the more specific deficits dealt with by behavioural methods.

Cognitive–behavioural approaches

Behavioural methods have been applied to such problems as aggression, sexual deviation, or deficient interpersonal skills in deviant populations likely to contain many with personality disorders, but very few of these programmes identify their clients in terms of psychopathic personality or personality disorder. It therefore seems likely that behaviour therapists commonly deal with personality disorders, but choose to call them something else. What are commonly identified as social skill deficits, for example, include social avoidance and anxiety, lack of assertiveness, and inappropriate anger expression, which appear among the criteria for personality disorders. Anger problems, for example, are among the criteria defining passive–aggressive, borderline, and antisocial personality disorders.

Despite their aversion to dispositional concepts, some behaviour therapists attempt to incorporate clinical concepts of personality disorder into a behavioural framework, usually by translating them into terms of skill deficits. Marshall and Barbaree (1984), for example, conceptualise personality disorders as unskillful social behavioural repertoires which fail to engender rewarding or nonaversive outcomes from others. A few behavioural programmes for undifferentiated personality disorders have been described which successfully reduced social dysfunction. Jones et al. (1977), for example, describe a short-term token economy ward for military personnel diagnosed as personality disorder. A combination of individualised contingency contracting and the reinforcement with points for appearance, work, and educational achievement led to significantly more of those treated remaining on active duty than untreated controls. Moyes, Tennent and Bedford (1985) also found that a programme combining a token economy, individualised contingency management, and social skills training reduced aggressive and disruptive behaviour and self-mutilation in youths described as behaviour and character disordered. It also delayed subsequent involvement with the police. However, an ambitious token economy programme described by Cavior and Schmidt (1978), in which offenders were also assigned to differential treatment on the basis of Quay's behaviour classification system, failed to produce any significant reduction in recidivism, or any differential effects for psychopaths.

Applications of cognitive–behavioural methods to personality disorders have received some attention, but outcome data are currently few. Temple and Wollersheim (1979) described a programme for psychopaths which employed fixed role therapy and problem-solving training through self-instruction to teach clients to obtain their goals of obtaining sensation and self gratification in socially acceptable ways, but reported no outcome data. A different approach was taken by Frederiksen and Rainwater (1981), who conceptualised explosive personality disorder (an impulse control disorder in DSM-III) in terms of negative interpersonal expectations and deficient assertion. They treated voluntary patients with a short but intensive programme of social skills training, cognitive restructuring, and self control of problem drinking, and found reductions in explosive outbursts for those followed up, although some continued to have social problems and drop-out rate was high. Only one controlled study of anger management training with personality disordered patients appears to have been reported, most of them APD (Stermac, 1986). This produced effects on self-reported anger and coping strategies, but longer-term behavioural effects were not examined.

Cognitive–behavioural approaches which redescribe personality disorders in terms of skill deficits follow the peripheralist, molecular emphasis of traditional learning theory based therapies, and eschew any broader conceptualisation of personality. However, the treatment literature suggests that the presence of personality disorder reduces the effectiveness of programmes which focus on skills training alone (Beck and Freeman, 1990). Beck and Freeman argue for a more molar approach, proposing that personality traits are overt expressions of tacit or deep cognitive schemata which dictate a generalised behavioural strategy. Each personality disorder is held to be characterised by a distinct cognitive profile reflecting a composite of beliefs, attitudes, affects, and strategies organised around a general theme of the nature of the self and others. For example, passive–aggressive personalities are held to be dominated by beliefs that others interfere with their freedom of action, and that they must do things their own way. In the case of antisocial personalities, core beliefs relate to looking out for oneself and an entitlement to break rules, which result in a strategy of attacking or exploiting others. Beck and Freeman give less weight to an absence of "superego" than to an egocentric level of moral development in which self-serving beliefs minimise future consequences. Therapy aims to enhance cognitive functioning by utilising self-serving motivation. The clinician attempts to guide the client from a strategy of unqualified self-interest to one of qualified self-interest which takes account of the needs of others, by means of guided discussions, structured cognitive exercises, and behavioural experiments.

Beck and Freeman (1990) report experience of success of cognitive therapy with antisocial outpatients, but the only available empirical data are those of Woody et al. (1985), whose findings offer only qualified support. Beck and Freeman's approach rests on a straightforward translation of DSM-III descriptions of personality disorder categories into belief systems which would appear to underlie them, but is not based on any systematic theory of personality or empirical research. A broader view with some empirical support (Chapters 3 and 9) conceptualises personality disorders as dysfunctional *interpersonal* styles supported by biased schemata which function as self-fulfilling prophecies through their effects on others (Carson, 1979; Kiesler, 1983). Therapy therefore needs to focus on disconfirming interpersonal expectations, and Kiesler (1983) and Safran (1990) argue that this can be achieved by using the therapist–client relationship as a mechanism for change. In the case of institutionalised offenders, it suggests programming the environment to provide not only disconfirming experiences, but also opportunities for developing new interpersonal skills.

Few new findings have emerged from the treatment literature to add to the tentative observations of Suedfeld and Landon (1978), and the number of methodologically adequate studies which differentiate a specific category of psychopathic personality from other personality disorders remains so small that only two conclusions can be drawn. First, it has yet to be established that "nothing works" to change psychopaths. Second, some offenders with personality disorders do appear to change with psychological treatment. No particular approach has consistently been found to be beneficial, but procedures which structure the therapeutic environment, such as the token economy and the therapeutic community, and eclectic psychotherapy, group therapy, social skills training, and cognitive restructuring, can all claim examples of positive effects. Several of the cognitive–behavioural procedures being developed with offenders generally seem particularly relevant to personality disorders, such as interpersonal problem solving and moral reasoning training, but these remain to be investigated.

These conclusions are relevant to dangerous offenders generally, since although few programmes explicitly target personality disorders, the more successful appear to focus on the kinds of dysfunctional beliefs and interpersonal styles subsumed by the global concept of personality disorder. Given the range of programmes which have achieved effects, it may be that specific techniques are less important than certain conditions which promote change. Common ingredients of more successful programmes appear to be inpatient containment, treatment staff who are warm but directive and set limits, procedures which challenge egocentric and antisocial beliefs, the programming of new cognitive and interpersonal skills through prosocial modelling and skills training, intensive treatment, and structured support beyond programme termination. While evidence for the importance of these for the rehabilitation of dangerous offenders is no more than suggestive, recent evaluations discussed in the next chapter indicate that many of these conditions are basic to successful offender rehabilitation generally.

Chapter 15

The Effectiveness and Ethics of Intervention

INTRODUCTION

During the 1970s rehabilitation as a penal goal came under attack. Appraisals of outcome research suggested that "nothing works" in terms of reducing recidivism, and it was argued that reoffending has more to do with opportunity, peer pressure, lack of family support, or the deprivations of an urban environment than with the personal deficits dealt with by rehabilitation programmes. This was seized on as right wing political philosophies gained ground on both sides of the Atlantic, and rehabilitation was de-emphasised in favour of "get tough" policies.

However, as the last two chapters illustrate, the variety of psychological change methods applied with the aim of reducing reoffending has increased during the last two decades. While it is clear that none represents a panacea, and that dramatic successes are rare, it is also clear that many psychologists working with offenders continue to have faith in the efficacy of their procedures. In the light of widespread disenchantment with rehabilitation, this might be construed as professional myopia. This final chapter therefore examines the justification for this persisting faith in psychological interventions. However, since many interventions are concerned with preventing offending rather than rehabilitating convicted offenders, psychological contributions to these will first be reviewed.

PRIMARY AND SECONDARY PREVENTION

Preventive approaches to psychological disorder initially followed the public health model, which assumes that prevention of onset is ultimately more effective than secondary or tertiary intervention. Limitations of this analogy have been increasingly noted, and are particularly apparent in the context of delinquency prevention. For example, delinquency is not a discrete disorder, and in the absence of clear criteria of onset, the distinction between primary and secondary prevention is often difficult to maintain. Primary prevention generally means a focus on populations of "well" people, or on subgroups who are at risk but who are not dysfunctional, whereas secondary prevention refers to prompt intervention for early detected maladaptation (Durlak, 1985). However, the more consistently identified risk factors for delinquency, such as early behaviour disorders or family problems, are signs of dysfunction calling for intervention in themselves, even though a longer-term goal may be to prevent the emergence of criminal behaviour. Only a few prevention programmes in this area can therefore be considered primary in the usual sense.

A further issue is that limited knowledge of the salient causal processes in delinquency precludes identification of the appropriate targets for preventive attention. Some sociologists argue that social institutions rather than at-risk individuals are the relevant targets, but Farrington (1985) notes that the evidence does not permit a simple choice between individual and social determinants. In fact, both sociological and psychological approaches to prevention are ultimately concerned to influence individual functioning, and psychological approaches increasingly draw on transactional or ecological models which recognise the reciprocal interaction of multiple individual and social factors (Rosenberg and Repucci, 1985; Zigler and Hall, 1987). While some question whether what is known is sufficient to be translated into effective prevention, several recent developments assume that it is sufficient to identify promising targets. The most prominent focus on preventing delinquent development through early intervention, minimising recidivism through diversion from the courts, and situational prevention of criminal acts.

Preventing delinquent development

Evidence that antisocial behaviour is a relatively stable characteristic with identifiable childhood antecedents suggests that modification of individual and familial factors may prevent developmental progression to later delinquency. Since these antecedents can frequently be conceptualised as deficient skills, psychological approaches emphasise enhancing the competence of children or parents at risk, usually through direct intervention, but sometimes indirectly through changing the social environment. The aim of competence enhancement programmes is to build or strengthen competencies, personal resources, and coping skills as buffers against stress or dysfunction. As Nietzel and Himelein (1986) note, such interventions need to be aimed at those specific deficiencies most strongly correlated with delinquency at different age levels. They therefore vary in terms of developmental stage targeted and whether the locus of intervention is the community, school, or family.

The classic attempt to prevent delinquency is the Cambridge–Somerville Youth Study of the 1940s. Over 500 boys aged 5 to 13, who were "difficult" or "average" in their social behaviour, were randomly assigned to a control group who simply provided information, or to an experimental group who received personal and social counselling from social workers, academic tutoring, medical attention, and participated in youth programmes, on average for five years. At a 30-year follow-up, there were no differences between groups in adult criminal history, and more of the experimental group had committed at least two crimes (McCord, 1978). Moreover, the treated group showed signs of negative side effects in the form of more alcohol problems, serious mental illness, lower status jobs, and early death. Treatment integrity may not have been high, since meetings with counsellors were less frequent than planned. However, a similar smaller scale project employing social casework with antisocial schoolchildren also failed to influence the development of delinquent behaviour (Hodges and Tait, 1965).

Several school-based delinquency prevention programmes have attempted to improve academic performance and prosocial behaviour in predelinquent adolescents. For example, PREP (Preparation through Responsive Educational Programmes) was a well publicised behaviourally oriented project conducted in schools in Maryland in the early 1970s (Filipczak, Friedman and Reese, 1979). It utilised contingency contracts, social and tangible reinforcement in the classroom, social skills training, and training of parents, to enhance the academic and social skills of youths experiencing academic and/or social problems. The complex evaluation, including a four-year follow-up, is summarised by Burchard and Lane (1982), who concluded that although the programme had a temporary effect on academic performance, it had little impact on nonacademic areas such as school dropout or delinquency. Burchard and Lane consider the evidence for the efficacy of behavioural school-based prevention programmes to be lacking, and question their cost effectiveness. However, positive results were obtained by Bry (1982), who describes a successful preventive programme aimed at academic achievement among adolescents experiencing school failure. Youths were randomly assigned to a control group or to a two-year experimental group which offered systematic feedback to boys and parents about school performance, reinforcement for appropriate academic behaviour, and training in self-efficacy to master difficult situations. At five-year follow-up, experimental subjects showed significantly less chronic offending than controls (9% vs 27%), though little effect was found for substance abuse.

Competence enhancement has also been a goal of interventions with the families of delinquents (Chapter 13). As well as having an impact in terms of tertiary intervention, functional family therapy has also had some success as both secondary and primary prevention. In a three-year follow-up of the original programme, Klein, Alexander and Parsons (1977) found that siblings of referred delinquents had an offence rate of 20% compared with 40% to 63% for siblings in families treated by other methods. Gordon and Arbuthnot (1988) also report that in their replication, delinquents treated by this approach were not only less likely to recidivate than those receiving probation alone (11% vs 67%), they were also less likely to be criminal as adults (10% vs 45%).

A possible reason for the limited success of school-based programmes is that they intervene at a stage when delinquent propensities have become too entrenched. Primary interventions in the early school years or at preschool level may therefore be more effective. Attempts to reduce impulsivity by training young school children in social–cognitive skills represent one approach (Spivack, Platt and Shure, 1976), although evidence for long-term effectiveness is lacking. Hawkins et al. (1987) describe a project for first to third grade children in Seattle which is school based, but which focuses on parent training. Their social developmental model combines social learning and social control theories, and assumes that bonding and attachment in the family are the foundation for subsequent bonds to school and peer group. Bonding is seen to depend on opportunities and skills available for participation, and on what is reinforced and punished within a social unit, and their programme therefore targets parental skills in family management and family communication. Preliminary data from a large scale randomisation study indicated that parental attendance at training sessions was significantly related to reported improvements in parenting behaviour and reduced child aggression one year after training.

Interventions at an earlier stage attempt to accelerate cognitive development prior to school entry by providing educational stimulation assumed to be lacking among high risk families, best known being Head Start in the United States. Although this has been criticised for failure to produce lasting gains in cognitive performance, long-term follow-ups of such programmes provide evidence of enhanced social competence, including improved delay of gratification and reduced aggression (Zigler and Hall, 1987). However, few have examined effects on later delinquency. An exception is the Perry Preschool Project, an early form of Head Start, which was carried out in Michigan in the early 1960s, and for which 15- and 19-year follow-up data are available (Schweinhart, 1987). One hundred and twenty-three black children aged 3 to 4, of low IQ, and from a low socioeconomic neighbourhood, were randomly assigned to a no-preschool control group, or to a two-year preschool programme involving daily teaching and weekly home visits, with the aim of facilitating intellectual development and academic motivation. Although IQ gains were temporary, the preschool group subsequently showed significantly better school performance and postschool educational and employment status, and fewer of them were ever arrested (31% versus 51%). Effects on self-reported delinquency, however, were more selective, and confined to a few items, such as reduced involvement in gang violence and contacts with the police. The effects of the programme are seen in terms of social learning and control theory, and a transactional concept of development. Thus, initial intellectual gains appear to have promoted stronger commitment to school which was sustained by teacher reinforcement. While it is unclear whether the effective components were child involvement in planning class activities, small class sizes, or parental involvement, this project is one of the best demonstrations of the potential of early intervention to affect delinquent development. Schweinhart (1987) also emphasises its cost effectiveness in terms of reduced costs of special education, crime, and welfare payments.

Less attention has been paid to prevention through manipulating the environment (Durlak, 1985). However, attempts to prevent child abuse have included educational programmes in hospitals and the community focusing on child-rearing to improve the coping and interactional skills of parents, and community level programmes, such as media campaigns, telephone hotlines, and social support networks to prevent the onset of abuse (Rosenberg and Repucci, 1985). Recent work in the areas of domestic and sexual abuse also focuses on providing information and skills to professionals, such as teachers, medical practitioners or the police (Finkelhor, 1986). As with most recent efforts to prevent antisocial behaviour, long-term preventive effects have yet to be established.

While many now argue that early intervention programmes have the greatest potential for preventing delinquency, there is little empirical basis for identifying the most effective stage of intervention. For example, training school children in parenting skills might be as effective as training mothers of preschool children, and easier to implement. Primary prevention which targets high risk families also raises ethical problems of stigma and the self-fulfilling prophecy. Hawkins et al. (1987) attempted to make their prevention programme more acceptable by offering training to all eligible families. However, they encountered the common problem of recruitment, attracting 41% of high risk white families, but only 13% of high risk black families. These problems are pervasive in community intervention programmes (e.g. Weathers and Liberman, 1975).

Diversion

Diversion as a form of secondary prevention aims to abort the development of criminality by minimising legal intervention. The idea that reoffending may be prevented by avoiding the stigma of official processing is seen in police discretion to warn and release. However, diversion of juvenile offenders away from the courts became a popular option during the 1960s, reflecting the influence of the labelling theory view that official action produces secondary deviance by creating a criminal identity. Large scale diversion schemes have subsequently been developed in the United States (Gendreau and Ross, 1987), and the Children and Young Persons Act of 1969 created two prominent forms in Britain. In England, the juvenile court was provided with the option of imposing supervision orders under the control of the social and probation services, which may involve attendance at intermediate treatment (IT) schemes aimed to involve the child in recreational, educational, or social activities in the community, and which are intermediate to custodial placement and individual casework. Similar legislation in Scotland went further by setting up a system of children's hearings as an alternative to the juvenile court. This allows a panel of lay members to decide whether a child's interests are best served by discharge, social work supervision, or residential placement.

Labelling theory predicts that minimising official intervention should reduce recidivism, but evidence from the Cambridge study provides only limited support for this (Farrington, Osborn and West, 1978). McCord (1985) found contradictory evidence in her 30-year follow-up of the Cambridge–Somerville study, in which criminal careers of adolescents deflected from the court with a police warning following a first arrest were compared with those of youths taken to court. Contrary to labelling theory, 51% of diverted youths and 23% of convicted youths subsequently committed at least one index crime.

Most recent diversion projects entail some form of personal or family services as an alternative to legal penalties, and in this respect, diversion extends the rehabilitation philosophy underlying the creation of the juvenile court. However, diversion has not been an unequivocal success. In some instances, it has "widened the net" of official intervention by bringing in children who would not previously have been subject to it (Austin and Krisberg, 1981). American evaluations also find that services provided are frequently poorly planned or co-ordinated, and inadequately resourced and implemented, and suggest that the success of diversionary schemes in reducing recidivism has yet to be demonstrated (Gendreau and Ross, 1987; Blasta and Davidson, 1988). A review of IT in England similarly found it to be ambiguously conceived and lacking consistent goals or procedures (Bottoms and McWilliams, 1990). On the other hand, the Scottish system of childrens' hearings has significantly reduced the number of children receiving formal legal attention or custody, possibly because alternative service provision has been minimal (Erickson, 1984).

The failures of diversion may reflect "structure without content" (Gendreau and Ross, 1987), since some programmes providing high quality services and evaluation have demonstrated significant effects on recidivism. Collingwood and Genther (1980) describe a diversion scheme in the Dallas Police department. Police and civilian counsellors were trained in Carkhuff's Human Resources Development skills. Following an arrest, juveniles could be referred to either a short course of awareness lectures, or a six-month counselling programme focusing on physical fitness, interpersonal skills, and study skills, depending on offence seriousness. Those assigned to counselling made significant gains in skills, and during the first 17 months of the scheme, 24% of those treated reoffended, compared with 47% of a similar group who were offered the programme but who did not participate. In another study of diversion, Quay and Love (1977) randomly assigned referred delinquents to a programme offering academic tutoring and personal and vocational counselling, or to a control group who participated in other diversionary schemes. The experimental group had a lower recidivism rate than controls (32% vs 45%), although they were followed up for a shorter time (311 vs 450 days), allowing for greater opportunity for reoffending by controls.

A more recent report by Davidson et al. (1987) demonstrates the utility of employing well-trained paraprofessionals. Adolescent offenders referred from the court were randomly assigned to a control group referred back for court processing, an attention–placebo control, supervision by a member of the court staff, or one of three treatment conditions supervised by trained student volunteers for 18 weeks. Treatments were behavioural contracting and advocacy with the child, similar procedures with family members, and Rogerian relationship therapy. There were no effects on self-reported delinquency at two-year follow-up, but youths in all treatment conditions had lower levels of officially recorded recidivism, individual behavioural and relationship conditions producing the lowest rates. Since those in the attention–placebo control had a marginally lower recidivism than the control group, it is suggested that nonspecific treatment factors may have enhanced the effects of diversion.

The effects of IT on recidivism have yet to be reported. It provides opportunities for working with delinquents in their natural environment, but psychological involvement has been rare. However, Preston and Carnegie (1989) describe a psychologically structured IT programme in Birmingham which utilised a points economy, individual goal-setting and contracting, and work experience to develop work-related skills in delinquents nearing school leaving. At one year follow-up, more of the group were in employment, and fewer had reoffended compared with a previous group who had experienced a less structured IT programme.

While diversion schemes have generally been focused on juveniles, attention is currently been paid in Britain to the diversion of mentally disordered offenders to community based facilities. This move is based on humanitarian considerations rather than appeal to any criminological theory. Cooke (1991b) describes a Scottish scheme for diverting adults with psychological problems, which permits offenders to be offered referral for psychological or psychiatric treatment rather than prosecution. Cooke found that those selected were an unusual group who did not have a traditional criminal career, and were more likely to be older first offenders who had committed minor property or sexual offences. Anxiety, depression, and alcohol abuse were the most common problems, and following treatment, reoffending was rare.

It would appear that diversion programmes *can* have an impact on recidivism when the intermediate objectives of intervention are clearly specified, and their implementation by appropriately trained staff is ensured. However, high quality schemes such as that reported by Davidson et al. (1987) are demonstration projects which are unlikely to represent usual practice.

Situational crime prevention

While preventive efforts have traditionally aimed to influence the dispositions of individuals, situational approaches aim to reduce the opportunities for criminal acts by changing the relationship between the offender, the victim, and the environment (Nietzel and Himelein, 1986). These approaches derive from rational choice models (Chapter 4), but have also been influenced by recent attention to victims of crime (Young and Matthews, 1992). Preventive attempts involve changing the physical environment, changing the behaviour of potential victims, or strengthening the social control of crime by the community.

Crime prevention through environmental design is not new, the invention of locks being an early example of target hardening, and many forms of situational crime prevention continue to have a pragmatic flavour. However, the development of rational choice models in the 1970s provided a theoretical focus for new initiatives (Clarke and Cornish, 1985; Cornish and Clarke, 1986). The most common form of environmental prevention is target hardening, which changes the balance of perceived benefits and costs of committing an offence. Examples include the strengthening of coin boxes in public telephone booths, the prominent display of burglar alarms on property, the introduction of steering locks on cars, the use of metal detectors in airport security, and property marking. A related development is the increased use of surveillance through TV cameras in vulnerable areas, such as shops or subways. The design of buildings and housing estates has also recently emphasised opportunity reduction through attention to access and surveillance (Newman, 1972). Although the preventive impact of such measures is not always established, reduced frequencies of specific criminal acts in specific locations have been demonstrated in several instances. For example, McNees et al. (1976) established experimentally that the introduction of signs in a department store indicating that shoplifting is a crime had a modest effect in reducing shoplifting, but identifying items frequently stolen by means of stars and signs reduced shoplifting to a near zero level. An example of an unintended effect observed in several countries is a reduction of motor cycle thefts following legislation making compulsory the wearing of protective helmets by motor cyclists, presumably reflecting increased risk of detection to a potential thief not equipped with such headgear (Clarke, 1980).

There are, however, several criticisms of this approach to crime prevention. First, the costs of target hardening are often considerable, but efforts directed at crimes such as criminal damage or vandalism may be of limited value in mitigating the concerns of the public associated with inner city crime (Trasler, 1986). Second, such attempts often have ambiguous goals, and rest on untested assumptions about criminal decision-making. Bennett (1986), for example, notes that property marking is not simply aimed at preventing theft but also at facilitating police action after property is stolen. From interviews with burglars, he also found that cues attended to by criminals, such as signs of house occupancy, are not always those given priority in crime prevention programmes. Third, a more general criticism is that situational measures making crimes more difficult may result in *displacement*, reflected in changes in the time, place, method, or form of criminal activity (Trasler, 1986). For example, thefts of new cars in London were reduced following the requirement that steering locks be fitted in 1971, but concomitantly, thefts of older cars increased (Mayhew, Clarke and Hough, 1980). However, Mayhew et al. (1980) suggest that displacement may be maximal for highly motivated "professional" crimes, such as bank robbery, but minimal for opportunistic crimes, and that its occurrence should be predictable from rational choice analyses of criminal decision processes.

Some components of situational prevention aim to influence the behaviour of potential victims, for example through police campaigns encouraging property marking or house security. Alternative approaches developed recently in the areas of domestic and sexual abuse aim to reduce vulnerability to crime by employing competence building strategies which promote skills of avoidance and coping (Rosenberg and Repucci, 1985; Finkelhor, 1986). Educational programmes using films, books, or lectures focusing on personal safety skills have been increasingly used in American schools to reduce the risk of sexual abuse. These teach recognition of inappropriate situations, resistance to inducements, escape, and the need to inform someone. The impact of these methods on knowledge and skills is only rarely investigated, but a study by Wurtele et al. (1986) compared behavioural skills training with use of an educational film. They found the former to be more effective in promoting relevant personal safety knowledge, compared with a control condition, although only marginal differences were found on a role-play test. Behavioural methods have also been used to teach coping skills to women to reduce vulnerability to rape (Nietzel and Himelein, 1986).

A third approach to situational crime prevention involves organised efforts by the community to reduce criminal opportunities and to strengthen informal social controls. One form now widespread in the United States and increasingly popular in other western countries is neighbourhood watch. This consists of schemes organised with police encouragement to facilitate surveillance of a neighbourhood by its members, who may provide patrols, escorts, and mutual assistance, and who may also function as pressure groups on the police to act against visible encouragements to crime, such as the presence of drug pushers or prostitutes. Kelling (1986) notes that such groups have existed in the United States for at least the past three decades, and traces their origins to social and political traditions of collective self-help. He suggests that the evidence supports their efficacy in reducing both crime and fear of crime, and that their claimed potential for vigilantism, intolerance of minorities, or anti-police attitudes has not been realised.

THE "NOTHING WORKS" DEBATE

In his influential review, Martinson (1974) examined 231 controlled outcome studies appearing between 1945 and 1967, which covered the range of correctional interventions from individual counselling to probation and parole. He concluded that "With few and isolated exceptions, the rehabilitative efforts that have been reported so far have had no appreciable effect on recidivism". Other reviewers have reached similar conclusions (Bailey, 1966; Logan, 1972; Brody, 1976), but Martinson's review, and the book which it summarised, appears to have reached a wider audience. "Nothing works", which Martinson (1979) claimed was a media slogan, appealed to the *zeitgeist* following the social unrest and rising crime rates of the 1960s (Cullen and Gendreau, 1989). It was therefore seized on by both liberals disenchanted with rehabilitation and conservatives favouring retribution and deterrence.

Martinson's conclusion did not go unchallenged. Palmer (1975) questioned whether it was justified by the data, since 48% of the studies reviewed showed positive or "partly positive" effects. He argued that insufficient account had been taken of interactions between offender characteristics and those of treaters and settings. It was also suggested that Martinson's criteria were too stringent, given that rehabilitation services in the criminal justice system are typically "perfunctory, underfunded, understaffed, and carried out in settings certainly not ideal" (Halleck and Witte, 1977). However, further appraisal by the Panel on Research in Rehabilitative Techniques (Sechrest, White and Brown, 1979; Martin, Sechrest and Redner, 1981) endorsed Martinson's review, while noting that poor methodology and frequent lack of programme integrity precluded a definitive conclusion.

Evaluations of outcome studies reported during the 1970s, however, reached more optimistic conclusions. Gendreau and Ross (1979) reviewed 95 reports of interventions with a variety of correctional populations, including programmes for alcoholism, drug abuse, and sexual deviation, and found that 86% described successful outcomes. In an appraisal of 40 psychological programmes for offenders appearing during the 1970s, Blackburn (1980) also found that of those which reported follow-up, half demonstrated significant reductions in recidivism. Moreover, Martinson (1979) recanted his more sweeping criticisms, noting that some programmes were clearly effective, and that "the critical fact seems to be the *conditions* under which the program is delivered". Palmer (1983) suggested that by 1980 there was "an unsettled atmosphere" between the *sceptic* and *sanguine* camps. The former took the view that insufficiently few programmes were successful to warrant any priority for rehabilitation. The latter argued that some offenders are amenable to a range of interventions, or that some treatments are effective for some offenders.

This polarisation has persisted as proponents of deterrence have attempted to fill the hiatus left by the apparent collapse of the rehabilitation ideal (van den Haag, 1982; Clarke, 1985; Wilkins, 1985). However, examples of successful interventions have continued to appear. Gendreau and Ross (1987) extended their earlier review, and found that while many interventions remain poorly evaluated, significant effects have been demonstrated for several approaches, notably early intervention, behavioural family therapy, and the use of cognitive programmes. Reviewing interventions with juvenile offenders reported during the 1980s, Basta and Davidson (1988) also found sufficient evidence of positive outcomes to reject the "nothing works" view. They nevertheless caution that any conclusions must be qualified because of continuing methodological deficiencies, such as small samples, limited use of random assignment, inadequate follow-up, and reliance on crude recidivism criteria.

These qualitative "evaluations of evaluations" follow the traditional ballot box approach in which the efficacy of an intervention is judged by the proportion of reported outcomes meeting a statistical criterion of success. They are inevitably limited by journal publication biases in favour of positive findings, by qualitative variations in the methodological adequacy of interventions within a category, and by frequently arbitrary categorisation of types of intervention. Some recent appraisals have attempted to overcome limitations of qualitative reviews by meta-analysis, which compares outcomes against a common metric of effect size (ES), although it should be emphasised that this approach is equally limited by the quality of studies entering the analysis. In comparing outcomes, ES can be estimated from a variety of summary statistics, but a basic form is a standard deviation measure (post-treatment mean of the experimental group minus the mean of the control group, divided by the control group standard deviation). It is instructive to recall that in their meta-analysis of psychotherapy outcomes, Smith and Glass (1977) found a mean ES of +0.68, indicating that the average client receiving therapy is better off than 75% of untreated controls.

Garrett (1985) describes a meta-analysis of 111 intervention studies covering 13 000 juvenile offenders, although only a third reported recidivism data. Across all outcome measures, mean ES was +0.37, largest ESs being found for academic improvement (+0.78), community adjustment (+0.63) and psychological adjustment (+0.52). That for recidivism was more modest (+0.13). Behavioural approaches were more effective (+0.63) than psychodynamic methods (+0.17), but when rigour of design was considered, neither approach had a positive effect on recidivism. On the other hand, contingency management and cognitive programmes produced consistently positive effects. Garrett concludes that the results are encouraging, since despite modest effects of some interventions, the direction was overwhelmingly positive. However, a later meta-analysis of 50 juvenile programmes focusing on recidivism measures concluded that "correctional treatment has little effect on recidivism" (Whitehead and Lab, 1989). Since 32% of the programmes included met the criterion of a positive effect, this conclusion is puzzling. It was also found that behavioural programmes showed no advantage over nonbehavioural, although given the different settings and populations involved, it is questionable whether a comparison of token economies with police cautioning is meaningful.

Andrews et al. (1990) argue that interventions which disregard clinically relevant parameters of client need or the conditions required for change cannot realistically be expected to be effective. They added further studies of juvenile and adult offenders to those employed by Whitehead and Lab (1989), and coded them according to type of intervention (criminal sanction only, inappropriate service, appropriate service, and unspecified). Magnitude of ES (phi coefficient) correlated significantly with type of treatment, appropriate programmes having a significantly greater effect than inappropriate or criminal sanction (mean phi of +0.30. −0.06, and −0.07, respectively). Since appropriate programmes reduced recidivism by 50%, on average, the results contradict the "nothing works" view. In a similar meta-analysis, Izzo and Ross (1990) analysed appropriateness in terms of adequacy of programme conceptualisation. Programmes based on an articulated theory of criminal behaviour (social learning, behaviour modification, modelling, systems theory, reality therapy, I-level, sociological) were five times more effective in reducing recidivism than atheoretical programmes. Although there were no differences between the theoretical models, programmes including a cognitive component were twice as effective as those without, consistent with earlier findings of Ross and Fabiano (1985).

TOWARDS SUCCESSFUL INTERVENTION

No review of interventions with offenders has unequivocally demonstrated that "nothing works", or even that "almost nothing works". Many programmes have been found to be weak or ineffective, but examples of interventions which have an impact on offender behaviour have now been identified too frequently to be dismissed as "isolated exceptions". Cullen and Gendreau (1989) suggest that resistance to this evidence reflects ideological biases, but it may also reflect professional roles. Practitioners clearly interpret the evidence more optimistically than academic criminologists, either because of personal investment in rehabilitation or because of close contact with the constraints on clinical practice in the penal system, and an awareness that like politics, rehabilitation is the art of the possible. From this perspective, the finding that some programmes reduce recidivism by 50% may be seen as a considerable achievement. Andrews, Bonta and Hoge (1990) also showed that appropriate service provision has effects on recidivism which are not found for conventional penal sanctions. While few would now argue that rehabilitation should be a primary purpose of imprisonment, the case for offering rehabilitation to offenders can therefore be justified on empirical as well as moral grounds.

Findings from meta-analyses indicate that interventions focusing on noncriminal targets, such as community or academic adjustment, are as effective as interventions with mental health problems more generally (e.g. Garrett, 1985). In this respect, the widely held view that most treatments are better than no treatment (Smith and Glass, 1977; Frank, 1985) seems as applicable in the correctional field as in mental health services more generally. However, this is less clearly the case with recidivism, on which many interventions have little impact, and some may actually increase it. Possible reasons for this limited success include methodological deficiencies, differential treatment effects, and conditions of service delivery.

Methodological issues

Reviewers frequently note that methodological shortcomings in rehabilitation research preclude firm conclusions (Logan, 1972; Sechrest, White and Brown, 1979; Blasta and Davidson, 1988: Furby, Weinrott and Blackshaw, 1989). These fall under the broad headings of problems of implementation, and problems of evaluation (Martin, Sechrest and Redner, 1981). Problems of implementation include both the strength and integrity of intervention (Kazdin, 1987). Strength refers to the potential of a treatment to achieve behavioural change, and is dependent on factors such as the theoretical rationale, the qualifications of treatment staff, the intensity of the treatment applied (cf. "dosage"), and the clarity of the planned intervention. Integrity relates to the extent to which the plan was actually implemented. A continuing problem is that these factors are infrequently evaluated or reported.

Problems of evaluation arise from failures to meet conventional requirements of research design. Prominent among these are sampling and design problems, and the psychometric properties of outcome measures (Blasta and Davidson, 1988). Samples are often too small or unrepresentative for statistical power and logical generalisability, and demographic, criminal, and personal attributes are not always adequately described. Designs may be limited by the absence of a control group or random allocation, and reports often fail to specify the experimental procedures sufficiently to permit replication or to ensure treatment integrity.

A pervasive problem is the use of criteria of "success" of unknown reliability and validity. Outcome measures need to be selected to reflect the goals of the programme, and to be assessed by unbiased data collectors. They therefore need to include intermediate within-programme targets as well as longer-term effects (Andrews, 1983). Where the latter are evaluated, however, they continue to be mainly crude all-or-none measures of reoffending, whose reliability is questionable. Not only are there issues about the reliability of official data as a measure of reoffending, investigators use different criteria, such as arrest, conviction, or parole violation, which do not yield equivalent results, and the use of self-report or other alternative data sources remains rare. There are also questions about the validity of recidivism as a measure of "success". Dichotomies of offending–nonoffending conceal variations in offence frequency or seriousness, which may signal partial success, and it was argued earlier that recidivism is not a sufficient criterion of the success of a rehabilitation programme. Reoffending may, for example, reflect factors not addressed by the programme, such as unanticipated changes in the social environment. Evaluation of effectiveness therefore requires not only appropriately scaled and multiple measures of further criminal behaviour, but also that these be demonstrated to covary with the personal or social changes targetted by the programme.

Commitment to methodological purity is an ideal on which scientific advances depend. However, it may not be shared by penal administrators, and the exigencies of the criminal justice system rarely allow for the niceties of random assignment or samples without attrition. As Adams (1977) suggests, the concerns of policy makers may more readily be addressed by weaker quasi-experimental designs, or by attention to system rather than outcome issues. The most pressing problem may be not so much the purity of evaluations, but rather to ensure that evaluations are carried out at all.

Differential treatment

Comparative outcome research has suggested that all psychotherapies have positive benefits, and none can lay claim to inherent advantages (Smith and

Glass, 1977; Frank, 1985). While the proposal that positive effects are achieved by common "nonspecific" factors to which specific techniques add nothing more than a ritual structure remains too ecumenical to be congenial (Parloff, 1984; Kazdin, 1986), this may well apply to offender rehabilitation, since no single approach can yet claim superiority (Blasta and Davidson, 1988; Izzo and Ross, 1990). Nevertheless, overall failure of an offender treatment programme to affect outcome may mask interactions, beneficial effects for some offenders being cancelled out by detrimental results for others. An increasingly voiced view is that clients therefore need to be matched with therapy and therapists (Warren, 1971; Palmer, 1975, 1983; Goldstein et al., 1989; Andrews et al., 1990).

As yet, little attempt has been made to move on from the professional sectarianism of "Which is better?" to the question of "Which technique works best for whom, and under what conditions?", and studies of differential treatment, or "prescriptive programing" (Goldstein et al., 1989) remain few. Reluctance to explore this approach may reflect the commitment of most therapists to a single theoretical model, and there is also little agreement on the most appropriate classifications of offenders, treatments, or treaters (Sechrest, 1987). Moreover, a comprehensive analysis requires examination of a daunting number of interactions, and it is perhaps not surprising that few studies have gone beyond varying one of the relevant factors.

One variant of the matching approach assumes that characteristics of offenders mediate treatment response, and that some offenders are *amenable* to a variety of treatment methods. For example, a serendipitous finding in a study of prison welfare officer casework by Sinclair, Shaw, and Troop (1974) was that introverted prisoners responded more favourably than extraverts in terms of reduced recidivism. In the PICO (Pilot Intensive Counselling Organisation) project (Adams, 1970), counsellors identified offenders as amenable or nonamenable to therapy, and assigned them to treatment or no-treatment controls. Nonamenable offenders who participated in treatment subsequently did worse than their untreated counterparts, but amenable youths exhibited less recidivism than their controls. While "amenable" was not clearly defined, Adams notes that amenable youths were more intelligent, articulate, anxious, and desirous of change. Outcome research on the therapeutic community suggests that those responding most favourably have similar characteristics, notably, emotional expressiveness, anxiety, intropunitiveness, some ability to relate, and persistence in treatment (Copas et al., 1984). Conversely, unsuccessful patients are more likely to be extrapunitive, aggressive, self-damaging, and recidivist. This parallels the common finding that psychotherapy clients who are more psychologically healthy to begin with have the more successful outcomes, regardless of treatment method (Frank, 1985). While amenability has been little explored among offenders, psychopathic personalities are generally seen as the least amenable.

Therapist variables may be equally relevant. Frank (1985) suggests that therapist relationship skills are crucial to any therapy, and some studies of offender interventions, including behavioural programmes, have found these to account for as much of the outcome variance as treatment method (Jesness,

1975; Jesness et al., 1975; Alexander et al., 1976). An interaction of offender and therapist characteristics was shown in the Camp Elliott project (Grant and Grant, 1959). Naval delinquents underwent intensive group therapy for up to nine weeks, while supervised in closed living units. More mature offenders, as classified by the I-level system, were more likely to have returned to duty at a six-month follow-up, but there was also a significant interaction of I-level with supervisor effectiveness, more mature offenders doing better with more effective supervisors. Effective supervisers were those who were less authoritarian and more interpersonally mature, and other studies also find that treatment staff who are "firm but fair" have a more favourable influence on offenders (Craft, Stephenson and Granger, 1964; Clarke, 1985).

A few studies have varied both offender characteristics and treatment method or setting. Much of the relevant research comes from the use of I-level classification, particularly in the California Youth Authority's Community Treatment Project (CTP: Palmer, 1974). The initial phase compared the effects of intensive community supervision and treatment within small parole caseloads with institutional placement, while a later phase examined the effects of initial residential placement followed by community supervision. The results are complex, but suggest that neurotic delinquents (I-4) do better with community supervision, power-oriented (I-3) youths with institutional placement. However, the CTP has been criticised for biases in the reporting of reoffending by counsellors (Wilson, 1980). Other studies in California have examined the relationship of I-level to varying institutional regimes. In the Preston study (Jesness, 1971), an experimental programme which assigned youths to units with different treatment goals according to I-level was subsequently found to have no effects on parole violation in comparison with a control institution. However, a re-analysis of the data indicated lower recidivism for I-3 and I-4 level youths who had been assigned to a psychiatric treatment unit, supporting the differential treatment approach (Austin, 1977). In his comparative study of institutions offering transactional analysis (Close) or behaviour modification (Holton), Jesness (1975) also found that effects varied according to I-level. Anxious and acting-out neurotics (I-4) had the lowest failure rates at both institutions, but unsocialised passives (I-2) benefitted more from Holton, manipulators (I-3) from Close.

Some research has employed Quay's behaviour classification. In one study, youths were assigned to an experimental programme at the R. F. Kennedy Youth Center or to a conventional institution (Cavior and Schmidt, 1978). The experimental prison utilised a token economy, and all inmates received educational and vocational training, but different treatment objectives and methods were specified for different groups. Neurotic delinquents, for example, received counselling, psychopaths behaviour modification. However, a three-year follow-up revealed no effect of the experimental programme on recidivism, and no effects for type of offender. On the other hand, Quay's dimensions predicted outcome in a study of diversion, in which delinquents were assigned to vocational and personal counselling or to a control group (Quay and Love, 1977). Psychopathic and neurotic adolescents were more likely to be rearrested, regardless of type of intervention.

Matching of client and therapist on conceptual level (Chapter 3) improves clinical outcome in psychotherapy (Frank, 1985), while educational achievement is similarly enhanced by matching student with teaching environment (Reitsma-Street and Leschied, 1988). Leschied and Thomas (1985) obtained evidence supporting the utility of matching conceptual level of delinquents with the structure of correctional programmes. "Hard to serve" adolescents in structured residential treatment showed a significant decline in the number of charges during the year following exposure to the programme, and also had lower re-incarceration rates than similar juveniles from conventional placements.

Little attention has been paid to treatment matching among adult or female offenders, but Annis and Chan (1983) report a study employing an empirical classification of young male adults. Offenders with drug and alcohol problems were randomly assigned to intensive confrontational group therapy or a control group. The experimental programme had no overall effect on recidivism at one-year follow-up. However, there was a significant interaction between exposure to treatment and an empirical typology derived from self-esteem and interpersonal measures. Offenders with a high self-image and low trust had fewer and less serious convictions with treatment than without, while those with a low self image and low interpersonal warmth did worse with treatment. Like the PICO findings, these results underscore the need to distinguish those who are amenable to particular approaches from those who might benefit from alternatives.

Since few studies have crossed offender classes with different types of treatment or treatment staff, there is little basis for distinguishing which kinds of offender might benefit from which kinds of intervention or by whom. Nevertheless, the logic of differential treatment is compelling. Andrews, Bonta and Hoge (1990) argue that differential responsivity of offenders to treatment regimes has been sufficiently demonstrated to suggest some basic guidelines. For example, those with low levels of cognitive and interpersonal maturity require highly structured programmes, while nondirective, unstructured therapies should be confined to those offenders possessing good levels of verbal, cognitive and interpersonal skills.

Characteristics of successful programmes

Effective rehabilitation depends not only on the techniques of intervention and the characteristics of service recipients and providers, but also on the conditions under which it is delivered. For example, failures to maintain treatment integrity may result from inadequate resources and inappropriately trained personnel, but they may also represent obstacles which are endemic in the penal system, such as low priorities for treatment, authoritarian management, and poor interdisciplinary and interagency communication. Three factors which may be critical to successful outcome are the location of an intervention, the targets, and the models of change (Blackburn, 1980).

Many programmes are carried out in institutions, but some argue that these are not the optimal *setting* in which to achieve change. Ross and Price (1976), for example, suggest that the social climate and organisational structure of prisons inevitably militate against the successful execution of behavioural programmes. A related argument is that the most potent influence on antisocial behaviour is the current environment, and that recidivism therefore has more to do with the post-institutional setting than with what happens to an offender during confinement (Gunn et al., 1978; Clarke, 1985). This, however, ignores the contribution of the offender to his environment. Some institutional programmes have, in fact, achieved success in reducing recidivism, while some community programmes fail. Blackburn (1980) observed that failures in both were often for similar reasons, such as lack of control by therapists of administrative resources, poor motivation or sabotage on the part of primary change agents, or failure to gain control over other sources of influence, such as the peer group or the reinforcement value of many deviant activities themselves. While recent data appear to favour community based programmes (Izzo and Ross, 1990), institutional programmes which equip the offender with coping skills are likely to be a necessary first step for many if they are to survive or avoid problems with peers, the family, or at work.

Successful interventions also depend on the relevance of treatment targets to criminal behaviour. Psychological approaches to crime typically disavow a sickness model, but most rehabilitation programmes focus on personal inadequacies or deficits. While some sociologists argue that the implicit assumption of personal inadequacy is misplaced, since criminals are merely responding to the facts and conditions of society (Martinson, 1974), it is apparent that deficits in academic, interpersonal, and cognitive skills characterise many offenders (Chapter 8). Nevertheless, many programmes attend to factors whose relation to offending is obscure. Traditional vocational training in prisons, for example, is often unrelated to the employment market, and does not attend to the job placement problems which offenders are likely to encounter (Dale, 1976). Again, indiscriminate use of psychodynamic counselling is inappropriate when many offenders do not have the neurotic problems for which such approaches were designed, and for whom such treatment may be detrimental. Similarly, many behavioural programmes have targeted behaviours which have not been shown to have anything to do with crime in the community (Chapter 13). A related issue, which is frequently neglected, is whether the goals of the therapist are congruent with those of the client.

An overriding issue is the *model of change* underlying an intervention, which rests ultimately on a theory of criminal behaviour. The criterion of success is typically what happens after treatment terminates, further offending being seen as a sign of programme failure. However, as was noted earlier, this approach is analogous to the medical model of treatment of infectious diseases, in which the relevant therapy is applied, and the "cure" awaited (Kazdin, 1987). For some offenders, the model of a systemic disease, such as diabetes, for which continuous intervention is necessary, may have more relevance for the prevention of reoffending. Currently, this is implicit in the application of relapse prevention methods to sex offenders. Zigler and Hall (1987) similarly suggest that the success of early interventions depends on follow through to enhance effects, rather than reliance on "inoculation".

Despite pessimistic arguments to the contrary (Sechrest et al., 1979), the outcome literature contains several pointers as to the kinds of procedures and targets which are likely to characterise successful offender rehabilitation programmes. Andrews, Bonta and Hoge (1990) suggest that these will contain a high degree of structure, will be operated by staff who use authority in a "firm but fair" fashion and who model and reinforce anticriminal values, will target attributes shown to mediate criminal behaviour, such as procriminal attitudes, psychopathic personality traits, and criminal associates, and will employ problem-solving procedures based on cognitive and social learning principles. At the same time, programmes need to be matched to offender characteristics. In particular, level of *risk of recidivism* should dictate the level of service delivery, more intense services being provided for high risk offenders, and type of *criminogenic need* which affects the chances of recidivism should determine the targets of services. Finally, *responsivity* of offenders should guide the choice of treatment option. This may be indicated by classifications such as I-level or conceptual level, but it is hypothesised that cognitive interpersonal skills, anxiety, psychopathy, sensation seeking, motivation for change, and social support are likely to be particularly relevant variables.

ROLE CONFLICTS AND ETHICAL ISSUES FOR PSYCHOLOGISTS IN CRIMINAL JUSTICE

Psychologists who intervene in the lives of offenders face a number of role ambiguities and ethical dilemmas. Employment in any organisation implies acceptance of its aims, but the punitive, custodial, and rehabilitative goals of the criminal justice system are frequently incompatible. For example, retribution may demand a custodial sentence, but the best rehabilitative strategy may be to keep the offender at home and in a job. While the aim of psychologists is typically to help offenders, and they are professionally obliged "...to hold the interest and welfare of those in receipt of their services to be paramount at all times..." (British Psychological Society, 1985), they are simultaneously the employees of a system whose primary purpose is social control. This is an explicit function of prisons, but it is also a latent function of institutions for mentally disordered offenders. Ethical dilemmas therefore centre on the question "Who is the client?" (Monahan, 1980). Similar issues also arise in health care and education, but they become particularly acute when individual liberty is at stake.

Models of psychological change applied to offenders have been imported from mental health and educational contexts, but authoritarian custodial settings impose particular constraints on service delivery. Conflicts arise in penal institutions between the demands for security and control and the treatment priorities of the psychologist, and attempts to introduce novel treatment programmes not infrequently encounter institutional inertia, staff conservatism, and hostility, which have to be dealt with by compromise (Laws, 1974; Ross and Price, 1976). Custodial staff often assign a low priority to treatment, sometimes taking a simplistic moral view that an offender does not "deserve" help, or that treatment is a soft option, and may sabotage the efforts of psychologists. Corsini and Miller (1954), for example, noted that staff often failed to ensure that inmates were available for treatment sessions, and this problem currently persists in some settings. Therapy for disruptive inmates may also be expected to serve the goals of management. For example, crisis interventions in the case of suicide attempts or assaults may be directed to changing the individual when changes in institutional conditions may be more appropriate.

A common ethical problem is the question of *confidentiality* arising from information revealed by an offender client to a psychologist but not to others. Clinicians are accustomed to treating such information as privileged, but it is doubtful whether confidentiality can ever be absolute. In a multidisciplinary context, for example, the psychologist is professionally obliged to share information with other members. Moreover, despite the dismay with which the *Tarasoff* decision was greeted by American mental health professionals (Chapter 12), a duty to warn third parties of risk is consistent with professional codes of conduct (Monahan, 1980). The British Psychological Society (1985), for example, enjoins psychologists to take all reasonable steps to preserve confidentiality, but recognises exceptions when the safety or interests of either the recipient of services or others is threatened. Dilemmas in this area can be avoided by declaring the limits of confidentiality to the client in advance. This also applies to any situation where a psychologist produces a report on an offender for a court or tribunal (Committee on Ethical Guidelines for Forensic Psychologists, 1991).

A perennial dilemma is whether interventions with clients who are involuntarily detained serve the interests of the institution or society or those of the individual offender. One issue is the potential for coercion, and some psychologists decline to accept court ordered treatment referrals on the grounds that the client cannot enter into a voluntary contract. Robinson (1974) argued that behavioural scientists have no warrant for mediating in conflict between the individual and society, and that psychological treatment for involuntary clients should be restricted to those who are physically harmful, or who request help. Others, he argues, retain a "right not to be changed". Under such conditions, compulsory therapy is offered as an "evil" of lesser gravity than the ultimate evil of loss of life or life in prison. It is, however, unclear why those who are physically harmful should not also retain such a right, even though they may forfeit the right to liberty.

The Council for Science and Society (1981) alternatively advocates that treatments for the compulsorily detained which affect personal autonomy should only be introduced when a "recognisable disorder" has been diagnosed, and when it is for the benefit of the individual and not the institution. This is an unduly narrow medical perspective which ignores the fact that personal autonomy is often restricted by psychological stress or dysfunction which does not amount to illness. Personality disorders, for example, are among the most commonly identified problems of offenders, but they are not discretely defined diseases. Psychological therapies normally demand informed consent, and require a willing participant for effectiveness, and there is no reason why these conditions should not obtain with a convicted offender. The problem is that motivation for change must be inferred from verbal statements, and it is never certain that an offender wishes to avoid repetition of his acts or merely reconviction (Feldman and Peay, 1982). However, voluntariness is never absolute, and the problem is no different in principle from that obtaining when people seek help for psychological problems which threaten their job or relationships.

Nevertheless, the question of defining a psychological problem is highlighted when the "problem" is identified as the deviant behaviour itself, since intervention may entail the imposition of a particular ideology or set of values. The rhetoric of rehabilitation as a liberal and liberating enterprise conceals the contradiction that it is a strategy aimed at changing the individual to conform with prevailing societal norms. Participation in this enterprise assumes that these norms are consensually agreed, but they may not be shared by the recipients of therapy. Evaluations for purposes of predicting dangerousness or parole outcome are also undertaken in the interests of society, while interventions in inmate management problems may similarly serve the goal of institutional compliance. The question is "Who has the problem?" (Feldman and Peay, 1982). Identifying socially unacceptable behaviour itself as the target of treatment uncritically equates psychological abnormality with social deviance, and implies that all offences, including "political" and victimless crimes, are grist to the psychologist's mill. This is clearly an ideological position, and mental health professionals who give primacy to their role as agent of social control risk not only violating their professional code, but also colluding with unjust laws and oppressive regimes.

The opposite stance is that compliance should never be a target of intervention, and that recidivism or institutional adjustment are inappropriate outcome criteria for psychological treatment. However, Brodsky (1980) notes that this is itself a value-driven position, and it is doubtful whether any therapy can avoid imposing *someone's* values. Moreover, to limit services to helping the offender survive the ordeals of incarceration would be to condone "benign warehousing" (Halleck and Witte, 1977). In practice, attempts to help offenders cannot avoid considering their future welfare. While conflict with society is not itself an adequate justification for psychological intervention, it is an occasion for offering services when psychological dysfunctions or deficits limit the individual's behavioural options, and in the United States, both the right of offenders to psychological treatment and the right to refuse it have been recognised for some years. As Feldman and Peay (1982) suggest, psychologists can retain their traditional role as agent of the client rather than the state by concentrating on the problems of offenders rather than on the problems caused by offenders to others. This does not mean opting out of responsibilities to the criminal justice system, but rather recognising that the offender, the institution, and society are all clients, but with differing priorities over time (Clingempeel, Mulvey and Repucci, 1980).

While ethical dilemmas arise when principles are in conflict, and there can rarely ever be absolute agreement or resolutions, a number of guiding principles have been proposed which appear to have some professional consensus. In the context of behavioural treatments, Feldman and Peay (1982) propose that the client has primacy in decisions concerning which behavioral repertoires should be added, maintained, or removed, and that this can only be achieved through fully informed consent. Where the interests of one client have consequences for another, and these are not congruent, the guiding principles should be maximum benefit and least harm, with pride of place going to those interested parties whose lives are most negatively affected by the problem behaviour. Finally the monitoring of professional activities should be undertaken by external review bodies (see also Brodsky, 1980). These guidelines seem applicable to the range of psychological interventions. A more general set of ethical principles covering assessment, professional competence, service evaluation, prediction, treatment, and training, was produced by the American Psychological Association Task Force on the Role of Psychologists in the Criminal Justice System (Monahan, 1980).

Psychologists may seek to confine themselves to apparently safe roles of therapist, administrator, or researcher, but it is doubtful whether there is any role in criminal justice settings which is free of value conflicts, or whether psychologists can escape the ambiguities of being agents of both offenders and society. Brodsky (1972) suggested that roles of psychologists vary along a system professional–system challenger continuum. The system professional accepts offender compliance and self-control as the primary target of intervention, does not question that treatment is in the service of society, and seeks to work with the system through establishing good working relationships. The system challenger sees offender problems in the context of social deprivation and discrimination, views both professional and agency goals as potentially inimical to inmates, and seeks to sabotage those which may be harmful. These roles are not mutually exclusive, and many psychologists struggle to maintain a balance between them. Brodsky notes that the wider interests of offenders are unlikely to be served by the psychologist who works all the time with individual offenders or by the fiery radical concerned with liberating a few institutions. Rather is there a need for multiple goals and commitments, with a recognition that psychology does not have all the answers. A minimal requirement is for psychologists to be aware of the social and legal context of criminal justice and behaviour problems.

References

Abel, G. G., and Rouleau, J. L. (1990). The nature and extent of sexual assault. In W. L. Marshall, D. R. Laws, and H. E. Barbaree (eds), *Handbook of Sexual Assault: Issues, Theories, and Treatment of the Offender*. New York: Plenum.

Abel, G. G., Becker, J. V., and Cunningham-Rathner, J. (1984). Complications, consent and cognitions in sex between children and adults. *International Journal of Law and Psychiatry*, **7**, 89–103.

Abel, G. G., Blanchard, E. B., and Becker, J. V. (1978). An integrated treatment program for rapists. In R. T. Rada (ed.), *Clinical Aspects of the Rapist*. New York: Grune and Stratton.

Abel, G. G., Barlow, D. H., Blanchard, E. B., and Guild, D. (1977). The components of rapists' sexual arousal. *Archives of General Psychiatry*, **34**, 895–903.

Abel, G. G., Becker, J. V., Murphy, W. D., and Flanagan, B. (1981). Identifying dangerous child molesters. In R. B. Stuart (ed.), *Violent Behavior: Social Learning Approaches to Prediction, Management and Treatment*. New York: Brunner/Mazel.

Abelson, R. P. (1981). Psychological status of the script concept. *American Psychologist*, **36**, 715–729.

Achenbach, T. M., and Edelbrock, C. S. (1978). The classification of child psychopathology: A review and analysis. *Psychological Bulletin*, **85**, 1275–1301.

Adams, R. (1973). Differential association and learning principles revisited. *Social Problems*, **20**, 458–470.

Adams, S. (1970). The PICO project. In N. Johnston, L. Savitz and M. Wolfgang (eds), *The Sociology of Punishment and Correction*. New York: Wiley.

Adams, S. (1977). Evaluating correctional treatments: Toward a new perspective. *Criminal Justice and Behavior*, **4**, 323–339.

Adler, F. (1975). *Sisters in Crime*. New York: McGraw-Hill.

Ageton, S., and Elliott, D. (1974). The effects of legal processing on self concept. *Social Problems*, **22**, 87–100.

Agee, V. (1986). Institutional treatment programs for the violent juvenile. In S. Apter and A. Goldstein (eds), *Youth Violence: Programs and Prospects*. New York:Pergamon.

Agnew, R.(1984). Appearance and delinquency. *Criminology*, **22**, 421–440.

Agnew, R. (1985). Social control theory and delinquency: A longitudinal test. *Criminology*, **23**, 47–60.

Agnew, R., and Peters, A. A. R. (1986). The techniques of neutralisation: An analysis of predisposing and situational factors. *Criminal Justice and Behavior*, **13**, 81–97.

Agnew, R., and Petersen, D. M. (1989). Leisure and delinquency. *Social Problems*, **36**, 332–350.

Ainsworth, M. D. S., and Bowlby, J. (1991). An ethological approach to personality development. *American Psychologist*, **46**, 333–341.

Ajzen, I. (1987). Attitudes, traits, and actions: dispositional prediction of behavior in personality and social psychology. In L. Berkowitz (ed.), *Advances in Experimental Social Psychology* Volume 20. San Diego: Academic Press.

Akers, R. (1977). *Deviant Behavior: A Social Learning Approach* Second Edition. Belmont, Ca. Wadsworth.

Akers, R. (1990). Rational choice, deterrence, and social learning theories in criminology: The path not taken. *Journal of Criminal Law and Criminology*, **81**, 653–676.

Akers, R., Krohn, M. D., Lanza-Kaduce, L., and Radesovich, M. (1979). Social learning and deviant behavior. *American Sociological Review*, **44**, 635–655.

Akhtar, S., and Thomson, A. (1982). Overview of narcissistic personality disorder. *American Journal of Psychiatry*, **139**, 12–20.

Alder, C. (1985). An exploration of self-reported sexually aggressive behavior. *Crime and Delinquency*, **31**, 306–331.

Aldrich, C. K. (1987). Acting out and acting up: the superego lacuna revisited. *American Journal of Orthopsychiatry*, **57**, 402–406.

Alexander, J. F., and Parsons. B. V. (1973). Short-term behavioral intervention with delinquent families: Impact on family process and recidivism. *Journal of Abnormal Psychology*, **81**, 219–225.

Alexander, J. F., Waldron, H. B., Barton, C., and Mas, C. H. (1989). The minimising of blaming attributions in delinquent families. *Journal of Consulting and Clinical Psychology*, **57**, 19–24.

Alker, II. A. (1972). Is personality situationally specific or intrapsychically consistent? *Journal of Personality*, **40**, 1–16.

Allan, E. A., and Steffensmeier, D. J. (1989). Youth, underemployment, and property crime: Differential effects of job availability and job quality on juvenile and young adult arrest rates. *American Sociological Review*, **54**, 107–123.

Allen, F. A. (1959). Criminal justice, legal values and the rehabilitative ideal. *Journal of Criminal Law, Criminology and Police Science*, **50**, 226–232.

Allsopp, J. F., and Feldman, M. P. (1976). Personality and antisocial behaviour in schoolboys. *British Journal of Criminology*, **16**, 337–351.

Alston, W.P. (1975). Traits, consistency, and conceptual alternatives for personality theory. *Journal for the Theory of Social Behaviour*, **5**, 17–48.

American Association of Correctional Psychologists (1980). Standards for psychological services in adult prisons and jails. *Criminal Justice and Behavior*, **7**, 81–127.

American Psychiatric Association (1983). American Psychiatric Association statement on the insanity defense. *American Journal of Psychiatry*, **140**, 681–688.

American Psychiatric Association (1987). *Diagnostic and Statistical Manual of Mental Disorders*, Third Edition (Revised). Washington, DC: American Psychiatric Association.

American Psychological Association (1984). Text of position on insanity defense. *APA Monitor*, **15** (March), 11.

American Psychological Association.(1990). The Seville statement on violence. *American Psychologist*, **45**, 1167–1168.

Amir, M. (1971). *Patterns in Forcible Rape*. Chicago: University of Chicago Press.

Andenaes, J. (1974). *Punishment and Deterrence*. Ann Arbor: University of Michigan Press.

Anderson, C. A. (1989). Temperature and aggression: Ubiquitous effects of heat on occurrence of human violence. *Psychological Bulletin*, **106**, 74–96.

Andrews, D. A. (1980). Some experimental investigations of the principles of differential association through deliberate manipulation of the structure of service systems. *American Sociological Review*, **45**, 448–462.

Andrews, D. A. (1983). The assessment of outcome in correctional samples. In M. L. Lambert, E. R. Christensen, and S. S. DeJulio (eds), *The Measurement of Psychotherapy Outcome*. New York: Wiley.

Andrews, D. A., Bonta, J., and Hoge, R. D. (1990). Classification for effective rehabilitation: Rediscovering psychology. *Criminal Justice and Behavior*, **17**, 19–52.

Andrews, D. A., Zinger, I., Hoge, R. D., Bonta, J., Gendreau, P., and Cullen, F. T. (1990). Does correctional treatment work? A clinically relevant and psychologically informed meta-analysis. *Criminology*, **28**, 369–404.

Annis, H., and Chan, D. (1983). The differential treatment model: Empirical evidence from a personality typology of adult offenders. *Criminal Justice and Behavior*, **10**, 159–173.

Appelbaum, P. S. (1988). The new preventive detention: Psychiatry's problematic responsibility for the control of violence. *American Journal of Psychiatry*, **145**, 779–785.

Arboleda-Flórez, J. (1980). Post-homicide psychotic reaction. *International Journal of Offender Therapy and Comparative Criminology*, **24**, 47–52.

Arboleda-Flórez, J. (1990). Two solitudes: Mental health and law. *Journal of Forensic Psychiatry*, **1**, 143–165.

Arbuthnot, J., and Gordon, D. A. (1986). Behavioral and cognitive effects of a moral reasoning development intervention for high-risk behavior disordered adolescents. *Journal of Consulting and Clinical Psychology*, **54**, 208–216.

Arbuthnot, J., and Gordon, D. A. (1988). Crime and Cognition: Community applications of sociomoral reasoning development. *Criminal Justice and Behavior*, **15**, 379–393.

Arbuthnot, J., Gordon, D. A., and Jurkovic, G. J. (1987). Personality. In H. C. Quay (ed.), *Handbook of Juvenile Delinquency*. Chichester: Wiley.

Armentrout, J. A., and Hauer, A. L. (1978). MMPIs of rapists of adults, rapists of children and nonrapist sex offenders. *Journal of Clinical Psychology*, **34**, 330–332.

Armstrong, J. S. (1980). The relationship of sex-role identification, self-esteem, and aggression in delinquent males. *Dissertation Abstracts International*, **40**, 3900-B.

Arnkoff, D. B. (1980). Psychotherapy from the perspective of cognitive theory. In M. Mahoney (ed.), *Psychotherapy Process: Current Issues and Future Directions*. New York: Plenum.

Aronfreed, J. (1968). *Conduct and Conscience*. New York: Academic Press.

Asarnow, J. R., and Callan, J. W. (1985). Boys with peer adjustment problems: social cognitive processes. *Journal of Consulting and Clinical Psychology*, **53**, 80–87.

Aultman, M. G. (1980). Group involvement in delinquent acts: A study of offense types and male–female participation. *Criminal Justice and Behavior*, **7**, 185–192.

Austin, J., and Krisberg, B. (1981). Wider, stronger and different nets: The dialectics of criminal justice reform. *Journal of Research in Crime and Delinquency*, **18**, 165–196.

Austin, R. (1975). Construct validity of I-level classification. *Criminal Justice and Behavior*, **2**, 113–129.

Austin, R. (1977). Differential treatment in an institution: Re-examining the Preston study. *Journal of Research in Crime and Delinquency*, **14**, 177–194.

Austin, R. (1978). Intelligence and adolescent theft. *Criminal Justice and Behavior*, **5**, 212–225.

Ausubel, D. P. (1961). Personality disorder *is* disease. *American Psychologist*, **16**, 69–74.

Averill, J. (1982). *Anger and Aggression*. New York: Springer-Verlag.

Avery-Clark, C. A., and Laws, D. R. (1984). Differential erection response patterns of sexual child abusers to stimuli describing activities with children. *Behavior Therapy*, **15**, 71–83.

Ayllon, T., and Milan, M. A. (1979). *Correctional Rehabilitation and Management: A Psychological Approach*. New York: Wiley.

Bach-Y-Rita, G., Lion, J., Climent, C., and Ervin, F. (1971). Episodic dyscontrol: A study of 130 violent patients. *American Journal of Psychiatry*, **127**, 1473–1478.

Bacon, M. K., Child, I., and Barry, L. H. (1963). A cross-cultural study of correlates of crime. *Journal of Abnormal and Social Psychology*, **66**, 2910-300.

Bailey, W. C. (1966). Correctional outcome: An evaluation of 100 reports. *Journal of Criminal Law, Criminology and Police Science*, **57**, 153–160.

Balay, J., and Shevrin, H. (1988). The subliminal psychodynamic activation method: A critical review. *American Psychologist*, **43**, 161–174.

Baldwin, J. D. (1985). Thrill and adventure seeking and the age distribution of crime: Comment on Hirschi and Gottfredson. *American Journal of Sociology*, **90**, 1326–1330.

Balch, R. W. (1975). The medical model of delinquency: Theoretical, practical and ethical implications. *Crime and Delinquency*, **21**, 116–129.

Ball, R. A. (1983). Development of basic norm violation: Neutralisation and self-concept within a male cohort. *Criminology*, **21**, 75–94.

Ball-Rokeach, S. (1973). Values and violence: A test of the subculture of violence thesis. *American Sociological Review*, **38**, 736–749.

Bandura, A. (1974). Behavior theory and the models of man. *American Psychologist*, **29**, 859–869.

Bandura, A. (1982). The psychology of chance encounters and life paths. *American Psychologist*, **37**, 747–755.

Bandura, A. (1983). Psychological mechanisms of aggression. In R. G. Geen and E. I. Donnerstein (eds), *Aggression: Theoretical and Experimental Reviews*. Volume One. New York: Academic Press.

Bandura, A. (1986). *Social Foundations Of Thought and Action*. Englewood Cliffs, NJ: Prentice-Hall.

Bandura, A. (1989). Human agency in social cognitive theory. *American Psychologist*, **44**, 1175–1184.

Bandura, A., and Walters, R. H. (1959). *Adolescent Aggression*. New York: Ronald Press.

Bandura, A., and Walters, R. H. (1963). *Social Learning and Personality Development*. New York: Holt, Rinehart and Winston.

Banister, P. A., Smith, F. V., Heskin, K. J., and Bolton, N. (1973). Psychological correlates of long-term imprisonment. 1. Cognitive variables. *British Journal of Criminology*, **13**, 312–323.

Barbaree, H. E. (1990). Stimulus control of sexual arousal: Its role in sexual assault. In W. L. Marshall, D. R. Laws, and H. E. Barbaree (eds), *Handbook of Sexual Assault: Issues, Theories, and Treatment of the Offender*. New York: Plenum.

Barbaree, H. E., Marshall, W. L., and Lanthier, R. D. (1979). Deviant sexual arousal in rapists. *Behaviour Research and Therapy*, **17**, 215–222.

Barbour-McMullen, J., Coid, J., and Howard, R. (1988). The psychometric identification of psychopathy in mentally abnormal offenders. *Personality and Individual differences*, **9**, 817–823.

Barlow, D. H., and Agras, W. S. (1973). Fading to increase heterosexual responsiveness in homosexuals. *Journal of Applied Behavior Analysis*, **6**, 355–367.

Bartol, C. R., and Bartol, A. M. (1987). History of forensic psychology. In I. B. Weiner and A. K. Hess (eds), *Handbook of Forensic Psychology*. New York: Wiley.

Bartollas, C. (1990). The prison: Disorder personified. In J. W. Murphy and J. E. Dison (eds), *Are Prisons Any Better? Twenty Years of Correctional Reform*. Newbury Park, Ca: Sage.

Barton, C., and Alexander, J. F. (1981). Functional family therapy. In A. S. Gurman and D. P. Kniskern (eds), *Handbook of Family Therapy*. New York: Brunner/Mazel.

Barton, C., Alexander, J. F., Waldron, H., Turner, C. W., and Warburton, J. (1985). Generalisation of treatment effects of functional family therapy: Three replications. *American Journal of Family Therapy*, **13**, 16–26.

Basta, J. M., and Davidson, W. S. (1988). Treatment of juvenile offenders: Study outcomes since 1980. *Behavioral Sciences and the Law*, **6**, 355–384.

Baxter, D. J., Barbaree, H. E., and Marshall, W. L. (1986). Sexual responses to consenting and forced sex in a large sample of rapists and nonrapists. *Behaviour Research and Therapy*, **24**, 513–520.

Bazelon, D. L. (1978). The role of the psychiatrist in the criminal justice system. *Bulletin of the American Academy of Psychiatry and the Law*, **6**, 139–146.

Bean, P. (1981). *Punishment: A Philosophical and Criminological Inquiry*. Oxford: Robertson.

Bean, P. (1983). The nature of psychiatric theory. In P. Bean (ed.), *Mental Illness: Changes and Trends*. Chichester: Wiley.

Bean, P. (1985). Social control and social theory in secure accommodation. In L. Gostin (ed.), *Secure Provision: A Review of Special Services for the Mentally Ill and Mentally Handicapped in England and Wales*. London: Tavistock.

Beck, A. T. (1976). *Cognitive Therapy and the Emotional Disorders*. New York: International Universities Press.

Beck, A. T., and Freeman, A. (1990). *Cognitive Therapy of Personality Disorders*. New York: Guilford.

Becker, H. (1963). *Outsiders*. New York: Free Press.

Becker, J. V., and Hunter, J. A. (1992). Evaluation of treatment outcome for adult child molesters. *Criminal Justice and Behavior*, **19**, 74–92.

Becker, W. C. (1960). The matching of behavior rating and questionnaire personality factors. *Psychological Bulletin*, **57**, 201–212.

Beidel, D. C., and Turner, S. M. (1986). A critique of the theoretical bases of cognitive–behavioral theories and therapies. *Clinical Psychology Review*, **6**, 177–197.

Bell, C. R., Mundy, P., and Quay, H. C. (1982). Modifying impulsive responding in conduct-disordered institutionalised boys. *Psychological Reports*, **52**, 307–310.

Bell, R. Q. (1968). A reinterpretation of the direction of effects in studies of socialisation. *Psychological Review*, **75**, 81–95.

Bellak, A. S. (1983). Recurrent problems in the behavioural assessment of social skill. *Behaviour Research and Therapy*, **21**, 29–41.

Bennett, T. (1986). Situational crime prevention from the offenders' perspective. In K. Heal and G. Laycock (eds), *Situational Crime Prevention: From Theory into Practice*. London: HMSO.

Bennight, K. (1975). A model program for counseling and placement of offenders. *Journal of Employment Counseling*, **12**, 168–173.

Benton, D., Kumari, N., and Brain, P. F. (1982). Mild hypoglycemia and questionnaire measures of aggression. *Biological Psychology*, **14**, 129–135.

Berkowitz, L. (1986). Some varieties of human aggression: Criminal violence as coercion, rule-following, impression management, and impulsive behaviour. In A. Campbell and J. J. Gibbs (eds), *Violent Transactions: The Limits of Personality*. Oxford: Blackwell.

Berkowitz, L. (1989). Frustration–aggression hypothesis: Examination and reformulation. *Psychological Bulletin*, **106**, 59–73.

Berkowitz, L. (1990). On the formation and regulation of anger and aggression: A cognitive-neoassociationist analysis. *American Psychologist*, **45**, 494–503.

Berkowitz, L., and Donnerstein, E. (1982). External validity is more than skin deep: Some answers to criticisms of laboratory experiments. *American Psychologist*, **37**, 245–257.

Berlyne, D. E. (1960). *Conflict, Arousal, and Curiosity*. New York: McGraw-Hill.

Berman, A., and Siegal, A. M. (1976). Adaptive and learning skills in juvenile delinquents: A neuropsychological analysis. *Journal of Learning Disabilities*, **9**, 583–590.

Berman, T., and Paisey, T. (1984). Personality in assaultive and nonassaultive juvenile male offenders. *Psychological Reports*, **54**, 527–530.

Bernal, M. E., Klinnert, M. D., and Schultz, L. A. (1980). Outcome evaluations of behavioral parent training and client-centred parent counselling for children with conduct problems. *Journal of Applied Behavior Analysis*, **13**, 677–691.

Bernard, T. J. (1984). Control criticisms of strain theories: An assessment of theoretical and empirical adequacy. *Journal of Research in Crime and Delinquency*, **21**, 353–372.

Bertilson, H. S. (1983). Methodology in the study of aggression. In R. G. Geen and E. I. Donnerstein (eds), *Aggression: Theoretical and Experimental Reviews* Volume One. New York: Academic Press.

Beyleveld, D. (1979). Identifying, explaining and predicting deterrence. *British Journal of Criminology*, **19**, 205–224.

Beyleveld, D. (1982). Ehrlich's analysis of deterrence. *British Journal of Criminology*, **22**, 101–123.

Bhagat, M., and Fraser, W. I. (1970). Young offenders' images of self and surroundings: A semantic enquiry. *British Journal of Psychiatry*, **117**, 381–387.

Bhaskar, R. (1979). *The Possibility of Naturalism*. Brighton: Harvester Press.

Binder, A. (1987). An historical introduction. In H. C. Quay (ed.), *Handbook of Juvenile Delinquency*. Chichester: Wiley.

Binder, A. (1988). Juvenile delinquency. *Annual Review of Psychology*, **39**, 253–282.

Binder, R. L., and McNiel, D. E. (1988). Effects of diagnosis and context on dangerousness. *American Journal of Psychiatry*, **145**, 728–732.

Bishop, D. M. (1984). Legal and extralegal barriers to delinquency. *Criminology*, **22**, 403–419.

Bishop, D. V. M. (1977). The P scale and psychosis. *Journal of Abnormal Psychology*, **86**, 127–134.

Bistline, J. L., and Frieden, F. P. (1984). Anger control: A case study of a stress inoculation treatment for a chronic aggressive patient. *Cognitive Therapy and Research*, **8**, 551–556.

Black, D. A., and Spinks, P. (1985). Predicting outcomes of mentally disordered and dangerous offenders. In D. P. Farrington and R. Tarling (eds), *Prediction in Criminology*. Albany: State University of New York Press.

Black, D. A., Blackburn, R., Blackler, C. D., and Haward, L. R. C. (1973). Memorandum of evidence to the Butler Committee on the law relating to the mentally abnormal offender. *Bulletin of the British Psychological Society*, **26**, 331–342.

Black, D. J., and Reiss, A. (1970). Police control of juveniles. *American Sociological Review*, **35**, 63–77.

Blackburn, R. (1968a). The scores of Eysenck's criterion groups on some MMPI scales related to emotionality and extraversion. *British Journal of Social and Clinical Psychology*, **7**, 3–12.

Blackburn, R. (1968b). Personality in relation to extreme aggression in psychiatric offenders. *British Journal of Psychiatry*, **114**, 821–828.

Blackburn, R. (1968c). Emotionality, extraversion and aggression in paranoid and nonparanoid schizophrenic offenders. *British Journal of Psychiatry*, **114**, 1301–1302.

Blackburn, R. (1969). Sensation seeking, impulsivity, and psychopathic personality. *Journal of Consulting and Clinical Psychology*, **33**, 571–574.

Blackburn, R. (1971a). Personality types among abnormal homicides. *British Journal of Criminology*, **11**, 14–31.

Blackburn, R. (1971b). MMPI dimensions of sociability and impulse control. *Journal of Consulting and Clinical Psychology*, **37**, 166.

Blackburn, R. (1972). Dimensions of hostility and aggression in abnormal offenders. *Journal of Consulting and Clinical Psychology*, **38**, 20–26.

Blackburn, R. (1975a). An empirical classification of psychopathic personality. *British Journal of Psychiatry*, **127**, 456–460.

Blackburn, R. (1975b). Aggression and the EEG: A quantitative analysis. *Journal of Abnormal Psychology*, **84**, 358–365.

Blackburn, R. (1978). Psychopathy, arousal, and the need for stimulation. In R. D. Hare and D. Schalling (eds), *Psychopathic Behaviour: Approaches to Research*. Chichester: Wiley.

Blackburn, R. (1979a). Psychopathy and Personality: The dimensionality of self-report and behaviour rating data in abnormal offenders. *British Journal of Social and Clinical Psychology*, **18**, 111–119.

Blackburn, R. (1979b). Cortical and autonomic arousal in primary and secondary psychopaths. *Psychophysiology*, **16**, 143–150.

Blackburn, R. (1980a). Personality and the criminal psychopath. In Facolto di Giurizprudentia, Universita di Messina *Lo Psicopatico Delinquente*. Milan: Giuffre.

Blackburn, R. (1980b). Still not working? A look at recent outcomes in offender rehabilitation. Paper presented at the Scottish Branch of the British Psychological Society's Conference on "Deviance" University of Stirling.

Blackburn, R. (1982). *The Special Hospitals Assessment of Personality and Socialisation.* Unpublished Manuscript, Park Lane Hospital, Liverpool.

Blackburn, R. (1984). The person and dangerousness. In D. J. Müller, D. E. Blackman, and A. J. Chapman (eds), *Psychology and Law*. Chichester: Wiley.

Blackburn, R. (1986). Patterns of personality deviation among violent offenders: Replication and extension of an empirical taxonomy. *British Journal of Criminology*, **26**, 254–269.

Blackburn, R. (1987). Two scales for the assessment of personality disorder in antisocial populations. *Personality and Individual Differences*, **8**, 81-93.

Blackburn, R. (1988a). Psychopathy and personality disorder. In E. Miller and P. J. Cooper (eds), *Adult Abnormal Psychology*. Edinburgh: Churchill Livingstone.

Blackburn, R. (1988b). On moral judgements and personality disorders: The myth of the psychopathic personality revisited. *British Journal of Psychiatry*, **153**, 505–512.

Blackburn, R. (1989). Psychopathy and personality disorder in relation to violence. In K. Howells and C. R. Hollin (eds), *Clinical Approaches to Violence*. Chichester: Wiley.

Blackburn, R. and Lee-Evans, J. M. (1985). Reactions of primary and secondary psychopaths to anger evoking situations. *British Journal of Clinical Psychology*, **24**, 93–100.

Blackburn, R. and Maybury, C. (1985). Identifying the psychopath: the relation of Cleckley's criteria to the interpersonal domain. *Personality and Individual Differences*, **6**, 375–386.

Blackburn, R., Crellin, M. C., Morgan, E. M., and Tulloch, R. M. B. (1990). Prevalence of personality disorders in a special hospital population. *Journal of Forensic Psychiatry*, **1**, 43–52.

Blackman, D. E. (1981). On mental elements and their place in psychology and law. In J. Shapland (ed.), Lawyers and Psychologists—The Way Forward. *Issues in Criminological and Legal Psychology, No. 1*. Leicester: British Psychological Society.

Blackman, D. E., Müller, D. J., and Chapman, A. J. (1984). Perspectives in psychology and law. In D. J. Müller, D. E. Blackman, and A. J. Chapman (eds.). *Psychology and Law*. Chichester: Wiley.

Blader, J. C., and Marshall, W. L. (1989). Is assessment of sexual arousal in rapists worthwhile? A critique of current methods and the development of a response compatibility approach. *Clinical Psychology Review*, **9**, 569–587.

Blair, C. D., and Lanyon, R. I. (1981). Exhibitionism: Etiology and treatment. *Psychological Bulletin*, **89**, 439–463.

Blakely, C. H., and Davidson, W. S. (1984). Behavioral approaches to delinquency. In P. Karoly and J. J. Steffen (eds), *Adolescent Behavior Disorders: Foundations and Contemporary Concerns*. Lexington, Mass: Lexington Books.

Blashfield, R. K. (1980). Propositions regarding the use of cluster analysis in clinical research. *Journal of Consulting and Clinical Psychology*, **48**, 456–459.

Blashfield, R. K., and Draguns, J. G. (1976). Toward a taxonomy of psychopathology: The purpose of psychiatric classification. *British Journal of Psychiatry*, **129**, 574–583.

Blasi, A. (1980). Bridging moral cognition and moral action: A critical review of the literature. *Psychological Bulletin*, **88**, 1–45.

Blaske, D. M., Borduin, C. M., Henggeler, S. W., and Mann, B.J. (1989). Individual, family, and peer characteristics of adolescent sex offenders and assaultive offenders. *Developmental Psychology*, **25**, 846–855.

Blau, P. (1981). Behavioral *sociology* or *behavioral* sociology? *American Sociologist*, **16**, 170–171.

Blau, T. H. (1984). Psychological tests in the courtroom. *Professional Psychology: Research and Practice*, **15**, 176–186.

Blau, T. H. (1985). The psychologist as expert in the courts. *The Clinical Psychologist*, **38**, 76–78.

Block, C. R., and Block, R. L. (1984). Crime definition, crime measurement, and victim surveys. *Journal of Social Issues*, **40**, 137–159.

Block, R. (1977). *Violent Crime*. Lexington, Ma: Lexington Books.

Blumstein, A. (1983). Selective incapacitation as a means of crime control. *American Behavioral Scientist*, **27**, 87–108.

Blumstein, A., Cohen, J., and Farrington, D. P. (1988). Criminal career research: Its value for criminology. *Criminology*, **26**, 1–35.

Blumstein, A., Farrington, D. P., and Moitra, S. (1985). Delinquency careers: Innocents, desistors, and persisters. In M. Tonry and N. Morris (eds), *Crime and Justice: An Annual Review of Research*, Volume 6. Chicago: University of Chicago Press.

Bohman, M., Cloninger, C. R., Sigvardsson, S., and von Knorring, A. (1982). Predisposition to petty criminality in Swedish adoptees: I. Genetic and environmental heterogeneity. *Archives of General Psychiatry*, **39**, 1233–1241.

Bolles, R. C. (1972). Reinforcement, expectancy, and learning. *Psychological Review*, **79**, 394–409.

Bonta, J. L. (1986). Prison crowding: Searching for the functional correlates. *American Psychologist*, **41**, 99–101.

Bonta, J. L., and Motiuk, L. L. (1985). Utilisation of an interview-based classification instrument: A study of correctional halfway houses. *Criminal Justice and Behavior*, **12**, 333–352.

Bornstein, P. H., Hamilton. S. B., and McFall, M. E. (1981). Modification of adult aggression: A critical review of theory, research and practice. In M. Hersen, R. M. Eisler and P. M. Miller (eds), *Progress in Behavior Modification*, Volume 12. New York: Academic Press.

Booraem, D., Flowers, V., Bodner, E., and Satterfield, D. A. (1977). Personal space variations as a function of criminal behavior. *Psychological Reports*, **41**, 1115–1121.

Boorse, C. (1975). On the distinction between disease and illness. *Philosophy and Public Affairs*, **5**, 49–68.

Boorse, C. (1976). What a theory of mental health should be. *Journal for the Theory of Social Behaviour*, **6**, 61–84.

Boren, J. J., and Colman, A. D. (1970). Some experiments on reinforcement principles within a psychiatric ward for delinquent soldiers. *Journal of Applied Behavior Analysis*, **3**, 29–37.

Bottoms, A., and McWilliams, W. (1990). Evaluating intermediate treatment. In D. Robbins and A. Walters (eds), *Department of Health Yearbook of Research and Development*. London: HMSO.

Bottomley, A. K. (1979). *Criminology in Focus*. Oxford: Robertson.

Bottomley, K., and Pease, K. (1986). *Crime and Punishment: Interpreting the Data*. Milton Keynes: Open University Press.

Bouchard, T. J., Lykken, D. T., McGue, M., Segal, N. L., and Tellegen, A. (1990). Sources of human psychological differences: The Minneapolis study of twins reared apart. *Science*, **250**, 223–228.

Bowden, P. (1985). Psychiatry and dangerousness: A counter renaissance? In L. Gostin (ed.), *Secure Provision: A Review of Special Services for the Mentally Ill and Mentally Handicapped in England and Wales*. London: Tavistock.

Bowlby, J. (1944). Forty-four juvenile thieves. *International Journal of Psychoanalysis*, **25**, 1–57.

Bowman, P. C., and Auerbach, S. M. (1982). Impulsive youthful offenders: A multimodal cognitive–behavioral treatment program. *Criminal Justice and Behavior*, **9**, 432–454.

Box, S. (1981). *Deviance, Reality and Society*, Second Edition. London: Holt, Rinehart and Winston.

Box, S. (1983). *Power, Crime, and Mystification*. London: Tavistock.

Bradford, J. M. V. (1985). Organic treatments for the male sexual offender. *Behavioral Sciences and the Law*, **3**, 355–375.

Brain, P. F. (1986). Alcohol and aggression—the nature of a presumed relationship. In P. F. Brain (ed.), *Alcohol and Aggression*. London: Croom Helm.

Braithwaite, J. (1981). The myth of social class and criminology reconsidered. *American Sociological Review*, **46**, 36–57.

Braukmann, C. J., and Wolf, M. M. (1987). Behaviorally based group homes for juvenile offenders. In E. K. Morris and C. J. Braukmann (eds), *Behavioral Approaches to Crime and Delinquency: A Handbook of Application, Research, and Concepts*. New York: Plenum.

Braukmann, C. J., Kirigin, K. A., and Wolf, M. M. (1980). Group home treatment research: Social learning and social control perspectives. In T. Hirschi and M. Gottfredson (eds), *Understanding Crime: Current Theory and Research*. Beverly Hills, Ca: Sage.

Brennan, T. (1987a). Classification: An overview of selected methodological issues. In D. M. Gottfredson and M. Tonry (eds), *Prediction and Classification: Criminal Justice Decision Making*. Chicago: University of Chicago Press.

Brennan, T. (1987b). Classification for control in jails and prisons. In D. M. Gottfredson and M. Tonry (eds), *Prediction and Classification: Criminal Justice Decision Making*. Chicago: University of Chicago Press.

Breslow, N. (1987). Locus of control, desirability of control, and sadomasochists. *Psychological Reports*, **61**, 995–1001.

Brewin, C. R. (1989). Cognitive change processes in psychotherapy. *Psychological Review*, **96**, 379–394.

Bridges, G. S., and Stone, J. A. (1986). Effects of criminal punishment on perceived threat of punishment: Toward an understanding of specific deterrence. *Journal of Research in Crime and Delinquency*, **23**, 207–239.

British Psychological Society (1985). A code of conduct for psychologists. *Bulletin of the British Psychological Society*, **38**, 41–43.

British Psychological Society (1986). Report of the working group on the use of the polygraph in criminal investigation and personnel screening. *Bulletin of the British Psychological Society*, **39**, 81–94.

Brittain, R. P. (1970). The sadistic murderer. *Medicine, Science and the Law*, **10**, 198–207.

Brodsky, S. L. (1972). *Psychologists in the Criminal Justice System*. Carbondale, Ill: American Association of Correctional Psychologists.

Brodsky, S. L. (1980). Ethical issues for psychologists in corrections. In J. Monahan (ed.), *Who is the Client? The Ethics of Psychological Intervention in the Criminal Justice System*. Washington, DC: American Psychological Association.

Brodsky, S. L., and Robey, A. (1973). On becoming an expert witness. *Professional Psychology*, **3**, 173–176.

Brodsky, S. L., and Smitherman, H. O. (1983). *Handbook of Scales for Research in Crime and Delinquency*. New York: Plenum.

Brody, S. R. (1976). *The Effectiveness of Sentencing*. Home Office Research Study No. 35. London: HMSO.

Brody, S. R., and Tarling, R. (1980). *Taking Offenders out of Circulation*. Home Office Research Study No. 64. London: HMSO.

Brown, B. J. (1985a). The involvement of psychologists in sentencing. *Bulletin of the British Psychological Society*, **38**, 180–182.

Brown, B. J. (1985b). An application of social learning methods in a residential programme for young offenders. *Journal of Adolescence*, **8**, 321–331.

Brown, D., Fenwick, P., and Howard, R. (1989). The contingent negative variation in a go/no go avoidance task: Relationships with personality and subjective state. *International Journal of Psychophysiology*, **7**, 35–45.

Brown, H. I. (1977). *Perception, Theory and Commitment*. Chicago: University of Chicago Press.

Brown, S. E. (1984). Social class, child maltreatment, and delinquent behavior. *Criminology*, **22**, 259–278.

Brownell, K. D., Marlatt, G. A., Lichtenstein, E., and Wilson, G. T. (1986). Understanding and preventing relapse. *American Psychologist*, **41**, 765–782.

Brownfield, D. (1986). Social class and violent behavior. *Criminology*, **24**, 421–438.

Brownmiller, S. (1975). *Against Our Will: Men, Women and Rape*. New York: Bantam.

Bry, B. H. (1982). Reducing the incidence of adolescent problems through preventive intervention: One- and five-year follow-up. *American Journal of Community Psychology*, **10**, 265–276.

Bryant, E, T., Scott, M. L., Golden, C. J., and Tori, C. D. (1984). Neuropsychological deficits, learning disability and violent behavior. *Journal of Consulting and Clinical Psychology*, **52**, 323–324.

Brynner, J., O'Malley, P., and Bachman, J. (1981). Self-esteem and delinquency revisited. *Journal of Youth and Adolescence*, **10**, 407–441.

Buikhuisen, W., and Hoekstra, H. A. (1974). Factors related to recidivism. *British Journal of Criminology*, **14**, 63–69.

Buikhuisen, W., Van Der Plas-Korenhoff, C., and Bontekoe, E. H. M. (1988). Alcohol and violence. In T. E. Moffitt and S. A. Mednick (eds), *Biological Contributions to Crime Causation*. Dordrecht: Martinus Nijhoff.

Bukstel, L. H., and Kilmann, P. R. (1980). Psychological effects of imprisonment on confined individuals. *Psychological Bulletin*, **88**, 469–493.

Bull, R. (1982). Physical appearance and delinquency. *Current Psychological Reviews*, **2**, 269–282.

Bull, R. (1984). Psychology's contribution to policing. In D. J. Müller, D. E. Blackman, and A. J. Chapman (eds), *Psychology and Law*. Chichester: Wiley.

Burchard, J. D., and Lane, T. W. (1982). Crime and delinquency. In A. S. Bellak, M. Hersen, and A. E. Kazdin (eds), *International Handbook of Behavior Modification*. New York: Plenum.

Burgess, A. W., Hartmen, C. R., Ressler, R. K., Douglas, J. E., and McCormack, A. (1986). Sexual homicide: A motivational model. *Journal of Interpersonal Violence*, **1**, 251–272.

Burgess, P. K. (1972). Eysenck's theory of criminality: A test of some objections to disconfirmatory evidence. *British Journal of Social and Clinical Psychology*, **11**, 248–256.

Burgess, R. L., and Akers, R. L. (1966). A differential association–reinforcement theory of criminal behaviour. *Social Problems*, **14**, 128–147.

Burgess, R. L., and Youngblade, L. M. (1988). Social incompetence and the intergenerational transmission of abusive parental practices. In G. T. Hotaling, D. Finkelhor, J. T. Kirkpatrick, and M. A. Straus (eds), *Family Abuse and its Consequences: New Directions in Research*. Beverly Hills: Sage.

Bursik, R. J. (1980). The dynamics of specialisation in juvenile offenses. *Social Forces*, **58**, 851–864.

Bursik, R. J., and Webb, J. (1982). Community change and patterns of delinquency. *American Journal of Sociology*, **88**, 24–42.

Burt, C. (1925). *The Young Delinquent*. London: University of London Press.

Burt, M. R. (1980). Cultural myths and support for rape. *Journal of Personality and Social Psychology*, **38**, 217–230.

Burton, R. V. (1984). A paradox in theories and research in moral development. In W. M. Kurtines and J. L. Gewirtz (eds), *Morality, Moral Behaviour, and Moral Development*. Chichester: Wiley.

Busch, K. G., Zagar, R., Hughes, J. R., Arbit, J., and Bussell, R. E. (1990). Adolescents who kill. *Journal of Clinical Psychology*, **46**, 472–485.

Bushman, B. J., and Cooper, H. M. (1990). Effects of alcohol on human aggression: An integrative research review. *Psychological Bulletin*, **107**, 341–354.

Buss, A. H. (1961). *The Psychology of Aggression*. New York: Wiley.

Cadoret, R. J. (1978). Psychopathology in adopted-away offspring of biologic parents with antisocial behavior. *Archives of General Psychiatry*, **35**, 176–184.

Cairns, R. B., Cairns, B. D., Neckerman, H. J., Gest, S. D., and Gariépy, J-L. (1988). Social networks and aggressive behavior: peer support or peer rejection? *Developmental Psychology*, **24**, 815–823.

Camp, B. W., Blom, G. E., Herbert, F., and Van Doorninck, W. J. (1977). "Think Aloud":

A program for developing self-control in young aggressive boys. *Journal of Abnormal Child Psychology*, **5**, 157–169.

Canter, D. (1989). Offender profiling. *The Psychologist*, **2**, 12–16.

Canter, D., and Heritage, R. (1990). A multivariate model of sexual offence behaviour: Developments in offender profiling. *Journal of Forensic Psychiatry*, **1**, 185–212.

Canter, R. J. (1982a). Sex differences in self-report delinquency. *Criminology*, **20**, 373–393.

Canter, R. J. (1982b). Family correlates of male and female delinquency. *Criminology*, **20**, 149–167.

Cantor, N. (1990). From thought to behavior: "having" and "doing" in the study of personality and cognition. *American Psychologist*, **45**, 735–750.

Cantor, N., Smith, E. E., French, R., and Mezzich, J. (1980). Psychiatric diagnosis as prototype categorisation. *Journal of Abnormal Psychology*, **89**, 181–193.

Caplan, N. S., and Siebert, L. A. (1964). Distribution of juvenile delinquent intelligence test scores over a thirty-four year period. *Journal of Clinical Psychology*, **20**, 242–247.

Carbonell, J. L. (1983). Inmate classification systems: a cross-tabulation of two methods. *Criminal Justice and Behavior*, **10**, 285–292.

Carney, F. L. (1977). Outpatient treatment of the aggressive offender. *American Journal of Psychotherapy*, **31**, 265–274.

Carney, F. L. (1978). Inpatient treatment programs. In W. H. Reid (ed.), *The Psychopath: A Comprehensive Study of Antisocial Disorders and Behaviors*. New York: Brunner/Mazel.

Carrigan, P. M. (1960). Extraversion–introversion as a dimension of personality: a reappraisal. *Psychological Bulletin*, **57**, 329–360.

Carroll, D. (1988). How accurate is polygraph lie detection? In A. Gale (ed.), *The Polygraph Test: Lies, Truth and Science*. London: Sage.

Carroll, J. S. (1978). A psychological approach to deterrence: The evaluation of crime opportunities. *Journal of Personality and Social Psychology*, **36**, 1512–1520.

Carroll, J. S. (1982). Committing a crime: the offender's decision. In V. J. Konecni and E. Ebbeson (eds), *The Criminal Justice System: A Social–Psychological Analysis*. San Francisco: Freeman.

Carroll, J. S., and Weaver, F. M. (1986). Shoplifters' perceptions of crime opportunities: A process-tracing study. In D. B. Cornish and R. V. G. Clarke (eds), *The Reasoning Criminal: Rational Choice Perspectives on Offending*. New York: Springer-Verlag.

Carroll, J. S., Perkowitz, W. T., Lurigio, A. J., and Weaver, F. M. (1987). Sentencing goals, causal attributions, ideology, and personality. *Journal of Personality and Social Psychology*, **52**, 107–118.

Carson, D. (1984). Putting the expert in expert witness. In D. J. Müller, D. E. Blackman, and A. J. Chapman (eds), *Psychology and Law*. Chichester: Wiley.

Carson, R. C. (1979). Personality and exchange in developing relationships. In R. L. Burgess and T. L. Huston (eds), *Social Exchange in Developing Relationships*. New York: Academic Press.

Carter, D. L., Prentky, R. A., Knight, R. A., Vanderveer, P. L., and Boucher, R. J. (1987). Use of pornography in the criminal and developmental histories of sex offenders. *Journal of Interpersonal Violence*, **2**, 196–211.

Caspi, A., Bem, D. J., and Elder, G. H. (1989). Continuities and consequences of interactional styles across the life course. *Journal of Personality*, **57**, 375–406.

Cattell, R. B. (1966). *The Scientific Analysis of Personality*. Harmondsworth: Penguin.

Cattell, R. B., Eber, H. W., and Tatsuoka, M. M. (1970). *Handbook for the Sixteen Personality Factor Questionnaire*. Champaign, Ill: Institute for Personality and Ability Testing.

Cavior, H. E. and Schmidt, A. A. (1978). Test of the effectiveness of a differential treatment strategy at the Robert F. Kennedy Centre. *Criminal Justice and Behavior*, **5**, 131–139.

Cernkovich, S. A., and Giordano, P. C. (1979). A comparative analysis of male and female delinquency. *Sociological Quarterly*, **20**, 131–145.

Cernkovich, S. A., and Giordano, P. C. (1987). Family relationships and delinquency. *Criminology*, **25**, 295–321.

Chaiken, M. R., and Chaiken, J. M. (1984). Offender types and public policy. *Crime and Delinquency*, **30**, 195–226.

Chambliss, W. (1969). *Crime and the Legal Process*. New York: McGraw-Hill.

Chappell, D. (1989). Sexual criminal violence. In N. A. Weiner and M. E. Wolfgang (eds), *Pathways to Criminal Violence*. Newbury Park, Ca: Sage.

Chandler, M. (1973). Egocentrism and antisocial behavior: The assessment and training of social perspective-taking skills. *Developmental Psychology*, **9**, 326–332.

Chess, S., and Thomas, A. (1984). *Origins and Evolution of Behavior Disorders*. New York: Brunner/Mazel.

Chilton, R. J., and Markle, G. E. (1972). Family disruption, delinquent conduct and the effect of sub-classification. *American Sociological Review*, **37**, 93–99.

Chiswick, D. (1978). Insanity in bar of trial in Scotland: A State Hospital study. *British Journal of Psychiatry*, **132**, 598–601.

Christiansen, K. O. (1977a). A review of studies of criminality among twins. In S. A. Mednick and K. O. Christiansen (eds), *Biosocial Bases of Criminal Behavior*. New York: Gardiner Press.

Christiansen, K. O. (1977b). A preliminary study of criminality among twins. In S. A. Mednick and K. O. Christiansen (eds), *Biosocial Bases of Criminal Behavior*. New York: Gardiner Press.

Christie-Brown, J. R. W. (1983). Paraphilias: Sadomasochism, fetishism, transvestism and transsexuality. *British Journal of Psychiatry*, **143**, 227–231.

Clarke, R. V. G. (1977). Psychology and crime. *Bulletin of the British Psychological Society*, **30**, 280–283.

Clarke, R. V. G. (1980). "Situational" crime prevention: Theory and practice. *British Journal of Criminology*, **20**, 136–147.

Clarke, R. V. G. (1985). Jack Tizard Memorial Lecture: Delinquency, environment and intervention. *Journal of Child Psychology and Psychiatry*, **26**, 505–523.

Clarke, R. V. G., and Cornish, D. B. (1985). Modeling offenders' decisions: A framework for research and policy. In M. Tonry and N. Morris (eds), *Crime and Justice: An Annual Review of Research*, Volume 6. Chicago: University of Chicago Press.

Claster, D. S. (1967). Comparison of risk perception between delinquents and nondelinquents. *Journal of Criminal Law, Criminology, and Police Science*, **58**, 80–86.

Cleckley, H. (1976). *The Mask of Sanity*, Sixth Edition. St. Louis: Mosby.

Clemmer, D. (1958). *The Prison Community*. New York: Holt, Rinehart and Winston.

Clinard, M. B., and Quinney, R. (1973). *Criminal Behavior Systems*. New York: Holt, Rinehart and Winston.

Clingempeel, W. G., Mulvey, E., and Repucci, N. D. (1980). A national study of ethical dilemmas of psychologists in the criminal justice system. In J. Monahan (ed.), *Who is the Client? The Ethics of Psychological Intervention in the Criminal Justice System*. Washington, DC: American Psychological Association.

Cloninger, C. R., Christiansen, K. O., Reich, T., and Gottesman, I. I. (1978). Implications of sex differences in the prevalence of antisocial personality, alcoholism, and criminality for familial transmission. *Archives of General Psychiatry*, **35**, 941–951.

Cloward, R. A., and Ohlin, L. E. (1961). *Delinquency and Opportunity*. Glencoe: Free Press.

Coccaro, E. (1989). Central serotonin and impulsive aggression. *British Journal of Psychiatry*, **155**, 52–56.

Cochrane, R. (1971). The structure of value systems in male and female prisoners. *British Journal of Criminology*, **11**, 73–79.

Cochrane, R. (1974). Crime and personality: Theory and evidence. *Bulletin of the British Psychological Society*, **27**, 19–22.

Cocozza, J. J., and Steadmen, H. J. (1974). Some refinements in the measurement and prediction of dangerous behavior. *American Journal of Psychiatry*, **131**, 1012–1014.

Cocozza, J. J., and Steadmen, H. J. (1978). Prediction in psychiatry: An example of misplaced confidence in experts. *Social Problems*, **25**, 265–276.

Cohen, A. K. (1955). *Delinquent Boys*. Glencoe: Free Press.

Cohen, H. L., and Filipczak, J. (1971). *A New Learning Environment*. San Francisco: Jossey-Bass.

Cohen, L. E., and Felson. M. (1979). Social change and crime rate trends: A routine activity approach. *American Sociological Review*, **44**, 588–608.

Cohen, L. E., and Klugel, J. R. (1978). Determinants of juvenile court dispositions. *American Sociological Review*, **43**, 162–176.

Cohen, L. E., and Land, K. C. (1987). Age structure and crime: Symmetry versus asymmetry and the projection of crime through the 1990s. *American Sociological Review*, **52**, 170–183.

Cohen, L. E., and Machalek, R. (1989). A general theory of expropriative crime: An evolutionary ecological approach. *American Journal of Sociology*, **94**, 465–501.

Cohen, M., Seghorn, T., and Calmas, W. (1969). Sociometric study of the sex offender. *Journal of Abnormal Psychology*, **74**, 249–255.

Coid, J. (1982). Alcoholism and violence. *Drug and Alcohol Dependence*, **9**, 1–13.

Coid, J. (1983). The epidemiology of abnormal homicide and murder followed by suicide. *Psychological Medicine*, **13**, 855–860.

Coid, J. (1984). How many psychiatric patients in prison? *British Journal of Psychiatry*, **145**, 78–86.

Colby, A., and Kohlberg, L. (1987). *The Measurement of Moral Judgment*. Cambridge: University of Cambridge Press.

Collingwood, T. R., and Genther, R. W. (1980). Skills training as treatment for juvenile delinquents. *Professional Psychology*, **11**, 591–598.

Collins, J. J. (1989). Alcohol and interpersonal violence: Less than meets the eye. In N. A. Weiner and M. E. Wolfgang (eds), *Pathways to Criminal Violence*. Newbury Park, Ca: Sage.

Collins, J. J., and Bailey, S. L. (1990a). Traumatic stress disorder and violent behavior. *Journal of Traumatic Stress*, **3**, 203–220.

Collins, J. J., and Bailey, S. L. (1990b). Relationship of mood disorders to violence. *Journal of Nervous and Mental Disease*, **178**, 44–47.

Colman, A. D., and Baker, S. L. (1969). Utilisation of an operant conditioning model for the treatment of character and behavior disorders in a military setting. *American Journal of Psychiatry*, **125**, 101–109.

Colman, A. M., and Gorman, L. P. (1982). Conservatism, dogmatism and authoritarianism in British police officers. *Sociology*, **16**, 1–11.

Colvin, M., and Pauly, J. (1983). A critique of criminology: Toward an integrated structural-Marxist theory of delinquency production. *American Journal of Sociology*, **89**, 513–551.

Committee on Ethical Guidelines for Forensic Psychologists (1991). Specialty guidelines for forensic psychologists. *Law and Human Behavior*, **15**, 655–665.

Como, P. G. (1977). The use of multiple personality variables to predict recidivism in prisoners. Unpublished M. A. Thesis, University of Texas.

Conaway, L. P., and Hansen, D. J. (1989). Social behavior of physically abused and neglected children: A critical review. *Clinical Psychology Review*, **9**, 627–652.

Conger, R. D. (1976). Social control and social learning models of delinquent behavior: A synthesis. *Criminology*, **14**, 17–40.

Connolly, K., and McKellar, P. (1963). Forensic psychology. *Bulletin of the British Psychological Society*, **16**, 16–24.

Conrad, S. R., and Wincze, J. P. (1976). Orgasmic reconditioning: A controlled study of its effects upon the sexual arousal and behavior of adult male homosexuals. *Behavior Therapy*, **7**, 155–166.

Convit, A., Jaeger, J., Lin, S. P., Meisner, M., Brizer, D., and Volavka, J. (1988). Prediction of violence in psychiatric patients. In T. E. Moffitt and S. A. Mednick (eds), *Biological Contributions to Crime Causation*. Dordrecht: Martinus Nijhoff.

Cook, P. J. (1980). Research in criminal deterrence: Laying the groundwork for the second decade. In M. Tonry and N. Morris (eds), *Crime and Justice: An Annual Review of Research*, Volume 2. Chicago: University of Chicago Press.

Cooke, D. (1989). Containing violent prisoners: An analysis of the Barlinnie Special Unit. *British Journal of Criminology*, **29**, 129–143.

Cooke, D. (1990). Being an "expert" in court. *The Psychologist*, **3**, 216–221.

Cooke, D. (1991a). Violence in prisons: The influence of regime factors. *Howard Journal*, **30**, 95–109.

Cooke, D. (1991b). Treatment as an alternative to prosecution: Offenders diverted for treatment. *British Journal of Psychiatry*, **158**, 785–791.

Cooper, B., and Shepherd, M. (1973). Epidemiology and abnormal psychology. In H. J. Eysenck (ed.), *Handbook of Abnormal Psychology*. London: Pitman.

Cooper, R. P., and Werner, P. D. (1990). Predicting violence in newly admitted inmates: A lens model analysis of staff decision making. *Criminal Justice and Behavior*, **17**, 431–447.

Copas, J. B., O'Brien, M., Roberts, J., and Whiteley, S. (1984). Treatment outcome in personality disorder: The effects of social, psychological, and behavioural measures. *Personality and Individual Differences*, **5**, 565–573.

Copeland, T. F., and Parish, T. S. (1979). Attempt to enhance moral judgments of offenders. *Psychological Reports*, **45**, 831–834.

Cornish, D. B., and Clarke, R. V. G. (1975). *Residential Treatment and its Effects on Delinquency*. London: HMSO.

Cornish, D. B., and Clarke, R. V. G. (eds) (1986). *The Reasoning Criminal: Rational Choice Perspectives on Offending*. New York: Springer-Verlag.

Corsini, R. J., and Miller, G. A. (1954). Psychology in prisons, 1952. *American Psychologist*, **9**, 184–185.

Cortés, J. B., and Gatti, F. M. (1972). *Delinquency and Crime: A Biopsychosocial Approach*. New York: Seminar Press.

Costin, F., and Schwartz, N. (1987). Beliefs about rape and women's social roles: A four-nation study. *Journal of Interpersonal Violence*, **2**, 46–56.

Council for Science and Society. (1981). *Treating the Troublesome*. London: Calverts North Star Press.

Court, J. H. (1984). Sex and violence: A ripple effect. In N. M. Malamuth and E. Donnerstein (eds), *Pornography and Sexual Aggression*. New York: Academic Press.

Cowie, J., Cowie, V., and Slater, E. (1968). *Delinquency in Girls*. London: Heinemann.

Cox, M. (1980). Personal reflections upon 3,000 hours in therapeutic groups with sex offenders. In D. J. West (ed.), *Sex Offenders in the Criminal Justice System*. Cropwood Conferences Series No. 12. Cambridge: Institute of Criminology.

Cox, V. C., Paulus, P. B., and McCain, G. (1984). Prison crowding research. *American Psychologist*, **39**, 1148–1160.

Craft, M., Stephenson, G., and Granger, C. (1964). A controlled trial of authoritarian and self-governing regimes with adolescent psychopaths. *American Journal of Orthopsychiatry*, **64**, 543–554.

Crawford, D. A. (1979). Modification of deviant sexual behaviour: the need for a comprehensive approach. *British Journal of Medical Psychology*, **52**, 151–156.

Crawford, D. A., and Allen, J. V. (1979). A social skills training program with sex offenders. In M. Cook and G. Wilson (eds), *Love and Attraction*. Oxford: Pergamon.

Crawford, D. A., and Howells, K. (1982). The effect of sex education with disturbed adolescents. *Behavioural Psychotherapy*, **10**, 339–345.

Crepault, C., and Couture, M. (1980). Men's erotic fantasies. *Archives of Sexual Behavior*, **9**, 565–581.

Cressey, D. R. (1969). Role theory, differential association, and compulsive crimes. In D. R. Cressey and D. Ward (eds), *Delinquency, Crime, and Social Process*. New York: Harper and Row.

Critchlow, B. (1986). The powers of John Barleycorn: Beliefs about the effects of alcohol on social behavior. *American Psychologist*, **41**, 751–764.

Crombag, H. F. M. (1984). Some psychological observations on *mens rea*. In D. J. Müller,

D. E. Blackman, and A. J. Chapman (eds), *Psychology and Law*. Chichester: Wiley.

Crow, I. (1987). Black people and criminal justice in the UK. *Howard Journal*, **26**, 303–314.

Crowe, R. R. (1972). The adopted offspring of women criminal offenders. *Archives of General Psychiatry*, **27**, 600–603.

Cullen, F. T., and Gendreau, P. (1989). The effectiveness of correctional rehabilitation: Reconsidering the "nothing works" debate. In L. Goodstein and D. L. MacKenzie (eds), *The American Prison: Issues in Research Policy*. New York: Plenum.

Cullen, F. T., Link, B. G., Travis, L. F., and Wozniack, J. F. (1985). Consensus of crime seriousness: Empirical reality or methodological artifact? *Criminology*, **23**, 99–118.

Cunnien, A. J. (1985). Pathological gambling as an insanity defense. *Behavioral Sciences and the Law*, **3**, 85–102.

Curtis, E. W. (1971). Predictive value compared to predictive validity. *American Psychologist*, **26**, 908–914.

Curtis, L. A. (1974). Victim precipitation and violent crime. *Social Problems*, **21**, 594–605.

Cusson, M., and Pinsonneault, P. (1986). The decision to give up crime. In D. B. Cornish and R. V. G. Clarke (eds), *The Reasoning Criminal: Rational Choice Perspectives on Offending*. New York: Springer-Verlag.

Daitzman, R., and Zuckerman, M. (1980). Disinhibitory sensation-seeking, personality and gonadal hormones. *Personality and Individual Differences*, **1**, 103–110.

Dale, M. W. (1976). Barriers to the rehabilitation of ex-offenders. *Crime and Delinquency*, **22**, 322–337.

Dalgaard, O. S., and Kringlen, E. (1976). A Norwegian twin study of criminality. *British Journal of Criminology*, **16**, 213–233.

Dalton, K. (1961). Menstruation and crime. *British Medical Journal*, **2**, 1752–1753.

Daum, J. M., and Bieliauskas, V. J. (1983). Fathers' absence and moral development of male delinquents. *Psychological Reports*, **53**, 223–228.

Davidson, W. S., Redner, R., Blakely, C. H., Mitchell, C. M., and Emshoff, J. G. (1987). Diversion of juvenile offenders: An experimental comparison. *Journal of Consulting and Clinical Psychology*, **55**, 68–75.

Davies, W., and Burgess, P. W. (1988). The effects of management regime on disruptive behaviour: An analysis within the British prison system. *Medicine, Science and the Law*, **28**, 243–247.

Davis, C., Cowles, M., and Kohn, P. (1983). Strength of the nervous system and augmenting-reducing: Paradox lost. *Personality and Individual Differences*, **4**, 491–498.

Davis, G. E., and Leitenberg, H. (1987). Adolescent sex offenders. *Psychological Bulletin*, **101**, 417–427.

Davis, H. M. (1974a). What does the P scale measure? *British Journal of Psychiatry*, **125**, 161–167.

Davis, H. M. (1974b). Psychometric prediction of institutional adjustment. *British Journal of Social and Clinical Psychology*, **13**, 239–246.

Davis, J. C., and Cropley, A. J. (1976). Psychological factors in juvenile delinquency. *Canadian Journal of Behavioural Science*, **8**, 68–77.

Davison, G. C. (1980). And now for something completely different: Cognition and little r. In M. J. Mahoney (ed.), *Psychotherapy Process: Current Issues and Future Directions*. New York: Plenum.

Deffenbacher, J. L., Demm, P. M., and Brandon, A. D. (1986). High general anger: Correlates and treatment. *Behaviour Research and Therapy*, **24**, 481–489.

DeFleur, M. C., and Quinney, R. (1966). A reformulation of Sutherland's differential association theory and a strategy for empirical intervention. *Journal of Research in Crime and Delinquency*, **3**, 1–22.

Dekker, J., and Everaerd, W. (1989). Psychological determinants of sexual arousal: A review. *Behaviour Research and Therapy*, **27**, 353–364.

Delgado-Escueta, A. V., Mattson, R. H., King, L., Goldensohn, E. S., Spiegel, H., Madsen, J., Crandall, P., Dreifuss, F., and Porter, R. J. (1981). The nature of aggression during epileptic seizures. *New England Journal of Medicine*, **305**, 711–716.

Dell, S., and Robertson, G. (1988). *Sentenced to Hospital: Offenders in Broadmoor*. Maudsley Monographs No. 32. Oxford: Oxford University Press.

Dell, S., and Smith, A. (1983). Changes in the sentencing of diminished responsibility homicides. *British Journal of Psychiatry*, **142**, 20–34.

Diener, E. (1977). Deindividuation: Causes and characteristics. *Social Behavior and Personality*, **5**, 143–156.

Dietrich, S. G., and Berger, L. S. (1978). The MMPI in criminology: Abuses of application. *Journal of Psychiatry and Law*, **2**, 453–480.

Dietz, P. (1978). Social factors in rapist behavior. In R. T. Rada (ed), *Clinical Aspects of the Rapist*. New York: Grune and Stratton.

Dietz, P. (1985). Sex offender profiling by the FBI: A preliminary conceptual model. In M. H. Ben-Aron, S. J. Hucker and C. D. Webster (eds), *Clinical Criminology*. Toronto: Clarke Institute of Psychiatry.

Dishion, T. J., Patterson, G. R., Stoolmiller, M., and Skinner, M. L. (1991). Family, school, and behavioral antecedents to early adolescent involvement with antisocial peers. *Developmental Psychology*, **27**, 172–180.

Dishion, T. J., Loeber, R., Stouthamer-Loeber, M., and Patterson, G. R. (1984). Skills deficits and male adolescent delinquency. *Journal of Abnormal Child Psychology*, **12**, 37–53.

Dixon, N. F., and Henley, S. H. A. (1980). Without awareness. In M. Jeeves (ed.), *Psychology Survey, No. 3*. London: Allen and Unwin.

Dobash, R. E., and Dobash, R. P. (1984). The nature and antecedents of violent acts. *British Journal of Criminology*, **24**, 269–288.

Dodge, K. A. (1986). A social-information processing model of social competence in children. In M. Perlmutter (ed.), *Minnesota Symposium on Child Psychology*. Hillsdale, NJ: Erlbaum.

Dodge, K. A., and Somberg, D. R. (1987). Hostile attributional biases among aggressive boys are exacerbated under conditions of threats to the self. *Child Development*, **58**, 213–224.

Dollard, J., Miller, N., Doob, L., Mowrer, O. H., and Sears, R. R. (1939). *Frustration and Aggression*. New Haven, Conn: Yale University Press.

Dombrose, L. A., and Slobin, B. S. (1958). The IES test. *Perception and Motor Skills*, **8**, 347–389.

Donnerstein, E. (1983). Erotica and human aggression. In R. G. Geen and E.I. Donnerstein (eds), *Aggression: Theoretical and Empirical Reviews*, Volume 2. New York: Academic Press.

Donnerstein, E. (1984). Pornography: Its effect on violence against women. In N. M. Malamuth and E. Donnerstein (eds), *Pornography and Sexual Aggression*. New York: Academic Press.

Donovan, D. M., and Marlatt, G. A. (1982). Personality subtypes among driving-while-intoxicated offenders: Relation to drinking behavior and driving risk. *Journal of Consulting and Clinical Psychology*, **50**, 241–249.

Dooley, E. (1990). Prison suicide in England and Wales, 1972–1987. *British Journal of Psychiatry*, **156**, 40–45.

d'Orban, P. T., and Dalton, K. (1980). Violent crime and the menstrual cycle. *Psychological Medicine*, **10**, 353–359.

Dorus, E. (1978). The findings of a higher frequency of long Y chromosomes in criminals: does the Y chromosome play a role in human behaviour? *Clinical Genetics*, **13**, 96–98.

Douglas, J. W. B., Ross, J. M., Hammond, W. A., and Mulligan, D. G. (1966). Delinquency and social class. *British Journal of Criminology*, **6**, 294–302.

Dreher, R. H. (1967). Origin, development and present status of insanity as a defense to criminal responsibility in the common law. *Journal of the History of the Behavioral Sciences*, **3**, 47–57.

Drinkwater, J., and Gudjonsson, G. H. (1989). The nature of violence in psychiatric hospitals. In K. Howells and C. R. Hollin (eds), *Clinical Approaches to Violence*. Chichester: Wiley.

Duguid, S. (1981). Moral development, justice, and democracy in prison. *Canadian Journal of Criminology*, **23**, 147–162.

Dunford, F. W., and Elliott, D. S. (1984). Identifying career offenders using self-report data. *Journal of Research in Crime and Delinquency*, **21**, 57–86.

Durlak, J. A. (1985). Primary prevention of school maladjustment. *Journal of Consulting and Clinical Psychology*, **53**, 623–630.

Dutton, D. G., and Browning, J. J. (1988). Concern for power, fear of intimacy, and aversive stimuli for wife assault. In G. T. Hotaling, D. Finkelhor, J. T. Kirkpatrick and M. A. Straus (eds), *Family Abuse and its Consequences: New Directions in Research*. Beverly Hills, Ca: Sage.

D'Zurilla, T., and Goldfried, M. (1971). Problem solving and behavior modification. *Journal of Abnormal Psychology*, **78**, 107–126.

Eastwood, L. (1985). Personality, intelligence and personal space among violent and nonviolent delinquents. *Personality and Individual Differences*, **6**, 717–723.

Ebbesen, E. B., and Konecni, V. J. (1982). Social psychology and the law: A decision-making approach to the criminal justice system. In V. J. Konecni and E. B. Ebbesen (eds), *The Criminal Justice System: A Social–Psychological Analysis*. San Francisco: Freeman.

Edwards, G., Hensman, C., and Peto, J. (1971). Drinking problems amongst recidivist prisoners. *Psychological Medicine*, **1**, 388–399.

Egeland, B., Jacobvitz, D., and Sroufe, L. A. (1988). Breaking the cycle of abuse. *Child Development*, **59**, 1080–1088.

Ehrenkranz, J., Bliss, E., and Sheard, M. H. (1974). Plasma testosterone: correlation with aggressive behavior and social dominance in man. *Psychosomatic Medicine*, **36**, 469–475.

Ehrlich, I. (1975). The deterrent effects of capital punishment: A question of life and death. *American Economic Review*, **65**, 397–417.

Ehrlich, I. (1981). On the usefulness of controlling individuals: An economic analysis for rehabilitation, incapacitation, and deterrence. *American Economic Review*, **71**, 307–322.

Eisen, M. (1972). Characteristic self-esteem, sex, and resistance to temptation. *Journal of Personality and Social Psychology*, **24**, 68–72.

Eisenberg, N., and Lennon, R. (1983). Sex differences in empathy and related capacities. *Psychological Bulletin*, **94**, 100–131.

Elifson, K. W., Peterson, D. M., and Hadaway, C. K. (1983). Religiosity and delinquency. *Criminology*, **21**, 505–527.

Elliott, D. S., and Ageton, S. S. (1980). Reconciling race and class differences in self-reported and official estimates of delinquency. *American Sociological Review*, **45**, 95–110.

Elliott, D. S., and Huizinga, D. (1983). Social class and delinquent behavior in a national youth panel, 1976–1980. *Criminology*, **21**, 149–177.

Elliott, D. S., and Voss, H. L. (1974). *Delinquency and Dropout*. Lexington: Heath and Co.

Elliott, D. S., Huizinga, D., and Ageton, S. S. (1985). *Explaining Delinquency and Drug Use*. Beverly Hills, Ca: Sage.

Elliott, F. A. (1982). Neurological findings in adult minimal brain dysfunction and the dyscontrol syndrome. *Journal of Nervous and Mental Disease*, **170**, 680–687.

Ellis, A. (1977). The basic clinical theory of Rational–Emotive Therapy. In A. Ellis and R. Grieger (eds), *Handbook of Rational–Emotive Therapy*. New York: Springer.

Ellis, L. (1987). Relationships of criminality and psychopathy with eight other apparent behavioural manifestations of sub-optimal arousal. *Personality and Individual Differences*, **8**, 905–925.

Ellis, L. (1988). Criminal behaviour and r/K selection: An extension of gene based evolutionary theory. *Personality and Individual Differences*, **9**, 697–708.

Ellis, P. L. (1982). Empathy: A factor in antisocial behavior. *Journal of Abnormal Child Psychology*, **2**, 123–133.

Emery, R. E. (1989). Family violence. *American Psychologist*, **44**, 321–328.

Emery, R. E., and Marholin, D. (1977). An applied behavior analysis of delinquency: The irrelevancy of relevant behavior. *American Psychologist*, **32**, 860–873.

Emery, R. E., and O'Leary, D. (1982). Children's perceptions of marital discord and behavior problems of boys and girls. *Journal of Abnormal Child Psychology*, **10**, 11–24.

Emler, N. (1984). Differential involvement in delinquency: Toward an interpretation in terms of reputation management. In B. A. Maher and W. B. Maher (eds), *Progress in Experimental Personality Research*, Volume 13. New York: Academic Press.

Emler, N., Heather, N., and Winton, M. (1978). Delinquency and the development of moral reasoning. *British Journal of Social and Clinical Psychology*, **17**, 325–331.

Engel, G. L. (1977). The need for a new medical model: A challenge for biomedicine. *Science*, **196**, 129–136.

Ennis, B. J., and Litwak, T. R. (1974). Psychiatry and the presumption of expertise: Flipping coins in the courtroom. *California Law Review*, **62**, 694–753.

Epps, P., and Parnell, R. W. (1952). Physique and temperament of women delinquents compared with women undergraduates. *British Journal of Medical Psychology*, **25**, 249–255.

Epstein, S. (1973). The self-concept revisited: Or a theory of a theory. *American Psychologist*, **28**, 404–416.

Epstein, S. and O'Brien, E. J. (1985). The person–situation debate in historical and current perspective. *Psychological Bulletin*, **98**, 513–537.

Erdelyi, M. (1985). *Psychoanalysis: Freud's Cognitive Psychology*. San Francisco: Freeman.

Erickson, P. G. (1984). Diversion—a panacea for delinquency? Lessons from the Scottish experience. *Youth and Society*, **16**, 29–45.

Erlanger, H. (1974). The empirical status of the subculture of violence thesis. *Social Problems*, **22**, 280–292.

Eron, L. D. (1987). The development of aggressive behavior from the perspective of a developing behaviorism. *American Psychologist*, **42**, 435–443.

Eron, L. D., and Huesmann, L. R. (1986). The role of television in the development of antisocial and prosocial behavior. In D. Olweus, J. Block and M. Radke-Yarrow (eds), *Development of Antisocial and Prosocial Behavior: Research, Theories, and Issues*. New York: Academic Press.

Eyo, I. D. (1981). British delinquents and nondelinquents on seven domains of the self-concept. *Journal of Psychology*, **109**, 137–145.

Eysenck, H. J. (1960). Classification and the problem of diagnosis. In H. J. Eysenck (ed.), *Handbook of Abnormal Psychology*. London: Pitman.

Eysenck, H. J. (1974). Crime and personality reconsidered. *Bulletin of the British Psychological Society*, **27**, 23–24.

Eysenck, H. J. (1977). *Crime and Personality*, Third Edition. London: Paladin.

Eysenck, H. J., and Eysenck, S. B. G. (1975). *Manual for the Eysenck Personality Questionnaire*. London: Hodder and Stoughton.

Eysenck, H. J., and Gudjonsson, G. H. (1989). *The Causes and Cures of Criminality*. New York: Plenum Press.

Eysenck, S. B. G., and Eysenck, H. J. (1963). On the dual nature of extraversion. *British Journal of Social and Clinical Psychology*, **2**, 46–55.

Eysenck, S. B. G., and Eysenck, H. J. (1977). Personality differences between prisoners and controls. *Psychological Reports*, **40**, 1023–1028.

Eysenck, S. B. G., and Eysenck, H. J. (1978). Impulsiveness and venturesomeness: Their position in a dimensional system of personality description. *Psychological Reports*, **43**, 1247–1255.

Eysenck, S. B. G., and McGurk, B. J. (1980). Impulsiveness and venturesomeness in a detention centre population. *Psychological Reports*, **47**, 1299–1306.

Eysenck, S. B. G., Rust, J., and Eysenck, H. J. (1977). Personality and the classification of adult offenders. *British Journal of Criminology*, **17**, 169–179.

Fagan, J., and Wexler, S. (1987). Family origins of violent delinquents. *Criminology*, **25**, 643–669.

Farley, F. H. (1986). The big T in personality. *Psychology Today*, **20** (May), 44–52.

Farley, F. H., and Farley, S. V. (1970). Impulsiveness, sociability, and the preference for varied experience. *Perception and Motor Skills*, **31**, 47–50.

Farley, F. H., and Farley, S. V. (1972). Stimulus-seeking motivation and delinquent behavior among institutionalised delinquent girls. *Journal of Consulting and Clinical Psychology*, **39**, 94–97.

Farley, F. H., and Sewell, T. (1976). Test of an arousal theory of delinquency: Stimulation-seeking in delinquent and nondelinquent black adolescents. *Criminal Justice and Behavior*, **3**, 315–320.

Farrington, D. P. (1972). Delinquency begins at home. *New Society*, **21**, 495–497.

Farrington, D. P. (1981). The prevalence of convictions. *British Journal of Criminology*, **21**, 173–175.

Farrington, D. P. (1985). Delinquency prevention in the 1980s. *Journal of Adolescence*, **8**, 3–16.

Farrington, D. P. (1989). Early predictors of adolescent aggression and adult violence. *Violence and Victims*, **4**, 79–100.

Farrington, D. P. (1990). Implications of criminal career research for the prevention of offending. *Journal of Adolescence*, **13**, 93–113.

Farrington, D. P. (1992). Explaining the beginning, progress, and ending of antisocial behavior from birth to adulthood. In J. McCord (ed.), *Facts, Frameworks, and Forecasts: Advances in Criminological Theory, Volume 3*. New Brunswick: Transactional Publishers.

Farrington, D. P., and Bennett, T. (1981). Police cautioning of juveniles in London. *British Journal of Criminology*, **21**, 123–135.

Farrington, D. P., and Dowds, E. A. (1985). Disentangling criminal behaviour and police reaction. In D. P. Farrington and J. Gunn (eds), *Reactions to Crime: The Public, The Police, Courts and Prisons*. Chichester: Wiley.

Farrington, D. P., and Tarling, R. (1985). Criminological prediction: An introduction. In D. P. Farrington and R. Tarling (eds), *Prediction in Criminology*. Albany: State University of New York Press.

Farrington, D. P., and West, D. J. (1990). The Cambridge study in delinquent development: a long-term follow-up of 411 London males. In G. Kaiser and H-J. Kerner (eds), *Criminality: Personality, Behaviour, Life History*. Heidelberg: Springer-Verlag.

Farrington, D. P., Biron, L., and Le Blanc, M. (1982). Personality and delinquency in London and Montreal. In J. Gunn and D. P. Farrington (eds), *Abnormal Offenders, Delinquency, and the Criminal Justice System*. Chichester: Wiley.

Farrington, D. P., Osborn, S. G., and West, D. J. (1978). The persistence of labelling effects. *British Journal of Criminology*, **18**, 277–284.

Farrington, D. P., Ohlin, L. E., and Wilson, J. Q. (1986). *Understanding and Controlling Crime*. New York: Springer-Verlag. Farrington, D. P., Gallagher, B., Morley, L., St Ledger, R. J., and West, D. J. (1988). Are there any successful men from criminogenic backgrounds? *Psychiatry*, **51**, 116–130.

Faust, D. (1986). Research on human judgment and its application to clinical practice. *Professional Psychology: Research and Practice*, **17**, 420–430.

Faust, D., and Miner, R. A., (1986). The empiricist in his new clothes: DSM-III in perspective. *American Journal of Psychiatry*, **143**, 962–967.

Faust, D., and Ziskin, J. (1988). The expert witness in psychology and psychiatry. *Science*, **241**, 31–35.

Feild, H. S. (1978). Attitudes toward rape: A comparative analysis of police, rapists, crisis counsellors, and citizens. *Journal of Personality and Social Psychology*, **36**, 156–179.

Feindler, E. L., Marriott, S. A., and Iwata, M. (1984). Group anger control training for junior high school delinquents. *Cognitive Therapy and Research*, **8**, 299–311.

Feldhusen, J. F., Thurston, J. R., and Benning, J. J. (1973). A longitudinal study of delinquency and other aspects of children's behaviour. *International Journal of Criminology and Penology*, **1**, 341–351.

Feldman, D. (1964). Psychoanalysis and crime. In B. Rosenberg, I. Gerver and F. W. Howton. (eds), *Mass Society in Crisis*. New York: Macmillan.

Feldman, M. P. (1977). *Criminal Behaviour: A Psychological Analysis*. Chichester: Wiley.

Feldman, M. P., and Peay, J. (1982). Ethical and legal issues. In A. S. Bellak, M. Hersen and A. E. Kazdin (eds), *International Handbook of Behavior Modification*. New York: Plenum.

Felson R. B. (1978). Aggression as impression management. *Social Psychology*, **41**, 205–213.

Felson R. B., and Steadman, H. J. (1983). Situational factors in disputes leading to criminal violence. *Criminology*, **21**, 59–74.

Felson M. (1986). Linking criminal choices, routine activities, informal control, and criminal outcomes. In D. B. Cornish and R. V. G. Clarke (eds), *The Reasoning Criminal: Rational Choice Perspectives on Offending*. New York: Springer-Verlag.

Felthous, A. R., and Kellert, S. R. (1987). Childhood cruelty to animals and later aggression against people: A review. *American Journal of Psychiatry*, **144**, 710–717.

Fenton, G. W., Fenwick, P. B. C., Fergusom, W., and Lamb, C. T. (1978). The contingent negative variation in antisocial behaviour: A pilot study of Broadmoor patients. *British Journal of Psychiatry*, **132**, 368–377.

Fenwick, P. (1990). Automatism. In R. Bluglas and P. Bowden (eds), *Principles and Practice of Forensic Psychiatry*. Edinburgh: Churchill Livingstone.

Ferguson, T. J. and Rule, B. G. (1983). An attributional perspective on anger and aggression. In R. G. Geen and E. I. Donnerstein (eds), *Aggression: Theoretical and Empirical Reviews*, Volume 1. New York: Academic Press.

Fergusson, D. M., Horwood, L. J., Kershaw, K. L., and Shannon, F. T. (1986). Factors associated with reports of wife assault in New Zealand. *Journal of Marriage and the Family*, **48**, 407–412.

Fersch, E. A. (1980). Ethical issues for psychologists in court settings. In J. Monahan (ed.), *Who is the Client: The Ethics of Psychological Intervention In the Criminal Justice System*. Washington, DC: American Psychological Association.

Feshbach, S. and Price, J. (1984). The development of cognitive competencies and the control of aggression. *Aggressive Behaviour*, **10**, 185–200.

Field, E. (1967). A validation study of Hewitt and Jenkins' hypothesis. *Studies in the Causes of Delinquency and the Treatment of Offenders, No. 10*. London: HMSO.

Figuera-McDonough, J. (1984). Feminism and delinquency. *British Journal of Criminology*, **24**, 325–342.

Filipczak, J., Friedman, R. M., and Reese, S. C. (1979). PREP: Educational programming to prevent juvenile problems. In J. S. Stumphauzer (ed.), *Progress in Behavior Therapy with Delinquents*. Springfield, Ill: Charles C. Thomas.

Fincham, F. D., and Jaspars, J. M. (1980). Attribution of responsibility: From man the scientist to man as lawyer. In L. Berkowitz (ed.), *Advances in Experimental Social Psychology*, Volume 13. New York: Academic Press.

Fingarette, H., and Hasse, A. F. (1979). *Mental Disabilities and Criminal Responsibility*. Berkeley: University of California Press.

Finkelhor, D. (1986). *A Sourcebook on Child Sex Abuse*. Newbury Park, Ca: Sage.

Finlayson, D. S., and Loughran, J. L. (1976). Pupils' perceptions in high and low delinquency schools. *Educational Research*, **18**, 138–145.

Fischer, D. (1984). Family size and delinquency. *Perception and Motor Skills*, **58**, 527–534.

Fitch, F. S., and Papantonio, A. (1983). Men who batter: Some pertinent characteristics. *Journal of Nervous and Mental Disease*, **171**, 190–192.

Fitzgerald, E. (1987). Psychologists and the law of evidence: Admissibility and confidentiality. In G. Gudjonsson and J. Drinkwater (eds), *Psychological Evidence in Court: Issues in Criminological and Legal Psychology, No. 11*. Leicester: British Psychological Society.

Fixsen, D. L., Phillips, E. L., and Wolf, M. M. (1973). Achievement Place: Experiments in self-government with pre-delinquents. *Journal of Applied Behavior Analysis*, **6**, 31–47.

Flor-Henry, P., Lang, R. A., Koles, Z. J., and Frenzel, R. R. (1991). Quantitative EEG studies of pedophilia. *International Journal of Psychophysiology*, **10**, 253–258.

Fo, W. S. O., and O'Donnell, C. R. (1975). The buddy system: Effect of community intervention on delinquent offences. *Behavior Therapy*, **6**, 522–524.

Fodor, E. (1973). Moral development and parent behavior antecedents in adolescent psychopaths. *Journal of Genetic Psychology*, **122**, 37–43.

Forbes, G. B., and Lebo, G. R. (1977). Antisocial behavior and lunar activity: A failure to validate the lunacy myth. *Psychological Reports*, **40**, 1309–1310.

Forgas, J. P. (1986). Cognitive representations of aggressive situations. In A. Campbell and J. J. Gibbs (eds), *Violent Transactions: The Limits of Personality*. Oxford: Blackwell.

Fottrell, E. (1980). A study of violent behaviour among patients in psychiatric hospitals. *British Journal of Psychiatry*, **136**, 216–221.

Foucault, M. (1978). About the concept of the dangerous individual in 19th century legal psychiatry. *International Journal of Law and Psychiatry*, **1**, 1–18.

Foulds, G. A. (1971). Personality deviance and personal symptomatology. *Psychological Medicine*, **1**, 222–233.

Fowles, D. C. (1988). Psychophysiology and psychopathology: A motivational approach. *Psychophysiology*, **25**, 373–391.

Frank, J. D. (1985). Therapeutic components shared by all psychotherapies. In M. J. Mahoney and A. Freeman (eds), *Cognition and Psychotherapy*. New York: Plenum.

Frederiksen, L. W. and Rainwater, N. (1981). Explosive behavior: A skill development approach to treatment. In R. B. Stuart (ed.), *Violent Behavior: Social Learning Approaches to Prediction, Management and Treatment*. New York: Brunner/Mazel.

Freedman, B. J., Rosenthal, L., Donahoe, C. P., Schlundt, D. G., and McFall, R. M. (1978). A social–behavioral analysis of skill deficits in delinquent and nondelinquent adolescent boys. *Journal of Consulting and Clinical Psychology*, **46**, 1448–1462.

Freedman, J. L. (1984). Effects of television on aggressiveness. *Psychological Bulletin*, **96**, 227–246.

Freeman-Longo, R. E., and Wall, R. V. (1986). Changing a lifetime of sexual crime: Can sex offenders ever alter their ways? *Psychology Today*, **20** (March), 58–64.

Freud, S. (1915/1957). Criminals from a sense of guilt. In J. Strachey (ed.), *The Complete Psychological Works of Sigmund Freud*, Volume 14. London: Hogarth Press.

Freud, S. (1920/1955). Beyond the pleasure principle. In J. Strachey (ed.), *The Complete Psychological Works of Sigmund Freud*, Volume 18. London: Hogarth Press.

Freund, K. (1967). Erotic preference in pedophilia. *Behaviour Research and Therapy*, **5**, 339–348.

Freund, K. (1980). Therapeutic sex drive reduction. *Acta Psychiatrica Scandinavica*, **62**, 5–38.

Freund, K. (1990). Courtship disorder. In W. L. Marshall, D. R. Laws and H. E. Barbaree (eds), *Handbook of Sexual Assault: Issues, Theories, and Treatment of the Offender*. New York: Plenum.

Freund, K., McKnight, C. K., Langevin, R., and Cibiri, S. (1972). The female child as a surrogate object. *Archives of Sexual Behavior*, **2**, 119–133.

Friedrich, W., and Boriskin, J. (1976). The role of the child in abuse. *American Journal of Orthopsychiatry*, **46**, 580–590.

Friedrich-Cofer, L., and Huston, A. C. (1986). Television violence and aggression: The debate continues. *Psychological Bulletin*, **100**, 363–371.

Fromm, E. (1973). *The Anatomy of Human Destructiveness*. New York: Holt, Rinehart and Winston.

Frosch, J. P. (1983). The treatment of antisocial and borderline personality disorders. *Hospital and Community Psychiatry*, **34**, 243–248.

Furby, L., Weinrott, M. R., and Blackshaw, L. (1989). Sex offender recidivism: A review. *Psychological Bulletin*, **105**, 3–30.

Gabrielli, W. F., and Mednick, S. A. (1980). Sinistrality and delinquency. *Journal of Abnormal Psychology*, **89**, 654–661.

Gaes, G. G. (1985). The effects of overcrowding in prison. In M. Tonry and N. Morris (eds), *Crime and Justice: An Annual Review of Research*, Volume 6. Chicago: University of Chicago Press.

Gaffney, L. R. (1984). A multiple choice test to measure social skills in delinquent and nondelinquent adolescent girls. *Journal of Consulting and Clinical Psychology*, **52**, 911–912.

Gagnon, J. H. (1974). Sexual conduct and crime. In D. Glaser (ed.), *Handbook of Criminology*. Chicago: Rand McNally.

Gale, A. (1976). Psychopathy and the EEG: A critical review. Paper presented at the Annual Conference of the British Psychological Society, York.

Gale, A. (ed.)(1988). *The Polygraph Test: Lies, Truth and Science*. London: Sage.

Gale, A., and Edwards, J. A. (1983). EEG and human behaviour. In A. Gale and J. A. Edwards (eds), *Physiolological Correlates of Human Behaviour*, Volume 2. New York: Academic Press.

Ganzer, V. T., and Sarason, I. G. (1973). Variables associated with recidivism among juvenile delinquents. *Journal of Consulting and Clinical Psychology*, **40**, 1–5.

Garabedian, P. G. (1963). Social roles and processes of socialisation in the prison community. *Social Problems*, **11**, 139–152.

Garland, D. (1985). *Punishment and Welfare: A History of Penal Strategies*. Aldershot: Gower.

Garrett, C. J. (1985). Effects of residential treatment on adjudicated delinquents: A meta-analysis. *Journal of Research in Crime and Delinquency*, **22**, 287–308.

Garrett, M., and Short, J. F. (1975). Social class and delinquency: Predictions and outcome of police juvenile encounters. *Social Problems*, **22**, 368–382.

Gavaghan, M. P., Arnold, K. D., and Gibbs, J. C. (1983). Moral judgment in delinquents and nondelinquents: recognition versus production measures. *Journal of Psychology*, **114**, 267–274.

Gayford, J. J. (1975). Battered wives. *Medicine, Science and the Law*, **15**, 237–245.

Gearing, M. L. (1979). The MMPI as a primary differentiator and predictor of behavior in prison: A methodological critique and review of the recent literature. *Psychological Bulletin*, **79**, 929–963.

Gecas, V. (1979). The influence of social class on the family. In W. R. Burt, R. Hill, F. I. Nye, and I. L. Reiss (eds), *Contemporary Theories About The Family*, Volume 1. New York: Free Press.

Geen, R. G. (1983). Aggression and television violence. In R. G. Geen and E.I. Donnerstein (eds), *Aggression: Theoretical and Empirical Reviews*, Volume 2. New York: Academic Press.

Geen, R. G., and Quanty, M. B. (1977). The cartharsis of aggression: An evaluation of a hypothesis. In L. Berkowitz (ed.), *Advances in Experimental Social Psychology*. Volume 10. New York: Academic Press.

Gelles, R. (1973). Child abuse as psychopathology: A sociological critique and reformulation. *American Journal of Psychiatry*, **43**, 611–621.

Gendreau, P. (1985). Critical comments on the practice of clinical criminology. In M. H. Ben-Aron, S. J. Hucker and C. D. Webster (eds), *Clinical Criminology*. Toronto: Clarke Institute of Psychiatry.

Gendreau, P., and Ross, R. R. (1979). Effective correctional treatment: Bibliotherapy for cynics. *Crime and Delinquency*, **25**, 463–489.

Gendreau, P., and Ross, R. R. (1987). Revivication of rehabilitation: Evidence from the 1980s. *Justice Quarterly*, **4**, 349–407.

Gendreau, P., Freedman, N. L., Wilde, G. J. S., and Scott, G. D. (1972). Changes in EEG alpha frequency and evoked response latency during solitary confinement. *Journal of Abnormal Psychology*, **79**, 54–59.

Gendreau, P., Grant, B. A., Leipciger, M., and Collins, S. (1979). Norms and recidivism risks for MMPI and selected scales on a Canadian delinquent sample. *Canadian Journal of Behavioural Science*, **11**, 21–31.

George, W. H., and Marlatt, G. A. (1986). The effects of alcohol and anger on interest in violence, erotica, and deviance. *Journal of Abnormal Psychology*, **95**, 150–158.

Getsinger, S. H. (1976). Sociopathy, self-actualisation and time. *Journal of Personality Assessment*, **40**, 398–402.

Gibbens, T. C. N. (1963). *Psychiatric Studies of Borstal Lads*. Maudsley Monographs No. 11. London: Oxford University Press.

Gibbens, T. C. N. (1981). Shoplifting. *British Journal of Psychiatry*, **138**, 346–347.

Gibbens, T. C. N., and Robertson, G. (1983). A survey of the criminal careers of restriction order patients. *British Journal Of Psychiatry*, **143**, 370–375.

Gibbons, D. C. (1965). *Changing the Lawbreaker*. Englewood Cliffs, NJ: Prentice-Hall.

Gibbons, D. C. (1971). Observations on the study of crime causation. *American Journal of Sociology*, **77**, 262–278.

Gibbons, D. C. (1988). Some critical observations on criminal types and criminal careers. *Criminal Justice and Behavior*, **15**, 8–23.

Gibbs, J. C., and Schnell, S. V. (1985). Moral development "versus" socialisation: A critique. *American Psychologist*, **40**, 1071–1080.

Gibbs, J. C., Arnold, K. D., Ahlborn, H. H., and Cheesman, F. L. (1984). Facilitation of sociomoral reasoning in delinquents. *Journal of Consulting and Clinical Psychology*, **52**, 37–43.

Gibbs, J. P. (1972). Issues in defining deviant behavior. In J. Douglas (ed.), *Theoretical Perspectives on Deviance*. New York: Basic Books.

Gibbs, J. P. (1985). Review essay. *Criminology*, **23**, 381–388.

Gibbs, L. E. (1974). Effects of juvenile legal procedures on juvenile offenders' self-attitudes. *Journal of Research in Crime and Delinquency*, **11**, 51–55.

Gibson, E. (1975). *Homicide in England and Wales 1967–1971*. London: HMSO.

Gibson, H. B. (1964). The Spiral Maze: A psychomotor test with implications for the study of delinquency. *British Journal of Psychology*, **55**, 219–225.

Gibson, H. B. (1969). Early delinquency in relation to broken homes. *Journal of Child Psychology and Psychiatry*, **10**, 195–204.

Gibson, H. B. (1971). The factorial structure of juvenile delinquency; a study of self-reported acts. *British Journal of Social and Clinical Psychology*, **10**, 1–9.

Gibson, H. B. (1975). Correspondence. *Bulletin of the British Psychological Society*, **28**, 212–213.

Gifford, R., and O'Connor, B. (1987). The interpersonal circumplex as a behavioral map. *Journal of Personality and Social Psychology*, **52**, 1019–1026.

Gillan, P. W. (1965). The measurement of impulsiveness in female delinquents. Unpublished M. A. Thesis, University of London.

Gilligan, C. (1982). *In a Different Voice: Psychological Theory and Women's Development*. Cambridge, Ma: Harvard University Press.

Gillmore, M. R., Hawkins, J. D, Catalano, R. F., Day, L. E., Moore, M., and Abbott, R. (1991). Structure of problem behaviors in preadolescence. *Journal of Consulting and Clinical Psychology*, **59**, 499–506.

Giordano, P. C., Cernkovich, S. A., and Pugh, M. D. (1986). Friendship and delinquency. *American Journal of Sociology*, **91**, 1170–1202.

Given, J.B. (1977). *Society and Homicide in Thirteenth Century England*. Stanford, Ca: Stanford University Press.

Glaser, D. (1956). Criminality theories and behavioral images. *American Journal of Sociology*, **61**, 433–444.

Glaser, D. (1977). The compatibility of free will and determinism in criminology: Comments on an alleged problem. *Journal of Criminal Law and Criminology*, **67**, 486–490.

Glaser, D. (1987). Classification for risk. In D. M. Gottfredson and M. Tonry (eds), *Prediction and Classification: Criminal Justice Decision Making*. Chicago: University of Chicago Press.

Glasser, W. (1975). *Reality Therapy: A New Approach to Psychiatry*. New York: Harper and Row.

Glover, E. (1960). *The Roots of Crime*. London: Imago.

Glueck, S., and Glueck, E. (1950). *Unravelling Juvenile Delinquency*. New York: The Commonwealth Fund.

Glueck, S., and Glueck, E. (1964). Potential juvenile delinquents can be identified: What next? *British Journal of Criminology*, **4**, 215–226.

Goddard, H. H. (1914). *Feeble-Mindedness: Its Causes and Consequences*. New York: Macmillan.

Gold, M. (1978). Scholastic experiences, self-esteem, and delinquent behavior: A theory for alternative schools. *Crime and Delinquency*, **24**, 290–308.

Golden, K., Twentyman, C. T., Jensen, M., Karan, J., and Kloss, J. D. (1980). Coping with authority: Social skills training for the complex offender. *Criminal Justice and Behavior*, **7**, 147–159.

Goldstein, A. P. (1986). Psychological skill training and the aggressive adolescent. In S. J. Apter and A. P. Goldstein (eds), *Youth Violence: Programs and Prospects*. New York: Plenum.

Goldstein, A. P., Glick, B., Irwin, M. J., Pask-McCartney, C., and Rubama, I. (1989). *Reducing Delinquency: Intervention in the Community*. New York: Pergamon.

Goldstein, M. Brain research and violent behavior. *Archives of Neurology*, **30**, 1–35.

Goldstein, P. J. (1989). Drugs and violent crime. In N. A. Weiner and M. E. Wolfgang (eds), *Pathways to Criminal Violence*. Newbury Park, Ca: Sage.

Goma, M., Perez, J., and Torrubia, R. (1988). Personality variables in antisocial and prosocial inhibitory behaviour. In T. E. Moffitt and S. A. Mednick (eds), *Biological Contributions to Crime Causation*. Dordrecht: Martinus Nijhoff.

Goodman, J., and Loftus, E. F. (1988). The relevance of expert testimony on eyewitness testimony. *Journal of Interpersonal Violence*, **3**, 115–121.

Goodstein, L. (1979). Inmate adjustment to prison and the transition to community life. *Journal of Research in Crime and Delinquency*, **16**, 246–272.

Gordon, D. A., and Arbuthnot, J. (1987). Individual, group, and family interventions. In H. C. Quay (ed.), *Handbook of Juvenile Delinquency*. New York: Wiley.

Gordon, D. A., and Arbuthnot, J. (1988). The use of paraprofessionals to deliver home-based family therapy to juvenile delinquents. *Criminal Justice and Behavior*, **15**, 364–378.

Gordon, D. A., Arbuthnot, J., Gustafson, K., and McGreen, P. (1988). Home-based behavioral systems family therapy with disadvantaged juvenile delinquents. *American Journal of Family Therapy*, **16**, 243–255.

Gordon, R. A. (1977). A critique of the evaluation of Patuxent Institution, with particular attention to the issues of dangerousness and recidivism. *Bulletin of the American Academy of Psychiatry and the Law*, **5**, 210–255.

Gorenstein, E. E. (1982). Frontal lobe function in psychopaths. *Journal of Abnormal Psychology*, **91**, 368–379.

Gorenstein, E. E. (1984). Debating mental illness: Implications for science, medicine, and social policy. *American Psychologist*, **39**, 50–56.

Gosselin, C., and Wilson, G. (1980). *Sexual Variations: Fetishism, Transvestism and Sadomasochism*. London: Faber and Faber.

Gostin, L. (1977). *A Human Condition*. London: MIND.

Gottesman, I. I., Carey, G., and Hanson, D. R. (1983). Pearls and perils in epigenetic psychopathology. In S. B. Guze, E. J. Earls and J. E. Barrett (eds), *Childhood Psychopathology and Development*. New York: Raven Press.

Gottfredson, M. R., and Hirschi, T. (1987). The positive tradition. In M. R. Gottfredson and T. Hirschi (eds), *Positive Criminology*. Beverly Hills, Ca: Sage.

Gottfredson, M. R., and Hirschi, T. (1990). *A General Theory of Crime*. Stanford: Stanford University Press.

Gottfredson, S. D. (1987). Prediction: An overview of selected methodological issues. In D. M. Gottfredson and M. Tonry (eds), *Prediction and Classification: Criminal Justice Decision Making*. Chicago: University of Chicago Press.

Gottschalk, R., Davidson, W. S., Mayer, J., and Gensheimer, L. K. (1987). Behavioral approaches with young offenders: A meta-analysis of long-term treatment efficacy. In E. K. Morris and C. J. Braukmann (eds), *Behavioral Approaches to Crime and Delinquency: A Handbook of Application, Research, and Concepts*. New York: Plenum.

Gough, H. G. (1948). A sociological theory of psychopathy. *American Journal of Sociology*, **53**, 359–366.

Gough, H. G. (1969). *Manual for the California Psychological Inventory*. Palo Alto, Ca: Consulting Psychologists Press.

Gough, H. G., Wenk, E. A., and Rozynko, V. V. (1965). Parole outcome as predicted from CPI, MMPI, and a base expectancy table. *Journal of Abnormal Psychology*, **70**, 432–441.

Graham, J. (1988). *Schools, Disruptive Behaviour and Delinquency*. Home Office Research Study, No. 96. London: HMSO.

Graham, K. (1980). Theories of intoxicated aggression. *Canadian Journal of the Behavioural Sciences*, **12**, 141–158.

Graham, K., La Rocque, L., Yetman, R., Ross, T. J., and Guistra, E. (1980). Aggression and bar-room environments. *Journal of Studies on Alcohol*, **41**, 277–292.

Grant, J. D., and Grant, M. Q. (1959). A group dynamics approach to the treatment of nonconformists in the navy. *Annals of the American Academy of Political and Social Science*, **322**, 126–135.

Grasmick, H. G., and Green, D. E. (1980). Legal punishment, social disapproval and internalisation as inhibitors of illegal behavior. *Journal of Criminal Law and Criminology*, **71**, 325–335.

Gray, J. A. (1981). A critique of Eysenck's theory of personality. In H. J. Eysenck (ed.), *A Model of Personality*. New York: Springer-Verlag.

Greene, E., Schooler, J. W., and Loftus, E. F. (1985). Expert psychological testimony. In S. M. Kassin and L. S. Wrightsman (eds), *The Psychology of Evidence and Trial Procedure*. Beverly Hills: Sage.

Greenwald, A. G., and Pratkanis, A. R. (1984). The self. In R. S. Wyer and T. K. Scrull (eds), *Handbook of Social Cognition*, Volume 3. Hillsdale, NJ: Erlbaum.

Griew, E. (1986). Reducing murder to manslaughter: Whose job? *Journal of Medical Ethics*, **12**, 18–23.

Grisso, T. (1987). The economic and scientific future of forensic psychological assessment. *American Psychologist*, **42**, 831–839.

Groth, A. N. (1977). The adolescent sex offender and his prey. *International Journal of Offender Therapy and Comparative Criminology*, **21**, 249–254.

Groth, A. N. (1983). Treatment of the sexual offender in a correctional institution. In J. G. Greer and I. R. Stuart (eds), *The Sexual Aggressor*. New York: Van Nostrand Reinhold.

Groth, A. N., and Burgess, A. W. (1977a). Rape: A sexual deviation. *American Journal of Orthopsychiatry*, **47**, 400–406.

Groth, A. N., and Burgess, A. W. (1977b). Motivational intent in the sexual assault of children. *Criminal Justice and Behavior*, **4**, 253–271.

Groth, A. N., Burgess, A. W., and Holstrom, L. L. (1977). Rape: Power, anger and · sexuality. *American Journal of Psychiatry*, **134**, 1239–1243.

Groth, A. N., Longo, R. E., and McFadin, J. B. (1982). Undetected recidivism among rapists and child molesters. *Crime and Delinquency*, **28**, 450–458.

Grubin, D. H. (1991). Unfit to plead in England and Wales, 1976–1988: A survey. *British Journal of Psychiatry*, **158**, 540–548.

Grunfeld, B., and Noreik, K. (1986). Recidivism among sex offenders: A follow-up study of 541 Norwegian sex offenders. *International Journal of Law and Psychiatry*, **9**, 95–102.

Guilford, J. P. (1977). Will the real factor of extraversion–introversion please stand up? A reply to Eysenck. *Psychological Bulletin*, **84**, 412–416.

Gudjonsson, G. H. (1984). Interrogative suggestibility: Comparison between "false confessors" and "deniers" in criminal trials. *Medicine, Science and the Law*, **24**, 56–60.

Gudjonsson, G. H. (1985). Psychological evidence in court: Results from the BPS survey. *Bulletin of the British Psychological Society*, **38**, 327–330.

Gudjonsson, G. H. (1986). Criminal court proceedings in England: The contribution of the psychologist as an expert witness. *Medicine and Law*, **5**, 395–404.

Gudjonsson, G. H. (1988). Interrogative suggestibility: Its relationship with assertiveness, social–evaluative anxiety, state anxiety and method of coping. *British Journal of Clinical Psychology*, **27**, 159–166.

Guerra, N. G., and Slaby, R. G. (1990). Cognitive mediators of aggression in adolescent offenders: 2. Intervention. *Developmental Psychology*, **26**, 269–277.

Guidano, V. F., and Liotti, G. (1985). A constructivist foundation for cognitive therapy. In M. J. Mahoney and A. Freeman (eds), *Cognition and Psychotherapy*. New York: Freeman.

Gunn, J. (1977). Criminal behaviour and mental disorder. *British Journal of Psychiatry*, **130**, 317–329.

Gunn, J., and Bonn, J. (1971). Criminality and violence in epileptic prisoners. *British Journal of Psychiatry*, **118**, 337–343.

Gunn, J., and Fenton, G. (1971). Epilepsy, automatism, and crime. *Lancet*, **1**, 1173–1176.

Gunn, J., Maden, A., and Swinton, M. (1991). Treatment needs of prisoners with psychiatric disorders. *British Medical Journal*, **303**, 338–341.

Gunn, J. Robertson, G., Dell, S. and Way, C. (1978). *Psychiatric Aspects of Imprisonment*. London: Academic Press.

Gurucharri, C., Phelps, E., and Selman, R. (1984). Development of interpersonal understanding: A longitudinal and comparative study of normal and disturbed youths. *Journal of Consulting and Clinical Psychology*, **52**, 26–36.

Guze, S. B. (1976). *Criminality and Psychiatric Disorders*. New York: Oxford University Press.

Häfner, H., and Böker, W. (1982). *Crimes of Violence by Mentally Abnormal Offenders*. Cambridge: Cambridge University Press.

Hagan, J. (1975). The social and legal construction of criminal justice: a study of the pre-sentencing process. *Social Problems*, **22**, 620–637.

Hagan, J., and Leon, J. (1977). Rediscovering delinquency: Social history, political ideology and the sociology of law. *American Sociological Review*, **42**, 587–598.

Hains, A. A., and Hains, A. H. (1987). The effects of a cognitive strategy intervention on the problem-solving abilities of delinquent youths. *Journal of Adolescence*, **10**, 399–413.

Hains, A. A., and Ryan, E. B. (1983). The development of social cognitive processes among juvenile delinquents and nondelinquent peers. *Child Development*, **54**, 1536–1544.

Halbasch, K. (1979). Differential reinforcement theory examined. *Criminology*, **17**, 217–229.

Hall, C. S., and Lindzey, G. (1970). *Theories of Personality*, Second Edition. New York: Wiley.

Hall, G. C. N. (1988). Criminal behavior as a function of clinical and actuarial variables in a sex offender population. *Journal of Consulting and Clinical Psychology*, **56**, 773–775.

Hall, G. C. N. (1990). Prediction of sexual aggression. *Clinical Psychology Review*, **10**, 229–245.

Hall, G. C. N., and Proctor, W. C. (1987). Criminological predictors of recidivism in a sexual offender population. *Journal of Consulting and Clinical Psychology*, **55**, 111–112.

Hall, G. C. N., Proctor, W. C., and Nelson, G. M. (1988). Validity of physiological measures of pedophilic sexual arousal in a sexual offender population. *Journal of Consulting and Clinical Psychology*, **56**, 118–122.

Hall, G. C. N., Maiuro, R. D., Vitaliano, P. P., and Proctor, W. C. (1986). The utility of the MMPI with men who have sexually assaulted children. *Journal of Consulting and Clinical Psychology*, **54**, 493–496.

Hall, G. S. (1904). *Adolescence*. New York: Appleton.

Hall, H. V. (1987). *Violence Prediction: Guidelines for the Forensic Practitioner*. Springfield, Ill: Charles C. Thomas.

Halleck, S. L. (1987). *The Mentally Ill Offender*. Washington, DC: American Psychiatric Press.

Halleck, S. L., and Witte, A. D. (1977). Is rehabilitation dead? *Crime and Delinquency*, **23**, 372–382.

Haller, R. M., and Deluty, R. H. (1988). Assaults on staff by psychiatric inpatients. *British Journal of Psychiatry*, **152**, 174–179.

Hands, J., Herbert, V., and Tennent, G. (1974). Menstruation and behaviour in a special hospital. *Medicine, Science and the Law*, **14**, 32–35.

Haney, C. W. (1983). The good, the bad, and the lawful: An essay on psychological injustice. In W, S. Laufer and J. M. Day (eds), *Personality Theory, Moral Development, and Criminal Behaviour*. Lexington: Lexington Books.

Hanks, S. E., and Rosenbaum, C. D. (1977). Battered women: A study of women who live with violent alcohol-abusing men. *American Journal of Orthopsychiatry*, **47**, 291–306.

Hanson, C. L., Hengeller, S. W., Haefele, W. F., and Rodick, J. D. (1984). Demographic, individual, and family relationship correlates of serious and repeated crime among adolescents and their siblings. *Journal of Consulting and Clinical Psychology*, **52**, 528–538.

Hanson, N. R. (1958). *Patterns of Discovery*. Cambridge: Cambridge University Press.

Hardt, R. G., and Peterson-Hardt, S. (1977). On determining the quality of the delinquency self-report method. *Journal of Research in Crime and Delinquency*, **14**, 247–261.

Hare, R. D. (1965). Temporal gradient of fear arousal in psychopaths. *Journal of Abnormal Psychology*, **70**, 442–445.

Hare, R. D. (1968). Psychopathy, autonomic functioning, and the orienting response. *Journal of Abnormal Psychology Monograph Supplements*, **73**, No. 3, 1–24.

Hare, R. D. (1978). Electrodermal and cardiovascular correlates of psychopathy. In R. D. Hare and D. Schalling (eds), *Psychopathic Behaviour: Approaches to Research*. Chichester: Wiley.

Hare, R. D. (1979). Psychopathy and laterality of cerebral function. *Journal of Abnormal Psychology*, **88**, 605–610.

Hare, R. D. (1980). A research scale for the assessment of psychopathy in criminal populations. *Personality and Individual Differences*, **1**, 111–119.

Hare, R. D. (1982). Psychopathy and the personality dimensions of psychoticism, extraversion and neuroticism. *Personality and Individual Differences*, **3**, 35–42.

Hare, R. D. (1983). Diagnosis of antisocial personality disorder in two prison populations. *American Journal of Psychiatry*, **140**, 887–890.

Hare, R. D. (1984). Performance of psychopaths on cognitive tasks related to frontal lobe function. *Journal of Abnormal Psychology*, **93**, 133–140.

Hare, R. D. (1985). A comparison of procedures for the assessment of psychopathy. *Journal of Consulting and Clinical Psychology*, **53**, 7–16.

Hare, R. D. (1986). Twenty years of experience with the Cleckley psychopath. In W. H. Reid, D. Dorr, J. Walker and J. W. Bonner (eds), *Unmasking the Psychopath: Antisocial Personality and Related Syndromes*. New York: Norton.

Hare, R. D., and McPherson, L. M. (1984). Violent and aggressive behaviour by criminal psychopaths. *International Journal of Law and Psychiatry*, **7**, 35–50.

Hare, R. D., and Quinn, M. (1971). Psychopathy and autonomic conditioning. *Journal of Abnormal Psychology*, **77**, 223–235.

Hare, R. D., McPherson, L. M., and Forth, A. E. (1988). Male psychopaths and their criminal careers. *Journal of Consulting and Clinical Psychology*, **56**, 710–714.

Hare, R. D., Williamson, S. E., and Harpur, T.J. (1988). Psychopathy and language.

In T. E. Moffitt and S. A. Mednick (eds), *Biological Contributions to Crime Causation*. Dordrecht: Martinus Nijhoff.

Hare, R. D., Harpur, T. J., Hakstian, A. R., Forth, A. E., Hart, S. D., and Newman, J. P. (1990). The revised Psychopathy Checklist: Reliability and factor structure. *Psychological Assessment: A Journal of Consulting and Clinical Psychology*, **2**, 338–341.

Hargreaves, D. H. (1980). Classrooms, schools, and juvenile delinquency. *Educational Analysis*, **2**, 75–87.

Hariton, E. B., and Singer, J. L. (1974). Women's fantasies during sexual intercourse: Normative and theoretical implications. *Journal of Consulting and Clinical Psychology*, **42**, 313–322.

Harper, L. V. (1975). The scope of offspring effects: From care giver to culture. *Psychological Bulletin*, **82**, 784–801.

Harpur, T. J., Hare, R. D., and Hakstian, A. R. (1989). Two-factor conceptualisation of psychopathy: Construct validity and assessment implications. *Psychological Assessment: A Journal of Consulting and Clinical Psychology*, **1**, 6–17.

Harpur, T. J., Williamson, S. E., Forth, A. E., and Hare, R. D. (1986). A quantitative assessment of the resting EEG in psychopathic and nonpsychopathic criminals. *Psychophysiology*, **23**, 439.

Harré. R. (1985). *The Philosophies of Science*. Oxford: Oxford University Press.

Harris, G. T., and Varney, G. W. (1986). A ten-year study of assaults and assaulters on a maximum security psychiatric unit. *Journal of Interpersonal Violence*, **1**, 173–191.

Harris, G. T., Rice, M. E., and Cormier, C. A. (1989). Violent recidivism among psychopaths and nonpsychopaths treated in a therapeutic community. *Research Reports*, Volume 6, No. 1. Mental Health Centre, Penetanguishene, Ontario.

Harris, P. W. (1983). The interpersonal maturity of delinquents and nondelinquents. In W. S. Laufer and J. M. Day (eds), *Personality Theory, Moral Development, and Criminal Behaviour*. Lexington: Lexington Books.

Harris, P. W. (1988). The interpersonal maturity level classification system: I-level. *Criminal Justice and Behavior*, **15**, 58–77.

Hart, H. L. A. (1968). *Punishment and Responsibility: Essays in the Philosophy of Law*. Oxford: Clarendon Press.

Hart, S. D., and Hare, R. D. (1989). Discriminant validity of the Psychopathy Checklist in a forensic psychiatric population. *Psychological Assessment: A Journal of Consulting and Clinical Psychology*, **2**, 338–341.

Hartjen, C. A. (1972). Legalism and humanism: A reply to the Schwendingers. *Issues in Criminology*, **7**, 59–69.

Hartl, E. M., Monnelly, E. P., and Elderkin, R. (1982). *Physique and Delinquent behaviour: A Thirty Year Follow-up of William H. Sheldon's Varieties of Delinquent Youth*. New York: Academic Press.

Hartmann, H., Kris, E., and Lowenstein, R. (1949). Notes on the theory of aggression. In A. Freud (ed.), *The Psychoanalytic Study of the Child*, Volume 3. New York: International Universities Press.

Hartshorne, H., and May, M. A. (1928). *Studies in Deceit*. New York: Macmillan.

Harvey, O. J., Hunt, D. E., and Schroder, H. M. (1961). *Conceptual Systems and Personality Organisation*. New York: Wiley.

Haward, L. R. C. (1981). *Forensic Psychology*. London: Batsford.

Haward, L. R. C. (1987). The uses and misuses of psychological evidence. In G. Gudjonsson and J. Drinkwater (eds), *Psychological Evidence in Court. Issues in Criminological and Legal Psychology, No. 11*. Leicester: British Psychological Society.

Hawk, S., and Peterson, R. A. (1974). Do MMPI psychopathic deviancy scores reflect psychopathic deviancy or just deviancy? *Journal of Personality Assessment*, **38**, 362–368.

Hawkins, J. D., Catalano, R. F., Jones, G., and Fine, D. (1987). Delinquency prevention through parent training: Results and issues from work in progress. In J. Q. Wilson and G. C. Loury (eds), *From Children to Citizens: Volume Three: Families, Schools, and Delinquency Prevention*. New York: Springer-Verlag.

Hayes, L. M. (1983). And darkness closes in... A national study of jail suicides. *Criminal Justice and Behavior*, **10**, 461–484.

Hayes, S. C., Brownell, K. D., and Barlow, D. H. (1978). The use of self-administered covert sensitisation in the treatment of exhibitionism and sadism. *Behavior Therapy*, **9**, 283–289.

Haynes, J. P., and Bensch, M. (1981). The P>V sign on the WISC-R and recidivism in delinquents. *Journal of Consulting and Clinical Psychology*, **49**, 480–481.

Healy, W., and Bronner, A. (1936). *New Light on Delinquency and its Treatment*. New Haven, Conn.: Yale University Press.

Hearnshaw, L. S. (1964). *A Short History of British Psychology 1840-1940*. London: Methuen.

Heath, L., Kruttschnitt, C., and Ward, D. (1986). Television and violent criminal behavior: Beyond the Bobo doll. *Violence and Victims*, **1**, 177–190. Heather, N. (1976). *Radical Perspectives in Psychology*. London: Methuen.

Heather, N. (1977). Personal illness in lifers and the effects of long-term indeterminate sentences. *British Journal of Criminology*, **17**, 378–386.

Heather, N. (1979). The structure of delinquent values: A repertory grid investigation. *British Journal of Social and Clinical Psychology*, **18**, 263–275.

Hebb, D. O. (1946). On the nature of fear. *Psychological Review*, **53**, 259–276.

Heilbrun, A.B. (1982). Cognitive models of criminal violence based on intelligence and psychopathy levels. *Journal of Consulting and Clinical Psychology*, **50**, 546–557.

Heilbrun, A. B., and Heilbrun, M. R. (1985). Psychopathy and dangerousness: Comparison, integration, and extension of two psychopathic typologies. *British Journal of Clinical Psychology*, **24**, 181–195.

Heilbrun, K. S., and Annis, L. V. (1988). Research and training in forensic psychology: National survey of forensic facilities. *Professional Psychology: Research and Practice*, **19**, 211–215.

Heilbrun, K., Bennett, W. S., Evans, J. H., Offult, R. A., Reiff, H. J., and White, A. J. (1988). Assessing treatability in mentally disordered offenders: A conceptual and methodological note. *Behavioral Sciences and the Law*, **6**, 479–486.

Heim, N., and Hursch, C. J. (1979). Castration for sex offenders: Treatment or punishment? A review and critique of recent European literature. *Archives of Sexual Behavior*, **8**, 281–304.

Hellman, D. S., and Blackman, N. (1966). Enuresis, firesetting and cruelty to animals: A triad predictive of adult crime. *American Journal of Psychiatry*, **122**, 1431–1435.

Hempel, G. C. (1965). *Aspects of Scientific Explanation*. New York: Free Press.

Henderson, M. (1982). An empirical classification of convicted violent offenders. *British Journal of Criminology*, **22**, 1–20.

Henderson, M., and Hewstone, M. (1984). Prison inmates explanations for interpersonal violence: Accounts and attributions. *Journal of Consulting and Clinical Psychology*, **52**, 789–794.

Henderson, M., and Hollin, C. R. (1986). Social skills training and delinquency. In C. R. Hollin and P. Trower (eds), *Handbook of Social Skills Training. Volume 1: Applications Across the Life Span*. Oxford: Pergamon.

Henggeler, S. W. (1989). *Delinquency in Adolescence*. Newbury Park, Ca: Sage.

Henker, B., and Whalen, C. K. (1989). Hyperactivity and attention deficits. *American Psychologist*, **44**, 216–223.

Henn, F. A., Bardwell, R., and Jenkins, R. L. (1980). Juvenile delinquents revisited: Adult criminal activity. *Archives of General Psychiatry*, **37**, 1160–1163.

Henn, F., Herjanic, M., and Vanderpearl, R. (1976). Forensic psychiatry: Diagnosis and criminal responsibility. *Journal of Nervous and Mental Disease*, **162**, 423–429.

Hennigan, K. M., DelRosario, M. L., Heath, L., Cook, T. D., Wharton, J. D., and Calder, B. J. (1982). Impact of the introduction of television on crime in the United States: Empirical findings and theoretical implications. *Journal of Personality and Social Psychology*, **42**, 461–477.

Herman, J. L. (1990). Sex offenders: A feminist perspective. In W. L. Marshall, D. R. Laws and H. E. Barbaree (eds), *Handbook of Sexual Assault: Issues, Theories, and Treatment of the Offender*. New York: Plenum.

Herzberg, J. L., and Fenwick, P. B. C. (1988). The aetiology of aggression in temporal lobe epilepsy. *British Journal of Psychiatry*, **153**, 50–55.

Herzberger, S. D., Potts, D. A., and Dillon, M. (1981). Abusive and nonabusive parental treatment from the child's perspective. *Journal of Consulting and Clinical Psychology*, **49**, 81–90.

Hetherington, E. M., and Martin, B. (1979). Family interaction. In H. C. Quay and J. S. Werry (eds), *Psychopathological Disorders of Childhood*, Second Edition. New York: Wiley.

Hetherington, E. M., Stouwie, R. J., and Ridberg, E. H. (1971). Patterns of family interaction and child-rearing attitudes related to three dimensions of juvenile delinquency. *Journal of Abnormal Psychology*, **78**, 160–176.

Hewitt, L., and Jenkins, R. L. (1946). *Fundamental Patterns of Maladjustment*. Illinois: State of Illinois.

Hickey, J. E. (1972). The effects of guided moral discussion upon youthful offenders' level of moral reasoning. *Dissertation Abstracts International*, **33**, 1551A.

Higgins, J. P., and Thies, A. P. (1981). Social effectiveness and problem-solving thinking of reformatory inmates. *Journal of Offender Counselling Services and Rehabilitation*, **5**, 93–98.

Hill, A. M., and Griffiths, R. C. (1982). English law and the psychologist. In J. Shapland (ed.), Lawyers and Psychologists—Gathering and Giving Evidence. *Issues in Criminological and Legal Psychology*, No. 3. Leicester: British Psychological Society.

Hill, D. (1947). Amphetamine in psychopathic states. *British Journal of Addiction*, **44**, 50–54.

Hill, D., and Watterson, D. (1942). Electroencephalographic studies of the psychopathic personality. *Journal of Neurology and Psychiatry*, **5**, 47–64.

Hindelang, M. J. (1974a). The Uniform Crime Reports revisited. *Journal of Criminal Justice*, **2**, 1–17.

Hindelang, M. J. (1974b). Moral evaluations of illegal behaviors. *Social Problems*, **21**, 370–385.

Hindelang, M. J. (1978). Race and involvement in common law personal crimes. *American Sociological Review*, **43**, 93–109.

Hindelang, M. J. (1979). Sex and involvement in criminal activity. *Social Problems*, **27**, 143–156.

Hindelang, M. J., and Weis, J. G. (1972). Personality and self-reported delinquency: An application of cluster analysis. *Criminology*, **10**, 268–294.

Hindelang, M. J., Hirschi, T., and Weis, J. G. (1979). Correlates of delinquency: The illusion of discrepancy between self-report and official measures. *American Sociological Review*, **44**, 995–1014.

Hindelang, M. J., Hirschi, T., and Weis, J. G. (1981). *Measuring Delinquency*. Beverly Hills, Ca: Sage.

Hinshaw, S. P. (1987). On the distinction between attention deficits/hyperactivity and conduct problems/aggression in child psychopathology. *Psychological Bulletin*, **101**, 443–463.

Hirschi, T. (1969). *Causes of Delinquency*. Berkeley: University of California Press.

Hirschi, T. (1978). Causes and prevention of juvenile delinquency. *Sociological Inquiry*, **47**, 322–341.

Hirschi, T. (1986). On the compatibility of rational choice and social control theories of crime. In D. B. Cornish and R. V. G. Clarke (eds), *The Reasoning Criminal: Rational Choice Perspectives on Offending*. New York: Springer-Verlag.

Hirschi, T., and Hindelang, M. J. (1977). Intelligence and delinquency: A revisionist review. *American Sociological Review*, **42**, 571–587.

Hirschi, T., and Gottfredson, M. (1988). Towards a general theory of crime. In

W. Buikhuisen and S. A. Mednick (eds), *Explaining Criminal Behaviour*. Leiden: Brill.

Hobbs, T. R., and Holt, M. M. (1976). The effects of token reinforcement on the behavior of delinquents in cottage settings. *Journal of Applied Behavior Analysis*, **9**, 189–198.

Hodges, E. F., and Tait, C. D. (1965). A follow-up study of potential delinquents. *American Journal of Psychiatry*, **120**, 449–453.

Hodges, E. G. (1971). Crime prevention by the Indeterminate Sentencing Law. *American Journal of Psychiatry*, **128**, 291–295.

Hodgens, J. B., and McCoy, J. F. (1989). Distinctions among rejected children on the basis of peer-nominated aggression. *Journal of Child Clinical Psychology*, **18**, 121–128.

Hodgins, S. (1992). Mental disorder, intellectual deficiency and crime. *Archives of General Psychiatry*, **49**, 476–483.

Hoffman, M. L. (1971). Father absence and conscience development. *Developmental Psychology*, **4**, 400–406.

Hoffman, M. L. (1977). Moral internalisation: Current theory and research. In L. Berkowitz (ed.), *Advances in Experimental Social Psychology*, Volume 10. New York: Academic Press.

Hoffman, M. L. (1982). Development of prosocial motivation: Empathy and guilt. In N. Eisenberg (ed.), *The Development of Prosocial Behavior*. New York: Academic Press.

Hoffman, M. L., and Saltzstein, H. D. (1967). Parent discipline and the child's moral development. *Journal of Personality and Social Psychology*, **5**, 45–57.

Hoffman-Plotkin, D., and Twentyman, C. T. (1984). A multimodal assessment of behavioral and cognitive deficits in abused and neglected preschoolers. *Child Development*, **55**, 794–802.

Hogan, R. (1969). Development of an empathy scale. *Journal of Consulting and Clinical Psychology*, **33**, 307–316.

Hogan, R. (1973). Moral conduct and moral character: A psychological perspective. *Psychological Bulletin*, **79**, 217–232.

Hogan, R. (1975). Theoretical egocentrism and the problem of compliance. *American Psychologist*, **30**, 533–540.

Hogan, R., and Jones, W. H. (1983). A role-theoretical model of criminal conduct. In W. S Laufer and J. M. Day (eds), *Personality Theory, Moral Development, and Criminal Behavior*. Lexington: Lexington Books.

Hogan, R., DeSoto, C. B. and Solano, C. (1977). Traits, tests, and personality research. *American Psychologist*, **32**, 255–264.

Hoghughi, M. (1979). The Aycliffe token economy. *British Journal of Criminology*, **19**, 384–399.

Hokanson, J. E. (1970). Psychophysiological evaluation of the catharsis hypothesis. In E. I. Megargee and J. E. Hokanson (eds), *The Dynamics of Aggression*. New York: Harper and Row.

Holcomb, W. R., Adam, N. A., and Ponder, H. N. (1985). The development and cross-validation of an MMPI typology of murderers. *Journal of Personality Assessment*, **49**, 240–244.

Holder, T. (1978). A review and perspective of human resource development programs in corrections. *Criminal Justice Review*, **2**, 7–16.

Holland, T. R., and Holt, N. (1975). Personality patterns among short-term prisoners undergoing presentence evaluation. *Psychological Reports*, **37**, 827–836.

Holland, T. R., and McGarvey, B. (1984). Crime specialisation, seriousness progression, and Markov chains. *Journal of Consulting and Clinical Psychology*, **52**, 837–840.

Holland, T. R., Holt, N., and Beckett, G. E. (1982). Prediction of violent versus nonviolent recidivism from prior violent and nonviolent criminality. *Journal of Abnormal Psychology*, **91**, 178–182.

Hollander, H. E., and Turner, F. D. (1985). Characteristics of incarcerated delinquents: Relationships between developmental disorders, environmental and family factors, and patterns of offence and recidivism. *Journal of the American Academy of Child Psychiatry*, **24**, 221–226.

Hollin, C. R. (1990). *Cognitive–Behavioral Interventions with Young Offenders*. New York: Pergamon.

Hollin, C. R., and Henderson, M. (1984). Social skills training with young offenders: False expectations and the "failure of treatment". *Behavioural Psychotherapy*, **12**, 331–341.

Hollin, C. R., Huff, G. J., Clarkson, F., and Edmondson, A. C. (1986). Social skills training with young offenders in a Borstal: An evaluative study. *Journal of Community Psychology*, **14**, 289–299.

Holmes, R. M. (1989). *Profiling Violent Crimes: An Investigative Tool*. Newbury Park, Ca: Sage.

Holmes, R. M., and De Burger, J. (1988). *Serial Murder*. Newbury Park, Ca: Sage.

Holt, R. R. (1962). Individuality and generalisation in the psychology of personality. *Journal of Personality*, **30**, 377–404.

Home Office (1986a). *The Sentence of the Court*. London: HMSO.

Home Office (1986b). *The Ethnic Origin of Prisoners: The Prison Population on 30 June, 1985, and Persons Received July 1984–March 1985*. Home Office Statistical Bulletin 17/86. London: Home Office.

Home Office (1987). *Criminal Careers of those Born in 1953: Persistent Offenders and Desistance*. Home Office Statistical Bulletin 35/87. London: Home Office.

Home Office (1989a). *Criminal Statistics England and Wales 1988*. London: HMSO.

Home Office (1989b). *Crime Statistics for the Metropolitan Police District by Ethnic Group, 1987: Victims, Suspects, and Those Arrested*. Home Office Statistical Bulletin 23/89. London: Home Office.

Home Office/Department of Health and Social Security (1975). *Report of the Committee on Abnormal Offenders*. London: HMSO.

Hooper, F. A., and Evans, R. G. (1984). Screening for disruptive behavior of institutionalised juvenile offenders. *Journal of Personality Assessment*, **48**, 159–161.

Hope, K., Philip, A. E., and Loughran, J. M. (1967). Psychological characteristics associated with XYY sex-chromosome complement in a state mental hospital. *British Journal of Psychiatry*, **113**, 495–498.

Hough, M., and Mayhew, P. (1983). *The British Crime Survey: First Report*. Home Office Research Study, No. 76. London: HMSO.

Hough, M., and Mayhew, P. (1985). *Taking Account of Crime: Findings From The Second British Crime Survey*. Home Office Research Study, No. 85. London: HMSO.

Hough, M., Clarke, R. V. G., and Mayhew, P. (1980). Introduction. In R. V. G. Clarke and P. Mayhew (eds), *Designing Out Crime*. London: HMSO.

Howard, R. C. (1984). The clinical EEG and personality in mentally abnormal offenders. *Psychological Medicine*, **14**, 569–580.

Howard, R. C., Fenton, G. W., and Fenwick, P. B. C. (1984). The contingent negative variation, personality, and antisocial behaviour. *British Journal of Psychiatry*, **144**, 463–474.

Howarth, E. (1986). What does Eysenck's Psychoticism scale really measure? *British Journal of Psychology*, **77**, 223–227.

Howells, K. (1978). The meaning of poisoning to a person diagnosed as a psychopath. *Medicine, Science and the Law*, **18**, 179–184.

Howells, K. (1979). Some meanings of children for pedophiles. In M. Cook and G. Wilson (eds), *Love and Attraction*. Oxford: Pergamon.

Howells, K. (1981). Adult sexual interest in children: Considerations relevant to theories of etiology. In M. Cook and K. Howells (eds), *Adult Sexual Interest in Children*. London: Academic Press.

Howells, K. (1982). Mental disorder and violent behaviour. In P. Feldman (ed.), *Developments in The Study of Criminal Behaviour*, Volume 2. Chichester: Wiley.

Howells, K. (1986). Social skills training and criminal and antisocial behaviour in adults. In C. R. Hollin and P. Trower (eds), *Handbook of Social Skills Training. Volume 1: Applications Across the Life Span*. Oxford: Pergamon.

Hsu, L. K. G., Wisner, K., Richey, E. T., and Goldstein, C. (1985). Is juvenile delinquency related to an abnormal EEG? A study of EEG abnormalities in juvenile delinquents and adolescent psychiatric inpatients. *Journal of the American Academy of Child Psychiatry*, **24**, 310–315.

Hubble, L. M., and Groff, M. (1982). WISC-R verbal-performance IQ discrepancies among Quay-classified adolescent male delinquents. *Journal of Youth and Adolescence*, **11**, 503–508.

Hucker, S. J., and Bain, J. (1990). Androgenic hormones and sexual assault. In W. L. Marshall, D. R. Laws and H. E. Barbaree (eds), *Handbook of Sexual Assault: Issues, Theories, and Treatment of the Offender*. New York: Plenum.

Hucker, S. J., Langevin, R., Wortzman, G., Bain, J., Handy, L., Chambers, J., and Wright, S. (1986). Neuropsychological impairment in pedophiles. *Canadian Journal of Behavioral Science*, **18**, 440–448.

Hucker, S. J., Langevin, R., Dickey, R., Handy, L., Chambers, J., Wright, S., Bain, J., and Wortzman, G. (1988). Cerebral damage and dysfunction in sexually aggressive men. *Annals of Sex Research*, **1**, 33–47.

Hudgins, W., and Prentice, N. (1973). Moral judgment in delinquent and nondelinquent adolescents and their mothers. *Journal of Abnormal Psychology*, **82**, 145–152.

Hudson, B. (1987). *Justice Through Punishment: A Critique of The Justice Model of Corrections*. London: Gower.

Huesmann, L. R., and Eron, L. D. (1984). Cognitive processes and the persistence of aggressive behavior. *Aggressive Behavior*, **10**, 243–251.

Huesmann, L. R., Eron, L. D., and Yarmel, P. W. (1987). Intellectual functioning and aggression. *Journal of Personality and Social Psychology*, **52**, 232–240.

Huesmann, L. R., Eron, L. D., Lefkowitz, M. M. and Walder, L. O. (1984). Stability of aggression over time and generations. *Developmental Psychology*, **20**, 1120–1134.

Huizinga, D., and Elliott, D. S. (1986). Reassessing the reliability and validity of self-report delinquency measures. *Journal of Quantitative Criminology*, **2**, 293–327.

Hunt, D. E., and Hardt, R. H. (1965). Developmental stage, delinquency, and differential treatment. *Journal of Research in Crime and Delinquency*, **2**, 20–31.

Hunt, J. McV. (1965). Intrinsic motivation and its role in psychological development. In D. Levine (ed.), *Nebraska Symposium on Motivation*. Lincoln: University of Nebraska Press.

Hunter, N., and Kelley, C. K. (1986). Examination of the validity of the Adolescent Problem Inventory among incarcerated juvenile delinquents. *Journal of Consulting and Clinical Psychology*, **54**, 301–302.

Hutchings, B., and Mednick, S. A. (1975). Registered criminality in the adoptive and biological parents of registered male criminal adoptees. In R. R. Fieve, D. Rosenthal and H. Brill (eds), *Genetic Research in Psychiatry*. Baltimore: Johns Hopkins University Press.

Iacono, W. G., and Patrick, C. J. (1987). What psychologists should know about lie detection. In I. B. Weiner and A. K. Hess (eds), *Handbook of Forensic Psychology*. New York: Wiley.

Irving, B. L., and Hilgendorf, E. L. (1980). *Police Interrogation: The Psychological Approach*. Royal Commission on Criminal Procedure. Research Study No. 1. London: HMSO.

Izzo, R. L., and Ross, R. R. (1990). Meta-analysis of rehabilitation programs for juvenile delinquents: A brief report. *Criminal Justice and Behavior*, **17**, 134–142.

Jackson, E. F., Tittle, C. R., and Burke, M. J. (1985). Offense-specific models of the differential association process. *Social Problems*, **33**, 335–356.

Jackson, H. F., Glass, C., and Hope, S. (1987). A functional analysis of recidivist arson. *British Journal of Clinical Psychology*, **26**, 175–185.

Jackson, P. R., and Warr, P. B. (1984). Unemployment and psychological ill-health: The moderating role of duration and age. *Psychological Medicine*, **14**, 605–614.

James, D. V., Fineberg, N. A., Shah, A. J., and Priest, R. G. (1990). An increase in violence on an acute psychiatric ward: a study of associated factors. *British Journal of Psychiatry*, **156**, 846–852.

Jarvik, L. F., Klodin, V., and Matsuyama, S. S. (1973). Human aggression and the extra Y chromosome: Fact or fantasy? *American Psychologist*, **28**, 674–682.

Jeffery, C. R. (1965). Criminal behavior and learning theory. *Journal of Criminal Law, Criminology, and Police Science*, **56**, 294–300.

Jeffery, C. R. (1976). Criminal behavior and physical environment: A perspective. *American Behavioral Scientist*, **20**, 149–174.

Jenkins, P. (1988). Serial murder in England 1940-1985. *Journal of Criminal Justice*, **16**, 1–15.

Jenkins, R. L. (1960). The psychopathic or antisocial personality. *Journal of Nervous and Mental Disease*, **131**, 318–334.

Jennings, W. S., Kilkenny, R., and Kohlberg, L. (1983). Moral-development theory and practice for youthful and adult offenders. In W. S. Laufer and J. M. Day (eds), *Personality Theory, Moral Development, and Criminal Behavior*. Lexington: Lexington Books.

Jensen, G. F. (1972). Parents, peers and delinquent action: A test of the differential association perspective. *American Journal of Sociology*, **78**, 562–575.

Jensen, G. F., Erickson, M. L., and Gibbs, J. P. (1978). Perceived risk of punishment and self-reported delinquency. *Social Forces*, **57**, 57–78.

Jesness, C. F. (1971). The Preston typology study: An experiment with differential treatment in an institution. *Journal of Research in Crime and Delinquency*, **8**, 38–52.

Jesness, C. F. (1975). Comparative effectiveness of behavior modification and transactional analysis programs for delinquents. *Journal of Consulting and Clinical Psychology*, **43**, 758–779.

Jesness, C. F. (1988). The Jesness Inventory classification system. *Criminal Justice and Behavior*, **15**, 78–91.

Jesness, C. F., and Wedge, R. F. (1984). Validity of a revised Jesness Inventory I-level classification with delinquents. *Journal of Consulting and Clinical Psychology*, **52**, 997–1010.

Jesness, C. F., Allison, T. S., McCormick, P. M., Wedge, R. F., and Young, M. L. (1975). *The Cooperative Behavior Demonstration Project*. California Youth Authority.

Jessor, R., and Jessor, S. L. (1977). *Problem Behavior and Psychosocial Development: A Longitudinal Study*. New York: Academic Press.

Jew, C. C., Clanon, T. L., and Mattocks, A. L. (1972). The effectiveness of group psychotherapy in a correctional institution. *American Journal of Psychiatry*, **129**, 602–605.

Johnson, A. M. (1959). Juvenile delinquency. In S. Arieti (ed), *American Handbook of Psychiatry*. New York: Basic Books.

Johnson, E., and Payne, J. (1986). The decision to commit a crime: An information processing analysis. In D. B. Cornish and R. V. G. Clarke (eds), *The Reasoning Criminal: Rational Choice Perspectives on Offending*. New York: Springer-Verlag.

Johnson, V. S. (1977). Behavior modification in the correctional setting. *Criminal Justice and Behavior*, **4**, 397–428.

Johnston, J. M. (1972). Punishment of human behavior. *American Psychologist*, **27**, 1033–1054.

Johnston, M. (1976). Responsiveness of delinquents and nondelinquents to social reinforcement. *British Journal of Social and Clinical Psychology*, **15**, 41–49.

Johnston, M. E. (1988). Correlates of early violence experience among men who are abusive toward female mates. In G. T. Hotaling, D. Finkelhor, J. T. Kirkpatrick and M. A. Straus (eds), *Family Abuse and Its Consequences: New Directions in Research*. Beverly Hills, Ca: Sage.

Jones, A. (1969). Stimulus seeking behavior. In J. P. Zubek (ed.), *Sensory Deprivation: Fifteen Years of Research*. New York: Appleton-Century-Crofts.

Jones, E. E. (1986). Interpreting interpersonal behavior: The effects of expectancies. *Science*, **234**, 41–46.

Jones, F. D., Stayer, S. J., Wichlacz, C. R., Thomes, L., and Livingstone, B. L. (1977).

Contingency management of hospital diagnosed character and behavior disorder soldiers. *Journal of Behavior Therapy and Experimental Psychiatry*, **8**, 33.

Jones, M. (1963). The treatment of character disorders. *British Journal of Criminology*, **3**, 276–282.

Jurkovic, G. J. (1980). The juvenile delinquent as a moral philosopher: A structural developmental approach. *Psychological Bulletin*, **88**, 709–727.

Jurkovic, G. J., and Prentice, N. M. (1977). Relation of moral and cognitive development to dimensions of juvenile delinquency. *Journal of Abnormal Psychology*, **86**, 414–420.

Jussim, L. (1986). Self-fulfilling prophecies: A theoretical and integrative review. *Psychological Review*, **93**, 429–445.

Justice, B., Justice, R., and Kraft, J. (1974). Early warning signs of violence: Is a triad enough? *American Journal of Psychiatry*, **131**, 457–459.

Kahn, J., Reed, F. S., Bates, M., Coates, T., and Everitt, B. (1976). A survey of Y chromosome variants and personality in 436 borstal lads and 254 controls. *British Journal of Criminology*, **16**, 233–244.

Kahneman, D., and Tversky, A. (1984). Choices, values, and frames. *American Psychologist*, **39**, 341–350.

Kandel, D. B. (1978). Homophily, selection and socialisation in adolescent friendships. *American Journal of Sociology*, **84**, 427–436.

Kandel, E., Mednick, S. A., Kierkegaard-Sorensen, L., Hutchings, B., Knop, J., Rosenberg, R., and Schulsinger, F. (1988). IQ as a protective factor for subjects at high risk for antisocial behavior. *Journal of Consulting and Clinical Psychology*, **56**, 224–226.

Kanfer, F.H. (1980). Self-management methods. In F. H. Kanfer and A. P. Goldstein (eds), *Helping People Change*. New York: Pergamon.

Kaplan, H.B. (1980). *Deviant Behavior in Defense of Self*. New York: Pergamon.

Kaplan, P.J., and Arbuthnot, J. (1985). Affective empathy and cognitive role-taking in delinquent and nondelinquent youth. *Adolescence*, **20**, 323–333.

Karli, P. (1981). Conceptual and methodological problems associated with the study of brain mechanisms underlying aggressive behaviour. In P. F. Brain and D. Benton (eds), *The Biology of Aggression*. Alphen aan der Rijn: Sijthoff and Noordhoff.

Karpman, B. (1948). The myth of the psychopathic personality. *American Journal of Psychiatry*, **104**, 523–534.

Karpman, B. (1949). Criminality, insanity and the law. *Journal of Criminal Law*, **39**, 584–605.

Kassebaum, G. G., Couch, A. S., and Slater, P. E. (1959). The factorial dimensions of the MMPI. *Journal of Consulting Psychology*, **23**, 226–236.

Kassebaum, G. G., Ward, D., and Wilner, D. (1971). *Prison Treatment and Parole Survival: An Empirical Assessment*. New York: Wiley.

Kaufman, J., and Zigler, E. (1987). Do abused children become abusive parents? *American Journal of Orthopsychiatry*, **57**, 186–192.

Kazdin, A. E. (1986). Comparative outcome studies of psychotherapy: Methodological issues and strategies. *Journal of Consulting and Clinical Psychology*, **54**, 95–105.

Kazdin, A. E. (1987). Treatment of antisocial behavior in children: Current status and future directions. *Psychological Bulletin*, **102**, 187–203.

Kazdin, A. E., Esveldt-Dawson, K., French, N. H., and Unis, A. S. (1987). Problem-solving skills training and relationship therapy in the treatment of antisocial child behavior. *Journal of Consulting and Clinical Psychology*, **55**, 76–85.

Keat, R. (1971). Positivism, naturalism and anti-naturalism in the social sciences. *Journal for the Theory of Social Behaviour*, **1**, 3–17.

Kegan, R. G. (1986). The child behind the mask: Sociopathy as developmental delay. In W. H. Reid, D. Dorr, J. I. Walker and J. W. Bonner (eds), *Unmasking the Psychopath: Antisocial Personality and Related Syndromes*. New York: Norton.

Keller, D. J., and Goldstein, A. (1978). Orgasmic reconditioning reconsidered. *Behaviour Therapy and Research*, **16**, 299–301.

Kelling, G. (1986). Neighbourhood crime control and the police: A view of the American experience. In K. Heal and G. Laycock (eds), *Situational Crime Prevention: From Theory into Practice*. London: HMSO.

Kellner, R. (1978). Drug treatment of personality disorders and delinquents. In W. H. Reid (ed.), *The Psychopath: A Comprehensive Study of Antisocial Disorders and Behaviors*. New York: Brunner/Mazel.

Kelly, F., and Veldman, D. J. (1964). Delinquency and school dropout as a function of impulsivity and nondominant values. *Journal of Abnormal and Social Psychology*, **69**, 190-194.

Kempe, C. H., Silverman, F. H., Steele, B. F., Droegemuller, W., and Silver, H. K. (1962). The battered child syndrome. *Journal of the American Medical Association*, **181**, 17-24.

Kempf, K. (1986). Offense specialisation: Does it exist? In D. B. Cornish and R. V. Clarke (eds), *The Reasoning Criminal: Rational Choice Perspectives on Offending*. New York: Springer-Verlag.

Kendall, P. C. (1984). Cognitive–behavioral self-control therapy for children. *Journal of Child Psychology and Psychiatry*, **25**, 173-179.

Kendall, P. C. (1989). The generalisation and maintenance of behavior change: Comments, considerations, and the "no cure" criticism. *Behavior Therapy*, **20**, 357-364.

Kendall, P. C, Deardorff, P., and Finch, A. (1977). Empathy and socialisation in first and repeat offenders and normals. *Journal of Abnormal Child Psychology*, **5**, 93-97.

Kendall, P. C., Reber, M., McLeer, S., Epps, J., and Ronan, K. R. (1990). Cognitive–behavioral treatment of conduct-disordered children. *Cognitive Therapy and Research*, **14**, 279-297.

Kendell, R. E. (1975). *The Role of Diagnosis in Psychiatry*. Oxford: Blackwell.

Kennard, D. (1983). *An Introduction to Therapeutic Communities*. London: Routledge and Kegan Paul.

Kenrick, D. T., and Funder, D. C. (1988). Profiting from controversy: Lessons from the person–situation debate. *American Psychologist*, **43**, 23-34.

Kernberg, O. (1975). *Borderline Conditions and Pathological Narcissism*. New York: Aronson.

Kernis, M. H., Grannemann, B. D., and Barclay, L. C. (1989). Stability and level of self-esteem as predictors of anger arousal and hostility. *Journal of Personality and Social Psychology*, **56**, 1013-1022.

Kerr, C. A., and Roth, J. H. (1986). Populations, practices, and problems in forensic psychiatric facilities. *Annals of the American Academy of Political and Social Science*, **484**, 127-143.

Khantzian, E. J., and Treece, C. (1985). DSM-III psychiatric diagnosis of narcotic addicts: Recent findings. *Archives of General Psychiatry*, **42**, 1067-1071.

Kiesler, D. J. (1983). The 1982 interpersonal circle: A taxonomy for complementarity in human transactions. *Psychological Review*, **90**, 185-214.

Kiesler, D. J., Denburg, T. F. V., Sikes-Nova, V. E., Larus, J. P., and Goldston, C. S. (1990). Interpersonal behavior profiles of eight cases of DSM-III personality disorder. *Journal of Clinical Psychology*, **46**, 440-453.

Kifer, R. E., Lewis, M. A., Green, D. R., and Phillips, E. (1974). Training predelinquent youth and their parents to negotiate conflict situations. *Journal of Applied Behavior Analysis*, **7**, 357-364.

Kilpatrick, D. G., Best, C. L., Veronen, L. J., Amick, A. E., Villeponteaux, L. A., and Ruff, G. A. (1985). Mental health correlates of criminal victimisation: A random community survey. *Journal of Consulting and Clinical Psychology*, **53**, 866-873.

Kinzel, A. F. (1970). Body-buffer zone in violent prisoners. *American Journal of Psychiatry*, **127**, 59-64.

Kipnis, D. (1971). *Character Structure and Impulsiveness*. New York: Academic Press.

Kirchner, E, Kennedy, R., and Draguns, J. (1979). Assertion and aggression in adult offenders. *Behavior Therapy*, **10**, 452-471.

Kirigin, K. A., Braukmann, C. J., Atwater, J. D., and Wolf, M. M. (1982). An evaluation of teaching family (Achievement Place) group homes for juvenile offenders. *Journal of Applied Behavior Analysis*, **15**, 1–16.

Klassen, D., and O'Connor, W. A. (1989). Assessing the risk of violence in released mental patients: A cross-validation study. *Psychological Assessment: A Journal of Consulting and Clinical Psychology*, **1**, 75–81.

Klein, M. W. (1984). Offense specialisation and versatility among juveniles. *British Journal Of Criminology*, **24**, 185–194.

Klein, M. W. (1986). Labelling theory and delinquency policy: An experimental test. *Criminal Justice and Behavior*, **13**, 47–79.

Klein, N. C., Alexander, J. F., and Parsons, B. V. (1977). Impact of family systems intervention on recidivism and sibling delinquency: A model of primary prevention and program evaluation. *Journal of Consulting and Clinical Psychology*, **45**, 469–474.

Kleinmuntz, B. (1990). Why we still use our heads instead of formulas: Toward an integrative approach. *Psychological Bulletin*, **107**, 296–310.

Kline, P. (1987). Psychoanalysis and crime. In B. J. McGurk, D. M. Thornton and M Williams (eds), *Applying Psychology to Imprisonment: Theory and Practice*. London: HMSO.

Knight, B. J., Osborn, S. G., and West, D. J. (1977). Early marriage and criminal tendency in males. *British Journal Of Criminology*, **15**, 43–50.

Knight, R. A., and Prentky, R. A. (1990). Classifying sexual offenders: The development and corroboration of taxonomic models. In W. L. Marshall, D. R. Laws, and H. E. Barbaree (eds), *Handbook of Sexual Assault: Issues, Theories, and Treatment of the Offender*. New York: Plenum.

Kohlberg, L. (1976). Moral stages and moralisation: The cognitive–developmental approach. In T. Lickona (ed.), *Moral Development and Behavior*. New York: Holt, Rinehart and Winston.

Kohlberg, L., and Candee, D. (1984). The relationship of moral judgment to moral action. In W. M. Kurtines and J. W. Gewirtz (eds), *Morality, Moral Behavior, and Moral Development*. Chichester: Wiley.

Kolvin, I., Miller, F. J. W., Fleeting, M., and Kolvin, P. A. (1988). Social and parenting factors affecting criminal offence rates: Findings from the Newcastle Thousand Family Study (1947–1980). *British Journal of Psychiatry*, **152**, 80–90.

Konecni, V. J., and Ebbesen, E. B. (eds), (1982). *The Criminal Justice System: A Social Psychological Analysis*. San Francisco: Freeman.

Kornhauser, R. R. (1978). *Social Sources of Delinquency: An Appraisal of Analytic Models*. Chicago: University of Chicago Press.

Koss, M. P., and Leonard, K. E. (1984). Sexually aggressive men: Empirical findings and theoretical implications. In N. M. Malamuth and E. Donnerstein (eds), *Pornography and Sexual Aggression*. New York: Academic Press.

Koss, M. P., Gidycz, C. A., and Wisniewski, N. (1987). The scope of rape: Incidence and prevalence of sexual aggression and victimisation in a national sample of higher education students. *Journal of Consulting and Clinical Psychology*, **55**, 162–170.

Kozol, H., Boucher, R., and Garofalo, R. (1972). The diagnosis and treatment of dangerousness. *Crime and Delinquency*, **18**, 371–392.

Krakowski, M., Volavka, J., and Brizer, D. (1986). Psychopathology and violence: A review of the literature. *Comprehensive Psychiatry*, **27**, 131–148.

Krauss, H. H., Robinson, I., Janzen, W., and Cauthen, N. (1972). Predictions of ethical risk taking by psychopathic and nonpsychopathic criminals. *Psychological Reports*, **30**, 83–88.

Kremsdorf, R. B., Holmen, M. L., and Laws, D. R. (1980). Orgasmic reconditioning without deviant imagery: A case report with a pedophile. *Behaviour Research and Therapy*, **18**, 203–207.

Kroll, J., and McKenzie, T. B. (1983). When psychiatrists are liable: Risk management and violent patients. *Hospital and Community Psychiatry*, **34**, 29–37.

Kruppa, I. (1991). Perpetrators suffer trauma too. *The Psychologist*, **4**, 401–403.

Krus, D. J., Sherman, J. L., and Krus, P. H. (1977). Changing values over the last half century: The story of Thurstone's crime scales. *Psychological Reports*, **40**, 207–211.

Krynicki, Y. (1978). Cerebral dysfunction in repetitively assaultive adolescents. *Journal of Nervous and Mental Disease*, **166**, 59–67.

Kurtines, W. M. (1984). Moral behavior as rule-governed behavior: A psychosocial role-theoretical approach to moral behavior and development. In W. M. Kurtines and J. W. Gewirtz (eds), *Morality, Moral Behavior, and Moral Development*. Chichester: Wiley.

Kurtines, W. M., and Hogan, R. (1972). Sources of conformity in unsocialised college students. *Journal of Abnormal Psychology*, **80**, 49–51.

Kurtines, W. M., Alvarez, M., and Azmitia, M. (1990). Science and morality: The role of values in science and the scientific study of moral phenomena. *Psychological Bulletin*, **107**, 283–295.

Kutash, S. B. (1978). Psychoanalytic theories of aggression. In I. L. Kutash, S. B. Kutash, L. B. Schlesinger and others (eds), *Violence: Perspectives on Murder and Aggression*. San Francisco: Jossey-Bass.

Lahey, B. B., Conger, R. D., Atkeson, B. M., and Treiber, F. A. (1984). Parenting behavior and emotional status of physically abusive mothers. *Journal of Consulting and Clinical Psychology*, **52**, 1062–1071.

Lahey, B. B., Hartdagen, S. E., Frick, P. J., McBurnett, K., Connor, R., and Hynd, G. W. (1988). Conduct disorder: Parsing the confounded relation to parental divorce and antisocial personality. *Journal of Abnormal Psychology*, **97**, 334–337.

Lambert, N. M. (1988). Adolescent outcomes for hyperactive children: Perspectives on general and specific patterns of childhood risk for adolescent educational, social, and mental health problems. *American Psychologist*, **43**, 786–799.

Landau, S. F. (1976). Delinquency, institutionalisation, and time orientation. *Journal of Consulting and Clinical Psychology*, **44**, 745–759.

Landau, S. F. (1981). Juveniles and the police. *British Journal of Criminology*, **21**, 27–46.

Lane, D. A. (1987). Personality and antisocial behaviour: A long term study. *Personality and Individual Differences*, **8**, 797–806.

Lane, P. J. and Kling, J. (1979). Construct validity of the Overcontrolled hostility scale of the MMPI. *Journal of Consulting and Clinical Psychology*, **47**, 781–782.

Lane, R. (1974). Crime and the industrial revolution: British and American views. *Journal of Social History*, **7**, 287–303.

Lang, R. A., Holden, R., Langevin, R., Pugh, G. M., and Wu, R. (1987). Personality and criminality in violent offenders. *Journal of Interpersonal Violence*, **2**, 179–195.

Lange, J. S. (1931). *Crime as Destiny*. London: Allen and Unwin.

Langevin, R. (ed.), (1985). *Erotic Preference, Gender Identity and Aggression*. Hillsdale, NJ: Erlbaum.

Langevin, R., Paitich, D., and Russon, A. E. (1985). Are rapists sexually anomalous, aggressive, or both. In R. Langevin (ed.), *Erotic Preference, Gender Identity and Aggression*. Hillsdale, NJ: Erlbaum.

Langevin, R., Ben-Aron,M. H., Coulthard, R., Heasman, G., Purins, J. E., Handy, L., Hucker, S.J., Russon, A. E., Day, D., Roper, V., Bain, J., Wortzman, G., and Webster, C. D. (1985). Sexual aggression: Constructing a predictive equation. A controlled pilot study. In R. Langevin (ed.), *Erotic Preference, Gender Identity and Aggression*. Hillsdale, NJ: Erlbaum.

Lanyon, R. I. (1986a). Theory and treatment in child molestation. *Journal of Consulting and Clinical Psychology*, **54**, 176–182.

Lanyon, R. I. (1986b). Psychological assessment procedures in court related settings. *Professional Psychology: Research and Practice*, **17**, 260–268.

Larrance, D. T., and Twentyman, C. I. (1983). Maternal attributions and child abuse. *Journal of Abnormal Psychology*, **92**, 449–457.

Latimer, P. R., and Sweet, A. A. (1984). Cognitive versus behavioral procedures in cognitive-behavior therapy: A critical review of the evidence. *Journal of Behavior Therapy and Experimental Psychiatry*, **15**, 9–22.

Laub, J. H. (1987). Data for positive criminology. In M. R. Gottfredson and T. Hirschi (eds), *Positive Criminology*. Beverly Hills, Ca: Sage.

Laufer, W, S., Johnson, J. A., and Hogan, R. (1981). Ego control and criminal behavior. *Journal of Personality and Social Psychology*, **41**, 179–184.

Laufer, W, S., Skoog, D. K., and Day, J. M. (1982). Personality and criminality: A review of the California Psychological Inventory. *Journal of Clinical Psychology*, **38**, 562–573.

Laws, D. R. (1974). The failure of a token economy. *Federal Probation*, **38**, 33–38.

Laws, D. R. (1984). The assessment of diverse sexual behaviour in humans: A critical review of the major methodologies. In K. Howells (ed.), *The Psychology of Sexual Diversity*. Oxford: Blackwell.

Laws, D. R. (ed.) (1989). *Relapse Prevention With Sex Offenders*. New York: Guilford Press.

Laws, D. R., and Marshall, W. M. (1990). A conditioning theory of the etiology and maintenance of deviant sexual preference and behavior. In W. L. Marshall, D. R. Laws, and H. E. Barbaree (eds), *Handbook of Sexual Assault: Issues, Theories, and Treatment of the Offender*. New York: Plenum.

Laws, D. R., and Osborn, C. A. (1983). Setting up shop: How to build and operate a laboratory to evaluate and treat sexual deviance. In J. G. Greer and I. Stuart (eds), *The Sexual Aggressor: Current Perspectives on Treatment*. New York: Van Nostrand Reinhold.

Laws, D. R., and Rubin, H. B. (1969). Instructional control of an autonomic sexual response. *Journal of Applied Behavior Analysis*, **2**, 93–99.

Laws, D. R., Meyer, J., and Holmen, M. L. (1978). Reduction of sadistic sexual arousal by olfactory aversion: A case study. *Behaviour Research and Therapy*, **16**, 281–285.

Lazarus, R. S. (1980). Cognitive behavior therapy as psychodynamics. In M. J. Mahoney (ed.), *Psychotherapy Process: Current Issues and Future Directions*. New York: Plenum.

Lazarus, R. S. (1991). Cognition and motivation in emotion. *American Psychologist*, **46**, 352–367.

Leary, T. (1957). *Interpersonal Diagnosis of Personality*. New York: Ronald Press.

Lee, M., and Prentice, N. M. (1988). Interrelations of empathy, cognition, and moral reasoning with dimensions of juvenile delinquency. *Journal of Abnormal Child Psychology*, **16**, 127–139.

LeFlore, L. (1988). Delinquent youths and family. *Adolescence*, **23**, 629–642.

Lemert, E. M. (1967). *Human Deviance, Social Problems and Social control*. Englewood Cliffs, NJ: Prentice-Hall.

Leschied, A. W., and Thomas, K. E. (1985). Effective residential programming for "hard to serve" delinquent youth: A description of the Craigwood program. *Canadian Journal of Criminology*, **27**, 161–177.

Levander, S. E., Schalling, D. S., Lidberg, L., Bartfai, A., and Lidberg, Y. (1980). Skin conductance recovery time and personality in a group of criminals. *Psychophysiology*, **17**, 105–111.

Levey, A. B., and Martin, I. (1981). Personality and conditioning. In H. J. Eysenck (ed.), *A Model for Personality*. New York: Springer-Verlag.

Levey, S., and Howells, K. (1990). Anger and its management. *Journal of Forensic Psychiatry*, **1**, 305–327.

Levine, W. R., and Bornstein, P. E. (1972). Is the sociopath treatable? The contribution of psychiatry to a legal dilemma. *Washington University Law Quarterly*, 693-717.

Levinson, R. B. (1988). Developments in the classification process: Quay's AIMS approach. *Criminal Justice and Behavior*, **15**, 24–38.

Levy, L. H. (1983). Trait approaches. In M. Hersen, A. E. Kazdin and A. S. Bellak (eds), *The Clinical Psychology Handbook*. New York: Pergamon.

Lewis, D. O., Shanok, S. S., and Balla, D. A. (1979). Perinatal difficulties, head and face trauma, and child abuse in the medical histories of seriously disturbed delinquent children. *American Journal of Psychiatry*, **136**, 419–423.

Lewis, D. O., Pincus, J. H., Shanok, S. S., and Glaser, G. H. (1982). Psychomotor epilepsy and violence in a group of incarcerated adolescent boys. *American Journal of Psychiatry*, **139**, 882–887.

Lewis, G., and Appleby, L. (1988). Personality disorder: The patients psychiatrists dislike. *British Journal of Psychiatry*, **153**, 44–49.

Lewis, R. V. (1983). Scared straight—California style. *Criminal Justice and Behavior*, **10**, 209–226.

Liazos, A. (1978). School, alienation, and delinquency. *Crime and Delinquency*, **24**, 355–370.

Lickona, T. (1976). Critical issues in the study of moral development. In T. Lickona (ed.), *Moral Development and Behavior*. New York: Holt, Rinehart and Winston.

Lidberg, L., Levander, S. E., Schalling, D., and Lidberg, Y. (1976). Excretion of adrenaline and noradrenaline as related to real life stress and psychopathy. *Reports from the Laboratory for Clinical Stress Research*, Stockholm, No. 50.

Lieber, A., and Sherin, C. (1972). Homicides and the lunar cycle: Toward a theory of lunar influence on human emotional disturbance. *American Journal of Psychiatry*, **129**, 69–74.

Linden, E., and Hackler, J. C. (1973). Affective ties and delinquency. *Pacific Sociological Review*, **16**, 27–46.

Lindqvist, P., and Allebeck, P. (1990). Schizophrenia and crime: A longitudinal follow-up of 644 schizophrenics in Stockholm. *British Journal of Psychiatry*, **157**, 345–350.

Linz, D., Donnerstein, E., and Penrod, S. (1987). The findings and recommendations of the Attorney General's Commission on Pornography: Do the psychological facts fit the political fury? *American Psychologist*, **42**, 946–953.

Lilly, J. R., Cullen, F. T., and Ball, R. A. (1989). *Criminological Theory: Context and Consequences*. Newbury Park, Ca: Sage.

Lion, J. R. (1978). Outpatient treatment of psychopaths. In W. H. Reid (ed.), *The Psychopath: A Comprehensive Study of Antisocial Disorders and Behaviors*. New York: Brunner/Mazel.

Lipton, D. N., McDonel, E. C., and McFall, R. M. (1987). Heterosexual perception in rapists. *Journal of Consulting and Clinical Psychology*, **55**, 17–21.

Liska, A. E., and Tausig, M. (1979). Theoretical interpretations of social class and race differentials in legal decision-making for juveniles. *Sociological Quarterly*, **20**, 197–207.

Litwack, T. R., and Schlesinger, L. B. (1987). Assessing and predicting violence: Research, law, and applications. In I. B. Weiner and A. K. Hess (eds), *Handbook of Forensic Psychology*. New York: Wiley.

Lloyd, C., and Walmsley, R. (1989). *Changes in Rape Offences and Sentencing*. Home Office Research Study, No. 105. London: HMSO.

Lobitz, G. K., and Johnson, S. M. (1975). Normal versus deviant children: A multimethod comparison. *Journal of Abnormal Child Psychology*, **3**, 353–374.

Lochman, J. E., Burch, P. R., Curry, J. F., and Lampron, L. B. (1984). Treatment and generalisation effects of cognitive–behavioral and goal-setting interventions with aggressive boys. *Journal of Consulting and Clinical Psychology*, **52**, 915–916.

Locke, E. A. (1972). Critical analysis of the concept of causality in behavioristic psychology. *Psychological Reports*, **31**, 175–197.

Loeber, R. (1982). The stability of antisocial and delinquent child behavior: A review. *Child Development*, **53**, 1431–1446.

Loeber, R. (1990). Development and risk factors of juvenile antisocial behavior and delinquency. *Clinical Psychology Review*, **10**, 1–41.

Loeber, R., and Dishion, T.J. (1984). Boys who fight at home and school: Family conditions influencing cross-setting consistency. *Journal of Consulting and Clinical Psychology*, **52**, 759–768.

Loeber, R., and Stouthamer-Loeber, M. (1986). Family factors as correlates and predictors of juvenile conduct problems and delinquency. In N. Morris and M. Tonry (eds), *Crime and Justice: An Annual Review of Research*, Volume 7. Chicago: University of Chicago Press. Logan, C. H. (1972). Evaluation research in crime and delinquency: A reappraisal. *Journal of Criminal Law, Criminology and Police Science*, **63**, 378–387.

London, H., Schubert, D. S. P., and Washburn, D. (1972). Increase of autonomic arousal by boredom. *Journal of Abnormal Psychology*, **80**, 29–36.

Longo, R. E. (1982). Sexual learning and experience among adolescent sexual offenders. *International Journal of Offender Therapy and Comparative Criminology*, **26**, 235–241.

Lopatto, D., and Williams, J. L. (1976). Self-control: A critical review and an alternative interpretation. *The Psychological Record*, **26**, 3–12.

Lorenz, K. (1966). *On Aggression*. London: Methuen.

Lorr, M. (1982). On the use of cluster analytic techniques. *Journal of Clinical Psychology*, **38**, 461–462.

Lowe, C. F., and Higson, P. J. (1980). Self-instructional training and cognitive behaviour modification: A behavioural analysis. In G. Davey (ed.), *Applications of Conditioning Theory*. London: Methuen.

Luckenbill, D. (1977). Criminal homicide as a situated transaction. *Social Problems*, **25**, 176–186.

Luckenbill, D., and Best, J. (1981). Careers in deviance and respectability: The analogy's limitations. *Social Problems*, **29**, 197–206.

Lund, N. L., and Salary, H. M. (1980). Measured self-concept in adjudicated juvenile offenders. *Adolescence*, **15**, 65–74.

Lundman, R. J., Sykes, R. E., and Clark, J. P. (1978). Police control of juveniles: A replication. *Journal of Research in Crime and Delinquency*, **15**, 74–91.

Lurigio, A. J., and Lewis, D. A. (1987). The criminal mental patient: A descriptive analysis and suggestions for future research. *Criminal Justice and Behavior*, **14**, 268–287.

Lykken, D. T. (1957). A study of anxiety in the sociopathic personality. *Journal of Abnormal and Social Psychology*, **55**, 6–10.

Lykken, D. T. (1988). The case against polygraph testing. In A. Gale (ed.), *The Polygraph Test: Lies, Truth and Science*. London: Sage.

Maccoby, E. E., and Martin, J. A. (1983). Socialisation in the context of the family: Parent–child interaction. In E. M. Hetherington (ed.), *Handbook of Child Psychology*, Volume 4. New York: Wiley. Maccoby, E. E., Johnson, J. P., and Church, R. M. (1958). Community integration and the control of juvenile delinquency. *Journal of Social Issues*, **14**, 38–51.

MacCulloch, M. J., Snowden, P. R., Wood, P. J. W., and Mills, H. E. (1983). Sadistic fantasy, sadistic behaviour, and offending. *British Journal of Psychiatry*, **143**, 20–29.

MacDonald, J. (1967). Homicidal threats. *American Journal of Psychiatry*, **124**, 61–68.

MacDonald, J. E. (1955). The concept of responsibility. *Journal of Mental Science*, **101**, 704–717.

Mack, J. L. (1969). The MMPI and recidivism. *Journal of Abnormal Psychology*, **74**, 612–614.

Mackay, R. D. (1990). Fact and fiction about the insanity defence. *Criminal Law Review*, 247–255.

MacKenzie, D. L., and Goodstein, L. (1985). Long-term incarceration impacts and characteristics of long-term offenders: An empirical analysis. *Criminal Justice and Behavior*, **12**, 395–414.

MacNamara, E. J. (1977). The medical model in corrections. *Criminology*, **14**, 439–448.

Madden, D. J. (1986). Psychotherapeutic approaches in the treatment of violent persons. In L. H. Roth (ed.), *Clinical Treatment of the Violent Person*. New York: Guilford.

Mahoney, M. J. (1974). *Cognition and Behavior Modification*. Cambridge: Ballinger.

Mahoney, M. J., and Arnkoff, D. B. (1978). Cognitive and self-control therapies. In S. L. Garfield and A. E. Bergin (eds), *Handbook of Psychotherapy and Behavior Change*, Second Edition. New York: Wiley.

Magnusson, D. (1988). Antisocial behaviour of boys and autonomic reactivity. In T. E. Moffitt and S. A. Mednick (eds), *Biological Contributions to Crime Causation*. Dordrecht: Martinus Nijhoff.

Malamuth, N.M. (1984). Aggression against women: Cultural and individual causes. In N. M. Malamuth and E. Donnerstein (eds), *Pornography and Sexual Aggression*. New York: Academic Press.

Malamuth, N.M. (1986). Predictors of naturalistic sexual aggression. *Journal of Personality and Social Psychology*, **50**, 953–962.

Malamuth, N. M., and Check, J. V. P. (1983). Sexual arousal to rape depictions: Individual differences. *Journal of Abnormal Psychology*, **92**, 55–67.

Maletzky, B. M. (1980). Self-referred versus court-referred sexually deviant patients: Success with assisted covert sensitisation. *Behavior Therapy*, **11**, 306–314.

Maletzky, B. M. (1991). *Treating the Sex Offender*. Newbury Park, Ca: Sage.

Maliphant, R., Watson, S. A., and Daniels, D. (1990). Disruptive behaviour in school, personality characteristics and heart rate (HR) levels in 7- to 9-year-old boys. *Educational Psychology*, **10**, 199–205.

Malmquist, C. P. (1968). Conscience development. *Psychoanalytic Study of the Child*, **23**, 301-331.

Manicas, P. T. (1987). *A History and Philosophy of the Social Sciences*. Oxford: Blackwell.

Manicas, P. T., and Secord, P. F. (1983). Implications for psychology of the new philosophy of science. *American Psychologist*, **38**, 399–413.

Mannheim, H. (1965). *Comparative Criminology*. London: Routledge and Kegan Paul.

Mannheim, H., and Wilkins, L. T. (1955). *Prediction Methods in Relation to Borstal Training*. London: HMSO.

Mannuzza, S., Klein, R. G., Konig, P. H., and Giampino, T. L. (1989). Hyperactive boys almost grown up: IV. Criminality and its relation to psychiatric status. *Archives of General Psychiatry*, **46**, 1073–1079.

Marceil, J. C. (1977). Implicit dimensions of idiography and nomothesis: A reformulation. *American Psychologist*, **32**, 1046–1055.

Margolin, G. (1979). Conjoint marital therapy to enhance anger management and reduce spouse abuse. *American Journal of Family Therapy*, **7**, 13–23.

Margolin, G. (1988). Interpersonal factors associated with marital violence. In G. T. Hotaling, D. Finkelhor, J. T. Kirkpatrick and M. A. Straus (eds), *Family Abuse and its Consequences: New Directions in Research*. Beverly Hills, Ca: Sage.

Mark, V. H., and Ervin, F. R. (1970). *Violence and the Brain*. New York: Harper and Row.

Marques, J. K. (1981). Effects of victim resistance strategies on the sexual arousal and attitudes of violent rapists. In R. B. Stuart (ed.), *Violent Behavior: Social Learning Approaches to Prediction, Management and Treatment*. New York: Brunner/Mazel.

Marsh, P. (1985). Patterns of aggression—not unnaturally. In E. Karas (ed.), *Current Issues in Clinical Psychology*, Volume 2. London: Plenum.

Marsh, P., Rosser, E., and Harré, R. (1978). *The Rules of Disorder*. London: Routledge and Kegan Paul.

Marshall, R. J. (1983). A psychoanalytic perspective on the diagnosis and development of juvenile delinquency. In W. S. Laufer and J. M. Day (eds) *Personality Theory, Moral Development, and Criminal Behavior*. Lexington: Heath.

Marshall, W. L. (1979). Satiation therapy: A procedure for reducing deviant sexual arousal. *Journal of Applied Behavior Analysis*, **12**, 377–389.

Marshall, W. L. (1989). Intimacy, loneliness and sexual offenders. *Behaviour Research and Therapy*, **27**, 491–503.

Marshall, W. L., and Barbaree, H. E. (1984). Disorders of personality, impulse, and adjustment. In S. M. Turner and M. Hersen (eds), *Adult Psychopathology and Diagnosis*. New York: Wiley.

Marshall, W. L., and Barbaree, H. E. (1990a). An integrated theory of the etiology of sexual offending. In W. L. Marshall, D. R. Laws, and H. E. Barbaree (eds), *Handbook of Sexual Assault: Issues, Theories, and Treatment of the Offender*. New York: Plenum.

Marshall, W. L., and Barbaree, H. E. (1990b). Outcome of comprehensive cognitive–behavioral treatment programs. In W. L. Marshall, D. R. Laws, and H. E. Barbaree (eds), *Handbook of Sexual Assault: Issues, Theories, and Treatment of the Offender*. New York: Plenum.

Martin, H., and Rodeheffer, M. (1976). The psychological impact of abuse on children. *Journal of Pediatric Psychology*, **1**, 12–16.

Martin, S. E., Sechrest, L. B., and Redner, R. (1981). *New Directions in the Rehabilitation of Criminal Offenders*. Washington, DC: National Academy Press.

Martinson, R. (1974). What works? Questions and answers about prison reform. *The Public Interest*, **35**, 22–54.

Martinson, R. (1979). New findings, new views: A note of caution regarding sentencing reform. *Hofstra Law Review*, **7**, 242–258.

Mason, S. T. (1984). The noradrenergic locus coeruleus—the centre of attention? *The Behavioral and Brain Sciences*, **7**, 445.

Matarazzo, J. D. (1990). Psychological assessment versus psychological testing. Validation from Binet to the school, clinic, and courtroom. *American Psychologist*, **45**, 999–1017.

Matsueda, R. L. (1982). Testing control theory and differential association: A causal modelling approach. *American Sociological Review*, **47**, 489–504.

Matsueda, R. L., Piliavin, I., and Gartner, R. (1988). Economic assumptions versus empirical research. *American Sociological Review*, **53**, 305–309.

Matthews, V. M. (1968). Differential identification: An empirical note. *Social Problems*, **14**, 376–383.

Mattson, A., Schalling, D., Olweus, D., Löw, H., and Svensson, M. A. (1980). Plasma testosterone, aggressive behavior, and personality dimensions in young male delinquents. *Journal of the American Academy of Child Psychiatry*, **19**, 476–490.

Matza, D. (1964). *Delinquency and Drift*. New York: Wiley.

Mawby, R. I., McCulloch, J. W., and Batta, I. D. (1979). Crime among Asian juveniles in Bradford. *International Journal of Sociology of Law*, **7**, 297–306.

Mawson, A. R., and Mawson, C. D. (1977). Psychopathy and arousal: A new interpretation of the psychophysiological literature. *Biological Psychiatry*, **12**, 49–74.

Mayhew, P., Clarke, R. V. G., and Hough, J. M. (1980). Steering column locks and car theft. In R. V. G. Clarke and P. Mayhew (eds), *Designing Out Crime*. London: HMSO.

Mayhew, P., Elliott, D., and Dowds, L. (1989). *The 1988 British Crime Survey*. London: HMSO.

Mazur, A. (1983). Physiology, dominance, and aggression in humans. In A. P. Goldstein (ed.), *Prevention and Control of Aggression*. New York: Pergamon.

McCaghy, C. H. (1968). Drinking and deviance disavowal: The case of child molesters. *Social Problems*, **16**, 43–49.

McCallum, C. (1973). The CNV and conditionability in psychopaths. *Electroencephalography and Clinical Neurophysiology Supplement 33*, 337–343.

McCandless, B. R., Persons, W. S., and Roberts, A. (1972). Perceived opportunity, delinquency, race and body-build among delinquent youth. *Journal of Consulting and Clinical Psychology*, **38**, 281–287.

McClintock, F. H., and Gibson, E. (1961). *Robbery in London*. London: Macmillan.

McCloskey, M., and Egeth, H. E. (1983). Eyewitness identification: What can a psychologist tell a jury? *American Psychologist*, **38**, 550–563.

McCord, J. (1978). A thirty-year follow-up of treatment effects. *American Psychologist*, **33**, 284–289.

McCord, J. (1979). Some childrearing antecedents of criminal behavior in adult men. *Journal of Personality and Social Psychology*, **37**, 1477–1486.

McCord, J. (1985). Deterrence and the light touch of the law. In D. P. Farrington and J. Gunn (eds), *Reactions to Crime: The Public, The Police, Courts, and Prisons*. Chichester: Wiley.

McCord, J. (1986). Instigation and insulation: How families affect antisocial aggression. In D. Olweus, J. Block and M. Radke-Yarrow (eds), *Development of Antisocial and Prosocial Behavior: Research, Theories, and Issues*. New York: Academic Press.

McCord, J., McCord, W. M., and Thurber, E. (1962). Some effects of paternal absence on male children. *Journal of Abnormal and Social Psychology*, **64**, 361–369.

McCord, W. M. (1983). *The Psychopath and Milieu Therapy*. New York: Academic Press.

McCord, W. M., and McCord, J. (1964). *The Psychopath: An Essay on The Criminal Mind*. New York: Van Nostrand.

McCrae, R. R., and Costa, P. T. (1985). Comparison of EPI and Psychoticism scales with measures of the five factor model of personality. *Personality and Individual Differences*, **5**, 587–597.

McCrae, R. R., and Costa, P. T. (1986). Clinical assessment can benefit from recent advances in personality psychology. *American Psychologist*, **41**, 1001–1003.

McCullough, J. P., Huntsinger, G. M., and Nay, W. R. (1977). Self-control treatment of aggression in a 16-year old male. *Journal of Consulting and Clinical Psychology*, **45**, 322–331.

McDougall, C., Barnett, R. M., Ashurst. B., and Willis, B. (1987). Cognitive control of anger. In B. J. McGurk, D. M. Thornton, and M. Williams (eds), *Applying Psychology to Imprisonment: Theory and Practice*. London: HMSO.

McEwan, A. W. (1983). Eysenck's theory of criminality and the personality types and offences of young delinquents. *Personality and Individual Differences*, **4**, 201–204.

McEwan, A. W., and McGurk, B. J. (1981). The professionalism of prison psychologists. *Bulletin of the British Psychological Society*, **34**, 415–417.

McFall, R. M. (1982). A review and reformulation of the concept of social skills. *Behavioral Assessment*, **4**, 1–33.

McGarry, A. L., and Parker, L. L. (1974). Massachusetts' Operation Baxstrom: A follow-up. *Massachusetts Journal of Mental Health*, **4**, 27–41.

McGarvey, B., Gabrielli, W., Bentler, P. M., and Mednick, S. (1981). Rearing social class, education, and criminality: A multiple indicative model. *Journal of Abnormal Psychology*, **90**, 354–364.

McGee, R., Williams, S., and Silva, P. A. (1985). Factor structure and correlates of ratings of inattention, hyperactivity, and antisocial behavior in a large sample of 9 year-old children from the general population. *Journal of Consulting and Clinical Psychology*, **53**, 480–490.

McGinn, C. (1979). Action and its explanation. In N. Bolton (ed.), *Philosophical Problems in Psychology*. London: Methuen.

McGuire, J., and Priestley, P. (1985). *Offending Behaviour: Skills and Strategems for Going Straight*. London: Batsford.

McGuire, R. J., Carlisle, J. M., and Young, B. G. (1965). Sexual deviations as conditioned behaviour: A hypothesis. *Behaviour Research and Therapy*, **2**, 185–190.

McGurk, B. J. (1978). Personality types among normal homicides. *British Journal of Criminology*, **18**, 146–161.

McGurk, B. J., and McGurk, R. E. (1979). Personality types among prisoners and prison officers. *British Journal of Criminology*, **19**, 31–49.

McGurk, B. J., and McDougall, C. (1981). A new approach to Eysenck's theory of criminality. *Personality and Individual Differences*, **2**, 338–340.

McManus, M., Alessi, N. E., Grapentine, W. L., and Brickman, A. (1984). Psychiatric disturbance in serious delinquents. *Journal of the American Academy of Child Psychiatry*, **3**, 602–615.

McMurran, M., and Hollin, C. R. (1989). Drinking and delinquency: Another look at young offenders and alcohol. *British Journal of Criminology*, **29**, 386–394.

McMurran, M., and Shapland, P. (1989). What do prison psychologists do? *The Psychologist*, **2**, 287–289.

McNees, M. P., Egli, D. S., Marshall, R. S., and Risley, T. R. (1976). Shoplifting prevention: Providing information through signs. *Journal of Applied Behavior Analysis*, **9**, 399–406.

McNeil, D. E., and Binder, R. L. (1987). Predictive validity of judgments of dangerousness in emergency civil commitment. *American Journal of Psychiatry*, **144**, 197–200.

McReynolds, P. (1987). Lightner Witmer: Little known founder of clinical psychology. *American Psychologist*, **42**, 849–858.

Mednick, S. A. (1975). Autonomic nervous system recovery and psychopathology. *Scandinavian Journal of Behaviour Therapy*, **4**, 55–66.

Mednick, S. A., and Kandel, E. (1988). Genetic and perinatal factors in violence. In T. E.

Moffitt and S. A. Mednick (eds), *Biological Contributions to Crime Causation*. Dordrecht: Martinus Nijhoff.

Mednick, S. A., Gabrielli, W. F., and Hutchings, B. (1984). Genetic influences in criminal convictions: Evidence from an adoption cohort. *Science*, **234**, 891–894.

Mednick, S. A., Volavka, J., Gabrielli, W. F., and Itil, T. M. (1981). EEG as a predictor of antisocial behavior. *Criminology*, **19**, 219–229.

Meehl, P. E. (1954). *Clinical Versus Statistical Prediction*. Minneapolis: University of Minnesota Press.

Meehl, P. E. (1986). Causes and effects of my disturbing little book. *Journal of Personality Assessment*, **50**, 370–375.

Meehl, P. E., and Rosen, A. (1955). Antecedent probability and the efficiency of psychometric signs, patterns, or cutting scores. *Psychological Bulletin*, **52**, 194–216.

Megargee, E. I. (1966). Undercontrolled and overcontrolled personality types in extreme antisocial aggression. *Psychological Monographs*, **80**, Whole No. 611.

Megargee, E. I. (1970). The prediction of violence with psychological tests. In C. D. Spielberger (ed.), *Current Topics in Clinical and Community Psychology*, Volume 2. New York: Academic Press.

Megargee, E. I. (1976). The prediction of dangerous behavior. *Criminal Justice and Behavior*, **3**, 1–22.

Megargee, E. I. (1977). A new classification system for criminal offenders: I. The need for a new classification system. *Criminal Justice and Behavior*, **4**, 107–114.

Megargee, E. I., and Bohn, M. J. (1979). *Classifying Criminal Offenders*. Beverly Hills, Ca: Sage.

Megargee, E. I., Parker, G. V. C., and Levine, R. V. (1971). Relationship of familial and social factors to socialisation in middle-class college students. *Journal of Abnormal Psychology*, **77**, 76–89.

Meichenbaum, D. (1977). *Cognitive–Behavior Modification: An Integrative Approach*. New York: Plenum.

Meichenbaum, D., and Gilmore, J. B. (1984). The nature of unconscious processes: A cognitive–behavioral perspective. In K. S. Bowers and D. Meichenbaum (eds), *The Unconscious Reconsidered*. New York: Wiley.

Mellsop, G., Varghese, F., Joshua, S., and Hicks, A. (1982). The reliability of Axis II of DSM-III. *American Journal of Psychiatry*, **139**, 1360–1361.

Melton, G., Petrila, J., Pythress, N., and Slobogin, C. (1987). *Psychological Evaluation for the Courts: A Handbook for Mental Health Professionals and Lawyers*. New York: Guilford.

Meltzer, L. J., Roditi, B. N., and Fenton, T. (1986). Cognitive and learning profiles of delinquent and learning-disabled adolescents. *Adolescence*, **21**, 581–591.

Menard, S., and Morse, B. J. (1984). A structuralist critique of the IQ–delinquency hypothesis: Theory and evidence. *American Journal of Sociology*, **89**, 1347–1378.

Menzies, R. J., and Webster, C. D. (1989). Mental disorder and violent crime. In N. A. Weiner and M. E. Wolfgang (eds), *Pathways to Criminal Violence*. Newbury Park, Ca: Sage.

Menzies, R. J., Webster, C. D., and Butler, B. T. (1981). Perceptions of dangerousness among forensic psychiatrists. *Comprehensive Psychiatry*, **22**, 387–396.

Merton, R. K. (1939). Social structure and anomie. *American Sociological Review*, **3**, 672–682.

Metfessel, M., and Lovell, C. (1942). Recent literature on individual correlates of crime. *Psychological Bulletin*, **39**, 133–164.

Milan, M. A. (1987). Token economy programs in closed institutions. In E. K. Morris and C. J. Braulmann (eds), *Behavioral Approaches to Crime and Delinquency: A Handbook of Applications, Research, and Concepts*. New York: Plenum.

Milan, M. A., and Evans, J. H. (1987). Intervention with incarcerated offenders. In I. B. Weiner and A. K. Hess (eds), *Handbook of Forensic Psychology*. New York: Wiley.

Miller, L. (1988). Neuropsychological perspectives on delinquency. *Behavioral Sciences and the Law*, **6**, 409–428.

Miller, W. B. (1958). Lower class culture as a generating milieu of gang delinquency. *Journal of Social Issues*, **14**, 5–19.

Millon, T. (1981). *Disorders of Personality: DSM-III, Axis II*. New York: Wiley.

Mills, C. M., and Walter, T. L. (1979). Reducing juvenile delinquency: A behavioral–employment intervention. In J. S. Stumphauzer (ed.), *Progress in Behavior Therapy with Delinquents*. Springfield, Ill: Charles C. Thomas.

Minor, W. W. (1980). The neutralisation of criminal offense. *Criminology*, **18**, 103–120.

Mischel, T. (1964). Personal constructs, rules, and the logic of clinical activity. *Psychological Review*, **71**, 180–192.

Mischel, W. (1961). Preference for delayed reinforcement and social responsibility. *Journal of Abnormal Psychology*, **62**, 1–7.

Mischel, W. (1968). *Personality and Assessment*. New York: Wiley.

Mischel, W. (1984). Convergences and challenges in the search for consistency. *American Psychologist*, **39**, 351–364.

Mischel, W., and Mischel, H. (1976). A cognitive social-learning approach to morality and self-regulation. In T. Lickona (ed.), *Moral Development and Behavior*. New York: Holt, Rinehart and Winston.

Mischel, W., Shoda, Y., and Rodriguez, M. I. (1989). Delay of gratification in children. *Science*, **244**, 933–938.

Moffitt, T. E. (1983). The learning theory model of punishment. *Criminal Justice and Behavior*, **10**, 131–158.

Moffitt, T. E. (1988). Neuropsychology and self-reported early delinquency in an unselected birth cohort: A preliminary report from New Zealand. In T. E. Moffitt and S. A. Mednick (eds), *Biological Contributions to Crime Causation*. Dordrecht: Martinus Nijhoff.

Moffitt, T. E., and Silva, P. A. (1987). WISC-R verbal and performance IQ discrepancy in an unselected cohort: Clinical significance and longitudinal stability. *Journal of Consulting and Clinical Psychology*, **55**, 768–774.

Moffitt, T. E., and Silva, P. A. (1988). IQ and delinquency: A direct test of the differential detection hypothesis. *Journal of Abnormal Psychology*, **97**, 330–333.

Moffitt, T. E., Gabrielli, W. F., Mednick, S., and Schulsinger, F. (1981). Socioeconomic status, IQ, and delinquency. *Journal of Abnormal Psychology*, **90**, 152–156.

Monachesi, E. D., and Hathaway, S. R. (1969). The personality of delinquents. In J. N. Butcher (ed.) *MMPI: Research Developments and Clinical Applications*. New York: McGraw-Hill.

Monahan, J. (ed.) (1980). *Who is the Client? The Ethics of Psychological Intervention in the Criminal Justice System*. Washington, DC: American Psychological Association.

Monahan, J. (1981). *Predicting Violent Behavior: An Assessment of Clinical Techniques*. Beverly Hills, Ca: Sage.

Monahan, J. (1984). The prediction of violent behavior: Toward a second generation of theory and policy. *American Journal of Psychiatry*, **141**, 10–15.

Monahan, J. (1988). Risk assessment of violence among the mentally disordered: Generating useful knowledge. *International Journal of Law and Psychiatry*, **11**, 249–257.

Monahan, J. (1992). Mental disorder and violent behavior: Perceptions and evidence. *American Psychologist*, **47**, 511–521.

Monahan, J., and Loftus, E. F. (1982). The psychology of law. *Annual Review of Psychology*, **33**, 441–475.

Monahan, J., and Steadman, H. J. (1983). Crime and mental disorder: An epidemiological approach. In N. Morris and M. Tonry (eds), *Crime and Justice: An Annual Review of Research*, Volume 3. Chicago: University of Chicago Press.

Monahan, J., Novaco, R. W., and Geis, G. (1979). Corporate violence: Research strategies for community psychology. In T. R. Sarbin (ed.), *Challenges to the Criminal Justice System: The Perspective of Community Psychology*. New York: Human Services Press.

Money, J. (1990). Forensic sexology: Paraphilic serial rape (biastophilia) and lust murder (erotophonophilia). *American Journal of Psychotherapy*, **44**, 26–36.

Monroe, R. (1978). *Brain Dysfunction in Aggressive Criminals*. Lexington: Heath.

Moon, J. R., and Eisler, R. M. (1983). Anger control: An experimental comparison of three behavioral treatments. *Behavior Therapy*, **14**, 493–505.

Moore, D. R., Chamberlain, P., and Mukai, L. H. (1979). Children at risk for delinquency: A follow-up comparison of aggressive children and children who steal. *Journal of Abnormal Child Psychology*, **7**, 345–355.

Moore, L. R., and Finn, P. E. (1986). Forensic psychology: An empirical review of experimental research. *Journal of Clinical Psychology*, **42**, 675–679.

Moore, M. (1984). *Law and Psychiatry*. Cambridge: University of Cambridge Press.

Moos, R. H. (1975). *Evaluating Correctional and Community Settings*. New York: Wiley.

Moran, R. (1985). The modern foundation for the insanity defense: The cases of James Hadfield (1800) and Daniel McNaughtan (1843). *Annals of the American Academy of Political and Social Science*, **477**, 31-42.

Morash, M. (1982). Juvenile reaction to labels: An experiment and an exploratory study. *Sociology and Social Research*, **67**, 76–88.

Morey, L. C. (1988). The categorical representation of personality disorder: A cluster analysis of DSM-III-R personality features. *Journal of Abnormal Psychology*, **97**, 314–321.

Morris, A. (1965). The comprehensive classification of adult offenders. *Journal of Criminal Law, Criminology and Police Science*, **56**, 197–202.

Morris, E. K., Higgins, S. T., Bickel, W. K., and Braukmann, C. J. (1987). An introduction to contemporary behaviorism: History, concepts, and a systematic analysis. In E. K. Morris and C. J. Braukmann (eds), *Behavioral Approaches to Crime and Delinquency: A Handbook of Application, Research, and Concepts*. New York: Plenum.

Morris, N. (1974). *The Future of Imprisonment*. Chicago: University of Chicago Press.

Morris, N. (1983). Mental illness and the criminal law. In P. Bean (ed.), *Mental Illness: Changes and Trends*. Chichester: Wiley.

Motandon, C., and Harding, T. (1984). The reliability of dangerousness assessments: A decision making exercise. *British Journal of Psychiatry*, **144**, 149–155.

Mowat, R. R. (1966). *Morbid Jealousy and Murder*. London: Tavistock.

Moyer, K. (1981). Biological substrates of aggression: Implications for control. In P. F. Brain and D. Benton (eds), *The Biology of Aggression*. Alphen aan der Rijn: Sijthoff and Noordhoff.

Moyes, T., Tennent, T. G. and Bedford, A.P. (1985). Long-term follow-up study of a ward-based behaviour modification programme for adolescents with acting-out and conduct problems. *British Journal of Psychiatry*, **147**, 300–305.

Mueller, C. W. (1983). Environmental stressors and aggressive behavior. In R. G. Geen and E. I. Donnerstein (eds), *Aggression: Theoretical and Empirical Reviews*, Volume 2. New York: Academic Press.

Mullen, P. E. (1990). The long-term influence of sexual assault on the mental health of victims. *Journal of Forensic Psychiatry*, **1**, 13–34.

Müller, D. J., Blackman, D. E., and Chapman, A. J. (eds) (1984). *Psychology and Law*. Chichester: Wiley.

Mulvey, E. P., and Larosa, J. F. (1986). Delinquency cessation and adolescent development: Preliminary data. *American Journal of Orthopsychiatry*, **56**, 212–224.

Mulvey, E. P., and Lidz, C. W. (1984). Clinical considerations in the prediction of dangerousness in mental patients. *Clinical Psychology Review*, **4**, 379–401.

Mungas, D. (1983). An empirical analysis of specific syndromes of violent behavior. *Journal of Nervous and Mental Disease*, **171**, 354–361.

Munsterberg, H. (1908). *On the Witness Stand*. New York: Doubleday.

Murphy, J. E. (1988). Date abuse and forced intercourse among college students. In G. T. Hotaling, D. Finkelhor, J. T. Kirkpatrick and M. A. Straus (eds), *Family Abuse and its Consequences: New Directions in Research*. Beverly Hills, Ca: Sage.

Murphy, W. D. (1990). Assessment and modification of cognitive distortions in sex offenders. In W. L. Marshall, D. R. Laws, and H. E. Barbaree (eds), *Handbook of Sexual Assault: Issues, Theories, and Treatment of the Offender*. New York: Plenum.

Murray, C. A. (1976). *The Link Between Learning Disabilities and Juvenile Delinquency.* Washington, DC: Office of Juvenile Justice and Delinquency.

Murray, D. J. (1989). *Review of Research on Re-offending of Mentally Disordered Offenders.* Research and Planning Unit Paper 55. London: Home Office.

Myers, R. G., and Berah, E. F. (1983). Some features of Australian exhibitionists compared with paedophiles. *Archives of Sexual Behavior*, **12**, 541–547.

Myers, T. (1982). Alcohol and violent crime re-examined: Self-reports from two sub-groups of Scottish male prisoners. *British Journal of Addictions*, **77**, 399–413.

Nass, M. L. (1966). The superego and moral development in the theories of Freud and Piaget. *Psychoanalytic Study of the Child*, **21**, 51–68.

Nassi, A. J., and Abramowitz, S. I. (1976). From phrenology to psychosurgery and back again: Biological studies of criminality. *American Journal of Orthopsychiatry*, **46**, 591-607.

Nelson, J. R., Smith, D. J., and Dodd, J. (1990). The moral reasoning of juvenile delinquents: A meta-analysis. *Journal of Abnormal Child Psychology*, **18**, 231–239.

Newman, D. J. (1956). Pleading guilty for considerations: A study of bargain justice. *Journal of Criminal Law, Criminology and Police Science*, **46**, 780–790.

Newman J. P., and Kosson, D. S. (1986). Passive avoidance learning in psychopathic and nonpsychopathic offenders. *Journal of Abnormal Psychology*, **95**, 252–256.

Newman, J. P., Widom, C. S., and Nathan, S. (1985). Passive avoidance in syndromes of disinhibition: Psychopathy and extraversion. *Journal of Personality and Social Psychology*, **48**, 1316–1327.

Newman, O. (1972). *Defensible Space: Crime Prevention Through Urban Design.* New York: Macmillan.

Newton, A. (1980). The effects of imprisonment. *Criminal Justice Abstracts*, **12**, 134–151.

Nicholson, R. C. (1970). Transactional analysis: A new method for helping offenders. *Federal Probation*, **34**, 29–39.

Nietzel, M. T. (1979). *Crime and its Modification: A Social Learning Perspective.* New York: Pergamon.

Nietzel, M. T., and Dillehay, R. C. (1986). *Psychological Consultation in the Courtroom.* New York: Pergamon.

Nietzel, M. T., and Himelein, M. J. (1986). Prevention of crime and delinquency. In B. A. Edelstein and L. Michelson (eds), *Handbook of Prevention.* New York: Plenum.

Nietzel, M. T., and Himelein, M. J. (1987). Probation and parole. In E. K. Morris and C. J. Braukmann (eds), *Behavioral Approaches to Crime and Delinquency: A Handbook of Application, Research, and Concepts.* New York: Plenum.

Nietzel, M. T., and Moss, C. S. (1972). The role of the psychologist in the criminal justice system. *Professional Psychology*, **3**, 259–270.

Noble, P., and Rodgers, S. (1989). Violence by psychiatric in-patients. *British Journal of Psychiatry*, **155**, 384–390.

Nomellini, S., and Katz, R. C. (1983). Effects of anger control training on abusive parents. *Cognitive Therapy and Research*, **7**, 57–68.

Normandeau, A. (1969). Robbery in Philadelphia and London. *British Journal of Criminology.* **9**, 71–79.

Normandeau, A. (1970). A comparative study of the weighted crime indices for eight countries. *International Criminal Police Review*, **25**, 15–18.

Norrie, A. (1986). Practical reasoning and criminal responsibility: A jurisprudential approach. In D. B. Cornish and R. V. Clarke (eds), *The Reasoning Criminal: Rational Choice Perspectives on Offending.* New York: Springer-Verlag.

Norris, M. (1983). Changes in patients during treatment at the Henderson Hospital therapeutic community during 1971–1981. *British Journal of Medical Psychology*, **56**, 135–143.

Novaco, R. W. (1978). Anger and coping with stress. In J. P. Foreyt and D. P. Rathjen (eds), *Cognitive Behavior Therapy.* New York: Plenum.

Novaco, R. W., and Welsh, W. N. (1989). Anger disturbances: Cognitive mediation and clinical prescriptions. In K. Howells and C. R. Hollin (eds), *Clinical Approaches to Violence*. Chichester: Wiley.

Nunner-Winkler, G. (1984). Two moralities?: A critical discussion of the ethic of care and responsibility versus the ethic of rights and justice. In W. M. Kurtines and J. L. Gewirtz (eds), *Moral Behaviour and Moral Development*. Chichester: Wiley.

Nurco, D. N., Ball, J. C., Shaffer, J. W., and Hanlon, T. E. (1985). The criminality of narcotic addicts. *Journal of Nervous and Mental Disease*, **173**, 94–102.

O'Callaghan, M. A. J. (1988). Bio-social influences on the control of aggression/aggressive behaviour in mental health settings. In T. E. Moffitt and S. A. Mednick (eds), *Biological Contributions to Crime Causation*. Dordrecht: Martinus Nijhoff.

O'Connor, A. A. (1987). Female sex offenders. *British Journal of Psychiatry*, **150**, 615–620.

Offord, D. R. (1982). Family backgrounds of male and female delinquents. In J. Gunn and D. P. Farrington (eds), *Abnormal Offenders, Delinquency, and the Criminal Justice System*. Chichester: Wiley.

Ogloff, J. R. P., Wong, S., and Greenwood, A. (1990). Treating criminal psychopaths in a therapeutic community program. *Behavioral Sciences and the Law*, **8**, 181–190.

O'Keefe, E., J. (1975). Porteus Maze Q score as a measure of impulsivity. *Perceptual and Motor Skills*, **41**, 675–678.

O'Leary, K., D., Barling, J., Arias, I., Rosenbaum, A., and Tyree, A. (1989). Prevalence and stability of physical aggression between spouses: A longitudinal analysis. *Journal of Consulting and Clinical Psychology*, **57**, 263–268.

Olejnik, A. (1980). Adults' moral reasoning with children. *Child Development*, **51**, 1285–1288. Ollendick, T. H., and Hersen, M. (1979). Social skills training for juvenile delinquents. *Behaviour Research and Therapy*, **17**, 547–554.

Olweus, D. (1979). Stability of aggressive reaction patterns in males: A review. *Psychological Bulletin*, **86**, 852–875.

Olweus, D. (1981). Continuity in aggressive and withdrawn, inhibited patterns. *Psychiatry and Social Science*, **1**, 141–159.

Olweus, D. (1986). Aggression and hormones: Behavioral relationship with testosterone and adrenaline. In D. Olweus, J. Block and M. Radke-Yarrow (eds), *Development of Antisocial and Prosocial Behavior*. New York: Academic Press.

Olweus, D., Mattson, A., Schalling, D., and Low, H. (1980). Testosterone, aggression, physical and personality dimensions in normal adolescent males. *Psychosomatic Medicine*, **42**, 263–269.

O'Neal, E., Brunault, M., Marquis, J., and Carifio, M. (1979). Anger and the body buffer zone. *Journal of Social Psychology*, **108**, 135–136.

Opton, E. M. (1975). Institutional behavior modification as a fraud and sham. *Arizona Law Review*, **17**, 20–28.

Orcutt, J. (1970). Self-concept and insulation against delinquency: some critical notes. *Sociological Quarterly*, **11**, 381–390.

Osborn, S. G., and West, D. J. (1980). Do adolescents really reform? *Journal of Adolescence*, **3**, 99–114.

Osgood, D. W., Johnson, L. D., O'Malley, P. M., and Bachman, J. G. (1988). The generality of deviance in late adolescence and early adulthood. *American Sociological Review*, **53**, 81–93.

Ostapiuk, E. (1982). Strategies for community intervention in offender rehabilitation: An overview. In M. P. Feldman (ed.), *Developments in the Study of Criminal Behaviour. Volume 1. Prevention and Control of Offending*. Chichester: Wiley.

Ostrom, T. M., Steele, C. M., Rosenblood, L. K., and Mirrels, H. L. (1971). Modification of delinquent behavior. *Journal of Applied Social Psychology*, **1**, 118–136.

Otterbein, K. F. (1979). A cross-cultural study of rape. *Aggressive Behavior*, **5**, 425–435.

Ounsted, C. (1969). Aggression and epilepsy. *Journal of Psychosomatic Research*, **13**, 237–242.

Ouston, J. (1984). Delinquency, family background and educational attainment. *British Journal of Criminology*, **24**, 2–26.

Overholser, J. C., and Beck, S. (1986). Multimethod assessment of rapists and child molesters and three control groups on behavioral and psychological measures. *Journal of Consulting and Clinical Psychology*, **54**, 682–687.

Overton, W. F. (1973). On the assumptive base of the nature–nurture controversy: Additive versus interactive conceptions. *Human Development*, **16**, 74–89.

Owen, D. R. (1972). The 47,XYY male: A review. *Psychological Bulletin*, **18**, 209–233.

Owens, R. G., and Ashcroft, J. B. (1982). Functional analysis in applied psychology. *British Journal of Clinical Psychology*, **21**, 181–190.

Ozer, D. J. (1985). Correlation and the coefficient of determination. *Psychological Bulletin*, **97**, 307–315.

Pachella, R. G. (1988). On the admissibility of psychological testimony in criminal justice proceedings. *Journal of Interpersonal Violence*, **3**, 111–114.

Palmer, J. (1977). Economic analyses of the deterrent effect of punishment: a review. *Journal of Research in Crime and Delinquency*, **14**, 4–21.

Palmer, T. (1974). The Youth Authority's Community Treatment Project. *Federal Probation*, **38**, 3–14.

Palmer, T. (1975). Martinson revisited. *Journal of Research in Crime and Delinquency*, **12**, 133–152.

Palmer, T. (1983). The effectiveness issue: An overview. *Federal Probation*, **47**, 3–10.

Palmstierna, T., and Wisredt, B. (1990). Risk factors for aggressive behaviour are of limited value for predicting the violent behaviour of acute involuntarily admitted patients. *Acta Psychiatrica Scandinavica*, **81**, 152–155.

Palys, T. S., and Divorski, S. (1984). Judicial decision-making: An examination of sentencing disparity among Canadian provincial court judges. In D. J. Müller, D. E. Blackman, and A. J. Chapman (eds), *Psychology and Law*. Chichester: Wiley.

Panton, J. J. (1958). MMPI profile configurations among crime classification groups. *Journal of Clinical Psychology*, **14**, 305–308.

Panton, J. J. (1979a). MMPI profile configurations associated with incestuous and non-incestuous child molesters. *Psychological Reports*, **45**, 335–338.

Panton, J. J. (1979b). Longitudinal post-validation of the MMPI Escape (Ec) and Prison Adjustment (Ap) scales. *Journal of Clinical Psychology*, **35**, 101–103.

Parke, R. D. (1974). Rules, roles, and resistance to deviation: Recent advances in punishment, discipline, and self control. *Minnesota Symposia on Child Psychology*. Volume 8. Minneapolis: University of Minnesota Press.

Parke, R. D. (1977). Socialisation into child abuse. In J. Tapp and F. Levine (eds), *Law, Justice, and the Individual in Society*. New York: Holt, Rinehart and Winston.

Parker, E. (1985). The development of secure provision. In L. Gostin (ed.), *Secure Provision: A Review of Special Services for the Mentally Ill and Mentally Handicapped in England and Wales*. London: Tavistock.

Parker, H., and Giller, H. (1981). More and less the same: British delinquency research since the sixties. *British Journal of Criminology*, **21**, 230–245.

Parker, J. G., and Asher, S. R. (1987). Peer relations and later personal adjustment: Are low accepted children at risk? *Psychological Bulletin*, **102**, 357–389.

Parloff, M. B. (1984). Psychotherapy research and its incredible credibility crisis. *Clinical Psychology Review*, **4**, 95–109.

Parrott, C. A., and Strongman, K. I. (1984). Locus of control and delinquency. *Adolescence*, **19**, 459–471.

Parsons, O. A., and Hart, R. P. (1984). Behavioral disorders associated with central nervous dysfunction. In H. E. Adams and P. B. Sutker (eds), *Comprehensive Handbook of Psychopathology*. New York: Plenum.

Pasewark, R. A. (1986). A review of research on the insanity defense. *Annals of the American Academy of Political and Social Science*, **484**, 100–114.

Pasewark, R. A., and Pantle, M. L. (1979). Insanity plea: Legislator's view. *American Journal of Psychiatry*, **136**, 222–223.

Pasewark, R. A., Pantle, M. L., and Steadman, H. J. (1982). Detention and rearrest rates of persons found not guilty by reason of insanity and convicted felons. *American Journal of Psychiatry*, **139**, 892–897.

Passingham, R. E. (1972). Crime and personality: A review of Eysenck's theory. In V. D. Nebylitsin and J. A. Gray (eds), *Biological Bases of Individual Behaviour*. New York: Academic Press.

Patterson, G. R. (1974). Interventions for boys with conduct problems: Multiple settings, treatments, and criteria. *Journal of Consulting and Clinical Psychology*, **42**, 471–481.

Patterson, G. R. (1982). *Coercive Family Process*. Eugene, Or: Castalia.

Patterson, G. R. (1986). Performance models for antisocial boys. *American Psychologist*, **41**, 432–444.

Patterson, G. R., and Stouthamer-Loeber, M. (1984). The correlation of family management practices and delinquency. *Child Development*, **55**, 1299–1307.

Patterson, G. R., Chamberlain, P., and Reid, J. B. (1982). A comparative evaluation of a parent-training program. *Behavior Therapy*, **13**, 638–650.

Patterson, G. R., DeBarsyshe, B. D., and Ramsey, E. (1989). A developmental perspective on antisocial behavior. *American Psychologist*, **44**, 329–335.

Pearson, M., Wilmot, E., and Padi, M. (1986). A study of violent behaviour among in-patients in a psychiatric hospital. *British Journal of Psychiatry*, **149**, 232–235.

Pease, K. (1985). Obscene telephone calls to women in England and Wales. *Howard Journal*, **24**, 275–281.

Pendleton, L. (1980). Treatment of persons found incompetent to stand trial. *American Journal of Psychiatry*, **137**, 1098–1100.

Penrose, L. S. (1939). Mental disease and crime: Outline of a comparative study of European statistics. *British Journal of Medical Psychology*, **18**, 1–15.

Perkins, D. E. (1987). A psychological treatment programme for sex offenders. In B. J. McGurk, D. M. Thornton and M. Williams (eds), *Applying Psychology to Imprisonment: Theory and Practice*. London: HMSO.

Pernanen, K. (1991). *Alcohol in Human Violence*. New York: Guilford.

Perry, D. G., Perry, L. C., and Rasmussen, P. (1986). Cognitive social learning mediators of aggression. *Child Development*, **57**, 700–711.

Persky, H., Smith, K. D., and Basu, G. (1971). Relation of psychologic measures of aggression and hostility to testosterone production in man. *Psychosomatic Medicine*, **33**, 265–277.

Persons, R. W. (1967). Relationship between psychotherapy with institutionalised boys and subsequent community adjustment. *Journal of Consulting and Clinical Psychology*, **31**, 137–141.

Petersen, K. G. I., Matousek, M., Mednick, S. A., Volavka, J., and Pollock, V. (1982). EEG antecedents of thievery. *Acta Psychiatrica Scandinavica*, **65**, 331–338.

Peterson, R., and Hagan, J. (1984). Changing conceptions of race: Towards an account of anomalous findings of sentencing research. *American Sociological Review*, **49**, 56–71.

Petrella, R. C., and Poythress, N. G. (1983). The quality of forensic evaluations: An interdisciplinary study. *Journal of Consulting and Clinical Psychology*, **51**, 76–85.

Petrie, A. (1967). *Individuality in Pain and Suffering*. Chicago: University of Chicago Press.

Phillips, D. P. (1983). The impact of mass media on homicide. *American Sociological Review*, **48**, 560–568.

Phillips, E. L. (1968). Achievement Place: Token reinforcement procedures in a home-style rehabilitation setting for pre-delinquent boys. *Journal of Applied Behavior Analysis*, **1**, 213–223.

Piaget, J. (1959). *Language and Thought of the Child*. London: Routledge and Kegan Paul.

Pichot, P. (1978). Psychopathic behaviour: A historical overview. In R. D. Hare and D. Schalling (eds), *Psychopathic Behaviour: Approaches to Research*. Chichester: Wiley.

Piliavin, I., and Briar, S. (1964). Police encounters with juveniles. *American Journal of Sociology*, **70**, 206–214.

Piliavin, I., Hardyck, A. J., and Vadum, A. C. (1968). Constraining effects of personal costs on the transgressions of juveniles. *Journal of Personality and Social Psychology*, **10**, 227–231.

Piliavin, I., Thornton, C., Gartner, R., and Matsueda, R. L. (1986). Crime, deterrence, and rational choice. *American Sociological Review*, **51**, 101–119.

Pithers, W. D. (1990). Relapse prevention with sexual aggressors: A method for maintaining therapeutic gain and enhancing external supervision. In W. L. Marshall, D. R. Laws and H. E. Barbaree (eds), *Handbook of Sexual Assault: Issues, Theories, and Treatment of the Offender*. New York: Plenum.

Pittman, D., and Handy, W. (1964). Patterns in criminal aggravated assault. *Journal of Criminal Law, Criminology and Police Science*, **55**, 462–470.

Planasky, K., and Johnson, R. (1977). Homicidal aggression in schizophrenic men. *Acta Psychiatrica Scandinavica*, **55**, 65–73.

Platt, J. J., and Prout, M. F. (1987). Cognitive–behavioral theory and interventions for crime and delinquency. In E. K. Morris and C. J. Braukmann (eds), *Behavioral Approaches to Crime and Delinquency: A Handbook of Application, Research, and Concepts*. New York: Plenum.

Platt, J. J., Scura, W., and Hannon, J. R. (1973). Problem-solving thinking of youthful incarcerated heroin addicts. *Journal of Community Psychology*, **1**, 278–281.

Plummer, K. (1979). Misunderstanding labelling perspectives. In D. Downes and P. Rock (eds), *Deviant Interpretations*. Oxford: Robertson.

Pokorny, A. D. (1965). Human violence: A comparison of homicide, aggravated assault and attempted suicide. *Journal of Criminal Law, Criminology and Police Science*, **56**, 488–497.

Pollock, N., McBain, I., and Webster, C. D. (1989). Clinical decision making and the assessment of dangerousness. In K. Howells and C. R. Hollin (eds), *Clinical Approaches to Violence*. Chichester: Wiley.

Porteus, S. D. (1959). *The Maze Test and Clinical Psychology*. Palo Alto: Pacific Books.

Powell, G. E., and Stewart, R. A. (1983). The relationship of personality to antisocial and neurotic behaviours as observed by teachers. *Personality and Individual Differences*, **4**, 97–100.

Power, M. J., Alderson, M. R., Phillipson, C. M., and Morris, J. N. (1967). Delinquent schools? *New Society*, **10**, 542–543.

Prentice-Dunn, S., and Rogers, R. W. (1983). Deindividuation in aggression. In R. G. Geen and E. I. Donnerstein (eds), *Aggression: Theoretical and Empirical Reviews*, Volume 2. New York: Academic Press.

Prentky, R. A., Cohen, M. L., and Seghorn, T. K. (1985). Development of a rational taxonomy for the classification of sexual offenders: Rapists. *Bulletin of the American Academy of Psychiatry and the Law*, **13**, 39–70.

Prentky, R. A., Burgess, A. W., Rokous, F., Lee, A., Hartman, C., Renler, R., and Douglas, J. (1989). The presumptive role of fantasy in serial sexual homicide. *American Journal of Psychiatry*, **146**, 887–891.

Preston, M. A., and Carnegie, J. (1989). Intermediate treatment: Working with offenders in the community. In C. Hollin and K. Howells (eds), *Clinical Approaches to Working With Offenders. Issues in Criminological and Legal Psychology. No. 14*. Leicester: British Psychological Society.

Price, R. H. (1978). *Abnormal Behavior: Perspectives in Conflict*. New York: Holt, Rinehart and Winston.

Price, W. H., Strong, J. A., Whatmore, P. B., and McClemont, W. F. (1966). Criminal patients with XYY sex-chromosome complement. *Lancet*, **1**, 565–566.

Prins, H. (1986). *Dangerous Behaviour, The Law, and Mental Disorder*. London: Tavistock.

Pritchard, D. A. (1979). Stable predictors of recidivism: A summary. *Criminology*, **17**, 15–21.

Ptacek, J. (1988). The clinical literature on men who batter: A review and critique. In

G. T. Hotaling, D. Finkelhor, J. T. Kirkpatrick and M. A. Straus (eds), *Family Abuse and Its Consequences: New Directions in Research*. Beverly Hills, Ca: Sage.

Pulkinnen, L. (1986). The role of impulse control in the development of antisocial and prosocial behavior. In D. Olweus, J. Block and M. Radke-Yarrow (eds), *Development of Antisocial and Prosocial Behavior: Research, Theories, and Issues*. New York: Academic Press.

Pyle, G. F. (1976). Spatial and temporal aspects of crime in Cleveland, Ohio. *American Behavioral Scientist*, **20**, 175–198.

Quay, H. C. (1965). Psychopathic personality as pathological stimulation seeking. *American Journal of Psychiatry*, **122**, 180–183.

Quay, H. C. (1977a). Measuring dimensions of deviant behavior: The Behavior Problem Checklist. *Journal of Abnormal Child Psychology*, **5**, 277–287.

Quay, H. C. (1977b). Psychopathic behavior: Reflections on its nature, origins, and treatment. In F. Weizmann and I. Uzigiris (eds), *The Structuring of Experience*. New York: Plenum.

Quay, H. C. (1977c). The three faces of evaluation: What can be expected to work. *Criminal Justice and Behavior*, **4**, 341–354.

Quay, H. C. (1984). *Managing Adult Inmates*. American Correctional Association.

Quay, H. C. (1986). The behavioral reward and inhibition systems in childhood behavior disorder. In L. M. Bloomingdale (ed.), *Attention Deficit Disorder*. Volume 3. New York: Spectrum.

Quay, H. C. (1987a). Patterns of delinquent behavior. In H. C. Quay (ed.), *Handbook of Juvenile Delinquency*. New York: Wiley.

Quay, H. C. (1987b). Intelligence. In H. C. Quay (ed.), *Handbook of Juvenile Delinquency*. New York: Wiley.

Quay, H. C., and Love, C. T. (1977). The effects of a juvenile diversion program on rearrests. *Criminal Justice and Behavior*, **4**, 377–396.

Quinn, J. T., Harbison, J. J., and McAllister, H. (1970). An attempt to shape penile response. *Behaviour Research and Therapy*, **8**, 212–216.

Quinney, R. (1974). *Critique of Legal Order*. Boston: Little, Brown.

Quinsey, V. L. (1984). Sexual aggression: Studies of offenders against women. In D. Weisstub (ed.), *Law and Mental Health: International Perspectives*, Volume 1. New York: Pergamon.

Quinsey, V. L. (1986). Men who have sex with children. In D. Weisstub (ed.), *Law and Mental Health: International Perspectives*. Volume 2. New York: Pergamon.

Quinsey, V. L. (1988). Assessment of the treatability of forensic patients. *Behavioral Sciences and the Law*, **6**, 443–452.

Quinsey, V. L., and Abtman, R. (1979). Variables affecting psychiatrists' and teachers' assessments of the dangerousness of mentally ill offenders. *Journal of Consulting and Clinical Psychology*, **47**, 353–362.

Quinsey, V. L., and Earls, C. M. (1990). The modification of sexual preferences. In W. L. Marshall, D. R. Laws and H. E. Barbaree (eds), *Handbook of Sexual Assault: Issues, Theories, and Treatment of the Offender*. New York: Plenum.

Quinsey, V. L., and Laws, D. R. (1990). Validity of physiological measures of sexual arousal in a sexual offender population: A critique of Hall, Proctor, and Nelson. *Journal of Consulting and Clinical Psychology*, **58**, 886–888.

Quinsey, V. L., and Maguire, A. (1986). Maximum security psychiatric patients: Actuarial and clinical prediction of dangerousness. *Journal of Interpersonal Violence*, **1**, 143–171.

Quinsey, V. L., and Marshall, W. L. (1983). Procedures for reducing inappropriate sexual arousal: An evaluative review. In J. G. Greer and I. R. Stuart (eds), *The Sexual Aggressor*. New York: Van Nostrand Reinhold.

Quinsey, V. L., Chaplin, T. C., and Upfold, D. (1984). Sexual arousal to non-sexual violence and sadomasochistic themes among rapists and non-sex offenders. *Journal of Consulting and Clinical Psychology*, **52**, 651–657.

Quinsey, V. L., Maguire, A., and Varney, G. W. (1983). Assertion and overcontrolled hostility among mentally disordered murderers. *Journal of Consulting and Clinical Psychology*, **51**, 550–556.

Quinsey, V. L., Warneford, A., Pruesse, M., and Link, N. (1975). Released Oak Ridge patients: A follow-up study of review board discharges. *British Journal of Criminology*, **15**, 264–270.

Rabkin, J. G. (1979). Criminal behavior of discharged mental patients: A critical appraisal of the literature. *Psychological Bulletin*, **86**, 1–29.

Rachlin, S., Halpern, A. L., and Portnow, S. L. (1984). The volitional rule, personality disorders and the insanity defense. *Psychiatric Annals*, **14**, 139–147.

Rachman, S. (1977). The conditioning theory of fear-acquisition: A critical examination. *Behaviour Research and Therapy*, **15**, 375–387.

Rada, R. T. (1978). *Clinical Aspects of the Rapist*. New York: Grune and Stratton.

Rada, R. T., Laws, D. R., and Kellner, R. (1976). Plasma testosterone levels in the rapist. *Psychosomatic Medicine*, **38**, 257–268.

Radden, J. (1985). *Madness and Reason*. London: Allen and Unwin.

Rader, C. M. (1977). MMPI profile types of exposers, rapists and assaulters in a court service population. *Journal of Consulting and Clinical Psychology*, **45**, 61–69.

Raine, A. (1986). Effect of early environment on electrodermal and cognitive correlates of schizotypy and psychopathy in criminals. *International Journal of Psychophysiology*, **4**, 277–287.

Raine, A. (1989). Evoked potentials and psychopathy. *International Journal of Psychophysiology*, **4**, 277–287.

Raine, A., and Venables, P. H. (1981). Classical conditioning and socialisation—a biosocial interaction. *Personality and Individual Differences*, **2**, 273–283.

Raine, A., and Venables, P. H. (1984). Tonic heart rate level, social class and antisocial behaviour in adolescents. *Biological Psychology*, **18**, 123–132.

Raine, A., and Venables, P. H. (1987). Contingent negative variation, P3 evoked potentials, and antisocial behavior. *Psychophysiology*, **24**, 191–199.

Rankin, J. H. (1983). The family context of delinquency. *Social Problems*, **30**, 466–479.

Rankin, R. J., and Wikoff, R. L. (1964). The IES Arrow Dot performance of delinquents and nondelinquents. *Perceptual Motor Skills*, **18**, 207–210.

Rapaport, K., and Burkhart, B. R. (1984). Personality and attitude characteristics of sexually coercive college males. *Journal of Abnormal Psychology*, **93**, 216–221.

Rasch, W. (1981). The effects of indeterminate detention: A study of men sentenced to life imprisonment. *International Journal of Law and Psychiatry*, **4**, 417–431.

Raskin, D. C. (1988). Does science support polygraph testing? In A. Gale (ed.), *The Polygraph Test: Lies, Truth and Science*. London: Sage.

Rathus, S. A., and Siegel, L. J. (1980). Crime and personality revisited: Effects of MMPI response sets in self-report studies. *Criminology*, **18**, 245–251.

Rauma, D., and Berk, R. A. (1987). Remuneration and recidivism: The long-term impact of unemployment compensation on ex-offenders. *Journal of Quantitative Criminology*, **3**, 3–28.

Raush, H. L. (1965). Interaction sequences. *Journal of Personality and Social Psychology*, **2**, 487–499.

Reckless, W. C. (1961). *The Crime Problem*. New York: Appleton-Century-Crofts.

Reckless, W. C., and Dinitz, S. (1967). Pioneering with self-concept as a vulnerability factor in delinquency. *Journal of Criminal Law, Criminology and Police Science*, **58**, 515–523.

Reicher, S., and Emler, N. (1986). Managing reputations in adolescence: The pursuit of delinquent and non-delinquent identities. In H. Beloff (ed.), *Getting into Life*. London: Methuen.

Reid, I. D. (1982). The development and maintenance of a behavioural regime in a secure youth treatment centre. In M. P. Feldman (ed.), *Developments in the Study of Criminal Behaviour. Volume 1: The Prevention and Control of Offending*. Chichester: Wiley.

Reis, D. J. (1974). Central neurotransmitters in aggression. *Research Publications of the Association for Research in Nervous and Mental Diseases*, **52**, 119–148.

Reitsma-Street, M., and Leschied, A. W. (1988). The concept-level matching model in corrections. *Criminal Justice and Behavior*, **15**, 92–108.

Reitsma-Street, M., Offord, D. R., and Finch, T. (1985). Pairs of same-sexed siblings discordant for antisocial behaviour. *British Journal of Psychiatry*, **146**, 415–423.

Remington, B., and Remington, M. (1987). Behavior modification in probation work: A review and evaluation. *Criminal Justice and Behavior*, **14**, 156–174.

Renwick, S., and Emler, N. (1984). Moral reasoning and delinquent behaviour among students. *British Journal of Social Psychology*, **23**, 281–283.

Renwick, S., and Emler, N. (1991). The relationship between social skills deficits and juvenile delinquency. *British Journal of Clinical Psychology*, **30**, 61–72.

Repucci, N. D., and Clingempeel, W. G. (1978). Methodological issues in research with correctional populations. *Journal of Consulting and Clinical Psychology*, **46**, 727–746.

Rescorla, R. A. (1988). Pavlovian conditioning: It's not what you think it is. *American Psychologist*, **43**, 151–160.

Ressler, R. K., Burgess, A. W., Douglas, J. E., Hartman, C. R., and D'Agostino, R. B. (1986). Sexual killers and their victims: Identifying patterns through crime scene analysis. *Journal of Interpersonal Violence*, **1**, 288–308.

Ressler, R. K., Burgess, A. W., Hartman, C. R., Douglas, J. E., and McCormack, A. (1986). Murderers who rape and mutilate. *Journal of Interpersonal Violence*, **1**, 273–287.

Rettig, S. (1964). Ethical risk-taking sensitivity in male prisoners. *British Journal of Criminology*, **4**, 582–590.

Rettig, S., and Rawson, H. E. (1963). The risk hypothesis in predictive judgments of unethical behavior. *Journal of Abnormal and Social Psychology*, **66**, 243–248.

Reynolds, D. (1976). The delinquent school. In M. Hammersley and P. Woods (eds), *The Process of Schooling*. London: Routledge and Kegan Paul.

Rice, M. E., Quinsey, V. L., and Houghton, R. (1990). Predicting treatment outcome and recidivism among patients in a maximum security token economy. *Behavioral Sciences and the Law*, **8**, 313–326.

Richard, B. A., and Dodge, K. A. (1982). Social maladjustment and problem-solving in school aged children. *Journal of Consulting and Clinical Psychology*, **50**, 226–233.

Richards, B. (1978). The experience of long-term imprisonment. *British Journal of Criminology*, **18**, 162–169.

Richman, C., Brown, K., and Clark, M. (1984). The relationship between self-esteem and maladaptive behaviors in high school students. *Social Behavior and Personality*, **12**, 177–185.

Riddle, M., and Roberts, A. H. (1977). Delinquency, delay of gratification, recidivism, and the Porteus Maze Tests. *Psychological Bulletin*, **84**, 417–425.

Riess, A. J., and Rhodes, A. L. (1964). An empirical test of differential association theory. *Journal of Research in Crime and Delinquency*, **1**, 5–18.

Rimé, B., Bouvy, H., LeBorgne, B., and Rouillon, F. (1978). Psychopathy and nonverbal behavior in an interpersonal situation. *Journal of Abnormal Psychology*, **87**, 636–643.

Roberts, A. H., Erikson, R. V., Riddle, M., and Bacon, J. G. (1974). Demographic variables, base rates, and personality characteristics associated with recidivism in male delinquents. *Journal of Consulting and Clinical Psychology*, **42**, 833–841.

Roberts, R. J., and Weerts, T. C. (1982). Cardiovascular responding during anger and fear imagery. *Psychological Reports*, **50**, 219–230.

Robertson, G. (1989). Treatment for offender patients: How should success be measured? *Medicine, Science, and the Law*, **29**, 303–307.

Robertson, G., and Gunn, J. (1987). A ten year follow-up of men discharged from Grendon prison. *British Journal of Psychiatry*, **151**, 674–678.

Robins, L. (1978). Sturdy predictors of adult antisocial behaviour: Replications from longitudinal studies. *Psychological Medicine*, **8**, 611–622.

Robins, L., West, P. A., and Herjanic, B. L. (1975). Arrests and delinquency in two generations: A study of black urban families and their children. *Journal of Child Psychology and Psychiatry*, **16**, 125–140.

Robins, L., Helzer, J. E., Weissner, M. M., Orvaschel, H., Gruenberg, E., Burke, J. D., and Regier, D. A. (1984). Lifetime prevalence of specific psychiatric disorder in three sites. *Archives of General Psychiatry*, **41**, 949–958.

Robinson, N. (1974). Harm, offence, and nuisance. *American Psychologist*, **29**, 233–238.

Robinson, W. S. (1950). Ecological correlations and the behavior of individuals. *American Sociological Review*, **15**, 351–357.

Rock, P. (1979). The sociology of crime, symbolic interactionism, and some problematic qualities of radical criminology. In D. Downes and P. Rock (eds), *Deviant Interpretations*. Oxford: Robertson.

Rodin, E. A. (1973). Psychomotor epilepsy and aggressive behavior. *Archives of General Psychiatry*, **28**, 210–213.

Roesch, R., and Golding, S. L. (1987). Defining and assessing competency to stand trial. In I. B. Weiner and A. K. Hess (eds), *Handbook of Forensic Psychology*. New York: Wiley.

Rogers, R. (1987). APA's position on the insanity defense: Empiricism versus emotionalism. *American Psychologist*, **42**, 840–848.

Rojek, D. G., and Erickson, M. L. (1982). Delinquent careers: A test of the escalation model. *Criminology*, **20**, 5–28.

Rohrbeck, C. A., and Twentyman, C. T. (1986). Multimodal assessment of impulsiveness in abusing, neglecting, and nonmaltreating mothers and their preschool children. *Journal of Consulting and Clinical Psychology*, **54**, 231–236.

Rollin, H. R. (1969). *The Mentally Abnormal Offender and the Law*. Oxford: Pergamon.

Rooth, G.(1973). Exhibitionism, sexual violence and paedophilia. *British Journal of Psychiatry*, **122**, 705–710.

Rosch, E. (1978). Principles of categorisation. In E. Rosch and B. B. Lloyd (eds), *Cognition and Categorisation*. Hillsdale, NJ: Erlbaum.

Rose, S. (1987). *Molecules and Minds: Essays on Biology and the Social Order*. Milton Keynes: Open University Press.

Rose, S., Kamin, L. J., and Lewontin, R. C. (1984). *Not in Our Genes: Biology, Ideology and Human Nature*. Harmondsworth: Penguin.

Rosen, A., and Schalling, D. (1974). On the validity of the California Psychological Inventory Socialisation scale: A multivariate approach. *Journal of Consulting and Clinical Psychology*, **42**, 757–765.

Rosenbaum. A., and O'Leary, K. D. (1981). Marital violence: characteristics of abusive couples. *Journal of Consulting and Clinical Psychology*, **49**, 63–71.

Rosenberg, F., and Rosenberg, M. (1978). Self-esteem and delinquency. *Journal of Youth and Adolescence*, **7**, 279–291.

Rosenberg, M. S., and Repucci, N. D. (1985). Primary prevention of child abuse. *Journal of Consulting and Clinical Psychology*, **53**, 576–585.

Ross, H. L. (1973). Law, science, and accidents: The British Road Safety Act of 1967. *Journal of Legal Studies*, **2**, 1–78.

Ross, H. L., and Glaser, E. M. (1973). Making it out of the ghetto. *Professional Psychology*, **4**, 347–356.

Ross, R. R., and Fabiano, E. A. (1985). *Time to Think: A Cognitive Model of Delinquency Prevention and Offender Rehabilitation*. Johnson City, Ten: Institute of Social Sciences and Arts.

Ross, R. R., and Mackay, H. B. (1976). A study of institutional treatment programs. *International Journal of Offender Therapy and Comparative Criminology*, **20**, 165–173.

Ross, R. R., and Price, M. J. (1976). Behavior modification in corrections: Autopsy before mortification. *International Journal of Criminology and Penology*, **4**, 305–315.

Ross, R. R., Fabiano, E. A., and Ewles, C. D. (1988). Reasoning and rehabilitation. *International Journal of Offender Therapy and Comparative Criminology*, **20**, 29–35.

Rossi, P. H., Waite, E., Bose, C. E., and Berk, R. E. (1974). The seriousness of crimes, normative structure and individual differences. *American Sociological Review*, **39**, 224–237.

Rotenberg, M. (1974). Conceptual and methodological notes on affective and cognitive role-taking (sympathy and empathy): An illustrative experiment with delinquent and nondelinquent boys. *Journal of Genetic Psychology*, **125**, 177–185.

Rotter, J. B. (1975). Some problems and misconceptions related to the construct of internal versus external control of reinforcement. *Journal of Consulting and Clinical Psychology*, **43**, 56–67.

Rotton, J., and Frey, J. (1985). Air pollution, weather, and violent crimes: Concomitant time-series analysis of archival data. *Journal of Personality and Social Psychology*, **49**, 1207–1220.

Rourke, B. P. (1988). Socioemotional disturbances of learning disabled children. *Journal of Consulting and Clinical Psychology*, **56**, 801–810.

Rowe, D. (1983). Biometric genetic models of self-reported delinquent behavior: A twin study. *Behavioral Genetics*, **13**, 473–489.

Rowe, D. C., and Osgood, D. W. (1984). Heredity and sociological theories of delinquency: A reconsideration. *American Sociological Review*, **49**, 526–540.

Rule, B. G., and Nesdale, A. R. (1976). Emotional arousal and aggressive behavior. *Psychological Bulletin*, **83**, 851–863.

Ruma, E. H., and Mosher, D. L. (1967). Relationship between moral judgment and guilt in delinquent boys. *Journal of Abnormal Psychology*, **72**, 122–127.

Rushton, J. F., and Christjohn, R. D. (1981). Extraversion, neuroticism, psychoticism and self-reported delinquency: Evidence from eight separate samples. *Personality and Individual Differences*, **2**, 11–20.

Rushton, J. P. (1990). Race and crime: A reply to Roberts and Gabor. *Canadian Journal of Criminology*, **32**, 315–334.

Rushton, J. P., Fulker, D. W., Neale, M. C., Nias, D. K. B. and Eysenck, H. J. (1986). Altruism and aggression: The heritability of individual differences. *Journal of Personality and Social Psychology*, **50**, 1192–1198.

Russell, D. E. H. (1984). *Sexual Exploitation: Rape, Child Sexual Abuse, and Workplace Harrassment*. Beverly Hills, Ca: Sage.

Rutter, M. (1971). Parent–child separation: Psychological effects on the children. *Journal of Child Psychology and Psychiatry*, **12**, 233–260.

Rutter, M. (1982). Syndromes attributable to "minimal brain dysfunction" in childhood. *American Journal of Psychiatry*, **139**, 21–33.

Rutter, M. (1987). Psychosocial resilience and protective mechanisms. *American Journal of Orthopsychiatry*, **57**, 316-331.

Rutter, M., and Giller, H. (1983). *Juvenile Delinquency: Trends and Perspectives*. Harmondsworth: Penguin.

Rutter, M., Maugham, B., Mortimore, P., and Ouston, J. (1979). *Fifteen Thousand Hours: Secondary Schools and Their Effects on Children*. London: Open Books.

Safran, J. D. (1990). Toward a refinement of cognitive therapy in light of interpersonal theory: 1. Theory. *Clinical Psychology Review*, **10**, 87–105.

Saklofse, D. H. (1977). Antisocial behavior and psychoticism in adolescent schoolboys. *Psychological Reports*, **41**, 425–526.

Salter, A. C. (1988). *Treating Child Sex Offenders and Victims: A Practical Guide*. Newbury Park, Ca: Sage.

Sanday, P. R. (1981). The sociocultural context of rape. *Journal of Social Issues*, **37**, 5–27.

Sandhu, H. J. (1970). Therapy with violent psychopaths in an Indian prison community. *International Journal of Offender Therapy*, **14**, 138–144.

Santrock, J. W. (1975). Father absence, perceived maternal behavior, and moral development in boys. *Child Development*, **46**, 753–757.

Sapp, A. D., and Vaughn, M. S. (1990). Juvenile sex offender treatment at state-operated correctional institutions. *International Journal of Offender Therapy and Comparative Criminology*, **34**, 131–146.

Sappington, A. A. (1990). Recent psychological approaches to the free will versus determinism issue. *Psychological Bulletin*, 108, 19–29.

Sapsford, R. (1983). *Life Sentence Prisoners: Reaction, Response and Change*. Milton Keynes: Open University Press.

Sarason, I. G. (1968). Verbal learning, modeling, and juvenile delinquency. *American Psychologist*, 23, 254–266.

Sarason, I. G. (1978). A cognitive social learning approach to juvenile delinquency. In R. D. Hare and D. Schalling (eds), *Psychopathic Behaviour: Approaches to Research*. Chichester: Wiley.

Sarason, I. G., and Ganzer, V. J. (1968). Concerning the medical model. *American Psychologist*, 23, 507–510.

Sarbin, T. R. (1967). On the futility of the proposition that some people be labelled "mentally ill". *Journal of Consulting Psychology*, 31, 447–453.

Sarbin, T. R. (1979). The myth of the criminal type. In T. R. Sarbin (ed.), *Challenges to the Criminal Justice System: The Perspective of Community Psychology*. New York: Human Services Press.

Satterfield, J. H. (1978). The hyperactive child syndrome: A precursor of adult psychopathy? In R. D. Hare and D. Schalling (eds), *Psychopathic Behaviour: Approaches to Research*. Chichester: Wiley.

Satterfield, J. H., Hoppe, C. M., and Schell, A. M. (1982). A prospective study of delinquency in 110 adolescent boys with attention deficit disorder and 88 normal adolescent boys. *American Journal of Psychiatry*, 139, 795–798.

Saulnier, K., and Perlman, D. (1981). Inmates' attributions: Their antecedents and effects on coping. *Criminal Justice and Behavior*, 8, 159–172.

Saunders, J. T., Repucci, N. D., and Sarata, B. P. (1973). An examination of impulsivity as a trait characterising delinquent youth. *American Journal of Orthopsychiatry*, 43, 789–795.

Saunders, W. M., and Kershaw, P. W. (1978). The prevalence of problem drinking and alcoholism in the West of Scotland. *British Journal of Psychiatry*, 133, 493–499.

Sawyer, J. (1966). Measurement and prediction, clinical and statistical. *Psychological Bulletin*, 66, 178–200.

Scarr, S., and Carter-Saltzman, L. (1979). Twin method: Defense of a critical assumption. *Behavior Genetics*, 9, 527–542.

Scarr, S., and McCartney, K. (1983). How people make their own environments: A theory of genotype -> environment effects. *Child Development*, 54, 424–435.

Schacter, S. (1964). The interaction of cognitive and physiological determinants of emotional state. In L. Berkowitz (ed.), *Advances in Experimental Social Psychology*, Volume 1. New York: Academic Press.

Schacter, S., and Latané, B. (1964). Crime, cognition, and the autonomic nervous system. In D. Levine (ed.), *Nebraska Symposium on Motivation*. Lincoln: University of Nebraska Press.

Schalling, D. (1978). Psychopathy-related personality variables and the psychophysiology of socialisation. In R. D. Hare and D. Schalling (eds), *Psychopathic Behaviour: Approaches to Research*. Chichester: Wiley.

Schalling, D., and Rosen, A. S. (1968). Porteus Maze differences between psychopathic and non-psychopathic criminals. *British Journal of Social and Clinical Psychology*, 7, 224–228.

Schalling, D., Asberg, M., Adman, G., and Oreland, L. (1987). Markers for vulnerability to psychopathology: Temperament traits associated with platelet MAO activity. *Acta Psychiatrica Scandinavica*, 76, 172–182.

Schalling, D., Lidberg, L., Levander, S. E., and Dahlin, Y. (1973). Spontaneous autonomic activity as related to psychopathy. *Biological Psychology*, 1, 83–97.

Scharf, P., and Hickey, J. (1976). The prison and the inmate's conception of legal justice: An experiment in democratic education. *Criminal Justice and Behavior*, 3, 107–122.

Schiavi, R. C., Thielgaard, A., Owen, D. R., and White, D. (1984). Sex chromosome anomalies, hormones and aggressivity. *Archives of General Psychiatry*, **41**, 93–99.

Schichor, D. (1980). The new criminology: Some critical issues. *British Journal of Criminology*, **20**, 1–19.

Schlichter, K. J., and Horan, J. J. (1981). Effects of stress inoculation on the anger and aggression management skills of institutionalised juvenile delinquents. *Cognitive Therapy and Research*, **5**, 359–365.

Schmideberg, M. (1961). Psychotherapy of the criminal psychopath. *Archives of Criminal Dynamics*, **4**, 724–735.

Schmauk, F. J. (1970). Punishment, arousal, and avoidance learning in sociopaths. *Journal of Abnormal Psychology*, **76**, 325–335.

Schneider, K. (1950). *Psychopathic Personalities*, Ninth Edition. London: Cassell.

Schoenthaler, S. J. (1983). Diet and delinquency: A multi-state replication. *International Journal of Biosocial Research*, **5**, 70–78.

Schroeder, M. L., Wormworth, J. A., and Livesley, W. J. (1992). Dimensions of personality disorder and their relationships to the big five dimensions of personality. *Psychological Assessment*, **4**, 47–53.

Schwartz, R. A., and Schwartz, I. K. (1976). Are personality disorders diseases? *Diseases of the Nervous System*, **86**, 613–617.

Schwartz, R. D., and Orleans, S. (1967). On legal sanctions. *University of Chicago Law Review*, **34**, 274–300.

Schweinhart, L. (1987). Can preschool programs help prevent delinquency? In J. Q. Wilson and G. C. Loury (eds), *From Children to Citizens. Volume 3. Families, Schools, and Delinquency Prevention*. New York: Springer-Verlag.

Schwendinger, H., and Schwendinger, J. (1970). Defenders of order or guardians of human rights? *Issues in Criminology*, **5**, 123–157.

Schwitzgebel, R. L. (1967). Short-term operant conditioning of adolescent offenders on socially relevant variables. *Journal of Abnormal Psychology*, **72**, 134–142.

Scott, W. A. (1958). Research definitions of mental health and mental illness. *Psychological Bulletin*, **55**, 29–46.

Scully, D., and Marolla, J. (1985). Riding the bull at Gilley's: Convicted rapists describe the rewards of rape. *Social Problems*, **32**, 233–251.

Sechrest, L. (1987). Classification for treatment. In D. M. Gottfredson and M. Tonry (eds), *Prediction and Classification: Criminal Justice Decision Making*. Chicago: University of Chicago Press.

Sechrest, L., White, S. O., and Brown, E. D. (1979). *The Rehabilitation of Criminal Offenders: Problems and Prospects*. Washington, DC: National Academy of Sciences.

Secord, P. F. (1983). Explanation in the social sciences and in life situations. Paper presented at a conference on Potentialities of Knowledge in the Social Sciences, University of Chicago.

Secord, P. F. (1986). Social psychology as a science. In J. Margolis, P. Manicas, R. Harré and P. F. Secord (eds), *Psychology: Designing the Discipline*. Oxford: Blackwell.

Segal, Z. V., and Marshall, W. L. (1985). Heterosexual social skills in a population of rapists and child molesters. *Journal of Consulting and Clinical Psychology*, **53**, 55–63.

Segal, Z. V., and Stermac, L. E. (1990). The role of cognition in sexual assault. In W. L. Marshall, D. R. Laws and H. E. Barbaree (eds), *Handbook of Sexual Assault: Issues, Theories, and Treatment of the Offender*. New York: Plenum.

Selby, M. J. (1984). Assessment of violence potential using measures of anger, hostility, and social desirability. *Journal of Personality Assessment*, **48**, 531–544.

Sellin, T. (1938). *Culture Conflict and Crime*. New York: Social Science Research Council.

Sellin, T., and Wolfgang, M. E. (1964). *The Measurement of Delinquency*. New York: Wiley.

Sepejak, D. S., Webster, C. D., and Menzies, R. J. (1984). The clinical prediction of dangerousness: Getting beyond the basic questions. In D. J. Müller, D. E. Blackman and A. J. Chapman (eds), *Psychology and Law*. Chichester: Wiley.

Serber, M. (1970). Shame aversion therapy. *Journal of Behavior Therapy and Experimental Psychiatry*, **1**, 213–215.

Serin, R. C. (1991). Psychopathy and violence in criminals. *Journal of Interpersonal Violence*, **6**, 423–431.

Serna, L. A., Schumaker, J. B., Hazel, J. S., and Sheldon, J. B. (1986). Teaching reciprocal social skills to parents and their delinquent adolescents. *Journal of Clinical Child Psychology*, **15**, 64–77.

Shah, S. A. (1978). Dangerousness: A paradigm for exploring some issues in law and psychology. *American Psychologist*, **33**, 224–238.

Shah, S. A., and Roth, L. H. (1974). Biological and psychophysiological factors in criminality. In D. Glaser (ed.), *Handbook of Criminology*. Chicago: Rand McNally.

Shanok, S. S., and Lewis, D. O. (1981). Medical histories of female delinquents. *Archives of General Psychiatry*, **38**, 211–213.

Shapiro, D. (1965). *Neurotic Styles*. New York: Basic Books.

Shaw, C. R., and McKay, H. D. (1942). *Juvenile Delinquency and Urban Areas*. Chicago: University of Chicago Press.

Sheard, M. H., Marini, J. L., Bridges, C. I., and Wagner, E. (1976). The effect of lithium on impulsive aggressive behavior in man. *American Journal of Psychiatry*, **133**, 1409–1413.

Sheldon, W. H. (1949). *Varieties of Delinquent Youth*. New York: Harper.

Shields, N. M., and Hanneke, C. R. (1988). Multiple sexual victimisation: The case of incest and marital rape. In G. T Hotaling, D. Finkelhor, J. T. Kirkpatrick and M. A. Straus (eds), *Family Abuse and its Consequences: New Directions in Research*. Beverly Hills, Ca: Sage.

Shinohara, M., and Jenkins, R. L. (1967). MMPI study of three types of delinquents. *Journal of Clinical Psychology,* **23**, 156–163.

Shore, M. F., and Massimo, J. L. (1979). Fifteen years after treatment: A follow-up study to comprehensive vocationally oriented psychotherapy. *American Journal of Orthopsychiatry*, **49**, 240–245.

Short, R. J., and Simeonsson, R. J. (1986). Social cognition and aggression in delinquent adolescent males. *Adolescence*, **21**, 159–176.

Shover, N. (1983). The later stages of ordinary property offender careers. *Social Problems*, **31**, 208–218.

Shupe, L. M. (1954). Alcohol and crime: A study of the urine alcohol concentration found in 882 persons arrested during 8 hours immediately after commission of a felony. *Journal of Criminal Law, Criminology and Police Science*, **44**, 661–664.

Siddle, D. A. T., Mednick, S. A., Nicol, A. R., and Foggit, R. H. (1976). Skin conductance recovery in antisocial adolescents. *British Journal of Social and Clinical Psychology*, **15**, 425–428.

Siegel, R. A. (1978). Probability of punishment and suppression of behavior in psychopathic and nonpsychopathic offenders. *Journal of Abnormal Psychology*, **87**, 514–522.

Siegman, A. W. (1966). Effects of auditory stimulation and intelligence on time estimation in delinquents and nondelinquents. *Journal of Consulting Psychology*, **30**, 320–328.

Silva, F., Martorell, C., and Clemente, A. (1986). Socialisation and personality: Study through questionnaires in a preadult Spanish population. *Personality and Individual Differences*, **7**, 355–372.

Silverman, D. C., Kalich, S. M., Bowie, S. I., and Edbiel, S. E. (1988). Blitz rape and confidence rape: A typology applied to 1,000 consecutive cases. *American Journal of Psychiatry*, **145**, 1438–1441.

Silverman, J., Buchsbaum, M. S., and Stierlin, H. (1973). Sex differences in perceptual differentiation and stimulus intensity control. *Journal of Personality and Social Psychology*, **25**, 309–318.

Simon, F. H. (1971). *Prediction Methods in Criminology*. London: HMSO.

Simon, H. A. (1978). Rationality as a process and product of thought. *American Economic Review*, **8**, 1–11.

Simon, R. J., and Baxter, S. (1989). Gender and violent crime. In N. A. Weiner and M. E. Wolfgang (eds), *Violent Crime, Violent Criminals*. Newbury Park, Ca: Sage.

Simon, W. T., and Schouten, P. G. W. (1991). Plethysmography in the assessment and treatment of sexual deviance. *Archives of Sexual Behavior*, **20**, 75–91.

Sinclair, I. A. C., Shaw, M. J., and Troop, J. (1974). The relationship between introversion and response to casework in a prison setting. *British Journal of Social and Clinical Psychology*, **13**, 51–60.

Singer, J. L. (1955). Delay of gratification and ego development: Implications for clinical and experimental research. *Journal of Consulting Psychology*, **19**, 259–266.

Singh, A. (1979). Reliability and validity of self-reported delinquency studies. *Psychological Reports*, **44**, 987–993.

Skinner, B. F. (1953). *Science and Human Behavior*. New York: Free Press.

Skinner, B. F. (1978). *Reflections on Behaviorism and Society*. Englewood Cliffs, NJ: Prentice-Hall.

Skogan, W. G. (1977). Dimensions of the dark figure of unreported crime. *Crime and Delinquency*, **23**, 41–50.

Slaby, R. G., and Guerra, N. G. (1988). Cognitive mediators of aggression in adolescent offenders: 1. Assessment. *Developmental Psychology*, **24**, 580–588.

Slaikeu, K. (1973). Evaluation studies on group treatment of juvenile and adult offenders in correctional institutions: A review of the literature. *Journal of Research in Crime and Delinquency*, **10**, 87–100.

Smith, B. D., Davidson, R. A., Smith, D. L., Goldstein, H., and Perlstein, W. (1989). Sensation-seeking and arousal: Effects of strong stimulation on electrodermal and memory task performance. *Personality and Individual Differences*, **10**, 671–679.

Smith, D. A., and Visher, C. A. (1980). Sex and involvement in deviance/crime: A quantitative review of the empirical literature. *American Sociological Review*, **45**, 691–701.

Smith, D. A., and Visher, C. A. (1982). Street level justice: Situational determinants of police arrest decisions. *Social Problems*, **29**, 167–177.

Smith, D. E. (1974). Relationship between the Eysenck and Jesness personality inventories. *British Journal of Criminology*, **14**, 376–384.

Smith, M. L., and Glass, G. V. (1977). Meta-analysis of psychotherapy outcome studies. *American Psychologist*, **32**, 752–760.

Snarey, J. R. (1985). Cross-cultural universality of socio-moral development. *Psychological Bulletin*, **97**, 202–232.

Snyder, J., and Patterson, G. (1987). Family interaction and delinquent behavior. In H. C. Quay (ed.), *Handbook of Juvenile Delinquency*. Chichester: Wiley.

Snyder, J., and White, J. J. (1979). The use of cognitive self-instruction in the treatment of behaviorally disturbed adolescents. *Behavior Therapy*, **10**, 227–235.

Snyder, J. J., Dishion, T. J., and Patterson, G. R. (1986). Determinants and consequences of associating with deviant peers during preadolescence and adolescence. *Journal of Early Adolescence*, **6**, 29–43.

Soloman, G. S., and Ray, J. B. (1984). Irrational beliefs of shoplifters. *Journal of Clinical Psychology*, **40**, 1075–1077.

Solomon, R. L. (1964). Punishment. *American Psychologist*, **19**, 239–253.

Solursh, L. P. (1989). Combat addiction: Overview of implications in symptom maintenance and treatment planning. *Journal of Traumatic Stress*, **2**, 451–462.

Soothill, K. L., and Gibbens, T. C. N. (1978). Recidivism of sex offenders: A re-appraisal. *British Journal of Criminology*, **18**, 267–276.

Soothill, K. L., Way, C. K., and Gibbens, T. C. N. (1980). Rape acquittals. *Modern Law Review*, **43**, 159–172.

Sosowsky, L. (1980). Explaining the arrest rate among mental patients: A cautionary note. *American Journal of Psychiatry*, **137**, 1602–1605.

Spence, S. H. (1981). Differences in social skills performance between institutionalised juvenile male offenders and a comparable group of boys without offence records. *British Journal of Clinical Psychology*, **20**, 163–171.

Spence, S. H. (1982). Social skills training with young offenders. In M. P. Feldman (ed.), *Developments in the Study of Criminal Behaviour. Volume 1: The Prevention and Control of Offending*. Chichester: Wiley.

Spence, S. H., and Marzillier, J. S. (1981). Social skills training with adolescent male offenders: II. Short-term, long-term and generalisation effects. *Behaviour Research and Therapy*, **19**, 349–368.

Spinetta, J., and Rigler, D. (1972). The child-abusing parent. *Psychological Bulletin*, **77**, 296–304.

Spivack, G., Platt, and Shure, M. (1976). *The Problem-Solving Approach to Adjustment*. San Francisco: Jossey-Bass.

Spruill, J., and May, J. (1988). The mentally retarded offender: Prevalence rates based on individual versus group tests. *Criminal Justice and Behavior*, **15**, 489–491.

Sroufe, L. A., and Fleeson, J. (1986). Attachment and the construction of relationships. In W. Hartup and Z. Rubin (eds), *Relationships and Development*. Hillsdale, NJ: Erlbaum.

Stattin, H., and Magnusson, D. (1989). The role of early aggressive behavior in the frequency, seriousness, and types of later crime. *Journal of Consulting and Clinical Psychology*, **57**, 710–718.

Stattin, H., and Magnusson, D. (1991). Stability and change in criminal behaviour up to age 30. *British Journal of Criminology*, **31**, 327–346.

Steadman, H. J. (1977). A new look at recidivism among Patuxent patients. *Bulletin of the American Academy of Psychiatry and the Law*, **5**, 200–209.

Steadman, H. J. (1985). Empirical research on the insanity defense. *Annals of the American Academy of Political and Social Science*, **477**, 58–71.

Steadman, H. J., and Keveles, G. (1972). The community adjustment and criminal activity of the Baxstrom patients: 1966–1970. *American Journal of Psychiatry*, **129**, 304–310.

Steadman, H. J., Cocozza, J. J., and Melick, M. E. (1978). Explaining the increased arrest rate among mental patients: The changing clientele of state hospitals. *American Journal of Psychiatry*, **135**, 816–820.

Steadman, H. J., Monahan, J., Hartstone, E., Davis, S. K., and Robbins, D. C. (1982). Mentally disordered offenders: A national survey of patients and facilities. *Law and Human Behavior*, **6**, 31–38.

Steffensmeier, D. J. (1980). Sex differences in patterns of adult crime, 1965-1977: A review and assessment. *Social Forces*, **58**, 1080–1108.

Steffensmeier, D. J., Allan, E. A., Harer, M. D., and Streifel, C. (1989). Age and the distribution of crime. *American Journal of Sociology*, **94**, 803–831.

Stein, K. B., Sarbin, T. R., and Kulik, J. A. (1968). Future time perspective: Its relation to the socialisation process and the delinquent role. *Journal of Consulting and Clinical Psychology*, **32**, 257–264.

Steinberg, L. (1986). Latch-key children and susceptibility to peer pressure: An ecological analysis. *Developmental Psychology*, **22**, 433–439.

Stermac, L. E. (1986). Anger control treatment for forensic patients. *Journal of Interpersonal Violence*, **1**, 446–457.

Stermac, L. E., and Quinsey, V. L. (1986). Social competence among rapists. *Behavioral Assessment*, **8**, 171–185.

Stermac, L. E., and Segal, Z. V. (1989). Adult sexual contact with children: An examination of cognitive factors. *Behavior Therapy*, **20**, 573–584.

Stevens, J. R., and Hermann, B. P. (1981). Temporal lobe epilepsy, psychopathology, and violence: The state of the evidence. *Neurology*, **31**, 1127–1132.

Stewart, D. J. (1972). Effects of social reinforcement on dependency and aggressive responses of psychopathic, neurotic, and subcultural delinquents. *Journal of Abnormal Psychology*, **79**, 76–83.

Stokes, T. F., and Baer, D. M. (1977). An implicit technology of generalisation. *Journal of Applied Behavior Analysis*, **10**, 349–367.

Stone, A. A. (1984). *Law, Psychiatry, and Morality: Essays and Analysis*. Washington, DC: American Psychiatric Press.

Stott, D. (1982). *Delinquency: The Problem and its Prevention*. London: Batsford.

Straus, M. A., and Gelles, R. J. (1988). How violent are American families? Estimates from the National Family Violence Resurvey and other studies. In G. T. Hotaling, D. Finkelhor, J. T. Kirkpatrick and M. A. Straus (eds), *Family Abuse and its Consequences: New Directions in Research*. Beverly Hills, Ca: Sage.

Straus, M. A., Gelles, R. J., and Steinmetz, S. K. (1980). *Behind Closed Doors: Violence in the American Family*. New York: Anchor/Doubleday.

Strauss, J. S. (1973). Diagnostic models and the nature of psychiatric disorder. *Archives of General Psychiatry*, **29**, 445–449.

Stringer, A.Y., and Josef, N. C. (1983). Methylphenidate in the treatment of aggression in two patients with antisocial personalty disorder. *American Journal of Psychiatry*, **140**, 1365–1366.

Strong, S. R., Hills, H. I., Kilmartin, C. T., DeVries, H., Lanier, K., Nelson, B. N., Strickland, D., and Meyer, C. W. (1988). The dynamic relations among interpersonal behaviors: A test of complementarity and anticomplementarity. *Journal of Personality and Social Psychology*, **54**, 798–810.

Stuart, R. B. (1971). Behavioral contracting with the families of delinquents. *Journal of Behavior Therapy and Experimental Psychiatry*, **2**, 1–11.

Stuart, R. B. (1972). Situational versus self-control. In R. D. Rubin, H. Fensterheim, J. D. Henderson and L. P. Ullmann (eds), *Advances in Behavior Therapy*, Volume 3. New York: Academic Press.

Stuart, R. B., Jayaratne, S., and Tripodi, T. (1976). Changing adolescent deviant behavior through reprogramming the behavior of parents and teachers. *Canadian Journal of Behavioral Science*, **8**, 132–144.

Stumphauzer, J. S. (1976). Elimination of stealing by self-reinforcement of alternative behavior and family contracting. *Journal of Behavior Therapy and Experimental Psychiatry*, **7**, 265–268.

Stumphauzer, J. S. (1986). *Helping Delinquents Change: A Treatment Manual of Social Learning Approaches*. New York: Haworth Press.

Stumphauzer, J. S., Veloz, E. V., and Aiken, T. W. (1981). Behavioral analysis of communities: A challenge. *Psychological Reports*, **49**, 343–346.

Sturman, A. (1980). Damage on buses: The effects of supervision. In R. V. G. Clarke and P. Mayhew (eds), *Designing Out Crime*. London: HMSO.

Suedfeld, P. and Landon, P. B. (1978). Approaches to treatment. In R. D. Hare and D. Schalling (eds), *Psychopathic Behavior: Approaches to Research*. New York: Wiley.

Sullivan, C., Grant, J. D., and Grant, M. Q. (1956). The development of interpersonal maturity: Application to delinquency. *Psychiatry*, **20**, 373–385.

Sutherland, E. H. (1945). Is "white collar crime" crime? *American Sociological Review*, **10**, 132–139.

Sutherland, E. H. (1950). The diffusion of sexual psychopath laws. *American Journal of Sociology*, **56**, 142–148.

Sutherland, E. H. (1951). Critique of Sheldon's varieties of delinquent youth. *American Sociological Review*, **16**, 10–13.

Sutherland, E. H., and Cressey. D. R. (1970). *Criminology*, Eighth Edition. Philadelphia: Lippincott.

Sutker, P. B., Moan, C. E., and Swanson, W. C. (1972). Porteus Maze qualitative performance in pure sociopaths, prison normals, and antisocial psychotics. *Journal of Clinical Psychology*, **28**, 349–353.

Sykes, G. (1966). *The Society of Captives*. New York: Atheneum.

Sykes, G., and Matza, D. (1957). Techniques of neutralisation: A theory of delinquency. *American Sociological Review*, **22**, 664–673.

Syndulko, K., Parker, D. A., Jens, R., Maltzman, I., and Ziskind, E. (1975). Psychophysiology of sociopathy: Electrocortical measures. *Biological Psychology*, **3**, 185–200.

Szasz, T. S. (1960). The myth of mental illness. *American Psychologist*, **15**, 113–118.

Szasz, T. S. (1979). Insanity and responsibility. In H. Toch (ed.), *The Psychology of Crime and Criminal Justice*. New York: Holt, Rinehart and Winston.

Tappan, P. (1947). Who is the criminal? *American Sociological Review*, **12**, 96–102.

Tarling, R. (1979). *Sentencing Practice in Magistrates' Courts*. Home Office Research Study No. 56. London: HMSO.

Tarter, R. E., Hegedus, A. M., Alterman, A. I., and Katz-Garris, L. (1983). Cognitive capacities of juvenile violent, nonviolent, and sexual offenders. *Journal of Nervous and Mental Disease*, **171**, 564–567.

Tarter, R. E., Hegedus, A. M., Winsten, S. T., and Alterman, A. I. (1987). Intellectual profiles of violent behavior in juvenile delinquents. *Journal of Psychology*, **119**, 125–128.

Taylor, I., Walton, P., and Young, J. (1973). *The New Criminology: For a Social Theory of Deviance*. New York: Harper and Row.

Taylor, P. (1982). Schizophrenia and violence. In J. Gunn and D. P. Farrington (eds), *Abnormal Offenders, Delinquency, and the Criminal Justice System*. Chichester: Wiley.

Taylor, P. (1985). Motives for offending among violent and psychotic men. *British Journal of Psychiatry*, **147**, 491–498.

Taylor, P. (1986). Psychiatric disorder in London's life-sentenced offenders. *British Journal of Criminology*, **26**, 63–78.

Taylor, P., and Gunn, J. (1984). Risk of violence among psychotic men. *British Medical Journal*, **288**, 1945–1949.

Taylor, S. P., and Leonard, K. E. (1983). Alcohol and human physical aggression. In R. G. Geen and E. I. Donnerstein (eds), *Aggression: Theoretical and Empirical Reviews*, Volume 2. New York: Academic Press.

Tedeschi, J. T. (1983). Social influence theory and aggression. In R. G. Geen and E. I. Donnerstein (eds), *Aggression: Theoretical and Empirical Reviews*, Volume 1. New York: Academic Press.

Templeman, T. L. and Wollersheim, J. P. (1979). A cognitive–behavioral approach to the treatment of psychopathy. *Psychotherapy: Theory, Research and Practice*, **16**, 132–139.

Tennent, G., and Gath, D. (1975). Bright delinquents: A three year follow-up study. *British Journal of Criminology*, **15**, 386–390.

Teplin, L. A. (1984). Criminalising mental disorder: The comparative arrest rate of the mentally ill. *American Psychologist*, **39**, 794–803.

Teplin, L. A. (1985). The criminality of the mentally ill: *American Journal of Psychiatry*, **142**, 593–598.

Thomas, C. W. (1977). Theoretical perspectives on prisonisation: A comparison of the importation and deprivation models. *Journal of Criminal Law and Criminology*, **68**, 135–145.

Thomas, C. W., and Cage, R. (1977). The effect of social characteristics on juvenile court dispositions. *Sociological Quarterly*, **18**, 237–252.

Thomas, M. H., Horton, R. W., Lippincott, E. C., and Drabman, R. S. (1977). Desensitisation to portrayals of real-life aggression as a function of exposure to television violence. *Journal of Personality and Social Psychology*, **35**, 450–458.

Thompson, W. E., and Dodder, R. A. (1986). Containment theory and juvenile delinquency: A reevaluation through factor analysis. *Adolescence*, **21**, 365–376.

Thornberry, T. P., and Farnworth, M. (1982). Social correlates of criminal involvement: Further evidence on the relationship between social status and criminal behavior. *American Sociological Review*, **47**, 505–518.

Thornberry, T., and Jacoby, J. (1979). *The Criminally Insane: A Community Follow-up of Mentally Ill Offenders*. Chicago: University of Chicago Press.

Thorne, F. C. (1959). The etiology of sociopathic reactions. *American Journal of Psychotherapy*, **13**, 319–330.

Thorne, G. L., Tharp, R. G., and Wetzel, R. J. (1967). Behavior modification techniques: New tools for probation officers. *Federal Probation*, **31**, 21–27.

Thornton, D. (1987a). Moral development theory. In B. J. McGurk, D. M. Thornton and M. Williams (eds), *Applying Psychology to Imprisonment: Theory and Practice*. London: HMSO.

Thornton, D. (1987b). Assessing custodial adjustment. In B. J. McGurk, D. M. Thornton and M. Williams (eds), *Applying Psychology to Imprisonment: Theory and Practice*. London: HMSO.

Thornton, D., and Reid, R. L. (1982). Moral reasoning and type of criminal offence. *British Journal of Social Psychology*, **21**, 231–238.

Thornton, D., Curran, L., Grayson, D., and Holloway, V. (1984). *Tougher Regimes in Detention Centres: Report of an Evaluation by the Young Offender Psychology Unit*. London: HMSO.

Thurstone, L. L. (1927). The method of paired comparisons for social values. *Journal of Abnormal and Social Psychology*, **21**, 384–400.

Tisdelle, D. A., and Lawrence, J. S. St. (1986). Interpersonal problem-solving competency: Review and critique of the literature. *Clinical Psychology Review*, **6**, 337–356.

Tittle, C. R. (1977). Sanction fear and the maintenance of social order. *Social Forces*, **55**, 579–596.

Tittle, C. R. (1983). Social class and criminal behavior: A critique of the theoretical foundation. *Social Forces*, **62**, 334–358.

Tittle, C. R., Villemez, W. J., and Smith, D. A. (1978). The myth of social class and criminality: An empirical assessment of the empirical evidence. *American Sociological Review*, **43**, 643–656.

Toch, H. (1969). *Violent Men*. Harmondsworth: Penguin Books.

Toch, H. (1975). Reducing violence in the criminal justice system. In D. Chappell and J. Monahan (eds), *Violence and Criminal Justice*. Lexington, Mass: Heath.

Toch, H. (1987). Supplementing the positivistic perspective. In M. R. Gottfredson and T. Hirschi (eds), *Positive Criminology*. Beverly Hills, Ca: Sage.

Toch, H., and Adams, K. (1989). *The Disturbed Violent Offender*. New Haven: Yale University Press.

Tong, J. E. (1959). Stress reactivity in relation to delinquent and psychopathic behavior. *Journal of Mental Science*, **105**, 935–956.

Tracy, P., Wolfgang, M., and Figlio, R. (1986). *Delinquency in a Birth Cohort 2: A Comparison of the 1945 and 1958 Philadelphia Birth Cohorts*. Washington, DC: National Institute of Juvenile Justice and Delinquency (Final Report).

Trasler, G. B. (1962). *The Explanation of Criminality*. London: Routledge and Kegan Paul.

Trasler, G. B. (1978). Relations between psychopathy and persistent criminality. In R. D. Hare and D. Schalling (eds), *Psychopathic Behavior: Approaches to Research*. New York: Wiley.

Trasler, G. B. (1979). Delinquency, recidivism and desistance. *British Journal of Criminology*, **19**, 314–322.

Trasler, G. B. (1986). Situational crime control and rational choice: A critique. In K. Heal and G. Laycock (eds), *Situational Crime Prevention: From Theory into Practice*. London: HMSO.

Tremblay, R. E., Masse, B., Perron, D., LeBlanc, M., Schwartzman, A. E., and Ledingham, J. E. (1992). Early disruptive behavior, poor school achievement, delinquent behavior, and delinquent personality: Longitudinal analyses. *Journal of Consulting and Clinical Psychology*, **60**, 64–72.

Trower, P. (1984). A radical reformulation and critique: From organism to agent. In P. Trower (ed.), *Radical Approaches to Social Skills Training*. London: Croom Helm.

Truscott, D. (1990). Assessment of overcontrolled hostility in adolescence. *Psychological Assessment: A Journal of Consulting and Clinical Psychology*, **2**, 145–148.

Tsujimoto, R. N., and Nardi, P. M. (1978). A comparison of Kohlberg's and Hogan's theories of moral development. *Social Psychology*, **41**, 235–245.

Tullock, G. (1974). Does punishment deter crime? *The Public Interest*, **36**, 103–111.

Tunstall, O., Gudjonsson, G., Eysenck, H., and Haward, L. (1982). Professional issues arising from psychological evidence presented in court. *Bulletin of the British Psychological Society*, **35**, 329–331.

Tupin, J. P. (1986). Psychopharmacology and aggression. In L. H. Roth (ed.), *Clinical Treatment of the Violent Person*. New York: Guilford.

Turco, R. N. (1990). Psychological profiling. *International Journal of Offender Therapy and Comparative Criminology*, **34**, 147–154.

Turk, D. C., and Salovey, P. (1985). Cognitive structures, cognitive processes, and cognitive–behavior modification. *Cognitive Therapy and Research*, **9**, 1–17.

Turner, S. M., Turner, J. H., and Fix, A. B. (1976). Throwing the beast back out: A closer look at Van Den Berghe's "beast". *American Sociological Review*, **41**, 551–555.

Tutt, N. (1973). Achievement motivation and delinquency. *British Journal of Social and Clinical Psychology*, **12**, 225–230.

Tutt, N. (1984). Contemporary approaches to the understanding, assessment and treatment of delinquency. In J. Nicholson and H. Beloff (eds), *Psychology Survey 5*. Leicester: British Psychological Society.

Tversky, A., and Kahneman, D. (1974). Judgment under uncertainty: Heuristics and biases. *Science*, **185**, 1124–1131.

Twain, D. C. (1957). Factor analysis of a particular aspect of behavioral control: Impulsivity. *Journal of Clinical Psychology*, **13**, 133–136.

Twentyman, C. T., Jensen, M., and Kloss, J. D. (1978). Social skills training for the complex offender: Employment seeking skills. *Journal of Clinical Psychology*, **34**, 320–326.

Tyrer, P. (1988). *Personality Disorders: Diagnosis, Management and Course*. London: Wright.

Tyrer, T. R. (1990). *Why People Obey the Law*. New Haven: Yale University Press.

Ulbrich, P., and Huber, J. (1981). Observing parental violence: Distribution and effects. *Journal of Marriage and the Family*, **43**, 623–631.

United Nations (1988). *Demographic Year-Book*. New York: United Nations Publishing Division.

US Department of Justice, Federal Bureau of Investigation (1989). *Uniform Crime Reports 1988*. Washington, DC: U. S. Government Printing Office.

Vaillant, G. E. (1975). Sociopathy as a human process: A viewpoint. *Archives of General Psychiatry*, **32**, 178–183.

Valenstein, E. S. (1976). Brain stimulation and the origin of violent behavior. In W. L. Smith and A. Kling (eds), *Issues in Brain/Behavior Control*. New York: Spectrum.

Valliant, P. M., Asu, M. E., and Howitt, R. (1983). Cognitive styles of Caucasian and native Indian juvenile offenders. *Psychological Reports*, **52**, 87–92.

Vambery, R. (1941). Criminology and behaviorism. *Journal of Criminal Law, Criminology and Police Science*, **32**, 158–165.

Van den Haag, E. (1982). Could successful rehabilitation reduce the crime rate? *Journal of Criminal Law and Criminology*, **73**, 1022–1035.

Van Eyken, A. (1987). Aggression: myth or model? *Journal of Applied Philosophy*, **4**, 165–176.

Van Hoorhis, P. (1988). A cross classification of five offender typologies. *Criminal Justice and Behavior*, **15**, 109–124.

Van Ness, S. (1984). Rape as instrumental violence: A study of youthful offenders. *Journal of Offender Counselling, Service, and Rehabilitation*, **9**, 161–170.

Venables, P. H. (1988). Psychophysiology and crime: Theory and data. In T. E. Moffitt and S. A. Mednick (eds), *Biological Contributions to Crime Causation*. Dordrecht: Martinus Nijhoff.

Venables, P. H., and Raine, A. (1987). Biological theory. In B. J. McGurk, D. M. Thornton and M. Williams (eds), *Applying Psychology to Imprisonment: Theory and Practice*. London: HMSO.

Veneziano, C., and Veneziano, L. (1988). Knowledge of social skills among institutionalised juvenile delinquents. *Criminal Justice and Behavior*, **15**, 152–171.

Virkunnen, M. (1988). Cerebrospinal fluid: Monoamine metabolites among habitually violent and impulsive offenders. In T. E. Moffitt and S. A. Mednick (eds), *Biological Contributions to Crime Causation*. Dordrecht: Martinus Nijhoff.

Virkunnen, M., DeJong, J., and Bartko, J. (1989). Relationship of psychobiological variables to recidivism in violent offenders and impulsive firesetters. *Archives of General Psychiatry*, **46**, 600–603.

Virkunnen, M., Nuutila, A., and Huusko, S. (1976). Effect of brain injury on social adaptability. *Acta Psychiatrica Scandinavica*, **53**, 168–172.

Von Hirsch, A. (1976). *Doing Justice: The Choice of Punishments*. New York: Hill and Wang.

Wadsworth, M. E. J. (1976). Delinquency, pulse rates and early emotional deprivation. *British Journal of Criminology*, **16**, 245–256.

Wakefield, J. C. (1992). The concept of mental disorder: On the boundary between biological facts and social values. *American Psychologist*, **47**, 373–388.

Waldo, G. P., and Dinitz, S. (1967). Personality attributes of the criminal: An analysis of research studies, 1950–1965. *Journal of Research in Crime and Delinquency*, **2**, 185–202.

Walker, J. L., Lahey, B. B., Hynd, G. W., and Frame, C. L. (1987). Comparison of specific patterns of antisocial behavior in children with conduct disorder with or without coexisting hyperactivity. *Journal of Consulting and Clinical Psychology*, **55**, 910–913.

Walker, L. E. (1988). The battered woman syndrome. In G. T. Hotaling, D. Finkelhor, J. T. Kirkpatrick and M. A. Straus (eds), *Family Abuse and its Consequences: New Directions in Research*. Beverly Hills, Ca: Sage.

Walker, L. J. (1986). Sex differences in the development of moral reasoning: A rejoinder to Baumrind. *Child Development*, **57**, 522–526.

Walker, M. A. (1978). Measuring the seriousness of crimes. *British Journal of Criminology*, **18**, 348–364.

Walker, N. (1983). Side-effects of incarceration. *British Journal of Criminology*, **23**, 61–71.

Walker, N. (1985). The insanity defense before 1800. *Annals of the American Academy of Political and Social Science*, **477**, 25–30.

Walker, N. (1987). *Crime and Criminology: A Critical Introduction*. Oxford: Oxford University Press.

Walker, N., and Farrington, D. P. (1981). Reconviction rates of adult males after different sentences. *British Journal of Criminology*, **21**, 357–360.

Walsh, A., Petee, T. A., and Beyer, J. A. (1987). Intellectual imbalance and delinquency: Comparing high verbal and high performance IQ delinquents. *Criminal Justice and Behavior*, **14**, 370–379.

Walters, G. D., Greene, R. L. and Solomon, G. S. (1982). Empirical correlates of the Overcontrolled Hostility Scale and the MMPI 4 3 highpoint pair. *Journal of Consulting and Clinical Psychology*, **50**, 213–218.

Ward, C. I., and McFall, R. M. (1986). Further validation of the Problem Inventory for Adolescent Girls: Comparing caucasian and black delinquents and nondelinquents. *Journal of Consulting and Clinical Psychology*, **50**, 213–218.

Ward, D. (1987). *The Validity of the Reconviction Prediction Score*. Home Office Research Study, No. 94. London: HMSO.

Warren, M. Q. (1971). Classification of offenders as an aid to efficient management and effective treatment. *Journal of Criminal Law, Criminology and Police Science*, **62**, 239–258.

Warren, M. Q. (1983). Applications of interpersonal-maturity theory of offender populations. In W. S. Laufer and J. M. Day (eds), *Personality Theory, Moral Development, and Criminal Behavior*. Lexington: Lexington Books.

Waterman, A. S. (1981). Individualism and interdependence. *American Psychologist*, **36**, 762–773.

Watkins, J. T. (1977). The rational–emotive dynamics of impulsive disorders. In A. Ellis and R. Grieger (eds), *Handbook of Rational–Emotive Therapy*. New York: Springer.

Watson, D. and Clark, L. A. (1984). Negative affectivity: The disposition to experience aversive emotional states. *Psychological Bulletin*, **96**, 465–490.

Weathers, L., and Liberman, R. P. (1975). Contingency contracting with families of delinquent adolescents. *Behavior Therapy*, **6**, 356–366.

Webster, C. D. (1984). On gaining acceptance: Why the courts accept only reluctantly findings from experimental and social psychology. *International Journal of Law and Psychiatry*, **7**, 407–414.

Weinberg, R. A. (1989). Intelligence and IQ: Landmark issues and great debates. *American Psychologist*, **44**, 98–104.

Weiner, B. (1986). *An Attributional Theory of Motivation and Emotion*. New York: Springer-Verlag.

Weiner, I. B. (1987). Writing forensic reports. In I. B. Weiner and A. K. Hess (eds), *Handbook of Forensic Psychology*. New York: Wiley.

Weiner, I. B., and Hess, A. K. (eds), (1987). *Handbook of Forensic Psychology*. New York: Wiley.

Weiner, N. A. (1989). Violent criminal careers and "violent career criminals": An overview of the research literature. In N. A. Weiner and M. E. Wolfgang (eds), *Violent Crime, Violent Criminals*. Newbury Park, Ca; Sage.

Weintraub, K. J., and Gold, M. (1991). Monitoring and delinquency. *Criminal Behaviour and Mental Health*, **1**, 268–281.

Weis, J. G. (1987). Social class and crime. In M. R. Gottfredson and T. Hirschi (eds), *Positive Criminology*. Beverly Hills, Ca: Sage.

Weiss, G., Hechtman. L., Milroy, T., and Perlman, T. (1985). Psychiatric status of hyperactives as adults: A controlled prospective 15-year follow-up of 63 hyperactive children. *Journal of the American Academy of Child Psychiatry*, **24**, 211–220.

Welford, C. (1975). Labelling theory and criminology: An assessment. *Social Problems*, **22**, 332–345.

Weller, M. P. I., and Weller, B. G. A. (1988). Crime and mental illness. *Medicine, Science and the Law*, **28**, 38–46.

Wells, L. E. (1978). Theories of deviance and the self-concept. *Social Psychology*, **41**, 189–204.

Wells, L. E., and Rankin, J. H. (1983). Self-concept as a mediating factor in delinquency. *Social Psychology Quarterly*, **46**, 11–22.

Wells, L. E., and Rankin, J. H. (1986). The broken homes model of delinquency: Analytic issues. *Journal of Research in Crime and Delinquency*, **23**, 68–93.

Wenk, E. A., Robison, J. O., and Smith, G. B. (1972). Can violence be predicted? *Crime and Delinquency*, **18**, 393–402.

Werner, E. E. (1989). High-risk children in young adulthood: A longitudinal study from birth to 32 years. *American Journal of Orthopsychiatry*, **59**, 72–81.

Werner, E. E., and Smith, R. S. (1982). *Vulnerable but Invincible*. New York: McGraw-Hill.

Werner, J. S., Minkin, N., Minkin, B. L., Fixsen, D. L., Phillips, E. L., and Wolf, M. M. (1975). "Intervention Package": An analysis to prepare juvenile delinquents for encounters with police officers. *Criminal Justice and Behavior*, **2**, 55–83.

Werner, P. D., Rose, T. L., and Yesavage, J. A. (1983). Reliability, accuracy and decision-making strategy in clinical predictions of imminent dangerousness. *Journal of Consulting and Clinical Psychology*, **51**, 815–825.

Werner, P. D., Yesavage, J. A., Becker, J. M. T., Brunsting, D. W., and Isaacs, J. S. (1983). Hostile words and assaultive behavior on an acute inpatient psychiatric unit. *Journal of Nervous and Mental Disease*, **171**, 385–387.

Wessely, S., and Taylor, P. J. (1991). Madness and crime: Criminology versus psychiatry. *Criminal Behaviour and Mental Health*, **1**, 193–228.

West, D. J. (1980). The clinical approach to criminology. *Psychological Medicine*, **10**, 619–632.

West, D. J. (1982). *Delinquency: Its Roots, Careers and Prospects*. Cambridge, Mass: Harvard University Press.

West, D. J., and Farrington, D. P. (1973). *Who Becomes Delinquent?* London: Heinemann.

Wetherick, N. E. (1979). The foundations of psychology. In N. Bolton (ed.), *Philosophical Problems In Psychology*. London: Methuen.

Wettstein, R. M. (1984). The prediction of violent behavior and the duty to protect third parties. *Behavioral Science and the Law*, **2**, 291–316.

Wexler, H. K., Falkin, G. P., and Lipton, D. S. (1990). Outcome evaluation of a prison therapeutic community for substance abuse treatment. *Criminal Justice and Behavior*, **17**, 71–92.

Wheeler, S. (1961). Socialisation in correctional communities. *American Sociological Review*, **26**, 697–712.

Wheeler, S. (1962). The social sources of criminology. *Sociological Inquiry*, **32**, 139–159.

White, H. R., LaBouvie, E. W., and Bates, M. E. (1985). The relationship between sensation-seeking and delinquency: A longitudinal study. *Journal of Research in Crime and Delinquency*, **22**, 197–211.

White, J. L., Moffitt, T. E., and Silva, P. A. (1989). A prospective replication of the protective effects of IQ in subjects at high risk for juvenile delinquency. *Journal of Consulting and Clinical Psychology*, **57**, 719–724.

White, J. W. (1983). Sex and gender issues in aggression research. In R. G. Geen and E. I. Donnerstein (eds), *Aggression: Theoretical and Empirical Reviews*, Volume 2. New York: Academic Press.

Whitehead, J. T., and Lab, S. P. (1989). A meta-analysis of juvenile correctional treatment. *Journal of Research in Crime and Delinquency*, **26**, 276–295.

Whitman, S., Coleman, T. E., Patmon, C., Desai, B. T., Cohen, R., and King, L. N. (1984). Epilepsy in prison: Elevated prevalence and no relationship to violence. *Neurology*, **34**, 774–782.

Wiatrowski, M. D., Hansell, S., Massey, C. R., and Wilson, D. L. (1982). Curriculum tracking and delinquency. *American Sociological Review*, **47**, 151–160.

Widiger, T. A., and Frances, A. (1985a). The DSM-III personality disorders: Perspectives from psychology. *Archives of General Psychiatry*, **42**, 615–623.

Widiger, T. A., and Frances, A. (1985b). Axis II personality disorders: Diagnostic and treatment Issues. *Hospital and Community Psychiatry*, **36**, 619–627.

Widiger, T. A., and Frances, A. (1987). Interviews and inventories for the measurement of personality disorders. *Clinical Psychology Review*, **7**, 47–75.

Widiger, T. A., Frances, A., Spitzer, R. L., and Williams J. B. W. (1988). The DSM-III personality disorders: An overview. *American Journal of Psychiatry*, **145**, 786–795.

Widom, C. S. (1978a). Toward an understanding of female criminality. In B. A. Maher (ed.), *Progress in Experimental Personality Research*, Volume 8. New York: Academic Press. Widom, C. S. (1978b). An empirical classification of the female offender. *Criminal Justice and Behavior*, **5**, 35–52.

Widom, C. S. (1989a). Does violence beget violence? A critical examination of the literature. *Psychological Bulletin*, **106**, 3–28.

Widom, C. S. (1989b). The cycle of violence. *Science*, **244**, 160–166.

Widom, C. S., and Ames, A. (1988). Biology and female crime. In T. E. Moffitt and S. A. Mednick (eds), *Biological Contributions to Crime Causation*. Dordrecht: Martinus Nijhoff.

Wiggins, J. S. (1981). Clinical and statistical prediction: Where are we and where do we go from here? *Clinical Psychology Review*, **1**, 3–18.

Wiggins, J. S. (1982). Circumplex models of interpersonal behaviour in clinical psychology. In P. C. Kendall and J. N. Butcher (eds), *Handbook of Research Methods in Clinical Psychology*. New York: Wiley.

Wiggins, J. S., and Broughton, R. (1985). The Interpersonal Circle: A structural model for integrating personality research. In R. Hogan and W. H. Jones (eds), *Perspectives in Personality*, Volume 1. Greenwich, CT: JAI Press.

Wiggins, J. S., and Pincus, A. L. (1989). Conceptions of personality disorders and dimensions of personality. *Psychological Assessment: A Journal of Consulting and Clinical Psychology*, **1**, 305–316.

Wilkins, L. T. (1985). The politics of prediction. In D. P. Farrington and R. Tarling (eds), *Prediction in Criminology*. Albany: State University of New York Press.

Williams, D. (1969). Neural factors related to habitual aggression. *Brain*, **92**, 503–520.

Williams, G. (1978). *Textbook of Criminal Law*. London: Stevens and Sons.

Williams, J. R., and Gold, M. (1972). From delinquent behavior to official delinquency. *Social Problems*, **20**, 209–229.

Williams, L. M., and Finkelhor, D. (1990). The characteristics of incestuous fathers: A review of recent studies. In W. L. Marshall, D. R. Laws and H. E. Barbaree (eds), *Handbook of Sexual Assault: Issues, Theories, and Treatment of the Offender*. New York: Plenum.

Williams, M. (1987). Radical behaviourism. In B. J. McGurk, D. M. Thornton and M. Williams (eds), *Applying Psychology to Imprisonment: Theory and Practice*. London: HMSO.

Williams, W., and Miller, K. (1977). The role of personal characteristics in perceptions of dangerousness. *Criminal Justice and Behavior*, **4**, 241–252.

Wilson, E. O. (1978). *On Human Nature*. Cambridge, Mass: Harvard University Press.

Wilson, G. D., and Cox, D. N. (1983). Personality of pedophile club members. *Personality and Individual Differences*, **4**, 323–329.

Wilson, H. (1980). Parental supervision: A neglected aspect of delinquency. *British Journal of Criminology*, **20**, 203–235.

Wilson, H. (1987). Parental supervision re-examined. *British Journal of Criminology*, **27**, 275–293.

Wilson, J. Q. (1980). "What works?" revisited: New findings on criminal rehabilitation. *The Public Interest*, **61**, 3–17.

Wilson, J. Q., and Herrnstein, R. S. (1985). *Crime and Human Nature*. New York: Simon and Schuster.

Wilson, S. (1980). Vandalism and "defensible space" on London housing estates. In R. V. G. Clarke and P. Mayhew (eds), *Designing Out Crime*. London: HMSO.

Witkin, H. A., Mednick, S. A., Schulsinger, F., Bakkestrom, E., Christiansen, K. O., Goodenough, D. R., Hirschhorn, K., Lundsteen, C., Owen, D. R., Philip, J., Rubin, D. B., and Stocking, M. M. (1976). Criminality in XYY and XXY men. *Science*, **193**, 547–555.

Wober, J. M. (1989). Screen violence: A psychologist's view. *The Psychologist*, **2**, 162–165.

Wolfe, D. A. (1987). *Child Abuse: Implications for Child Development and Psychopathology*. Beverly Hills, Ca: Sage.

Wolfe, D. A., Jaffe, P., Wilson, S. K., and Zak, L. (1985). Children of battered women: The relation of child behavior to family violence and maternal stress. *Journal of Consulting and Clinical Psychology*, **53**, 657–665.

Wolfgang, M. E. (1957). Victim-precipitated criminal homicide. *Journal of Criminal Law, Criminology and Police Science*, **48**, 1–11.

Wolfgang, M. E. (1958). *Patterns in Criminal Homicide*. Philadelphia: University of Pennsylvania Press.

Wolfgang, M. E. (1983). Delinquency in two birth cohorts. *American Behavioral Scientist*, **27**, 75–86.

Wolfgang, M. E., and Ferracutti, F. (1967). *The Subculture of Violence*. London: Tavistock.

Wolfgang, M. E., Figlio, R. M., and Sellin, T. (1972). *Delinquency in a Birth Cohort*. Chicago: University of Chicago Press.

Woody, G.E., McLellan, A. T., Luborsky, L. and O'Brien, C. P. (1985). Sociopathy and psychotherapy outcome. *Archives of General Psychiatry*, **42**, 1081–1086.

Wootton, B. (1959). *Social Science and Social Pathology*. London: Allen and Unwin.

Wootton, B. (1980). Psychiatry, ethics and the criminal law. *British Journal of Psychiatry*, **136**, 525–532.

Wright, J. C., and Mischel, W. (1987). A conditional approach to dispositional constructs: The local predictability of social behavior. *Journal of Personality and Social Psychology*, **53**, 1159–1177.

Wright, K. N. (1985). Developing the Prison Environment Inventory. *Journal of Research in Crime and Delinquency*, **22**, 257–277.

Wright, R., and West, D. J. (1981). Rape: A comparison of group offences and lone assaults. *Medicine, Science and the Law*, **21**, 25–30.

Wulach, J. (1988). The criminal personality as a DSM-III-R antisocial, narcissistic, borderline, and histrionic personality disorder. *International Journal of Offender Therapy and Comparative Criminology*, **32**, 185–199.

Wurtele, S. K., Saslawsky, D. A., Miller, C. l., Marrs, S. L., and Britcher, J. C. (1986). Teaching personal safety skills for potential prevention of sexual abuse: A comparison of treatments. *Journal of Consulting and Clinical Psychology*, **54**, 688–692.

Wylie, R. C. (1968). The present status of self theory. In E. F. Borgatta and Lambert (eds), *Handbook of Personality Theory and Research*. Chicago: Rand McNally.

Yaryura-Tobias, J. A., and Neziroglu, F. A. (1975). Violent behavior, brain dysrhythmia, and glucose function: A new syndrome. *Journal of Orthomolecular Psychiatry*, **4**, 182–188.

Yates, E., Barbaree, H. E., and Marshall, W. L. (1984). Anger and deviant sexual arousal. *Behavior Therapy*, **15**, 287–294.

Yesavage, J. A. (1983). Bipolar illness: Correlates of dangerous inpatient behavior. *British Journal of Psychiatry*, **143**, 554–557.

Yeudall, L. T., and Fromm-Auch, D. (1979). Neuropsychological impairments in various psychopathological populations. In J. Gruzelier and P. Flor-Henry (eds), *Hemisphere Asymmetries of Function in Psychopathology*. Amsterdam: Elsevier.

Yeudall, L. T., Fromm-Auch, D., and Davies, P. (1982). Neuropsychological impairment of persistent delinquency. *Journal of Nervous and Mental Disease*, **170**, 257–265.

Yochelson, S., and Samenow, S. (1976). *The Criminal Personality. Volume 1. A Profile for Change*. New York: Jason Aronson.

Young, J. (1986). The failure of criminology: The need for a radical realism. In R. Matthews and J. Young (eds), *Confronting Crime*. London: Sage.

Young, J., and Matthews, R. (1992). Questioning left realism. In R. Matthews and J. Young (eds), *Issues in Realist Criminology*. London: Sage.

Yule, W., and Brown, B. J. (1987). Some behavioral applications with juvenile offenders outside North America. In E. K. Morris and C. J. Braukmann (eds), *Behavioral Approaches to Crime and Delinquency: A Handbook of Application, Research, and Concepts*. New York: Plenum.

Zager, L. D. (1988). The MMPI-based criminal classification system: A review, current status, and future directions. *Criminal Justice and Behavior*, **15**, 39–57.

Zamble, E. (1990). Behavioral and psychological considerations in the success of prison reform. In J. W. Murphy and J. E. Dison (eds), *Are Prisons Any Better? Twenty Years of Prison Reform*. Newbury Park, Ca: Sage.

Zamble, E., and Porporino, F. J. (1988). *Coping, Behavior, and Adaptation in Prison Inmates*. Berlin: Springer-Verlag.

Zeleny, L. (1933). Feeblemindedness and criminal conduct. *American Journal of Sociology*, **38**, 564–576.

Zigler, E., and Hall, N. W. (1987). The implications of early intervention for the primary prevention of juvenile delinquency. In J. Q. Wilson and G. C. Loury (eds), *From Children to Citizens. Volume 3. Families, Schools, and Delinquency Prevention*. New York: Springer-Verlag.

Zillmann, D. (1979). *Hostility and Aggression*. Hillsdale, NJ: Erlbaum.

Zimbardo, P. G. (1970). The human choice: Individuation, reason, and order versus deindividuation, impulse and chaos. In W. J. Arnold and D. Levine (eds), *Nebraska Symposium on Motivation*. Lincoln: University of Nebraska Press.

Zimmerman, J. Rich, W. D., Keilitz, I., and Broder, P. K. (1981). Some observations on the link between learning disabilities and juvenile delinquency. *Journal of Criminal Justice*, **9**, 1–17.

Zimring, F. E. (1981). Kids, groups, and crime: Some implications of a well-known secret. *Journal of Criminal Law and Criminology*, **72**, 867–885.

Zuckerman, M. (1969). Variables affecting deprivation results. In J. P. Zubek (ed.), *Sensory Deprivation: Fifteen Years of Research*. New York: Appleton-Century-Crofts.

Zuckerman, M. (1984). Sensation seeking: A comparative approach to a human trait. *The Behavioral and Brain Sciences*, **7**, 413–471.

Zuckerman, M., and Como, P. (1983). Sensation seeking and arousal systems. *Personality and Individual Differences*, **4**, 381–386.

Zuckerman, M., Kuhlman, M., and Camac, K. (1988). What lies beyond E and N? Factor analysis of scales believed to measure basic dimensions of personality. *Journal of Personality and Social Psychology*, **54**, 96–107.

Zuriff, G. E. (1985). *Behaviorism: A conceptual Reconstruction*. New York: Columbia University Press.

Index